CU00267511

Collins
School
Thesaurus

HarperCollins Publishers
Westerhill Road
Bishopbriggs
Glasgow
G64 2QT

First Edition 2005

© HarperCollins Publishers 2005

ISBN 0-00-718372-0

Collins® is a registered trademark of
HarperCollins Publishers Limited

www.collins.co.uk

A catalogue record for this book is
available from the British Library.

Typeset by Wordcraft

Printed and bound by Legoprint S.P.A.

Acknowledgements
We would like to thank those authors
and publishers who kindly gave
permission for copyright material to
be used in the Collins Word Web.
We would also like to thank Times
Newspapers Ltd for providing
valuable data.

EDITORIAL STAFF

EDITORS
Sandra Anderson
Lorna Gilmour
Imogen Kerr
Cordelia Lilly

FOR THE PUBLISHERS
Morven Dooner
Elaine Higgleton
Lorna Knight

CONTENTS

William Collins' dream of knowledge for all began with the publication of his first book in 1819. A self-educated mill worker, he not only enriched millions of lives, but also founded a flourishing publishing house. Today, staying true to this spirit, Collins books are packed with inspiration, innovation, and practical expertise. They place you at the centre of a world of possibility and give you exactly what you need to explore it.

Language is the key to this exploration, and at the heart of Collins Dictionaries is language as it is really used. New words, phrases, and meanings spring up every day, and all of them are captured and analysed by the Collins Word Web. Constantly updated, and with over 2.5 billion entries, this living language resource is unique to our dictionaries.

Words are tools for life. And a Collins Dictionary makes them work for you.

Collins. Do more

When Collins New School Thesaurus was first published in 20001, it proved itself to be a vital language and literacy tool for today's students. It was created to meet their needs and aspirations, and through research among teachers, many samples were tested so Collins could establish exactly what featureswould be considered most helpful. Now these features have been incorporated into this first edition of **Collins School Gem Thesaurus**, giving students even more language and study help.

What exactly does this book offer that isn't featured in other school thesauruses? Each entry is followed by a short explanation of its meaning, which is then followed by an example of real English showing the context in which the word may be used. Furthermore, each synonym given for the entry word is also accompanied by an example showing context; this makes it clearer for the student to see which synonyms can be directly substituted for the entry word, and which involve a slight shift in sense.

Collins Gem School Thesaurus helps you further, with a 40-page Word Studies section at the back of the book. This section gives helpful advice on how to avoid using the most over-used words, such as nice, and offers detailed groups of alternatives for every context.

Collins Gem School Thesaurus is very straightforward, with an accessible layout that's easy on the eye, guiding students quickly to want they want. The perfect companion volume to **Collins Gem School Dictionary**, it's accessible and student friendly, and offers essential help on the route to success.

USING THIS THESAURUS

Main Entry Words   are printed in large bold type:

object

All main entry words, are in alphabetical sequence, with phrases including the main word coming directly after the entry for that word:

object
object to
objection
objectionable

Parts of Speech   shown in italics

object *noun*

When a word can be used as more than one part of speech, the change of part of speech is shown after an arrow:

▷ *verb* **3**

Meanings   A helpful definition of each word is given in normal type:

anything solid or non-living

Examples	are given for the main words, in italic, and after the meaning, to show use. They are introduced with a colon:
	: everyday objects such as wooden spoons
Alternative words (synonyms)	each alternative word starts on a new line after the entry word they refer to. They are shown in bold, and are indented. They are followed with examples to help with context:
	article: *household articles*
Cross References	shown in bold type, eg
	see also **article, disagree, goal**

a

abandon verb **1** to leave someone or something: *His parents had abandoned him*

  desert: *Medical staff have deserted the city's main hospital*

  jilt: *She was jilted by her first fiancé*

  leave: *My husband has left me*

  leave behind: *He walked out and left behind a wife and two young children*

  ▷ noun **2** lack of restraint: *He began to laugh with abandon*

  recklessness: *the headstrong recklessness of youth*

  wildness: *Her wildness just needed to be channelled properly*

  see also **cancel, leave**

abandoned *see* **derelict**

abate verb to become less: *The four-day flood at last abated*

  decrease: *The pain had decreased considerably*

  diminish: *The attacks on the village did not diminish*

  ebb: *Her strength was ebbing fast*

  lessen: *After a while, the cramps lessened*

  subside: *Their enthusiasm was beginning to subside*

  wane: *His popularity shows no sign of waning*

  see also **ease, lessen, moderate**

abbreviate *see* **shorten**

abdicate *see* **resign**

abduct *see* **kidnap**

abhor *see* **dislike, hate**

abhorrence *see* **horror**

abhorrent *see* **hateful**

abide *see* **bear, put up with**

abide by *see* **obey**

abiding *see* **permanent**

ability noun the skill needed to do something: *the ability to get on with others*

  capability: *We have the capability of going out and winning*

  competence: *They have a high level of competence*

  expertise: *legal expertise*

  skill: *the skill to play at a higher level*

  talent: *a talent for music*

  see also **capacity, gift, potential, qualification, skill, talent**

able adjective good at doing something: *He proved himself to be an able politician*

  accomplished: *an accomplished pianist*

  capable: *a very capable manager*

  efficient: *a team of efficient workers*

  expert: *My mother was an expert baker*

  first-rate: *This run is only suitable for first-rate skiers*

  skilled: *a skilled craftsman*

  talented: *a talented actor*

  see also **capable, expert, proficient, skilful, skilled**

ably *see* **well**

abnormal *see* **strange**

abode *see* **home, house**

abolish verb to do away with something: *Their objective was to abolish capital gains tax*

  annul: *The marriage was annulled last month*

  do away with: *the proposal to do*

away with nuclear weapons
overturn: *criminals seeking to overturn their convictions*
put an end to: *efforts to put an end to the traffic in drugs*

abortive *see* **futile, vain**

about *preposition* **1** of or concerning: *anxiety about his sick son*
concerning: *documents concerning the estate*
on: *his book on Picasso*
regarding: *strict rules regarding the disposal of food*
relating to: *the rules relating to transfer fees*
▷ *adverb* **2** not exactly: *The procedure takes about thirty minutes*
almost: *Their wages have almost doubled*
approximately: *It was approximately three times the size of a domestic cat*
around: *The crowd here is around 12,000*
nearly: *a tradition going back nearly 20 centuries*
roughly: *One unit is roughly equivalent to half a pint of beer*
see also **almost**

above *preposition* **1** over or higher than something: *above the clouds*
higher than: *There are no hotels higher than four storeys*
over: *the picture over the fireplace*
2 greater than a certain level or amount: *The death toll will rise above 50*
beyond: *I expect to live way beyond 100*
exceeding: *a floor area exceeding 50,000 square feet*
see also **over**

abrasion *see* **graze**

abrupt *adjective* **1** sudden or unexpected: *the abrupt resignation of the prime minister*

sudden: *this week's sudden thaw*
unexpected: *His career came to an unexpected end*
unforeseen: *unforeseen difficulties*
2 unfriendly and impolite: *He was taken aback by her abrupt manner*
curt: *'The matter is closed,' was the curt reply*
rude: *He was frequently rude to waiters and servants*
short: *She seemed tense and was definitely short with me*
terse: *He received a terse one-line rejection from the Ministry*
see also **rude, sharp, sudden**

absence *see* **lack, want**

absent *adjective* not present: *absent from work*
away: *She is away on a business trip*
elsewhere: *Four witnesses can prove he was elsewhere at the time*
gone: *I'll only be gone for ten minutes*
missing: *Another 44 passengers are still missing*

absent-minded *adjective* forgetful or not paying attention: *Her absent-minded stepfather left the camera under the carriage seat*
distracted: *He seems distracted, giving the impression of being elsewhere*
forgetful: *She's getting rather forgetful, and living mostly in the past*
random *New Zealand*: *I'm sorry, I'm a bit random these days*

absolute *adjective* **1** total and complete: *He is talking absolute nonsense*
complete: *The operation was a complete success*
total: *the total destruction of the city*
downright: *That's a downright lie!*
pure: *a work of pure genius*
sheer: *It would be sheer madness to carry on after this*
thorough: *He has a thorough*

knowledge of the subject

utter: *He stared at me in utter disbelief*

2 having total power: *an absolute ruler*

dictatorial: *a dictatorial system of government*

supreme: *humble subjects of her supreme rule*

tyrannical: *popular uprisings against tyrannical rulers*

see also **complete, final, perfect, pure, rank, sheer, total, utter**

absolutely see **exactly, quite, really**

absolutely not see **no**

absolve see **clear, forgive**

absorb verb to soak up or take in something: *plants absorb carbon dioxide*

digest: *Fats are hard to digest*

soak up: *Stir until the wheat has soaked up all the water*

take in: *A growing tree takes in light and processes it for food*

see also **busy, fascinate, grasp, take in**

absorbed see **preoccupied**

absorbing see **interesting**

abstain verb to choose not to do something: *The patients had to abstain from alcohol*

avoid: *Heartburn sufferers should try to avoid fatty foods*

deny oneself: *I won't deny myself some celebration tonight*

forgo: *My wife and I have to forgo holidays now*

give up: *She gave up smoking last year*

refrain: *He appealed to all factions to refrain from violence*

see also **decline, refuse**

absurd adjective ridiculous or nonsensical: *an absurd waste of money*

crazy informal: *It would be crazy to*

tinker with a winning team

illogical: *his completely illogical arguments*

ludicrous: *It was ludicrous to suggest that the visit could be kept secret*

nonsensical: *He says many diets are harmful and nonsensical*

ridiculous: *The programme is too ridiculous to take seriously*

see also **impossible, incredible, irrational, ridiculous, silly, stupid**

absurdity see **stupidity**

abundance noun a great amount of something: *an abundance of wildlife*

affluence: *Pockets of affluence coexist with poverty*

bounty: *autumn's bounty of fruit, seeds, and berries*

plenty: *Allow plenty of time to get home*

see also **lot** or **lots, wealth**

abundant adjective present in large quantities: *an abundant supply of cheap labour*

ample: *ample space for a good-sized kitchen*

copious: *copious amounts of red wine*

full: *a full tank of petrol*

plentiful: *a plentiful supply of vegetables*

see also **ample, generous, plentiful, rich**

abuse noun 1 cruel treatment of someone: *child abuse*

exploitation: *Most human life involves the exploitation of animals*

harm: *The smokers willingly do to their own health*

hurt: *The victims suffer mental scars as well as physical hurt*

ill-treatment: *the ill-treatment of political prisoners*

oppression: *the oppression of black people throughout history*

2 unkind remarks directed towards someone: *I was left shouting abuse as* the car sped off

censure: *a controversial policy which has attracted international censure*

derision: *He was greeted with shouts of derision*

insults: *They shouted insults at each other*

invective: *A woman had hurled racist invective at the family*

▷ **verb 3** to speak insultingly to someone: *He was verbally abused by other soldiers*

curse: *We started cursing them under our breath*

insult: *I did not mean to insult you*

scold: *Later she scolded her daughter for having talked to her father like that*

slate *British informal*: *Willis's acting skills have been slated, yet again*
see also **impose on, harm, insult, mistreat, wrong**

abused see **oppressed**

abusive *adjective* rude and unkind: *abusive language*

disparaging: *He made some disparaging remarks about the team*

insulting: *She was charged with insulting behaviour to a police officer*

offensive: *The book was seen by many Muslims as being deeply offensive to Islam*

rude: *He is rude to her friends*

scathing: *He made some particularly scathing comments about the design*
see also **offensive**

abysmal see **terrible**

abyss *noun* a very deep hole: *He crawled to peer over the edge of the abyss*

chasm: *The climbers strung a rope across the chasm and crawled along it*

fissure: *The earthquake opened large fissures in the ground*

gorge: *The valley narrowed to a gorge with cascading crags*

pit: *Eric lost his footing and began to slide into the pit*

void: *His feet dangled in the void*
see also **hell**

academic see **learned**

accelerate *verb* to go faster: *She accelerated away from the kerb*

hurry: *He shouted at me to hurry*

quicken: *Her pulse quickened in alarm*

speed up: *It is designed to speed up credit-card transactions*
see also **hurry**

accelerated see **fast**

accent see **emphasis, emphasize**

accentuate see **emphasize, stress**

accept *verb* to receive or agree to something: *All those invited to next week's conference have accepted*

acknowledge: *He was willing to acknowledge her as his child*

agree to: *Hours before the deadline, the Chinese agreed to the conditions*

concur with: *I concur with her opinion*

consent to: *The Russians consented to the peace treaty*

take: *He took the job*
see also **resign oneself, admit, assume, believe, grant, receive, tolerate**

acceptable *adjective* good enough to be accepted: *an acceptable standard of living*

adequate: *a lack of adequate facilities*

all right: *The meal was all right for the price*

fair: *He is a fair player, but not outstanding*

good enough: *I'm afraid that excuse just isn't good enough*

passable: *She can speak fluent Spanish and passable French*

satisfactory: *The workmen have done a satisfactory job*

tolerable: *a tolerable level of noise*

see also **adequate, all right, correct, okay, right, satisfactory, suitable, tolerable**

accepted *see* **general, proper, standard**

access *see* **entrance**

accessible *see* **available, ready**

accessory *see* **attachment, extra, fitting**

accident *see* **chance, crash, luck**

accidental *adjective* happening by chance: *The fire was accidental*
casual: *a casual remark*
chance: *a chance meeting*
inadvertent: *She giggled at the inadvertent pun*
random: *the random nature of death in war*
see also **casual**

accolade *see* **honour, praise, prize, tribute**

accommodate *verb* to provide someone with a place to stay: *a hotel built to accommodate guests for the wedding*
house: *The building will house 12 boys*
put up: *I wanted to know if she could put me up for a few days*
shelter: *There were no facilities for sheltering the refugees*

accommodating *adjective* willing to help: *his polite, accommodating manner*
considerate: *I try to be considerate to non-smokers*
helpful: *The staff in the Newcastle office are very helpful*
hospitable: *He was very hospitable to me when I came to New York*
kind: *It was very kind of you to come*
obliging: *an extremely pleasant and obliging man*
see also **helpful**

accommodation *noun* a house or room for living in: *Travel and overnight accommodation are included*

digs *British informal*: *I was studying and living in digs all round the country*
house: *He sold his house in London and moved to the country*
housing: *a serious housing shortage*
lodgings: *At the moment the house provides lodgings for Oxford students*
quarters: *the officers' quarters*
see also **space**

accompany *verb* **1** to go somewhere with someone: *Children must be accompanied by an adult*
conduct *formal*: *He asked if he might conduct us to the ball*
escort: *They were escorted by police to their plane*
go with: *I haven't asked my friend to go with me yet*
usher: *I ushered him into the office*
2 to occur with something: *severe pain accompanied by fever*
come with: *Stress comes with this job*
go together with: *Poverty and illiteracy go together with high birth rates*
see also **guide**

accomplish *verb* to manage to do something: *If we'd all work together, I think we'd accomplish our goal*
achieve: *Achieving our aims makes us feel good*
bring about: *the only way to bring about political change*
complete: *She has just completed her first novel*
do: *Have you done it yet?*
fulfil: *All the necessary conditions were fulfilled*
manage: *40% of children managed the required standard in reading*
see also **achieve, carry out, fulfil**

accomplished *see* **able, capable, practical, proficient, skilful, skilled**

accomplishment *see* **achievement, act, action, qualification**

accord see agree, understanding

account see bill, note, report, statement, story

accountability see blame

accumulate see collect, concentrate, gather, stockpile

accurate adjective correct to a detailed level: Quartz watches are very accurate

correct: The correct answers can be found at the bottom of the page

exact: an exact copy

faithful: a faithful translation

precise: precise sales figures

right: That clock never tells the right time

strict: He has never been a playboy in the strict sense of the word

true: a true account of what happened

see also correct, exact, faithful, precise, right, strict, true

accurately see exactly

accuse verb to charge someone with doing something wrong: He accused her of having an affair

blame: The police blamed the explosion on terrorists

censure: The Stock Exchange took the unusual step of censuring him in public

charge: Police have charged Mr Smith with murder

cite: He was banned for 30 days after being cited for foul play

denounce: He publicly denounced government nuclear policy

see also blame

accustomed adjective used to something: The manager has become accustomed to abuse of late

adapted: The camel's feet, well adapted for dry sand, are useless on mud

familiar: He was very familiar with contemporary music

used: I'm used to having my sleep interrupted

see also usual

ace see expert

ache see long, pain

ache for see be dying for

achieve verb to gain by hard work or ability: She has achieved her best tournament result for years

accomplish: halfway towards accomplishing an important career goal

carry out: debate about how such reforms should be carried out

complete: The commission completed this task in March

do: I have done what I came here to do

fulfil: The army has fulfilled its objective

perform: He has not performed his administrative duties properly

see also accomplish, carry out, fulfil, gain, win

achievement noun something which someone has succeeded in doing: His presence here is an achievement in itself

accomplishment: The list of her accomplishments is staggering

deed: His heroic deeds were celebrated in every corner of India

exploit: His wartime exploits were later made into a TV series

feat: A racing car is an extraordinary feat of engineering

see also act, action, qualification

aching see painful, tender

acid see bitter, sour

acknowledge see accept, admit, confess, grant, recognize

acknowledgment see confession, reaction

acquaintance see contact

acquainted with see aware of, familiar

acquire verb to get something: I have recently acquired a digital camera

attain: students who attain the

required grades
gain: *He gained valuable experience from the job*
get: *My video's broken – I'll have to get a new one*
obtain: *I couldn't obtain a ticket at any price*
pick up: *You can pick up some real bargains at the January sales*
procure: *It was still difficult to procure food and fuel*
secure: *The team have secured a place in the semi-finals*
see also **buy, earn, gain, get, obtain, possess, secure**

acquit *see* **clear**
acquittal *see* **forgiveness**
acrid *see* **bitter**
acrimonious *see* **bitter**
across *see* **discover**

act *verb* **1** to do something: *The bank acted properly in the best interests of the depositors*
function: *All the computer systems functioned properly*
operate: *In the first half he operated effectively in defence*
perform: *He performed well in a World Cup match last summer*
work: *All sides will work towards a political solution*
2 to perform in a play or film: *He acted in 91 films altogether*
act out: *It was made using real people to act out the scene*
perform: *She performed the role on television twice*
play: *He plays agent Lillian Scully in a spoof of The X-Files*
play the part of: *She agreed to play the part of Evita*
portray: *His mean, moody looks are perfect for the cynical anti-hero he portrays*
▷ *noun* **3** a single thing someone does: *an act of disloyalty to the King*

accomplishment: *Winning the tournament would be an incredible accomplishment*
achievement: *She was honoured for her achievements as a filmmaker*
deed: *forgotten deeds of heroism*
feat: *an outstanding feat of athleticism*
undertaking: *Organizing the show has been a massive undertaking*
see also **appear, behave, conduct yourself, law, perform**

act against *see* **counteract**
act on *see* **affect**
act out *see* **act**
act towards *see* **treat**

action *noun* **1** the process of doing something: *He had to take evasive action to avoid being hit*
activity: *the electrical activity of the brain*
operation: *It is quite a tricky operation*
process: *the peace process*
2 something that is done: *He did not like his actions questioned*
accomplishment: *sporting accomplishments*
achievement: *If we can win the league it will be a great achievement for me*
deed: *daring and heroic deeds*
exploit: *the stories of his wartime exploits*
feat: *prodigious feats of engineering*
see also **activity, case, fight**

active *adjective* **1** full of energy: *Having an active child around the house can be exhausting*
energetic: *an energetic, happy young girl*
lively: *a lively and attractive teenager*
restless: *On Christmas Eve the kids are too restless to sleep*
sprightly: *a small, sprightly 60-year-old*

vivacious: He was very vivacious and great fun to work with

2 busy and hardworking: people who are active in local politics

busy: My husband lived a full and busy life

engaged: The contenders are now fully engaged in their campaigns

enthusiastic: As a student he was an enthusiastic member of the Communist party

hardworking: a team of hardworking and dedicated volunteers

industrious: It is a happy and industrious community

involved: She is heavily involved in local fundraising projects

occupied: A busy social life will keep you fully occupied in February

see also **alive**, **busy**, **healthy**, **lively**, **vital**

activist see **fanatic**

activity noun **1** a situation in which lots of things are happening: There is an extraordinary level of activity in the office

action: a film full of action and excitement

bustle: the hustle and bustle of a busy hospital

energy: I love the energy you find in big cities

liveliness: a restaurant with a wonderful atmosphere of liveliness

2 something you do for pleasure: sports and other leisure activities

hobby: My hobby is birdwatching

interest: Amongst his many interests are angling and painting

pastime: You need a more active pastime than playing computer games

pursuit: I like art, cooking and outdoor pursuits

see also **action**, **bustle**, **excitement**, **exercise**, **interest**, **pastime**

actual adjective real, rather than imaginary or guessed at: That is the official figure: the actual figure is much higher

authentic: music played on authentic medieval instruments

genuine: a store selling genuine army clothing

realistic: a realistic picture of Dublin life

true: The film is based on a true story

verified: verified reports of serious human rights violations

see also **precise**, **real**

actually see **really**

acute adjective **1** severe or intense: an acute shortage of supplies

critical: suffering from a critical illness

extreme: a crippling disease which causes extreme pain

grave: His country faces grave problems

great: He died in great agony

intense: I felt an intense loneliness

serious: It increases the risk of serious injuries

severe: Nuts can trigger off a severe allergic reaction

2 very intelligent: an acute mind

alert: He is old, but he has a very quick and alert mind

astute: He has a remarkably astute brain

bright: You don't need to be very bright to figure that one out

keen: a competent economist with a keen intellect

perceptive: a perceptive analysis of the situation

quick: a child with an enquiring mind and a quick intelligence

sharp: His gentle manner disguised a sharp mind

shrewd: He demonstrated a shrewd understanding of human nature

see also **brilliant**, **extreme**, **grave**,

intelligent, intense, perceptive, serious, severe, uncommon, violent

ad see **advertisement**

adage see **saying**

adamant see **firm**

adapt *verb* to alter for a new use: *Shelves were built to adapt the library for use as an office*

adjust: *He had to adjust the seat*

alter: *The government has altered the rules*

change: *The law needs to be changed*

convert: *a table that converts into an ironing board*

modify: *Our workshop is busy modifying the tanks for desert conditions*
see also **fit**

adaptable see **flexible**

adapted see **accustomed**

add *verb* **1** to put something with something else: *Add the grated cheese to the sauce*

attach: *Don't forget to attach the completed entry form*

augment: *a way to augment the family income*

supplement: *I suggest supplementing your diet with vitamin A*

2 to combine numbers or quantities: *Banks add all the interest and other charges together*

add up: *adding up calories on a calculator*

count up: *They counted up all the hours the villagers worked*

total: *They will compete for prizes totalling nearly £300*

add to see **augment, enlarge, extend, supplement**

add up see **add, count**

add up to see **total**

added see **extra, more**

addiction see **habit**

addition *noun* something that has

been added to something else: *recent additions to their range of cars*

increase: *a substantial increase in workload*

supplement: *a supplement to their basic pension*
see also **extra, supplement**

additional see **extra, more**

address see **lecture, speech, talk**

adept see **capable, expert, proficient, skilful**

adequate *adjective* enough in amount or quality for a purpose: *an adequate diet*

acceptable: *a company which offers an acceptable benefits package*

ample: *You've had ample time to discuss this matter*

enough: *enough money to live on*

satisfactory: *a satisfactory bid for the company*

sufficient: *One teaspoon of salt should be sufficient*
see also **acceptable, all right, decent, satisfactory, sufficient, tolerable**

adequately see **well**

adhere see **stick**

adhere to see **obey**

adherent see **fan, supporter**

adhesive see **sticky**

adjacent see **near, next**

adjacent to see **beside, near**

adjoining see **near, next**

adjourn see **postpone**

adjust see **adapt**

adjustment see **correction**

administer *verb* **1** to be responsible for managing something: *people who administer large companies*

be in charge of: *Who is in charge of this division?*

command: *Who would command the troops in the event of war?*

control: *He controls the largest publishing house in the country*

direct: Christopher will direct day-to-day operations

manage: Within two years he was managing the shop

run: This is no way to run a business

supervise: the men who supervised the project

2 to inflict or impose something on someone: He administered most of the blows

carry out: You are not authorized to carry out disciplinary action

deal: His attacker dealt him a severe blow to the face

dispense: They have set up military courts to dispense swift justice

execute: She leapt up and executed a spinning kick to his head

impose: The judge had no choice but to impose a death sentence

inflict: Inflicting punishment to stop crime is not the answer

perform: He had to perform emergency surgery

see also **control, handle, rule, run**

administration see **bureaucracy, management**

admirable see **fine**

admirably see **well**

admiration noun a feeling of great liking and respect: I have always had the greatest admiration for him

appreciation: gifts presented to them in appreciation of their work

approval: His son had an obsessive drive to gain his father's approval

esteem: Their public esteem has never been lower

regard: He has always been held in high regard

respect: We all have so much respect for her

see also **approval, esteem, respect, worship**

admire verb to like and respect someone or something: All those who

knew him will admire him for his work

appreciate: the need for children to appreciate their mother tongue

look up to: A lot of the younger girls look up to you

respect: I want him to respect me as a career woman

value: She genuinely values his opinion

see also **appreciate, approve, praise, respect**

admirer see **fan**

admission see **confession, entrance**

admit verb **1** to agree that something is true: The driver admitted to falling asleep at the wheel

accept: I accepted the truth of all that Nicola had told me

acknowledge: Belatedly the government has acknowledged the problem

grant: The magistrates granted that the RSPCA was justified in bringing the action

2 to allow to enter: He was admitted to university after the war

accept: Stephen was accepted into the family

let in: Turnstile operators were accused of letting in fans without tickets

receive: He was received into the priesthood

take in: The monastery has taken in 26 refugees

see also **confess, grant**

adolescent see **young**

adorable see **lovable**

adoration see **love, worship**

adore see **like, love, worship**

adored see **beloved**

adoring see **fond**

adorn see **decorate**

adornment see **ornament**

adrift see **lost**

adulation see **flattery, worship**

adult noun a grown-up person:
Becoming a father signified he was
now an adult

grown-up: Las Vegas is the ultimate
playground for grown-ups

man: He is now a man of 42

woman: A woman of 38
see also **mature**

adulterous see **unfaithful**

advance verb **1** to move forward or
develop: Rebel forces are advancing
on the capital

make inroads: They have made
impressive inroads in the movie
business

press on: Poland pressed on with
economic reform

proceed: He proceeded down the
spiral stairway

progress: the ability to progress from
one step to the next
▷ noun **2** progress in something:
scientific advance

breakthrough: a breakthrough in
cancer treatment

development: the development
of the car

gain: a gain of nearly 10%

progress: signs of progress in his
reading

step: the first step towards peace
see also **develop, early, gain, go,
improve, improvement, loan,
payment, proceed, produce,
progress, raise**

advance warning see **notice**

advanced see **sophisticated**

advantage noun a more favourable
position or state: We have a
competitive advantage

ascendancy: The extremists are
gaining ascendancy

benefit: For maximum benefit use
your treatment every day

dominance: the battle for high-street
dominance

superiority: military superiority
see also **beauty, benefit, merit,
value, virtue**

advantageous see **beneficial,
favourable, helpful**

advent see **appearance**

adventure see **excitement,
experience**

adventurous see **bold, daring**

adversary see **competitor, enemy,
rival**

adversity see **hardship, misfortune**

advert see **advertisement**

advertise verb to present
something to the public in order to
sell it: Bookmakers cannot advertise
on television

plug informal: If I hear another actor
plugging his latest book I will scream

promote: What are you doing to
promote your new film?

publicize: He never publicized his
plans

push: a publisher who knows how to
push a product
see also **announce, promote,
publicize**

advertisement noun a public
announcement to sell or publicize
something: She recently placed an
advertisement in the local newspaper

ad informal: an ad for a minicab
company

advert British informal: She appeared
in a coffee advert

commercial: She has turned down a
small fortune to do TV commercials

notice: The request is published in
notices in today's national newspapers

plug informal: a shameless plug for
his new film
see also **announcement, notice**

advertising see **publicity**

advice noun a suggestion as to what
to do: Take my advice and stay away
from him!

counsel formal: He had always been able to count on her wise counsel

drum Australian informal: What's the drum on this?

guidance: The nation looks to them for guidance

opinion: You should seek a medical opinion

suggestion: She made suggestions as to how I could improve my diet
see also **help, hint**

advise verb **1** to offer advice to someone: The minister advised him to leave as soon as possible

caution: The researchers caution against drawing general conclusions from this study

counsel: My advisers counselled me to do nothing

recommend: We strongly recommend reporting the incident to the police

suggest: He suggested a visit to the Cézanne exhibition

urge: We urge that vigorous action be taken immediately

2 to notify someone: I think it best that I advise you of my decision to retire

inform: My daughter informed me that she was pregnant

make known: The details will be made known by the end of August

notify: The skipper notified the coastguard of the tragedy
see also **brief, inform, notify, suggest**

adviser noun a person whose job is to give advice: The President and his advisers spent the day in meetings

aide: a former aide to Ronald Reagan

consultant: a management consultant

guru: He became Britain's modern design guru

mentor: He is my friend and musical mentor

tutor: my college tutor

advocate verb to publicly support a plan or course of action: Mr Smith advocates corporal punishment for young offenders

back: The newspaper is backing the residents' campaign

champion: He passionately champions our cause

endorse: We are reluctant to endorse such drastic measures

favour: judges who favour the death penalty

promote: He promoted the idea of Scottish independence

recommend: I can't recommend such a course of action

support: people who supported his policies

uphold: We uphold the capitalist free economy
see also **back, champion, defender, lawyer, suggest, supporter**

afar see **far**

affable see **pleasant**

affair noun **1** an event or series of events: This business has really upset me

business: This business has really upset me

event: A wedding should be a joyous event

issue: a major political issue

matter: I never interfere in these business matters

question: the difficult question of unemployment

situation: The whole situation is now under control

subject: a subject which had worried him for some time

2 a secret and romantic relationship: He had an affair with someone he met on holiday

fling: We had a brief fling, but it was nothing serious

liaison: He denied that he had a sexual liaison with his secretary

relationship: She went public on her relationship with a Hollywood star

romance: Our company discourages office romances

see also **business, concern, event, experience, matter, occasion, relationship, undertaking**

affect verb to influence something or someone: More than 7 million people have been affected by the drought

act on: This drug acts very fast on the central nervous system

alter: The earth's climate appears to have been altered by pollution

change: It was to change the course of my life

impinge on: My private life does not impinge on my professional life

see also **concern, infect, influence, move, touch**

affected see **pretentious**

affecting see **moving, touching**

affection noun a feeling of fondness for someone or something: She thought of him with affection

attachment: Mother and child form a close attachment

fondness: his fondness for cats

liking: a liking for flashy cars

love: My love for all my children is unconditional

warmth: He greeted us both with warmth and affection

see also **attachment, friendship, love**

affectionate adjective full of fondness for someone: She gave me a long affectionate hug

caring: a loving, caring husband

fond: She gave him a fond smile

loving: The children were very loving to me

tender: a tender kiss

see also **fond, friendly, loving, tender, warm**

affiliation see **association, connection, link, tie**

affinity see **relationship, tie**

affirm see **declare, state**

affirmation see **declaration**

affirmative see **favourable**

affix see **attach, connect**

affliction see **disorder, evil, illness**

affluence see **abundance, luxury, wealth**

affluent see **rich, wealthy**

afford see **spare**

affront see **insult, offend**

afraid adjective scared of something unpleasant happening: I was afraid of the other boys

apprehensive: People are still terribly apprehensive about the future

fearful: Bankers were fearful of a world banking crisis

frightened: She was frightened of flying

nervous: Emotionally, he left me a wreck, nervous of everyone

scared: I was too scared to move

see also **frightened**

afresh see **again**

after adverb at a later time: Shortly after, police arrested five suspects

afterwards: He was taken to hospital but died soon afterwards

following: We shared so much, not only during the war, but in the many years following

later: He resigned ten years later

subsequently: She subsequently became honorary secretary

afterwards see **after, next**

again adverb happening one more time: He kissed her again

afresh: The couple moved abroad to start life afresh

anew: She's ready to start anew

once more: Rage overcame him

once more

against *preposition* **1** in opposition to: *I am against animal cruelty*

averse to: *He's not averse to a drink*

hostile to: *countries that were once hostile to South Africa*

in opposition to: *radio stations set up in opposition to the BBC*

versus: *Portugal versus England*

2 in preparation for or in case of something: *precautions against fire*

in anticipation of: *His school was one of several which closed in anticipation of Arctic conditions*

in expectation of: *The hotel was being renovated in expectation of a tourist boom*

in preparation for: *The army massed troops and guns in preparation for a counter-attack*

agenda *see* **programme**

agent *see* **representative**

aggregate *see* **total, whole**

aggressive *adjective* full of hostility and violence: *These fish are very aggressive*

hostile: *The prisoner eyed him in a hostile silence*

quarrelsome: *He had been a wild boy and a quarrelsome young man*

see also **fierce, pushy**

aggrieved *see* **hurt, resentful**

agile *adjective* able to move quickly and easily: *He is as agile as a cat*

lithe: *He is a strong young gymnast*

nimble: *He built his career around quick reflexes and nimble footwork*

sprightly: *She is alert and sprightly despite her 85 years*

supple: *She is as supple as a dancer*

agitate *verb* **1** to campaign energetically for something: *They began to agitate for better conditions*

campaign: *an organization which campaigns for better consumer rights*

demonstrate: *marchers*

demonstrating for political reform

protest: *country dwellers who were protesting for the right to hunt*

push: *Some board members are pushing for the merger*

2 to worry or distress someone: *Everything she said was beginning to agitate me*

bother: *It really bothers me when you talk like that*

distress: *sudden noises which distressed the animals*

disturb: *These dreams disturb me for days afterwards*

trouble: *Are you troubled by thoughts of the future?*

upset: *The whole incident upset me dreadfully*

worry: *I didn't want to worry you with my own problems*

see also **disturb, excite, shake, trouble, upset**

agitated *see* **excited, uneasy, upset**

agitation *see* **excitement, frenzy, fuss**

agony *see* **hell, pain**

agree *verb* **1** to have the same opinion as someone: *So we both agree there's a problem?*

assent: *I assented to the request of the publishers to write this book*

be of the same opinion: *All the other players are of the same opinion*

concur: *Four other judges concurred*

see eye to eye: *He has not always seen eye to eye with his brother*

2 to match or be the same as something: *His second statement agrees with facts as stated by the other witness*

accord: *I cannot support policies that no longer accord with my principles*

conform: *It doesn't conform with current building regulations*

match: *Attendances do not match the*

ticket sales
square: Does that explanation square with the facts?
tally: The figures don't seem to tally
see also **correspond, match, settle, submit, suit**

agree to *see* **accept**

agree with *see* **side with**

agreeable *adjective* **1** pleasant or enjoyable: I found it a most agreeable experience
delightful: I've had a delightful time
enjoyable: an enjoyable meal
lovely: I hope you have a lovely holiday
nice: It would be very nice to get away from it all for a few days
pleasant: This restaurant offers good food in pleasant surroundings
pleasurable: the pleasurable task of deciding where to go on holiday
2 willing to allow or do something: She said she was agreeable to this plan
game: Are you game to try something a little bit different?
happy: I'm happy to go along with what everyone else thinks
prepared: Would you be prepared to queue for hours for a ticket?
ready: I'm ready to take over if he resigns
willing: Are you willing to take part in a survey?
see also **pleasant, ready, willing**

agreement *noun* a decision reached by two or more people: The two countries have signed agreements on fishing and oil
arrangement: Eventually we came to an arrangement that suited us both
contract: She has signed an exclusive solo-album contract
deal *informal*: The company recently won a five-year deal to build runways
pact: He ruled out any formal pact with the government

settlement: She accepted an out-of-court settlement of £4000
treaty: negotiations over a 1992 treaty on global warming
see also **approval, bond, understanding**

ahead *see* **in front**

ahead of time *see* **early**

aid *see* **benefit, encourage, help**

aide *see* **adviser, assistant, helper**

ailing *see* **ill, sick, unhealthy, unwell**

ailment *see* **illness**

aim *verb* **1** to plan to do something: The company aims to sign 1 million customers within five years
aspire: people who aspire to public office
attempt: He will attempt to win the title for the second year running
intend: I intend to remarry
plan: Mr Beach was planning to sue over injuries he received
propose: And where do you propose building such a huge thing?
strive: He strives hard to keep himself very fit
▷ *noun* **2** what someone intends to achieve: Our main aim is to offer a superior product
ambition: His ambition is to sail round the world
goal: I have to keep setting goals for myself
intention: It was always my intention to stay in Italy
objective: His objective was to play golf and win
plan: His plan was to acquire paintings by the best artists in Italy
target: his target of 20 goals this season
see also **cause, focus, goal, intend, intention, mean, object, point, purpose, seek**

aimed *see* **calculated**

aimless *see* **random**

aimlessly see **at random**

air see **look, show**

aisle see **passage**

ajar see **open**

akin see **like**

alarm noun **1** a feeling of fear: *The cat sprang back in alarm*
anxiety: *anxiety about crime*
apprehension: *I tensed every muscle in my body in apprehension*
fright: *The birds smashed into the top of their cages in fright*
nervousness: *I smiled warmly so he wouldn't see my nervousness*
panic: *There was panic in the streets of the capital*
scare: *Despite the scare there are no plans to withdraw the drug*
2 a device used to warn people of something: *a burglar alarm*
distress signal: *The pilot was trying to send a distress signal when the aircraft crashed*
siren: *a police siren*
warning: *A second air raid warning sounded over the capital*
▷ verb **3** to fill with fear: *We could not see what had alarmed him*
distress: *He is very distressed by what happened*
frighten: *The future frightens me*
panic: *He was panicked by his wife's behaviour*
scare: *Horses scare me*
startle: *startled by a gunshot*
unnerve: *Investors had been unnerved by the country's ailing stockmarket*
see also **acute, frighten, horror, panic, scare, warning**

alarmed see **frightened**

alarming see **frightening, scary, serious**

alcohol noun a drink that can make you drunk: *There wasn't even any alcohol at the party*

booze *informal*: *clutching a bottle of booze*
drink: *Too much drink is bad for you*
grog *Australian, New Zealand informal*: *They demanded a bottle of grog*
liquor: *I could smell liquor on his breath*
spirits: *a voluntary ban on advertising spirits on TV*

alcoholic see **drunk**

alert adjective **1** paying full attention: *apprehended by alert security staff*
attentive: *an attentive audience*
observant: *an observant policeman*
on guard: *on guard against the threat of invasion*
vigilant: *letter bombs intercepted by vigilant post office staff*
wary: *He kept a wary eye on the dog as he passed the gate*
▷ verb **2** to warn of danger: *I was hoping he'd alert the police*
forewarn: *The guide had forewarned me what to expect*
inform: *The patient was not properly informed of the risks*
notify: *The passengers were notified of the bomb threat*
warn: *They warned him of the dangers of sailing alone*
see also **acute, alive, astute, scare, sharp, warn, warning**

alien see **strange, unfamiliar**

alight see **land**

alike adjective **1** similar in some way: *You and your father are so alike*
analogous: *a ritual analogous to those of primitive cultures*
close: *a creature close in appearance to a panther*
identical: *Nearly all the houses were identical*
similar: *These two wines are very similar in taste*
the same: *products which are almost*

the same in every respect

▷ adverb **2** in a similar way: *I punish all my pupils alike if they misbehave*

equally: *Democracy calls for all people to be treated equally*

in the same way: *He speaks in the same way to his boss as to his own employees*

similarly: *All the children were dressed similarly*

uniformly: *The rules apply uniformly to everyone*

see also **like, same, similar**

alive adjective **1** having life: *They kept her alive on a life support machine*

animate: *animate beings*

breathing: *Not only is he still breathing, but he lives right here in New York*

living: *The blue whale is the largest living thing on the planet*

2 lively and active: *I never expected to feel so alive in my life again*

active: *half an hour's physical activity, five times a week, will keep you active*

alert: *A brisk walk will make you feel more alert*

animated: *He becomes animated when talking about his work*

energetic: *a vital and energetic man*

full of life: *She was so chatty and full of life*

lively: *Cheryl was a very lively and attractive girl*

vivacious: *a vivacious personality*

see also **live**

all pronoun the whole of something: *Why did you have to go and say all that?*

each: *Each of us received a free gift*

every one: *Every one of you must take a share of the blame*

everything: *Sit down and tell me everything*

the whole amount: *Have you paid the whole amount of the fine?*

the (whole) lot: *The whole lot of you are under arrest*

see also **whole**

allegation see **claim**

allege see **claim**

alleged see **supposed**

alliance see **party**

allocate see **allow, distribute, grant**

allocation see **grant**

allot see **allow, distribute**

allotment see **share**

allow verb **1** to permit someone to do something: *Smoking will not be allowed*

approve: *The Housing Minister approved the building of the flats*

authorize: *authorized to carry weapons*

let: *They won't let her leave the country*

permit: *Unauthorized personnel are not permitted to enter*

stand for: *I won't stand for it any more*

tolerate: *I won't tolerate sloppiness*

2 to set aside for a particular purpose: *Allow four hours for the paint to dry*

allocate: *an efficient method of allocating resources*

allot: *We were allotted just 15 minutes*

assign: *the full amount of economic aid assigned for the year*

grant: *Funding had been granted for the project*

set aside: *money set aside for education*

see also **grant, let, permit, sanction**

allowance see **grant**

alloy see **blend, mixture**

all right adjective acceptable: *It was all right but nothing special*

acceptable: *We've made an acceptable start, but it could have been better*

adequate: Our accommodation was adequate

average: I was only average academically

fair: The overall standard of the entries was fair

okay or **OK** informal: The prices here are okay

see also **acceptable, okay, safe, satisfactory, sound**

allude see **refer**

allude to see **mention**

allure see **charm**

allusion see **mention**

ally see **assistant, connect, supporter**

almost adverb very nearly: Over the past decade their wages have almost doubled

about: I was about nine at the time

approximately: The family owns approximately 8% of the company

close to: He spent close to 30 years in prison

nearly: The beach was very nearly empty

not quite: It's more than a hill but not quite a mountain

practically: I've known him practically all my life

see also **about, barely, nearly**

alone adjective not with other people or things: He was all alone in the middle of the hall

detached: a 'counter-culture' detached from the rest of the world

isolated: Talking things over in a group meant none of us felt isolated

separate: They were kept separate from the other prisoners

single: I get depressed on Valentine's Day because I'm still single

see also **lonely, on your own**

alongside see **beside, near**

aloof see **cold, distant, impersonal, remote, unfriendly**

aloud adverb out loud: Our father read aloud to us

audibly: Hugh sighed audibly

out loud: I tried not to laugh out loud

also adverb in addition: He is also an army doctor

as well: She published historical novels as well

besides: You get to sample lots of baked things and take home masses of cookies besides

furthermore: Furthermore, they claim that any such interference is completely ineffective

into the bargain: The machine can play ordinary cassettes into the bargain

moreover: They have accused the government of corruption. Moreover, they have named names

too: I was there too

alter see **adapt, affect, change, transform, vary**

alteration see **change, variation**

altercation see **disagreement, row, squabble**

alternate see **vary**

alternative see **choice**

although see **but**

always adverb all the time or forever: She's always moaning

continually: Malcolm was continually changing his mind

every time: You can't get it right every time

forever: He was forever attempting to arrange deals

invariably: Their teamwork was invariably good

perpetually: The two groups are perpetually at loggerheads

amalgamate see **combine, mix**

amalgamation see **blend, combination, mixture, union**

amass see **gather, stockpile**

amaze verb to surprise greatly: He

amazed us by his knowledge of Welsh history

astonish: I was astonished by his stupidity

astound: I am astounded at the comments made by the Chief Superintendant

shock: She was shocked by the appalling news

stagger: He was staggered by the sheer size of the crowd

stun: Many cinema-goers were stunned by the film's tragic end

surprise: We'll solve the case ourselves and surprise everyone

see also **surprise**

amazement noun complete surprise: Much to my amazement, he arrived on time

astonishment: They looked at each other in astonishment

shock: I am still getting over the shock of winning

surprise: To my surprise, I found I liked it

wonder: Cross shook his head in wonder

see also **surprise**

amazing adjective very surprising or remarkable: some of the most amazing stunts you're ever likely to see

astonishing: an astonishing display of physical strength

astounding: The results are quite astounding

staggering: a staggering 17% leap in sales

startling: startling new evidence

stunning: a stunning piece of news

surprising: A surprising number of customers order the same sandwich every day

see also **extraordinary, incredible, wonderful**

ambiguous see **uncertain, unclear**

ambition see **aim, dream, drive, hope**

ambitious see **pushy**

amble see **ramble**

amend see **correct, reform, revise**

amendment see **correction, reform**

amends see **compensation**

amiable see **friendly, pleasant, warm**

amicable see **favourable**

amid see **among**

amidst see **among**

amok see **on the rampage**

among preposition **1** surrounded by: The bike lay among piles of chains and pedals

amid: a tiny bungalow amid clusters of trees

amidst: His parents were found dead amidst the wreckage of the plane

in the middle of: a tiny island in the middle of the Pacific

in the thick of: a restaurant built on stilts in the thick of a vast mangrove swamp

surrounded by: surrounded by bodyguards

2 between more than two: The money will be divided among seven charities

between: Proceeds from the auction will be shared between the artists

to each of: £2,000 to each of the five winners

amorous see **romantic**

amount noun how much there is of something: I still do a certain amount of work for them

expanse: a vast expanse of grassland

quantity: vast quantities of food

volume: the sheer volume of traffic and accidents

see also **figure, measure, price, quantity**

amount to see **total**

ample adjective of an amount: more than enough: There is ample space for *a good-sized kitchen*

abundant: *providing abundant food for local wildlife*

enough: *Do you have enough money for a taxi home?*

plenty of: *You've had plenty of time to make up your mind*

sufficient: *The police have sufficient evidence to charge him*

see also **abundant, adequate, generous, handsome, plentiful, spacious, sufficient**

amply see **well**

amuse see **delight, entertain, please**

amuse oneself see **play**

amusement see **entertainment, fun, pleasure**

amusing see **funny, witty**

analogous see **alike, like, similar**

analogy see **resemblance, similarity**

analyse see **examine, research**

analysis see **examination, research, review**

anarchy see **riot**

ancestor noun a person from whom someone is descended: *He could trace his ancestors back 700 years*

forebear: *our Victorian forebears*

forefather: *the land of their forefathers*

ancestry see **origin, stock**

ancient see **former, past**

anecdote see **story**

anew see **again**

angel see **dear**

anger noun **1** extreme annoyance: *She vented her anger at the umpire*

fury: *She screamed, her face distorted in fury*

outrage: *The decisions provoked outrage from human rights groups*

rage: *An intense rage was burning inside her*

wrath: *He incurred the wrath of the referee*

▷ verb **2** to make someone angry: *remarks which will anger his critics*

enrage: *He enraged the government by renouncing the agreement*

infuriate: *Peter's presence had infuriated Gordon*

outrage: *Customers are outraged by the bank's soaring profits*

see also **irritate, provoke, rage, resentment**

angle see **tilt**

angry adjective very annoyed: *He gets angry when I'm late*

cross: *She was rather cross about having to trail across London*

enraged: *The enraged crowd stoned the car, then set it on fire*

furious: *He is furious at the way his wife has been treated*

mad informal: *I'm pretty mad about it, I can tell you*

see also **cross, mad, resentful**

anguish see **hell, pain**

animal noun a living creature: *He was attacked by wild animals*

beast: *the threat our ancestors faced from wild beasts*

creature: *sea creatures*

animate see **alive, excite, live**

animated see **alive, energetic, lively**

animation see **spirit**

animosity noun a feeling of strong dislike towards someone: *There is no animosity between these two players*

antagonism: *a history of antagonism between the two sides*

antipathy: *our growing antipathy towards our manager*

dislike: *She looked at him with dislike*

hatred: *He didn't bother to conceal his hatred towards my mother*

hostility: *unacceptable hostility toward minority groups*

ill will: *He didn't bear anyone any ill will*

malice: There was no malice in her voice

resentment: There is growing resentment towards newcomers
see also **dislike, hate, hatred, hostility, resentment**

ankle-biter see **baby, child**

annex see **seize**

annihilate see **destroy**

annihilation see **destruction**

anniversary see **festival**

announce verb to make known something publicly: He will announce tonight that he is resigning from office

advertise: He did not want to advertise his presence in the town

make known: Details will be made known tomorrow

proclaim: He loudly proclaimed his innocence

reveal: They were now free to reveal the truth

tell: She was relieved that she'd finally told the full story
see also **declare, reveal**

announcement noun a statement giving information about something: There has been no formal announcement by either government

advertisement: an advertisement placed in the local newspaper

broadcast: In a broadcast on state radio the government announced its plans

bulletin: At 3.30pm a bulletin was released announcing the decision

declaration: a public declaration of support

report: Local press reports estimate that at least sixteen people have died

statement: a short statement by her solicitors
see also **statement, word**

annoy verb to irritate or displease someone: Try making a note of the things which annoy you

bother: I didn't think it would bother me so much to see Brian again

displease: Not wishing to displease her, he avoided answering the question

get on someone's nerves informal: That song gets on my nerves

hack off British, New Zealand slang: This will just hack people off more

hassle informal: Then my husband started hassling me

irritate: The flippancy in her voice seemed to irritate him

plague: We were plagued by mosquitoes

vex: Cassandra was vexed at not having noticed it herself
see also **bother, irritate, pester, provoke**

annoyance noun **1** a feeling of irritation: He made no secret of his annoyance

displeasure: She voiced her displeasure at her treatment

irritation: He tried not to let his irritation show

2 something that causes irritation: Snoring can be more than an annoyance

bore: It's a bore to be off sick

drag informal: A dry sandwich is a drag to eat

nuisance: He could be a bit of a nuisance when he was drunk

pain informal: The peacocks are a pain – beautiful but noisy

pain in the neck informal: Traffic jams are a pain in the neck

pest: He climbed on the table, pulled my hair, and was generally a pest
see also **bother, nuisance**

annoyed see **cross**

annul see **abolish, cancel**

anoint see **bless**

another see **different**

answer verb **1** to reply to someone: I knew Ben was lying when he *answered me*

reply: *He replied that this was absolutely impossible*

respond: *'Mind your manners, lady!' I responded*

retort: *Was he afraid, he was asked. 'Afraid of what?' he retorted*

▷ noun 2 a reply given to someone: *Without waiting for an answer, he turned and went in through the door*

reply: *I called out a challenge but there was no reply*

response: *There has been no response to his remarks from the government*

retort: *His sharp retort clearly made an impact*

see also **meet, reaction, reply**

antagonism *see* **animosity, conflict, hostility**

antagonist *see* **enemy, rival**

antagonistic *see* **hostile, unfriendly**

anticipate *see* **expect**

anticipated *see* **likely**

antipathy *see* **animosity, dislike, hatred**

antiquated *see* **old-fashioned, out of date**

antiquity *see* **the past**

antiseptic *see* **clean, sterile**

antithesis *see* **foil, opposite**

anxiety noun nervousness or worry: *our growing anxiety about their safety*

apprehension: *a feeling of apprehension about the future*

concern: *growing concern about the environment*

fear: *His fears might be groundless*

misgiving: *She had some misgivings about what she had been asked to do*

nervousness: *I smiled, trying to hide my nervousness*

unease: *a deep sense of unease about the coming interview*

worry: *a major source of worry to us all*

see also **alarm, burden, care,**

concern, strain, stress, worry

anxious noun nervous or worried: *He admitted he was still anxious about the situation*

apprehensive: *Their families are apprehensive about the trip*

bothered: *I'm still bothered about what she's going to say*

concerned: *a phone call from a concerned neighbour*

fearful: *We are all fearful for the security of our jobs*

nervous: *I still get nervous before a visit to the dentist's*

troubled: *He was troubled about his son's lifestyle*

uneasy: *an uneasy feeling that something was wrong*

worried: *His parents are worried about his lack of progress*

see also **eager, nervous, tense, uneasy, worried**

any minute now *see* **soon**

apart from *see* **except**

apartment *see* **flat**

apathetic adjective not interested in anything: *apathetic about politics*

cool: *The idea met with a cool response*

indifferent: *People have become indifferent to the sufferings of others*

passive: *His passive attitude made things easier for me*

uninterested: *unhelpful and uninterested shop staff*

see also **uninterested**

apathy *see* **boredom**

ape *see* **copy, imitate**

apex *see* **top**

aplomb *see* **confidence**

apologetic *see* **sorry**

apologize verb to say sorry for something: *I apologize for being late*

ask forgiveness: *He fell to his knees asking for forgiveness*

beg someone's pardon: *I was*

impolite and I do beg your pardon

express regret see regret: *Mr Galloway expressed regret that he had caused any offence*

say sorry: *I wanted to say sorry to you*

appal see horrify, shock

appalling see awful, dreadful, horrible, terrible

apparatus see equipment, machine, stuff

apparent see clear, conspicuous, evident, obvious, probable, visible

apparition see ghost, spirit, vision

appeal verb 1 to make an urgent request for something: *The police appealed for witnesses to come forward*

beg: *I begged him to leave me alone*

call upon: *Frequently he was called upon to resolve conflicts*

plead: *I pleaded to be allowed to go*

request: *She had requested that the door to her room be left open*

2 to attract or interest: *The idea appealed to him*

attract: *What attracted you to research work?*

fascinate: *Classical music had fascinated him since the age of three*

interest: *It was the garden that really interested me*

please: *It pleased him to talk to her*

▷ noun 3 a formal request for something: *an appeal for peace*

petition: *The court rejected their petition*

plea: *his emotional plea for help in solving the killing*

request: *France had agreed to his request for political asylum*

see also ask, charm, interest, plead, request

appeal to see attract

appealing see attractive, cute

appear verb 1 to become visible or present: *A woman appeared at the far end of the street*

come into view: *Nearly fifty gliders came into view to the south of the plateau*

crop up informal: *Problems will crop up and hit you before you are ready*

emerge: *The postman emerged from his van soaked to the skin*

show up informal: *He failed to show up at the ceremony*

surface: *The same old problems would surface again*

turn up: *This is like waiting for a bus that never turns up*

2 to begin to exist: *small white flowers which appear in early summer*

become available: *In 1950, legal aid became available in Britain*

be invented: *The lawn mower was invented in 1830*

come into being: *Fireworks first came into being with the invention of gunpowder*

come into existence: *before our solar system came into existence*

come out: *This book first came out in 1992*

3 to take part in a show or play: *He is soon to appear in two more films*

act: *She has also been acting in a sitcom*

perform: *He is currently performing in the West End show "Grease"*

play: *He played Hamlet to packed houses*

play a part: *His ambition is to play the part of Dracula*

see also come, look, occur, seem

appearance noun 1 the time when something begins to exist: *the appearance of computer technology*

advent: *the advent of satellite and cable channels*

arrival: *the arrival of modern technologies*

coming: *the coming of the railways*

debut: *the debut of the new channel*

emergence: the emergence of pay-per-view TV
introduction: the introduction of the minimum wage
2 the way that a person looks: She used to be so fussy about her appearance
bearing: a man of iron will and military bearing
image: He urged the rest of the band to update their image
look: She is so much happier with her new look
looks: a young woman with wholesome good looks
see also **entrance, entry, front, look**

appease see **pacify**
appendix see **supplement**
appetite see **desire, taste**
appetizing see **delicious, tasty**
applaud see **praise**
appliance see **gadget, machine**
applicable see **relevant**
applicant see **candidate**
application see **effort, request, use**
applied see **practical**
apply see **spread, use**
apply to see **concern**
appoint see **employ, hire**
appointment noun **1** an arrangement to meet someone: She has an appointment with her accountant
date: I have a date with Wendy
interview: a job interview
meeting: Can we have a meeting to discuss that?
rendezvous: I had almost decided to keep my rendezvous with Tony
2 the choosing of a person to do a job: his appointment as manager
election: the election of the government in 1997
naming: the naming of the new captain
nomination: They opposed the nomination of a junior officer to the position
selection: his selection as a parliamentary candidate
3 a job: He applied for an appointment in Russia
assignment: my first assignment for The New York Times
job: He's trying for a job in the Civil Service
place: All the candidates won places on the ruling council
position: She took up a position at the Arts Council
post: He has held several senior military posts

apposite see **relevant**
appraisal see **estimate, judgment**
appraise see **judge, rate, value**
appreciable see **respectable**
appreciate verb **1** to value something highly: He appreciates fine wines
admire: All those who knew him will admire him for his work
prize: Military figures made out of lead are prized by collectors
rate highly: The four-year-old mare is rated highly by her trainer
respect: I respect his talent as a pianist
treasure: She treasures her memories of those joyous days
value: I value the work he gives me
2 to understand a situation or problem: I didn't appreciate the seriousness of it at the time
be aware of: I am well aware of the arguments on the other side
perceive: to get pupils to perceive for themselves the relationship between success and effort
realize: People don't realize how serious this is
recognize: They have been slow to recognize it as a problem

understand: They are too young to understand what is going on
see also **admire, comprehend, enjoy, grasp, like, love, realize, recognize, see, take in, understand, value**

appreciation see **admiration, gratitude, understanding**

appreciative see **grateful**

apprehend see **arrest, capture, catch, know**

apprehension see **alarm, anxiety, arrest, concern, worry**

apprehensive see **afraid, anxious, nervous, suspicious**

apprentice see **beginner**

approach see **contact, method, style, way**

approaching see **future, near**

appropriate adjective suitable or acceptable for a given situation: Jeans are not appropriate wear for work
apt: an apt title for his memoirs
correct: the importance of correct behaviour and social niceties
fitting: a fitting tribute to a great man
proper: the proper course for the court to take
suitable: a suitable location
see also **correct, fitting, proper, relevant, right, seize, steal, suitable**

approval noun 1 agreement given to something: The plan will require approval from the local authority
agreement: The clubs are seeking agreement for a provisional deal
authorization: We didn't have authorization to go
blessing: Mr Ryabov appeared to give his blessing to Mr Yeltsin's plan
endorsement: His endorsement has been fervently sought by all the main presidential candidates
permission: They cannot leave the country without permission
sanction: The King cannot enact laws without the sanction of Parliament
2 liking and admiration of a person or thing: He wanted to gain his father's approval
admiration: a strategy that is winning admiration from around the world
esteem: Their public esteem has never been lower
favour: He has won favour with a wide range of groups
praise: She is full of praise for the range of excellent services available
respect: We all have so much respect for her
see also **admiration, blessing, favour, permission, praise, sanction**

approve verb 1 to think something or someone is good: Not everyone approves of the festival
admire: I admire him for his work
favour: The opposition parties favour constitutional reform
praise: He praised the fans for their continued support
respect: I want him to respect me as a career woman
think highly of: He thought highly of his brother
2 to agree formally to something: The court approved the compensation plan
authorize: to authorize the use of military force
consent to: His parents consented to an autopsy
endorse: I can endorse their opinion wholeheartedly
permit: The doorman is not allowed to permit them entry to the film
sanction: He may now be ready to sanction the use of force
see also **allow, praise, sanction**

approved see **formal**

approving see **favourable**

approximate adjective close but not exact: We believe that an approximate figure of 20% is nearer the mark

estimated: Our estimated time of arrival is 3.30

inexact: Forecasting is an inexact science

loose: a loose translation

rough: a rough estimate
see also **broad, rough**

approximately see **about, almost**

apt see **appropriate, proper, relevant, suitable**

aptitude see **gift, head, potential, talent**

arbitrarily see **at random**

arbitrary see **random**

arbitrate see **intervene**

arc see **bend, curve**

arcane see **mysterious, obscure**

arch see **bend, curve**

archaic see **old-fashioned, out of date**

archives see **record**

arctic see **cold, frozen**

ardent adjective full of enthusiasm and passion: an ardent supporter of capital punishment

avid: an avid follower of the team

devoted: surrounded by devoted fans

enthusiastic: enthusiastic collectors of Elvis memorabilia

fervent: a fervent admirer of his

intense: his intense love of football

keen: a keen supporter of the cause

passionate: He developed a passionate interest in motor racing
see also **eager, enthusiastic, fervent, intense, keen, passionate**

ardour see **love**

arduous see **difficult, hard, stiff, tough**

area noun 1 a particular part of a place: a built-up area of the city

district: I drove around the business district

locality: All other factories in the locality went on strike in sympathy

neighbourhood: She no longer takes evening strolls around her neighbourhood

region: a remote mountainous region of Afghanistan

zone: a war zone

2 the size of a two-dimensional surface: The islands cover a total area of 625 square kilometres

expanse: a huge expanse of blue-green sea

extent: the extent of the rain forest

range: a driver's range of vision

size: a country nearly three times the size of ours
see also **field, place, region, stretch, territory**

arena see **scene**

argue verb 1 to disagree with someone in an angry way: They argued over the cost of the taxi fare

bicker: They bickered endlessly about procedure

disagree: They can communicate even when they strongly disagree

fall out informal: Mum and I used to fall out a lot

feud: feuding neighbours

fight: We're always fighting about money

quarrel: My brother quarrelled with my father

row: We started rowing about whose turn it was next

squabble: The children were squabbling over the remote control

wrangle: Delegates wrangled over the future of the organization

2 to try to prove: She argued that her client had been wrongly accused

assert: The defendants continue to assert their innocence

claim: *Statisticians claim that the book contains inaccuracies*
debate: *Parliament will debate the issue today*
maintain: *He had always maintained his innocence*
reason: *I reasoned that if he could do it, so could I*
see also **quarrel, squabble**
argument *noun* **1** an angry disagreement: *She got into an argument with one of the marchers*
barney *British, Australian, New Zealand informal*: *We had such a barney that we nearly split up*
blue *Australian slang*: *He gets into more blues with authority than I do*
clash: *clashes between police and demonstrators*
dispute: *a dispute over ticket allocation*
feud: *a two-year feud between neighbours*
fight: *We had another fight about money*
row: *Maxine and I had a terrible row*
squabble: *a family squabble over Sunday lunch*
2 a set of reasons presented for something: *There's a strong argument for lowering the price*
case: *the case for his dismissal*
grounds: *facts providing grounds for an unfair dismissal complaint*
logic: *The logic is that, without more growth, the deficit will rise*
reasoning: *the reasoning behind the decision*
see also **defence, disagreement, dispute, fight, quarrel, row, squabble**
arid see **barren, dry**
arise see **occur, result, start**
aristocrat see **noble**
aristocratic see **posh**
arm see **equip**

armistice see **peace**
aroma see **fragrance, smell**
aromatic see **fragrant, sweet**
around see **about**
arouse see **excite**
arrange *verb* **1** to make plans to do something: *Why don't you arrange to meet him later?*
fix up: *I fixed up an appointment to see her*
organize: *She organized the trip to the museum*
plan: *She planned to leave in August*
schedule: *Our appointment is scheduled for Tuesday*
2 to set things out in a particular order: *He started to arrange the books in piles*
classify: *Weathermen classify clouds into several different groups*
group: *The fact sheet is grouped into seven sections*
order: *The French order things differently*
organize: *He began to organize his materials*
sort: *The students are sorted into three ability groups*
see also **classify, determine, fit, group, lay, organize, plan, position, set, settle, sort, stage**
arranged see **set**
arrangement see **agreement, layout, sequence, structure, system**
array see **variety**
arrest *verb* **1** to take someone into custody: *Police arrested five men in connection with the attack*
apprehend: *Police have not apprehended her killer*
capture: *Her accomplice was captured by Dutch police*
nick *British slang*: *Keep quiet or we'll all get nicked*
seize: *Two military observers were*

seized by rebels yesterday

take prisoner: He was taken prisoner in 1940 at the fall of Dunkirk

▷ **noun 2** the act of arresting someone: The police made two arrests

apprehension: information leading to the apprehension of the killer

capture: He was trying to evade capture by security forces

seizure: the mass seizure of terrorists

see also **capture, catch, stop**

arrival see **appearance, entrance, entry**

arrive see **come**

arrive at see **reach**

arrogance see **pride**

arrogant see **bossy, cocky, haughty, pompous, stuck-up**

arsenal see **stockpile**

artful see **crafty, cunning**

article noun **1** a piece of writing in a newspaper or magazine: There's an article about it in today's paper

feature: a feature about GulfWar syndrome

item: I read an item about this only last week

piece: I disagree with your recent piece about Australia

story: The newspapers had a story about the film's premiere

2 a particular item: household articles

item: Various items have gone missing from my desk

object: everyday objects such as wooden spoons

thing: I have a few things to buy for the trip

see also **feature, item, object, piece, thing**

articulate see **fluent, state**

artificial see **fake, false, mock**

as see **because**

as a result see **therefore**

as a result of see **by virtue of**

as a rule see **on average**

as good as see **nearly**

as one see **together**

as well see **also, too**

ascend see **climb, rise**

ascendancy see **advantage, power**

ascertain see **determine, hear, learn, prove, see**

ashamed adjective feeling embarrassed or guilty: He was not even ashamed of what he had done

embarrassed: I'm not embarrassed to admit I cried

guilty: When she realized I was watching, she looked guilty

humiliated: I felt humiliated at the scene he was causing

sheepish: "I'm afraid it was my idea," he admitted, looking sheepish

sorry: She's really sorry for all the trouble she's caused

see also **embarrassed, guilty**

ashen see **pale**

ask verb **1** to put a question to someone: She asked me if I'd enjoyed my dinner

inquire: I rang up to inquire about train times

interrogate: I interrogated everyone even slightly involved

query: He queried whether sabotage could have been involved

question: He was questioned by police

quiz: He was quizzed about his eligibility for benefits

2 to make a request to someone: We had to ask him to leave

appeal: The police appealed for witnesses to come forward

beg: I begged him to leave me alone

demand: I demanded an explanation from him

implore: I implored him not to give it up

plead: She pleaded to be allowed to go

seek: *Always seek legal advice before entering into any agreement*
3 to invite someone: *Not everybody had been asked to the wedding*
bid *literary*: *They all smiled at him and bade him eat*
invite: *She invited him to her 26th birthday party*
see also **plead, pose, request**
ask (for) *see* **charge**
ask for advice *see* **consult**
ask forgiveness *see* **apologize**
ask oneself *see* **wonder**
asleep *see* **unconscious**
aspect *noun* a feature of something: *Exam results are only one aspect of a school's success*
   consideration: *The cost involved will be a chief consideration in our choice*
   element: *Fitness is now an important element in our lives*
   factor: *an important factor in a child's development*
   feature: *the most significant feature of his childhood*
   part: *Respect is an important part of any relationship*
   point: *There is another point to remember when making your decision*
   side: *He had a darker side to his character*
   see also **detail, face, factor, feature, quality, view**
aspiration *see* **dream**
aspire *see* **aim**
aspire to *see* **seek**
assassinate *see* **kill, murder**
assassination *see* **murder**
assault *see* **attack, raid**
assemble *verb* **1** to gather together in a group: *a convenient place for students to assemble between classes*
   collect: *We all collected round him to listen*
   come together: *a common room where we can come together and relax*
congregate: *Youngsters love to congregate here in the evenings*
convene: *A grand jury has convened to gather evidence*
gather: *We all gathered in the board room*
mass: *Troops were massing on both sides of the border*
2 to fit the parts of something together: *Workers were assembling planes*
   build: *A carpenter built the shelves for us*
   construct: *He had constructed a crude explosive device*
   erect: *Stagehands are employed to erect the scenery*
   make: *I like making model aeroplanes*
   put together: *You can buy the parts and put it together yourself*
   see also **build, collect, construct, form, gather, make, manufacture, mass, meet, piece together**
assembly *see* **company, convention, council, gathering, hui, making, manufacture**
assent *see* **agree, permission**
assert *see* **argue, claim, declare, state**
assertion *see* **claim**
assertive *see* **pushy**
assess *see* **judge, test, value**
assessment *see* **estimate, judgment, opinion, test**
asset *see* **beauty, benefit, merit, virtue**
assets *see* **possessions, property**
assign *see* **allow**
assignation *see* **meeting**
assignment *see* **appointment, duty, task, work**
assimilate *see* **grasp, take in**
assist *see* **benefit, help**
assistance *see* **help**
assistant *noun* a person who helps someone: *His assistant took over*

while he went out
aide: *a presidential aide*
ally: *her political allies*
colleague: *a business colleague*
helper: *volunteer helpers*
right-hand man: *the resignation of the manager's right-hand man*
see also **helper**

associate verb **1** to connect one thing with another: *Poverty is associated with old age*
connect: *a common problem directly connected with stress*
couple: *The papers coupled the Gulf crisis with the problems facing the former Soviet Union*
identify: *Candidates want to identify themselves with reform*
link: *Liver cancer is linked to the hepatitis B virus*
2 to spend time with a person: *I began associating with different crowds of people*
hang out *informal*: *People want to hang out with you for the wrong reasons*
mingle: *reporters who mingled freely with the crowd*
mix: *local youths who want to mix with the foreign tourists*
run around *informal*: *What's he doing running around with a teenager?*
socialize: *She made little effort to socialize with other staff*
▷ noun **3** a person known through work: *the restaurant owner's business associates*
colleague: *learning from more experienced colleagues*
co-worker: *Their Chinese co-workers often worked seven days a week*
workmate: *employees who expose dishonest workmates*
see also **colleague, connect**

associate with see **identify with**

association noun **1** an organization:

a research association
body: *the chairman of the policemen's representative body*
club: *the local Young Conservatives' club*
company: *a major motor company*
confederation: *the Confederation of British Industry*
group: *an environmental group*
institution: *a member of various financial institutions*
league: *the World Muslim League*
society: *the Royal Society for the Protection of Birds*
syndicate: *a syndicate of international banks*
2 a connection or involvement with a person or group: *his association with a terrorist group*
affiliation: *He has no affiliation with any political party*
attachment: *Mother and child form a close attachment*
bond: *There is a special bond between us*
connection: *He has denied any connection with the organization*
relationship: *Ours was strictly a professional relationship*
tie: *I had very close ties with the family*
see also **body, club, connection, fellowship, link, organization, relationship, society, union**

assorted see **several, various**
assortment see **collection, range, variety**

assume verb **1** to accept that something is true: *I assumed that he would turn up*
believe: *I believe she'll be back next week*
guess *informal*: *I guess she thought that was pretty smart*
imagine: *You tend to imagine that you cannot put a foot wrong*
suppose: *I see no reason to suppose*

that it isn't working
think: *They thought that they had won*
2 to take responsibility for something: *Mr Cross will assume the role of Chief Executive*
accept: *He accepted the role of player-captain*
shoulder: *He has had to shoulder the responsibility of his father's mistakes*
take on: *Don't take on more responsibilities than you can handle*
undertake: *He undertook to edit the text himself*
see also **believe, expect, gather, imagine, reckon, suppose**
assumed *see* **supposed**
assurance *see* **confidence, guarantee, promise, word**
assure *see* **convince, promise**
assured *see* **confident, definite**
astonish *see* **amaze, surprise**
astonishing *see* **amazing, incredible, unexpected**
astonishment *see* **amazement, surprise**
astound *see* **amaze, surprise**
astounding *see* **amazing, incredible, wonderful**
astray *see* **lost**
astringent *see* **bitter**
astute *adjective* very intelligent or perceptive: *an astute judge of character*
alert: *He is old, but he has a very quick and alert mind*
clever: *a clever business move*
keen: *a keen understanding of politics*
perceptive: *his perceptive analysis of the situation*
quick: *He has an enquiring mind and a quick intelligence*
sharp: *His gentle manner disguised a sharp mind*
shrewd: *He demonstrated a shrewd understanding of human nature*

smart: *a very smart move*
see also **acute, keen, perceptive, sharp, shrewd, smart**
asylum *see* **refuge, shelter**
asymmetrical *see* **irregular**
at an end *see* **over**
at ease *see* **comfortable, relaxed**
at fault *see* **responsible**
at hand *see* **available, handy, present**
at home *see* **comfortable**
at large *see* **free**
at last *see* **finally**
at liberty *see* **free**
at no time *see* **never**
at once *see* **immediately, now, together**
at someone's disposal *see* **available**
at the last moment *see* **finally**
at times *see* **sometimes**
at your fingertips *see* **handy**
atone *see* **compensate**
atonement *see* **compensation**
atrocious *see* **dreadful, wicked**
attach *verb* to join or fasten things together: *The gadget can be attached to any surface*
affix: *His name was affixed to the wall of his cubicle*
connect: *Connect the pipe to the tap*
couple: *The engine is coupled to a gearbox*
fasten: *The shelves are fastened to the wall with screws*
join: *two sticks joined together by a chain*
link: *tree houses linked by ropes*
tie: *He tied the dog to a post with its leash*
see also **add, connect, fasten, fix, hang, join, link, secure, stick**
attachment *noun* **1** a feeling of love and affection: *Mother and child form a close attachment*
affection: *the affection between a pet*

and its owner

bond: *There has always been a strong bond between us*

fondness: *I have a great fondness for all animals*

liking: *He has never shown any liking for his colleagues*

love: *A deep love gradually developed between them*

2 a part attached to something else: *The drill comes with a wide range of attachments*

accessory: *a range of accessories for your mobile phone*

fitting: *bathroom fittings*

fixture: *The box can be adapted to take a light fixture*

component: *Additional components are available as listed*

part: *Extra parts can be added later*

unit: *The unit plugs into any TV set*
see also **affection, association, bond, fitting, friendship, link**

attack verb **1** to use violence against someone or something: *I thought he was going to attack me*

assault: *The gang assaulted him with iron bars*

charge: *He ordered us to charge*

invade: *The allies invaded the Italian mainland at Anzio*

raid: *He was found guilty of raiding a bank*

set upon: *As the lorry drove east it was set upon by bandits*

storm: *The refugees decided to storm the embassy*

2 to criticize someone strongly: *She attacked the government's economic policies*

blast: *He blasted the referee for his inconsistency*

censure: *The bank has been censured and fined by the authority*

criticize: *The regime has been harshly criticized*

have a go British informal: *If they made a mistake the crowd would have a go at them*

put down informal: *He was always putting me down*

vilify formal: *He was vilified, hounded, and forced into exile*

▷ noun **3** violent physical action against someone or something: *a vicious attack on an unarmed man*

assault: *The rebels are poised for a new assault*

charge: *a bayonet charge*

invasion: *the Roman invasion of Britain*

offensive: *the government's military offensive against the rebels*

onslaught: *civilians trying to flee from the military onslaught*

raid: *a raid on a house by armed police*
see also **bomb, invade, raid, savage**

attain see **acquire, earn, reach, win**

attainable see **possible**

attempt verb **1** to try to do something: *They attempted to escape*

endeavour: *I will endeavour to arrange it*

seek: *We have never sought to impose our views*

strive: *The school strives to treat pupils as individuals*

try: *I tried hard to persuade him to stay*

try your hand at: *He'd always wanted to try his hand at writing*

▷ noun **2** an act of trying to do something: *one of his rare attempts at humour*

bid: *a bid to save the newspaper*

crack informal: *his third crack at the world heavyweight title*

go informal: *My mum suggested I should have a go at becoming a jockey*

shot informal: *We'd like a shot at winning the league*

stab informal: *Several tennis stars*

have had a stab at acting
try: *That makes the scheme worth a try*
see also **aim, effort, go, seek, strive, try**

attend *see* **frequent, listen**

attend to *see* **deal, take care of**

attention *see* **care, consideration, heed, interest**

attentive *see* **alert, observant, thoughtful**

attire *see* **clothes, dress**

attitude noun *someone's way of thinking and behaving: negative attitudes to work*
  outlook: *behaviour that seems contrary to his whole outlook*
  perspective: *It gave me a new perspective on life*
  point of view: *Try to look at this from my point of view*
  position: *What's your position on this issue?*
  stance: *the Church's stance on contraception*
  see also **conduct, outlook, view, viewpoint**

attorney *see* **lawyer**

attract verb *to appeal to or interest: The trials have attracted many leading riders*
  appeal to: *The idea appealed to him*
  draw: *The match drew a large crowd*
  entice: *She resisted attempts to entice her into politics*
  lure: *They were being lured into a trap*
  pull *informal*: *They have to employ performers to pull a crowd*
  tempt: *Can I tempt you with some wine?*
  see also **appeal, lure**

attraction *see* **beauty, charm, lure, pull**

attractive adjective *pleasant, especially to look at: an attractive woman*
  appealing: *a sense of humour that I found very appealing*
  charming: *a charming little village*
  fetching: *a fetching outfit*
  handsome: *a handsome man*
  lovely: *a lovely island*
  pretty: *a shy, pretty girl*
  see also **beautiful, cute, handsome, lovely, pretty**

attractiveness *see* **beauty**

attribute noun *a quality or feature: a normal attribute of human behaviour*
  characteristic: *their physical characteristics*
  feature: *the most striking feature of his music*
  property: *the magnetic properties of iron*
  quality: *His humility is one of his most endearing qualities*
  trait: *personality traits*
  see also **characteristic, feature, point, property, virtue**

audacious *see* **daring**

audacity *see* **cheek, daring, impudence**

audibly *see* **aloud**

audience *see* **meeting**

augment verb *to add something to something else: a good way to augment your basic wage*
  add to: *A fitted kitchen adds to the value of your house*
  boost: *people who boost their earnings by working part-time from home*
  complement: *an in-work benefit that complements earnings*
  increase: *He is eager to increase his income by any means*
  reinforce: *measures which will reinforce their current strengths*
  supplement: *I suggest supplementing your diet with vitamin A*
  top up: *compulsory contributions to top up pension schemes*

see also **add, supplement**

austere see **harsh, plain**

authentic adjective real and genuine: an authentic French recipe
bona fide: We are happy to donate to bona fide charities
dinkum Australian, New Zealand informal: a place which serves dinkum Aussie tucker
genuine: Experts are convinced the manuscript is genuine
real: It's a real Rembrandt
true: Of course she's not a true blonde
see also **actual, exact, genuine, real, realistic, true**

authenticity see **reality**

authoritarian see **bossy, strict**

authority see **control, expert, influence, mana, power**

authorization see **approval, permission, permit, power, sanction**

authorize see **allow, approve, permit, sanction**

authorized see **legal, official**

automated see **automatic**

automatic adjective **1** operating mechanically by itself: Modern trains have automatic doors
automated: highly automated production lines
mechanical: the oldest working mechanical clock in the world
robot: a robot telescope
self-propelled: self-propelled artillery
2 without conscious thought: automatic body functions
instinctive: an instinctive reaction
involuntary: involuntary muscle movements
natural: the insect's natural instinct to feed
reflex: Blushing is a reflex action linked to the nervous system

automobile noun American a

vehicle for carrying a few people: the Japanese automobile manufacturer
car: My dad's promised me a car if I pass my finals
motor: He's bought himself a flash new motor
vehicle: A child ran straight out in front of the vehicle
see also **car**

autonomous see **independent**

available adjective ready for use: There are three small boats available for hire
accessible: This information is accessible on the Internet
at hand: Having the right equipment at hand will be enormously useful
at someone's disposal: Do you have all the facts at your disposal?
free: There was only one seat free on the train
handy: Keep your keys handy so you can get into your car quickly
to hand: Keep your insurance details to hand when driving
see also **ready**

avenge see **revenge**

average adjective **1** standard or normal: the average American teenager
normal: I am now back to leading a perfectly normal life
regular: He's just a regular guy
standard: the standard price of a CD
typical: A typical day begins at 8.30
usual: This isn't the usual kind of mail-order catalogue
on average adverb for the most part: Men are, on average, taller than women
as a rule: As a rule, the fee is roughly equal to the savings you have made
generally: A glass of fine wine generally costs about £4
normally: Normally, the transport system carries 50,000 passengers

a day
typically: *In America, estate agents typically charge 5-6% of the sale price*
usually: *In good condition, these models usually fetch up to 300 dollars at auction*
see also **all right, common, medium, moderate, normal, typical**

averse *see* **reluctant, unwilling**

averse to *see* **against**

aversion *see* **dislike, hate, hatred, horror**

avert *see* **prevent**

avid *see* **ardent, eager, enthusiastic, keen**

avoid *verb* **1** to make an effort not to do something: *We economists always try to avoid giving a straight answer*
dodge: *dodging military service by feigning illness*
duck out of *informal*: *ducking out of the post-match press conference*
fight shy of: *She fought shy of confronting her critics*
refrain from: *Mrs Hardie refrained from making any comment*
shirk: *We won't shirk our responsibility*
2 to keep away from someone or something: *She thought he was trying to avoid her*
dodge: *He refuses to dodge his critics*
elude: *an attempt to elude photographers*
eschew *formal*: *He eschewed publicity and avoided nightclubs*
evade: *He managed to evade the police*
shun: *Everybody shunned him*
sidestep: *Rarely does she sidestep a question*
steer clear of: *It would be best to steer clear of her*
see also **abstain, dodge, escape**

awake *see* **wake**

award *see* **give, grant, present,**

prize

award-winning *see* **prize**

aware of *adjective* conscious of something: *She was acutely aware of the noise of the city*
acquainted with: *He was well acquainted with American literature*
conscious of: *She was very conscious of Max studying her*
familiar with: *I am not familiar with your work*
mindful of: *Everyone should be mindful of the dangers*
2 knowing about something: *Keep me aware of any developments*
informed: *the importance of keeping the public properly informed*
in the picture: *He's always kept me in the picture*
knowledgeable: *He's very knowledgeable about new technology*
see also **perceptive**

aware of *see* **familiar**

awareness *see* **grasp**

away *see* **absent**

awe *see* **fear**

awesome *see* **impressive**

awful *adjective* very unpleasant or very bad: *the same awful jokes*
appalling: *living under the most appalling conditions*
dreadful: *They told us the dreadful news*
frightful: *a frightful ordeal*
ghastly: *a mother accompanied by her ghastly unruly child*
horrendous: *The violence used was horrendous*
terrible: *Her French is terrible*
see also **dreadful, horrible, terrible**

awkward *see* **clumsy, embarrassed, uncomfortable**

awkwardness *see* **clumsiness, embarrassment**

axiom *see* **principle, saying**

aye *see* **yes**

babalas see **drunk**

babble verb to talk in an excited way:
He babbled on and on
burble: *He burbles on about the goals
he has scored*
chatter: *Jane chattered about the
children*
gabble: *I started to gabble in the
interview*
prattle: *Alan is prattling on again*
see also **ramble, rave**

babies see **young**

baby noun a very young child: *I've had
this birthmark since I was a baby*
ankle-biter Australian, New
Zealand slang: *I knew him when he
was just an ankle-biter*
bairn Scottish: *My wife's expecting
a bairn*
child: *They celebrated the birth of their
first child*
infant: *young mums with infants
in prams*
see also **child**

back noun 1 the part that is behind
the front: *the back of a postcard*
end: *the end of the corridor*
rear: *the rear of the building*
reverse: *the reverse of the sheet*
stern: *the stern of a boat*

▷ verb 2 to support a person
or organization: *His friends are
backing him*
advocate: *Mr Jones advocates longer
school days*
encourage: *The government is
encouraging better child care*
endorse: *Do you endorse his opinion?*
favour: *I favour a different approach*
promote: *Ann is promoting Alan's
ideas*
support: *We supported his political
campaign*
see also **advocate, finance, gamble,
promote, sanction, support**

back away see **retreat**

back off see **retreat**

back out see **withdraw**

background noun where you come
from: *a rich background*
culture: *people from different cultures*
environment: *the environment I
grew up in*
history: *She has an interesting history*
upbringing: *a strict upbringing*
see also **foil, record, surroundings**

backing see **blessing, sanction**

backlash see **reaction**

backside see **bottom**

bad adjective 1 harmful, unpleasant,
or upsetting: *I have some bad news*
2 of poor quality: *bad roads*
3 evil in character: *a bad person*
see **word studies bad**
see also **evil, naughty, rotten,
serious, unpleasant, wicked,
wrong**

bad for you see **unhealthy**

bad luck see **misfortune**

badger see **hassle, pester**

badly adverb in an inferior way: *This
essay is badly written*
see **word studies badly**

badness see **evil**

bad-tempered see **irritable**

baffle see **confuse, puzzle**

baffled see **confused**

baffling see **confusing, hard, mysterious**

baggy see **full, loose**

bairn see **baby, child**

bait noun something used to tempt someone: *Charles isn't taking the bait*
  bribe: *a politician who took bribes*
  decoy: *He acted as a decoy to trap the murderer*
  inducement: *financial inducements to talk to the newspapers*
  lure: *the lure of a huge salary*
  temptation: *the temptation of easy money*
  see also **incentive, lure, pick on**

bake see **cook, harden**

balance verb 1 to make or remain steady: *Balancing on one leg is difficult*
  level: *House prices have levelled*
  stabilize: *attempts to stabilize the economy*
  steady: *He steadied himself and shot at goal*
  ▷ noun 2 a stable relationship between things: *the chemical balance of the brain*
  equilibrium: *the political equilibrium of Europe*
  equity: *plans for greater equity of incomes*
  equivalence: *the lack of equivalence between film and radio*
  parity: *She won pay parity with male colleagues*
  see also **compensate, difference, remainder, rest**

ball noun a round object: *a ball of wool*
  drop: *a drop of blood*
  globe: *the globe of the eyeball*
  pellet: *an airgun pellet*
  sphere: *a sphere the size of the Earth*
  see also **lump**

ballot see **vote**

balmy see **calm, mild, warm**

ban verb 1 to disallow something: *I am banned from taking part*
  bar: *The press will be barred from the talks*
  disqualify: *He was disqualified from driving*
  exclude: *They were excluded from the maths class*
  forbid: *The rules forbid the use of force*
  outlaw: *regulations outlawing child labour*
  prohibit: *a law that prohibits alcohol*
  ▷ noun 2 a rule disallowing something: *a ban on smoking*
  disqualification: *a four-year disqualification from athletics*
  embargo: *an embargo on trade with the country*
  prohibition: *a prohibition on tobacco*
  suppression: *the suppression of anti-government protests*
  see also **exclude, forbid, prohibit, sanctions, veto**

banal see **corny, hackneyed**

band noun 1 a group of musicians who play together: *a singer in a rock and roll band*
  group: *They formed the group while they were still at school*
  orchestra: *the National Youth Orchestra*
  2 a group of people who share a common purpose: *a band of rebels*
  bunch: *A bunch of protesters were picketing the factory*
  company: *a company of actors*
  crowd: *A small crowd of onlookers had gathered*
  gang: *a gang of criminals*
  party: *a party of sightseers*
  troupe: *She toured with a professional dance troupe*
  see also **body, bunch, company, group, party, ring, team**

bandit see **thug**

bane see **pest**

bang verb **1** to hit or put something
down hard, with a loud noise: *a
toddler banging a saucepan with a
wooden spoon*
beat: *They sat in a circle, beating
small drums*
hammer: *The supporters hammered
on the windows of the bus*
hit: *They were hitting the sides of the
van with sticks*
knock: *I knocked on the door for ages,
but no-one answered*
pound: *We pounded on the walls*
slam: *I slammed down the receiver*
thump: *The children cheered and
thumped on their desks*
▷ noun **2** a sudden, short, loud noise:
The TV exploded with a bang
blast: *the ear-splitting blast of a
cannon*
boom: *There was a boom and a cloud
of smoke*
crack: *the crack of a pistol shot*
detonation: *We heard several loud
detonations coming from the building*
explosion: *the deafening explosion
of gunshots*
thump: *She dropped her case to the
floor with a loud thump*
3 a hard or painful bump against
something: *I got a nasty bang on
the elbow*
blow: *a blow to the side of the head*
clout *informal*: *She gave him a swift
clout on the ear*
knock: *Knocks like this can cause
damage to the spine*
thump: *Ralph got a thump on the
chest*
whack: *She gave the horse a whack
on the rump*
see also **blow, bump, crash,
explosion**

bang into see **hit**

banish verb **1** to exile someone: *She

banished him from the house*
deport: *Many fans are being deported
from Italy*
eject: *He was ejected from the club*
evict: *Police evicted ten families from
the building*
exile: *He was exiled from Russia*
expel: *patients expelled from
hospitals*
transport: *He was transported to a
prison camp*
2 to get rid of something or
someone: *to banish illness*
discard: *Read the instructions before
discarding the box*
dismiss: *I dismissed the idea from
my mind*
dispel: *The myths are being dispelled*
eliminate: *They eliminated him from
their enquiries*
eradicate: *projects to eradicate
certain diseases*
remove: *talks to remove the last
obstacles to the deal*

bank noun **1** a store of something:
a blood bank
fund: *a pension fund*
hoard: *a hoard of treasure*
reserve: *the world's oil reserves*
stock: *stocks of paper and ink*
store: *a secret store of sweets*
2 the edge of a river or lake: *He sat
fishing on the bank*
brink: *orchards near the brink of the
sea cliffs*
edge: *She stood too close to the edge
and fell in*
shore: *He swam towards the shore*
side: *a picnic by the side of the river*
see also **row**

bank on see **depend**
banking see **finance**
bankruptcy see **crash**
banned see **illegal**
banquet see **meal**
banter see **joke**

baptize see name
bar noun 1 a piece of metal: *bars across the windows*
  pole: *He was tied to a pole*
  rail: *a curtain rail*
  rod: *a fishing rod*
  shaft: *the shaft of a spear*
  ▷ verb 2 to stop someone: *His bodyguards barred the way*
  obstruct: *Vehicles have obstructed the entrance*
  prevent: *A fence prevents people from entering*
  see also **ban, block, close, exclude, obstruct, pub**
barbarian see savage
barbaric see savage
barbarity see cruelty
barbarous see cruel, savage
barbecue see cook
barbed see jagged
bare adjective 1 not covered: *bare legs*
  exposed: *His whole back is exposed*
  naked: *a naked body*
  nude: *a nude model*
  stripped: *I got stripped to have a shower*
  uncovered: *His arms were uncovered*
  undressed: *She got undressed in the bathroom*
  2 with nothing on top or inside: *a small bare office*
  empty: *an empty room*
  open: *open country*
  spartan: *spartan accommodation*
  vacant: *a vacant chair*
  see also **blank, empty, naked, plain**
barefaced see shameless
barely adverb only just: *She is barely sixteen*
  almost: *I almost didn't make it*
  hardly: *I could hardly believe it*
  just: *They only just won*
  scarcely: *I can scarcely hear her*
  see also **hardly**
bargain see cheap

barge see burst
bark see bay
barmy see mad
barney see argument, squabble
barrage see hail
barren adjective 1 with nothing growing on it: *a barren desert*
  arid: *the arid lands of Botswana*
  desert: *desert regions*
  desolate: *a desolate place*
  dry: *poor, dry countries*
  empty: *the empty desert*
  waste: *waste land*
  2 unable to produce babies: *women who are barren*
  childless: *childless couples*
  infertile: *infertile women*
  sterile: *sterile females*
  see also **sterile**
barricade see barrier
barrier noun 1 something preventing entry: *Demonstrators broke through the barriers*
  barricade: *a barricade of vehicles*
  fence: *a garden fence*
  obstruction: *Check the exhaust pipe is clear of obstructions*
  wall: *the huge city walls*
  2 something that prevents progress: *plans to reduce the barriers to trade*
  handicap: *It is a handicap not knowing a foreign language*
  hindrance: *a potential hindrance to the peace process*
  hurdle: *the first hurdle in a job search*
  impediment: *a serious impediment to free trade*
  obstacle: *the main obstacle to the takeover*
  see also **handicap, obstacle, protection, safeguard**
barrister see lawyer
barter see change, exchange, swap
base noun 1 the lowest part of something: *the base of the cliffs*
  bed: *the river bed*

bottom: the bottom of the lake
foot: the foot of the mountain
foundation: They have laid the foundations for the new building
pedestal: The statue is back on its pedestal
stand: a microphone stand
2 the place you work from: a military base
camp: refugee camp
centre: a health centre
headquarters: army headquarters in Colombo
post: a military post in the capital
station: the police station
▷ verb **3** to use as a foundation: The film is based on a true story
build: a reputation built on lies
derive: The name is derived from a Greek word
found: My hopes were founded on a mistake
ground: I like a film to be grounded in reality
hinge: The whole play hinges on one character
see also **bottom**

basement see **bottom**
bash see **club**
bashful see **shy, timid**
bashfulness see **embarrassment**
basic adjective most necessary: the basic requirements for the job
elementary: elementary computer training
essential: essential reading and writing skills
fundamental: fundamental rights
key: key skills such as communication and teamwork
necessary: They lack the necessary resources
vital: vital supplies
see also **essential, straightforward**
basics see **essentials**
basis noun the main principle of

something: The same theme is the basis of several poems
core: the core of Asia's problems
fundamental: the fundamentals of road safety
heart: the heart of the matter
premise: the premise of his argument
principle: the principles of Buddhism
see also **cause, grounds**

bass see **deep**
bat see **club, stick**
batch see **bunch, lot, set**
bathe see **soak, wash**
batter see **beat, club**
battle see **clash, conflict, contest, fight, war**
batty see **mad**
bauble see **ornament**
bawdy see **naughty, obscene**
bawl see **shout**
bay noun **1** a curve in a coastline: the Bay of Biscay
cove: a sandy cove with white cliffs
gulf: the Gulf of Mexico
inlet: a deep inlet on the west coast
sound: streams that run into the sound
▷ verb **2** to make a howling noise: wolves baying in the moonlight
bark: a small dog barking at a seagull
cry: I heard animals cry in the forest
howl: distant coyotes howling in the night
yelp: A dog snapped and yelped at them
see also **compartment**

bazaar see **fair, market**
be advantageous see **pay**
be afraid see **fear**
be after see **seek**
be alert see **watch out**
be aware of see **appreciate, know, sense**
beach noun an area beside the sea: making sandcastles on the beach
coast: a day at the coast

sands: *the long white sands of Goa*
seashore: *walks along the seashore*
seaside: *trips to the seaside*
shore: *He swam out from the shore*
strand: *collecting shells on the strand*
see also **coast**

beacon *see* **signal**
bead *see* **blob, drip, drop**
beak *see* **judge**
beam *see* **shine, smile**
bear *verb* **1** to carry something:
*The ice wasn't thick enough to bear
their weight*
  carry: *He always carried a gun*
  convey: *The taxi conveyed us to
  the centre*
  shoulder: *He had to shoulder the
  blame for the mistake*
  support: *Thick wooden posts support
  the ceiling*
  take: *You'd better take an umbrella*
2 to have or show something:
*The room bore the signs of a violent
struggle*
  exhibit: *He began to exhibit
  symptoms of the disease*
  harbour: *She still harbours feelings
  of resentment*
  have: *I have a grudge against her*
3 to accept something: *He can't bear
to talk about it*
  abide: *I can't abide arrogant people*
  endure: *The pain was hard to endure*
  stomach: *He could not stomach
  violence*
  suffer: *I had to suffer his company
  all day*
  tolerate: *Women tolerate pain better
  than men*
  see also **bring, carry, put up with,
  suffer, take, tolerate**
bear a resemblance to *see*
resemble
bear in mind *see* **consider**
bear out *see* **confirm**
bearable *see* **tolerable**

bearing *see* **appearance, look,
manner, relation**
beast *see* **animal, savage**
beat *verb* **1** to hit someone or
something hard: *He threatened to
beat her*
  batter: *The waves kept battering
  the life raft*
  buffet: *Their plane was buffeted
  by storms*
  hit: *He hit me on the head*
  pound: *Someone was pounding on
  the door*
  strike: *She struck him across the
  mouth*
  thrash: *He was thrashed by his father*
2 to defeat: *She was easily beaten
in the race*
  defeat: *The team hasn't been defeated
  all year*
  outdo: *One man was trying to outdo
  the other*
  outstrip: *The company is outstripping
  its rivals*
  overcome: *Molly had overcome her
  fear of flying*
  overwhelm: *One attack could
  overwhelm the enemy*
  vanquish: *the man who helped
  vanquish Napoleon*
▷ *noun* a rhythm: *the thumping
beat of rock music*
  cadence: *The pulsing cadences of
  his music*
  metre: *the strict metre of the poem*
  rhythm: *His foot tapped a rhythm
  on the floor*
  stress: *differences of stress in speech*
  time: *a song written in waltz time*
  see also **bang, club, defeat, rhythm,
  top, vanquish**
beaut *see* **excellent**
beautiful *adjective* attractive or
pleasing: *beautiful music*
  attractive: *an attractive woman*
  delightful: *The perfume is delightful*

fine: a fine summer's day
gorgeous: *a gorgeous man*
lovely: *You look lovely*
pleasing: *a pleasing appearance*
see also **fine, lovely, pretty**
beauty noun **1** the quality of being beautiful: *an area of outstanding beauty*
attractiveness: *the attractiveness of the region*
charm: *a woman of great charm*
elegance: *the elegance of the overall design*
loveliness: *the loveliness of the scene*
2 a good-looking person: *a dark-haired beauty*
hunk *informal*: *The Swedish hunk is back again*
stunner *informal*: *the 23-year-old stunner*
3 an attractive feature: *The beauty of the fund is its simplicity*
advantage: *the advantages of the new system over the old one*
asset: *The one asset the job provided was contacts*
attraction: *The main attraction of the place is the monument*
benefit: *Every age has its benefits*
because conjunction for the reason that: *I went home because I was tired*
as: *Don't cook for me as I'll be home late*
since: *Since you didn't listen, I'll repeat that*
because of see **by virtue of**
beckon see **lure, signal**
become see **get, grow**
bed see **base, bottom**
bedraggled see **untidy**
beefy see **plump**
before adverb at a previous time: *Have you been to Greece before?*
earlier: *Here is a cake I made earlier*
formerly: *He had formerly been in the army*

in advance: *We booked the room well in advance*
previously: *Previously she had little time to work*
sooner: *I wish I'd arrived sooner*
see also **in front**
before long see **soon**
beforehand see **early, first**
beg verb to ask anxiously for something: *I begged him to leave me alone*
beseech: *Her eyes beseeched him to show mercy*
implore: *I implore you not to say anything*
petition: *He petitioned the Court to let him go free*
plead: *She was pleading with me to stay*
see also **appeal, ask, implore, plead, press, request, scrounge, urge**
beg someone's pardon see **apologize**
begin verb to start or cause to start: *She began to move around the room*
commence *formal*: *He commenced his journey*
inaugurate: *The committee was inaugurated ten days ago*
initiate: *They wanted to initiate a discussion*
originate: *Mankind may have originated in Africa*
set about: *He set about tackling his problems*
start: *The meeting starts at 10 o'clock*
see also **proceed, start**
begin again see **renew**
beginner noun someone learning to do something: *a beginner's course*
apprentice: *an apprentice in a law firm*
learner: *young learners of French*
novice: *Many of us are novices on the computer*
starter: *new starters at school*

trainee: *a trainee in a newspaper office*
see also **recruit**

beginning noun where something starts: *the beginning of the city*
birth: *the birth of modern art*
commencement formal: *a date for the commencement of talks*
opening: *the opening of the trial*
origin: *the origins of civilization*
outset: *There were lots of problems from the outset*
start: *the start of all the trouble*
see also **head, opening, source, start**

begrudge see **envy**
begrudging see **bitter**

behave verb to act in a certain way: *They were behaving like animals*
act: *He is acting like a spoilt child*
function: *They are functioning as a team*
operate: *I know how Graham operates*
work: *My mind is working well today*
see also **conduct yourself**

behave towards see **treat**
behaviour see **conduct, manner**
behind see **bottom, late**
behind time see **late**
behold see **see**
belated see **late**

belief noun **1** the certainty something is true: *belief in reincarnation*
confidence: *I have every confidence that you'll do well*
conviction: *She speaks with conviction*
judgment: *My judgment is that he should leave*
opinion: *Robert has strong opinions*
trust: *She has complete trust that you'll help her*
view: *In my view, he is wrong*
2 a principle of a religion or system:

the culture and beliefs of ancient times
creed: *people of every race and creed*
doctrine: *Christian doctrine*
dogma: *religious dogma*
faith: *Do you practise any faith?*
ideology: *different political ideologies*
principle: *the principles of Jewish faith*
tenet: *the fundamental tenets of Islam*
see also **confidence, faith, idea, opinion, view, viewpoint**

believable adjective possible or likely to be the case: *The book is full of believable characters*
credible: *credible witnesses*
imaginable: *It is scarcely imaginable that it happened here*
likely: *It's more likely that she forgot*
plausible: *a plausible explanation*
possible: *It's quite possible that I'm wrong*
probable: *the most probable outcome*

believe verb to accept something is true: *Don't believe everything you read in the papers*
accept: *He can't accept that he is wrong*
assume: *I assume these eggs are fresh*
presume: *The missing person is presumed to be dead*
swallow informal: *I found their story hard to swallow*
trust: *I trust that you will manage*
see also **assume, consider, expect, feel, imagine, reckon, suppose, suspect, think, understand**

believed see **supposed**
believer see **follower**

belittle verb to make someone or something seem less important: *He belittles my opinions*
deride: *He is derided as weak and incompetent*
detract from: *Her sour comments detracted from Meg's happiness*

downgrade: I fear failure, but I downgrade my successes

scorn: Eleanor scorns the work of others

undervalue: We must never undervalue freedom

see also **put down**

belligerent see **hostile**

bellow see **shout**

belly see **stomach**

belong see **fit**

belongings see **possessions, property, stuff, things**

beloved adjective dearly loved: He lost his beloved wife last year

adored: an adored father

cherished: his most cherished possession

darling: our darling child

dearest: my dearest Maria

precious: I love my precious cat

treasured: treasured memories

see also **dear**

below preposition or adverb lower down: six centimetres below soil level

beneath: She hid the letter beneath her mattress

down: I fell down to the bottom

lower: The price will fall lower than this

under: tunnels under the ground

underneath: He crawled underneath the table

see also **under**

bench see **court**

bend verb **1** to make or become curved: Bend the bar into a horseshoe

buckle: A wave buckled the ship's deck

curve: The wall curves to the left

turn: The road turns right at the end

twist: glass twisted into elaborate patterns

warp: The wood had started to warp **2** to move forwards and downwards: I bent over and kissed her cheek

arch: Don't arch your back!

bow: He turned and bowed to her

crouch: We were crouching in the bushes

incline: The woman inclined her head to one side

lean: She leant out of the window

stoop: Stooping down, he picked up a stone

▷ noun **3** a curve in something: a bend in the road

arc: the full arc of a rainbow

corner: He drove round the corner

curve: the curve of the stream

loop: The river curves in a loop

turn: a turn in the path

see also **curve, fold, twist**

bend down see **crouch**

beneath see **below, under**

beneficial adjective giving some benefit: Wine in moderation is beneficial to the health

advantageous: an advantageous arrangement

good for you: Regular exercise is good for you

healthy: trying to switch to a healthy lifestyle

helpful: This treatment is particularly helpful to hay fever sufferers

useful: a useful addition to your first aid kit

wholesome: food made with good, wholesome ingredients

see also **favourable, healthy, helpful, useful, valuable**

benefit noun **1** an advantage: the benefits of relaxation

advantage: The advantages of the new system far outweigh its disadvantages

asset: A second language is an asset in this job

boon: a great boon for busy housewives

gain: He used the knowledge for his personal gain

good: *Study for your own good!*
help: *It's no help to know I was right*
profit: *the profits of working hard*
use: *His training was of no use to him*
▷ *verb* **2** to help in something: *The experience will benefit you*
aid: *measures to aid working mothers*
assist: *The extra money will assist you*
enhance: *His injury does not enhance our chances*
further: *His support will further our cause*
help: *The new laws won't help the environment*
profit: *It won't profit us to complain*
see also **advantage, beauty, blessing, gain, value**

benevolence see **generosity, goodwill, kindness**
benevolent adjective kind and helpful: *a benevolent ruler*
benign: *a benign and loveable man*
charitable: *charitable organizations*
compassionate: *my compassionate friends*
humane: *humane treatment of prisoners*
kind: *You have been kind and helpful to us*
see also **humane, kind**

benign see **benevolent, gentle, kind**
bent see **crooked, set on**
bent on see **determined**
bequeath see **hand down, will**
bequest see **gift, inheritance, legacy**
berserk see **on the rampage**
beseech see **beg, implore, plead, urge**
beside preposition next to: *I stood beside my father and my uncle*
adjacent to: *a hotel adjacent to the beach*
alongside: *a house alongside the river*
close to: *The restaurant is close to their home*

near: *He stood very near the front door*
next to: *She sat down next to him*
besides see **also, too**
best adjective **1** of the highest standard: *the best film I have seen in a long time*
▷ *noun* **2** the preferred thing: *Of all my presents, this is the best*
see word studies **best**
see also **foremost, prime, senior, top**
best part see **majority**
best-loved see **favourite**
bestow see **present**
bet see **gamble**
betray verb **1** to do someone harm: *I was betrayed by someone I had thought a friend*
be unfaithful: *He's been unfaithful to his wife*
break your promise: *I broke my promise to help her*
double-cross informal: *I was angry that he double-crossed me*
inform on: *people who inform on their colleagues*
2 to show feelings: *Jeremy's voice betrayed little emotion*
expose: *She never exposed her hostile feelings*
manifest: *Fear can manifest itself in many ways*
reveal: *Her expression revealed nothing*
show: *His eyes showed his unhappiness*
see also **inform on**
better adjective **1** of more worth than another: *Today was much better than yesterday*
2 well after being ill: *I hope you feel better soon*
see word studies **better**
see also **improve, reform, senior, superior, top**
better part see **majority**

between see **among**

beware verb to be cautious: *Beware of the dog*
   be careful: *Be careful what you say to him*
   be cautious: *Doctors are cautious about using the treatment*
   be wary: *Michelle is wary of marriage*
   guard against: *We have to guard against thieves*
   look out: *Look out, there's a train coming*
   watch out: *Watch out for fog and ice*

bewilder see **confuse, puzzle**

bewildered see **confused, dazed**

bewildering see **confusing**

bewitch see **charm, entrance, fascinate**

bewitching see **magical**

beyond see **above, past**

bias noun prejudice for or against a person or group: *bias against women*
   bigotry: *religious bigotry*
   favouritism: *His promotion was due to favouritism*
   prejudice: *racial prejudice*
   see also **colour, favouritism, injustice, prejudice**

biased adjective showing prejudice: *biased attitudes*
   one-eyed Australian, New Zealand: *I may be a bit one-eyed because of the family connection*
   one-sided: *a one-sided argument*
   partial: *a very partial view of the situation*
   prejudiced: *Don't be prejudiced by what you say*
   slanted: *a slanted newspaper article*
   weighted: *a scheme weighted towards those in need*
   see also **narrow-minded**

bicker see **argue, quarrel, squabble**

bid see **ask, attempt, command, effort, tender**

bidding see **command**

big adjective **1** of a large size: *a big house*
   2 of great importance: *a big name*
   see **word studies big**
   see also **large**

big name see **celebrity, personality**

bigheaded see **conceited**

bigmouth see **braggart**

bigoted see **narrow-minded**

bigotry see **bias, prejudice**

bill noun a statement of how much is owed: *a huge restaurant bill*
   account: *Please charge it to my account*
   charges: *charges for eye tests*
   invoice: *They sent an invoice for the damage*
   statement: *a credit card statement*
   see also **charge, notice**

billow see **cloud**

bind see **bond, fix, secure, tie**

birth see **beginning, start**

bisect see **divide**

bit noun a small amount: *a bit of coal*
   crumb: *a crumb of comfort*
   fragment: *glittering fragments of broken glass*
   grain: *His story contains a grain of truth*
   part: *part of the problem*
   piece: *The vase was smashed to pieces*
   scrap: *a scrap of evidence*
   see also **part, piece, portion**

bitchy see **spiteful**

bite verb to cut into something with your teeth: *His cat bit me when I tried to pat it*
   chew: *a video of a man having his leg chewed off by a bear*
   gnaw: *The bones had been gnawed by wild animals*
   nibble: *She nibbled a biscuit*
   nip: *There were blotches where the mosquitoes had nipped him*
   see also **savage, taste**

biting see **cold**

bitter adjective **1** angry and resentful: a bitter row
  acrimonious: an acrimonious discussion
  begrudging: He gave me begrudging thanks
  embittered: an embittered old lady
  rancorous: the issue that has led to rancorous disputes
  resentful: She is resentful of others' success
  sour: a sour expression
2 tasting or smelling sharp: bitter lemons
  acid: the acid smell of sweat
  acrid: clouds of acrid smoke
  astringent: astringent disinfectant
  sharp: a clean, sharp taste
  sour: a rich, sour stew
  tart: the tart qualities of citrus fruit
  see also **cold, resentful, sour**
bitterness see **resentment**
bizarre adjective very strange or eccentric: He has some bizarre ideas about women
  curious: a curious mixture of ancient and modern
  eccentric: Her eccentric behaviour was beginning to attract attention
  extraordinary: What an extraordinary character he is!
  odd: a series of very odd coincidences
  outlandish: her outlandish style of dressing
  peculiar: a peculiar combination of flavours
  queer: A very queer thing happened to me tonight
  strange: She's been behaving in a very strange way lately
  weird: his weird theories about UFOs
  see also **curious, eccentric, extraordinary, odd, peculiar, strange, weird**
black out see **faint**
blacklist see **boycott**

blame verb **1** to believe someone caused something: Don't blame me for this trouble
  accuse: She accused him of causing the fire
  charge: He will be charged for murder
  hold responsible: I hold you responsible for this mess
  ▷ noun **2** the responsibility for something bad: I'm not going to take the blame for that!
  accountability: He escaped accountability for his crimes
  fault: The fault was all yours
  guilt: the sole guilt for the outbreak of war
  liability: He admitted liability for the crash
  rap slang: A maid took the rap for stealing the jewels
  responsibility: responsibility for the murder
  see also **accuse, censure, condemn, fault, responsibility**
blameless see **innocent**
bland see **tasteless**
blank adjective **1** with nothing on it: a blank sheet of paper
  bare: bare walls
  clean: a clean sheet of paper
  clear: a clear patch of floor
  empty: an empty page
  plain: a plain envelope
  unmarked: an unmarked board
2 showing no feeling: John just looked blank
  deadpan: a deadpan expression
  dull: a dull stare
  empty: She saw the empty look in his eyes
  impassive: her impassive smile
  vacant: the vacant expression on his face
  see also **empty, ignore, space**
blanket see **layer**
blaring see **loud**

blast see attack, bang, explosion

blatant see clear, conspicuous, manifest, naked, obvious

blaze see burn, fire, glare

bleached see light

bleak see cold

blemish see fault, flaw, spot

blend verb 1 to mix things so as to form a single item or substance: *Blend the butter with the sugar*

combine: *Combine the ingredients in a large bowl*

merge: *how to merge the graphics with the text*

mingle: *the mingled smells of flowers and cigar smoke*

mix: *Mix the two liquids together with a whisk*

2 to combine in a pleasing way: *The colours blend with the rest of the decor*

complement: *The flavours complement each other perfectly*

co-ordinate: *Choose accessories which co-ordinate with your outfit*

go well: *a wine which goes well with fish*

harmonize: *shades which harmonize with most skin tones*

match: *Those shoes don't match that dress*

suit: *glasses which suit the shape of your face*

▷ noun 3 a mixture or combination of things: *a blend of wine and sparkling water*

alloy: *an alloy of copper and tin*

amalgamation: *Bartók's rich amalgamation of musical styles*

combination: *a fantastic combination of colours*

compound: *a compound of water, sugar and enzymes*

fusion: *a fusion of cooking styles*

mix: *a delicious mix of exotic spices*

mixture: *a sticky mixture of flour and water*

see also **combination, combine, cross, mix, mixture, union**

bless verb to ask God's protection: *The bishop blessed the congregation*

anoint: *The priest anointed the child with oil*

consecrate: *ground that has been consecrated*

dedicate: *The well was dedicated to saints*

hallow: *A building could be hallowed by prayer*

blessed see holy, lucky

blessing noun 1 something good: *Good health is a blessing*

benefit: *the benefits of technology*

boon: *This service is a boon to the elderly*

gift: *A cheerful nature is a gift*

godsend: *The extra twenty dollars was a godsend*

help: *My computer is a real help in my work*

2 approval or permission to do something: *She got married with her parents' blessing*

approval: *Does this plan have your approval?*

backing: *We can't do anything without his backing*

consent: *He gave his consent to the article*

leave: *She gave us leave to start*

permission: *You have my permission to go*

support: *My manager has given his full support to my project*

see also **approval, sanction**

blight see infect, pest

bliss see ecstasy, heaven, joy

blister see boil

blob noun a small amount of a thick or sticky substance: *He had a blob of chocolate mousse on his tie*

bead: *Beads of blood spattered the counter*

dab: You've got a dab of glue on your nose

drop: a few thick drops of fluid

droplet: droplets of congealed fat

block noun **1** a large piece: a block of wood

bar: a bar of soap

brick: concrete bricks

chunk: chunks of meat

ingot: a gold ingot

lump: lumps of metal

piece: a big piece of cake

▷ verb **2** to close by putting something across: Mud blocked the river

choke: The town was choked with cars

clog: Dishes clogged the sink

obstruct: The crash obstructed the road

plug: Have you plugged the leaks?

3 to prevent something happening: The council blocked his plans

bar: He was barred from entering

check: a policy to check population growth

halt: attempts to halt the spread of disease

obstruct: Lack of funds obstructed our progress

stop: measures to stop the rising crime rate

thwart: My plans were thwarted by Taylor

see also **blockage, close, frustrate, hinder, impede, obstruct, plug**

blockage noun a thing that clogs something: a blockage in the pipe

block: a block in the blood vessel

obstruction: an obstruction on the track

stoppage: We have to clear the stoppage

bloke see **man**

blond see **fair, light**

blonde see **fair, light**

bloodshed see **violence**

bloodthirsty see **violent**

bloom see **flourish**

blooming see **well**

blossom see **progress**

blot see **spot, stain**

blotch see **spot**

blot out verb to cover and prevent from being seen: The smoke blotted out the sky

eclipse: The moon eclipsed the sun

obliterate: Our view was obliterated by mist

obscure: My way was obscured by fog

shadow: Her veil shadowed her face

blow verb **1** to move or cause to move in the wind: The wind blew his papers away

buffet: The ship was buffeted by gales

drive: The strong wind drove us forward

flutter: The flags are fluttering

sweep: A sudden blast swept away the cloth

waft: His hair wafted in the breeze

whirl: The fallen leaves whirled around

▷ noun **2** a hit from something: a blow to the head

bang: He suffered some bangs and bumps

clout informal: a clout on the head

knock: Knocks can cause damage to the spine

smack: She gave the child a smack

thump: Ralph got a thump on the chest

whack: The horse got a whack from its rider

3 something disappointing or upsetting: Marc's death was a terrible blow

bombshell: His departure was a bombshell for the team

disappointment: My exam results were a real disappointment

misfortune: a series of misfortunes

setback: *We faced many setbacks before we got the house*
shock: *The news came as a shock*
upset: *The defeat caused an upset*
see also **bang, disappointment, hit, shock, sound**

blow up *see* **bomb, explode**
bludge *see* **scrounge**
bludgeon *see* **club**
blueprint *see* **plan**
bluff *see* **blunt, con**
blunder *see* **err, error, mistake, slip**
blunt *adjective* **1** having rounded edges: *blunt scissors*
  dull: *a dull knife*
  rounded: *rounded edges*
  unsharpened: *an unsharpened pencil*
  2 saying what you think: *a blunt speaker*
  bluff: *a bluff old man*
  brusque: *His response was brusque*
  forthright: *a forthright reply*
  frank: *I'll be frank with you*
  outspoken: *an outspoken critic*
  straightforward: *She has a straightforward manner*
  see also **candid, direct, frank, straight**

blush *verb* **1** to go red in the face: *I felt myself blushing*
  colour: *I found myself colouring as I spoke*
  crimson: *He looked at her and she crimsoned*
  flush: *I saw her face flush*
  go red: *His face went red as a beetroot*
  turn red: *He turned red with embarrassment*
  turn scarlet: *She turned scarlet with humiliation*
  ▷ *noun* **2** a red colour: *Ann took the gift with a blush*
  colour: *The walk will bring colour to your cheeks*
  flush: *A slow flush spread over the man's face*
  glow: *a healthy glow*

board *see* **council, management, sign**
boast *verb* to talk proudly: *Carol boasted about her costume*
  brag: *I don't mind bragging about my talents*
  crow: *Stop crowing about your success*
  skite *Australian, New Zealand informal*: *That's nothing to skite about*
  see also **brag**

boaster *see* **braggart**
boastful *adjective* tending to brag about things: *a boastful liar*
  bragging: *bragging stories about his time in the navy*
  cocky: *The boxer is cocky and brash*
  conceited: *Young men tend to be conceited*
  crowing: *crowing remarks*
  egotistical: *egotistical fibs*
  swaggering: *He has a swaggering arrogance*

bob *see* **bounce, float**
body *noun* **1** all your physical parts: *My whole body hurt*
  build: *He is of medium build*
  figure: *Janet has a nice figure*
  form: *clothes that flatter your form*
  frame: *their bony frames*
  physique: *a powerful physique*
  shape: *his trim shape*
  2 a dead body: *Police found a body hidden in the forest*
  carcass: *a sheep's carcass*
  corpse: *the corpse of a young man*
  dead body: *He'd never seen a dead body*
  remains: *human remains*
  3 an organized group of people: *local voluntary bodies*
  association: *the Football Association*
  band: *a band of rebels*

company: the Royal Shakespeare Company
confederation: a confederation of workers
organization: student organizations
society: I joined the local opera society
see also **association**, **build**, **figure**, **organization**

boggle see **wonder**
bogus see **false**, **mock**, **phoney**
boil verb **1** to bubble: The water is boiling
bubble: Potatoes bubbled in the pot
fizz: The liquid fizzed and bubbled
foam: When the butter foams, add the onions
froth: The milk frothed over in the pan
▷ noun **2** a swelling on the skin: five boils on his face
blister: a blister on my index finger
swelling: a swelling under the eye
tumour: The tumours had all disappeared
see also **cook**

boiling see **hot**
boisterous see **rowdy**, **wild**
bold adjective **1** confident and not shy: a bold question
brash: a brash young sergeant
brazen: a brazen young woman
cheeky: a cheeky grin
confident: I felt confident confronting him
forward: It was forward of you to ask him
impudent: an impudent child
2 unafraid of risk or danger: a bold attempt
adventurous: an adventurous spirit
brave: a brave woman
courageous: courageous firefighters
daring: daring feats
fearless: a fearless warrior
intrepid: an intrepid explorer
3 clear and noticeable: bold colours

bright: bright light
flashy: flashy clothes
loud: a loud tie
striking: a striking tartan pattern
strong: dressed in strong reds and yellows
vivid: vivid green and purple
see also **brave**, **daring**

boldness see **bravery**, **daring**, **impudence**
bolster see **reassure**, **strengthen**, **support**
bolt verb to escape or run away: I bolted towards the exit
dash: He dashed out of the room in a panic
escape: They escaped across the frontier
flee: We fled before the police arrived
fly: She flew down the stairs with her attacker in hot pursuit
run away: I called to him but he just ran away
run off: The children ran off when they spotted me
rush: They all rushed away as we approached
see also **catch**, **dash**, **flee**, **gobble**, **run**

bomb noun **1** an explosive device: The bomb exploded in the centre of the city
device: Experts defused the device
explosive: a block of plastic explosive
missile: long-range missiles
rocket: a rocket launcher
shell: Shells began to fall
torpedo: The torpedo struck the ship
▷ verb **2** to attack with bombs: His house was bombed
attack: We are being attacked!
blow up: He attempted to blow up the building
bombard: Warships began to bombard the coast
destroy: Helicopters destroyed his village

shell: They shelled the troops heavily

torpedo: His ship was torpedoed in the Channel

bombard see **bomb**

bombardment see **hail**

bombshell see **blow, shock, surprise**

bona fide see **authentic, genuine, real, true**

bond noun **1** a close relationship: *a special bond between us*

attachment: *Mother and child form a close attachment*

connection: *a family connection*

link: *the links of friendship*

relation: *the relation between husband and wife*

tie: *the ties of blood*

union: *the union of father and son*
2 an obligation to do something: *the social bonds of community*

agreement: *He has broken our agreement*

contract: *He signed a two-year contract*

obligation: *your obligation to your father*

pledge: *a pledge of support*

promise: *You must keep your promises*

word: *I give you my word*

▷ verb **3** to attach separate things: *Strips of wood are bonded together*

bind: *Tape was used to bind the files*

fasten: *I fastened the picture to the wall*

fuse: *The pieces to be joined are melted and fused together*

glue: *Glue the pieces together*

paste: *He pasted posters to the wall*

see also **association, attachment, connection, link, relation, relationship, stick, tie**

bonds see **stock**

bonsela see **gift, present**

bonus see **extra, reward**

bony see **skinny**

book noun **1** a number of pages in a cover: *I'm reading a great book just now*

publication: *publications about job hunting*

textbook: *He wrote a textbook on law*

title: *We publish a range of titles*

tome: *a heavy tome*

volume: *small volumes of poetry*

work: *my favourite work by this author*

▷ verb **2** to arrange to have or use: *The tickets are booked*

charter: *A plane was chartered for them*

engage: *We engaged the services of a plumber*

organize: *I have organized our flights*

reserve: *Hotel rooms have been reserved*

schedule: *A meeting is scheduled for Monday*

booklet see **leaflet**

boom see **bang, flourish**

boon see **benefit, blessing**

boost see **augment, encourage**

booty see **loot**

booze see **alcohol, drink**

boozer see **drunk, pub**

border noun **1** a dividing line between things or places: *the border between two countries*

borderline: *the borderline between health and sickness*

boundary: *national boundaries*

frontier: *the American frontier*

line: *the line between fact and fiction*
2 an edge of something: *plain tiles with a bright border*

bounds: *the bounds of good taste*

edge: *the edge of town*

limits: *the city limits*

margin: *the western margins of the island*

rim: *the rim of the lake*

▷ verb **3** to form an edge: *Tall trees bordered the fields*
  edge: *the woods that edge the lake*
  fringe: *Street lights fringe the bay*
  hem: *dresses hemmed with feathers*
  rim: *the restaurants rimming the harbour*
  trim: *coats trimmed with fur collars*
  see also **coast, edge**

borderline *see* **border**

bore *see* **annoyance, pest, pierce**

bored adjective impatient and not interested in something: *I am bored with this business*
  fed up: *He is fed up with this country*
  tired: *I am tired of this music*
  uninterested: *He seems uninterested in politics*
  wearied: *He spoke in a wearied voice*
  see also **sick of, uninterested**

boredom noun a lack of interest: *the boredom of long trips*
  apathy: *political apathy*
  dullness: *a period of dullness*
  flatness: *a feeling of flatness*
  monotony: *the monotony of winter*
  tedium: *the tedium of unemployment*
  weariness: *a sense of weariness*

boring adjective dull and uninteresting: *a boring job*
  dull: *dull tasks*
  flat: *a flat performance*
  humdrum: *humdrum lives*
  monotonous: *the monotonous prison routine*
  tedious: *The work is tedious*
  tiresome: *a tiresome old man*
  see also **dreary, dull, flat**

boss noun a person in charge of something: *He can't stand his boss*
  chief: *the police chief*
  director: *the directors of the bank*
  employer: *He was sent to Rome by his employer*
  head: *Heads of government met in New York*

leader: *The party's leader has resigned*
  manager: *the company's marketing manager*
  see also **chief, employer, head, leader, manager, superior**

bosses *see* **management**

bossy adjective telling people what to do: *a rather bossy little girl*
  arrogant: *arrogant behaviour*
  authoritarian: *He has an authoritarian approach to parenthood*
  dictatorial: *a dictatorial management style*
  domineering: *She is domineering and ruthless*
  imperious: *He has an imperious manner*
  overbearing: *an overbearing mother*
  see also **pushy**

botch verb to do something badly: *a botched operation*
  bungle: *inefficient people who bungled the job*
  mar: *She marred her exit by twisting her ankle*
  mess up: *He manages to mess up his life*

botch up *see* **mess**

bother verb **1** to cause worry or concern: *His lack of money bothers him*
  annoy: *The things that annoy me*
  concern: *The future concerns me*
  disturb: *It disturbs me to see you unhappy*
  get on someone's nerves *informal*: *This place gets on my nerves*
  trouble: *Are you troubled by nightmares?*
  worry: *I'm worried by the amount he is drinking*
▷ noun **2** trouble and difficulty: *I hate the bother of shopping*
  annoyance: *Snoring can be an annoyance*
  difficulty: *The strikes are causing*

difficulties for commuters

inconvenience: a minor inconvenience

irritation: Noise is an irritation

trouble: You've caused me a lot of trouble

worry: It was a time of worry for us
see also **agitate, annoy, concern, distress, disturb, fuss, hassle, irritate, nuisance, pester, trouble, upset, worry**

bothered see **anxious, worried**

bottom noun 1 the lowest part of something: the bottom of the stairs

base: the base of the spine

bed: the river bed

depths: the depths of the earth

floor: the ocean floor

foot: the foot of the bed

2 the part of the body you sit on: Sit on your bottom!

backside informal: the muscles in your backside

behind informal: He kicked me on the behind

buttocks: exercises for your buttocks

posterior humorous: He fell on his posterior

rear: I was thrown out on my rear

▷ adjective 3 in the lowest place or position: the bottom drawer

base: the base edge of the curtain

basement: a basement flat

ground: ground level

lowest: the lowest part of the brain
see also **base**

bottomless see **deep**

bounce verb to spring back or move up and down: I bounced a ball against the wall

bob: The raft bobbed along

bound: He bounded up the stairway

bump: My bicycle bumped along the rough ground

jump: They jumped up and down to keep warm

ricochet: The bullets ricocheted off the jeep
see also **glance, leap**

bound see **bounce, jump, leap**

boundary see **border, edge, extreme**

boundless see **infinite**

bounds see **border, limit, range**

bountiful see **plentiful**

bounty see **abundance, reward, wealth**

bouquet see **bunch, fragrance**

bout see **event, fight**

boutique see **shop**

bovine see **cow**

bow see **resign oneself, bend, submit**

box noun a container with a firm base and sides: All her possessions were packed in boxes

carton: cartons full of books

case: It is still in its original case

chest: She kept her heirlooms in a carved wooden chest

container: substances kept in heavy metal containers

trunk: a trunk full of toys
see also **case**

boy noun a male child: I knew him when he was a boy

fellow: a fine little fellow

lad: I remember being a lad his age

schoolboy: a group of schoolboys

youngster: I was only a youngster in 1970

youth: gangs of youths who cause trouble

boycott verb to refuse to have anything to do with: Some parties are boycotting the elections

blacklist: He has been blacklisted by various societies

embargo: Imports of fruit were embargoed

exclude: I exclude animal products from my diet

reject: *She rejected her parents' religion*
spurn: *You spurned his last offer*
see also **sanctions**

brace *see* **refresh, steady, strengthen, support**

bracing *see* **healthy**

brag *verb* to boast about something: *I hate people who brag about their achievements*
boast: *She kept boasting about how many guys she'd been out with*
crow: *Stop crowing about your victory*
skite or **skite** *Australian, New Zealand informal*: *That's nothing to skite about*
see also **boast**

braggart *noun* a person who boasts: *He was a braggart and a liar*
bigmouth *slang*: *He's nothing but a bigmouth*
boaster: *an idle boaster after the main chance*
bragger: *He was quite a bragger*
show-off: *I've always been a show-off*
skite or **skiter** *Australian, New Zealand informal*: *a bit of a skite*

bragger *see* **braggart**

bragging *see* **boastful**

brain *see* **genius, head, mind**

brains *see* **genius, sense**

brain-teaser *see* **puzzle**

brainy *see* **bright, brilliant, clever, intelligent**

brak *see* **dog, salty**

brake *see* **curb**

brand *see* **kind, make, sort, type**

brandish *see* **flourish, shake, wave**

brash *see* **bold, cocky**

brave *adjective* **1** willing to do dangerous things: *a brave attempt to stop the attack*
bold: *Amrita became a bold rebel*
courageous: *a courageous decision*
fearless: *his fearless campaigning for justice*

heroic: *The heroic sergeant risked his life*
plucky: *The plucky schoolgirl amazed the doctors*
valiant: *a valiant attempt to keep going*
▷ *verb* **2** to face something without fear: *Fans braved the rain to hear him sing*
face: *I can't face another three years of this*
stand up to: *I have tried to stand up to the bullies*
see also **bold, daring**

bravery *noun* the quality of being courageous: *He deserves praise for his bravery*
boldness: *an outward display of boldness*
courage: *They do not have the courage to apologize*
fortitude: *He suffered with tremendous fortitude*
heroism: *acts of heroism*
pluck: *He has pluck and presence of mind*
valour: *He won a medal for valour*
see also **courage, daring**

brawl *see* **fight**

brawn *see* **power, strength**

brazen *see* **bold, shameless**

breach *noun* **1** a breaking of an agreement or law: *a breach of contract*
infringement: *an infringement of the rules*
offence: *criminal offences*
trespass: *a campaign of trespasses and demonstrations*
violation: *a violation of the peace agreement*
2 a gap in something: *the breach in the Berlin Wall*
crack: *a large crack in the ice*
gap: *a narrow gap in the curtains*
hole: *We cut holes in the fabric*

opening: an opening in the fence
rift: The earthquake caused a deep rift
split: There's a split in my mattress
see also **break, division, split**

break verb **1** to separate into pieces: I broke a plate
see **word studies break**
2 to fail to keep a rule or promise: He broke his promise to attend
breach: breaches of discipline
contravene: His behaviour contravenes our code of conduct
infringe: The judge ruled that he had infringed no rules
violate: They violated the peace agreement
▷ noun **3** a short period of rest or change: I took a five-minute break from work
interlude: a happy interlude in my life
interval: a long interval when no-one spoke
pause: After a pause Alex spoke
recess: The court adjourned for a recess
respite: They have had no respite from bombing
rest: I'll start again after a rest
see also **burst, crack, dash, disobey, gap, holiday, interrupt, interval, pause, rest, ruin**

break free see **escape**
break into see **raid**
break out see **escape**
break up see **disintegrate, separate**
break your promise see **betray**
breakable see **fragile**
breakdown see **failure**
breaker see **wave**
breakfast see **eat**
break-in see **raid**
breakneck see **furious**
breakthrough see **advance, progress**
breakup see **split**
breathing see **alive**

breathtaking see **superb**
breed noun **1** a type of animal: rare breeds of cattle
kind: What kind of horse is that?
species: Pandas are an endangered species
stock: cattle of Highland stock
strain: a special strain of rat
type: What type of dog should we get?
variety: many varieties of birds
▷ verb **2** to produce and look after: He breeds dogs for the police
cultivate: She cultivates fruit and vegetables
develop: A new variety of potato is being developed
keep: He keeps guinea pigs
nurture: trimming and nurturing plants and saplings
raise: He raises birds of prey as a hobby
rear: the difficulties of rearing children
3 to produce offspring: Frogs can breed in most ponds
multiply: Rats multiply quickly
produce: She produced a son
propagate: This plant is difficult to propagate
reproduce: the natural desire to reproduce
see also **kind, type**

bribe see **bait, corrupt**
bribery see **corruption**
brick see **block**
brief adjective **1** lasting for a short time: a brief appearance on television
fleeting: a fleeting glance
momentary: There was a momentary silence
quick: a quick look at the newspaper
short: a short holiday
swift: a swift glance at John's face
▷ verb **2** to give necessary information: A spokesman briefed reporters
advise: I must advise you of my

decision to retire

fill in *informal:* Can you fill me in on Wilbur's visit?

inform: They would inform him of their progress

instruct: He instructed us in first aid

prepare: I will prepare you for this exam

prime: Arnold primed him for his duties

see also **concise, quick, short**

bright *adjective* **1** strong and startling: a bright light

brilliant: brilliant green eyes

dazzling: a dazzling white shirt

glowing: the glowing windows of the Cathedral

luminous: a luminous star

radiant: eyes as radiant as sapphires

vivid: strong, vivid colours

2 clever and alert: my brightest student

brainy: I don't consider myself brainy

brilliant: She has a brilliant mind

clever: a clever child

ingenious: an ingenious idea

intelligent: Dolphins are an intelligent species

smart: He thinks he's as smart as Sarah

3 cheerful and lively: a bright smile

cheerful: Jack sounded quite cheerful about the idea

happy: a confident, happy child

jolly: a jolly nature

light-hearted: They are light-hearted and enjoy life

lively: He has a lively personality

merry: bursts of merry laughter

see also **acute, bold, brilliant, cheerful, clever, colourful, gaudy, glossy, intelligent, sharp, shining, smart**

brighten see **light**

brightness see **light**

brilliance see **genius, gloss, light**

brilliant *adjective* **1** very bright: a brilliant light

bright: a bright star

dazzling: a dazzling white shirt

gleaming: gleaming headlights

glowing: glowing colours

luminous: luminous orange paint

radiant: a figure surrounded by a radiant glow

sparkling: a choker of sparkling jewels

vivid: the vivid hues of tropical flowers

2 very clever: a brilliant pupil

acute: His relaxed exterior hides an acute mind

brainy *informal:* You don't have to be too brainy to work that one out

bright: an exceptionally bright child

clever: What a clever idea!

intelligent: a lively and extremely intelligent woman

perceptive: a perceptive analysis of the situation

sharp: a sharp intellect

smart: He's the smartest student we've ever had

3 wonderful or superb: It's a brilliant film

first-class: a first-class violinist

great: one of the greatest novels of the century

magnificent: a magnificent display

marvellous: I've had a marvellous time

outstanding: He's an outstanding actor

superb: a superb artist

tremendous: a tremendous performance

wonderful: the most wonderful music I've ever heard

see also **bright, colourful, excellent, glossy, grand, keen, marvellous, outstanding, shining, witty**

brim see **edge**

bring *verb* **1** to take somewhere:

Bring a friend to the party
bear: *They bore the box into the kitchen*
carry: *She carried her son to the car*
convey: *Emergency supplies were conveyed by truck*
lead: *She led him into the house*
take: *He took cakes to the party*
transport: *The troops were transported to Moscow*
2 to cause to happen: *Bring the vegetables to the boil*
cause: *My mistake caused me some worry*
create: *The new factory will create more jobs*
inflict: *The attack inflicted heavy casualties*
produce: *The drug produces side effects*
result in: *Many accidents result in serious injuries*
wreak: *Violent storms wreaked havoc*
see also **take**
bring about *verb* to cause something to happen: *It was his arrogance which brought about his downfall*
cause: *This may cause delays*
create: *The new scheme will create even more confusion*
generate: *the excitement generated by this film*
make happen: *If you want change, you have to make it happen yourself*
produce: *His comments produced a furious response*
provoke: *a move that has provoked a storm of protest*
see also **accomplish, cause, create, occasion, result in**
bring back *see* **remind**
bring down *see* **overthrow**
bring forward *see* **produce**
bring in *see* **earn**
bring out *see* **publish**

bring round *see* **persuade, reason**
bring to a standstill *see* **cripple**
bring to an end *see* **end**
bring to bear *see* **employ**
bring to light *see* **expose, produce, reveal, uncover**
bring up *see* **mention, raise, refer, vomit**
brink *see* **bank**
briny *see* **salty**
brisk *see* **hasty, quick, swift**
bristling *see* **thick**
broach *see* **mention, raise**
broad *adjective* **1** large, especially from side to side: *His shoulders were broad and his waist narrow*
expansive: *There are also several swing sets and an expansive grassy play area*
extensive: *The palace grounds were more extensive than the town itself*
large: *He was a large man with a thick square head*
thick: *a finger as thick as a sausage*
vast: *rich families who own vast stretches of land*
wide: *a sunhat with a wide brim*
2 including or affecting many different things or people: *A broad range of issues was discussed*
comprehensive: *This book is a comprehensive guide to the region*
extensive: *extensive research into public attitudes to science*
general: *The project should raise general awareness about bullying*
sweeping: *sweeping economic reforms*
universal: *the universal problem of pollution*
wide: *A major event which brought together a wide range of interest groups*
wide-ranging: *The aims of our campaign are wide-ranging but simple*
3 general rather than detailed: *These*

documents provided a broad outline of the Society's development

approximate: They did not have even an approximate idea of what the word meant

general: The figures represent a general decline in employment

non-specific: I intend to use these terms in a deliberately non-specific way

rough: I've got a rough idea of what he looks like

sweeping: a sweeping statement about women drivers

vague: They have only a vague idea of the amount of water available

see also **extensive, general, spacious, widespread**

broadcast see **announcement, programme, send**

broad-minded see **tolerant**

brochure see **leaflet**

broke see **poor**

broken adjective **1** in pieces: a broken window

  burst: a burst pipe

  demolished: a demolished house

  fractured: He suffered a fractured skull

  fragmented: fragmented images

  shattered: shattered glass

  smashed: smashed windows

  2 not kept: a broken promise

  infringed: a case of infringed human rights

  violated: a series of violated agreements

see also **imperfect**

broken-down see **worn-out**

broker see **trader**

brood see **ponder, worry, young**

brotherhood see **fellowship**

bruised see **tender**

brumby see **horse**

brush see **glance, touch**

brush up see **polish**

brusque see **blunt, impatient**

brutal see **cruel, savage, violent**

brutality see **cruelty, violence**

brute see **oaf, savage**

bubble see **boil, foam**

bubbles see **foam**

buckle see **bend, clasp, give**

budding see **in the making**

buddy see **china**

budgetary see **economic**

budgeting see **finance**

buff see **expert, polish**

buffer see **protection**

buffet see **beat, blow**

bug see **pester**

build verb **1** to make something: The house was built last year

  assemble: Workers were assembling planes

  construct: plans to construct a temple on the site

  erect: The building was erected in 1900

  fabricate: All the tools are fabricated from steel

  form: hotels formed from cheap cement

  make: a wall made of bricks

  2 to develop gradually: I want to build a relationship with them

  develop: These battles could develop into war

  extend: Three new products extend the range

  increase: The population continues to increase

  intensify: The conflict is bound to intensify

  strengthen: Cycling strengthens the muscles

  ▷ noun **3** the size of a body: He is of medium build

  body: a body of average size

  figure: Janet has a nice figure

  form: clothes that flatter your form

  frame: their bony frames

physique: *a powerful physique*
shape: *his trim shape*
see also **assemble, base, body, construct, figure, make**

build up see **reconstruct**

building noun *a structure with walls*: *a glass building*
edifice: *historic edifices in the area*
structure: *The museum is an impressive structure*
see also **house, making, structure**

bulge verb **1** to swell out: *He bulges out of his black T-shirt*
expand: *The pipes expanded in the heat*
protrude: *His blue eyes protruded from his head*
stick out: *His stomach stuck out under his jacket*
swell: *My ankles swelled*
▷ noun **2** *a lump in something*: *My purse made a bulge in my pocket*
bump: *a bump in the road*
hump: *a camel's hump*
lump: *itchy red lumps on the skin*
protrusion: *a strange protrusion on his forehead*
swelling: *a swelling on my foot*
see also **bump, lump**

bulk see **majority, size**

bulky see **heavy**

bull see **nonsense**

bulletin see **announcement, message, news, statement, word**

bully noun **1** *someone who deliberately frightens or hurts others*: *I fell victim to the class bully*
oppressor: *They were powerless against their oppressors*
persecutor: *Eventually he stood up to his persecutors*
▷ verb **2** *to frighten or hurt someone deliberately and repeatedly*: *I wasn't going to let him bully me*
intimidate: *Jones had set out to intimidate and dominate Paul*

oppress: *men who try to dominate and oppress women*
persecute: *Tom was persecuted by his sisters*
pick on: *I don't like to see you pick on younger children*
tease: *The boys in the village had set on him, teasing him*
torment: *My older brother and sister used to torment me*
3 *to make someone do something by using force*: *She used to bully me into doing my schoolwork*
force: *I cannot force you in this. You must decide*
intimidate: *attempts to intimidate people into voting for the governing party*
pressurize: *Do not be pressurized into making your decision immediately*

bump verb **1** *to hit something*: *He bumped his head on the wall*
bang: *I banged my shin on the edge of the table*
collide: *The car collided with a tree*
hit: *She hit the last barrier and fell*
jolt: *We hit the wall with a jolt*
knock: *He knocked on the door*
strike: *His head struck the windscreen*
▷ noun **2** *a dull noise*: *He heard a bump outside*
bang: *I heard four or five loud bangs*
knock: *They heard a knock at the door*
thud: *She tripped and fell with a thud*
thump: *There was a loud thump against the house*
3 *a raised part of something*: *a bump in the road*
bulge: *My purse made a bulge in my pocket*
hump: *a camel's hump*
knob: *a door with a brass knob*
lump: *itchy red lumps on the skin*
swelling: *a swelling on my foot*
see also **bounce, bulge, crash, hit, lump**

bump into see meet
bumpy see irregular, rough, uneven
bunch noun 1 a group of people: *The players were a great bunch*
  band: *Bands of criminals were roaming some neighbourhoods*
  crowd: *All the old crowd have come out for this occasion*
  gaggle: *A gaggle of journalists sit in a hotel foyer waiting impatiently*
  gang: *Come on over – we've got lots of the old gang here*
  group: *The trouble involved a small group of football supporters*
  lot: *Future generations are going to think that we were a pretty boring lot*
  multitude: *surrounded by a noisy multitude*
2 several cut flowers held together: *He had left a huge bunch of flowers in her hotel room*
  bouquet: *She laid a bouquet on his grave*
  posy: *a posy of wild flowers*
  spray: *a small spray of freesias*
3 a group of things: *George took out a bunch of keys and went to work on the lock*
  batch: *She brought a large batch of newspaper cuttings*
  bundle: *a bundle of sticks tied together with string*
  cluster: *a cluster of shops, cabins and motels*
  heap: *a heap of old boxes for the bonfire*
  load: *His people came up with a load of embarrassing stories*
  pile: *I've got a pile of questions afterwards for you*
  set: *Only she and Mr Cohen had complete sets of keys to the shop*
  see also band, group, lot
bundle see bunch
bung see plug
bungle see botch, mess

bungling see incompetent
buoyant see cheerful, optimistic
burble see babble
burden noun 1 a load that is carried: *My wet clothes were an added burden*
  load: *a big load of hay*
  weight: *straining to lift heavy weights*
2 something that worries you: *the burden of looking after a sick parent*
  anxiety: *He expressed his anxieties to me*
  care: *Forget all the cares of the day*
  strain: *I find the travelling a strain*
  stress: *the stress of exams*
  trouble: *The Sullivans have money troubles*
  worry: *My son is a worry to me*
  see also handicap
bureaucracy noun complex rules and procedures: *Is there too much bureaucracy in government?*
  administration: *high administration costs*
  officialdom: *Officialdom is against us*
  red tape: *Our application was delayed by red tape*
  regulations: *absurd regulations about opening hours*
burglar see thief
burgle see rob
burly see plump
burn verb 1 to be on fire: *a fire burning in the fireplace*
  be ablaze: *The houses were ablaze*
  be on fire: *The ship was on fire*
  blaze: *The wreckage blazed*
  flame: *We watched as the house flamed*
  flare: *The match flared in the dark*
  flicker: *The fire flickered and crackled*
2 to destroy with fire: *They burned the house down*
  char: *charred bodies*
  incinerate: *Hospitals incinerate*

waste

scorch: The bonfire scorched the grass

shrivel: The papers shrivelled in the flames

singe: Her hair was singed and her coat burnt

burrow see dig

burst verb 1 to split apart: The balloon burst

break: He broke the box open

crack: A water pipe had cracked

explode: The glass exploded

puncture: The glass punctured the tyre

rupture: His appendix ruptured

split: The seam of my dress split

2 to happen or appear suddenly: to burst into flames

barge: He barged into the room

break: Her face broke into a smile

erupt: Violence could erupt soon

rush: Water rushed out of the hole
▷ noun 3 a short period of something: a burst of energy

fit: a fit of rage

outbreak: an outbreak of violence

rush: a sudden rush of excitement

spate: a spate of attacks on horses

surge: a surge of emotion

torrent: a torrent of words
see also broken, explode, flash, split

bush see country

bushie see yokel

bushy see yokel

business noun 1 the buying and selling of goods: a career in business

commerce: commerce between Europe and South America

dealings: All dealings with the company were suspended

industry: the American car industry

trade: French trade with the West Indies

trading: trading between the two countries

transaction: We settled the transaction over lunch

2 an organization selling goods or services: a family business

company: the Ford Motor Company

corporation: international corporations

enterprise: small industrial enterprises

establishment: shops and other commercial establishments

firm: a firm of engineers

organization: a well-run organization

3 any event or situation: This business has upset me

affair: He handled the affair badly

issue: What is your view on this issue?

matter: This is a matter for the police

problem: solutions to the drug problem

question: the whole question of TV censorship

subject: He raised the subject of money
see also affair, company, concern, enterprise, event, firm, matter, profession, scene, trade, undertaking, work

businesslike see efficient

bustle verb 1 to move hurriedly: My mother bustled about the room

dash: We dashed about purposefully

fuss: Waiters were fussing round the table

hurry: Claire hurried along the road

rush: I'm rushing to finish the cooking

scurry: rats scurrying around

scuttle: Crabs scuttle along the bank
▷ noun 2 busy and noisy activity: the bustle of modern life

activity: a burst of activity in the building

commotion: He heard a commotion outside

excitement: The news created great excitement

flurry: *a flurry of activity*
fuss: *He works without any fuss*
hurry: *the hurry and excitement of the city*
see also **activity, fuss, rush**

busy *adjective* **1** *doing something*: *What is it? I'm busy*
active: *He is active in local politics*
employed: *He was employed helping me*
engaged: *He was engaged in conversation*
engrossed: *She is engrossed in her work*
occupied: *He is occupied with the packing*
working: *I am working on a novel*
2 *full of activity*: *a busy tourist resort*
active: *an active, independent country*
full: *a full life*
hectic: *my hectic work schedule*
lively: *a lively restaurant*
restless: *a restless mind*
▷ *verb* **3** *to occupy or keep busy*: *Kathryn busied herself in the kitchen*
absorb: *Her career absorbed her completely*
employ: *You'd be better employed helping me*
engage: *He was engaged in a meeting when I called*
immerse: *She immersed herself in her book*
occupy: *Try to occupy yourself with something*
see also **active, industrious**

but *conjunction* **1** *although*: *Heat the cider until it is very hot but not boiling*
although: *He was in love with her, although he had not yet admitted it to himself*
though: *He's very attractive, though not exactly handsome*
while: *The first two services are free, while the third costs £35*
yet: *It is completely waterproof, yet light and comfortable*
▷ *preposition* **2** *with the exception of*: *The crew gave them nothing but bread to eat*
except: *I don't take any drugs except aspirin*
except for: *No-one had complained except for you*
save: *The people had no water at all save that brought up from bore holes*
other than: *This route is not recommended to anyone other than the most experienced cyclist*
see also **except**

butcher *see* **kill**

butt in *see* **interfere, interrupt, intrude**

buttocks *see* **bottom**

buy *verb* *to obtain with money*: *I'd like to buy him lunch*
acquire: *I have acquired a new car*
invest in: *I invested in a house*
obtain: *She went to obtain a ticket*
pay for: *He let me pay for his drink*
procure: *attempts to procure more food*
purchase: *He purchased a sandwich for lunch*

buy off *see* **corrupt**

buyer *see* **customer**

by *see* **past**

by degrees *see* **slowly**

by design *see* **on purpose**

by dint of *see* **by virtue of**

by oneself *see* **on your own**

bygone *see* **former, past**

bystander *see* **spectator, witness**

C

cache see hide, hoard, reserve, stockpile, store, supply

cadence see beat

cadge see scrounge

cagey see secretive

cajole see coax

cake see harden, lump

calamitous see fatal

calamity see disaster

calculate verb to work out a number or amount: *how to calculate the cost of setting up a business*

count: *Shareholders are counting the cost of the slump*

determine: *calculations to determine the rate of tax*

reckon: *an amount reckoned at 140 billion marks*

work out: *Work out the distance of the journey*

see also **count, reckon, work out**

calculated adjective deliberately planned: *Everything they said was calculated to wound*

aimed: *The restructuring is aimed at reducing costs*

designed: *a scheme designed to help poorer families*

intended: *the intended effect of the revised guidelines*

planned: *a carefully planned campaign*

see also **deliberate**

calculating see devious

calculation see count

calibre see quality, standard

call verb 1 to give a name: *a man called Jeffrey*

2 to telephone: *He called me at my office*

3 to say loudly: *I heard someone calling my name*

see word studies **call**

▷ noun **4** an instance of someone shouting out: *a call for help*

cry: *the cry of a seagull*

shout: *I heard a distant shout*

yell: *He let out a yell*

see also **cry, hail, name, request, shout, visit**

call off see cancel

call on see visit

call upon see appeal

callous adjective not concerned about other people: *his callous disregard for human life*

cold: *What a cold, unfeeling woman she was*

heartless: *It was a heartless thing to do*

indifferent: *indifferent to the suffering of others*

insensitive: *insensitive remarks*

see also **cruel, merciless**

callousness see cruelty

calm adjective **1** not worried or excited: *Try to keep calm*

collected: *She was cool and collected during her interrogation*

composed: *a very composed, business-like woman*

cool: *We have to keep a cool head in this situation*

impassive: *He remained impassive as his sentence was passed*

relaxed: *a relaxed manner*

2 still because there is no wind:
Tuesday was a fine, clear and calm day
balmy: *balmy summer evenings*
mild: *a mild winter climate*
still: *The air was still*
tranquil: *a tranquil lake*
▷ noun **3** the state of being peaceful:
He liked the calm of the evening
calmness: *an aura of calmness*
peace: *a wonderful feeling of peace*
peacefulness: *the peacefulness of
the gardens*
quiet: *a quiet, relaxing holiday*
serenity: *the peace and serenity of a
tropical sunset*
stillness: *the stillness of the summer
night*
▷ verb **4** to make less upset or
excited: *We were trying to calm him*
quieten: *trying to quieten the restless
horses*
relax: *This music is supposed to
relax you*
soothe: *I think a bath may soothe me*
see also **cool, ease, pacify, patient,
peace, peaceful, quiet, relaxed,
silence, still**
calmness see **calm, patience, quiet**
camaraderie see **fellowship**
camp see **base, side**
campaign noun actions planned to
get a certain result: *a campaign to
educate people*
crusade: *the crusade for human
rights*
movement: *the human rights
movement*
operation: *a full-scale military
operation*
push: *an all-out push to promote
the show*
see also **agitate, movement**
cancel verb **1** to stop something from
happening: *We're going to have to
cancel our picnic*
abandon: *He had to abandon his*

holiday plans
call off: *The union has called off
the strike*
2 to stop something from being
valid: *They were forced to cancel their
contract*
annul: *The marriage was annulled*
quash: *His jail sentence was quashed
when new evidence came to light*
repeal: *The new law was repealed
within the year*
revoke: *His licence was immediately
revoked*
see also **lift**
cancel out see **compensate**
candid adjective honest and frank: *a
candid interview*
blunt: *She is blunt about his faults*
frank: *They had a frank discussion
about the issue*
honest: *What is your honest opinion?*
open: *He had always been open with
her and she would know if he lied*
truthful: *We've all learnt to be fairly
truthful about our personal lives*
straightforward: *I was impressed by
his straightforward manner*
see also **direct, frank, natural, open,
straight, straightforward**
candidate noun a person being
considered for a position: *a candidate
for the presidency*
applicant: *one of thirty applicants for
the manager's post*
competitor: *several competitors for
the contract*
contender: *a strong contender for
the chairmanship*
candy see **sweet**
cane see **stick**
canine see **dog**
canny see **shrewd, smart**
canon see **principle**
cantankerous see **irritable**
cap see **top**
capability see **ability, capacity,**

potential, qualification

capable *adjective* able to do something well: *a capable leader*
able: *a very able businessman*
accomplished: *an accomplished painter*
adept: *an adept diplomat*
competent: *a competent and careful driver*
efficient: *efficient administration*
proficient: *proficient with computers*
skilful: *the country's most skilful politician*
see also **able, proficient**

capable of see **equal to**

capacity *noun* 1 the maximum amount that something holds or produces: *the vehicle's fuel capacity*
dimensions: *a car of compact dimensions*
room: *There wasn't enough room in the baggage compartment for all the gear*
size: *My bedroom is half the size of yours*
space: *There is space in the back for two people*
volume: *a container with a volume of two litres*
2 a person's power or ability to do something: *Our capacity for giving care, love and attention is limited*
ability: *The public never had faith in his ability to handle the job*
capability: *a country with the capability of launching a nuclear attack*
facility: *Humans have lost the facility to use their sense of smell properly*
gift: *As a youth he discovered a gift for making people laugh*
potential: *the economic potentials of Eastern and Western Europe*
power: *Human societies have the power to solve the problems confronting them*

see also **part, potential, room, space, talent**

capital see **fund, money**

capitalize on see **profit**

capitulate see **give in, submit, surrender**

capitulation see **surrender**

capsize see **overturn, upset**

captain see **leader**

captivate see **charm, delight, entrance, fascinate, interest**

captive see **prisoner**

capture *verb* 1 to take prisoner: *He was captured by rebels*
apprehend: *Police have not yet apprehended the killer*
arrest: *Seven people were arrested*
catch: *The thief was caught and the money was returned*
seize: *seized by armed police*
take: *An army unit took the town*
▷ *noun* 2 the act of capturing: *He evaded capture for eight years*
arrest: *Police made two arrests*
seizure: *the taking of territory*
taking: *the taking of hostages*
trapping: *The trapping of these animals is illegal*
see also **arrest, catch, kidnap**

car *noun* a vehicle for carrying a few people: *I finally left the car at the garage*
automobile *American formal*: *the Japanese automobile manufacturer, Nissan*
motor: *Patricia's new motor*
vehicle: *She managed to scramble out of the vehicle*
see also **automobile**

carcass see **body**

cardinal see **essential, main**

care *verb* 1 to be concerned about something: *a company that cares about the environment*
be bothered: *I am not bothered what others think about me*

be concerned: *We are concerned about the problem*

be interested: *He's not interested in what anyone else says*

mind: *I do not mind who wins*

▷ *noun* **2** something that causes you to worry: *without a care in the world*

anxiety: *anxieties about money*

concern: *Their main concern is unemployment*

stress: *the stresses of modern life*

trouble: *She has had her share of troubles*

woe: *They blame the government for all their woes*

worry: *My biggest worry is how I will cope on my own*

3 close attention when doing something: *We took great care in choosing a location*

attention: *medical attention*

caution: *Proceed with caution*

pains: *She takes great pains with her appearance*

see also **burden, caution, mind**

care for see **keep, look after, take care of, tend, treat**

career see **profession, record, speed**

carefree see **easy**

careful *adjective* **1** acting with care: *Be careful what you say to him*

cautious: *a cautious approach*

prudent: *prudent management*

2 complete and well done: *It needs careful planning*

meticulous: *meticulous attention to detail*

painstaking: *a painstaking search*

precise: *precise instructions*

thorough: *a thorough examination*

see also **cautious, deliberate, economical, thrifty**

careless *adjective* **1** not taking enough care: *careless driving*

irresponsible: *an irresponsible attitude*

neglectful: *neglectful parents*

sloppy *informal*: *sloppy work*

2 relaxed and unconcerned: *careless laughter*

casual: *a casual remark*

nonchalant: *a nonchalant attitude*

offhand: *his usual offhand way*

see also **casual, irresponsible**

cargo see **load**

caring see **affectionate, compassionate, humane, tender, thoughtful**

cark it see **die**

carnal see **lustful**

carnival see **fair, festival**

carp see **complain, grumble**

carping see **critical**

carriage see **compartment, walk**

carry *verb* to hold and take something somewhere: *He was carrying a briefcase*

bear: *He arrived bearing gifts*

convey *formal*: *The minibus conveyed us to the station*

lug: *lugging boxes of books around*

take: *Don't forget to take your camera*

transport: *goods being transported abroad*

see also **bear, bring, hold, take, transport**

carry off see **wash**

carry on see **continue, last, proceed**

carry out *verb* to do and complete something: *the surgeon who carried out the operation*

accomplish: *the desire to accomplish a task*

achieve: *We have achieved our objective*

fulfil: *to fulfil a promise*

perform: *people who have performed acts of bravery*

see also **achieve, administer, commit, conduct, do, fulfil, keep, perform**

carton see **box**

carve verb to make something by cutting: *He carves his figures from pine*
 chisel: *the mason chiselling his stone*
 cut: *a figure cut from marble*
 engrave: *an engraved crystal goblet*
 inscribe: *the words inscribed on his monument*
 sculpt: *a sculpted clay figure*
 see also **model**

case noun 1 a particular situation or example: *a case of mistaken identity*
 example: *an example of what can go wrong*
 illustration: *a clear illustration of this point*
 instance: *a serious instance of corruption*
 occasion: *the last occasion on which he appeared*
 occurrence: *a frequent occurrence*
 2 a container for holding something: *a spectacle case*
 box: *a chocolate box*
 container: *a huge plastic container*
 3 a trial or inquiry: *a libel case*
 action: *a civil action for damages*
 lawsuit: *the rising cost of defending a lawsuit*
 proceedings: *criminal proceedings against the former leader*
 trial: *Police lied at the trial*
 see also **argument, box, cover, patient, situation**

cash see **money**

cast see **throw**

cast a vote see **vote**

cast aside see **discard**

castle see **fort**

casual adjective 1 happening by chance: *a casual remark*
 accidental: *a verdict of accidental death*
 chance: *a chance meeting*
 incidental: *an incidental effect*
 2 showing no concern or interest: *a casual look over his shoulder*
 careless: *careless remarks*
 cursory: *a cursory glance*
 nonchalant: *his nonchalant attitude to life*
 offhand: *a deceptively offhand style*
 relaxed: *a relaxed manner*
 see also **accidental, careless, informal, relaxed**

cat noun a small animal kept as a pet: *sharing his flat with four cats*
 feline: *Even the most cuddly feline has claws*
 kitty: *a kitty stuck up a tree*
 moggy or **moggie** *British, New Zealand slang*: *a grey, long-haired moggy*
 pussy, puss, or **pussycat** *informal*: *a fluffy little pussycat*

catalogue see **list**

catastrophe see **disaster**

catastrophic see **fatal**

catch verb 1 to capture something: *another technique for catching criminals*
 apprehend: *the force necessary to apprehend a suspect*
 arrest: *Police arrested the gunman*
 capture: *Poachers had captured a gorilla*
 snare: *He'd snared a rabbit*
 trap: *Their aim was to trap drug-dealers*
 ▷ noun 2 a device that fastens something: *windows fitted with safety catches*
 bolt: *the sound of a bolt being slid open*
 clasp: *the clasp of her handbag*
 clip: *She took the clip out of her hair*
 latch: *You left the latch off the gate*
 3 a hidden difficulty: *The catch is that you have to fly via Paris*
 disadvantage: *The disadvantage is that this plant needs frequent watering*
 drawback: *The flat's only drawback*

was its size

snag: The snag is that you have to pay in advance

see also **capture, clasp, develop, hear, snag, stick, tangle, trap**

catch on see **understand**

catching see **infectious**

catchy see **memorable**

categorize see **class, classify, sort**

category noun a set of things with something in common: The items were organized into six different categories

class: dividing the stars into six classes of brightness

classification: There are various classifications of genres or types of book

group: She is one of the most promising players in her age group

set: Pupils are divided into sets according to ability

sort: What sort of school did you go to?

type: The majority of complaints received are of this type

see also **class, kind, sort, variety**

cattle see **cow**

catty see **spiteful**

cause noun 1 what makes something happen: the most common cause of back pain

origin: the origin of the present war

root: We need to get to the root of the problem

source: the source of the leak

2 an aim supported by a group: dedication to the cause of peace

aim: political aims

ideal: socialist ideals

movement: the women's movement

3 the reason for something: They gave us no cause to believe that

basis: There is no basis for this assumption

grounds: discrimination on the grounds of race or religion

justification: There was no justification for what he was doing

motivation: the motivation for his actions

motive: Police have ruled out robbery as a motive

reason: You have every reason to be upset

▷ verb 4 to make something happen: This may cause delays

bring about: We must try to bring about a better world

create: The scheme may create even more confusion

generate: the excitement generated by this film

produce: His comments produced a furious response

provoke: a move that has provoked a storm of protest

see also **bring, bring about, create, factor, grounds, lead to, prompt, provoke, reason, result in, source**

caustic see **sarcastic**

caution noun 1 great care taken in order to avoid danger: Drivers are urged to exercise extreme caution in icy weather

care: Scissors can be safe for young children if used with care

prudence: A lack of prudence may lead to problems

▷ verb 2 to scold or warn someone against doing something: The two men were cautioned but police say they will not be charged

reprimand: He was reprimanded by a teacher for talking in the corridor

tick off informal: Traffic police ticked off a pensioner for jumping a red light

warn: My mother warned me not to talk to strangers

see also **advise, care, warn, warning**

cautious adjective acting very carefully to avoid danger: a cautious approach

careful: *Be extremely careful when on holiday abroad*

guarded: *a guarded response*

tentative: *a tentative approach*

wary: *small firms remain wary of committing themselves to debt*

see also **careful**, **deliberate**, **wary**

cavalcade see **parade**

cave in see **give**

cease verb **1** to stop happening: *Almost miraculously, the noise ceased*

be over: *The captured planes will be kept until the war is over*

come to an end: *The strike came to an end*

die away: *The sound died away and silence reigned*

end: *The college year ends in March*

finish: *The teaching day finished at around four o'clock*

stop: *The rain had stopped*

2 to stop doing something: *A small number of firms have ceased trading*

desist from: *His wife never desisted from trying to change his mind*

discontinue: *Do not discontinue the treatment without consulting your doctor*

finish: *As soon as he'd finished eating, he excused himself*

give up: *smokers who give up before 30*

stop: *Stop throwing those stones!*

suspend: *The union suspended strike action this week*

see also **disappear**, **end**, **fail**, **halt**, **stop**, **vanish**

cede see **surrender**

ceiling see **maximum**

celebrate verb to do something special to mark an event: *I was in a mood to celebrate*

commemorate: *The anniversary of the composer's death was commemorated with a concert*

party: *It's your birthday – let's party!*

rejoice: *My family rejoiced at the happy outcome to events*

see also **commemorate**, **rejoice**

celebrated see **famous**

celebration noun an event in honour of a special occasion: *his eightieth birthday celebrations*

festival: *a religious festival*

festivity: *the wedding festivities*

gala: *the Olympics' opening gala*

party: *a housewarming party*

see also **party**

celebrity noun a famous person: *At the age of twelve, he was already a celebrity*

big name: *all the big names in rock and pop*

name: *some of the most famous names in modelling and show business*

personality: *a well-known radio and television personality*

star: *Not all football stars are ill-behaved louts*

superstar: *a Hollywood superstar*

VIP: *such VIPs as Prince Charles and the former US President*

see also **personality**, **star**, **success**

cell see **ring**

censure noun **1** strong disapproval: *a controversial policy which has attracted international censure*

blame: *I'm the one who'll get the blame if things go wrong*

condemnation: *There was widespread condemnation of Saturday's killings*

criticism: *This policy had repeatedly come under strong criticism*

disapproval: *His action had been greeted with almost universal disapproval*

reproach: *Those in public life should be beyond reproach*

▷ verb **2** to criticize severely: *I would not presume to censure him* for his views

condemn: *He condemned the players for lack of ability and application*

criticize: *The regime has been harshly criticized for its human rights violations*

denounce: *The letter called for civil rights, but did not openly denounce the regime*

reproach: *She had not even reproached him for breaking his promise*

see also **abuse, accuse, attack, condemn, criticism, criticize, disapproval, fault**

central *see* **crucial, middle, vital**

centre *noun* **1** the middle of something: *the centre of the room*

core: *the earth's core*

focus: *Her children are the main focus of her life*

heart: *The heart of the problem*

hub: *The kitchen is the hub of most households*

middle: *in the middle of the back row*

▷ *verb* **2** to have as the main subject: *All his thoughts were centred around himself*

concentrate: *Scientists are concentrating their efforts on finding a cure*

focus: *Attention is likely to focus on sales growth*

revolve: *Since childhood, her life has revolved around tennis*

see also **base, focus, middle**

ceremony *noun* **1** formal actions done for a special occasion: *his recent coronation ceremony*

observance: *a Memorial Day observance*

pomp: *His departure was celebrated with suitable pomp*

rite: *a fertility rite*

ritual: *a Summer Solstice ritual*

service: *The President attended the morning service*

2 formal and polite behaviour: *He hung up without ceremony*

decorum: *a responsibility to behave with decorum*

etiquette: *the rules of diplomatic etiquette*

formality: *his lack of stuffy formality*

niceties: *social niceties*

protocol: *minor breaches of protocol*

certain *adjective* **1** definite or reliable: *One thing is certain – they respect each other*

definite: *It's too soon to give a definite answer*

established: *an established medical fact*

guaranteed: *Success is not guaranteed*

inevitable: *If she wins her case, it is inevitable that other people will sue the company*

known: *It is not known when the bomb was planted*

sure: *Sharpe's leg began to ache, a sure sign of rain*

undeniable: *undeniable proof of guilt*

2 having no doubt in your mind: *She's absolutely certain she's going to succeed*

clear: *It is important to be clear about what you are doing*

confident: *I am confident that everything will come out right*

convinced: *He was convinced that I was part of the problem*

definite: *Mary is very definite about this fact*

sure: *She was no longer sure how she felt about him*

positive: *I'm as positive as I can be about it*

satisfied: *People must be satisfied that the treatment is safe*

see also **confident, definite, necessary, positive, sure**

certainly adverb without any doubt:
I'll certainly do all I can to help

definitely: *Something should definitely be done*

undeniably: *Bringing up a baby is undeniably hard work*

undoubtedly: *He is undoubtedly a great player*

unquestionably: *He is unquestionably a star*

without doubt: *The refugees are, without doubt, extremely vulnerable*
see also **really**

certainly not *see* **no**

certainty *see* **fact**

certified *see* **official**

certify *see* **declare**

chaff *see* **joke**

chain *see* **sequence, series**

challenge noun 1 a suggestion to try something: *They issued a challenge to their rivals*

dare: *He'd do almost anything for a dare*

invite: *We were invited to have a try at the limbo*

▷ verb 2 to give someone a challenge: *He challenged his rival to a duel*

dare: *I dare you to ask him*

defy: *He looked at me as if he was defying me to argue*

3 to question the truth or value of something: *challenging the authority of the state*

dispute: *He disputed the charge*

question: *questioning the jury's verdict*
see also **contest, dare, dispute, query, question**

challenger *see* **competitor, rival**

challenging *see* **formidable**

chamber *see* **compartment, room**

champion noun 1 a person who wins a competition: *Kasparov became a world chess champion*

hero: *the goalscoring hero of the British hockey team*

title holder: *He became the youngest world title holder at the age of 22*

victor: *the British Grand Prix victors*

winner: *The winner was a horse called Baby Face*

2 someone who supports a group, cause, or principle: *He received acclaim as a champion of the oppressed*

advocate: *He was a strong advocate of free trade*

defender: *a strong defender of human rights*

guardian: *The party wants to be seen as a guardian of traditional values*

protector: *She sees him as a protector and provider*

▷ verb 3 to support a group, cause, or principle: *He passionately championed the poor*

defend: *his courage in defending religious and civil rights*

fight for: *Our Government should be fighting for an end to child poverty*

promote: *You don't have to sacrifice the environment to promote economic growth*

stick up for *informal*: *He has shown courage in sticking up for civil liberties*

support: *The vice president has always supported the people of New York*

uphold: *upholding the artist's right to creative freedom*
see also **advocate, defender, support, supporter, winner**

championship *see* **competition**

chance noun 1 a possibility of something happening: *a good chance of success*

likelihood: *the likelihood of infection*

odds: *What are the odds of that happening?*

possibility: *the possibility of pay cuts*

probability: *a probability of victory*
prospect: *There is little prospect of peace*
2 an opportunity to do something: *He didn't give me a chance to explain*
occasion: *I had no occasion to speak to her that day*
opening: *an opening for finding a peaceful outcome to the conflict*
opportunity: *an opportunity to go abroad to study*
time: *There was no time to think*
3 the way things happen without being planned: *events which were merely the result of chance*
accident: *a strange accident of fate*
coincidence: *It was no coincidence that she arrived just then*
fortune: *A change of fortune*
luck: *His injury was just bad luck*
see also **accidental, casual, fate, gamble, luck, occasion, possibility, risk, turn, unexpected, unpredictable**

chances *see* **probability**

change noun **1** an alteration in something: *a change in her attitude*
alteration: *some alterations in your diet*
difference: *a noticeable difference in his behaviour*
modification: *Some minor modifications were required*
transformation: *the transformation of a wilderness into a garden*
▷ *verb* **2** to make or become different: *Her views have changed since her husband's death*
alter: *There is no prospect of the decision being altered*
convert: *a plan to convert his spare room into an office*
moderate: *They persuaded him to moderate his views*
modify: *He refused to modify his behaviour*

reform: *his plans to reform the economy*
transform: *The landscape has been transformed*
3 to exchange one thing for another: *Can I change this sweater for one a size bigger?*
barter: *bartering wheat for cotton and timber*
exchange: *the chance to sell back or exchange goods*
interchange: *Meat can be interchanged with pulses as a source of protein*
replace: *His smile was replaced by a frown*
substitute: *You can substitute honey for the sugar*
swap: *Let's swap places*
trade: *They traded land for goods and money*
see also **adapt, affect, exchange, reverse, transform, turn, variation, vary**

changeable adjective likely to change all the time: *changeable weather*
erratic: *erratic driving*
fickle: *Fashion is a fickle business*
irregular: *an irregular heartbeat*
unpredictable: *unpredictable behaviour*
unstable: *The political situation is unstable*
variable: *a variable rate of interest*
volatile: *a volatile atmosphere*

channel *see* **medium, passage, route, way**

chaos *see* **confusion, disorder, mess, muddle**

chaotic *see* **confused, untidy**

chap *see* **man**

char *see* **burn**

character noun **1** the qualities of a person: *He has a dark side to his character*

make-up: Determination has always been a part of his make-up

nature: a sunny nature

personality: an outgoing personality

temperament: his impulsive temperament

2 an honourable nature: She showed real character in her attempt to win over the crowd

honour: He has acted with honour

integrity: a man of integrity

strength: He had the strength to turn down the offer

see also **eccentric, figure, individual, name, nature, personality, reputation, sign**

characteristic noun **1** a typical quality: His chief characteristic is honesty

attribute: a normal attribute of human behaviour

feature: a feature of the local culture

property: This liquid has many unique properties

quality: leadership qualities

trait: personality traits

▷ adjective **2** typical of a person or thing: He responded with characteristic generosity

distinctive: a distinctive voice

distinguishing: no distinguishing marks

typical: his typical British modesty

see also **attribute, feature, individual, point, property, quality, representative, special, typical**

charge verb **1** to ask someone for money as a payment: The majority of producers charged a fair price

ask (for): The artist was asking £6,000 for each painting

bill: Are you going to bill me for this?

levy: Taxes should not be levied without the authority of Parliament

2 to rush forward, often to attack

someone: He charged into the room

dash: She dashed in from the garden

rush: A schoolgirl rushed into the burning flat to help an old man

stampede: The crowd stampeded

storm: He stormed into the shop, demanding to see the manager

▷ noun **3** the price you have to pay for something: We can arrange this for a small charge

cost: Badges are available at a cost of £2.50

fee: Pay your solicitor's fees

payment: I'll do it in return for a small payment

price: We negotiated a price for the service

see also **accuse, attack, blame, cost, direction, price, rate, tear**

charges see **bill**

charitable see **benevolent, generous, humane, kind**

charity see **generosity, kindness, pity**

charlatan see **fraud**

charm noun **1** an attractive quality: a man of great personal charm

allure: the allure of Egypt

appeal: confident of his appeal to women

attraction: the attractions of living by the sea

fascination: It is hard to explain the fascination of this place

magnetism: a man of enormous magnetism

▷ verb **2** to use charm to please someone: He charmed his 2,000-strong audience

bewitch: bewitched by her beauty

captivate: The crowd was captivated by her honesty

delight: a style of music that has delighted audiences

entrance: entranced by her smile

see also **beauty, delight, entertain,**

entrance, please

charmed see **lucky**

charming see **attractive, cute, lovable, pleasant**

charter see **book, hire, law**

chase verb **1** to try to catch someone or something: *She chased the thief for a hundred yards*

hunt: *He fled to Portugal after being hunted by police*

pursue: *She pursued the man who had snatched her bag*

2 to force to go somewhere: *Angry demonstrators chased him away*

drive: *The troops drove the rebels into the jungle*

hound: *He was hounded out of his job*

chasm see **abyss, pit**

chat noun **1** a friendly talk: *We sat around and had a chat*

conversation: *a telephone conversation*

gossip: *Don't you enjoy a good gossip?*

natter informal: *Let's get together for a natter some time*

talk: *We will have a talk about it later*

▷ verb **2** to talk in a friendly way: *He was chatting to his father*

gossip: *We gossiped into the night*

natter informal: *His mother would natter to anyone*

talk: *She's very easy to talk to*

see also **talk, word**

chatter see **babble, ramble, talk**

chatty see **talkative**

chauvinism see **prejudice**

cheap adjective **1** costing very little: *Cheap flights are available*

bargain: *selling at bargain prices*

economical: *These cars are very economical to run*

inexpensive: *an inexpensive wine*

reasonable: *His fees were quite reasonable*

2 inexpensive but of poor quality: *a suit made of some cheap material*

inferior: *an inferior imitation*

second-rate: *second-rate equipment*

tawdry: *tawdry souvenirs*

see also **economical, petty, reasonable**

cheat verb to get something from someone dishonestly: *the people he cheated out of their life savings*

con informal: *He conned his way into a job*

deceive: *Investors were deceived by a scam*

defraud: *charges of conspiracy to defraud the government*

dupe: *Stamp collectors were duped into buying fakes*

fleece: *He fleeced her out of thousands of pounds*

rip off slang: *ticket touts ripping off soccer fans*

swindle: *two executives who swindled their employer*

see also **con, crook, dupe, fraud**

cheating see **dishonesty**

check verb **1** to examine something: *Check all the details first*

check out informal: *Check out the financial figures*

examine: *He examined her passport and stamped it*

inspect: *the right to inspect company files*

test: *The drug must be tested in clinical trials*

2 to reduce or stop something: *a policy to check fast population growth*

control: *a measure to control illegal mining*

curb: *reforms which aim to curb spending*

halt: *an attempt to halt the spread of the disease*

inhibit: *factors which inhibit growth*

restrain: *the need to restrain wage rises*

stop: *measures to stop the trade*

in ivory

▷ noun **3** an examination: *a thorough check of the equipment*

examination: *a medical examination*
inspection: *a routine inspection of the premises*
test: *a test for cancer*
see also **block, curb, delay, examination, examine, foil, frustrate, halt, hinder, inspect, slow (down), stop, test**

check out see **check, try**

checkup see **examination**

cheek noun speech or behaviour that is rude or disrespectful: *I'm amazed they had the cheek to ask in the first place*
audacity: *I was shocked at the audacity of the gangsters*
gall: *She had the gall to claim she had been victimized*
impudence: *My sister had the impudence to go out wearing my clothes*
insolence: *The pupil was excluded for insolence*
nerve: *He had the nerve to ask me to prove who I was*
rudeness: *Mother was cross at Tom's rudeness*
see also **impudence**

cheeky adjective rude and disrespectful: *cheeky teenagers*
impertinent: *an impertinent question*
impudent: *his rude and impudent behaviour*
insolent: *a defiant, almost insolent look*
rude: *She was often rude to her mother*
see also **bold**

cheer see **comfort, encourage**

cheer up see **reassure**

cheerful adjective in a happy mood: *She was very cheerful despite her illness*

bright: *"May I help you?" said a bright voice*
buoyant: *in a buoyant mood*
cheery: *a cheery nature*
happy: *a confident, happy child*
jaunty: *a jaunty tune*
jolly: *a jolly, easy-going man*
light-hearted: *They were light-hearted and enjoyed life*
merry: *a burst of merry laughter*
see also **bright, cheery**

cheery adjective happy and cheerful: *He is loved by everyone for his cheery disposition*
cheerful: *They are both very cheerful in spite of their circumstances*
chirpy: *She sounded quite chirpy on the phone*
good-humoured: *Charles was brave and remarkably good-humoured*
happy: *Marina was a confident, happy child*
jolly: *She was a jolly, kind-hearted woman*
upbeat: *Neil's colleagues said he was in a joking, upbeat mood*
sunny: *a nice lad with a sunny disposition*
see also **cheerful**

cherish see **love, prize, treasure, value**

cherished see **beloved, dear**

chest see **box**

chew verb to break food up with the teeth: *Eat slowly and chew your food properly*
crunch: *She crunched the ice cube loudly*
gnaw: *He sat and gnawed at an apple*
munch: *Sheep were munching the leaves*
see also **bite**

chic see **exclusive, smart, style**

chicken see **coward, cowardly**

chide see **scold**

chief noun **1** the leader of a group or

organization: *the deputy chief of the territory's defence force*
boss: *He cannot stand his boss*
chieftain: *the legendary British chieftain, King Arthur*
director: *the financial director of the company*
governor: *The incident was reported to the prison governor*
head: *heads of government from 100 countries*
leader: *the leader of the Conservative Party*
manager: *a retired bank manager*
▷ *adjective* **2** most important: *The job went to one of his chief rivals*
foremost: *one of the world's foremost scholars of ancient Indian culture*
key: *He is expected to be the key witness at the trial*
main: *one of the main tourist areas of Amsterdam*
prevailing: *the prevailing attitude towards women in this society*
primary: *His language difficulties were the primary cause of his other problems*
prime: *The police will see me as the prime suspect!*
principal: *The principal reason for my change of mind is this*
see also **boss, first, foremost, head, leader, leading, main, prime, principal, supreme, top**
chiefly see **mainly**
chieftain see **chief**
child *noun* a young person: *I lived in France as a child*
ankle-biter *Australian, New Zealand slang*: *I knew him when he was just an ankle-biter*
baby: *She took care of me when I was a baby*
bairn *Scottish*: *a two-year-old bairn*
infant: *young mums with infants in prams*

juvenile: *a prison for juveniles*
kid *informal*: *They've got three kids*
minor: *charged with selling cigarettes to minors*
offspring: *parents choosing shoes for their offspring*
toddler: *a toddler in a pushchair*
tot: *The tot was too young to know what was happening*
youngster: *I was only a youngster in 1965*
see also **baby**

childish *adjective* immature and foolish: *I don't have time for this childish behaviour*
immature: *She is emotionally immature*
infantile: *infantile jokes*
juvenile: *juvenile behaviour*
puerile: *a puerile sense of humour*
childless see **barren**
childlike see **innocent**
chill see **cool**
chilled see **cool, frozen**
chilling see **scary**
chilly see **cold, cool**
chime see **ring, sound**
china *noun* South African informal a friend: *How are you, my old china?*
buddy *informal*: *We've been buddies since we were kids*
chum *informal*: *He went on holiday with his two best chums*
crony *old-fashioned*: *She is always surrounded by her cronies*
friend: *lifelong friends*
mate *British informal*: *Come on mate, things aren't that bad*
pal *informal*: *He'd never let a pal down*
see also **friend**
chink see **gap, leak, opening**
chirpy see **cheery**
chisel see **carve**
choice *noun* **1** a range of things to choose from: *available in a choice of colours*

range: *a range of sun-care products*
selection: *an interesting selection of recipes*
variety: *a variety of candidates from which to choose*
2 *the power to choose*: *They had little choice in the matter*
alternative: *He said he could not see any alternative*
option: *He was given the option of going to jail or paying a fine*
say: *We don't have a say in the company's decisions*
see also **prime, select, superior, will**

choke see **block, gasp, obstruct**

choose verb *to decide to have or do something*: *a number of foods to choose from*
opt for: *He opted for early retirement*
pick: *She was picked for the debating team*
select: *She paused to select another cookie from the box*
take: *She took the option he offered her*
see also **decide, determine, pick, select**

choosy see **fussy, particular**

chop verb *to cut down or into pieces*: *I heard him chopping wood in the yard*
cut: *Cut the vegetables up*
fell: *43,000 square miles of tropical forest are felled each year*
hack: *They hacked away at the undergrowth*
lop: *Somebody had lopped the heads off our tulips*

chore see **task, work**
chortle see **laugh**
christen see **name**
chubby see **plump, tubby**
chuck see **throw**
chuckle see **laugh**
chum see **china**
chunder see **puke, vomit**
chunk see **block, lump, piece,**

portion
chunky see **stocky**
chutzpah see **impudence**
circle see **club, company, ring, society**
circular see **leaflet, round**
circulate verb *to pass around*: *He circulated rumours about everyone*
distribute: *distributing leaflets*
propagate: *They propagated their political ideas*
spread: *spreading malicious gossip*
see also **distribute, flow, spread**

circumstance see **event, incident**
circumstances see **situation, state**
citadel see **fort**
cite see **accuse, quote, refer**
citizen see **inhabitant**
citizens see **people**
city noun *a large town*: *the city of London*
metropolis: *a busy metropolis*
town: *the oldest town in Europe*

civic see **public**
civil see **polite**
civility see **courtesy, politeness**
civilization see **society**
civilized adjective *having an advanced society*: *a highly civilized country*
cultured: *a mature and cultured nation*
enlightened: *this enlightened century*
see also **refined**

claim verb **1** *to say something is the case*: *He claims to have lived here all his life*
allege: *He is alleged to have killed a man*
assert: *The defendants continued to assert their innocence*
hold: *She holds that these measures are unnecessary*
insist: *They insisted that they had no money*

maintain: I still maintain that I am not guilty

profess: She professed to hate her nickname

▷ noun **2** a statement that something is the case: He rejected claims that he had taken bribes

allegation: allegations of theft

assertion: his assertion that he did not plan to remarry

see also **argue**

clamber see **climb**

clammy see **damp, humid**

clamour see **racket**

clandestine see **private**

clang see **ring, sound**

clarification see **explanation**

clash verb **1** to fight or argue with another person: A group of 400 demonstrators clashed with police

battle: In one town thousands of people battled with police officers

fight: two rival gangs fighting in the streets

quarrel: My brother quarrelled with my father

wrangle: Delegates wrangled over the future of the organization

2 of two things: to be so different that they do not go together: Don't make policy decisions which clash with company thinking

conflict: He held opinions which sometimes conflicted with my own

contradict: Cut-backs like these surely contradict the Government's commitment to education

differ: The two leaders differed on several issues

disagree: Our managers disagreed on several policy issues

go against: Changes are being made which go against my principles

jar: They had always been good together and their temperaments seldom jarred

▷ noun **3** a fight or argument: a number of clashes between rival parties

battle: a gun battle between police and drug traffickers

conflict: attempts to prevent a conflict between workers and management

confrontation: This issue could lead to a military confrontation

fight: He had had a fight with Smith and bloodied his nose

struggle: a struggle between competing political factions

skirmish: informal: Border skirmishes between the two countries were common

squabble: There have been minor squabbles about phone bills

see also **argument, conflict, crash, dispute, game, quarrel, war**

clasp verb **1** to hold something tightly: Mary clasped the children to her desperately

clutch: She was clutching a photograph

embrace: People were crying for joy and embracing each other

grip: She gripped the rope

hold: He held the pistol in his right hand

hug: She hugged her legs tight to her chest

press: I pressed the child closer to my heart and prayed

squeeze: He longed to just scoop her up and squeeze her

▷ noun **2** a fastening such as a hook or catch: She undid the clasp of her hooded cloak

buckle: He wore a belt with a large brass buckle

catch: She fiddled with the catch of her bag

clip: She took the clip out of her hair

fastener: a product range which includes nails, woodscrews, and

fasteners
fastening: The sundress has a neat back zip fastening
see also **catch, grasp, grip, hold, hug**

class noun **1** a group of a particular type: a new class of vehicle
category: different categories of taxpayer
genre: films of the horror genre
grade: the lowest grade of staff
group: a plan to help people in this group
kind: the biggest prize of its kind in the world
set: The fashionable set all go to this club
sort: several articles of this sort
type: various types of vegetable
▷ verb **2** to regard as being in a particular group: They are officially classed as visitors
categorize: His films are hard to categorize
classify: Carrots are also classified as a fruit
designate: The house is designated as a national monument
grade: This ski-run is graded as easy
rank: She is ranked in the world's top 50 players
rate: He rates the film highly
see also **category, family, form, grade, group, kind, lesson, polish, range, rank, rate, sort, type, variety**

classes see **course**

classic see **ideal, simple**

classification see **category, family, kind**

classify verb to arrange similar things in groups: We can classify the differences into three groups
arrange: Arrange the books in neat piles
categorize: This film is hard to categorize

grade: musical pieces graded according to difficulty
rank: He was ranked among Britain's best-known millionaires
sort: sorting the material into folders
see also **arrange, class, grade, group, sort**

classy see **exclusive, posh**

clay see **earth, soil**

clean adjective **1** free from dirt or marks: clean shoes
immaculate: immaculate white flannels
impeccable: dressed in an impeccable trouser suit
laundered: freshly laundered shirts
spotless: The kitchen was spotless
washed: newly washed hair
2 free from germs or infection: a lack of clean water and sanitation
antiseptic: an antiseptic hospital room
hygienic: a hygienic kitchen
purified: Only purified water is used
sterilized: sterilized milk
uncontaminated: uncontaminated air
unpolluted: unpolluted beaches
▷ verb **3** to remove dirt from: She cleaned the house from top to bottom
cleanse: a lotion to cleanse the skin
dust: I vacuumed, dusted and polished the living room
scour: She scoured the sink
scrub: I started to scrub off the dirt
sponge: Sponge your face and body
swab: an old man swabbing the floor
wash: He got a job washing dishes in a restaurant
wipe: He wiped the sweat from his face
see also **blank, pure, simple**

cleanliness see **hygiene**

cleanse see **clean, wash**

clear adjective **1** easy to see or

understand: *He made it clear he did not want to talk*
apparent: *There is no apparent reason for the crime*
blatant: *a blatant piece of cheating*
conspicuous: *one conspicuous difference*
definite: *a definite advantage*
evident: *He ate with evident enjoyment*
explicit: *He was very explicit about his intentions*
obvious: *There are obvious dangers*
plain: *The results are plain to see*
2 easy to see through: *a clear liquid*
crystalline: *crystalline green waters*
glassy: *The water was a deep glassy blue*
translucent: *translucent stones*
transparent: *transparent glass walls*
▷ **verb 3** to prove someone is not guilty: *She was cleared of murder*
absolve: *He was absolved of all charges*
acquit: *acquitted of disorderly conduct*
see also **blank, certain, definite, empty, evident, innocent, jump, manifest, obvious, plain, positive, sure, transparent, visible**
clear up see **resolve, settle, solve**
clear-cut see **positive**
cleft see **crack, fissure, opening**
clever adjective very intelligent: *My sister was always a lot cleverer than I was*
brainy informal: *I don't consider myself to be especially brainy*
bright: *an exceptionally bright child*
intelligent: *a lively and intelligent woman*
shrewd: *a shrewd businessman*
smart: *a very smart move*
see also **astute, bright, brilliant, intelligent, smart, witty**
cleverness see **intelligence**
clichéd see **hackneyed**

client see **customer**
climax see **peak**
climb verb to move upwards over something: *Climbing the first hill took half an hour*
ascend: *He ascended the ladder into the loft*
clamber: *They clambered up the stone walls*
mount: *He mounted the steps*
scale: *the first British woman to scale Everest*
see also **rise**
climb to see **reach**
clinch see **hug**
cling see **stick**
clip see **catch, clasp**
clique see **party, ring**
cloak see **cover, obscure**
clog see **block, obstruct**
close verb **1** to shut something: *Close the gate behind you*
secure: *The shed was secured by a padlock*
shut: *Someone had forgotten to shut the door*
2 to block so that nothing can pass: *All the roads out are closed*
bar: *Protesters barred the way to his car*
block: *The road was blocked by debris*
obstruct: *buskers obstructing the pavement*
seal: *Soldiers had sealed the border*
▷ adjective **3** near to something: *a restaurant close to their home*
see **word studies** close
4 friendly and loving: *We became close friends*
see **word studies** close
see also **alike, conclude, conclusion, finish, friendly, halt, handy, immediate, imminent, near, shut, stuffy**
close to see **almost, beside, near**
closed see **shut**

closely see **immediately, well**

closeness see **friendship**

closest see **next**

closet see **secret**

closing see **final, last**

clot see **thicken**

cloth noun woven or knitted fabric: *a piece of red cloth*
fabric: *waterproof fabric*
material: *This material shrinks badly*
textiles: *a trader in clothes and textiles*
see also **material**

clothe see **dress**

clothes plural noun the things people wear: *She spends all her money on clothes*
attire: *formal attire*
clothing: *men's clothing*
costume: *national costume*
dress: *traditional dress*
garments: *winter garments*
gear informal: *trendy gear*
outfit: *a stunning scarlet outfit*
wardrobe: *next summer's wardrobe*
wear: *evening wear*
see also **dress**

clothing see **clothes, dress**

clotted see **thick**

cloud noun 1 a mass of vapour or smoke: *The sky was dark with clouds*
billow: *Smoke billowed from the engine*
fog: *a fog of cigar smoke*
haze: *a haze of exhaust fumes*
mist: *The valley was wrapped in thick mist*
vapour: *warm vapour rising from the ground*
▷ verb 2 to make something confusing: *Anger has clouded his judgement*
confuse: *You're just confusing the matter by bringing politics into it*
distort: *a distorted memory*
muddle: *The question muddles up two separate issues*
see also **obscure**

cloudy adjective 1 full of clouds: *a cloudy sky*
dull: *It's always dull and wet here*
gloomy: *gloomy weather*
leaden: *leaden skies*
overcast: *a damp, overcast morning*
2 difficult to see through: *a glass of cloudy liquid*
muddy: *a muddy duck pond*
murky: *murky waters*
opaque: *an opaque glass jar*
see also **dark, dull**

clout see **bang, blow**

cloying see **sweet**

club noun 1 an organization for people with a special interest: *a swimming club*
association: *the Women's Tennis Association*
circle: *a local painting circle*
group: *an environmental group*
guild: *the Screen Writers' Guild*
society: *a historical society*
union: *the International Astronomical Union*
2 a heavy stick: *armed with knives and clubs*
bat: *a baseball bat*
stick: *a crowd carrying sticks and stones*
truncheon: *a policeman's truncheon*
▷ verb 3 to hit with a heavy object: *Two thugs clubbed him with baseball bats*
bash: *They bashed his head with a spade*
batter: *battered to death*
beat: *beaten with rifle butts*
bludgeon: *bludgeoning his wife with a hammer*
see also **association, fellowship, society**

clue see **hint, idea, indication, lead, sign**

clumsiness noun awkwardness of movement: *The accident was entirely the result of his own clumsiness*
 awkwardness: *They moved with the awkwardness of mechanical dolls*
 ungainliness: *his physical ungainliness*

clumsy adjective moving awkwardly: *He is big and clumsy in his movements*
 awkward: *an awkward gesture*
 gauche: *He makes me feel stupid and gauche*
 lumbering: *a big, lumbering man*
 uncoordinated: *an uncoordinated dancer*
 ungainly: *As a youth he was lanky and ungainly*

cluster see **bunch**

clutch see **clasp, grab, grasp, grip, hold**

clutches see **grip**

clutter see **disorder, junk**

cluttered see **untidy**

coach see **instruct, teach, teacher, train**

coaching see **education, lesson**

coalition see **party, union**

coarse see **common, crude, vulgar**

coast noun the land next to the sea: *a holiday by the coast*
 beach: *a beautiful sandy beach*
 border: *the border of the Black Sea*
 coastline: *the stunning Caribbean coastline*
 seaside: *a day at the seaside*
 shore: *a bleak and rocky shore*
 strand: *boats fishing from the strand*
 see also **beach**

coastline see **coast**

coat noun an animal's fur or hair: *She gave the dog's coat a brush*
 fleece: *a blanket of lamb's fleece*
 fur: *a kitten with black fur*
 hair: *He's allergic to cat hair*
 hide: *rhino hide*
 pelt: *a wolf pelt*
 skin: *convicted of attempting to sell the skin of a Siberian tiger*
 wool: *Lanolin comes from sheep's wool*
 see also **coating, cover, layer, spread**

coating noun a layer of something: *a thin coating of ice*
 coat: *a coat of paint*
 covering: *a covering of dust*
 layer: *a layer of dead leaves*
 see also **cover, layer**

coax verb to persuade gently: *We coaxed her into coming with us*
 cajole: *Her sister cajoled her into playing*
 persuade: *My husband persuaded me to come*
 talk into: *They've talked him into getting a new car*
 see also **persuade, prompt**

cocky adjective cheeky or too self-confident: *He was a bit cocky because he was winning all the time*
 arrogant: *an air of arrogant indifference*
 brash: *On stage she seems hard and brash*
 conceited: *I thought him conceited*
 overconfident: *She couldn't cope with this new generation of noisy, overconfident teenage girls*
 ▷ noun **2** Australian, New Zealand a farmer, especially one whose farm is small: *He got some work with the cane cockies on Maroochy River*
 crofter Scottish: *the financial plight of crofters in the islands*
 farmer: *He was a simple farmer scratching a living from the soil*
 see also **boastful, conceited**

code see **convention, law**

coil verb to wind in loops: *a coiled spring*
 curl: *dark, curling hair*
 loop: *A rope was looped between*

his hands

spiral: vines spiralling up towards the roof

twine: This lily produces twining stems

twist: She twisted her hair into a bun

wind: a rope wound round her waist

coin see **create, invent**

coincide see **correspond**

coincidence see **chance**

cold adjective **1** having a low temperature: the coldest winter for ten years

arctic: arctic conditions

biting: a biting wind

bitter: driven inside by the bitter cold

bleak: The weather can be bleak on the coast

chilly: It's chilly for June

freezing: This house is freezing

icy: the icy north wind

raw: a raw December morning

wintry: wintry showers

2 not showing affection: a cold, unfeeling woman

aloof: He seemed aloof and detached

distant: She was polite but distant

frigid: a frigid smile

lukewarm: a lukewarm response

reserved: emotionally reserved

stony: He gave me a stony look

see also **callous, cool, impersonal, remote, stiff, unfriendly**

cold-blooded see **cruel**

collaborate verb **1** to fall down: The whole building is about to collapse

fall down: The ceiling fell down

give way: The bridge gave way beneath him

2 to fail: 50,000 small businesses collapsed last year

fail: His hotel business has failed

fold: We were laid off when the company folded

founder: a foundering radio station

▷ noun **3** the failure of something: the collapse of his marriage

downfall: the downfall of the government

failure: the failure of his business empire

see also **crash, downfall, faint, fall, give**

colleague noun a person someone works with: I'll have to consult my colleagues

associate: business associates

fellow worker: She started going out with a fellow worker

partner: her business partner

workmate: the nickname his workmates gave him

see also **assistant, associate**

collect verb to gather together: collecting signatures for a petition

accumulate: Most children enjoy accumulating knowledge

assemble: trying to assemble a team

gather: gathering information

raise: They've raised over £100 for charity

see also **assemble, concentrate, gather, stockpile**

collected see **calm, cool**

collection noun a group of things collected together: a collection of paintings

assortment: an assortment of pets

group: a group of songs

store: a vast store of knowledge

see also **group, number, variety**

collectively see **together**

collide see **bump, crash**

collide with see **hit**

collision see **crash**

colloquial adjective used in conversation: a colloquial expression

conversational: a conversational style

everyday: He used plain, everyday

English

informal: *an informal expression*
see also **informal**

colony noun **1** a country controlled by another country: *an American colony*

  dependency: *the tiny British dependency of Montserrat*

  dominion: *The Republic is a dominion of Brazil*

  territory: *territories under Israeli control*

2 a group of settlers in a place: *a colony of Scots*

  community: *the Sikh community in Britain*

  outpost: *a remote outpost*

  settlement: *a Muslim settlement*

colossal adjective very large indeed: *a colossal statue*

  enormous: *The main bedroom is enormous*

  gigantic: *a gigantic task*

  huge: *They are making huge profits*

  immense: *an immense cloud of smoke*

  mammoth: *This mammoth undertaking was completed in 18 months*

  massive: *a massive steam boat*

  vast: *farmers who own vast stretches of land*

see also **enormous, huge, immense, large, unbelievable, vast**

colour noun **1** a shade or hue: *Her favourite colour is blue*

  hue: *delicate pastel hues*

  pigmentation: *skin pigmentation*

  shade: *walls painted in two shades of green*

  tint: *a distinct orange tint*

2 a substance used to give colour: *food colour*

  dye: *hair dye*

  paint: *a pot of red paint*

  pigment: *a layer of blue pigment*

▷ verb **3** to give something a colour: *Many women colour their hair*

  dye: *Only dye clean garments*

  paint: *She paints her toenails red*

  stain: *Some foods can stain the teeth*

  tint: *tinted glass*

4 to affect the way you think: *Her upbringing has coloured her opinion of marriage*

  bias: *a biased opinion*

  distort: *The shock of the accident distorted my judgement*

  prejudice: *Criticism will prejudice the Government's decision*

  slant: *deliberately slanted news coverage*

see also **blush**

colourful adjective **1** full of colour: *colourful clothes*

  bright: *a bright green dress*

  brilliant: *The garden has burst into brilliant flower*

  intense: *an intense shade of blue*

  jazzy: *informal a jazzy tie*

  rich: *a rich blue glass bowl*

  vibrant: *vibrant orange shades*

  vivid: *vivid hues*

2 interesting or exciting: *a colourful character*

  graphic: *a graphic account of his career*

  interesting: *He has had an interesting life*

  lively: *a lively imagination*

  rich: *the rich history of the island*

  vivid: *a vivid description*

colourless see **pale**

column see **feature, line, rank, row**

comb see **search**

combat see **conflict, fight, war**

combination noun a mixture of things: *a combination of charm and skill*

  amalgamation: *an amalgamation of two organizations*

  blend: *a blend of wine and spring*

water

mix: *a mix of fantasy and reality*

mixture: *a mixture of horror, envy and awe*

see also **blend, cross, mixture, union**

combine verb to join or mix together: *trying to combine motherhood with work*

amalgamate: *a plan to amalgamate the two parties*

blend: *The band blends jazz and folk music*

fuse: *a performer who fuses magic and dance*

integrate: *integrating various styles of art*

merge: *The two countries have merged into one*

mix: *mixing business with pleasure*

unite: *people uniting to fight racism*

see also **blend, mix, unite**

combustion *see* **fire**

come verb 1 to move or arrive somewhere: *Two men came into the room*

appear: *He appeared at about 9 o'clock*

arrive: *My brother has just arrived*

enter: *The class fell silent as the teacher entered*

materialize: *The car just materialized from nowhere*

show up *informal*: *He showed up over an hour late*

turn up *informal*: *I'll call you when she turns up*

2 to happen or take place: *Christmas only comes once a year*

happen: *Nothing ever happens on a Sunday*

occur: *How did the accident occur?*

take place: *The meeting never took place*

come about *see* **happen, take place**

come across *see* **discover, find,**

meet

come after *see* **follow**

come apart *see* **split**

come back *see* **return**

come between *see* **divide**

come first *see* **win**

come on *see* **flourish**

come out *see* **appear**

come to *see* **cost, total, wake**

come together *see* **assemble**

come up with *see* **invent**

come upon *see* **meet**

come with *see* **accompany**

comedy *see* **humour, play**

comfort noun 1 a state of ease: *He settled back in comfort*

ease: *a life of ease*

luxury: *brought up in an atmosphere of luxury*

wellbeing: *a wonderful sense of wellbeing*

2 relief from worry or unhappiness: *Her words gave him some comfort*

consolation: *He knew he was right, but it was no consolation*

help: *Just talking to you has been a great help*

relief: *temporary relief from the pain*

satisfaction: *At least I have the satisfaction that I tried*

support: *His family were a great support to him*

▷ verb **3** to give someone comfort: *trying to comfort the screaming child*

cheer: *The thought did nothing to cheer him*

console: *"Never mind," he consoled me*

reassure: *He did his best to reassure her*

soothe: *She took him in her arms and soothed him*

see also **reassure**

comfortable adjective **1** physically relaxing: *a comfortable chair*

cosy: *a cosy living room*

easy: You've had an easy time of it
homely: a homely atmosphere
relaxing: a relaxing holiday
restful: a restful scene
2 feeling at ease: I don't feel
comfortable around him
at ease: He is not at ease in female
company
at home: We soon felt quite at home
contented: a contented life
happy: I'm not very happy with
that idea
relaxed: a relaxed attitude
see also **cosy, easy, homely,
leisurely, relaxed, wealthy**
comic see **funny**
comical see **funny, hysterical**
coming see **appearance, future,
imminent**
command verb **1** to order someone
to do something: She commanded me
to lie down
bid: The soldiers bade us turn and
go back
demand: They demanded that
he leave
direct: His doctor has directed him
to rest
order: He ordered his men to cease fire
2 to be in charge of: the general who
commanded the UN troops
control: He now controls the whole
company
head: Who heads the firm?
lead: He led the country between 1949
and 1984
manage: I manage a small team
of workers
supervise: He supervised more than
400 volunteers
▷ noun **3** an order to do something:
The execution was carried out at his
command
bidding: They refused to leave at
his bidding
decree: a presidential decree

directive: a government directive
injunction: He left her with the
injunction to go to sleep
instruction: They were just following
instructions
order: I don't take orders from you
4 knowledge and ability: a good
command of English
grasp: a good grasp of foreign
languages
knowledge: He has no knowledge
of law
mastery: a mastery of grammar
see also **administer, control,
direction, exact, instruct, lead,
manage, order, tell**
commander see **leader, ruler**
commanding see **powerful**
commemorate verb **1** to do
something in memory of: concerts
to commemorate the anniversary of
his death
celebrate: celebrating their golden
wedding
honour: celebrations to honour his
memory
see also **celebrate, honour**
commence see **begin, start**
commencement see **beginning,
opening, start**
commend see **honour**
commendation see **credit, honour,
praise**
comment verb **1** to make a remark:
He refused to comment on the rumours
mention: I mentioned that I didn't
like jazz
note: He noted that some issues
remained to be settled
observe: "You're very pale," he
observed
point out: I should point out that
these figures are approximate
remark: Everyone had remarked on
her new hairstyle
say: "Well done," he said

▷ noun **2** something you say: *sarcastic comments*

observation: *a few general observations*

remark: *snide remarks*

statement: *That statement puzzled me*

see also **observe, remark, word**

commentary *see* **review**

commerce *see* **business, finance, trade**

commercial *see* **advertisement, economic**

commission *see* **employ, hire**

commit *verb* to do something: *A crime has been committed*

carry out: *attacks carried out by terrorists*

do: *They have done a lot of damage*

perform: *people who have performed acts of bravery*

perpetrate: *A fraud has been perpetrated*

committed *see* **fervent**

committee *see* **council**

commodity *see* **product**

common *adjective* **1** of many people: *a common complaint*

general: *the general opinion*

popular: *a popular belief*

prevailing: *the prevailing atmosphere*

prevalent: *Smoking is becoming more prevalent among girls*

universal: *The desire to look attractive is universal*

widespread: *widespread support*

2 not special: *the common man*

average: *the average teenager*

commonplace: *a commonplace observation*

everyday: *your everyday routine*

ordinary: *an ordinary day*

plain: *My parents were just plain ordinary folks*

standard: *standard practice*

usual: *In a usual week I watch about*

15 *hours of television*

3 having bad taste or manners: *a common, rude woman*

coarse: *coarse humour*

rude: *It's rude to stare*

vulgar: *vulgar remarks*

see also **everyday, frequent, general, low, natural, popular, universal, usual, vulgar, widespread**

commonplace *see* **common**

common sense *noun* the ability to make good judgments: *Use your common sense*

good sense: *He had the good sense to call me at once*

judgment: *I respect your judgment*

level-headedness: *He prides himself on his level-headedness*

prudence: *His lack of prudence led to financial problems*

wit: *They don't have the wit to realize what's happening*

see also **head, sense**

commotion *see* **bustle, excitement, fuss, noise, racket**

communal *see* **public**

communicate *verb* **1** to be in touch with someone: *We communicate mainly by email*

be in contact: *I'll be in contact with him next week*

be in touch: *He hasn't been in touch with me yet*

correspond: *We correspond regularly*

2 to pass on information: *The results will be communicated by post*

convey: *They have conveyed their views to the government*

impart: *the ability to impart knowledge*

inform: *Will you inform me of any changes?*

pass on: *I'll pass on your good wishes*

spread: *She has spread the news to everyone*

transmit: He transmitted his enjoyment to the audience
see also **convey, express**

communicate with see **contact**

communication see **contact, message, note, word**

communicative see **talkative**

community see **colony, company, local, public**

companion noun someone you travel with or spend time with: He has been her constant companion for the last six years

comrade: Unlike so many of his comrades he survived the war

crony old-fashioned: a round of golf with his business cronies

friend: Sara's old friend, Charles

mate: A mate of mine used to play soccer for Liverpool

pal informal: We've been pals for years

partner: a partner in crime
see also **friend, partner**

companionship see **company, fellowship**

company noun 1 a business: a publishing company

business: a family business

corporation: multi-national corporations

establishment: a commercial establishment

firm: a firm of engineers

house: the world's top fashion houses

2 a group of people: the Royal Shakespeare Company

assembly: an assembly of citizens

band: bands of rebels

circle: a large circle of friends

community: a community of believers

crowd: I don't go around with that crowd

ensemble: an ensemble of young musicians

group: an environmental group

party: a party of sightseers

troupe: a troupe of actors

3 the act of spending time with someone: I could do with some company

companionship: He keeps a dog for companionship

presence: Your presence is not welcome here
see also **association, band, body, business, enterprise, firm, organization**

comparable see **similar**

compare verb to look at things for similarities or differences: Compare these two illustrations

contrast: In this section we contrast four possible approaches

juxtapose: art juxtaposed with reality

weigh: She weighed her options

compartment noun 1 a section of a railway carriage: We shared our compartment with a group of businessmen

carriage: Our carriage was full of drunken football fans

2 one of the separate parts of an object: the freezer compartment of the fridge

bay: the cargo bays of the aircraft

chamber: the chambers of the heart

division: Each was further split into several divisions

section: a toolbox with sections for various items

compassion see **kindness, mercy, pity, sympathy**

compassionate adjective feeling or showing sympathy and pity for others: My father was a deeply compassionate man

caring: He is a lovely boy, very gentle and caring

humane: She began to campaign for humane treatment of prisoners and their families

kind: I must thank you for being so kind to me

kind-hearted: He was a warm, generous and kind-hearted man

merciful: a merciful God

sympathetic: She was very sympathetic to their problems

tender: Her voice was tender, full of pity

see also **benevolent, humane, kind, merciful, tender, understanding**

compassionately see **well**

compatible adjective going together: Lifelong partners should be compatible

congenial: congenial company

consistent: injuries consistent with a car crash

harmonious: a harmonious partnership

in keeping: This behaviour was in keeping with his character

compel see **drive, force, make, require**

compelling see **interesting, powerful, urgent**

compensate verb 1 to repay someone for loss or damage: You will be properly compensated for your loss

atone: He felt he had atoned for what he had done

refund: The company will refund the full cost

repay: collateral with which to repay swindled investors

reward: Their patience was finally rewarded

2 to cancel out: His lack of skill was compensated for by his enthusiasm

balance: The pros balance the cons

cancel out: The two influences cancel each other out

counteract: pills to counteract high blood pressure

make up for: I'll make up for what

I've done

offset: The loss is being offset by a new tax

see also **pay**

compensation noun something that makes up for loss or damage: compensation for his injuries

amends: an attempt to make amends for his crime

atonement: an act of atonement for our sins

damages: damages for libel

payment: a redundancy payment

compete verb to try to win: companies competing for business

contend: two groups contending for power

contest: the candidates contesting in the election

fight: rivals fighting for supremacy

vie: The contestants vied to finish first

see also **play**

competence see **ability, skill**

competent see **capable, efficient, proficient, skilful, skilled**

competently see **well**

competition noun 1 an attempt to win: There's a lot of competition for places

contention: contention for the gold medal

contest: the contest between capitalism and socialism

opposition: They are in direct opposition for the job

rivalry: the rivalry between the two leaders

struggle: a power struggle

2 a contest to find the winner in something: a surfing competition

championship: a swimming championship

contest: a beauty contest

event: major sporting events

tournament: a judo tournament

see also **competitor, contest, event,**

match
competitive see **reasonable**
competitor *noun* a person who competes for something: *one of the youngest competitors in the event*
  adversary: *his political adversaries*
  challenger: *20 seconds faster than the nearest challenger*
  competition: *staying ahead of the competition*
  contestant: *contestants in the Miss World pageant*
  opponent: *the best opponent I've played all season*
  opposition: *They can outplay the opposition*
  rival: *a business rival*
  see also **candidate**
complacent see **smug**
complain *verb* to express dissatisfaction: *He came round to complain about the noise*
  carp: *She is constantly carping at him*
  find fault: *He's always finding fault with my work*
  grouse: *You're always grousing about something*
  grumble: *It's not in her nature to grumble*
  kick up a fuss *informal*: *He kicks up a fuss whenever she goes out*
  moan: *moaning about the weather*
  whine: *whining children*
  whinge *informal*: *Stop whingeing and get on with it*
  see also **grumble**, **moan**, **protest**
complaint *noun* an instance of complaining about something: *There have been a number of complaints about the standard of service*
  criticism: *The criticism that we do not try hard enough to learn other languages was voiced*
  grievance: *They had a legitimate grievance against the company*
  grumble: *Her main grumble is over*

the long hours she has to work
  objection: *I have no objections about the way I have been treated*
  protest: *Despite our protests, they went ahead anyway*
  see also **disorder**, **grumble**, **illness**, **protest**
complement see **augment**, **blend**, **foil**, **supplement**
complete *adjective* **1** to the greatest degree possible: *a complete transformation*
  absolute: *absolute nonsense*
  consummate: *a consummate professional*
  outright: *an outright victory*
  perfect: *a perfect stranger*
  thorough: *a thorough snob*
  total: *a total failure*
  utter: *an utter shambles*
  2 with nothing missing: *a complete set of tools*
  entire: *the entire plot*
  full: *a full report*
  intact: *the few buildings which have survived intact*
  undivided: *I want your undivided attention*
  whole: *I told him the whole story*
  ▷ *verb* **3** to finish: *He has just completed his first novel*
  conclude: *The judge concluded his summing-up*
  end: *The crowd was in tears as he ended his speech*
  finish: *I'll finish my report this week*
  see also **absolute**, **accomplish**, **achieve**, **finish**, **ideal**, **over**, **perfect**, **perform**, **pure**, **rank**, **sheer**, **thorough**, **total**, **utter**, **whole**
completely see **quite**, **well**
completion see **finish**
complex *adjective* **1** having many different parts: *complex issues*
  complicated: *a very complicated*

voting system
difficult: *the laborious and difficult process of adopting a child*
intricate: *intricate patterns*
involved: *a long, involved explanation*
tangled: *His personal life has become more tangled than ever*
▷ *noun* **2** *an emotional problem:*
I have never had a complex about my weight
fixation: *She has a fixation about men with beards*
obsession: *95% of patients know their obsessions are irrational*
phobia: *The man had a phobia about flying*
preoccupation: *his total preoccupation with neatness*
problem: *an eating problem*
thing: *He's got this thing about women's shoes*
see also **complicated, elaborate, hard, obsession, sophisticated, tricky**
complicated *adjective* complex and difficult: *a complicated situation*
complex: *a complex issue*
convoluted: *a convoluted plot*
elaborate: *an elaborate theory*
intricate: *an intricate process*
involved: *a long, involved explanation*
see also **complex, confusing, elaborate, hard, sophisticated, tricky**
complication see **difficulty**
compliment see **flatter, tribute**
complimentary see **free**
comply see **follow, submit**
comply with see **obey**
component see **attachment, fitting, ingredient**
compose *verb* to create or write: *He has composed a symphony*
create: *He has created a new ballet*
devise: *a play devised by the drama company*

invent: *the man who invented gangsta rap*
produce: *He has produced a book about the city*
write: *I've never been able to write poetry*
see also **create, form, make up, write**
composed see **calm, cool, patient**
composition see **piece**
composure see **patience**
compound see **blend, mixture**
comprehend *verb* to understand or appreciate something: *I just cannot comprehend your attitude*
appreciate: *She has never really appreciated the scale of the problem*
fathom: *I really couldn't fathom what Steiner was talking about*
grasp: *The Government has not yet grasped the seriousness of the crisis*
see: *I don't see why you're complaining*
take in: *I try to explain, but you can tell she's not taking it in*
understand: *They are too young to understand what's going on*
work out: *It took me some time to work out what was causing the problem*
see also **know, read, realize, see, take in, understand**
comprehensible see **plain**
comprehension see **grasp, intelligence, understanding**
comprehensive see **broad, extensive, full, general, thorough**
compress see **press**
compressed see **firm**
comprise see **consist of, contain, make up**
compromise see **endanger**
compulsion see **force, urge**
compulsory *adjective* required by law: *School attendance is compulsory*
mandatory: *the mandatory retirement age*

obligatory: an obligatory medical examination
required: the required reading for this course
requisite: the requisite documents
comrade see **companion**
con verb 1 to trick someone into doing or believing something: He claimed that the salesman had conned him out of his life savings
cheat: a deliberate attempt to cheat employees out of their pensions
deceive: She deceived us into giving her a job
mislead: Ministers must not knowingly mislead the public
swindle: A City businessman swindled investors out of millions of pounds
trick: They tricked him into parting with his life savings
▷ noun 2 a trick intended to mislead or disadvantage someone: Slimming snacks that offer miraculous weight loss are a con
bluff: The letter was a bluff
deception: You've been the victim of a rather cruel deception
fraud: an investigation into frauds in the world of horseracing
swindle: a tax swindle
trick: a cheap trick to encourage people to switch energy suppliers
see also **cheat, deceive, dupe, fool, rob, take in, trick**
conceal see **cover, hide, obscure, suppress**
concealed see **invisible**
concede see **give in, grant**
conceit noun excessive pride: his insufferable conceit
egotism: typical showbiz egotism
pride: a blow to his pride
self-importance: his bad manners and self-importance
vanity: her vanity about her long hair
see also **pride**

conceited adjective too proud: a conceited young idiot
bigheaded informal: an arrogant, bigheaded man
cocky: I was very cocky as a youngster
egotistical: an egotistical show-off
self-important: self-important pop stars
vain: a shallow, vain woman
see also **boastful, cocky, haughty, pretentious, smug, stuck-up, vain**
conceivable see **possible**
conceivably see **maybe, perhaps**
conceive see **imagine, invent**
conceive of see **picture**
concentrate verb 1 to give something all your attention: Concentrate on your studies
be engrossed in: He was engrossed in his work
focus your attention on: focusing his attention on the race
give your attention to: I gave my attention to the question
put your mind to: You could do it if you put your mind to it
2 to be found in one place: They are mostly concentrated in the urban areas
accumulate: Cholesterol accumulates in the arteries
collect: dust collecting in the corners
gather: residents gathered in huddles
see also **centre, essence, focus**
concentrated see **thick**
conception see **vision**
concern noun 1 a feeling of worry: public concern about violence
anxiety: anxiety about the economy
apprehension: apprehension about the future
disquiet: a growing sense of disquiet
worry: She has no worries about his health
2 someone's duty or responsibility: His private life is not my concern
affair: If you want to go, that's

your affair
business: This is none of my business
responsibility: He's not my
responsibility
▷ *verb* **3** to make someone worried:
It concerns me that he doesn't want
to go
bother: Nothing bothers me
distress: They are distressed by the
accusations
disturb: disturbed by the news
trouble: Is anything troubling you?
worry: an issue that had worried him
for some time
4 to affect or involve: This concerns
both of us
affect: the ways in which computers
affect our lives
apply to: This rule does not apply
to us
be relevant to: These documents are
relevant to the case
involve: meetings which involve most
of the staff
see also **anxiety, bother, care,
consideration, enterprise,
interest, issue, job, worry**
concerned *see* **anxious, worried**
concerning *see* **about**
concise *adjective* using no
unnecessary words: a concise guide
brief: a brief description
short: a short speech
succinct: a succinct explanation
terse: a terse statement
see also **short**
conclude *verb* **1** to decide
something: He concluded that she
had been right
decide: I decided he must be ill
deduce: She deduced that I had
written the letter
infer: His feelings were easily inferred
from his reply
judge: The doctor judged that he was
not fit enough to play

reckon *informal*: I reckon we should
wait a while
suppose: There's no reason to suppose
he'll be there
surmise: It is surmised that he must
have known
2 to finish something: He concluded
the letter with a postscript
close: They closed the show with
a song
end: His speech ended with a prayer
for peace
finish: We finished the evening with a
walk on the beach
round off: This rounded the afternoon
off perfectly
wind up: She quickly wound up her
conversation
see also **complete, end, finish,
gather, stop**
concluding *see* **final, last**
conclusion *noun* **1** a decision
made after thinking carefully
about something: I've come to the
conclusion that she was lying
deduction: a shrewd deduction about
what was going on
inference: There were two inferences
to be drawn from her letter
judgment: My judgment is that
things are going to get worse
verdict: The doctor's verdict was that
he was fine
2 the finish or ending of something:
the conclusion of the programme
close: bringing the talks to a close
end: The war is coming to an end
ending: a dramatic ending
finish: the finish of the race
termination: the termination of
their marriage
see also **decision, finish, judgment,
verdict**
conclusive *see* **convincing, final,
positive**
concoct *see* **invent, make up**

concrete see **positive, real**

concur see **agree**

concur with see **accept**

concurrently see **together**

condemn verb 1 to say that
something is bad or unacceptable:
He was condemned for his arrogance
blame: I blame television for the rise
in violence
censure: a motion censuring the
government
criticize: He was criticized for his
failure to act
damn: The report damns the
government's handling of the affair
denounce: He was denounced as
a traitor
2 to give a punishment: condemned
to death
damn: sinners damned to eternal
torment
doom: doomed to die for his crime
sentence: sentenced to ten years
in prison
see also **censure, criticize,
disapprove**

condemnation see **censure,
disapproval**

condemned see **doomed**

condense see **thicken**

condensed see **thick**

condescending see **superior**

condition noun 1 the state of
something: The house is in good
condition
form: The team are not in good form
this season
shape: He's in great shape for his age
state: Look at the state of my car!
2 something required for something
else to be possible: terms and
conditions of the contract
prerequisite: A science background is
a prerequisite for the job
provision: a provision in his will
forbidding the sale of the house

proviso: The answer is yes, with
one proviso
qualification: He agreed, but with
some qualifications
requirement: The product meets all
legal requirements
requisite: the main requisite for
membership
stipulation: The only dress
stipulation was "no jeans"
terms: the terms of the agreement
see also **disorder, health,
qualification, state**

conditions see **terms**

condone see **forgive**

conduct verb 1 to carry out an
activity or task: to conduct an
experiment
carry out: carry out a survey
direct: Christopher will direct day-to-
day operations
do: I'm doing a piece of important
research right now
manage: his ability to manage the
business
organize: The initial mobilization was
well organized
perform: Several grafts were
performed during the operation
run: Each teacher will run a different
workshop
▷ noun 2 the way someone behaves:
Other people judge you by your conduct
attitude: His attitude made me angry
behaviour: Make sure that good
behaviour is rewarded
manners: He dressed well and had
impeccable manners
ways: urged him to alter his ways
see also **accompany, handle, lead,
manner, take, way**

conduct yourself verb to behave in
a particular way: The way he conducts
himself reflects on the school
act: a gang of youths who were acting
suspiciously

behave: He'd behaved badly

confectionery see **sweet**

confederation see **association, body, organization, union**

confer with see **consult**

conference noun a meeting for discussion: *a conference on education*

congress: *a congress of coal miners*

convention: *the Geneva convention*

discussion: *a round of formal discussions*

forum: *a forum for trade negotiations*

meeting: *a meeting of shareholders*
see also **convention, hui, meeting**

confess verb to admit to something: *Your son has confessed to his crimes*

acknowledge: *He acknowledged that he was a drug addict*

admit: *I admit to feeling jealous*

own up: *The headmaster is waiting for someone to own up*

confession noun the act of confessing: *a confession of adultery*

acknowledgment: *an acknowledgment of his mistakes*

admission: *an admission of guilt*

confidant see **friend**

confidante see **friend**

confidence noun 1 a feeling of trust: *I have complete confidence in you*

belief: *his belief in his partner*

faith: *He has great faith in her judgment*

reliance: *I don't put much reliance on that idea*

trust: *He destroyed my trust in people*

2 sureness of yourself: *I've never had much confidence*

aplomb: *She handled the interview with aplomb*

assurance: *He led the orchestra with great assurance*

self-assurance: *his supreme self-assurance*

self-possession: *an air of self-possession*

see also **belief, faith**

confident adjective 1 sure about something: *confident of success*

certain: *certain of getting a place on the team*

convinced: *He is convinced it's your fault*

positive: *I'm positive it will happen*

satisfied: *We must be satisfied that the treatment is safe*

secure: *secure about his job prospects*

sure: *I'm not sure I understand*

2 sure of yourself: *a confident attitude*

assured: *His playing became more assured*

self-assured: *a self-assured young man*

self-possessed: *a self-possessed career woman*

see also **bold, certain, optimistic, positive, secure**

confidential see **private, secret**

confine verb 1 to limit to something specified: *They confined themselves to talking about the weather*

limit: *Limit yourself to six units of alcohol a week*

restrict: *The patient was restricted to a meagre diet*

2 to prevent from leaving: *confined to bed for two days*

hem in: *hemmed in by spectators*

imprison: *imprisoned in a tiny cell*

restrict: *We were restricted to the building*

shut up: *He can't stand being shut up in the house*

see also **imprison, limit, restrict**

confirm verb 1 to say or show that something is true: *Police confirmed that they had received a call*

bear out: *The figures bear out his words*

endorse: *This theory has been endorsed by research*

prove: The results prove his point

substantiate: no evidence to substantiate the claims

validate: It is difficult to validate this belief

verify: I was asked to verify this statement

2 to make something definite: Can we confirm the arrangements for tomorrow?

fix: The date for the election was fixed

settle: I've settled a time to see him

see also **determine, prove**

confirmation see **proof**

confiscate see **seize**

conflict noun **1** disagreement and argument: conflict between workers and management

antagonism: antagonism within the team

disagreement: The meeting ended in disagreement

discord: public discord

friction: friction between him and his father

hostility: hostility between parents and teachers

opposition: a wave of opposition

strife: a cause of strife in many marriages

2 a war or battle: the conflict in the Gulf

battle: a battle between two gangs

combat: men who died in combat

fighting: Villagers have left their homes to avoid the fighting

strife: civil strife

war: the war between Israel and Egypt

▷ verb **3** to differ or disagree: conflicting ideas

be at variance: His statements are at variance with the facts

be incompatible: These two principles are incompatible

clash: a decision which clashes with official policy

differ: The two leaders differ on several issues

disagree: Governments disagree over the need for action

see also **clash, dispute, interfere, war**

conflicting see **opposite**

conform see **agree, follow**

conform to see **suit**

conformist see **conventional**

confrontation see **clash**

confuse verb **1** to mix two things up: confusing fact with fiction

mistake: I mistook you for someone else

mix up: He sometimes mixes up his words

muddle up: I keep muddling him up with his brother

2 to puzzle or bewilder: Politics confuse me

baffle: Police are baffled by the murder

bewilder: His silence bewildered her

mystify: I was mystified by his attitude

puzzle: One thing still puzzles me

see also **cloud, mix up, muddle, puzzle**

confuse with see **mistake**

confused adjective **1** puzzled or bewildered: confused about health risks

baffled: He stared in baffled amazement

bewildered: bewildered holidaymakers

muddled: She was muddled about the date

perplexed: perplexed by recent events

puzzled: a puzzled expression

2 in an untidy mess: They lay in a confused heap

chaotic: the chaotic mess on his desk

disordered: a disordered pile of papers

disorganized: a disorganized lifestyle

untidy: an untidy room
see also **dazed, garbled, unclear**

confusing adjective puzzling or
bewildering: a confusing situation
  baffling: a baffling statement
  bewildering: a bewildering choice
  of products
  complicated: a complicated voting
  system
  puzzling: a puzzling problem

confusion noun an untidy mess: My
life is in confusion
  chaos: economic chaos
  disarray: The nation is in disarray
  disorder: The emergency room was
  in disorder
  disorganization: scenes of chaos
  and disorganization
  mess: He always leaves the bathroom
  in a mess
see also **disorder, fuss, muddle**

congeal see **thicken**
congealed see **firm**
congenial see **compatible**
congested see **crowded**
congratulate see **praise**
congratulation see **praise**
congregate see **assemble, crowd,
gather, mass, meet**
congregation see **gathering**
congress see **conference,
convention, hui, meeting**
conjecture see **theory**
connect verb 1 to join together:
Connect the pipe to the tap
  affix: His name was affixed to his
  cubicle
  attach: Attach the curtains to the
  rods with hooks
  couple: The engine is coupled to a
  gearbox
  fasten: A hatchet was fastened to
  his belt
  join: two springs joined together
  link: the Channel Tunnel linking
  Britain with France

2 to associate one thing with
another: evidence connecting him
with the robberies
  ally: The new government is allied
  with the military
  associate: symptoms associated with
  migraine headaches
  link: research which links smoking
  with cancer
  relate: the denial that unemployment
  is related to crime
see also **associate, attach, join, link**

connection noun 1 a link or
relationship: a connection between
drinking and liver disease
  affiliation: He has no affiliation with
  any political party
  association: the association between
  the two companies
  bond: the bond between a mother
  and child
  correlation: the correlation between
  unemployment and crime
  correspondence: the
  correspondence between Eastern and
  Western religions
  link: a link between smoking and
  lung cancer
  relation: This theory bears no relation
  to reality
  relationship: the relationship
  between humans and their
  environment

2 a point where things are joined:
The fault was just a loose connection
  coupling: The coupling between the
  railway carriages snapped
  fastening: a zip fastening
  junction: the junction between nerve
  and muscle
  link: a link between the city and the
  motorway
see also **association, bond, contact,
link, relation, relationship, tie**

conquer see **defeat, overcome,
vanquish**

conqueror see **winner**

conquest see **defeat**

conscience noun a sense of right and wrong: *He had a guilty conscience*

  principles: *It's against my principles to eat meat*

  scruples: *a man with no moral scruples*

  sense of right and wrong: *children with no sense of right and wrong* see also **principle**

conscientious see **industrious**

conscious see **deliberate**

conscious of see **aware of**

consciousness see **sense**

consecrate see **bless**

consecrated see **holy**

consent see **blessing, permission**

consent to see **accept, approve**

consequence see **effect, result**

consequently see **therefore**

conservationist see **green**

conservative adjective unwilling to change: *People get more conservative as they grow older*

  conventional: *conventional tastes*

  traditional: *a traditional school* see also **conventional, right-wing**

consider verb 1 to think of someone or something as: *They do not consider him a suitable candidate*

  believe: *I believe him to be innocent*

  judge: *His work was judged unsatisfactory*

  rate: *The film was rated excellent*

  regard as: *They regard the tax as unfair*

  think: *Many people think him arrogant*

  2 to think carefully: *I will consider your offer*

  contemplate: *He contemplated his fate*

  deliberate: *The jury deliberated for three days*

  meditate: *He meditated on the problem*

  muse: *She sat musing on how unfair life was*

  ponder: *pondering how to improve the team*

  reflect: *I reflected on the child's future*

  think about: *I've been thinking about what you said*

  3 to take into account: *We should consider her feelings*

  bear in mind: *There are a few points to bear in mind*

  make allowances for: *Remember to make allowances for delays*

  respect: *We will respect your wishes*

  take into account: *another factor to be taken into account*

  think about: *more important things to think about*

  see also **contemplate, feel, judge, ponder, rate, reckon, regard, think, view**

considerable see **extensive, handsome, respectable, significant**

considerably see **far**

considerate see **accommodating, kind, thoughtful, understanding**

considerately see **well**

consideration noun 1 careful thought about something: *a decision requiring careful consideration*

  attention: *I gave the question all my attention*

  contemplation: *The problem deserves serious contemplation*

  deliberation: *After much deliberation, he called the police*

  study: *The proposals need careful study*

  thought: *I've given the matter a great deal of thought*

  2 concern for someone: *Show some consideration for other passengers*

  concern: *concern for the homeless*

  kindness: *We have been treated with*

great kindness

respect: no respect for wildlife

tact: a master of tact and diplomacy

3 something to be taken into
account: Safety is a major
consideration

factor: an important factor in buying
a house

issue: Price is not the only issue

point: There is another point to
remember

see also **aspect, factor, thought**

consignment see **load**

consistency see **texture**

consistent see **compatible, logical,
regular, steady**

consist of verb to be made up of: The
brain consists of millions of nerve cells

be composed of: The committee is
composed of ten people

be made up of: The bouquet was
made up of roses and carnations

comprise: The show comprises 50
paintings and sketches

consolation see **comfort**

console see **comfort**

consolidate see **strengthen**

conspicuous adjective easy to see
or notice: Her conspicuous lack of
warmth confirmed her disapproval

apparent: It has been apparent that
someone has been stealing

blatant: a blatant disregard for rules

evident: He spoke with evident
emotion about his ordeal

noticeable: the most noticeable
effect of these changes

obvious: an obvious injustice

perceptible: a perceptible air of
neglect

see also **clear, manifest, noticeable,
prominent, visible**

conspiracy see **plot**

conspire see **plot**

constant adjective **1** going on all the
time: a city under constant attack

continual: continual pain

continuous: continuous gunfire

eternal: an eternal hum in the
background

nonstop: nonstop music

perpetual: her perpetual complaints

relentless: relentless pressure

2 staying the same: a constant
temperature

even: an even level of sound

fixed: a fixed salary

regular: a regular beat

stable: a stable condition

steady: travelling at a steady 50
miles per hour

uniform: a uniform thickness

see also **continual, continuous,
devoted, even, loyal, permanent,
regular, steadfast, steady**

constituent see **ingredient**

constitute see **form, make up**

constitution see **health, law**

constraint see **restriction**

constricted see **tight**

construct verb to build or make
something: The boxes are constructed
from rough-sawn timber

assemble: She had been trying to
assemble the bomb when it went off

build: Workers at the plant build the
F-16 jet fighter

create: We created a makeshift
platform for him to stand on

erect: The building was erected
in 1900

make: The company now makes cars
at two plants in Europe

put together: the mechanic whose
job was to put together looms within
the plant

put up: He was putting up a new
fence

see also **assemble, build, fashion,
make, produce**

construction see **making, structure**

constructive see **helpful, positive,**

productive

consult verb to go to for advice: Consult your doctor before undertaking exercise

ask for advice: Ask your bank manager for advice on mortgages

confer with: He is conferring with his lawyers

refer to: I had to refer to the manual see also **refer**

consultant see **adviser**

consultation see **discussion**

consume see **drain, exhaust**

consumer see **customer**

consummate see **complete, ideal, perfect, utter**

contact noun 1 the state of being in touch with someone: We must keep in contact

communication: The leaders were in constant communication

touch: I've lost touch with her over the years

2 someone you know: a contact in the music business

acquaintance: We met through a mutual acquaintance

connection: She had a connection in England

▷ verb **3** to get in touch with: We contacted the company to complain

approach: A journalist has approached me for a story

communicate with: We communicate mostly by email

get hold of: I've been trying to get hold of you all week

get in touch with: I will get in touch with my solicitors

reach: Where can I reach you in an emergency?

contagious see **infectious**

contain verb 1 to include as a part of: Alcohol contains sugar

comprise: The band comprises two singers and two guitarists

include: The price includes VAT

2 to keep under control: efforts to contain the disease

control: He could hardly control his rage

curb: measures to curb inflation

repress: people who repress their emotions

restrain: unable to restrain her anger

stifle: stifling the urge to scream see also **curb, include, restrain, restrict, suppress**

container noun something which holds things: a plastic container for food

holder: a cigarette holder

vessel: storage vessels see also **box, case**

contaminate see **infect, pollute**

contemplate verb 1 to think carefully about something: He cried as he contemplated his future

consider: She paused to consider her options

examine: I have examined all the possible alternatives

muse on: Many of the papers muse on the fate of the President

ponder: He didn't waste time pondering the question

reflect on: I reflected on the child's future

think about: Think about how you can improve the situation

2 to consider doing something: He contemplated a career as a doctor

consider: Watersports enthusiasts should consider hiring a wetsuit

envisage: He had never envisaged spending the whole of his life in that job

plan: I had been planning a trip to the West Coast

think of: Martin was thinking of taking legal action against his employers *see also* **consider, ponder, regard, study, think**

contemplation *see* **consideration, thought**

contemplative *see* **thoughtful**

contemporary *see* **current, modern**

contempt *noun* complete lack of respect: *I shall treat that remark with the contempt it deserves*

   derision: *He was greeted with shouts of derision*

   disdain: *Janet looked at him with disdain*

   disregard: *total disregard for the safety of the public*

   disrespect: *complete disrespect for authority*

   scorn: *They greeted the proposal with scorn*

   see also **scorn**

contemptible *see* **low, shabby**

contemptuous *see* **scornful**

contend *see* **compete**

contender *see* **candidate**

content *see* **satisfied**

contented *see* **comfortable, pleased, satisfied**

contention *see* **competition**

contest *noun* **1** a competition or game: *Few contests in the history of boxing have been as thrilling*

   competition: *a surfing competition*

   game: *the first game of the season*

   match: *He was watching a football match*

   tournament: *Here is a player capable of winning a world tournament*

   2 a struggle for power: *a bitter contest over who should control the state's future*

   battle: *the eternal battle between good and evil*

   fight: *the fight for the US Presidency*

   struggle: *locked in a power struggle with his Prime Minister*

▷ *verb* **3** to object formally to a statement or decision: *Your former employer has 14 days to contest the case*

   challenge: *The move was immediately challenged*

   dispute: *He disputed the allegations*

   oppose: *Many parents oppose bilingual education in schools*

   question: *It never occurs to them to question the doctor's decisions*

   see also **compete, competition, dispute, event, game, match**

contestant *see* **competitor**

continual *adjective* **1** happening all the time without stopping: *Despite continual pain, he refused all drugs*

   constant: *She suggests that women are under constant pressure to be abnormally thin*

   continuous: *a continuous stream of phone calls*

   endless: *her endless demands for attention*

   eternal: *In the background was that eternal hum*

   nagging: *a nagging pain between his shoulder blades*

   perpetual: *the perpetual thump of music from the flat downstairs*

   uninterrupted: *five years of uninterrupted growth*

   2 happening again and again: *She suffered continual police harassment*

   frequent: *He is prone to frequent bouts of depression*

   recurrent: *buildings in which staff suffer recurrent illness*

   regular: *He is a regular visitor to our house*

   repeated: *Mr Smith did not return the money, despite repeated reminders*

   see also **constant, frequent**

continually *see* **always**

continue *verb* **1** to keep doing something: *Will you continue working after you're married?*

carry on: *The assistant carried on talking*

go on: *Unemployment is likely to go on rising*

keep on: *He kept on trying*

persist: *She persists in using his nickname*

2 to go on existing: *The fighting continued after they'd left*

carry on: *My work will carry on after I'm gone*

endure: *Their friendship has endured for 30 years*

last: *Nothing lasts forever*

persist: *The problem persists*

remain: *The building remains to this day*

survive: *companies which survived after the recession*

3 to start doing again: *After a moment, she continued speaking*

carry on: *He took a deep breath, then carried on*

recommence: *He recommenced work on his novel*

resume: *Police will resume the search today*

see also **extend**, **last**, **proceed**, **remain**, **stretch**

continued see **continuous**

continuous adjective going on without stopping: *continuous growth*

constant: *under constant pressure*

continued: *a continued improvement*

extended: *conflict over an extended period*

prolonged: *a prolonged drought*

uninterrupted: *uninterrupted rule*

see also **constant**, **continual**, **gradual**, **steady**

contours see **form**, **outline**, **shape**

contract see **agreement**, **bond**, **develop**, **diminish**, **shrink**

contradict see **clash**, **deny**, **dispute**

contraption see **machine**

contrary see **opposite**, **reverse**

contrast see **compare**, **difference**, **foil**

contrasting see **different**, **opposite**

contravene see **break**

contribute see **provide**

contribute to see **lead to**

contribution see **gift**

control noun **1** power over something: *He was forced to give up control of the company*

authority: *You have no authority here*

command: *He was in command of the ceremony*

direction: *The team worked well under his direction*

government: *The entire country is under the government of one man*

management: *the day-to-day management of the business*

power: *a position of great power*

rule: *15 years of Communist rule*

supremacy: *The party has re-established its supremacy*

▷ verb **2** to be in charge of: *companies fighting to control the Internet*

administer: *the authorities who administer the island*

be in charge of: *She is in charge of the project*

command: *the general who commanded the troops*

direct: *He will direct day-to-day operations*

govern: *his ability to govern France*

have power over: *Her husband has total power over her*

manage: *the government's ability to manage the economy*

rule: *the dynasty which ruled China*

see also **administer**, **check**, **command**, **contain**, **curb**, **determine**, **direct**, **direction**, **grip**, **head**, **hold**, **influence**, **manage**, **management**, **possess**, **possession**, **power**, **restrain**, **restriction**, **run**

103 | **control**

conundrum see **mystery, problem**

convalesce see **recover**

convene see **assemble, meet**

convenient adjective helpful or easy to use: a convenient mode of transport

handy: Credit cards can be handy

helpful: a helpful fact sheet

useful: a useful invention

see also **handy, ready**

convention noun **1** an accepted way of behaving or doing something: It's just a social convention that men don't wear skirts

code: the code of the Shaolin monks

custom: The custom of lighting the Olympic flame goes back centuries

etiquette: the rules of diplomatic etiquette

practice: It is normal practice not to reveal the sex of the baby

tradition: different cultural traditions from ours

2 a large meeting of an organization or group: the annual convention of the Parapsychological Association

assembly: an assembly of women Olympic gold-medal winners

conference: a conference attended by 450 delegates

congress: A lot changed after the party congress

meeting: the annual meeting of company shareholders

see also **conference, custom, habit, hui, meeting, tradition**

conventional adjective **1** having or relating to a very ordinary lifestyle: a respectable married woman with conventional opinions

conformist: He may have to become more conformist if he is to prosper

conservative: The girl was well dressed in a rather conservative style

unadventurous: He was a strong player, but rather unadventurous

2 familiar, or usually used: These discs hold 400 times as much information as a conventional floppy disk

customary: the customary one minute's silence

ordinary: It has 25 per cent less fat than ordinary ice cream

orthodox: Many of these ideas are being incorporated into orthodox medical treatment

regular: This product looks and tastes like regular margarine

standard: It was standard practice for untrained clerks to deal with serious cases

traditional: traditional teaching methods

see also **conservative, formal, normal, ordinary, popular, proper, traditional**

conversation see **chat, discussion, talk, word**

conversational see **colloquial**

converse see **opposite, reverse**

convert see **adapt, change, recruit, transform, turn**

convey verb to cause information or ideas to be known: I tried to convey the wonder of the experience to my husband

communicate: They successfully communicate their knowledge to others

express: She did her best to express wordless disapproval by scowling

get across: I wanted to get my message across

impart: the ability to impart knowledge

see also **bear, bring, carry, communicate, take, transport**

convict see **prisoner**

convicted see **guilty**

conviction see **belief, idea, view, viewpoint**

convince verb to persuade that

something is true: *I convinced him of my innocence*

assure: *She assured me that there was nothing wrong*

persuade: *I had to persuade him of the advantages*

satisfy: *He had to satisfy the doctors that he was fit to play*

see also **satisfy**

convinced see **certain, confident, positive, sure**

convincing adjective persuasive: *a convincing argument*

conclusive: *conclusive proof*

effective: *an effective speaker*

persuasive: *persuasive reasons*

plausible: *a plausible explanation*

powerful: *a powerful speech*

telling: *a telling criticism*

see also **powerful**

convoluted see **complicated**

cook verb to prepare food for eating by heating it in some way: *I enjoy cooking for friends*

bake: *a machine for baking bread*

barbecue: *a Korean method of barbecuing meat*

boil: *Boil the fruit and syrup together for half an hour*

fry: *Garnish the rice with thinly sliced fried onion*

grill: *Grill the fish for five minutes*

microwave: *Microwaved vegetables have a fresher flavour*

poach: *I had ordered poached eggs on toast for breakfast*

roast: *Roast the aubergine in the oven for about one hour until soft*

steam: *mussels on a bed of steamed cabbage*

stew: *You can stew the vegetables in oil*

toast: *This currant loaf is delicious either fresh or toasted*

cool adjective **1** having a low temperature: *a gust of cool air*

chilled: *a chilled bottle of wine*

chilly: *a chilly afternoon*

cold: *Your dinner's getting cold*

refreshing: *a refreshing breeze*

2 staying calm: *He kept cool through the whole thing*

calm: *Try to stay calm*

collected: *She was cool and collected throughout the interview*

composed: *a composed player*

level-headed: *Simon is level-headed and practical*

relaxed: *a relaxed manner*

serene: *a serene smile*

▷ verb **3** to make or become cool: *Put the cookies on a wire rack to cool*

chill: *a glass of chilled champagne*

cool off: *Dip the carrots in water to cool them off*

freeze: *Make double the quantity and freeze half for later*

refrigerate: *Refrigerate the dough overnight*

see also **apathetic, calm, patience, relaxed**

cool off see **cool**

cooperate verb to work together: *The family cooperated with the author of the book*

collaborate: *They collaborated on an album*

join forces: *The two political parties are joining forces*

pull together: *The staff and management pull together*

work together: *industry and government working together*

see also **team**

cooperative see **helpful**

coordinate see **blend, oversee**

cope with see **deal, endure, manage, take care of**

copious see **abundant, plentiful**

copy noun **1** something made to look like something else: *He had kept a copy of the letter*

counterfeit: This credit card is a counterfeit
duplicate: I lost my key and had to get a duplicate made
fake: How do I know this painting isn't a fake?
forgery: The letter was a forgery
imitation: Beware of cheap imitations
replica: a replica of the Statue of Liberty
reproduction: a reproduction of a famous painting
▷ verb **2** to do the same thing as someone else: My little brother copies everything I do
ape: Generations of women have aped her style and looks
emulate: Sons are expected to emulate their fathers
follow: Where America goes, Britain will surely follow
imitate: Children imitate what they see on TV
mimic: He mimicked her accent
3 to make a copy of: documents copied by hand
counterfeit: These banknotes are very easy to counterfeit
duplicate: Videos are being illicitly duplicated all over the country
reproduce: a new method of reproducing oil paintings
see also **fake, imitate, issue**
cordial see **friendly, warm**
core see **basis, centre, essence**
cork see **plug**
corner see **bend, trap**
corny adjective unoriginal or sentimental: corny old love songs
banal: banal dialogue
hackneyed: a hackneyed plot
maudlin: a maudlin film
sentimental: a sentimental ballad
stale: stale ideas
stereotyped: a stereotyped image

of Britain
trite: a trite ending
corporation see **business, company, firm**
corpse see **body**
correct adjective **1** without mistakes: a correct diagnosis
accurate: an accurate description
exact: an exact copy
faultless: Hans's English was faultless
flawless: a flawless performance
precise: precise calculations
right: That clock never shows the right time
true: a true account
2 socially acceptable: correct behaviour
acceptable: It is becoming more acceptable for women to drink
appropriate: appropriate dress
fitting: behaving in a manner not fitting for a lady
okay or **OK** informal: Is it okay if I bring a friend with me?
proper: In those days it was not proper for women to go on the stage
seemly: It is not seemly to joke about such things
▷ verb **3** to make right: trying to correct his faults
amend: They want to amend the current system
cure: an operation to cure his limp
improve: We must improve the situation
rectify: attempts to rectify the problem
reform: He promised to reform his wicked ways
remedy: What is needed to remedy these deficiencies?
right: I intend to right these wrongs
see also **accurate, appropriate, fitting, fix, formal, precise, proper, reform, revise, right, standard,**

true

correction noun the act of making something right: *the correction of obvious mistakes*

  adjustment: *My car needs a brake adjustment*

  amendment: *He has made lots of amendments to the script*

  righting: *the righting of the country's domestic troubles*

  see also **reform**

correlate see **correspond**

correlation see **connection, relation, relationship**

correspond verb to be similar or connected to something else: *The two maps correspond closely*

  agree: *His statement agrees with those of other witnesses*

  be related: *These philosophical problems are closely related*

  coincide: *He was delighted to find that her feelings coincided with his own*

  correlate: *Obesity correlates with increased risk for diabetes*

  fit: *The punishment must always fit the crime*

  match: *Our value system does not match with theirs*

  tally: *This description did not tally with what we saw*

  see also **communicate, fit, match, suit, write**

correspondence see **connection, resemblance**

corridor see **passage**

corrode see **eat away, erode, wear**

corrosion see **wear**

corrupt adjective **1** acting dishonestly or illegally: *corrupt politicians*

  crooked: *a crooked cop*

  dishonest: *a dishonest scheme*

  fraudulent: *fraudulent trading*

  shady informal: *shady deals*

unscrupulous: *unscrupulous landlords*

  ▷ verb **2** to make dishonest: *Organized crime has corrupted local government*

  bribe: *accused of bribing officials*

  buy off: *Police were bought off by drugs dealers*

  fix informal: *He fixed the match by bribing the players*

  3 to make immoral: *TV is corrupting our children*

  deprave: *material likely to deprave those who watch it*

  pervert: *perverted by their contact with criminals*

  see also **criminal, crooked, dirty, dishonest**

corruption noun dishonest and illegal behaviour: *charges of corruption*

  bribery: *on trial for bribery*

  dishonesty: *She accused the government of dishonesty and incompetence*

  fraud: *jailed for fraud*

  see also **dishonesty**

cosmopolitan see **sophisticated**

cosset see **spoil**

cost noun **1** the amount of money needed: *The cost of petrol has increased*

  charge: *We can arrange this for a small charge*

  expense: *household expenses*

  outlay: *Buying wine in bulk is well worth the outlay*

  payment: *an initial payment of just $100*

  price: *House prices are expected to rise*

  rate: *specially reduced rates*

  2 loss or damage: *the total cost in human misery*

  detriment: *These changes are to the detriment of staff morale*

  expense: *I supported my husband's*

career at the expense of my own
penalty: *paying the penalty for someone else's mistakes*
▷ verb **3** to involve a cost of: *The air fares were going to cost a lot*
come to: *Lunch came to nearly 15*
sell at: *The books are selling at £1 per copy*
set someone back *informal*: *This wedding will set us back thousands of pounds*
see also **charge, price, rate, value**

cost-effective *see* **economical**

costly *see* **dear, expensive, valuable**

costume *see* **clothes, dress**

cosy *adjective* **1** warm and comfortable: *Guests can relax in the cosy bar*
comfortable: *a comfortable fireside chair*
snug: *a snug log cabin*
warm: *warm blankets*
2 pleasant and friendly: *a cosy chat between friends*
friendly: *a friendly little get-together*
informal: *The house was in an informal atmosphere*
intimate: *an intimate candlelit dinner for two*
relaxed: *a relaxed evening in*
see also **comfortable, homely**

couch *see* **express**

council *noun* a governing group of people: *the city council*
assembly: *the National Assembly*
board: *the Pakistan Cricket Board*
committee: *the management committee*
panel: *a panel of judges*

counsel *see* **advice, advise, guide, lawyer**

count *verb* **1** to add up: *I counted the money*
add up: *Add up the sales figures*
calculate: *First, calculate your monthly living expenses*

tally: *Computers now tally the votes*
2 to be important: *Our opinions don't count*
carry weight: *a politician whose words carry weight*
matter: *It doesn't matter what she thinks*
rate: *This does not rate as one of my main concerns*
signify: *His absence does not signify much*
weigh: *This evidence did not weigh with the jury*
▷ noun **3** a counting or number counted: *The count revealed that our party had the majority*
calculation: *I did a quick calculation in my head*
reckoning: *By my reckoning we were about two miles from camp*
sum: *I've never been good at sums*
tally: *They keep a tally of visitors to the castle*
see also **calculate, matter, rate, reckon**

count on *see* **depend, trust**

count up *see* **add**

countenance *see* **expression, face**

counter *see* **foil, reply**

counteract *verb* to reduce the effect of something: *pills to counteract high blood pressure*
act against: *The immune system acts against infection*
offset: *The slump was offset by a surge in exports*
see also **compensate**

counterbalance *see* **reaction**

counterfeit *see* **copy, fake, mock, phoney, pretend**

countless *adjective* too many to count: *the star of countless films*
infinite: *an infinite number of atoms*
innumerable: *innumerable problems*
myriad: *pop music in all its myriad forms*

untold: untold wealth
see also **many**

country noun **1** a political area: the boundary between the two countries
kingdom: The kingdom's power declined
land: America, land of opportunity
state: a communist state
2 land away from towns and cities: He lives right out in the country
bush New Zealand, South African: a trip out to the bush
countryside: surrounded by beautiful countryside
outback Australian, New Zealand: nostalgic paintings of the outback
outdoors: He loves the great outdoors
see also **land, state, territory**

countryman see **yokel**

countryside see **country**

couple see **associate, attach, connect, join, link**

coupling see **connection**

courage noun lack of fear: His courage impressed everyone
bravery: an act of bravery
daring: tales of daring and adventure
guts informal: He didn't have the guts to admit he was wrong
heroism: the young soldier's heroism
nerve: I didn't have the nerve to complain
pluck: You have to admire her pluck
valour: He was decorated for valour in the war
see also **bravery, daring**

courageous see **bold, brave**

courier see **messenger**

course noun **1** a series of lessons: a course in computing
classes: I go to dance classes
curriculum: the history curriculum
2 a policy of action: He took the only course left open to him
plan: Your best plan is to see your doctor
policy: She decided the best policy was to wait
procedure: He did not follow the correct procedure
3 a way taken to get somewhere: She sensed the plane had changed course
direction: He went off in the opposite direction
line: the birds' line of flight
path: the path of an oncoming car
route: the most direct route
trajectory: the trajectory of the missile
way: What way do you go home?
see also **direction, line, passage, path, pour, route, sequence, way**

course of action see **process**

court noun **1** a place where legal matters are decided: He ended up in court for theft
bench: He was brought before the bench
law court: prisoners tried by a law court
tribunal: The claim was thrown out by a European tribunal
▷ verb **2** old-fashioned to intend to marry: I was courting Billy at 19 and married him at 21
go steady: They've been going steady for six months now
woo: He wooed and married his first love

courteous see **polite**

courteousness see **courtesy**

courtesy noun polite and considerate behaviour: a lack of courtesy to other drivers
civility: Handle customers with tact and civility
courteousness: his courteousness and kindness
gallantry: He treated me with old-fashioned gallantry
good manners: the rules of good

manners

grace: He didn't even have the grace to apologize

graciousness: The team displayed graciousness in defeat

politeness: basic standards of politeness

see also **favour, politeness**

cove see **bay**

cover verb 1 to protect or hide: He covered his face

cloak: a land cloaked in mist

conceal: The hat concealed her hair

cover up: I covered him up with a blanket

hide: His sunglasses hid his eyes

mask: A cloud masked the sun

obscure: One wall was obscured by a huge banner

screen: The road was screened by a block of flats

shade: shading his eyes from the glare

2 to form a layer over: Tears covered his face

coat: Coat the fish with batter

overlay: The floor was overlaid with rugs

▷ noun **3** something which protects or hides: a duvet cover

case: a spectacle case

coating: steel covered with a coating of zinc

covering: a plastic covering

jacket: the jacket of a book

mask: a surgical mask

screen: They put a screen round me

wrapper: Take the product from its sealed wrapper

see also **defence, defend, include, protection, report, safeguard, shelter, spread, stretch**

cover up see **cover**

covering see **coating, cover, layer**

covert see **secret**

covet see **envy, long, want**

cow noun a farm animal kept for milk

or meat: a herd of dairy cows

bovine: a herd of deranged bovines

cattle: fields where cattle graze

coward noun someone who is easily scared: He's too much of a coward to fight

chicken slang: We called him a chicken

wimp informal: He seems like a wimp to me

cowardly adjective easily scared: too cowardly to tell the truth

chicken slang: I was too chicken to complain

faint-hearted: This is no time to be faint-hearted

gutless informal: a gutless coward

sookie New Zealand: a sookie thing to do

see also **timid**

cowboy see **incompetent**

cower verb to bend down with fear: The hostages cowered in their seats

cringe: I cringed in horror

quail: She quailed at the sight

shrink: He shrank back in terror

co-worker see **associate**

crack verb 1 to become damaged, with lines on the surface: A gas main has cracked

break: She broke her leg playing rounders

fracture: You've fractured a rib

snap: The mast snapped like a dry twig

2 to find the answer to something: We've managed to crack the problem

decipher: trying to decipher the code

solve: attempts to solve the mystery

work out: I've worked out where I'm going wrong

▷ noun **3** a line or gap caused by damage: a large crack in the wall

break: a train crash caused by a break in the rails

cleft: a cleft in the rocks

crevice: a crevice in the cliff-face

fracture: a hip fracture

see also **attempt, bang, breach, burst, fissure, gap, leak, opening, solve, split**

cracking see **excellent, splendid**

craft see **work**

craftsman see **worker**

crafty adjective clever and rather dishonest: That crafty old devil has taken us for a ride

artful: the smiles and schemes of an artful woman

cunning: I have a cunning plan to get us out of this mess

devious: By devious means she obtained the address

scheming: You're a scheming little devil, aren't you?

slippery: a slippery customer

sly: He is a sly old beggar if ever there was one

wily: the wily manoeuvring of the President

see also **cunning, shrewd, sly, sneaky**

craggy see **jagged, rough**

cram verb to stuff something into a container or place: She crammed her mouth with nuts

jam: The place was jammed with people

pack: The drawers were packed with clothes

squeeze: The two of us were squeezed into one seat

stuff: wallets stuffed with dollars

see also **fill, jam, stuff**

cramped see **tight, uncomfortable**

crank see **eccentric, weirdo**

crash noun 1 an accident involving a moving vehicle: a plane crash

accident: a serious car accident

bump: I had a bump in the car park

collision: a head-on collision

pile-up informal: a 54-car pile-up

smash: He nearly died in a car smash

2 a loud noise: There was a sudden crash outside

bang: The door slammed with a bang

clash: the clash of cymbals

din: the din of battle

smash: the smash of falling crockery

3 the failure of a business: a stock market crash

bankruptcy: Many firms are now facing bankruptcy

collapse: The economy is on the edge of collapse

depression: the Great Depression of the 1930s

failure: A major cause of business failure

ruin: Inflation has driven them to the brink of ruin

▷ verb 4 to have an accident: His car crashed into the rear of a van

bump: I've just bumped my car

collide: Two trains collided in London today

drive into: He drove his car into a tree

have an accident: My brother's had an accident on his moped

hurtle into: The racing car hurtled into the spectator enclosure

plough into: The plane had ploughed into the mountainside

wreck: He's wrecked his van

see also **dash**

crave see **desire, long, want**

craving see **desire, longing**

crawl verb to be full of: The place is crawling with drunks

be alive with: The river was alive with frogs

be full of: The place was full of insects

be overrun with slang: The area is overrun with tourists

swarm: The wood was swarming with police officers

teem: ponds teeming with fish

craze noun a brief enthusiasm for

something: *the latest fitness craze*

fad: *a new-age fad*

fashion: *the fashion for Seventies toys*

trend: *the latest trend among film stars*

vogue: *a vogue for so-called health drinks*

see also **fashion, whim**

crazy adjective **1** *informal* very strange or foolish: *People thought we were crazy when we told them our plans*

foolish: *It is foolish to risk skin cancer for the sake of a tan*

insane: *If you want my opinion, I think your idea is completely insane*

mad: *You'd be mad to work with him again*

ridiculous: *It was an absolutely ridiculous decision*

wild: *all sorts of wild ideas*

zany: *zany humour*

2 *informal* very keen on something: *He's crazy about football*

fanatical: *fanatical about computer games*

mad: *She's not as mad about sport as I am*

obsessed: *He was obsessed with American gangster movies*

passionate: *He is passionate about the project*

smitten: *They were totally smitten with each other*

wild: *I'm just wild about Peter*

see also **absurd, daft, idiotic, insane, irrational, mad**

crease see **crumple, fold**

create verb **1** to make something happen: *His reaction created a bad atmosphere*

bring about: *helping to bring about peace*

cause: *Sugar causes dental decay*

lead to: *The takeover led to widespread redundancies*

occasion: *the distress occasioned by her dismissal*

2 to invent something: *creating a new style of painting*

coin: *the man who coined the term "virtual reality"*

compose: *Vivaldi composed many concertos*

devise: *We devised a scheme to help him*

formulate: *He formulated his plan for escape*

invent: *He invented the first electric clock*

originate: *the designer who originated platform shoes*

see also **bring, bring about, cause, compose, construct, fashion, form, invent, make, produce, start**

creation see **making, piece**

creative adjective able to invent: *her creative talents*

fertile: *a fertile imagination*

imaginative: *an imaginative writer*

inspired: *his inspired use of colour*

inventive: *an inventive storyline*

creativity see **imagination**

creature see **animal**

credible see **believable**

credit noun praise for something: *He took all the credit for my idea*

commendation: *Both teams deserve commendation*

glory: *basking in reflected glory*

praise: *Praise is due to all concerned*

recognition: *She got no recognition for her work*

thanks: *He received no thanks for his efforts*

see also **loan**

creed see **belief, faith**

creep see **ease, edge, slip, steal**

creepy adjective *informal* strange and frightening: *This place is really creepy at night*

disturbing: *There was something*

about him she found disturbing

eerie: I walked down the eerie dark path

macabre: macabre stories

scary informal: We watched scary movies

sinister: There was something sinister about him

spooky: The whole place has a slightly spooky atmosphere

unnatural: The altered landscape looks unnatural and weird

see also **scary, spooky**

crest see **peak, top**

crevice see **crack, fissure**

crew see **party, team**

crime noun an act that breaks the law: the problem of organized crime

misdemeanour: a financial misdemeanour

offence: a serious offence

violation: tax law violations

wrong: I intend to right that wrong

see also **pity, sin, wrong**

criminal noun 1 someone who has committed a crime: the country's most dangerous criminals

crook informal: The man is a crook and a liar

culprit: the true culprit's identity

delinquent: juvenile delinquents

offender: a first-time offender

skelm South African: a skelm from the city

villain: He tackled an armed villain single-handed

▷ adjective 2 involving crime: criminal activities

corrupt: corrupt practices

crooked: crooked business deals

illegal: an illegal action

illicit: illicit dealings

unlawful: unlawful entry

see also **crooked, guilty, illegal**

crimson see **blush**

cringe see **cower, flinch**

cripple verb 1 to injure severely: crippled in a car accident

disable: disabled by polio

lame: He was lamed for life

maim: mines maiming and killing civilians

paralyse: paralysed in a riding accident

2 to prevent from working: The crisis may cripple the Irish economy

bring to a standstill: The strike brought France to a standstill

impair: Their actions will impair France's national interests

put out of action: The port has been put out of action

see also **paralyse**

crippled see **lame**

crisis see **emergency**

crisscross see **cross**

criterion see **standard**

critical adjective 1 very important: a critical point in history

crucial: a crucial election campaign

deciding: Price was a deciding factor

decisive: a decisive moment in my life

momentous: a momentous decision

pivotal: He played a pivotal role in the match

vital: vital information

2 very serious: a critical illness

grave: grave danger

precarious: a precarious financial situation

serious: His condition is said to be serious

3 finding fault with something or someone: critical remarks

carping: carping comments

derogatory: derogatory references to women

disapproving: a disapproving look

disparaging: He spoke in disparaging tones

scathing: a scathing attack

see also **acute, crucial, grave,**

major, serious, severe, vital

criticism noun expression of disapproval: *public criticism of his actions*

censure: *They deserve praise rather than censure*

disapproval: *a chorus of disapproval*

disparagement: *their disparagement of this book*

fault-finding: *her husband's constant fault-finding*

flak informal: *I got a lot of flak for that idea*

panning informal: *a panning from the critics*

see also **censure**, **complaint**, **disapproval**, **review**

criticize verb to find fault: *The regime has been harshly criticized*

censure: *a decision for which she was censured*

condemn: *He refused to condemn their behaviour*

find fault with: *She keeps finding fault with my work*

knock informal: *Don't knock it till you've tried it*

pan informal: *Critics panned the show*

put down: *She's always putting him down in front of the kids*

see also **attack**, **censure**, **condemn**, **fault**, **put down**

croaky see **hoarse**

crofter see **cocky**

crony see **china, companion, friend**

crook noun 1 informal a criminal: *The man is a crook and a liar*

cheat: *a rotten cheat*

rogue: *Mr Scott wasn't a rogue at all*

scoundrel old-fashioned: *He is a lying scoundrel*

shark: *Beware the sharks when you are deciding how to invest*

swindler: *Swindlers have cheated investors out of £12 million*

thief: *The thieves snatched the camera*

villain: *As a copper, I've spent my life putting villains behind bars*

▷ adjective 2 Australian, New Zealand informal ill: *He admitted to feeling a bit crook*

ill: *I was feeling ill*

nauseous: *The drugs may make the patient feel nauseous*

poorly: *Julie's still poorly*

queasy: *He was very prone to seasickness and already felt queasy*

sick: *The very thought of food made him feel sick*

under the weather: *I was still feeling a bit under the weather*

unwell: *He felt unwell as he was travelling home this afternoon*

see also **criminal**, **thief**, **unhealthy**, **unwell**

crooked adjective 1 bent or twisted: *a crooked tree*

bent: *a bent back*

deformed: *born with a deformed right leg*

distorted: *a distorted image*

irregular: *irregular and discoloured teeth*

out of shape: *The wires were bent out of shape*

twisted: *bits of twisted metal*

warped: *warped wooden shutters*

2 dishonest or illegal: *crooked business practices*

corrupt: *corrupt police officers*

criminal: *criminal activities*

dishonest: *dishonest salespeople*

fraudulent: *a fraudulent claim*

illegal: *illegal trading*

shady: *shady deals*

see also **corrupt**, **criminal**, **dirty**, **dishonest**, **dubious**, **wrong**

crop up see **appear**

cross verb 1 to go across: *the bridge which crosses the river*

ford: *trying to find a safe place to ford the stream*

go across: going across the road

span: the iron bridge spanning the railway

traverse: a valley traversed by streams

2 to meet and go across: the intersection where the roads cross

crisscross: Phone wires criss-cross the street

intersect: The circles intersect in two places

▷ noun **3** a mixture of two things: a cross between a collie and a retriever

blend: a blend of the old and the new

combination: a combination of fear and anger

mixture: a mixture of two factors

▷ adjective **4** rather angry: I'm very cross with him

angry: Are you angry with me?

annoyed: I'm annoyed with myself for being so stupid

fractious: The children were getting fractious

fretful: the fretful expression on her face

grumpy: a grumpy old man

in a bad mood: He's in a bad mood about something

irritable: She had been restless and irritable all day

see also **angry**

cross out see **delete**

crouch verb to squat down: A man was crouching behind the car

bend down: I bent down and touched the grass

squat: He squatted on his heels to talk to the children

see also **bend**

crow see **boast, brag**

crowd noun **1** a large group of people: A huge crowd gathered in the square

horde: hordes of tourists

host: a host of fans

mass: a heaving mass of people

mob: a mob of demonstrators

multitude: surrounded by a noisy multitude

swarm: swarms of visitors

throng: An official pushed through the throng

▷ verb **2** to gather close together: Hundreds of fans crowded into the hall

congregate: A large crowd congregated outside the stadium

gather: Dozens of people gathered to watch

swarm: Police swarmed into the area

throng: The crowds thronged into the mall

see also **band, bunch, company, group, jam, lot, mass, number**

crowded adjective full of people: a crowded room

congested: congested cities

full: The train was full

overflowing: buildings overflowing with students

packed: By 10.30 the shop was packed

crowing see **boastful**

crown see **top**

crucial adjective very important: a crucial moment in his career

central: central to the whole process

critical: a critical point in the campaign

decisive: ready to strike at the decisive moment

momentous: a momentous event

pivotal: He played a pivotal role in the match

vital: vital information

see also **critical, essential, major, serious, vital**

crude adjective **1** rough and simple: a crude weapon

primitive: They managed to make a primitive harness

rough: a rough sketch

rudimentary: some form of rudimentary heating

simple: *a simple stringed instrument*
2 rude and offensive: *a crude sense of humour*
coarse: *coarse speech*
dirty: *a dirty joke*
indecent: *indecent lyrics*
obscene: *obscene language*
tasteless: *a tasteless remark*
vulgar: *a vulgar phrase*
see also **indecent, primitive, vulgar**

cruel adjective deliberately causing hurt: *I hate people who are cruel to animals*
barbarous: *a barbarous attack*
brutal: *a brutal murder*
callous: *callous treatment*
cold-blooded: *a cold-blooded killer*
heartless: *It was a heartless thing to do*
inhumane: *He was kept under inhumane conditions*
sadistic: *mistreated by sadistic guards*
vicious: *a vicious blow*
see also **harsh, malicious, merciless, savage, spiteful, unkind, violent**

cruelty noun cruel behaviour: *an act of unbelievable cruelty*
barbarity: *the barbarity of war*
brutality: *police brutality*
callousness: *the callousness of his murder*
inhumanity: *man's inhumanity to man*
savagery: *scenes of unimaginable savagery*
viciousness: *the viciousness of the attacks*
see also **violence**

cruise see **wander**
crumb see **bit**
crumble see **crush, disintegrate**
crumple verb to squash and wrinkle: *She crumpled the paper in her hand*
crease: *Don't crease the material*
crush: *Andrew crushed his empty can*

screw up: *He screwed the letter up in anger*
wrinkle: *trying not to wrinkle her silk skirt*
see also **crush, fold**

crunch see **chew**
crusade see **campaign**
crush verb **1** to destroy the shape of by squeezing: *Their car was crushed by an army tank*
crumble: *Crumble the stock cubes into a jar*
crumple: *She crumpled the note up and threw it away*
mash: *Mash the bananas with a fork*
squash: *She squashed the wasp under her heel*
2 to defeat completely: *his bid to crush the uprising*
overcome: *working to overcome the enemy forces*
put down: *Soldiers moved in to put down the rebellion*
quell: *Troops eventually quelled the unrest*
stamp out: *steps to stamp out bullying in schools*
vanquish: *his vanquished foe*
see also **crumple, dash, defeat, jam, press, subdue, suppress, vanquish**

cry verb **1** to have tears coming from your eyes: *Stop crying and tell me what's wrong*
see **word studies cry**
2 to call out loudly: *"See you soon!" they cried*
call: *She called to me across the square*
exclaim: *'You must be mad!' she exclaimed*
shout: *"Over here!" they shouted*
yell: *He yelled out of the window*
▷ noun **3** a loud or high shout: *a cry of pain*
call: *the call of a seagull*
exclamation: *an exclamation of surprise*

shout: I heard a distant shout
yell: Bob let out a yell
see also **bay, call, scream, shout**
cryptic see **mysterious, obscure**
crystalline see **clear, transparent**
cuddle see **hug**
cue see **signal**
culminate see **peak**
culmination see **peak, top**
culprit see **criminal**
cultivate see **breed**
cultivated see **educated,
sophisticated**
culture see **background, society**
cultured see **civilized, educated,
polite, sophisticated**
cunning adjective **1** clever and
deceitful: a cunning and ruthless
businessman
artful: an artful old woman
crafty: a crafty plan
devious: a devious mind
sly: a sly trick
wily: a wily politician
▷ noun **2** cleverness and deceit: the
cunning of today's criminals
deviousness: the deviousness of drug
traffickers
guile: She was without guile or
pretence
see also **crafty, sly**
curb verb **1** to keep something within
limits: He must learn to curb that
temper of his
check: an attempt to check the spread
of the disease
contain: A hundred firefighters are
still trying to contain the fire
control: the need to control
environmental pollution
limit: He limited payments on the
country's foreign debt
restrain: efforts to restrain corruption
suppress: The Government is
suppressing inflation by devastating
the economy

▷ noun **2** an attempt to keep
something within limits: He called
for stricter curbs on immigration
brake: Illness had put a brake on his
progress
control: price controls
limit: limits on government spending
limitation: We need a limitation on
the powers of the government
restraint: new restraints on trade
unions
see also **check, contain, halt, limit,
moderate, restrain, restriction,
suppress**
curdled see **sour**
cure verb **1** to make well: a treatment
which cures eczema
heal: plants used to heal wounds
remedy: an operation to remedy a
blood clot on his brain
▷ noun **2** something that makes an
illness better: a cure for cancer
medicine: herbal medicines
remedy: a remedy for colds and flu
treatment: the most effective
treatment for malaria
see also **correct**
curiosity noun **1** the desire to know:
a curiosity about the past
inquisitiveness: the inquisitiveness
of children
interest: a lively interest in current
affairs
2 something unusual: a museum
displaying relics and curiosities
freak: a freak of nature
marvel: a marvel of science
novelty: in the days when a motor car
was a novelty
oddity: Tourists are still something of
an oddity here
rarity: Mexican restaurants are a
rarity here
see also **interest**
curious adjective **1** wanting to know:
He was curious about my family

inquiring: *He gave me an inquiring look*

inquisitive: *Cats are very inquisitive*

interested: *A crowd of interested villagers gathered*

nosy *informal*: *nosy neighbours*

2 strange and unusual: *a curious mixture of the old and the new*

bizarre: *his bizarre behaviour*

extraordinary: *an extraordinary story*

odd: *an odd coincidence*

peculiar: *a peculiar smell*

singular: *singular talent*

strange: *a strange taste*

unusual: *an unusual name*

see also **bizarre, nosy, odd, peculiar, strange, unusual, weird**

curl *see* **coil, twist**

current noun **1** a strong continuous movement of water: *swept away by the strong current*

flow: *the quiet flow of the olive-green water*

tide: *We will sail with the tide*

undertow: *Dangerous undertows make swimming unsafe along the coastline*

▷ *adjective* **2** happening, being done, or being used now: *current trends*

contemporary: *He has adopted a more contemporary style*

fashionable: *the fashionable theory about this issue*

ongoing: *an ongoing debate on inner city problems*

present: *skilfully renovated by the present owners*

present-day: *Even by present-day standards these are large aircraft*

today's: *In today's America, health care is big business*

up-to-the-minute: *up-to-the-minute information on sales and stocks*

see also **fashionable, flow, modern, recent**

currently *see* **now**

curriculum *see* **course**

curriculum vitae *see* **record**

curse *see* **abuse**

cursed *see* **unlucky**

cursory *see* **casual, quick**

curt *see* **abrupt, impatient**

curtail *see* **reduce**

curve noun **1** a bending line: *a curve in the road*

arc: *The ball rose in an arc*

bend: *a bend in the river*

trajectory: *the trajectory of an artillery shell*

turn: *every turn in the road*

▷ *verb* **2** to move in a curve: *The road curved sharply to the left*

arc: *A rainbow arced over the town*

arch: *a domed ceiling arching overhead*

bend: *The path bent to the right*

swerve: *His car swerved off the road*

see also **bend**

custody *see* **possession**

custom noun **1** a traditional activity: *an ancient Chinese custom*

convention: *the conventions of Western art*

practice: *an old Jewish practice*

ritual: *an ancient Shintoist ritual*

tradition: *different cultural traditions*

2 something a person always does: *It was his custom to start work at 8.30*

habit: *his habit of making tactless remarks*

practice: *her usual practice of attending church*

routine: *his daily routine*

wont: *Paul woke early, as was his wont*

see also **convention, habit, practice, tradition, way**

customary *see* **conventional, regular, standard, usual**

customer noun someone who buys something: *The shop was filled with* customers

buyer: *show homes to tempt potential buyers*

client: *a solicitor and his client*

consumer: *the increasing demands of consumers*

patron: *the restaurant's patrons*

purchaser: *a prospective purchaser*

shopper: *late-night shoppers on their way home*

cut *verb* **1** to mark or injure with something sharp: *The thieves cut a hole in the fence*

see **word studies cut**

2 to reduce something: *The department's first priority is to cut costs*

cut back: *The Government has decided to cut back on defence spending*

decrease: *calls to decrease income tax*

lower: *The Central Bank has lowered interest rates*

reduce: *Gradually reduce the dosage*

slash: *Holiday prices have been slashed*

▷ *noun* **3** a mark or injury made by cutting: *a cut on his left eyebrow*

gash: *There was a deep gash across his forehead*

incision: *a tiny incision in the skin*

slash: *jeans with slashes in the knees*

slit: *Make a slit along the stem*

4 a reduction in something: *another cut in interest rates*

cutback: *cutbacks in funding*

decrease: *a decrease in foreign investment*

lowering: *the lowering of taxes*

reduction: *reductions in staff*

saving: *household savings on energy use*

see also **carve, chop, lower, reduce, shorten**

cut back *see* **cut**

cut down *see* **decrease, reduce**

cut out *see* **eliminate, stop**

cut short *see* **halt**

cut up *see* **divide**

cutback *see* **cut, decrease**

cute *adjective* pretty or attractive: *You were such a cute baby!*

appealing: *an appealing kitten*

attractive: *I thought he was very attractive*

charming: *a charming little cottage*

dear: *Look at their dear little faces!*

good-looking: *Cassandra noticed him because he was so good-looking*

gorgeous: *All the girls think Ryan's gorgeous*

pretty: *She's a very pretty girl*

see also **pretty**

cycle *see* **sequence**

cylindrical *see* **round**

cynical *adjective* **1** always thinking the worst of people: *a cynical attitude*

distrustful: *distrustful of all politicians*

sceptical: *a sceptical response*

d

dab see **blob**

daft adjective **2** extremely silly: *Now there's a daft suggestion!*
 crazy: *He has this crazy idea about his neighbours*
 foolish: *It would be foolish to raise his hopes unnecessarily*
 ludicrous: *It was ludicrous to suggest that the visit could be kept a secret*
 preposterous: *their preposterous claim that they had discovered a plot*
 ridiculous: *It was an absolutely ridiculous decision*
 silly: *That's a silly question*
 stupid: *I made a stupid mistake*
 see also **idiotic, mad, silly, stupid, unwise**

daily see **everyday**

dainty see **fragile**

damage verb **1** to cause harm to something: *A fire had severely damaged the school*
 harm: *a warning that the product may harm the environment*
 hurt: *He had hurt his back in an accident*
 injure: *Several policemen were injured in the clashes*
 ▷ noun **2** harm that is done to something: *The bomb caused extensive damage to the restaurant*
 harm: *All dogs are capable of doing harm to human beings*
 injury: *He escaped without injury*
 see also **harm, injury, ruin, spoil**

damaged see **imperfect**

damages see **compensation**

damaging see **harmful**

dame see **woman**

damn see **condemn**

damp adjective **1** slightly wet: *a damp towel*
 clammy: *clammy hands*
 dank: *The kitchen was dank and cheerless*
 humid: *Visitors can expect hot and humid conditions*
 moist: *The soil is reasonably moist after the September rain*
 sodden: *We stripped off our sodden clothes*
 soggy: *soggy cheese sandwiches*
 wet: *My hair was still wet*
 ▷ noun **2** slight wetness: *There was damp all over the walls*
 dampness: *I could see big circles of dampness under each arm*
 humidity: *The heat and humidity were intolerable*
 moisture: *Compost helps the soil retain moisture*
 see also **wet**

dampen see **wet**

dampness see **damp**

danger noun the possibility of harm: *Your life is in danger*
 hazard: *a health hazard*
 jeopardy: *A series of setbacks have put the whole project in jeopardy*
 menace: *In my view you are a menace to the public*
 peril: *the perils of the sea*
 risk: *There is a small risk of brain damage*
 threat: *Some couples see single women as a threat to their relationship*

see also **risk**

dangerous *adjective* likely to cause harm: *It's dangerous to drive when you're tired*

hazardous: *They have no way to dispose of the hazardous waste they produce*

perilous: *a perilous journey across the war-zone*

risky: *Investing is risky*

treacherous: *Blizzards had made the roads treacherous*

see also **fierce, serious, treacherous**

dangle *see* **hang**

dank *see* **damp**

dare *verb* **1** to challenge someone to do something: *I dare you to ask him his name*

challenge: *He left a note at the scene of the crime, challenging detectives to catch him*

defy: *I defy you to watch it on your own*

throw down the gauntlet: *Jaguar has thrown down the gauntlet to competitors by giving the best guarantee on the market*

2 to have the courage to do something: *Nobody dared to complain*

risk: *The skipper was not willing to risk taking his ship through the straits*

venture: *the few Europeans who had ventured beyond the Himalayas*

see also **challenge, risk**

daring *adjective* **1** willing to take risks: *a daring escape by helicopter*

adventurous: *an adventurous skier*

audacious: *an audacious plan to win the presidency*

bold: *bold economic reforms*

brave: *He was not brave enough to report the loss of the documents*

fearless: *They were young and strong and fearless*

▷ *noun* **2** the courage to take risks: *His daring may have cost him his life*

audacity: *He had the audacity to make a 200-1 bet on himself to win*

boldness: *the boldness of his economic programme*

bravery: *He deserves the highest praise for his bravery*

courage: *He impressed everyone with his personal courage*

guts *informal*: *I haven't got the guts to tell him*

nerve *informal*: *He didn't have the nerve to meet me*

see also **bold, courage**

dark *adjective* **1** lacking light: *It was too dark to see what was happening*

cloudy: *a cloudy sky*

dim: *the dim outline of a small boat*

dingy: *a dingy bedsit*

murky: *the murky waters of the loch*

overcast: *a cold, windy, overcast afternoon*

shadowy: *a shadowy corner*

2 dull in colour: *a dark suit*

black: *a black leather coat*

swarthy: *a broad swarthy face*

▷ *noun* **3** lack of light: *I've always been afraid of the dark*

darkness: *The room was plunged into darkness*

dimness: *I squinted to adjust my eyes to the dimness*

dusk: *She disappeared into the dusk*

gloom: *the gloom of a foggy November morning*

see also **dim, gloomy**

darkness *see* **dark**

darling *see* **beloved, dear, favourite**

darn *see* **mend, repair**

dart *see* **fly, tear**

dash *verb* **1** to rush somewhere: *Suddenly she dashed out into the garden*

bolt: *I bolted for the exit*

fly: *She flew downstairs*

race: *The hares raced away out of sight*

run: The gunmen ran off into the woods

rush: Someone rushed out of the building

sprint: Sergeant Greene sprinted to the car

tear: He tore off down the road

2 to throw or be thrown violently against something: The waves dashed against the rocks

break: Danny listened to the waves breaking against the shore

crash: The door swung inwards and crashed against a cupboard behind it

hurl: He hurled the vase to the ground in rage

slam: They slammed me on to the ground

smash: smashing the bottle against a wall

3 to ruin or frustrate someone's hopes or ambitions: They had their hopes raised and then dashed

crush: My dreams of becoming an actor have been crushed

destroy: Even the most gifted can have their confidence destroyed by the wrong teacher

disappoint: His hopes have been disappointed many times before

foil: Our idea of building a water garden was foiled by the planning authorities

frustrate: The government has deliberately frustrated his efforts

shatter: A failure would shatter all our hopes

thwart: Her ambition to be an artist was thwarted by failing eyesight

▷ noun **4** a sudden movement or rush: a 160-mile dash to the hospital

bolt: He made a bolt for the door

race: a race for the finishing line

run: One of the gang made a run for it

rush: the mad rush not to be late for school

sprint: a last-minute sprint to catch the bus

stampede: There was a stampede for the exit

5 a small quantity of something: a dash of wine vinegar

drop: I'll have a drop of that milk in my tea

pinch: a pinch of salt

splash: add a splash of lemon juice

sprinkling: a light sprinkling of sugar

see also **bolt, bustle, charge, fly, hurry, race, rush, tear, trace**

data see **information**

date see **appointment**

dated see **old-fashioned**

daunt see **discourage**

daunting see **formidable**

dawn see **start**

dawn on see **occur**

daydream noun **1** a series of pleasant thoughts: He learnt to escape into daydreams

dream: My dream is to have a house in the country

fantasy: fantasies of romance and true love

▷ verb **2** to think about pleasant things: He daydreams of being a famous journalist

dream: She used to dream of becoming an actress

fantasize: I fantasized about writing music

see also **dream, vision**

days gone by see **the past**

day-to-day see **everyday**

dazed adjective unable to think clearly: At the end of the interview I was dazed and exhausted

bewildered: Some shoppers looked bewildered by the sheer variety

confused: Things were happening too quickly and Brian was confused

dizzy: Her head hurt and she felt dizzy

light-headed: If you miss breakfast,

you may feel light-headed

numbed: I'm so numbed with shock that I can hardly think

stunned: a stunned silence

dazzling see **bright, brilliant**

de luxe see **luxurious, superior**

dead adjective **1** no longer alive: My husband's been dead a year now

deceased: his recently deceased mother

departed: my dear departed father

extinct: the bones of extinct animals

late: my late husband

2 no longer functioning: a dead language

defunct: the now defunct Social Democratic Party

not working: The radio is not working

see also **late, numb**

dead body see **body**

dead ringer see **lookalike**

deaden see **silence**

deadline see **limit**

deadly adjective causing death: a deadly disease

destructive: the destructive power of nuclear weapons

fatal: a fatal heart attack

lethal: a lethal dose of sleeping pills

mortal: Our lives were in mortal danger

see also **fatal**

deadpan see **blank**

deafening see **loud, noisy**

deal verb to cope successfully with something: He must learn to deal with stress

attend to: You have business to attend to first

cope with: She has had to cope with losing all her money

handle: I have learned how to handle pressure

manage: As time passed I learned to manage my grief

see to: Sarah saw to the packing while Jim fetched the car

take care of: Malcolm took care of all the arrangements

see also **administer, agreement, trade**

deal in see **sell, stock**

deal with see **handle, process, take care of, treat**

dealer see **trader**

dealings see **business**

dear noun **1** a person for whom you have affection: What's the matter, dear?

angel: Be an angel and fetch my bag

beloved old-fashioned: He took his beloved into his arms

darling: Thank you, darling

treasure informal: Charlie? Oh, she's a treasure

▷ adjective **2** much loved: a dear friend of mine

beloved: He lost his beloved wife last year

cherished: his most cherished possession

darling: his darling daughter

esteemed: my esteemed colleagues

precious: Her family's support is very precious to her

prized: one of the gallery's most prized possessions

treasured: one of my most treasured memories

3 costing a lot: They're too dear

costly: Having curtains professionally made can be costly

expensive: Wine's so expensive in this country

pricey informal: Medical insurance is very pricey

see also **cute, expensive**

dearest see **beloved, favourite**

dearth see **shortage**

debacle see **defeat**

debatable see **doubtful**

debate see argue, deliberate, discuss, discussion

debris see garbage, remains

debut see appearance

decay see rot, ruin

decayed see rotten

deceased see dead, late

deceit see dishonesty, fraud, lie, lying

deceitful see dishonest, false, insincere, lying, sneaky, two-faced

deceive verb to make someone believe something untrue: I was really hurt that he had deceived me
con informal: The British motorist has been conned by the government
double-cross: They were frightened of being double-crossed
dupe: a plot to dupe stamp collectors into buying fake rarities
fool: They tried to fool you into coming after us
mislead: He was furious with his doctors for having misled him
take in: I wasn't taken in for one moment
trick: His family tricked him into going to Pakistan
see also cheat, con, dupe, fool, take in, trick

decelerate see slow (down)

decency see honour, politeness

decent adjective **1** of an acceptable standard: He gets a decent pension
adequate: an adequate diet
passable: She speaks passable French
reasonable: He couldn't make a reasonable living from his writing
respectable: investments that offer respectable rates of return
satisfactory: I never got a satisfactory answer
tolerable: to make life more tolerable
2 correct and respectable: the decent thing to do

proper: It is right and proper to do this
respectable: He came from a perfectly respectable middle-class family
see also respectable

deception see con, fraud, trick

deceptive adjective likely to make people believe something untrue: First impressions can be deceptive
false: 'Thank you,' she said with false enthusiasm
fraudulent: fraudulent claims about being a nurse
illusory: They argue that freedom is illusory
misleading: It would be misleading to say that we were friends
unreliable: His account is quite unreliable

decide verb to choose to do something: She decided to do a secretarial course
choose: The council chose to inform the public about the risks
come to a decision: Have you come to a decision about where you're going tonight?
determine formal: He determined to rescue his two countrymen
elect formal: I have elected to stay
make up your mind: He simply can't make his mind up whether he should stay
reach a decision: He demanded to know all the facts before reaching any decision
resolve formal: She resolved to report the matter to the authorities
see also conclude, determine, resolve, settle

decide on see select, settle

decide upon see pick

decided see definite

deciding see critical

decipher see crack, read, solve

decision noun a judgment about something: *The editor's decision is final*
  conclusion: *I've come to the conclusion that she's a great musician*
  finding: *It is the finding of this court that you are guilty*
  judgment: *a landmark judgment by the Court of Appeal*
  resolution: *a resolution condemning violence*
  ruling: *He tried to have the court ruling overturned*
  verdict: *The judges will deliver their verdict in October*
  see also **verdict**

decisive see **critical, crucial**

deck see **decorate**

declaration noun a forceful or official announcement: *a declaration of war*
  affirmation: *her first public affirmation of her decision*
  protestation: formal: *his protestations of innocence*
  statement: *He made a formal statement to the police*
  testimony: *His testimony was an important element in the case*
  see also **announcement, statement**

declare verb to state something forcefully or officially: *He declared that he was going to be famous*
  affirm: *a speech in which he affirmed a commitment to lower taxes*
  announce: *She was planning to announce her engagement*
  assert: *He asserted his innocence*
  certify: *The president certified that the project would receive $650m*
  proclaim: *He still proclaims himself a believer in the Revolution*
  profess: formal: *Why do organizations profess that they care?*
  pronounce: *The authorities took time to pronounce their verdict*
  state: *Please state your name*
  see also **state**

decline verb 1 to become smaller or weaker: *a declining birth rate*
  decrease: *The number of independent firms decreased from 198 to 96*
  diminish: *The threat of nuclear war has diminished*
  drop: *His blood pressure had dropped*
  fall: *Output will fall by six per cent*
  go down: *Crime has gone down 70 per cent*
  plummet: *The Prime Minister's popularity has plummeted to an all-time low*
  reduce: *The number of students fluent in Latin has been steadily reducing*
  2 to refuse politely to accept or do something: *He declined their invitation*
  abstain: *I will abstain from voting in the ballot*
  excuse yourself: *I was invited, but I excused myself*
  refuse: *He refused to comment after the trial*
  turn down: *I thanked him for the offer but turned it down*
  ▷ noun 3 a gradual weakening or decrease: *economic decline*
  decrease: *a decrease in the number of young people out of work*
  downturn: *a sharp downturn in the industry*
  drop: *a drop in support for the Conservatives*
  fall: *a sharp fall in the value of the pound*
  recession: *pull the economy out of recession*
  shrinkage: *a shrinkage in industrial output*
  slump: *a slump in property prices*
  see also **decrease, drop, fail, fall, recession, refuse, reject, wither, worsen**

decompose see rot

decomposed see rotten

decorate verb 1 to make more attractive: *He decorated his room with pictures*

adorn: *Several oil paintings adorn the walls*

deck: *The house was decked with flowers*

ornament: *a high ceiling, ornamented with plaster fruits and flowers*

2 to put paint or wallpaper on: *when they came to decorate the bedroom*

do up *informal*: *He spent the summer doing up the barn*

renovate: *The couple spent thousands renovating the house*
see also honour

decorated see fancy

decoration see ornament

decorum see ceremony

decoy see bait

decrease verb 1 to become or make less: *Population growth is decreasing by 1.4% each year*

cut down: *He cut down his coffee intake*

decline: *The number of staff has declined*

diminish: *The threat of nuclear war has diminished*

drop: *Temperatures can drop to freezing at night*

dwindle: *his dwindling authority*

lessen: *changes to their diet that would lessen the risk of disease*

lower: *The Central Bank has lowered interest rates*

reduce: *It reduces the risk of heart disease*

shrink: *The forests have shrunk to half their size*

▷ noun 2 a lessening in the amount of something: *a decrease in the number of unemployed*

cutback: *cutbacks in defence spending*

decline: *the rate of decline in tobacco consumption*

drop: *a drop in temperature*

lessening: *a lessening of tension*

reduction: *dramatic reductions in staff*
see also abate, cut, decline, diminish, drop, fall, lessen, lower, reduce

decree see command, law, order, rule

dedicate see bless

dedicated see devoted

deduce see conclude, reconstruct

deduct see subtract

deduction see conclusion

deed see achievement, act, action

deem see feel, think, view

deep adjective 1 having a long way to the bottom: *a deep hole*

bottomless: *a bottomless pit*

yawning: *a yawning chasm*

2 great or intense: *his deep love of Israel*

extreme: *extreme poverty*

grave: *a grave crisis*

great: *the great gulf between the two teams*

intense: *The pain was intense*

profound: *discoveries which had a profound effect on medicine*

serious: *a serious problem*

3 low in sound: *a deep voice*

bass: *a beautiful bass voice*

low: *Her voice was so low she was sometimes mistaken for a man*
see also extreme, far, heavy, intense, serious, severe

deeply see very

defeat verb 1 to win a victory over someone: *His guerrillas defeated the colonial army in 1954*

beat: *the team that beat us in the final*

conquer: During 1936, Mussolini conquered Abyssinia

crush: in his bid to crush the rebels

rout: the battle at which the Norman army routed the English

trounce: Australia trounced France by 60 points to 4

vanquish formal: after the hero had vanquished the dragon

▷ noun **2** a failure to win: a 2-1 defeat by Sweden

conquest: He had led the conquest of southern Poland

debacle formal: It will be hard for them to recover from this debacle

rout: The retreat turned into a rout

trouncing: after a 6-2 trouncing on Sunday

see also **beat, failure, foil, subdue, vanquish**

defect noun a fault or flaw: A defect in the aircraft caused the crash

deficiency: the most serious deficiency in NATO's air defence

failing: She blamed the country's failings on its culture of greed

fault: a minor technical fault

flaw: The only flaw in his character is a short temper

imperfection: my physical imperfections

shortcoming: The book has its shortcomings

weakness: His only weakness is his laziness

see also **fault, flaw, handicap, hole, weakness**

defective see **faulty, imperfect**

defence noun **1** action to protect something: The flat alone offered no scope for defence

cover: They could not provide adequate air cover for ground operations

protection: Such a diet is believed to offer protection against cancer

resistance: Most people have a natural resistance to the disease

safeguard: legislation that offers safeguards against discrimination

security: Airport security was tightened

2 an argument in support of something: Chomsky's defence of his approach

argument: There's a strong argument for lowering the price

excuse: There's no excuse for behaviour like that

explanation: The authorities have given no explanation for his arrest

justification: The only justification for a zoo is educational

plea: a plea of insanity

see also **safeguard**

defenceless see **helpless**

defend verb **1** to protect from harm: They would have killed him if he hadn't defended himself

cover: travel insurance covering you against theft

guard: A few men were left outside to guard her

protect: What can women do to protect themselves from heart disease?

safeguard: action to safeguard the ozone layer

shelter: a wooden house, sheltered by a low roof

shield: He shielded his head from the sun with an old sack

2 to argue in support of: I can't defend what he did

endorse: I can endorse their opinion wholeheartedly

justify: No argument can justify a war

stick up for informal: Why do you always stick up for her?

support: Would you support such a move?

uphold: upholding the artist's right to creative freedom *see also* **champion, guard, justify, protect, safeguard, support**

defender noun a person who argues in support of something: *a committed defender of human rights*

advocate: *a strong advocate of free market policies*

champion: *a champion of women's causes*

supporter: *a major supporter of the tax reform*

see also **champion**

defer *see* **delay, postpone, put off**

deferential *see* **meek**

deficiency noun a lack of something: *signs of vitamin deficiency*

deficit: *a staffing deficit*

deprivation: *sleep deprivation*

inadequacy: *the inadequacies of the current system*

lack: *a lack of people wanting to start new businesses*

want formal: *a want of manners and charm*

see also **defect, failure, fault, lack, shortage, want**

deficient adjective lacking in something: *a diet deficient in vitamins*

inadequate: *inadequate staffing*

lacking: *Why was military intelligence so lacking?*

poor: *soil that is poor in zinc*

short: *The proposals were short on detail*

wanting: *He analysed his game and found it wanting*

see also **inadequate, incomplete, insufficient, weak**

deficit *see* **deficiency**

define *see* **describe, explain**

definite adjective **1** unlikely to be changed: *It's too soon to give a definite answer*

assured: *Victory was still not assured*

certain: *Very little in life is certain*

decided: *Is anything decided yet?*

fixed: *a world without fixed laws*

guaranteed: *Success is not guaranteed*

settled: *Nothing is settled yet*

2 certainly true: *They had nothing definite against her*

clear: *It was a clear case of homicide*

positive: *We have positive proof that he was a blackmailer*

see also **certain, clear, final, sure**

definitely *see* **certainly**

definitely not *see* **no**

definition *see* **explanation**

definitive *see* **final**

deformed adjective abnormally shaped: *a deformed right leg*

disfigured: *the scarred, disfigured face*

distorted: *the distorted image caused by the projector*

see also **crooked**

defraud *see* **cheat, rob**

defunct *see* **dead**

defy *see* **challenge, dare, disobey, rebel, resist**

degenerate *see* **worsen**

degrade verb to humiliate someone: *the notion that pornography degrades women*

demean: *I wasn't going to demean myself by acting like a suspicious wife*

humiliate: *He enjoyed humiliating me*

see also **reduce**

degree *see* **extent, measure**

dehydrate *see* **dry**

dejected *see* **disappointed, down, gloomy, miserable, sad**

dejection *see* **despair, disappointment, sadness**

delay verb **1** to put something off until later: *the decision to delay the launch until tomorrow*

defer: *Customers often defer payment for as long as possible*

postpone: The visit has been postponed indefinitely

put off: women who put off having a baby

shelve: The project has now been shelved

suspend: Relief convoys will be suspended until the fighting stops
2 to slow or hinder something: Various setbacks delayed production

check: a policy to check fast population growth

hinder: Further investigation was hindered by the loss of all documentation

impede: Fallen rocks are impeding the progress of rescue workers

obstruct: The authorities are obstructing a UN investigation

set back: public protests that could set back reforms
▷ noun **3** a time when something is delayed: a 7-hour stoppage that caused delays on most flights

interruption: interruptions in the supply of food

obstruction: Obstruction of justice is a criminal offence

setback: a setback for the peace process
see also **hinder, impede, pause, postpone, put off, wait**

delayed see **late**

delectable see **delicious, lekker**

delegate see **representative**

delete verb to remove something written: The word 'exploded' had been deleted

cross out: He crossed out the first sentence and wrote it again

erase: It was unfortunate that she had erased the message

rub out: She rubbed out the marks in the margin
see also **remove**

deliberate adjective **1** done on

purpose: a deliberate act of sabotage

calculated: a calculated attempt to cover up her crime

conscious: a conscious decision not to hide

intentional: The kick was intentional

premeditated: a premeditated attack

studied: 'It's an interesting match,' he said with studied understatement
2 careful and not hurried: His movements were gentle and deliberate

careful: The trip needs careful planning

cautious: a cautious approach

measured: walking at the same measured pace

methodical: Da Vinci was methodical in his research
▷ verb **3** to think carefully about something: The jury deliberated for five days before reaching a verdict

debate: He was debating whether or not he should tell her

meditate: She meditated on the uncertainties of his future

mull over: McLaren had been mulling over an idea to make a movie

ponder: He was pondering the problem when Phillipson drove up

reflect: I reflected on the child's future
see also **consider, think**

deliberately see **on purpose**

deliberation see **consideration, thought**

delicacy see **tact**

delicate see **fine, fragile, sheer, tricky, weak**

delicious adjective tasting very nice: a wide selection of delicious meals

appetizing: the appetizing smell of freshly baked bread

delectable: delectable wine

luscious: luscious fruit

tasty: The food was very tasty
see also **lekker, tasty**

delight noun 1 great pleasure or joy:
To my great delight, it worked
glee: His victory was greeted with glee
by his supporters
happiness: Our happiness at being
reunited knew no bounds
joy: the joys of being a parent
pleasure: the pleasure of seeing
her face
rapture: gasps of rapture
satisfaction: I felt a glow of
satisfaction at my achievement
▷ verb 2 to give someone great
pleasure: The report has delighted
environmentalists
amuse: a selection of toys to amuse
your baby
captivate: captivated the world with
her radiant looks
charm: He charmed his landlady,
chatting and flirting with her
enchant: Dena was enchanted by
the house
please: It pleased him to talk to her
thrill: The electric atmosphere
thrilled him
see also **charm, ecstasy, entertain,
entrance, happiness, joy, please,
pride, rejoice**
delight in see **enjoy**
delighted see **glad, joyful, pleased**
delightful see **agreeable, beautiful,
lovely, pleasant**
delinquent see **criminal, hooligan**
deliver see **give, issue, release, save**
delude see **dupe**
deluded see **fond**
deluge see **flood, rain**
delusion see **illusion**
demand verb to need or require
something: This situation demands
hard work
involve: Running a kitchen involves a
great deal of discipline
need: a problem that needs careful
handling

require: Then he'll know what's
required of him
take: Walking across the room took all
her strength
want: The windows wanted cleaning
see also **ask, command, expect,
insist, need, require, requirement,
take, want**
demanding see **difficult**
demean see **degrade**
demeanour see **manner**
demolish see **destroy**
demolished see **broken**
demolition see **destruction**
demonstrate see **agitate, prove,
show**
demote see **reduce**
denote see **indicate, mean**
denounce see **accuse, censure,
condemn, inform on**
dense see **slow, thick**
deny verb 1 to say that something is
untrue: She denied both accusations
contradict: Her version contradicted
the Government's claim
refute: He angrily refutes the charge
2 to refuse to believe something: He
denied the existence of God
reject: children who rejected their
parents' religious beliefs
renounce: after she renounced
terrorism
3 to refuse to give something: His
ex-partner denies him access to the
children
refuse: The council had refused
permission for the march
withhold: Financial aid for Russia
has been withheld
see also **dispute, reject**
deny oneself see **abstain**
depart see **leave**
departed see **dead, late**
department noun a section of
an organization: the marketing
department

division: *the bank's Latin American division*

office: *Contact your local tax office*

section: *a top-secret section of the Foreign Office*

unit: *the health services research unit*
see also **division, field**

departure see **retreat, variation**

depend verb 1 to rely on: *You can depend on me*

bank on: *The government is banking on the Olympics to save the city money*

count on: *I can always count on you to cheer me up*

rely on: *They can always be relied on to turn up*

trust: *I knew I could trust him to meet a tight deadline*

2 to be affected by: *Success depends on the quality of the workforce*

be determined by: *Social status is largely disapprove by occupation*

hinge on: *Victory or defeat hinged on her final putt*

depend on see **require, trust**

dependable see **loyal, reliable, responsible, sure, trusty**

dependence see **habit**

dependency see **colony**

depict see **describe, represent**

deplete see **exhaust**

deplorable see **sorry**

deplore see **disapprove**

deport see **banish**

depose see **overthrow**

deposit verb to put down or leave somewhere: *The barman deposited a bottle in front of him*

drop: *He dropped me outside the hotel*

lay: *The table was spread with a cloth, and the box was laid on top*

leave: *Leave your key with a neighbour*

place: *I placed the book on the counter*

put down: *Mishka put down her heavy shopping bag*

see also **dump, keep, payment, place, put, set**

depot see **store**

deprave see **corrupt**

depraved see **evil, perverted, wicked**

depressed see **down, miserable, sad, unhappy**

depressing see **sad**

depression see **crash, misery, recession, sadness**

deprivation see **deficiency**

depth see **extreme**

depths see **bottom**

deputy see **helper, representative, substitute**

deranged see **insane, mad**

derelict adjective abandoned and in poor condition: *a derelict warehouse*

abandoned: *a network of abandoned mines*

dilapidated: *a dilapidated castle*

neglected: *a neglected garden*

ruined: *a ruined church*

deride see **belittle, make fun of, mock**

derision see **abuse, contempt, mockery, scorn**

derivation see **origin, source**

derive see **base, result**

derogatory see **critical**

descend verb to move downwards: *as we descend to the cellar*

dip: *The sun dipped below the horizon*

dive: *The shark dived down and under the boat*

fall: *Bombs fell in the town*

go down: *after the sun has gone down*

plummet: *as the plane plummeted through the air*

sink: *A fresh egg will sink and an old egg will float*

see also **drop**

descendants see **family**

descent see **origin, stock**

describe verb to give an account of something: We asked her to describe what she did in her spare time

define Culture can be defined in many ways

depict a novel depicting a gloomy, futuristic America

portray a writer who accurately portrays provincial life
see also **explain, report, represent**

description see explanation, report

desert see abandon, barren, leave

deserted see empty, lonely

deserve verb to have a right to something: He deserves a rest

be entitled to She is entitled to feel proud

be worthy of The bank might think you're worthy of a loan

earn You've earned this holiday

justify The decision was fully justified by economic conditions

merit Such ideas merit careful consideration

warrant no evidence to warrant a murder investigation
see also **merit**

design verb 1 to make a plan of something: They wanted to design a machine that was both attractive and practical

draft The legislation was drafted by Democrats

draw up a working party to draw up a formal agreement

plan when we plan road construction
▷ noun 2 a plan or drawing: his design for a new office

model an architect's model of a wooden house

plan when you have drawn a plan of the garden

3 the shape or style of something: a new design of clock

form the form of the human body

pattern a pattern of coloured dots

shape a kidney shape

style Several styles of hat were available
see also **intend, layout, pattern, plan, structure**

designate see class

designation see name, term

designed see calculated

desirable see right

desire verb 1 to want something: We can stay longer if you desire

crave I crave her approval

fancy She fancied living in Canada

long for He longed for the winter to be over

want I want a drink

wish We wished to return

yearn He yearned to sleep
▷ noun 2 a feeling of wanting something: I had a strong desire to help people

appetite She had lost her appetite for air travel

craving a craving for sugar

hankering a hankering to be an actress

longing her longing to return home

wish Her wish is to be in films

yearning a yearning for a child of my own

yen informal: Mike had a yen to try cycling
see also **longing, passion, urge, want, wish**

desist see stop

desist from see cease

desolate see barren, lonely

despair noun 1 a loss of hope: feelings of despair

dejection There was an air of dejection about her

despondency There's a mood of despondency in the country

gloom the deepening gloom over the economy

hopelessness She had a feeling of

hopelessness about the future
▷ verb **2** to lose hope: *I despair at the attitude with which their work is received*
feel dejected: *Everyone has days when they feel dejected*
feel despondent: *John often felt despondent after visiting the job centre*
lose heart: *He appealed to his countrymen not to lose heart*
lose hope: *You mustn't lose hope*
see also **misery**
despatch see **message**
desperate see **terrible**
despicable see **hateful, low, shabby**
despise see **hate, scorn**
despite preposition in spite of: *He fell asleep despite all the coffee he'd drunk*
in spite of: *In spite of all the gossip, Virginia stayed behind*
notwithstanding formal: *Notwithstanding his age, Sikorski had an important job*
regardless of: *He led from the front, regardless of the danger*
see also **in spite of**
despondency see **despair, disappointment, sadness**
despondent see **disappointed, pessimistic, unhappy**
destiny see **fate, luck**
destitute see **poor**
destitution see **hardship, poverty**
destroy verb to ruin something completely: *The building was completely destroyed*
annihilate: *The lava annihilates everything in its path*
demolish: *A storm moved over the island, demolishing buildings*
devastate: *A fire had devastated large parts of Windsor castle*
obliterate: *Whole villages were obliterated by fire*
raze: *The town was razed to the ground during the occupation*

ruin: *My wife was ruining her health through worry*
wreck: *the injuries which nearly wrecked his career*
see also **bomb, dash, eat away, erode, kill, put down, ruin, spoil**
destruction noun the act of destroying something: *the destruction of the ozone layer*
annihilation: *Leaders fear the annihilation of their people*
demolition: *the demolition of an old bridge*
devastation: *A huge bomb blast brought chaos and devastation*
obliteration: *the obliteration of three rainforests*
see also **ruin**
destructive see **deadly, harmful**
detach see **remove, separate**
detached see **alone, distant, impersonal, remote, separate**
detail noun an individual feature of something: *We discussed every detail of the performance*
aspect: *Climate affects every aspect of our lives*
element: *one of the key elements of the peace plan*
particular: *You will find all the particulars in Chapter 9*
point: *Many of the points in the report are correct*
respect: *At least in this respect we are equals*
detailed see **elaborate, full**
detain see **imprison, jail**
detect see **discern, find, notice, spot**
deter see **discourage**
deteriorate see **erode, worsen**
deterioration see **rot, wear**
determination noun a firm decision to do something: *the government's determination to beat inflation*
perseverance: *Adam's perseverance*

proved worthwhile

persistence: *She was determined to be a doctor and her persistence paid off*

resolution: *She acted with resolution and courage*

resolve: *formal: the American public's resolve to go to war if necessary*

tenacity: *Hard work and sheer tenacity are crucial to career success*

see also **drive, resolve, will**

determine verb 1 to cause or control a situation or result: *The size of the chicken pieces will determine the cooking time*

control: *Scientists may soon be able to control the ageing process*

decide: *The results will decide if he will win a place on the course*

dictate: *A number of factors will dictate how long the tree will survive*

govern: *the rules governing eligibility for unemployment benefit*

shape: *the role of key leaders in shaping the future of Europe*

2 to decide or settle something firmly: *The final wording had not yet been determined*

arrange: *It was arranged that the party would gather in the Royal Garden Hotel*

choose: *Houston was chosen as the site for the convention*

decide: *Her age would be taken into account when deciding her sentence*

fix: *The date of the election was fixed*

resolve: *She resolved to report the matter to the authorities*

settle: *That's settled then. We'll do it tomorrow*

3 to find out the facts about something: *The investigation will determine what really happened*

ascertain: *formal: We need to ascertain the true facts*

confirm: *X-rays have confirmed that he has not broken any bones*

discover: *It was difficult for us to discover the reason for the decision*

establish: *an autopsy to establish the cause of death*

find out: *one family's campaign to find out the truth*

verify: *A clerk verifies that the payment and invoice amount match*

see also **calculate, decide, learn, resolve, see, settle**

determined adjective firmly decided: *She was determined not to repeat her error*

bent on: *They seem bent on destroying the city*

dogged: *dogged persistence*

intent on: *He is intent on repeating his victory*

persistent: *He phoned again this morning. He's very persistent*

purposeful: *She had a purposeful air*

resolute: *formal: a decisive and resolute leader*

single-minded: *a single-minded determination to win*

tenacious: *a tenacious and persistent interviewer*

see also **firm, set on**

detest see **dislike, hate**

detested see **unpopular**

detonate see **explode, fire**

detonation see **bang**

detract from see **belittle**

detriment see **cost**

detrimental see **harmful**

devastate see **destroy, ruin**

devastation see **destruction, ruin**

develop verb 1 to grow or become more advanced: *Children develop at different rates*

advance: *tracing how medical technology has advanced to its present state*

evolve: *As scientific knowledge evolves, beliefs change*

grow: *The boys grew into men*

mature: *Other changes occur as the child matures physically*
progress: *His disease progressed quickly*
result: *Ignore the warnings and illness could result*
spring: *His anger sprang from his childhood suffering*
2 to become affected by an illness or fault: *He developed pneumonia*
catch: *catch a cold*
contract *formal*: *He contracted AIDS from a blood transfusion*
fall ill: *She fell ill with measles*
get: *When I was five I got mumps*
go down with: *Three members of the band went down with flu*
pick up: *They've picked up an infection from something they've eaten*
succumb: *I was determined not to succumb to the virus*
see also **breed, build, elaborate, enlarge on, expand, expand on, extend, form, grow, progress, result, work out**
development see **advance, growth, improvement**
deviant see **perverted**
deviation see **variation**
device see **bomb, gadget, machine**
devious *adjective* getting what you want by sly methods: *a devious politician*
  calculating: *a calculating businessman*
  scheming: *He was branded a "scheming liar"*
  underhand: *He used underhand tactics to win the election*
  wily: *a wily old statesman*
  see also **crafty, cunning, sly, sneaky**
deviousness see **cunning**
devise see **compose, create, plan**
devoted *adjective* very loving and loyal: *a devoted father*
  constant: *her constant companion*

dedicated: *dedicated followers of classical music*
doting: *His doting parents bought him a racing bike*
faithful: *I'm very faithful when I love someone*
loving: *Jim was a loving husband*
loyal: *a loyal friend*
true: *David was true to his wife*
see also **ardent, enthusiastic, faithful, fond, loving**
devotee see **fan, fanatic**
devotion see **love, worship**
devotional see **religious**
devour see **gobble**
devout see **fervent, holy, religious**
dexterity see **skill**
diagnose see **identify**
diagram see **pattern, plan**
dialect see **language**
dialogue see **discussion**
dictate see **determine, impose, order**
dictatorial see **absolute, bossy**
die *verb* **1** to stop living: *My mother died of cancer*
  cark it *Australian, New Zealand informal*: *You think you're about to cark it*
  expire *formal*: *before he finally expired*
  pass away: *He passed away last year*
  pass on: *My mother passed on four years ago*
  perish *formal*: *the ferry disaster in which 193 passengers perished*
2 to fade away: *My love for you will never die*
  fade away: *With time, they said, the pain will fade away*
  fade out: *Thanks to supermarkets, the corner shop is gradually fading out*
  peter out: *The six-month strike seemed to be petering out*
die away see **cease, fade**
die out *verb* to cease to exist: *That*

custom has died out now

disappear: Huge areas of the
countryside are disappearing

fade: Prospects for peace had already
started to fade

vanish: those species which have
vanished

see also **disappear, vanish**

diet see **food**

differ see **clash, conflict, disagree**

difference noun **1** a lack of similarity
between things: the vast difference
in size

contrast: the real contrast between
the two poems

discrepancy: discrepancies between
their statements

disparity: disparities between poor
and wealthy districts

distinction: a distinction between
the body and the soul

divergence: There's a substantial
divergence of opinion within the party

variation: a wide variation in the
prices charged

2 the amount by which two
quantities differ: The difference is 8532

balance: They were due to pay the
balance on delivery

remainder: They own a 75% stake.
The remainder is owned by the bank

see also **change, disagreement,
gap, variation**

difference of opinion see **division**

different adjective **1** unlike
something else: We have totally
different views

contrasting: painted in contrasting
colours

disparate formal: The republics are
very disparate in size and wealth

dissimilar: His methods were not
dissimilar to those used by Freud

divergent formal: divergent opinions

opposed: two opposed ideologies

unlike: This was a foreign country, so

unlike San Jose

2 unusual and out of the ordinary:
The result is interesting and different

special: a special variety of strawberry

unique: Each person's signature
is unique

3 distinct and separate: The lunch
supports a different charity each year

another: Her doctor referred her to
another therapist

discrete formal: two discrete sets
of nerves

distinct: A word may have two quite
distinct meanings

individual: Each family needs
individual attention

separate: The word 'quarter' has two
completely separate meanings

see also **various**

different from see **unlike**

differentiate see **distinguish**

difficult adjective **1** not easy to do or
solve: a difficult decision to make

arduous: a long, arduous journey

demanding: a demanding job

hard: He found it hard to get work

intractable formal: an intractable
problem

laborious: a laborious task

uphill: an uphill battle

2 not easy to deal with: I hope she
isn't going to be difficult

demanding: a demanding child

troublesome: a troublesome
teenager

trying: The whole business has been
very trying

see also **complex, formidable, hard,
rough, serious, stiff, tough, tricky**

difficulty noun **1** a problem: The
central difficulty is his drinking

complication: An added
complication is the growing concern
for the environment

hassle informal: all the usual hassles
at the airport

hurdle: preparing a CV, the first hurdle in a job search
obstacle: To succeed, you must learn to overcome obstacles
pitfall: the pitfalls of working abroad
problem: He left home because of family problems
snag: The only snag was that he had no transport
trouble: What seems to be the trouble?
2 the quality of being difficult: the difficulty of the problem
hardship: economic hardship
strain: the stresses and strains of a busy career
tribulation formal: the trials and tribulations of everyday life
see also **bother, distress, drawback, fix, hardship, obstacle, problem, snag, trouble**

diffident see **hesitant, timid**
diffuse see **distribute**
diffusion see **spread**

dig verb **1** to break up soil or sand: He dug a hole in the ground
burrow: The larvae burrow into cracks in the floor
excavate: A contractor was hired to excavate soil from the area
gouge: quarries which have gouged great holes in the hills
hollow out: They hollowed out crude dwellings from the soft rock
quarry: The caves are quarried for cement
till: freshly tilled fields
tunnel: The rebels tunnelled out of jail
2 to push something in: He could feel the beads digging into his palm
jab: A needle was jabbed into the baby's arm
poke: She poked a fork into the turkey skin
thrust: She thrust her hand into the sticky mess

▷ noun **3** a push or poke: She silenced him with a jab in the ribs
jab: a swift jab in the stomach
poke: a playful poke in the arm
prod: He gave the donkey a prod in the backside
thrust: knife thrusts
see also **poke, stick**

digest see **absorb, take in**
digit see **figure, number**
dignitary see **figure**
digs see **accommodation**
dilapidated see **derelict, shabby**
dilemma see **jam**
diligent see **industrious**
dilute see **thin**
diluted see **thin**

dim adjective **1** not bright or well-lit: a dim outline of a small boat
dark: a dark corridor
dull: The stamp was a dark, dull blue
grey: a grey, wet, April Sunday
murky: one murky November afternoon
poorly lit: a poorly lit road
shadowy: a shadowy corner
2 vague or unclear: a dim memory
faint: a faint recollection
hazy: Many details remain hazy
indistinct: the indistinct murmur of voices
obscure: The origin of the custom is obscure
shadowy: the shadowy world of spies
vague: I have a vague memory of shots being fired
3 informal slow to understand: He is rather dim
dumb informal: I've met a lot of dumb people
obtuse: I've really been very obtuse
slow: He got hit on the head and he's been a bit slow since
stupid: How could I have been so stupid?
thick informal: I must have seemed

incredibly thick
see also **dark, dumb, fade, faint, slow, soft, stupid**

dimensions see **capacity, size**

diminish verb to reduce or become reduced: *The threat of war has diminished*

contract: *Output fell last year and is expected to contract further*

decrease: *Gradually decrease the amount of vitamin C you are taking*

lessen: *The attention he gets will lessen when the new baby is born*

lower: *This drug lowers cholesterol levels*

reduce: *It reduces the risk of heart disease*

shrink: *the entertainment giant's intention to shrink its interest in the venture*

weaken: *The Prime Minister's authority has been fatally weakened*
see also **abate, decline, decrease, drop, fall, lessen, lower, reduce, shrink, weaken**

diminutive see **tiny**

dimness see **dark**

din see **crash, noise, racket, sound**

dine see **eat**

dingy see **drab, drab**

dinkum adjective Australian, New Zealand informal genuine or right: *a fair dinkum bloke with no pretensions*

genuine: *If this offer is genuine I will gladly accept*

guileless: *She was so guileless that he had to believe her*

honest: *My dad was the most honest man I ever met*

sincere: *a sincere desire to reform*
see also **authentic, genuine, real**

dinner see **function, meal**

dip see **descend**

diplomacy see **tact**

diplomatic see **tactful**

dire see **extreme, severe, terrible**

direct adjective 1 in a straight line or with nothing in between: *the direct route*

first-hand: *She has little first-hand knowledge of Quebec*

immediate: *his immediate superior*

personal: *I have no personal experience of this*

straight: *Keep the boat in a straight line*

uninterrupted: *an uninterrupted view*

2 open and honest: *He can be very direct sometimes*

blunt: *She is blunt about her personal life*

candid: *I haven't been completely candid with you*

forthright: *forthright language*

frank: *She is always very frank*

straight: *He never gives you a straight answer*

straightforward: *his straightforward manner*

▷ verb 3 to control and guide something: *Christopher will direct day-to-day operations*

control: *He now controls the entire company*

guide: *He should have let his instinct guide him*

lead: *He led the country between 1949 and 1984*

manage: *Within two years he was managing the store*

oversee: *an architect to oversee the work*

run: *Is this any way to run a country?*

supervise: *I supervise the packing of all mail orders*
see also **administer, command, conduct, control, express, focus, guide, head, immediate, influence, instruct, lead, manage, order, oversee, require, run, straightforward, supervise, tell**

direction noun **1** the line in which something is moving: *ten miles in the opposite direction*
course: *The captain altered course of a reversing car*
path: *He stepped into the path of a reversing car*
route: *We took the wrong route*
way: *Does anybody know the way to the bathroom?*
2 control and guidance of something: *He was chopping vegetables under the chef's direction*
charge: *A few years ago he took charge of the company*
command: *In 1942 he took command of 108 Squadron*
control: *The restructuring involves Ronson giving up control of the company*
guidance: *the reports which were produced under his guidance*
leadership: *The agency doubled in size under her leadership*
management: *The zoo needed better management*
see also **control, course, management, path**
directive *see* **command, order**
directly *see* **immediately**
director *see* **boss, chief, head, leader, manager**
directors *see* **management**
directory *see* **list**
dirt noun **1** dust or mud: *I started to scrub off the dirt*
dust: *The furniture was covered in dust*
filth: *tons of filth and sewage*
grime: *Kelly got the grime off his hands*
muck: *This congealed muck was interfering with the filter*
mud: *Their lorry got stuck in the mud*
2 earth or soil: *He drew a circle in the dirt with the stick*
earth: *a huge pile of earth*

soil: *an area with very good soil*
see also **earth, gossip, ground, soil**
dirty adjective **1** marked with dirt: *The kids have got their clothes dirty*
filthy: *a pair of filthy jeans*
grimy: *a grimy industrial city*
grubby: *kids with grubby faces*
mucky: *a mucky floor*
muddy: *his muddy boots*
soiled: *a soiled white apron*
unclean: *unclean water*
2 unfair or dishonest: *a dirty fight*
corrupt: *corrupt practices*
crooked: *crooked business deals*
3 sexually explicit: *a dirty joke*
blue: *a blue movie*
filthy: *a filthy book*
pornographic: *pornographic videos*
rude: *a rude joke*
see also **crude, indecent, obscene, scungy, shabby, soil, stain, vulgar**
disability *See* **handicap**
disable *see* **cripple, paralyse**
disadvantage noun an unfavourable circumstance: *the advantages and disadvantages of allowing their soldiers to marry*
drawback: *The apartment's only drawback was that it was too small*
handicap: *The tax issue was undoubtedly a handicap to Labour*
minus: *The pluses and minuses were about equal*
weakness: *the strengths and weaknesses of the argument*
see also **catch, handicap, snag**
disagree verb **1** to have a different opinion: *They can communicate even when they disagree*
differ: *They differ on lots of issues*
dispute: *Nobody disputed that Davey was clever*
dissent: *dissenting views*
2 to think that something is wrong: *I disagree with drug laws in general*
object: *We objected strongly but were*

outvoted

oppose: protesters opposing nuclear tests

take issue with: I take issue with much of what he said

see also **argue, clash, conflict, protest**

disagreeable adjective unpleasant in some way: a disagreeable odour

horrible: a horrible small boy

horrid: What a horrid smell!

nasty: What a nasty little snob you are!

objectionable: an objectionable, stuck-up young woman

obnoxious: One of the parents was a most obnoxious character

unfriendly: She spoke in a loud, rather unfriendly voice

unpleasant: The side-effects can be unpleasant

see also **horrible, nasty, sour, uncomfortable, unfriendly, unpleasant**

disagreement noun 1 a dispute about something: My driving instructor and I had a brief disagreement

altercation formal: an altercation with the referee

argument: an argument about money

difference: We have our differences but we get along

dispute: a pay dispute

quarrel: I had a terrible quarrel with my brother

row: a major diplomatic row

squabble: minor squabbles over phone bills

tiff: a lovers' tiff

2 an objection to something: Britain and France have expressed some disagreement with the proposal

dissent: voices of dissent

objection: I have no objection to

banks making money

opposition: their opposition to the scheme

see also **conflict, dispute, quarrel, squabble**

disappear verb 1 to go out of sight: The aircraft disappeared off the radar

be lost to view: They observed the comet for 70 days before it was lost to view

drop out of sight: After his first film he dropped out of sight

fade: We watched the harbour fade into the mist

recede: Luke receded into the distance

vanish: Anne vanished from outside her home the Wednesday before last

2 to stop existing: The pain has finally disappeared

cease formal: At 1 o'clock the rain ceased

die out: How did the dinosaurs die out?

go away: All she wanted was for the pain to go away

melt away: His anger melted away

pass: He told her the fear would pass

vanish: species which have vanished

see also **die out, melt, vanish**

disappoint see **dash**

disappointed adjective sad because something has not happened: I was disappointed that Kluge was not there

dejected: Her refusal left him feeling dejected

despondent: After the interview John was despondent

disenchanted: She has become very disenchanted with the marriage

disillusioned: I've become very disillusioned with politics

downcast: After his defeat Mr Rabin looked downcast

saddened: He is saddened that they did not win anything

disappointing see **unsatisfactory**

disappointment noun **1** a feeling of being disappointed: *Book early to avoid disappointment*

dejection: *There was an air of dejection about her*

despondency: *a mood of gloom and despondency*

regret: *my one great regret in life*

2 something that disappoints you: *The reunion was a bitter disappointment*

blow: *It was a terrible blow when he was made redundant*

setback: *a setback for the peace process*

see also **blow, failure**

disapproval noun the belief that something is wrong: *his mother's disapproval of his marriage*

censure: *He deserves support, not censure*

condemnation: *the universal condemnation of French nuclear tests*

criticism: *actions which have attracted fierce criticism*

see also **censure, criticism, opposition**

disapprove verb to think that something is wrong: *Everyone disapproved of their marrying so young*

condemn: *Political leaders condemned the speech*

deplore formal: *He deplores violence*

dislike: *Her father seemed to dislike all her boyfriends*

find unacceptable: *I find such behaviour totally unacceptable*

take a dim view of: *They took a dim view of local trade unionists*

see also **protest**

disapproving *see* **critical, severe**

disarray *see* **confusion, disorder, mess, muddle**

disaster noun a very bad accident: *another air disaster*

calamity formal: *It could only end in calamity*

catastrophe: *War would be a catastrophe*

misfortune: *She seemed to enjoy the misfortunes of others*

tragedy: *They have suffered an enormous personal tragedy*

disastrous *see* **fatal**

discard verb to get rid of something: *Read the instructions before discarding the box*

cast aside: *In America we seem to cast aside our elderly people*

dispose of: *how he disposed of the murder weapon*

dump informal: *The getaway car was dumped near the motorway*

jettison: *The crew jettisoned excess fuel*

shed: *a snake that has shed its skin*

throw away: *I never throw anything away*

throw out: *Why don't you throw out all those old magazines?*

see also **banish, dispose of**

discern verb to notice or understand something clearly: *trying to discern a pattern in his behaviour*

detect: *Arnold could detect a certain sadness in the old man's face*

make out: *I could just make out a shadowy figure through the mist*

notice: *Mrs Shedden noticed a bird sitting on the garage roof*

observe: *In 1664 Hooke observed a reddish spot on the planet's surface*

perceive: *Get pupils to perceive the relationship between success and effort*

see: *Supporters saw in him a champion of the oppressed*

spot: *I've spotted an error in your calculations*

see also **distinguish, notice, see, spot, tell**

discernment *see* **wisdom**

discharge verb **1** to send something

out: *The resulting salty water will be discharged at sea*
emit: *the amount of greenhouse gases emitted*
empty: *companies which empty toxic by-products into rivers*
expel: *Poisonous gas is expelled into the atmosphere*
flush: *Flush out all the sewage*
give off: *natural gas, which gives off less carbon dioxide than coal*
release: *a weapon which releases toxic nerve gas*
2 to allow someone to leave hospital or prison: *He has a broken nose but may be discharged today*
free: *The country is set to free more prisoners*
let go: *They held him for three hours and then let him go*
liberate: *They promised to liberate prisoners held in detention camps*
release: *He was released on bail*
set free: *More than ninety prisoners have been set free*
3 to dismiss someone from a job: *He was discharged from the military*
dismiss: *The military commander has been dismissed*
eject: *He was ejected from his first job for persistent latecoming*
fire *informal*: *If he wasn't so good at his job, I'd fire him*
sack *informal*: *The teacher was sacked for slapping a schoolboy*
▷ *noun* **4** a sending away from a job or institution: *They face a dishonourable discharge from the Army*
dismissal: *shock at the director's dismissal from his post*
ejection: *These actions led to his ejection from office*
expulsion: *his expulsion from the party in 1955*
the sack *informal*: *People who make mistakes can be given the sack*

see also **drain, dump, fire, free, release, sack, the sack**
disciple *see* **follower**
discipline *see* **punish**
disclose *see* **reveal**
disclosure *see* **news**
discolour *see* **fade**
discomfort *see* **pain**
disconcert *see* **embarrass**
disconnect *see* **separate**
disconnected *see* **separate**
discontinue *see* **cease, interrupt, quit, stop**
discord *see* **conflict**
discount *see* **ignore**
discourage *verb* to make someone lose enthusiasm: *Don't let these problems discourage you*
daunt: *He was not the type of man to be daunted by adversity*
deter: *Tougher sentences would do nothing to deter crime*
dissuade: *He considered emigrating, but his family managed to dissuade him*
put off: *I wouldn't let it put you off applying*
discourse *verb see* **discussion, lecture, speech, talk**
discover *verb* to find something or find out about something: *He discovered that she had a brilliant mind*
come across: *He came across the jawbone of a carnivorous dinosaur*
find: *The police also found a pistol*
find out: *Watch the next episode to find out what happens*
learn: *The Admiral, on learning who I was, wanted to meet me*
realize: *As soon as we realized something was wrong, we took action*
stumble on *or* **across**: *They stumbled on a magnificent waterfall*
unearth: *Researchers have unearthed documents implicating her in the crime*
see also **determine, find, hear,**

learn, observe, see

discredit see **disgrace, disprove, shame**

discreet see **tactful**

discrepancy see **difference**

discrete see **different, individual, separate**

discretion see **freedom, tact**

discretionary see **flexible**

discriminate see **distinguish**

discriminating see **fussy**

discrimination see **injustice, prejudice**

discuss verb to talk about something: *I will be discussing the situation with colleagues tomorrow*
  debate: *The UN Security Council will debate the issue today*
  exchange views on: *They exchanged views on a wide range of subjects*
  go into: *We didn't go into that*
  talk about: *What did you talk about?*

discussion noun a talk about something: *informal discussions*
  consultation: *consultations between lawyers*
  conversation: *I struck up a conversation with him*
  debate: *There has been a lot of debate among scholars about this*
  dialogue: *a direct dialogue between the two nations*
  discourse: *a long tradition of political discourse*
  talk: *We had a long talk about it*
  see also **conference, word**

disdain noun a talk about: *I will be discussing the situation with*
disdain noun a talk about contempt, scorn

disdainful see **haughty, scornful, stuck-up, superior**

disease see **disorder, illness**

disenchanted see **disappointed**

disfigured see **deformed**

disgrace noun 1 lack of respect: *She has brought disgrace upon the whole team*

scandal: *They often abandoned their children because of fear of scandal*

shame: *I don't want to bring shame on the family name*

▷ verb 2 to bring shame upon: *I have disgraced my family's name*

discredit: *He said such methods discredited the communist fight worldwide*

shame: *I wouldn't shame my father by doing that*
  see also **humble, humiliate, shame**

disgraceful adjective deserving of shame: *disgraceful behaviour*
  scandalous: *a scandalous waste of money*
  shameful: *the most shameful episode in US naval history*
  shocking: *a shocking invasion of privacy*

disguised see **invisible**

disgust noun 1 a strong feeling of dislike: *his disgust at the incident*
  nausea: *I was overcome with a feeling of nausea*
  repulsion: *a shudder of repulsion*
  revulsion: *They expressed their shock and revulsion at his death*
  ▷ verb 2 to cause someone to feel disgust: *He disgusted many with his behaviour*
  repel: *a violent excitement that frightened and repelled her*
  revolt: *The smell revolted her*
  sicken: *What he saw there sickened him*
  see also **horrify, horror, repel, shock**

disgusting adjective very unpleasant or unacceptable: *one of the most disgusting sights I had ever seen*
  foul: *a foul stench*
  gross: *Don't be so gross!*
  obnoxious: *a most obnoxious character*
  repellent: *a very large, repellent toad*
  revolting: *The smell was revolting*

sickening: a sickening attack on a pregnant woman
vile: a vile odour
see also **nasty**

dishonest adjective not truthful: It would be dishonest to mislead people
corrupt: corrupt police officers
crooked: crooked business deals
deceitful: The ambassador called the report deceitful and misleading
fraudulent: fraudulent claims about being a nurse
lying: He called her 'a lying little twit'
see also **corrupt, crooked, dubious, insincere, lying, sneaky, two-faced**

dishonesty noun dishonest behaviour: She accused the government of dishonesty
cheating: He was accused of cheating
corruption: The President faces 54 charges of corruption
deceit: the deceit and lies of the past
trickery: They resorted to trickery in order to impress their clients
see also **corruption, lying**

dishonour see **shame**
disillusioned see **disappointed**
disinclined see **reluctant**
disintegrate verb to break into many pieces: At 420 mph the windscreen disintegrated
break up: There was a danger of the ship breaking up completely
crumble: The flint crumbled into fragments
fall apart: Bit by bit the building fell apart
fall to pieces: The radio handset fell to pieces
fragment: The clouds fragmented and out came the sun
see also **erode**

disinterested see **neutral**
dislike verb 1 to consider something unpleasant: We don't serve it often

because many people dislike it
abhor formal: a man who abhorred violence
be averse to: He's not averse to a little publicity
detest: Jean detested being photographed
hate: Most people hate him
loathe: a play loathed by the critics
not be able to abide: I can't abide liars
not be able to bear: I can't bear people who speak like that
not be able to stand: He can't stand the sound of her voice
▷ noun **2** a feeling of not liking something: She looked at him with dislike
animosity: The animosity between the two men grew
antipathy: their antipathy to my smoking
aversion: I've always had an aversion to being part of a group
distaste: Roger looked at her with distaste
hatred: her hatred of authority
hostility: hostility to ethnic groups
loathing: He made no secret of his loathing of her
see also **animosity, disapprove, hate, hatred, resent**

disliked see **unpopular**
disloyal see **false, treacherous, two-faced**
dismal see **drab, gloomy, sad**
dismay see **horrify, panic**
dismiss see **banish, discharge, fire, sack**
dismissal see **discharge, the sack**
disobedient see **naughty**
disobey verb to deliberately refuse to follow instructions: He was forever disobeying the rules
break: drivers breaking speed limits
defy: the first time that I dared to defy

my mother

flout: *illegal campers who persist in flouting the law*

infringe: *He was adamant that he had infringed no rules*

violate: *They violated the ceasefire agreement*

disorder noun **1** a state of untidiness: *Inside, all was disorder*

clutter: *She prefers the worktop to be free of clutter*

disarray: *Her clothes were in disarray*

muddle: *a general muddle of pencils and boxes*

2 a lack of organization: *The men fled in disorder*

chaos: *Their concerts often ended in chaos*

confusion: *There was confusion when a man fired shots*

disarray: *The nation is in disarray following rioting*

turmoil: *the political turmoil of 1989*

3 a disease or illness: *a rare nerve disorder*

affliction: *an affliction which can ruin a young man's life*

complaint: *a common skin complaint*

condition: *a heart condition*

disease: *heart disease*

illness: *mental illness*

see also **confusion, illness, mess, muddle, riot**

disordered *see* **confused**

disorganization *see* **confusion, muddle**

disorganized *see* **confused, inefficient**

disown *see* **renounce**

disparagement *see* **criticism**

disparaging *see* **abusive, critical**

disparate *see* **different, various**

disparity *see* **difference, gap**

dispassionate *see* **neutral**

dispatch *see* **message, news, send**

dispel *see* **banish**

dispense *see* **administer, distribute**

dispense with *see* **dispose of**

disperse *see* **distribute, melt**

dispirited *see* **down**

display *see* **flourish, show, sight**

displease *see* **annoy**

displeasure *see* **annoyance**

disposed *see* **prone**

dispose of verb to get rid of something: *Fold up the nappy and dispose of it*

discard: *Read the instructions before discarding the box*

dispense with: *We got a CD-player and dispensed with our old-fashioned record-player*

dump: *The government declared that it did not dump radioactive waste at sea*

get rid of: *The owner needs to get rid of the car for financial reasons*

jettison: *The crew jettisoned excess fuel and made an emergency landing*

throw away: *I never throw anything away*

see also **discard, dump, get rid of, process, settle**

disprove verb to show that something is not true: *the statistics that will prove or disprove the hypothesis*

discredit: *There would be difficulties in discrediting the evidence*

give the lie to: *This survey gives the lie to the idea that the economy is recovering*

invalidate: *Some of the other criticisms were invalidated years ago*

prove false: *It is hard to prove such claims false*

refute: *the kind of rumour that is impossible to refute*

dispute noun **1** an argument: *The dispute between them is settled*

argument: *a heated argument*

clash: *the clash between trade union*

leaders and the government

conflict: *Avoid any conflict between yourself and your ex-partner*

disagreement: *disagreements among the member states*

feud: *a bitter feud between the state government and the villagers*

row: *a major diplomatic row with France*

wrangle: *a legal wrangle*

▷ *verb* **2** to question something's truth or wisdom: *He disputed the allegations*

challenge: *I challenge the wisdom of this decision*

contest: *Your former employer wants to contest the case*

contradict: *Her version contradicted the Government's claim*

deny: *She denied both accusations*

query: *No one queried my decision*

question: *It never occurred to me to question the doctor's diagnosis*

see also argument, challenge, contest, disagree, disagreement, fight, quarrel, query, question, squabble

disqualification *see* ban

disqualify *see* ban

disquiet *see* concern

disregard *see* contempt, ignore, neglect, overlook

disrepair *see* ruin

disreputable *see* low, notorious

disrespect *see* contempt

disrespectful *see* rude

disrupt *see* disturb, impede, interfere

dissent *see* disagree, disagreement

dissimilar *see* different

dissimilar to *see* unlike

dissolve *see* eat away, melt, vanish

dissuade *see* discourage

distance *see* length, space

distant *adjective* **1** far away in space or time: *a distant land*

far: *Is it very far?*

outlying: *outlying districts*

out-of-the-way: *an out-of-the-way spot*

remote: *a remote village*

2 cold and unfriendly: *He is polite but distant*

aloof: *He seemed aloof and detached*

detached: *He observed me with a detached curiosity*

reserved: *She's quite a reserved person*

withdrawn: *Her husband had become withdrawn and moody*

see also cold, far, foreign, remote

distaste *see* dislike

distasteful *see* unpleasant

distilled *see* refined

distinct *see* different, particular, plain

distinct from *see* unlike

distinction *see* difference, quality

distinctive *see* characteristic, individual, peculiar, special

distinguish *verb* **1** to see the difference between things: *Could he distinguish right from wrong?*

differentiate: *At this age your baby cannot differentiate one person from another*

discriminate: *He is unable to discriminate a good idea from a terrible one*

tell: *How do you tell one from another?*

tell apart: *I can only tell them apart by the colour of their shoes*

tell the difference: *I can't tell the difference between their policies and ours*

2 to recognize something: *I heard shouting but was unable to distinguish the words*

discern: *We could just discern a narrow ditch*

make out: *He couldn't make out what she was saying*

pick out: Through my binoculars I picked out a group of figures

recognize: He did not think he could recognize his car in the snow

distinguishable see **visible**

distinguished see **famous**

distinguishing see **characteristic, peculiar**

distort see **cloud, colour, misrepresent, twist**

distorted see **crooked, deformed, garbled**

distract verb to stop someone from concentrating: Playing video games distracts him from his homework

divert: They want to divert our attention from the real issues

draw away: to draw attention away from the crime

distracted see **absent-minded**

distraction see **escape**

distress noun 1 great suffering: Jealousy causes distress and painful emotions

heartache: the heartache of her divorce

pain: eyes that seemed filled with pain

sorrow: a time of great sorrow

suffering: to put an end to his suffering

2 the state of needing help: The ship might be in distress

difficulty: rumours about banks being in difficulty

need: When you were in need, I loaned you money

straits: The company's closure left them in desperate financial straits

trouble: a charity that helps women in trouble

▷ verb 3 to cause someone unhappiness: Her death had profoundly distressed me

bother: It bothered me that boys weren't interested in me

disturb: dreams so vivid that they disturb me for days

grieve: It grieved her to be separated from her son

pain: It pains me to think of you struggling all alone

sadden: The cruelty in the world saddens me deeply

trouble: He was troubled by the lifestyle of his son

upset: I'm sorry if I've upset you

worry: I didn't want to worry you

see also **agitate, alarm, concern, disturb, grief, grieve, hurt, pain, shake, shock, upset**

distress signal see **alarm**

distressed see **upset**

distressing see **painful, tragic**

distribute verb 1 to hand something out: They publish and distribute brochures

circulate: He has circulated a discussion document

hand out: One of my jobs was to hand out the prizes

pass around: Sweets were being passed around

pass round: She passed her holiday photos round

2 to spread something through an area: Distribute the topping evenly over the fruit

diffuse: Interest in books is more widely diffused than ever

disperse: The leaflets were dispersed throughout the country

scatter: She scattered the petals over the grave

spread: A thick layer of wax was spread over the surface

3 to divide and share something: Distribute chores evenly among all family members

allocate: funds allocated for nursery education

allot: The seats are allotted to the candidates who have won the most votes

dispense *formal: The Union had already dispensed £400 in grants*

divide *see* Paul divides his spare time between the bedroom and the study

dole out *You cut out my wallet and began to dole out the money*

share out *You could share out the money a bit more equally*
see also **circulate**

district *see* **area, local, region, territory**

distrust *see* **question, suspect, suspicion**

distrustful *see* **cynical, suspicious, wary**

disturb *verb* **1** to intrude on someone's peace: *She slept in a separate room so as not to disturb him*

bother *I'm sorry to bother you*

disrupt *Protesters disrupted the debate*

intrude on *I don't want to intrude on your parents*

2 to upset or worry someone: *Some scenes may disturb you*

agitate *The thought agitated her*

distress *Her death had profoundly distressed me*

shake *Well, it shook me quite a bit*

trouble *He was troubled by the lifestyle of his son*

unsettle *The presence of the two policemen unsettled her*

upset *I'm sorry if I've upset you*

worry *I didn't want to worry you*
see also **agitate, bother, concern, distress, shake, trouble, upset**

disturbance *see* **riot**

disturbing *see* **creepy**

dither *see* **hesitate**

dive *verb* **1** to jump or fall into water: *She was standing by the pool, about to dive in*

jump *He ran along the board and jumped in*

leap *as she leapt into the water*

submerge *Hippos are unable to submerge in the few remaining water holes*
see also **descend**

diverge *see* **split**

divergence *see* **difference, split**

divergent *see* **different**

divergent from *see* **unlike**

diverse *see* **various**

diversify *see* **vary**

diversion *see* **escape, hobby, pastime, variation**

divert *see* **distract**

divide *verb* **1** to split something up: *The idea is to divide the country into four sectors*

cut up *Halve the tomatoes, then cut them up*

partition *a plan to partition the country*

segregate *Police were used to segregate the two rival camps*

separate *Fluff the rice with a fork to separate the grains*

split *Split the chicken in half*

split up *He split up the company*

2 to form a barrier between things: *the frontier dividing Mexico from the USA*

bisect *The main street bisects the town*

separate *the fence that separated the yard from the paddock*

3 to cause people to disagree: *the enormous differences that still divide them*

come between *It's difficult to imagine anything coming between them*

set against one another *The case has set neighbours against one another in the village*

split *Women priests are accused of splitting the church*
see also **distribute, separate,**

share, sort
divine see **religious**
division noun **1** separation into parts: *the unification of Germany after its division into two states*
partition: *fighting which followed the partition of India*
separation: *the separation of church and state*
2 a disagreement: *There were divisions in the Party on economic policy*
breach: *a serious breach in relations between the two countries*
difference of opinion: *Was there a difference of opinion over what to do with the money?*
rupture: *a rupture of the family unit*
split: *They accused both sides of trying to provoke a split in the party*
3 a section of something: *the Research Division*
department: *the company's chemicals department*
section: *a top-secret section of the Foreign Office*
sector: *the nation's manufacturing sector*
see also **compartment, department, section, split**
divorce see **separate**
divorced see **separate**
divulge see **reveal**
dizzy adjective about to lose your balance: *He kept getting dizzy spells*
giddy: *She felt slightly giddy*
light-headed: *If you skip breakfast, you may feel light-headed*
see also **dazed, faint**
do verb **1** to carry out a task: *He just didn't want to do any work*
carry out: *Police believe the attacks were carried out by nationalists*
execute formal: *The landing was skillfully executed*
perform: *people who have performed*

outstanding acts of bravery
undertake: *She undertook the arduous task of monitoring the elections*
2 to be sufficient: *Home-made stock is best, but cubes will do*
be adequate: *The western diet should be perfectly adequate for most people*
be sufficient: *One teaspoon of sugar should be sufficient*
suffice formal: *Often a far shorter letter will suffice*
3 to perform well or badly: *Connie did well at school*
fare: *Some later expeditions fared better*
get on: *I asked him how he had got on*
manage: *How did your mother manage after your father died?*
see also **accomplish, achieve, commit, conduct, perform, practise, suit**
do away with see **abolish, eliminate**
do business see **trade**
do up see **decorate, renovate**
do well see **flourish, succeed, thrive**
do wrong see **sin**
do your best see **strive**
do your utmost see **strive**
docile see **meek, passive**
dock see **land**
doctrinal see **religious**
doctrine see **belief, principle**
document see **record**
dodge verb **1** to move out of the way: *We dodged behind a pillar out of sight of the tourists*
duck: *I wanted to duck down and slip past but they saw me*
swerve: *He swerved to avoid a truck*
2 to avoid doing something: *dodging military service by feigning illness*
avoid: *They managed to avoid paying their fares*

elude: *He eluded the police for 13 years*
evade: *by evading taxes*
get out of: *He'll do almost anything to get out of paying his share*
shirk: *We can't shirk our responsibility*
sidestep: *Rarely, if ever, does he sidestep a question*
see also **avoid, escape, manoeuvre**

dodgy see **suspect, suspicious**

dog *noun* an animal often kept as a pet: *a children's book about dogs*
brak *South African: a rabid brak*
canine: *a new canine was needed*
mongrel: *a rescued mongrel called Chips*
mutt *slang: the most famous mutts in the western world*
pooch *slang: Julian's pet pooch*

dogged see **determined, obstinate, stubborn**

dogma see **belief**

dole out see **distribute**

domain see **field, territory**

domestic see **home**

dominance see **advantage, hold**

dominant see **powerful**

domineering see **bossy**

dominion see **colony, power, territory**

don see **teacher, wear**

donate see **give, present**

donation see **gift, present**

done see **over, right**

doom see **condemn**

doomed *adjective* certain to fail: *a doomed attempt to rescue the children*
condemned: *Many women are condemned to poverty*
hopeless: *I don't believe your situation is as hopeless as you think*
ill-fated: *his ill-fated attempt on the world record*

door see **entrance, entry**

doorway see **entrance, entry**

dope see **fool**

dosh see **money**

doting see **devoted, fond, loving**

double *adjective* **1** twice the usual size: *a double whisky*
twice: *Unemployment in Northern Ireland is twice the national average*
twofold: *a twofold risk*
2 consisting of two parts: *a double album*
dual: *dual nationality*
twin: *twin beds*
twofold: *Their concern was twofold: personal and political*
see also **lookalike**

double-cross see **betray, deceive**

doubt *noun* **1** a feeling of uncertainty: *This raises doubts about the point of advertising*
misgiving: *I had misgivings about his methods*
qualm: *I have no qualms about recommending this approach*
scepticism: *The report has been greeted with scepticism*
uncertainty: *the uncertainties regarding the future funding of the company*
▷ *verb* **2** to feel uncertain about something: *No one doubted his ability*
be dubious: *I was dubious about the entire proposition*
be sceptical: *Other archaeologists are sceptical about his findings*
query: *No one queried my decision*
question: *It never occurs to them to question the doctor's decisions*
see also **question, suspect, suspicion**

doubtful *adjective* unlikely or uncertain: *It is doubtful whether he will appear again*
debatable: *Whether the Bank of England would do any better is highly debatable*
dubious: *This claim seems to us rather dubious*
questionable: *It is questionable*

whether the expenditure is justified

uncertain *see* **It's uncertain whether they will accept the plan**

see also **dubious, hesitant, improbable, suspect, suspicious, uncertain, unpredictable**

doubtless *see* **probably**

dough *see* **money**

dovetail *see* **fit**

down *adverb* **1** towards the ground, or in a lower place: *We went down in the lift*

downwards: *She gazed downwards*

downstairs: *Denise went downstairs and made some tea*

▷ *adjective* **2** depressed: *He sounded really down*

dejected: *Everyone has days when they feel dejected*

depressed: *She's been very depressed about this situation*

dispirited: *I left feeling utterly dispirited*

fed up *informal*: *I'm just fed up and I don't know what to do*

glum: *She was very glum and was missing her children*

melancholy: *It was in the afternoon that Tom felt most melancholy*

miserable: *My work was making me really miserable*

see also **below, gloomy, miserable, pile, sad, unhappy**

downcast *see* **disappointed, miserable, sad**

downfall *noun* the failure of a person or thing: *His lack of experience had led to his downfall*

collapse: *The medical system is facing collapse*

fall: *the fall of the military dictator*

ruin: *Inflation has driven them to the brink of ruin*

see also **collapse, failure, ruin**

downgrade *see* **belittle, reduce**

downpour *see* **flood, rain**

downright *see* **absolute, rank**

downstairs *see* **down**

down-to-earth *see* **realistic, sensible, sound**

downtrodden *see* **oppressed**

downturn *see* **decline, recession**

downwards *see* **down**

doze *see* **sleep**

drab *adjective* dull and unattractive: *the same drab grey dress*

dingy: *his rather dingy office*

dismal: *a dark dismal day*

dreary: *a dreary little town*

gloomy: *the gloomy days of winter*

grey: *a New Year that will be grey and cheerless*

sombre: *a worried official in sombre black*

see also **dreary, dull**

draft *see* **design, plan, recruit**

drag *verb* to pull something along the ground: *He dragged his chair towards the table*

draw: *He drew his chair nearer the fire*

haul: *A crane was used to haul the car out of the stream*

lug: *Nobody wants to lug around huge suitcases*

tow: *They threatened to tow away my car*

trail: *She came down the stairs slowly, trailing the coat behind her*

see also **annoyance, draw, pull, tug**

drain *verb* **1** to cause a liquid to flow somewhere: *Miners built the tunnel to drain water out of the lakes*

draw off: *The fluid can be drawn off with a syringe*

pump: *to get rid of raw sewage by pumping it out to sea*

2 to flow somewhere: *rivers that drain into lakes*

discharge: *Blood was discharging from its nostrils*

empty: *The Washougal empties into the Columbia River*

flow: The waters of Lake Erie now flow into the Niagara River

seep: Radioactive water has seeped into underground reservoirs

3 to use something up: The prolonged boardroom battle drained him of energy and money

consume: plans which will consume hours of time

exhaust: People are now living longer and exhausting natural resources

sap: The illness sapped his strength

tax: Overcrowding has taxed the city's ability to deal with waste

use up: They aren't the ones who use up the world's resources

see also **dry, empty, exhaust, tax, tire**

drained see **tired, weary**

drama see **play**

dramatic see **exciting**

drape see **hang**

drastic adjective severe and urgent: It's time for drastic action

extreme: I would rather die than do anything so extreme

harsh: harsh new measures to combat drink-driving

radical: radical economic reforms

severe: a severe shortage of drinking water

see also **extreme**

draw verb **1** to make a picture: He starts a drawing by painting simplified shapes

paint: He is painting a huge volcano

sketch: He sketched a map on the back of a menu

trace: He learned to draw by tracing pictures out of old storybooks

2 to move somewhere: as the car drew away

move: She moved away from the window

pull: He pulled into the driveway

3 to pull something: He drew his

chair nearer the fire

drag: He dragged his chair towards the table

haul: A crane was used to haul the car out of the stream

pull: a freight train pulling wagons

see also **attract, drag, earn, extract, lure, pull, tie, tug**

draw away see **distract**

draw back see **retreat**

draw off see **drain**

draw out see **withdraw**

draw up see **design, form, halt**

drawback noun a problem that makes something less than perfect: The only drawback was that the apartment was too small

difficulty: There is only one difficulty – I don't have the key

hitch: It's a great idea but I can see a serious hitch

problem: The main problem with the house is its inaccessibility

snag: It's a great school – the snag is the fees are £9,000 a year

trouble: The trouble is that he might not agree with our plans

see also **catch, disadvantage, fault, handicap, snag**

drawing see **picture**

dread see **fear, horror**

dreadful adjective very bad or unpleasant: He told us the dreadful news

appalling: living under the most appalling conditions

atrocious: The food here is atrocious

awful: Jeans look awful on me

frightful: The war had been so frightful he couldn't talk about it

ghastly: a ghastly pair of shoes

horrendous: the most horrendous experience of his life

terrible: Thousands more people suffered terrible injuries

see also **awful, horrible, terrible**

dream noun **1** mental pictures while sleeping: *He had a dream about Claire*
hallucination: *The drug induces hallucinations at high doses*
trance: *She seemed to be in a trance*
vision: *seeing the Virgin Mary in a vision*
2 something that you want very much: *his dream of winning the lottery*
ambition: *His ambition is to sail round the world*
aspiration: *one of his greatest aspirations*
daydream: *He learned to escape into daydreams of becoming a writer*
fantasy: *fantasies of romance and true love*
see also **daydream, hope, vision**

dreary adjective dull or boring: *the dreary winter months*
boring: *a boring job*
drab: *The rest of the day's activities often seem drab*
dull: *There was scarcely a dull moment*
humdrum: *The new government seemed rather humdrum*
monotonous: *It's monotonous work, like most factory jobs*
tedious: *Such lists are tedious to read*
uneventful: *her dull, uneventful life*
see also **drab, gloomy**

dregs *see* **remains**

drenched *see* **wet**

dress noun **1** a piece of clothing: *a black dress*
frock: *a party frock*
gown: *wedding gowns*
robe: *a fur-lined robe*
2 clothing in general: *evening dress*
attire formal: *women dressed in their finest attire*
clothes: *casual clothes*
clothing: *protective clothing*
costume: *women in traditional costume*
garb formal: *his usual garb of a*
dark suit
▷ verb **3** to put on clothes: *a tall woman dressed in black*
attire: *He was attired in a smart blue suit*
clothe: *He lay down on the bed fully clothed*
garb formal: *He was garbed in sweater, jacket and boots*
see also **clothes**

dribble *see* **drip**

dried-up *see* **dry**

drift *see* **float, flow, meaning, wander**

drill *see* **pierce, practice, teach, train**

drink verb **1** to swallow liquid: *He drank some tea*
gulp: *She quickly gulped her coffee*
guzzle: *She guzzled gin and tonics like they were lemonade*
sip: *She sipped from her coffee mug*
swig informal: *I swigged down two white wines*
2 to drink alcohol: *He drinks little and eats carefully*
booze informal: *drunken businessmen who had been boozing all afternoon*
tipple: *We saw a woman tippling from the sherry bottle*
see also **alcohol**

drip verb **1** to fall in small drops: *Rain dripped from the brim of his cap*
dribble: *Sweat dribbled down his face*
splash: *Tears splashed into her hands*
trickle: *A tear trickled down the old man's cheek*
▷ noun **2** a small amount of a liquid: *drips of water*
bead: *beads of sweat*
drop: *a drop of blue ink*
droplet: *water droplets*
see also **drop**

drive verb **1** to operate or power a machine or vehicle: *Don't drive a car or operate heavy machinery after taking this medication*

operate: *A rock fall trapped the men as they operated a tunnelling machine*

pilot: *He piloted his own plane to Washington*

power: *The flywheel's battery could be used to power an electric car*

propel: *Attached is a tiny rocket designed to propel the spacecraft towards Mars*

run: *I ran a Rover 100 from 1977 until 1983*

steer: *What is it like to steer a ship this size?*

work: *I learned how to work the forklift*

2 to force someone to do something: *Depression drove him to self-harm*

compel: *He felt compelled to speak out against their actions*

force: *A back injury forced her to withdraw from the tournament*

lead: *His abhorrence of racism led him to write his first book*

motivate: *What motivates people to behave like this?*

prompt: *The recession has prompted consumers to cut back on spending*

push: *James did not push her into stealing the money*

spur: *It's the money that spurs these fishermen to take such risks*

3 to force something pointed into a surface: *I used the sledgehammer to drive the pegs in*

hammer: *Hammer a wooden peg into the hole*

knock: *He knocked a couple of nails into the wall*

ram: *He rammed the stake with all his strength into the creature's heart*

sink: *He sinks the needle into my arm*

thrust: *thrusting a knife into his ribs*

▷ *noun* **4** a journey in a vehicle: *We might go for a drive on Sunday*

excursion: *an excursion to a local*

vineyard

jaunt: *Let's take a jaunt down to the beach*

journey: *The journey from Manchester to Plymouth took a few hours*

ride: *We took some friends for a ride in the family car*

run: *We went for a run in the new car to try it out*

spin: *I was thinking about going for a spin*

trip: *He went on a coach trip to the seaside*

5 energy and determination: *He is best remembered for his drive and enthusiasm*

ambition: *When I was young I never had any ambition*

determination: *her natural determination to succeed*

energy: *At 54 years old, her energy is magnificent*

enterprise: *the group's lack of enterprise*

initiative: *We were disappointed by his lack of initiative*

motivation: *His poor performance may be attributed to lack of motivation*

vigour: *He played with great vigour*

see also **blow**, **chase**, **energy**, **force**, **go**, **make**, **motivate**, **reduce**, **urge**

drive into *see* **crash**

drive off *see* **repel**

drive someone up the wall *see* **pester**

drivel *see* **garbage**, **nonsense**, **rubbish**

drizzle *see* **rain**

droop *see* **hang**, **wither**

drooping *see* **limp**

drop *verb* **1** to fall downwards: *She let her head drop*

descend: *as the aircraft descended*

fall: *Bombs fell in the town*

plummet: *His parachute failed to*

open and he plummeted to the ground
sink: She sank to her knees
tumble: The gun tumbled out of
his hand
2 to become less: Temperatures can
drop to freezing at night
decline: The number of staff has
declined
decrease: Population growth is
decreasing by 1.4% each year
diminish: diminishing resources
fall: Her weight fell to under seven
stone
plummet: Share prices have
plummeted
sink: Pay increases have sunk to
around 7%
slump: Net profits slumped by 41%
tumble: House prices have tumbled
by almost 30%
▷ noun **3** a small amount of a liquid:
a drop of blue ink
bead: beads of sweat
drip: drips of water
droplet: water droplets
see also **ball, blob, dash, decline,
decrease, deposit, drip, dump,
fall, lose, lower, trace**
drop out of sight see **disappear**
droplet see **blob, drip, drop**
drown see **flood**
drowsy see **sleepy, tired**
drug noun **1** a treatment for disease:
a new drug in the fight against AIDS
medication: She is not on any
medication
medicine: herbal medicines
2 an illegal substance: She was sure
Leo was taking drugs
narcotic: He was indicted for dealing
in narcotics
stimulant: the use of stimulants
in sport
see also **medicine**
drum see **advice, information**
drunk adjective **1** having consumed

too much alcohol: I got drunk
babalas South African: He was
babalas again last night
intoxicated formal: He appeared
intoxicated
tipsy: I'm feeling a bit tipsy
▷ noun **2** someone who consumes
too much alcohol: A drunk lay in
the alley
alcoholic: after admitting that he
was an alcoholic
boozer informal: He's a bit of a boozer
dry adjective **1** without any liquid: The
path was dry after the sunshine
arid: arid conditions
dried-up: a dried-up river bed
parched: parched brown grass
▷ verb **2** to remove liquid from
something: Wash and dry the lettuce
dehydrate: Avoid alcohol, which
dehydrates the body
drain: The authorities have mobilized
vast numbers of people to drain
flooded land
see also **barren**
dual see **double**
dub see **name**
dubious adjective **1** not entirely
honest or reliable: a rather dubious
claim
crooked: expose his crooked business
deals
dishonest: He had become rich by
dishonest means
questionable: allegations of
questionable business practices
suspect: The whole affair is highly
suspect
suspicious: two characters who
looked suspicious
unreliable: a notoriously unreliable
source of information
2 doubtful about something: My
parents were a bit dubious about it all
doubtful: I was still very doubtful
about our chances for success

nervous: The party has become nervous about its prospects of winning
sceptical: Other archaeologists are sceptical about his findings
suspicious: I'm a little suspicious about his motives
unconvinced: Most consumers seem unconvinced that the recession is over
undecided: After university she was still undecided as to what career she wanted
unsure: Fifty-two per cent were unsure about the idea
see also **doubtful, improbable, suspect, suspicious, uncertain**

duck see **dodge, escape**

duck out of see **avoid**

due see **outstanding**

duel see **fight**

dull adjective 1 not interesting: I found him rather dull
boring: a boring job
drab: The rest of the day's activities often seem drab
humdrum: The new government seemed rather humdrum
monotonous: It's monotonous work, like most factory jobs
tedious: Such lists are tedious to read
uninteresting: Their media has a reputation for being dull and uninteresting
2 not bright or clear: a dark, dull blue colour
drab: the same drab grey dress
gloomy: Inside it's gloomy after all that sunshine
muted: He likes sombre, muted colours
sombre: an official in sombre black
subdued: subdued lighting
3 covered with clouds: It's always dull and raining
cloudy: In the morning it was cloudy
leaden: a leaden sky
murky: one murky November

afternoon
overcast: For three days it was overcast
see also **blank, blunt, boring, cloudy, dim, dreary, fade, flat, gloomy, numb, sleepy, stuffy**

dullness see **boredom**

dumb adjective 1 unable to speak: We were all struck dumb for a minute
mute: a mute look of appeal
silent: Suddenly they both fell silent
speechless: Alex was almost speechless with rage
2 informal slow to understand: I've met a lot of pretty dumb people
dim: He is rather dim
obtuse formal: I've really been very obtuse
stupid: How could I have been so stupid?
thick informal: I must have seemed incredibly thick
see also **dim, idiotic, silent, slow**

dumbness see **silence**

dummy see **mock, model**

dump verb 1 to get rid of something: The getaway car was dumped near the motorway
discharge: The resulting salty water will eventually be discharged at sea
dispose of: how he disposed of the murder weapon
get rid of: The cat had kittens, which they got rid of
jettison: The crew jettisoned their excess fuel
throw away: You should have thrown the letter away
throw out: You ought to throw out those empty bottles
2 to put something down: We dumped our bags at the hotel and went for a walk
deposit: Imagine if you were suddenly deposited on a desert island
drop: Many children had been dropped

outside the stadium by their parents
see also **discard, dispose of, get
rid of**

dunce see **fool**

dungeon see **prison**

dupe verb to trick someone: *Some of
the offenders duped the psychologists*
cheat: *Many brokers were charged
with cheating customers*
con informal: *The British people have
been conned by the government*
deceive: *He has deceived us all*
delude: *Television deludes you into
thinking you are experiencing reality*
fool: *Art dealers fool a lot of people*
play a trick on: *She realized he had
played a trick on her*
trick: *He'll be upset when he finds out
you tricked him*
see also **cheat, deceive, fool, take
in, trap, trick**

duplicate see **copy**

durable see **sturdy, tough**

duration see **length**

duress see **force**

dusk see **dark**

dust see **clean, dirt**

duty noun 1 something that you
ought to do: *We have a duty as adults
to listen to children*
obligation: *He had not felt an
obligation to help save his old friend*
responsibility: *work and family
responsibilities*
2 a task associated with a job: *He
carried out his duties conscientiously
and with considerable skill*
assignment: *dangerous assignments*
job: *One of my jobs was to make
the tea*
responsibility: *He handled his
responsibilities as a counsellor
very well*
role: *Both sides had important roles
to play*
3 tax paid to the government:

customs duties
excise: *These products are excused
VAT and excise*
levy formal: *An annual motorway levy
is imposed on all drivers*
tariff: *America wants to eliminate
tariffs on such items as electronics*
tax: *the tax on new cars and
motorcycles*
see also **function, job, part,
responsibility, task, tax, work**

dwell see **inhabit, live**

dwelling see **home, house**

dwindle see **decrease, fall, lessen,
shrink**

dye see **colour**

dying be dying for verb to want
something very much: *I'm dying for a
breath of fresh air*
ache for: *She still ached for the lost
intimacy of marriage*
hunger for: *Jules hungered for
adventure*
long for: *He longed for the winter
to be over*
pine for: *I pine for the countryside*
yearn for: *He yearned for freedom*

dynamic see **energetic, vital**

e

each see **all**

eager *adjective* wanting very much to do or have something: *Robert is eager to earn some extra money*

anxious: *She was anxious to leave early*

ardent: *one of the government's most ardent supporters*

avid: *He's always been an avid reader*

enthusiastic: *Tom usually seems very enthusiastic*

keen: *Kirsty has always been a keen swimmer*

raring to go *informal*: *They're all ready and raring to go*

see also **enthusiastic, impatient, keen, ready, willing**

eagerness see **enthusiasm**

earlier see **before, first, previous**

earliest see **first**

early *adjective* **1** before the arranged or expected time: *You're not late – I'm early!*

advance: *We got an advance copy of her new book*

premature: *The injury put a premature end to his sporting career*

untimely: *her untimely death in a car crash at the age of 21*

2 near the beginning of a period of time: *the early 1970's*

primeval: *These insects first appeared in the primeval forests of Europe*

primitive: *We found a fossil of a primitive bird-like creature*

▷ *adverb* **3** before the arranged or expected time: *We left early so we wouldn't have to queue*

ahead of time: *The bus always arrives ahead of time*

beforehand: *If you'd let me know beforehand, you could have come with us*

in advance: *You need to book in advance to get a good seat*

in good time: *We arrived at the airport in good time*

prematurely: *men who go prematurely bald*

earmark see **intend**

earn *verb* **1** to get money in return for doing work: *He earns a lot more than I do*

bring in: *My job brings in just enough to pay the bills*

draw: *I draw a salary, so I can afford to run a car*

get: *How much do you get if you're a lorry driver?*

make: *She makes a lot of money*

obtain: *the profits obtained from buying and selling shares*

2 to receive something that you deserve: *He earned the respect of his troops*

acquire: *She has acquired a reputation as a liar and a cheat*

attain *formal*: *He finally attained his pilot's licence*

win: *She won the admiration of all her colleagues*

see also **deserve, gain, merit**

earnest see **intense, serious, solemn**

earnings see **income, pay, profit**

earth *noun* **1** the planet on which we

live: *the tallest mountain on earth*
globe: *from every corner of the globe*
planet: *the effects of pollution on the atmosphere of our planet*
world: *the first person to cycle round the world*
2 soil from the ground: *He filled a pot with earth and popped the seeds in it*
clay: *lumps of clay that stuck to his boots*
dirt: *kneeling in the dirt*
ground: *digging potatoes out of the ground*
soil: *We planted some bulbs in the soil around the pond*
see also **dirt**, **ground**, **soil**

ease *noun* **1** lack of difficulty or worry: *He passed his driving test with ease*
leisure: *living a life of leisure*
relaxation: *The town has a feeling of relaxation and tranquility about it*
simplicity: *The simplicity of the new scheme has made it popular with motorists*
▷ *verb* **2** to make or become less severe or intense: *The doctor gave him another injection to ease the pain*
abate: *By morning the storms had abated*
calm: *The government is taking steps to calm the situation*
relax: *He relaxed his grip on the axe and smiled*
relieve: *The pills will help relieve the pain for a while*
slacken: *Her grip on the rope slackened and she fell back*
3 to move slowly or carefully: *He eased the door open and peered outside*
creep: *The car crept down the ramp*
edge: *I edged the van slowly back into the garage*
guide: *Bob guided the plane out onto the tarmac*
inch: *The ambulance inched its way*

through the crowds of shoppers
lower: *He lowered himself into the armchair*
manoeuvre: *We attempted to manoeuvre his canoe towards the shore*
squeeze: *They squeezed him into his seat and strapped him in*
see also **comfort**, **moderate**

easily offended see **sensitive**, **touchy**

easily upset see **sensitive**

easy *adjective* **1** able to be done without difficulty: *The software is very easy to install*
light: *a few light exercises to warm up*
painless: *Finding somewhere to stay was pretty painless in the end*
simple: *All you have to do is answer a few simple questions*
smooth: *a smooth changeover to the new system*
straightforward: *The route is fairly straightforward so you shouldn't need a map*
2 comfortable and without worries: *He has not had an easy life*
carefree: *a carefree summer spent on the beach*
comfortable: *a comfortable teaching job at a small private school*
leisurely: *a leisurely weekend spent with a few close friends*
quiet: *a quiet weekend in the sun*
relaxed: *It's very relaxed here, you can do what you like*
see also **comfortable**, **fluent**, **informal**, **leisurely**, **relaxed**, **simple**, **straightforward**

easy to use see **handy**

eat *verb* **1** to chew and swallow food: *For lunch he ate a cheese sandwich*
see **word studies eat**
2 to have a meal: *We like to eat early*
breakfast *formal*: *The ladies like to breakfast in their rooms*
dine: *We usually dine at about six*

feed: Leopards only feed when they are hungry

have a meal: We could have a meal at Pizza Palace after the film

lunch formal: We lunched at El Greco's

picnic: After our walk, we picnicked by the river

eat away verb to destroy something slowly: The front of the car had been eaten away by rust

corrode: buildings corroded by acid rain

destroy: Areas of the coast are being destroyed by the sea

dissolve: Chemicals in the water are dissolving the bridge

erode: the floods that erode the dry, loose soil

rot: Too many sweets will rot your teeth

wear away: The weather soon wears away the paintwork
see also **erode**

eavesdrop see **hear**

eavesdropping see **nosy**

ebb see **abate**

eccentric adjective 1 regarded as odd or peculiar: His maths teacher was considered a bit eccentric

bizarre: He's quite a bizarre character

outlandish: his outlandish behaviour sometimes put people off

quirky: a quirky, delightful film that is full of surprises

strange: his strange views about UFOs

weird: His taste in music is a bit weird

whimsical: a whimsical old gentleman

▷ noun 2 someone who is regarded as odd or peculiar: He's always been regarded as a bit of an eccentric

character informal: a well-known character who lived in Johnson Street

crank: People regarded vegetarians as cranks in those days

see also **bizarre, weirdo**

echelon see **rank**

echo see **repeat**

eclipse see **blot out, top**

ecological see **green**

economic adjective 1 concerning the way money is managed: the need for economic reforms

budgetary: a summit meeting to discuss various budgetary matters

commercial: a purely commercial decision

financial: The financial pressures on the government are mounting

2 making a profit: goods that happen to be economic to produce

productive: the need to make these industries more productive

profitable: a new venture that has proved highly profitable

viable: businesses that are no longer viable

see also **economical, efficient, financial**

economical adjective 1 cheap to use and saving you money: Our car may not be fast, but it's very economical

cheap: This isn't a very cheap way of buying stationery

cost-effective: the most cost-effective way of shopping

economic: the most economic way to see the museum

inexpensive: There are several good inexpensive restaurants in town

2 careful and sensible with money or materials: He's never been very economical about housekeeping

careful: She's very careful with her pocket money

frugal: his frugal lifestyle

prudent: the prudent use of precious natural resources

thrifty: My mother was very thrifty because she had so little spare cash

see also **cheap, thrifty**

economics see **finance**

economy noun the careful use of things to save money: *improvements in the fuel economy of new cars*
  frugality formal: *We must live with strict frugality if we are to survive*
  prudence: *A lack of prudence could seriously affect his finances*
  restraint: *We need to exercise some restraint in our spending*
  thrift: *He was widely praised for his thrift and imagination*

ecstasy noun extreme happiness: *his feeling of ecstasy after winning the medal*
  bliss: *husband and wife living together in bliss and harmony*
  delight: *He squealed with delight when we told him*
  elation: *His supporters reacted to the news with elation*
  euphoria: *There was a sense of euphoria after our election victory*
  exaltation: *the mood of exaltation that affected everyone*
  joy: *her joy at finding him after so long*
  rapture: *His speech was received with rapture by a huge crowd*
  see also **happiness, heaven, joy**

edge noun **1** the place where something ends or meets something else: *on the edge of the forest*
  border: *a pillowcase with a lace border*
  boundary: *The area beyond the western boundary belongs to Denmark*
  brim: *He kept climbing until he reached the brim of the crater*
  fringe: *the rundown areas on the fringes of the city*
  lip: *The lip of the jug was badly cracked*
  margin: *standing on the margin of the land where it met the water*
  rim: *a large round mirror with a gold rim*
  ▷ verb **2** to move somewhere slowly: *He edged towards the phone, ready to grab it if it rang*
  creep: *The car crept forward a few feet, then stopped*
  inch: *The ambulance inched its way through the crowds*
  sidle: *A man sidled up to him and tried to sell him a ticket*
  see also **bank, border, ease, outskirts, side**

edgy see **nervous, restless, tense**

edifice see **building, structure**

edit see **revise**

edition see **issue**

educate see **instruct, teach, train**

educated adjective having a high standard of learning: *He is an educated, tolerant and reasonable man*
  cultivated: *His mother was an elegant, cultivated woman*
  cultured: *a cultured man with a wide circle of friends*
  intellectual: *He is the intellectual type*
  learned: *He was a scholar, a very learned man*

education noun the process of learning or teaching: *the importance of a good education*
  coaching: *extra coaching to help him pass his exams*
  instruction: *All instruction is provided by qualified experts*
  schooling: *He began to wish he'd paid more attention to his schooling*
  training: *His military training was no use to him here*
  tuition: *personal tuition in the basics of photography*
  see also **knowledge**

eerie see **creepy, scary, spooky**

effect noun a direct result of something: *the effect that divorce has on children*
  consequence: *aware of the consequences of their actions*

end result: The end result of this process is still unclear

fruit: The new software is the fruit of three years' hard work

result: The result of all this uncertainty is that no-one is happy

upshot: The upshot is that we have a very unhappy workforce

see also **influence, result**

effective see **convincing, efficient, powerful, useful**

effectively see **well**

effectiveness see **value**

effects see **possessions, property, things**

efficient adjective able to work well without wasting time or energy: The new hatchback has a much more efficient engine

businesslike: a highly businesslike approach that impressed everyone

competent: an extremely competent piece of work

economic: The new system is much more economic, and will save millions

effective: effective use of the time we have left

organized: Tony seemed very organized, and completely in control of the situation

productive: the need to make farmers much more productive

see also **able, capable, proficient**

efficiently see **well**

effort noun **1** physical or mental energy: It took a lot of effort, but we managed in the end

application: His talent, application and energy are a credit to the school

energy: He decided to devote his energy to writing another book

exertion: Is it really worth all the exertion?

trouble: It's not worth the trouble

work: All the work I put in has now been wasted!

2 an attempt or struggle: an unsuccessful effort to ban Sunday shopping

attempt: an attempt to obtain an interview with the President

bid: a last-minute bid to stop the trial going ahead

stab informal: his latest stab at acting

struggle: his struggle to clear his name

see also **enterprise, hassle, labour, struggle, try**

effortless see **fluent**

egoistic see **selfish**

egoistical see **selfish**

egotism see **conceit, pride**

egotistic see **selfish**

egotistical see **boastful, conceited, selfish, vain**

eject see **banish, discharge, get rid of, remove**

ejection see **discharge**

elaborate adjective **1** having many different parts: an elaborate research project

complex: a complex explanation

complicated: a complicated plan of the building's security system

detailed: the detailed plans that have been drawn up

intricate: an intricate system of levers and pulleys

involved: a very involved operation, lasting many hours

2 highly decorated: elaborate wooden carvings

fancy: the fancy plasterwork on the ceiling

fussy: a rather fussy design

ornate: an ornate wrought-iron staircase

▷ verb **3** to add more information about something: He promised to elaborate on what had been said last night

develop: Maybe we should develop

this idea

enlarge see *He was enlarging on proposals made earlier*

expand: *a view that I will expand on later*

see also **complicated, fancy, sophisticated**

elaborate on see **enlarge on, expand on**

elastic see **flexible**

elated see **joyful**

elation see **ecstasy, happiness, joy**

elbow see **poke**

elbow room see **room**

elect see **decide**

election see **appointment**

electrifying see **exciting**

elegance see **beauty, grace, polish, style**

elegant see **posh, smart**

element see **aspect, detail, factor, ingredient, substance**

elementary see **basic, simple, straightforward**

elevate see **lift, promote, raise**

elicit see **excite, extract**

eliminate verb 1 to get rid of someone or something: *We've eliminated two of the four options so far*

cut out: *His guilty plea cut out the need for a long, costly trial*

do away with: *the attempt to do away with nuclear weapons altogether*

eradicate: *Efforts to eradicate malaria seem to be failing*

get rid of: *Why don't we just get rid of the middlemen altogether?*

remove: *You should try and remove these fatty foods from your diet*

stamp out: *We need to stamp out this disgusting practice*

2 to beat someone in a competition: *His team was eliminated in the first round*

knock out: *We were knocked out by*

the Dutch champions

put out: *Decker finally put her fellow American out in the quarter final*

see also **banish, exclude, remove**

elite see **pick, top**

elsewhere see **absent**

elude see **avoid, dodge, escape**

emaciated see **skinny**

emancipation see **freedom, release**

embargo see **ban, boycott, sanctions**

embark upon see **start**

embarrass verb to make someone feel ashamed or awkward: *You always embarrass me in front of my friends!*

disconcert: *The way Anderson was smirking disconcerted her*

fluster: *Nothing could fluster him*

humiliate: *How dare you humiliate me like that!*

shame: *Her son's behaviour had upset and shamed her*

see also **humiliate, shame**

embarrassed adjective ashamed and awkward: *I'm not embarrassed about taking my clothes off*

ashamed: *I felt so ashamed I wanted to die*

awkward: *It was a very awkward occasion*

humiliated: *A humiliated Mr Stevens admitted that the concert had been cancelled*

red-faced: *Red-faced executives had to explain this fact*

self-conscious: *I always feel self-conscious when I'm having my picture taken*

sheepish: *He looked very sheepish when he finally appeared*

see also **ashamed, uncomfortable**

embarrassment noun shame and awkwardness: *I laughed loudly to cover my embarrassment*

awkwardness: *the awkwardness of*

our first meeting

bashfulness: *Overcome with bashfulness, he lowered his voice*

humiliation: *the humiliation of having to ask for money*

self-consciousness: *her painful self-consciousness*

shame: *the shame he felt at having let her down*

see also **shame**

embittered see **bitter, resentful, sour**

emblem see **sign, symbol**

embrace see **clasp, grasp, hold, hug, include**

emerge see **appear**

emergence see **appearance**

emergency noun an unexpected and difficult situation: *This is an emergency!*

crisis: *the economic crisis affecting parts of Africa*

pinch: *I don't mind working late in a pinch*

emergent see **in the making**

eminence see **fame, success**

eminent see **important, leading, prominent**

emit verb to give out or release something: *Polly blinked and emitted a long sigh*

exude: *a plant that exudes an extremely unpleasant smell*

give off: *The fumes it gives off are poisonous, so watch out*

give out: *The alarm gave out a series of bleeps, then stopped*

release: *The factory is still releasing toxic fumes*

send out: *The volcano has been sending out smoke for weeks*

utter: *He uttered a loud snort and continued eating*

see also **discharge**

emotion see **feeling, passion**

emotional see **moving, passionate**

empathize with see **identify with**

empathy see **sympathy**

emphasis noun special or extra importance: *too much emphasis on commercialism*

accent: *In the new government the accent will be on co-operation*

importance: *There's not enough importance being given to environmental issues*

prominence: *Crime prevention has to be given more prominence*

weight: *This adds more weight to the government's case*

emphasize verb to make something seem specially important or obvious: *He emphasized the need for everyone to remain calm*

accent: *a white dress accented by a coloured scarf*

accentuate: *His shaven head accentuates his round face*

highlight: *This disaster has highlighted the difficulty faced by the government*

play up: *He played up his bad-boy image*

stress: *I would like to stress that we are in complete agreement*

underline: *This underlines how important the new trade deal really is*

see also **feature, stress**

employ verb **1** to pay someone to work for you: *Mollison was employed by Mr Darnley as a bodyguard*

appoint: *We need to appoint a successor to Mr Stevens*

commission: *He has been commissioned to design a new bridge*

engage formal: *They have finally engaged a suitable nanny*

hire: *I was hired as a gardener on the estate*

take on: *the need to take on more workers for the summer*

2 to use something: *the tactics*

employed by the police

bring to bear: We can bring two very different techniques to bear on this

make use of: He makes use of several highly offensive terms to describe them

use: the methods used in the investigation

utilize: Engineers will utilize a range of techniques to improve the signal

see also **busy, hire, use**

employed see **busy**

employee noun someone who is paid to work for: the way they look after their employees

hand: He's been working as a farm hand down south

worker: Workers at the plant have been laid off

workman: A council workman finally arrived to fix the door

see also **worker**

employees see **labour, staff**

employer noun someone that other people work for: a meeting with her employer to discuss the issue

boss: My boss has always been very fair

gaffer informal: You'll need to speak to the gaffer about that

see also **boss**

employers see **management**

employment noun the fact of employing people: the employment of children to work in shops

engagement: the engagement of suitable staff

enlistment: Enlistment in the armed forces is falling

hiring: The hiring of new staff is our top priority

recruitment: new policies on recruitment and training

taking on: Taking on extra staff would make life a lot easier

see also **job, use, work**

empty adjective **1** having no people

or things in it: The roads were empty

bare: When she got there, the cupboard was bare

blank: all the blank pages in his diary

clear: The runway must be kept clear at all times

deserted: By nightfall, the square was deserted

unfurnished: The flat was unfurnished when we moved in

uninhabited: The house has remained uninhabited since she moved out

vacant: two vacant lots on the industrial estate

2 boring or without value or meaning: My life is empty without him

inane: a series of inane remarks

meaningless: the feeling that his existence was meaningless

worthless: a worthless film with nothing to say about anything

▷ verb **3** to remove people or things: He emptied all the cupboards before Tony arrived

clear: The police cleared the building just in time

drain: She drained the bottles and washed them out

evacuate: Fortunately the building had been evacuated

unload: It only took twenty minutes to unload the van

see also **bare, barren, blank, discharge, drain, fond**

emulate see **copy, imitate**

en masse see **together**

enable see **permit**

enchant see **delight**

enchanting see **lovable, magical**

encircle see **enclose, surround**

enclose verb to surround a thing or place completely: The book arrived enclosed in a red plastic bag

encircle: The area had been encircled

by barbed wire

fence off: We decided to fence off the land

hem in: We were hemmed in by walls and hedges

surround: the low wall that surrounded the rose garden

wrap: Wrap the chicken in foil and bake it in a medium oven

see also **surround**

encompass see **include, surround**

encounter see **experience, meet, meeting, receive**

encourage verb **1** to give someone confidence: We were very encouraged by the response

cheer: This news cheered us all and helped us keep going

hearten: I am heartened to hear that

reassure: He always reassures me when I'm feeling down

2 to support a person or activity: the need to encourage people to be sensible

aid: I tried to aid his creative efforts

boost: Efforts to boost investment seem to be succeeding

favour: conditions which favour growth in the economy

help: policies aimed at helping small businesses

incite: He incited his followers to attack the police station

support: Rowe will support me in this campaign

see also **back, push, reassure, strengthen, support**

encouragement see **incentive**

encroach see **intrude**

end noun **1** the last part of a period or event: the end of the 20th century

see **word studies end**

2 the furthest point of something: the room at the end of the corridor

see **word studies end**

3 the purpose for which something is done: The army is being used for

political ends

see **word studies end**

▷ verb **4** to come or bring to a finish: talks being held to end the fighting

bring to an end: The treaty brought to an end fifty years of conflict

cease: By one o'clock the storm had ceased

conclude: The evening concluded with the usual speeches

finish: waiting for the film to finish

stop: When is it all going to stop?

terminate: the decision to terminate their contract

see also **back, cease, complete, conclude, conclusion, extreme, finish, goal, halt, lift, stop, use**

end result see **effect**

endanger verb to put someone or something in danger: a dispute that could endanger the peace talks

compromise: We will not allow safety to be compromised

jeopardize: a scandal that could jeopardize his government

put at risk: those who were put at risk by her stupidity

risk: He is risking the lives of others

threaten: A breakdown in this system could threaten the whole project

see also **threaten**

endearing see **lovable**

endeavour see **attempt, enterprise, seek, strive, try, undertaking**

ending see **conclusion, finish**

endless see **continual**

endorse see **advocate, approve, back, confirm, defend, sanction**

endorsement see **approval**

endow see **equip**

endure verb **1** to experience something difficult: He had to endure hours of discomfort

cope with: We've had a lot to cope with in the last few weeks

experience: The company has

experienced heavy financial losses
go through: having to go through the
public humiliation of a court case
stand: I don't know how he stood it
for so long
suffer: Steven has suffered years of
pain from arthritis
2 to continue to exist: Our friendship
has endured through everything
last: a car that is built to last
live on: His name will live on as an
inspiration to others
remain: When all the rest is forgotten,
this fact will remain
survive: the few traces of their
civilization that have survived
see also **bear, continue, go through,
have, last, remain, suffer, survive,
tolerate, undergo**
enduring see **permanent**
enemy noun someone who is
against you: She has many enemies in
the government
adversary: face to face with his old
adversary
antagonist: He killed his antagonist
in a duel
foe: He plays Dracula's foe, Dr. Van
Helsing
opponent: Her political opponents
will be delighted at this news
energetic adjective full of energy:
an able, energetic and very determined
politician
animated: an animated conversation
about politics and sport
dynamic: a dynamic and ambitious
businessman
indefatigable: trying to keep up with
their indefatigable boss
spirited: a spirited defence of his new
tax proposals
tireless: a tireless campaigner for
the homeless
vigorous: a vigorous campaign
see also **active, alive, lively, vital**

energy noun the ability and strength
to do things: I'm saving my energy
for tomorrow
drive: a man with immense drive and
enthusiasm
life: At 96, she's still as full of life
as ever
spirit: Despite trailing 6-2, they played
with a lot of spirit
strength: She put all her strength
into finding a new job
vigour: They returned to their work
with renewed vigour
vitality: a woman with considerable
charm and endless vitality
see also **activity, drive, effort, spirit**
enforce see **impose**
engage see **book, busy, employ, hire**
engage in see **participate**
engaged see **active, busy**
engagement see **employment**
engineer see **stage**
engrave see **carve**
engrossed see **busy, preoccupied**
enhance see **benefit, flatter,
improve**
enhancement see **improvement**
enigma see **mystery**
enigmatic see **mysterious**
enjoy verb to find pleasure in
something: I haven't enjoyed a film as
much as that in ages!
appreciate: people who don't
appreciate Satie's music
delight in: He delights in playing
practical jokes
like: Kirsty likes shopping
love: He loves skiing
relish: She relished the opportunity to
get back at him
revel in: Stevens was revelling in the
attention
take pleasure from: He took no
pleasure from the knowledge that he
had won
take pleasure in: She seemed to take

pleasure in my discomfort
see also **have, like, love, possess**

enjoyable see **agreeable, lovely, pleasant**

enjoyment see **entertainment, fun, pleasure**

enlarge verb to make something larger: *plans to enlarge the 30,000 seat stadium*

add to: *We've decided to add to this house rather than move again*

expand: *If we want to stay in business, we need to expand*

extend: *They extended the house by adding a conservatory*

increase: *They have increased the peace-keeping force to 2000*

magnify: *A more powerful lens will magnify the image*

see also **elaborate, expand, extend, increase**

enlargement see **growth**

enlarge on verb to give more information about something: *I'd like you to enlarge on that last point*

develop: *Maybe I should develop this idea a little bit further*

elaborate on: *He refused to elaborate on what he had said earlier*

expand on: *an idea that I will expand on later*

see also **expand on**

enlighten see **inform**

enlightened see **civilized, rational**

enlist see **join, recruit**

enlistment see **employment**

enliven see **refresh**

enormous adjective very large in size or amount: *an enormous dust cloud*

colossal: *a colossal waste of public money*

gigantic: *The road is bordered by gigantic rocks*

huge: *Several painters were working on a huge piece of canvas*

immense: *an immense cloud of*

smoke

massive: *The scale of the problem is massive*

tremendous: *I felt a tremendous pressure on my chest*

vast: *vast stretches of land*

see also **colossal, excessive, huge, immense, large, vast**

enough see **adequate, ample, plenty, sufficient**

enrage see **anger, provoke**

enraged see **angry, furious, mad**

enrol see **join, recruit**

ensemble see **company**

ensue see **result**

ensuing see **next**

ensure verb to make sure about something: *We must ensure that this never happens again*

guarantee: *Further investment should guarantee that profits will rise*

make certain: *to make certain that he'll get there*

make sure: *I will personally make sure that the job gets done*

see also **guarantee**

enter see **come, insert, invade, record**

enter into see **participate**

enterprise noun **1** a business or company: *a small enterprise with a high turnover*

business: *a medium-sized business*

company: *a company that was doing very well*

concern: *It's not a large concern, but it makes a profit*

establishment: *a modest establishment dedicated to sailing*

firm: *a clothing firm*

operation: *a one-man operation*

2 a project or task: *a risky enterprise such as horse breeding*

effort: *her latest fund-raising effort for cancer research*

endeavour: *an endeavour that was*

bound to end in failure
operation: *He'd set up a small mining operation*
project: *a project that will attract a lot of media attention*
undertaking: *This undertaking will rely on the hard work of our volunteers*
venture: *a venture that few were willing to invest in*
see also **business, drive, firm, racket, undertaking**

entertain verb to keep people amused or interested: *things that might entertain children in the school holidays*
amuse: *He amused us all evening, singing and telling jokes*
charm: *He charmed Mrs Nisbet with his tales of life on the road*
delight: *a routine that will delight audiences*
enthral: *He enthralled audiences all over Europe*
please: *He certainly knows how to please a crowd*
see also **please, receive**

entertain oneself see **play**

entertaining see **interesting**

entertainment noun enjoyable activities: *Their main form of entertainment is the TV*
amusement: *looking for some amusement on a Saturday night*
enjoyment: *We need a bit of enjoyment to cheer us up*
fun: *It's not really my idea of family fun*
pleasure: *Hours of pleasure can be had with a pack of cards*
recreation: *a healthy and enjoyable form of recreation*
see also **festival, fun**

enthral see **entertain, entrance, fascinate**

enthuse see **rave**

enthusiasm noun eagerness

and enjoyment in something: *We were disappointed by their lack of enthusiasm*
eagerness: *He could barely contain his eagerness*
excitement: *Her excitement got the better of her*
interest: *He doesn't show much interest in football*
keenness: *I don't doubt his keenness; it's his ability that worries me*
warmth: *He greeted us with his usual warmth and affection*
see also **excitement, spirit**

enthusiastic adjective showing great excitement and eagerness for something: *He was very enthusiastic about the new scheme*
ardent: *one of the government's most ardent supporters*
avid: *an avid reader*
devoted: *a devoted Star Trek fan*
eager: *He is eager to learn more about computers*
excited: *We are very excited about getting a new dog*
keen: *Dave is a keen angler*
passionate: *a passionate opponent of the government*
see also **active, ardent, eager, excited, fervent, keen**

entice see **attract, lure, tempt**

entire see **complete, whole**

entirely see **quite**

entrails see **insides**

entrance noun 1 the way into a particular place: *I met Barry at the entrance to the station*
door: *She was waiting by the front door*
doorway: *the mass of people blocking the doorway*
entry: *Kevin had been hanging round the back entry for hours*
gate: *the security guard at the main gate*

way in: *Is this the way in?*

2 a person's arrival somewhere: *She had failed to notice her father's entrance*

appearance: *She had timed her appearance at the dinner to perfection*

arrival: *journalists awaiting the arrival of the team*

entry: *He was arrested on his entry into Mexico*

3 the right to enter somewhere: *He gained entrance to the hotel where the band were staying*

access: *We were denied access to the stadium*

admission: *no admission without a ticket*

entry: *I was unable to gain entry to the meeting*

▷ *verb* **4** to amaze and delight someone: *The audience were entranced by her voice*

bewitch: *Young Gordon's smile bewitched everyone*

captivate: *I was captivated by her piercing blue eyes*

charm: *He charmed Mr Darnley and made him feel young again*

delight: *a CD that will delight her many fans*

enthral: *Audiences were enthralled by his spectacular stage act*

fascinate: *She never failed to fascinate him*
see also **charm, entry**

entry *noun* **1** a person's arrival somewhere: *her dramatic entry*

appearance: *She made her appearance to tumultuous applause*

arrival: *He apologized for his late arrival*

entrance: *My entrance was spoiled when I tripped over the carpet*

2 the way into a particular place: *He was hanging around at the entry to the station*

door: *I'll meet you at the front door*

doorway: *A bicycle was blocking the doorway*

entrance: *The bomb had been left outside the entrance to the building*

gate: *Guards were posted at the main gate*

way in: *I can't find the way in*

3 something that has been written down: *the final entry in his journal*

item: *A number of interesting items appear in his diary*

note: *He grunted and made a note in his pocket book*

record: *There is no record for 13 October in the log book*
see also **entrance**

envelop *see* **surround**

envious *see* **jealous**

environment *see* **background, habitat, scene, surroundings**

envisage *see* **contemplate, imagine**

envoy *see* **messenger**

envy *noun* **1** a feeling of resentment about what someone else has: *his feelings of envy towards Kevin*

jealousy: *the jealousy people felt towards him because of his money*

resentment: *All the anger, bitterness and resentment suddenly melted away*

▷ *verb* **2** to want something that someone else has: *I don't envy you one bit*

be envious: *people who were envious of her good fortune*

begrudge: *Surely you don't begrudge me one night out*

be jealous: *I couldn't help being jealous when I knew he had won*

covet: *He coveted his job*

resent: *Anyone with money was resented and ignored*

ephemeral *see* **temporary**

epidemic *see* **rash**

episode *see* **event, experience, incident**

epithet see name

epitome see ideal, model, ultimate

equal adjective **1** the same in size, amount, or value: *equal numbers of men and women*

equivalent: *A kilogram is equivalent to 2.2 pounds*

identical: *glasses containing identical amounts of water*

the same: *different areas of research that have the same importance*

▷ verb **2** to be as good as something else: *a time that equalled the European record*

be equal to: *The final score is equal to his personal best*

match: *able to match her previous time for the 100m*

see also even, fair, rival, same

equally see alike

equal to adjective having the necessary ability for something: *She was equal to any task they gave her*

capable of: *I'm no longer capable of this kind of work*

up to: *He said he wasn't up to a long walk*

equilibrium see balance

equine see horse

equip verb to supply someone with something: *The boat was equipped with an outboard motor*

arm: *The children arrived armed with a range of gardening tools*

endow: *The male bird is endowed with a vicious-looking beak*

fit out: *the amount spent on fitting out their offices*

provide: *We provided them with waterproofs and sandwiches*

supply: *They supplied us with camping gear and a stove*

see also issue, provide, supply

equipment noun the things you need for a particular job: *a shed full of gardening equipment*

apparatus: *All the firemen were wearing breathing apparatus*

gear: *Police in riot gear have sealed off the area*

paraphernalia: *ashtrays, lighters and other paraphernalia associated with smoking*

stuff: *The builders had left all their stuff in the garden*

tackle: *Martin kept all his fishing tackle in the spare room*

see also stuff, supplies

equitable see fair

equity see balance, justice, right

equivalence see balance

equivalent see equal, same

eradicate see banish, eliminate

erase see delete, remove

erect see assemble, build, construct, straight

erode verb to wear something away and destroy it: *The cliffs were being eroded by the constant pounding of the sea*

corrode: *buildings corroded by acid rain*

destroy: *ancient monuments destroyed by pollution*

deteriorate: *The tapestry had deteriorated badly where the roof was leaking*

disintegrate: *Once they were exposed to light the documents rapidly disintegrated*

eat away: *The chemicals in the water had eaten away the cables*

wear away: *rocks worn away by the action of the wind*

wear down: *Some of her teeth were worn down with gnawing on the bars*

see also eat away, wash, wear

erosion see wear

erotic see sexy

err verb to make a mistake: *The builders had erred considerably in their original estimate*

blunder: Fletcher had obviously blundered

go wrong: We must have gone wrong somewhere in our calculations

make a mistake: Okay, I made a mistake, I'm only human

miscalculate: They miscalculated, and now they're in deep trouble

erratic see **changeable, irregular**

erroneous see **false, untrue**

error noun a mistake: a mathematical error

blunder: He made a tactical blunder by announcing his intentions

fault: It is a fault to think you can learn how to manage people in business school

lapse: a serious security lapse

mistake: spelling mistakes

slip: We must be careful – we can't afford any slips

see also **hole, mistake, slip**

erudite see **learned**

erupt see **burst**

eruption see **outbreak, rash**

escalate see **jump**

escape verb 1 to manage to get away: Three prisoners who escaped have given themselves up

break free: He was handcuffed to his bed, but somehow managed to break free

break out: two prisoners who broke out of the maximum security wing

get away: She got away from her guards

make your escape: We made our escape down a drainpipe using knotted sheets

run away: I called him but he just ran away

run off: The children ran off when they spotted me

2 to manage to avoid something: He was lucky to escape injury

avoid: She has managed to avoid

dodge: He dodged his military service by pretending to be ill

duck: a pathetic attempt to duck her responsibilities

elude: He managed to elude the police for 13 years

evade: He has now been charged with evading tax

▷ noun 3 something that distracts you from something unpleasant: Cycling gives me an escape from the routine of work

distraction: a distraction from his troubles

diversion: a pleasant diversion from my studies

relief: The piano provides relief from all the stress

see also **bolt, flee, leak**

eschew see **avoid**

escort see **accompany, guide, lead, take**

essence noun 1 the most basic and important part of something: The essence of good management is the ability to listen

core: the need to get to the core of the problem

heart: a problem that reaches to the very heart of the party

nature: the nature of what it is to be European

soul: a song that captures the soul of this proud nation

spirit: the spirit of modern manhood

2 a concentrated liquid: vanilla essence

concentrate: orange concentrate

extract: lemon extract

essential adjective 1 extremely important: Good ventilation is essential in a greenhouse

crucial: Her speech was a crucial part of the campaign

indispensable: She has become

indispensable to the department

vital: *a vital aspect of the plans that everyone has overlooked*

2 basic and important: *an essential part of any child's development*

basic: *the basic laws of physics*

cardinal: *He had broken one of the cardinal rules of physics*

fundamental: *the fundamental principles of democracy*

key: *Mollison had a key role to play in the negotiations*

main: *an attempt to analyse the main points of his theory*

principal: *the principal idea that underpins their argument*

see also **basic, necessary, requirement, vital**

essentials plural noun the things that are most important: *We only had enough food money for the essentials*

basics: *We need to get back to basics*

fundamentals: *the fundamentals of road safety*

necessities: *Water, food, and shelter are the necessities of life*

prerequisites: *Self-confidence is one of the prerequisites for a happy life*

rudiments: *teaching him the rudiments of car maintenance*

establish see **determine, form, organize, prove, set up, start**

established see **certain, set, traditional**

establishment see **business, company, enterprise, introduction**

estate see **grounds, land, legacy, possessions, property**

esteem noun admiration and respect for another person: *He is held in high esteem by his colleagues*

admiration: *I have always had the greatest admiration for him*

estimation: *He has gone down in my estimation*

regard: *I had a very high regard for*

him and his work

respect: *I have tremendous respect for Dean*

reverence: *He is still spoken of with reverence by those who knew him*

see also **admiration, approval, favour, prize, respect**

esteemed see **dear**

estimate noun a guess at an amount, quantity, or outcome: *This figure is five times the original estimate*

appraisal: *an appraisal of your financial standing*

assessment: *assessments of mortgaged property*

estimation: *The first group were correct in their estimation of the man's height*

guess: *He examined her and made a guess at her temperature*

quote: *Never agree to a job without getting a quote first*

reckoning: *By my reckoning we were seven kilometres from the town*

valuation: *The valuations reflect prices at the end of the fiscal year*

see also **guess, judge, price, reckon, tender, value**

estimated see **approximate, rough**

estimation see **esteem, estimate, opinion**

eternal adjective lasting forever: *the secret of eternal life*

everlasting: *everlasting love*

immortal: *your immortal soul*

unchanging: *the unchanging laws of the cosmos*

see also **constant, continual, infinite, permanent**

ethics see **standards**

ethnic group see **race**

etiquette see **ceremony, convention, politeness**

euphoria see **ecstasy**

evacuate see **empty**

evacuation see **retreat**

evade see **avoid, dodge, escape**

evaluate see **judge, value**

evaporate see **melt, vanish**

even adjective **1** flat and level: *I need an even surface to write on*

flat: *a small flat with a flat roof*

horizontal: *He drew a series of horizontal lines on the paper*

level: *checking the floor to make sure it was level*

smooth: *the smooth marble floor tiles*

2 without changing or varying: *an even flow of liquid*

constant: *The temperature remained more or less constant*

regular: *her quiet, regular breathing*

smooth: *He caught the ball and passed it in one smooth motion*

steady: *a steady stream of people*

uniform: *The price rises are not uniform across the country*

3 the same: *At half-time the scores were still even*

equal: *The two teams shared equal points into the second round*

identical: *At the end of the contest, our scores were identical*

level: *The scores were level at half-time*

neck and neck: *They're still neck and neck with two minutes to go*

see also **constant, regular, steady, straight**

even though see **in spite of**

event noun **1** something that happens: *still amazed at the events of last week*

affair: *He preferred to forget the whole affair*

business: *Do you remember that business with Jim?*

circumstance: *due to circumstances beyond our control*

episode: *a rather embarrassing episode at Yvonne's wedding*

experience: *an experience that*

changed his mind about going to university

incident: *the incident in the restaurant*

matter: *She doesn't seem to be taking this matter seriously*

2 a competition: *The next event is the long jump*

bout: *This is his fifth heavyweight bout in three months*

competition: *the first competition of the afternoon*

contest: *She's out of the contest for good*

see also **affair, competition, incident, occasion**

eventual see **final, ultimate**

eventually see **finally**

everlasting see **eternal, infinite**

every now and then see **sometimes**

every one see **all**

every so often see **sometimes**

every time see **always**

everyday adjective usual or ordinary: *the drudgery of everyday life*

common: *a common occurrence*

daily: *In our daily life we follow predictable patterns of behaviour*

day-to-day: *I use a lot of spices in my day-to-day cooking*

mundane: *the mundane realities of life*

ordinary: *ordinary tableware*

routine: *routine maintenance of the machine*

see also **colloquial, common, frequent, natural, regular, routine**

everything see **all, whole**

evict see **banish**

evidence see **proof, sign, trace**

evident adjective easily noticed or understood: *He spoke with evident emotion about his ordeal*

apparent: *He spoke with apparent nonchalance about his experience*

clear: It became clear that I hadn't convinced Mike

noticeable: a noticeable effect

obvious: It's obvious that he doesn't like me

palpable: The tension between Jim and Amy is palpable

plain: It was plain to him that she was having a nervous breakdown

visible: the most visible sign of her distress

see also **clear, conspicuous, naked, noticeable, obvious, plain, visible**

evil noun **1** the force that causes bad things to happen: the conflict between good and evil

badness: behaving that way out of sheer badness

immorality: the immorality that is typical of the arms trade

sin: The whole town is a den of sin and corruption

vice: a place long associated with vice and immorality

wickedness: the wickedness of his behaviour

2 something unpleasant or harmful: a lecture on the evils of alcohol

affliction: Hay fever is an affliction that affects thousands

ill: Many of the nation's ills are his responsibility

misery: the misery of drug addiction

sorrow: the joys and sorrows of family life

▷ adjective **3** morally wrong or bad: an utterly evil man

bad: He's not a bad man, he's just very unhappy

depraved: a throughly depraved film

malevolent: a malevolent influence on the whole school

sinful: He is a good person in a sinful world

vile: vile acts of brutality

wicked: a wicked attack on a helpless child

see also **sin, sinister, wicked, wrong**

evoke see **excite, provoke**

evolve see **develop**

exact adjective **1** correct in every detail: It's an exact reproduction of the first steam engine

accurate: an accurate description of the man

authentic: authentic Elizabethan costumes

faithful: faithful copies of ancient stone tools

faultless: She spoke with a faultless French accent

precise: It's difficult to give a precise date for the painting

true: Is this a true picture of life in the Middle Ages?

▷ verb **2** formal to demand and obtain something: They are certain to exact a high price for their cooperation

command: an excellent surgeon who commanded the respect of all his colleagues

extract: to extract the maximum political advantage from this situation

impose: the first council to impose a fine for dropping litter

insist on: She insisted on conducting all the interviews herself

insist upon: He insists upon good service

wring: attempts to wring concessions from the government

see also **accurate, correct, faithful, particular, precise, right, strict**

exacting see **fussy, particular, stiff, tough**

exactly adverb **1** with complete accuracy and precision: He arrived at exactly five o'clock

accurately: We cannot accurately predict where the missile will land

faithfully: I translated the play as faithfully as I could

just: There are no statistics about just how many people won't vote
on the dot: At nine o'clock on the dot, they have breakfast
precisely: No-one knows precisely how many people are in the camp
quite: That wasn't quite what I meant
▷ interjection **2** an expression implying total agreement: "We'll never know the answer." – "Exactly. So let's stop speculating."
absolutely: "It's worrying, isn't it?" – "Absolutely."
indeed: "That's a topic that's getting a lot of media coverage." – "Indeed."
precisely: "So, you're suggesting we do away with these laws?" – "Precisely."
quite: "It's your choice, isn't it?" – "Quite."
see also **prompt**

exaggerate verb to make things seem worse than they are: He thinks I'm exaggerating, but I'm not!
overdo: I think he's overdoing it a bit when he complains like that
overestimate: I think we're overestimating their desire to cooperate
overstate: It's impossible to overstate the seriousness of this situation

exaggerated see **excessive**
exaltation see **ecstasy**
exam noun a test to find out how much you know: a maths exam
examination: a three-hour written examination
oral: I got good marks for my French oral
test: I failed my history test again
examination noun **1** a careful inspection of something: The Navy is carrying out an examination of the wreck
analysis: An analysis of the ash revealed traces of lead oxide

inspection: The police inspection of the vehicle found no fingerprints
study: A study of the wreckage has thrown new light on the crash
2 a check carried out on someone by a doctor: The doctor suggested an immediate examination of his ear
check: a quick check just to make sure everything's working properly
checkup: my annual checkup at the clinic
medical: He had a medical before leaving England
see also **check, exam, research, review**

examine verb **1** to look at something very carefully: Police scientists are examining the scene of the crash
analyse: We haven't had time to analyse all the samples yet
go over: I'll go over your report tomorrow
go through: We went through his belongings and found a notebook
inspect: Customs officials inspected the vehicle
look over: Once we've looked the house over we should know what caused the fire
study: Experts are studying the frozen remains of a mammoth
▷ noun **2** to give someone a medical examination: I was examined by several specialists
check: Dr Mollison checked my nose and throat
inspect: I was inspected twice by Dr Stevens
look at: He said he wanted to look at my chest again just to make sure
test: They tested my eyes but my vision was fine
see also **check, contemplate, inspect, interrogate, investigate, question, research, scrutinize, study**

example noun 1 something that represents a group of things: some examples of medieval wood carving

illustration: Lo's success is an illustration of how well China is doing

sample: This drawing is a sample of his early work

specimen: I had to submit a specimen of my handwriting for analysis

2 something that people can imitate: His dedication is an example to us all

ideal: a woman who was the American ideal of beauty

model: His conduct at the talks was a model of dignity

paragon: She is a paragon of neatness and efficiency

prototype: He was the prototype of the English gentleman

see also **case, ideal, model**

exasperate see **irritate**

excavate see **dig**

exceed see **pass, top**

exceeding see **above, over**

excellence see **merit**

excellent adjective extremely good: It's an excellent book, one of my favourites

beaut Australian, New Zealand informal: a beaut spot to live

brilliant: What a brilliant film!

cracking British, Australian, New Zealand informal: You've done a cracking job in the garden!

fine: There's a fine view from the bedroom window

first-class: a first-class effort

great: He's a great player and we'll be sorry to lose him

outstanding: an outstanding performance

superb: a superb craftsman

see also **exceptional, fine, first-rate, marvellous, outstanding, splendid, superb, wonderful**

except preposition apart from: I don't drink, except for the occasional glass of wine

apart from: The room was empty apart from one man seated by the fire

but: He didn't speak anything but Greek

other than: She makes no reference to any research other than her own

save formal: We had almost nothing to eat, save the few berries and nuts we could find

with the exception of: Yesterday was a day off for everybody, with the exception of Tom

see also **but**

except for see **but**

exception see **qualification**

exceptional adjective 1 unusually excellent, talented, or clever: His piano playing is exceptional

excellent: The recording quality is excellent

extraordinary: He is an extraordinary musician

outstanding: an outstanding athlete

phenomenal: The performances have been absolutely phenomenal

remarkable: a remarkable achievement

talented: He is a talented violinist

2 unusual and likely to happen very rarely: The courts hold that this case is exceptional

isolated: They said the allegations related to an isolated case

out of the ordinary: I've noticed nothing out of the ordinary

rare: those rare occasions when he did eat alone

special: In special cases, an exception to this rule may be made

unheard-of: buying rum at the unheard-of rate of $2 per bottle

unusual: To be appreciated as a parent is unusual

see also **extreme, first-rate, outstanding, particular, rare, singular, special, superior, uncommon, unusual**

excerpt see **extract, passage**

excess noun **1** behaviour that goes beyond what is acceptable: *a life of excess*

extravagance: *Examples of her extravagance were everywhere*

indulgence: *a moment of sheer indulgence*

2 a larger amount than necessary: *An excess of houseplants made the room look like a jungle*

glut: *the current glut of dairy products in Europe*

overdose: *An overdose of sun can lead to skin problems later*

surfeit: *A surfeit of rich food did not help his digestive problems*

surplus: *Germany suffers from a surplus of teachers at the moment*

▷ adjective **3** more than is needed: *problems associated with excess weight*

extra: *Pour any extra liquid into a bowl and set aside*

superfluous: *all our superfluous belongings – things we don't need*

surplus: *Farmers have to sell off their surplus stock cheap*

see also **extra**

excessive adjective too great: *an excessive reliance on government funding*

enormous: *She spent an enormous amount on clothes*

exaggerated: *the exaggerated claims made by their supporters*

needless: *a film that is full of needless violence*

undue: *the need to avoid undue expense*

unreasonable: *unreasonable increases in the price of petrol*

see also **extreme, steep**

excessively see **too**

exchange verb **1** to give something in return for something else: *We exchanged phone numbers*

barter: *Traders came from everywhere to barter in the markets*

change: *Can you change these euros for pounds?*

swap: *I wouldn't swap places with her for anything!*

switch: *They switched cars and were away before the alarm was raised*

trade: *a secret deal to trade arms for hostages*

▷ noun **2** the act of giving something for something else: *a ceasefire to allow the exchange of prisoners*

interchange: *a meeting at which the interchange of ideas was encouraged*

swap: *They agreed to a swap and made the necessary arrangements*

switch: *The switch went ahead as planned*

trade: *I am willing to make a trade with you*

see also **change, substitute, swap**

exchange views on see **discuss**

excise see **duty, tax**

excite verb **1** to make someone feel enthusiastic or nervous: *The idea of visiting America really excited the kids*

agitate: *I've no idea what has agitated him*

animate: *There was plenty about this match to animate the capacity crowd*

thrill: *The reception he got at the meeting thrilled him*

titillate: *a meal that will titillate the taste buds of every gourmet*

2 to cause a particular feeling or reaction: *The meeting failed to excite strong feelings in anyone*

arouse: *a move that has aroused deep public anger*

elicit: *His proposal elicited a storm*

of protest

evoke: The film has evoked a sense of nostalgia in many older people

incite: a crude attempt to incite racial hatred

inspire: The handling of the new car quickly inspires confidence

provoke: The suggestion has provoked anger

stir up: He's just trying to stir up trouble

see also **thrill**

excited adjective happy and unable to relax: We are very excited about getting a new dog

agitated: in an excited and agitated state

enthusiastic: Tom usually seems very enthusiastic

feverish: a state of feverish anticipation

high informal: I was feeling really high after Lorraine's party

thrilled: The children were thrilled when the snow came

see also **enthusiastic**

excitement noun interest and enthusiasm: The release of his latest film has caused great excitement

activity: a scene of frenzied activity

adventure: setting off in search of adventure

agitation: He reacted to the news with considerable agitation

commotion: We decided to find out what all the commotion was about

enthusiasm: They greeted our arrival with enthusiasm

thrill: the thrill of scuba diving

see also **bustle, enthusiasm, heat, passion**

exciting adjective making you feel happy and enthusiastic: the most exciting race I've ever seen

dramatic: Their arrival was dramatic and exciting

electrifying: It was an electrifying performance

exhilarating: an exhilarating walk along the cliff tops

rousing: a rousing speech

stimulating: It's a stimulating book, full of ideas

thrilling: a thrilling opportunity to watch the lions as they feed

see also **impressive**

exclaim see **cry**

exclamation see **cry**

exclude verb 1 to decide not to include something: We cannot exclude this possibility altogether

eliminate: We can eliminate Mr Darnley from our list of suspects

ignore: We cannot afford to ignore this option

leave out: We can narrow it down by leaving out everywhere that's too expensive

omit: His name seems to have been omitted from the list

rule out: The police have already ruled out a retrial

2 to stop someone going somewhere or doing something: The university used to exclude women from all lectures

ban: Tony was banned from driving for three years

bar: She was barred from the tennis club

forbid: Carver was forbidden to attend any of the society's meetings

keep out: We need to keep out troublemakers

see also **ban, boycott, forbid, omit**

exclusive adjective available only to a few rich people: one of Britain's most exclusive golf clubs

chic: a chic nightclub in Monaco

classy: a very classy restaurant

posh informal: She took me to a posh hotel to celebrate

select: *a very lavish and very select party*
up-market: *The area is much more up-market than it used to be*
see also **posh, private, select**
excruciating see **painful**
excursion see **drive, journey, ramble, trip**
excuse *noun* **1** a reason or explanation: *Stop making excuses and get on with it!*
explanation: *You'd better have a good explanation for your conduct*
justification: *What possible justification can there be for this?*
pretext: *His pretext for leaving early was an upset stomach*
reason: *This gave me the perfect reason for visiting London*
▷ *verb* **2** to forgive someone or someone's behaviour: *Please excuse my late arrival*
forgive: *Forgive me, I'm so sorry*
overlook: *the need to overlook each other's failings*
pardon: *Pardon my ignorance, but who is Cliff Hanley?*
turn a blind eye to: *We can't be expected to turn a blind eye to this behaviour*
see also **defence, forgive, grounds, justify**
excuse yourself see **decline**
excused see **exempt**
execute see **administer, do, kill, perform**
executive see **manager, official**
exempt *adjective* excused from a duty or rule: *Teachers were exempt from military service*
excused: *Some MPs will have been officially excused attendance*
immune: *Members of the parliament are immune from prosecution*
not liable: *They are not liable to pay income tax*

see also **immune**
exemption see **freedom**
exercise *noun* activity that keeps you fit: *I need to get more exercise*
activity: *a bit of physical activity to get the heart going*
exertion: *I'm tired out by all this exertion*
training: *He needs to do a bit more training before the match*
work: *I'm doing a lot more work at the gym now I'm feeling better*
see also **practice**
exertion see **effort, exercise, labour**
exhaust *verb* **1** to make very tired: *I mustn't exhaust myself as I did last time*
drain: *My emotional turmoil had drained me*
fatigue: *He is easily fatigued*
tire out: *a great new job that tires me out*
wear out: *Living out of a suitcase wears you out*
2 to use something up completely: *She has exhausted all my patience*
consume: *plans which will consume hours of time*
deplete: *chemicals that deplete the earth's protective ozone shield*
run through: *The project ran through its funds in months*
use up: *The gas has all been used up*
see also **drain, tax, tire, wear out**
exhausted see **tired, weary, worn-out**
exhausting see **hard**
exhaustive see **full, thorough**
exhibit see **bear**
exhibition see **fair, show**
exhilarating see **exciting**
exile see **banish**
exist see **live, occur**
existence see **life**
exotic see **foreign, strange, unfamiliar**

expand verb to make or become larger: *The rails expanded and buckled in the fierce heat*

develop: *We need to develop the company's engineering division*

enlarge: *Plans to enlarge the stadium have been approved*

extend: *We're trying to extend our range of sports wear*

fill out: *The balloon had filled out and was already almost airborne*

grow: *The Japanese share of the market has grown dramatically*

increase: *We will need to increase our overseas operations*

swell: *The river had swollen rapidly*

see also **bulge, elaborate, enlarge, extend, grow, increase, spread**

expand on verb to give more information about something: *an idea that I will expand on later*

develop: *You should develop this theme a little bit further*

elaborate on: *He refused to elaborate on what he had said earlier*

enlarge on: *I'd like you to enlarge on that last point*

see also **enlarge on**

expanse see **amount, area, stretch**

expansion see **growth, spread**

expansive see **broad, extensive, spacious**

expect verb 1 to believe that something is going to happen: *The trial is expected to last several weeks*

anticipate: *We do not anticipate any problems*

assume: *He assumed that they would wait for him*

believe: *Experts believe the comet will pass close to the earth*

imagine: *The meal cost more than we had imagined*

presume: *I presume they'll be along shortly*

reckon: *We reckon it'll be a fairly quick journey*

think: *I thought the concert would be cancelled*

2 to believe that something is your right: *I was expecting to have a bit of time to myself*

demand: *a job that demands a lot of time and money*

rely on: *I'm relying on you to help me*

require: *They require a lot of her, maybe too much*

see also **figure, suppose**

expectation see **hope, prospect**

expected see **likely, supposed**

expedient see **measure**

expedition see **journey**

expel see **banish, discharge**

expense see **cost**

expensive adjective costing a lot of money: *a very expensive Italian suit*

costly: *a costly court case*

dear: *Those trainers are far too dear*

pricey: *Medical insurance can be very pricey*

see also **dear, precious, valuable**

experience noun 1 knowledge or skill in a particular activity: *We're looking for someone with engineering experience*

expertise: *They lack the expertise to deal with such a complex case*

know-how: *Her technical know-how was invaluable*

knowledge: *We need someone with knowledge of computing*

training: *His military training made the difference between life and death*

understanding: *someone with considerable understanding of the law*

2 something that happens to you: *a terrifying experience that she still talks about*

adventure: *a series of hair-raising adventures during the war*

affair: *He seemed keen to forget the affair and never discussed it*

encounter: his first encounter with alcohol

episode: The episode has proved deeply embarrassing for him

incident: an incident he would rather forget

ordeal: a painful ordeal that is now over

▷ verb **3** to have something happen to you: We are experiencing a few technical problems

encounter: The storms were the worst they had ever encountered

have: We're having a few difficulties with the computer

meet: The next time you meet a situation like this, be careful

undergo: The market is now undergoing a severe recession

see also **endure, event, feel, go through, have, suffer, undergo**

experienced adjective very skilful as a result of practice: an experienced diver

expert: an expert pilot

knowledgeable: He's very knowledgeable in this field

practised: a practised and accomplished surgeon

seasoned: a seasoned climber

well-versed: He is well-versed in many styles of jazz

see also **expert, practical, skilled**

expert noun **1** a skilled or knowledgeable person: A team of experts will be on hand to offer advice

ace informal: former motor-racing ace Stirling Moss

authority: an authority on ancient Egypt

buff informal: Cliff is a bit of a film buff

guru: fashion gurus who predicted a 70s revival

master: He is a master in the art of office politics

professional: He's widely respected in the theatre as a true professional

specialist: a specialist in tropical diseases

wizard: a financial wizard who made millions in the early 80s

▷ adjective **2** skilled and knowledgeable: Mollison's expert approach impressed everyone

able: an able and dedicated surgeon

adept: He's an adept guitar player

experienced: He was an experienced traveller and knew the area well

knowledgeable: He's very knowledgeable about Chinese pottery

proficient: Jackson is proficient in several European languages

skilful: the skilful use of light in his early paintings

skilled: Ian is a highly skilled photographer

see also **able, experienced, fundi, perfect, skilful, skilled**

expertise see **ability, experience, skill**

expertly see **well**

expire see **die**

explain verb to give extra information about something: He explained to us how the system worked

define: Can you define what you mean by 'excessive'?

describe: an attempt to describe the whole process

illustrate: Let me illustrate this point with an example

see also **justify**

explanation noun a helpful or clear description: his lucid explanation of Einstein's theories

clarification: Her clarification has done little to help matters

definition: a definition of what we actually mean by 'symbolism'

description: a fascinating description of how the pyramids were built

exposition: the fullest available exposition of Coleridge's ideas

see also **defence, excuse, statement**

explicit see **clear**

explode verb **1** to burst or cause to burst loudly: the sound of a bomb exploding nearby

blow up: Their boat blew up as they slept

burst: Joey blew up the balloon until it burst

detonate: Troops managed to detonate the mine safely

go off: The bomb went off without any warning

set off: No-one knows who planted the bomb, or how it was set off

2 to become angry suddenly: I asked him if he'd finished and he just exploded

blow up: When she finally told him, he blew up and walked out

go berserk: He'll go berserk if he ever finds out

go mad: He went mad when I mentioned the kids

3 to increase suddenly and rapidly: Sales of computer games have exploded in recent years

rocket: Inflation has rocketed in the last few months

shoot up: Prices shot up and the shelves were soon empty

soar: Demand for shares in his new company has soared

see also **burst, fire**

exploit see **achievement, action, profit**

exploitation see **abuse**

exploration see **research**

explore see **investigate, research**

explosion noun a violent burst of energy: The explosion shattered windows all along the street

bang: A loud bang made me run for cover

blast: Three people were killed in the blast

see also **bang, outbreak**

explosive see **bomb**

expose verb **1** to make something visible: The wreck was exposed by the action of the tide

reveal: His shirt was open, revealing his tattooed chest

show: a short skirt which showed too much of her legs

uncover: She removed her scarf and uncovered her head

2 to tell the truth about someone or something: He has been exposed as a liar and a cheat

bring to light: The truth will be brought to light eventually

reveal: an investigation that revealed widespread corruption

show up: She was finally shown up as a hypocrite

uncover: We uncovered evidence of fraud

unearth: Investigators have unearthed new evidence

see also **betray, subject, uncover**

exposed see **bare, vulnerable**

exposition see **explanation**

express verb **1** to say what you think: She expressed interest in the plans for the new dam

communicate: People must learn to communicate their feelings

couch: Their demands, though extreme, are couched in moderate language

phrase: It sounds fine, but I would have phrased it differently

put: Absolutely – I couldn't have put it better

put across: the need to put across your message without offending anyone

voice: Local people have voiced their concern over plans for a bypass

▷ adjective **2** very fast: *a special express delivery service*

direct: *There's also a direct train*

fast: *delays due to an accident in the fast lane*

high-speed: *the high-speed rail link between London and Paris*

nonstop: *the new nonstop service to New York*

see also **convey, particular, state, swift**

express regret see **apologize**

expression noun **1** the look on your face that shows your feelings: *an aggrieved expression*

countenance: *the beaming countenance of the prime minister*

face: *Why are you all wearing such long faces?*

2 a word or phrase used to communicate: *a good old American expression*

idiom: *idioms such as 'it's raining cats and dogs'*

phrase: *What is the origin of the phrase?*

remark: *her passing remark to the camera*

term: *a derogatory term for an Arab*

see also **look, term**

expulsion see **discharge**

exquisite see **superb**

extend verb **1** to have a particular size or position: *The region will extend way beyond the capital*

continue: *The caves continue for miles beneath the hills*

hang: *The branches hang down to the ground*

reach: *a long shirt that reached to her knees*

stretch: *an area of forest stretching as far as the eye could see*

2 to stick out: *a brass peg that extended from the end of the mast*

jut out: *The tip of the island juts out like a finger into the sea*

project: *the ruins of a fort which projected from the mud*

protrude formal: *a huge rock protruding from the surface of the lake*

stick out: *pieces of rough metal that stuck out like spikes*

3 to make something larger: *We'd like to extend the house and build a conservatory*

add to: *They will be adding to their range of children's wear*

develop: *He developed the US arm of the company*

enlarge: *plans to enlarge the conference centre*

expand: *an unsuccessful attempt to expand the store's range of footwear*

widen: *the need to widen the appeal of the scheme*

see also **build, enlarge, expand, increase, lengthen, range, spread, stretch**

extend to see **reach**

extended see **continuous**

extensive adjective **1** covering a large area: *a manor house set in extensive grounds*

broad: *a broad expanse of green lawn*

expansive: *an expansive grassy play area*

large: *a large country estate*

spacious: *a spacious dining area*

sweeping: *the sweeping curve of the bay*

vast: *vast stretches of land*

wide: *Worktops should be wide enough to allow food preparation*

2 very great in effect: *The blast caused extensive damage*

comprehensive: *comprehensive television coverage of last week's events*

considerable: *He has considerable powers within the party*

far-reaching: *a decision with far-reaching consequences*

great: great changes in British society

pervasive: the pervasive influence of the army in national life

untold: This might do untold damage to her health

widespread: There is widespread support for the proposals

see also **broad, full, spacious, widespread**

extent noun the length, area, or size of something: The full extent of the losses was revealed yesterday

degree: To what degree were you in control of these events?

level: the level of public concern over this issue

measure: The full measure of the government's dilemma has become apparent

scale: He underestimates the scale of the problem

size: the size of the task

see also **area, length, quantity, range, size, spread, stretch**

exterior see **face, front, outside**

exterminate see **kill**

external see **outside**

extinct see **dead**

extortionate see **steep**

extra adjective 1 more than is usual or expected: The company is taking on extra staff for the summer

added: The Tandoori Cottage has the added advantage of being cheap

additional: the need for additional funding

excess: If there's any excess sauce, you can freeze it

further: the introduction of further restrictions

more: We need three more places at the table

new: the burden of new legislation on top of all the recent changes

spare: There are spare blankets in the cupboard

▷ noun 2 something that is not included with other things: Air conditioning is an optional extra

accessory: the accessories you have to buy to make the place look good

addition: the latest addition to the team

bonus: The view from the hotel was an added bonus

see also **excess, luxury, more, spare, supplement**

extract verb 1 to take or get something out of somewhere: Citric acid can be extracted from orange juice

draw: Villagers still have to draw their water from wells

mine: the finest gems, mined from all corners of the world

obtain: Opium is obtained from poppies

pull out: I can pull that information out of the database for you

remove: Three bullets were removed from his wounds

take out: I got an abscess so he took the tooth out

2 to get information from someone: He tried to extract further information from the witness

draw: They finally drew a confession from him

elicit formal: the question of how far police should go to elicit a confession

get: How did you get an admission like that out of her?

glean: We're gleaning information from all sources

obtain: Police have obtained statements from several witnesses

▷ noun 3 a small section of music or writing: an extract from his latest novel

excerpt: an excerpt from Tchaikovsky's Nutcracker

passage: He read out a passage from Milton

reading: The author treated us to a

reading from his latest novel

section: Let's study a section of the text in more detail

snatch: We played them a snatch of a violin concerto

snippet: snippets of popular classical music

see also **essence, exact, passage, quote, remove, withdraw**

extraction see **origin, stock**

extraordinary adjective
unusual or surprising: He really is an extraordinary man

amazing: What an amazing coincidence!

bizarre: It's such a bizarre thing to happen

odd: It's an odd combination of colours

singular: Cathy gave me a smile of singular sweetness

strange: It's a strange piece of music

surprising: A surprising number of women prefer to wear trousers to work

unusual: It's a most unusual way to spend your holiday

see also **bizarre, curious, exceptional, incredible, singular, strange, uncommon, unusual, weird**

extravagance see **excess, luxury, waste**

extravagant see **extreme, fancy, ostentatious, wasteful**

extreme adjective 1 very great in degree or intensity: those people living in extreme poverty

acute: a mistake that caused acute embarrassment for everyone concerned

deep: a decision that caused deep resentment

dire: He is in dire need of hospital treatment

great: a change in the law that could cause many people great hardship

intense: A number of people collapsed in the intense heat that day

profound: feelings of profound shock and anger

severe: a business with severe financial problems

2 unusual or unreasonable: I think that's rather an extreme reaction

drastic: Let's not do anything too drastic

exceptional: I think this is an exceptional case

excessive: a newspaper feature about the use of excessive force by the police

extravagant: All that money being spent on hospitality seemed a bit extravagant

radical: The government is introducing a series of radical economic reforms

unreasonable: I don't think she's being the least bit unreasonable

▷ noun 3 the highest or furthest degree or point: We're just going from one extreme to the other

boundary: the boundaries of artistic freedom

depth: the beauty of the countryside in the depths of winter

end: There are extremist groups at both ends of the political spectrum

height: His behaviour was the height of bad manners

limit: The ordeal tested the limits of their endurance

ultimate: A Rolls-Royce is the ultimate in luxury

see also **acute, deep, drastic, intense, serious, severe, ultimate, uncommon**

extremely see **really, very**

extremist see **fanatic**

extricate see **release**

exude see **emit**

eye see **inspect, regard**

eye-catching see **prominent**

eyesight see **sight**

eyewitness see **spectator, witness**

f

fabric see **cloth, material, substance**

fabricate see **build, invent, make, make up, manufacture**

fabrication see **lie, lying, making, manufacture**

facade see **outside**

face noun **1** the front part of the head: *A strong wind was blowing in my face*

countenance: *He met each enquiry with an impassive countenance*

features: *Her features were strongly defined*

mug slang: *He managed to get his ugly mug on the telly*

2 a surface or side of something: *the north face of Everest*

aspect: *The house had a south-west aspect*

exterior: *The exterior of the building was made of brick*

front: *There was a large veranda at the front of the house*

side: *narrow valleys with steep sides*

surface: *tiny waves on the surface of the water*

▷ verb **3** to look towards something or someone: *a room that faces on to the street*

be opposite: *I was opposite her at the breakfast table*

look at: *She turned to look at the person who was speaking*

overlook: *The pretty room overlooks a beautiful garden*

see also **brave, expression, front, look, outside**

face down see **prone**

facility see **capacity, skill**

fact noun a piece of information that is true: *a statement of verifiable fact*

certainty: *A general election became a certainty three weeks ago*

reality: *Fiction and reality became increasingly blurred*

truth: *In the town, very few know the whole truth*

see also **reality, truth**

faction see **movement, party, side**

factor noun something that helps to cause a result: *Physical activity is an important factor in maintaining fitness*

aspect: *Exam results illustrate only one aspect of a school's success*

cause: *Smoking is the biggest preventable cause of death and disease*

consideration: *Money was also a consideration*

element: *Fitness has now become an important element in our lives*

influence: *Van Gogh was a major influence on the development of modern painting*

part: *Respect is a very important part of any relationship*

see also **aspect, consideration**

factory noun a building where goods are made: *He owned furniture factories in several areas*

mill: *a textile mill*

plant: *The plant produces most of the company's output*

works: *the steel works*

facts see **information**

factual see **real, right, true**

fad see **craze, fashion, whim**

fade verb to make or become less intense: *The fabric had faded in the bright sunlight*
die away: *The sound died away gradually*
dim: *The house lights dimmed*
discolour: *Exposure to bright light can cause wallpaper to discolour*
dull: *Repeated washing had dulled the bright finish*
wash out: *This dye won't wash out*
see also **die out, disappear, vanish, wither**

fade away see **die, vanish**
fade out see **die**
faded see **faint, pale**

fail verb **1** to be unsuccessful: *He failed in his attempt to take over the company*
be defeated: *The vote to change the law was defeated*
be in vain: *It became clear that his efforts had been in vain*
be unsuccessful: *My job application was unsuccessful*
come to grief: *Many marriages have come to grief over lack of money*
fall through: *Negotiations with business leaders fell through last night*
flunk informal: *He flunked all his exams*
2 to omit to do something: *They failed to phone her*
neglect: *They never neglect their duties*
omit: *He had omitted to tell her of the change in his plans*
3 to become less effective: *His eyesight began to fail*
cease: *The secrecy about his condition had ceased to matter*
decline: *His power declined as he grew older*
give out: *All machines give out eventually*
sink: *Her spirits sank lower and lower*

stop working: *The boat came to a halt when the engine stopped working*
wane: *my mother's waning strength*
see also **collapse, neglect, weaken**

fail to notice see **miss**
fail to remember see **forget**
failing see **defect, fault**
failure noun **1** a lack of success: *to end in failure*
breakdown: *a breakdown of the talks between the parties*
defeat: *It is important not to admit defeat*
downfall: *people wishing to see the downfall of the government*
fiasco: *The evening was a total fiasco*
miscarriage: *a miscarriage of justice*
2 an unsuccessful person or thing: *The venture was a complete failure*
disappointment: *a disappointment to his family*
flop informal: *The play turned out to be a flop*
loser: *He had always been a loser*
no-hoper Australian, New Zealand: *hanging around a group of no-hopers*
3 a weakness in something: *a failure in the insurance system*
deficiency: *a serious deficiency in their defence system*
shortcoming: *The book has many shortcomings*
see also **collapse, crash**

faint adjective **1** lacking in intensity: *a faint smell of tobacco*
dim: *dim lighting*
faded: *a faded sign on the side of the building*
indistinct: *The lettering was worn and indistinct*
low: *She spoke in a low voice*
muted: *some muted cheers from the gallery*
vague: *a vague memory*
2 feeling dizzy and unsteady: *Feeling faint is one of the symptoms*

dizzy: suffering from dizzy spells
giddy: He felt giddy after the ride
light-headed: She felt light-headed because she hadn't eaten
▷ *verb* **3** to lose consciousness temporarily: to faint from shock
black out: The blood drained from his head and he blacked out
collapse: I collapsed when I heard the news
pass out: to pass out with pain
swoon *literary*: Women in the '20s swooned over Valentino
see also **dim, slender, soft, weak**

faint-hearted *see* **cowardly**

fair *adjective* **1** reasonable and just: a fair trial
equal: the commitment to equal opportunities
equitable: an equitable allocation of resources
impartial: an impartial observer
legitimate: a legitimate claim to the money
proper: It's right and proper that he should be here
upright: an upright and trustworthy man
2 having light-coloured hair or pale skin: long fair hair
blonde or **blond**: a darker shade of blonde
light: He had a light complexion and blue eyes
▷ *noun* **3** an outdoor entertainment: a country fair
bazaar: a fundraising bazaar
carnival: the annual Antigua Carnival
exhibition: an international trade exhibition
festival: a rock festival
fete: The church fete was a popular attraction
show: an agricultural show
see also **acceptable, all right, festival, light, market, moderate,**
reasonable, respectable

fairly *see* **pretty, quite, rather**

fairness *see* **justice, right**

faith *noun* **1** trust in a thing or a person: to have great faith in something
confidence: They had no confidence in the police
trust: His trust in them was misplaced
2 a person's or community's religion: They believed in the old faith
belief: united by belief
creed: open to all, regardless of creed
persuasion: people of all religious persuasions
religion: the Christian religion
see also **belief, confidence**

faithful *adjective* **1** loyal to someone or something: a faithful dog
devoted: They are devoted to each other
loyal: a sign of true and loyal friendship
staunch: a staunch member of the party
true: a true believer
2 accurate and truthful: The film was faithful to the novel
accurate: an accurate description of the event
exact: an exact copy of the original
strict: We demand strict adherence to the rules
true: The film was quite true to life
see also **accurate, devoted, exact, loyal, realistic, reliable, steadfast, trusty**

faithfully *see* **exactly**

faithless *see* **treacherous**

fake *noun* **1** a deceitful imitation of a thing or person: These paintings are fakes
copy: It isn't real, just a copy
forgery: The signature was a forgery
fraud: Many psychics are frauds
imitation: The "antique" chair is in

fact a clever imitation

reproduction: a reproduction of a famous painting

sham: The election was denounced as a sham

▷ adjective **2** imitation and not genuine: fake fur

artificial: It's made with artificial sweeteners

counterfeit: a large number of counterfeit documents

false: a false passport

imitation: bound in imitation leather

phoney or **phony** informal: He used a phoney accent

▷ verb **3** to pretend to experience something: He faked his own death

feign: to feign illness

pretend: Todd shrugged with pretended indifference

simulate: writhing around in simulated agony

see also copy, **false**, fraud, mock, phoney, pretend

fall verb **1** to descend towards the ground: The tile fell from the roof

collapse: The bridge collapsed on to the road

drop: bombs dropping from the sky

plunge: A bus plunged into the river

topple: He toppled slowly backwards

trip: She tripped and broke her leg

2 to become lower or less: Output fell by more than half

decline: a declining birth rate

decrease: The number of bankruptcies decreased last year

diminish: Resources are diminishing steadily

dwindle: his dwindling authority

plummet: plummeting share prices

subside: The flood waters have subsided

▷ noun **3** a reduction in amount: a fall in the exchange rate

decline: signs of economic decline

decrease: an overall decrease of 10%

drop: the sharp drop in export sales

reduction: The bank announced a reduction in interest rates

slump: a slump in property prices

see also decline, descend, downfall, drop, ruin, slope

fall apart see disintegrate

fall behind see lag

fall down see collapse

fall ill see develop

fall out see argue, quarrel, squabble

fall over see trip

fall through see fail

fall to see reach

fall to pieces see disintegrate

fallacy see illusion

false adjective **1** not true or correct: He gave a false name and address

erroneous: to arrive at an erroneous conclusion

fictitious: the source of the fictitious rumours

incorrect: a decision based on incorrect information

mistaken: I had a mistaken view of what had happened

untrue: The remarks were completely untrue

2 not genuine but intended to seem so: false hair

artificial: an artificial limb

bogus: their bogus insurance claim

fake: a fake tan

forged: They crossed the frontier using forged documents

simulated: a simulated display of affection

3 unfaithful and deceitful: They turned out to be false friends

deceitful: deceitful and misleading remarks

disloyal: He was accused of being disloyal to the company

insincere: A lot of actors are insincere

unfaithful: left alone by her

unfaithful husband
see also **deceptive, fake, insincere, lying, mock, phoney, two-faced, untrue, wrong**

falsehood see **lie**

falsify see **misrepresent, pretend**

fame noun the state of being very well-known: *The film brought him international fame*
eminence: *to achieve eminence as a politician*
glory: *my moment of glory*
prominence: *He came to prominence with his bestselling novel*
renown: *a singer of great renown*
reputation: *the city's reputation as a place of romance*
see also **glory, success**

familiar adjective knowing something well: *Most children are familiar with stories*
acquainted with: *Peter was well acquainted with Wordsworth*
aware of: *aware of the dangers of smoking*
knowledgeable about: *They were very knowledgeable about gardening*
versed in: *She was well versed in company law*
see also **accustomed, informal**

familiar with see **aware of**

family noun 1 a group of relatives: *My family are always supportive of me*
descendants: *Their descendants lived there for centuries*
relations: *friends and relations*
relatives: *She had relatives in many countries*
2 a group of related species: *Tigers are members of the cat family*
class: *several classes of butterflies*
classification: *The classification includes conifers*
kind: *different kinds of roses*
see also **kin, young**

famished see **hungry**

famous adjective very well known: *the most famous woman of her time*
celebrated: *his most celebrated film*
distinguished: *a distinguished academic family*
illustrious: *the most illustrious scientists of the century*
legendary: *His skills are legendary*
noted: *He is noted for his generosity*
renowned: *The area is renowned for its cuisine*
see also **prominent**

famous name see **personality**

fan noun an enthusiast about something or someone: *a fan of the new band*
adherent: *The movement was gaining adherents everywhere*
admirer: *one of her many admirers*
devotee: *a devotee of chamber music*
lover: *an art lover*
supporter: *rival football supporters*
zealot: *a religious zealot*
see also **follower, supporter**

fan out see **spread**

fanatic noun someone who is extremely enthusiastic about something: *a football fanatic*
activist: *political activists*
devotee: *a devotee of the movement*
extremist: *groups of religious extremists*
militant: *The militants took over the organization*
zealot: *He was a supporter but not a zealot*

fanatical adjective showing extreme support for something: *a fanatical patriot*
fervent: *a fervent supporter*
obsessive: *obsessive about motor racing*
passionate: *a passionate interest*
rabid: *a rabid racist group*
wild: *I am wild about this band*
see also **crazy**

fancy verb 1 to want to have or do
something: *He fancied a drink*
  be attracted to: *I am attracted to
  the idea of emigrating*
  hanker after: *to hanker after a
  bigger car*
  have a yen for: *She had a yen for
  some new clothes*
  would like: *I would really like some
  ice cream*
  ▷ adjective 2 special and elaborate:
  dressed up in fancy clothes
  decorated: *She preferred decorated
  surfaces to plain ones*
  elaborate: *his elaborate costume
  ideas*
  extravagant: *the extravagant
  frescoes in the upper church*
  intricate: *covered with intricate
  patterns*
  ornate: *an ornate picture frame*
  see also **desire, elaborate, illusion,
  whim**

fantasize *see* **daydream, imagine**

fantastic *see* **splendid**

fantasy *see* **daydream, dream,
vision**

far adverb 1 at a great distance from
something: *The sea was far below us*
  afar: *seen from afar*
  a great distance: *They travelled a
  great distance*
  a long way: *The guy's lonely and a
  long way from home*
  deep: *deep into the jungle*
  miles: *He lived miles away*
  2 to a great extent or degree: *far
  better than the others*
  considerably: *The dinners were
  considerably less formal than before*
  incomparably: *South Africa seems
  incomparably richer than the rest of
  Africa*
  much: *I feel much better now*
  very much: *Things got very much
  worse*

  ▷ adjective 3 very distant: *in the far
  south of the country*
  distant: *the distant horizon*
  long: *a long distance from here*
  outlying: *The outlying areas are
  accessible only by air*
  remote: *a cottage in a remote village*
  see also **distant**

far from *see* **unlike**

fare *see* **do, food**

far-fetched *see* **improbable,
incredible**

farmer *see* **cocky**

far-off *see* **remote**

far-reaching *see* **extensive, serious**

fascinate verb to be of intense
interest to someone: *He was
fascinated by the new discovery*
  absorb: *totally absorbed by her career*
  bewitch: *Bill was bewitched by
  her charm*
  captivate: *Her looks captivated the
  whole world*
  enthral: *She sat enthralled by the
  actors*
  intrigue: *Her story intrigued them*
  see also **appeal, entrance, interest**

fascination *see* **charm, interest**

fashion noun 1 a popular style of
dress or behaviour: *changing fashions
in clothing*
  craze: *the latest health craze*
  fad: *just a passing fad*
  style: *a revival of an old style*
  trend: *the current trend in footwear*
  vogue: *a vogue for fitness training*
  2 a manner or way of doing
something: *It works in a similar
fashion*
  manner: *in a friendly manner*
  method: *He did it by his usual
  method*
  mode: *a different mode of living*
  way: *in her usual resourceful way*
  ▷ verb 3 to make and shape
something: *fashioned from rough*

wood
construct: *an inner frame constructed from timber*
create: *It was created from odds and ends*
make: *a doll made from fabric*
mould: *They moulded the cups from clay*
shape: *Shape the dough into a loaf*
work: *a machine for working the stone*
see also **craze, form, make, manner, model, shape**

fashionable adjective very popular: *a fashionable restaurant*
current: *the current thinking on the subject*
in informal: *Jogging was the in thing*
latest: *all the latest hairstyles*
popular: *the most popular movie*
prevailing: *contrary to prevailing attitudes*
see also **current, popular, posh, trendy**

fast adjective **1** moving at great speed: *a fast train*
accelerated: *at an accelerated pace*
hurried: *He ate a hurried breakfast*
quick: *a quick learner*
rapid: *a rapid rise through the company*
speedy: *best wishes for a speedy recovery*
swift: *as swift as an arrow*
▷ adverb **2** quickly and without delay: *You'll have to move fast*
hastily: *sheltering in hastily erected tents*
hurriedly: *students hurriedly taking notes*
quickly: *She worked quickly and methodically*
rapidly: *moving rapidly across the field*
swiftly: *They had to act swiftly to save him*
3 firmly and strongly: *She held fast*

to the rail
firmly: *with windows firmly shut*
securely: *The door was securely locked and bolted*
tightly: *held tightly in his arms*
see also **express, quick, quickly, swift**

fasten verb to close or attach something: *Fasten your seat belts*
attach: *He attached a label to the plant*
fix: *It was fixed on the wall*
join: *joined together by string*
lock: *a locked door*
secure: *The chest was secured with a lock and chain*
tie: *Tie your shoelaces*
see also **attach, bond, connect, fix, hang, join, link, secure, shut, tie**

fastened see **secure, shut**
fastener see **clasp**
fastening see **clasp, connection**
fastidious see **fine, fussy, particular**

fat adjective weighing too much: *a fat man*
see **word studies fat**
see also **overweight, plump, thick, tubby**

fatal adjective **1** causing death: *fatal injuries*
deadly: *a deadly disease*
incurable: *It was regarded as an incurable illness*
lethal: *a lethal dose of sleeping pills*
mortal: *They were in mortal danger*
terminal: *terminal cancer*
2 having an undesirable effect: *The mistake was fatal to my plans*
calamitous: *a calamitous air crash*
catastrophic: *The water shortage is potentially catastrophic*
disastrous: *This could have disastrous consequences for industry*
lethal: *a lethal left hook*
see also **deadly**

fate noun a power believed to control

events: *the fickleness of fate*
chance: *a victim of chance*
destiny: *We are masters of our own destiny*
fortune: *Remember, fortune favours the brave*
providence: *His death was an act of providence*
see also **luck**
father see **parent**
fathom see **comprehend, understand**
fatigue see **exhaust, tire**
fatigued see **tired, weary, worn-out**
fault noun **1** something for which someone is responsible: *It was all my fault*
blame: *They put the blame on her*
liability: *The company was forced to admit liability*
responsibility: *He accepted full responsibility for the error*
2 a defective quality in something: *a minor technical fault*
blemish: *a blemish on an otherwise outstanding career*
defect: *a manufacturing defect*
deficiency: *serious deficiencies in the system*
drawback: *The plan had one major drawback*
failing: *the country's many failings*
flaw: *serious character flaws*
imperfection: *small imperfections on the surface*
weakness: *his one weakness*
▷ verb **3** to find reasons to be critical of someone: *Her conduct cannot be faulted*
blame: *I don't blame him*
censure: *He was censured by the committee*
criticize: *The minister criticized the police*
see also **blame, defect, error, fissure, flaw, hole, responsibility**

fault-finding see **criticism**
faultless see **correct, exact, perfect**
faulty adjective containing flaws or errors: *Faulty goods should be sent back*
defective: *a lorry with defective brakes*
flawed: *The test results were seriously flawed*
imperfect: *an imperfect specimen*
invalid: *That's an invalid argument*
unsound: *a building that is structurally unsound*
see also **imperfect, weak, wrong**
favour noun **1** a liking or approval of something: *The proposals met with favour*
approval: *to gain his father's approval*
esteem: *in high esteem*
grace: *to fall from grace*
support: *They gave us their full support*
2 a kind and helpful action: *Can you do me a favour?*
courtesy: *the courtesy of a personal response*
good turn: *to do someone a good turn*
kindness: *She did me the kindness of calling*
service: *a service to your country*
▷ verb **3** to prefer something or someone: *They favoured the eldest child*
prefer: *the preferred candidate*
single out: *He is always being singled out for special treatment*
see also **advocate, approval, approve, back, encourage, goodwill, prefer**
favourable adjective **1** of advantage and benefit to someone: *favourable conditions*
advantageous: *the most advantageous course of action*
beneficial: *a beneficial effect on*

our health
good: He got a very good deal
opportune: an opportune moment to attack
suitable: Conditions were not suitable for life to flourish
2 positive and expressing approval: a positive response
affirmative: to give an affirmative answer
amicable: amicable discussions
approving: a warm, approving glance
friendly: The proposal was given a friendly reception
positive: a positive effect on the situation
sympathetic: He got a sympathetic hearing
welcoming: a welcoming atmosphere

favourably see **well**

favoured see **favourite**

favourite adjective **1** being someone's best-liked person or thing: my favourite hotel
best-loved: our best-loved music
dearest: Her dearest wish was fulfilled
favoured: the favoured child of elderly parents
preferred: his preferred method of exercise
▷ noun **2** the thing or person someone likes best: The youngest was always her favourite
darling: the spoilt darling of the family
idol: the idol of his fans
pet: the teacher's pet
pick: the pick of the bunch
see also **popular**

favouritism noun unfair favour shown to a person or group: There was never a hint of favouritism
bias: political bias in broadcasting
one-sidedness: The committee must show no one-sidedness
see also **bias**

fawn see **flatter**

fawning see **flattery**

fear noun **1** an unpleasant feeling of danger: shivering with fear
alarm: I looked at him with growing alarm
awe: in awe of his great powers
dread: She thought with dread of the coming storm
fright: He jumped with fright at the noise
panic: a moment of panic
terror: to shake with terror
▷ verb **2** to feel frightened of something: There is nothing to fear
be afraid: The dog was afraid of him
be frightened: I am frightened of thunder
be scared: Are you scared of snakes?
dread: He dreaded angry scenes
take fright: The horse took fright at the sudden noise
see also **anxiety**, **horror**, **panic**, **worry**

fearful see **afraid**, **anxious**

fearless see **bold**, **brave**, **daring**

feasible see **possible**, **probable**

feast see **meal**

feat see **achievement**, **act**, **action**

feature noun **1** a particular characteristic of something: an unusual feature of the room
aspect: every aspect of our lives
attribute: a normal attribute of human behaviour
characteristic: their physical characteristics
mark: distinguishing marks
property: the magnetic properties of iron
quality: skills and personal qualities
2 a special article or programme: a news feature
article: a travel article

column: the advice column

item: an item about chemical waste

piece: a specially-written piece

report: a film report on the scandal

story: front-page news stories

▷ verb **3** to include and draw attention to something: featuring an interview with the president

emphasize: to emphasize their differences

give prominence to: The Times is alone in giving prominence to the visit

spotlight: a book spotlighting female singers

star: starring a major Australian actor
see also **article, aspect, attribute, characteristic, item, point, property, quality**

features see **face**

fed up see **sick of, bored, down**

federation see **union**

fee see **charge, pay, price, rate**

feeble see **lame, pathetic, poor, puny, weak**

feed see **eat**

feedback see **reaction**

feel verb **1** to experience emotionally: I felt enormous happiness

experience: They seem to experience more distress than the others

suffer: suffering from pangs of conscience

undergo: to undergo a change of heart

2 to believe that something is the case: She feels she is in control of her life

believe: I believe they are right

consider: We consider them to be our friends

deem: I deemed it best to cancel the party

judge: She was judged to be capable of anything

think: I think I am very lucky

3 to touch something physically:

Feel this lovely material!

finger: He was fingering the coins in his pocket

fondle: She fondled the dog's ears

stroke: I stroked the smooth wooden surface

touch: He touched my face
see also **handle, have, sense, suspect, texture, touch**

feel dejected see **despair**

feel despondent see **despair**

feel for see **identify with, pity**

feel sorry for see **pity**

feel uneasy see **worry**

feeling noun **1** the experiencing of an emotion: feelings of envy

emotion: trembling with emotion

fervour: religious fervour

heat: He spoke with some heat about his experiences

passion: She argued with great passion

sentiment: I'm afraid I don't share your sentiments

2 a physical sensation: a feeling of pain

sensation: a very pleasant sensation

sense: a slight sense of heat at the back of my throat

3 an opinion on something: strong feelings on politics

inclination: neither the time nor the inclination

opinion: a consensus of opinion

point of view: an unusual point of view on the subject

view: Make your views known
see also **guess, impression, instinct, sense, view, viewpoint**

feign see **fake, pretend**

feigned see **mock**

feline see **cat**

fell see **chop**

fellow see **boy**

fellow worker see **colleague**

fellowship noun **1** a feeling of

friendliness within a group: *a sense of community and fellowship*
brotherhood: *a symbolic act of brotherhood*
camaraderie: *the camaraderie among soldiers*
companionship: *the companionship between old friends*
2 a group of people with a common interest: *a fellowship of writers*
association: *a trade association*
brotherhood: *a secret international brotherhood*
club: *a youth club*
league: *the League of Nations*
society: *the historical society*
see also **society**

female noun **1** a person or animal which can have babies: *Hay fever affects males more than females*
girl: *a girls' school*
lady: *a nice young lady*
sheila *Australian, New Zealand informal*: *her role as a sheila in her own play*
woman: *the number of women in the police force*
▷ adjective **2** relating to females: *the world's greatest female distance runner*
feminine: *the traditional feminine role*
girlish: *She gave a girlish giggle*
womanly: *a womanly shape*
see also **woman**

feminine see **female**
fence see **barrier**
fence off see **enclose**
ferocious see **fierce, savage**
ferry see **take**
fertile adjective capable of producing plants or offspring: *fertile soil*
fruitful: *The fruitful earth gave forth its treasures*
productive: *the most productive vineyards*
prolific: *Chinchillas are prolific*

breeders
rich: *This plant grows in moist rich ground*
see also **creative, productive, rich**

fervent adjective showing sincere and enthusiastic feeling: *a fervent admirer of her work*
ardent: *one of the most ardent supporters of the policy*
committed: *a committed socialist*
devout: *She was a devout Christian*
enthusiastic: *a huge and enthusiastic crowd*
impassioned: *an impassioned appeal for peace*
passionate: *I'm a passionate believer in public art*
zealous: *He was a recent convert, and very zealous*
see also **ardent, fanatical, intense**

fervour see **feeling, heat, violence**
fester see **rot**
festival noun **1** an organized series of events: *an arts festival*
carnival: *The carnival lasted for three days*
entertainment: *theatrical entertainments*
fair: *The book fair attracted many visitors*
fete: *a church fete*
gala: *the May Day gala*
2 a day or period of religious celebration: *open except on days of religious festivals*
anniversary: *The anniversary is celebrated each spring*
holiday: *the Easter holiday*
see also **celebration, fair**

festivity see **celebration**
fetch see **get, take**
fetching see **attractive**
fete see **fair, festival**
feud see **argue, argument, dispute, quarrel, squabble**
feverish see **excited**

few adjective small in number: *a few moments ago*
  infrequent: *at infrequent intervals*
  meagre: *a society with meagre resources*
  not many: *Not many people attended the meeting*
  scanty: *scanty memories of his childhood*
  scarce: *Resources are scarce*
  sparse: *a bare landscape with sparse trees*
  see also **rare, scarce, uncommon**

fewest see **least**

fiasco see **failure**

fib see **lie**

fibbing see **lying**

fickle see **changeable**

fiction see **lie**

fictional see **imaginary**

fictitious see **false, imaginary, untrue**

fiddle see **fidget**

fidget verb to move and change position restlessly: *fidgeting in his seat*
  fiddle informal: *She fiddled with her pencil*
  jiggle: *He's jiggling his keys*
  squirm: *He squirmed and wriggled with impatience*
  twitch: *Everybody twitched in their seats*
  see also **fuss**

fidgety see **restless**

field noun 1 an area of farm land: *a field full of sheep*
  green: *on the village green*
  meadow: *a grassy meadow*
  pasture: *cows grazing in the pasture*
  2 a particular subject or interest: *a breakthrough in the field of physics*
  area: *a politically-sensitive area*
  department: *Health care isn't my department*
  domain: *in the domain of art*

province: *This is the province of a different section*
  speciality: *His speciality was mythology*
  territory: *an expert in his own territory of history*
  see also **range**

fierce adjective 1 wild and aggressive: *a fierce lion*
  aggressive: *encouraging aggressive behaviour in later life*
  dangerous: *These birds are dangerous*
  ferocious: *two and a half days of ferocious violence*
  murderous: *a murderous attack*
  2 very intense: *a fierce contest*
  intense: *We found ourselves standing in intense heat*
  keen: *a keen interest in cars*
  relentless: *The pressure was relentless*
  strong: *a strong dislike*
  see also **furious, intense, wild**

fight verb 1 to take part in a battle or contest: *He fought the world champion*
  battle: *The gang battled with the police*
  brawl: *men brawling drunkenly in the street*
  grapple: *grappling with an alligator*
  struggle: *He was struggling with police outside the club*
  ▷ noun 2 an aggressive struggle: *a fight to the death*
  action: *wounded in action*
  battle: *a gun battle*
  bout: *a wrestling bout*
  combat: *the end of a long combat*
  duel: *He was killed in a duel*
  skirmish: *a minor border skirmish*
  3 an angry disagreement: *a fight with my mother*
  argument: *an argument over a boyfriend*

blue Australian slang: a bloke I'd had a blue with years ago

dispute: a dispute over ticket allocation

row: Maxine and I had a terrible row

squabble: a family squabble over Sunday lunch

see also argue, argument, clash, compete, contest, quarrel, resist, squabble, war

fight against see oppose

fight for see champion

fight shy of see avoid

fighter noun someone who physically fights another person: a tough street fighter

soldier: well-respected soldiers

warrior: a brave warrior

fighting see conflict, war

figure noun **1** a number, or amount represented by a number: No one really knows the true figures

amount: Postal money orders are available in amounts up to $700

digit: a code made up of letters and digits

number: A lot of marriages end in divorce, but we don't know the exact number

numeral: the numeral six

statistic: Official statistics show wages declining by 24%

total: Then he added everything together to arrive at the final total

2 Stuff, or the shape of someone's body: A figure appeared in the doorway

body: She's got nice hair and a great body

build: a tall woman with a naturally slim build

form: The shadowy form receded into the darkness

physique: He has the physique and energy of a man half his age

silhouette: Tuck the shirt in to give yourself a streamlined silhouette

shape: tall, dark shapes moving in the mist

3 a person: international political figures

character: What a sad character that Nigel is

dignitary: a visiting dignitary of great importance

person: My grandfather was a person of some influence

personality: The event was attended by many showbiz personalities

player: a key player in the negotiations

▷ verb **4** informal to guess or conclude something: I figure I'll learn from experience

expect: I expect you're just tired

guess: I guess he's right

reckon: informal: Toni reckoned that it must be about three o'clock

suppose: What do you suppose he's up to?

see also body, build, number, outline, price, shape, symbol

figure out see reckon, work out

file see line, rank, record

fill verb to make something full: Fill it up with water

cram: Mourners crammed the small church

gorge: gorged with food

pack: a lorry packed with explosives

stock: a lake stocked with carp

stuff: Stuff the pillow with feathers

see also load, plug, stuff

fill in see brief

fill out see expand

filled see full

film see layer

filtered see refined

filth see dirt

filthy see dirty, obscene, scungy

final adjective **1** being the last one in a series: the fifth and final day

closing: in the closing stages of

the race

concluding: *the concluding part of the serial*

eventual: *the eventual aim of their policies*

last: *his last chance*

ultimate: *The ultimate outcome will be different*

2 unable to be changed or questioned: *The judges' decision is final*

absolute: *absolute authority*

conclusive: *conclusive proof*

definite: *too soon to give a definite answer*

definitive: *the definitive account of the war*

see also **last, ultimate**

finale see **finish**

finalize see **finish**

finally *adverb* **1** happening after a long time: *It finally arrived*

at last: *He came at last*

at the last moment: *They changed their minds at the last moment*

eventually: *The flight eventually left in the end*

in the end: *It all turned out right in the end*

in the long run: *a success in the long run*

2 in conclusion of something: *Finally, I'd like to talk about safety measures*

in conclusion: *In conclusion, we have to agree*

in summary: *It was, in summary, a satisfactory outcome*

lastly: *Lastly, I would like to thank my agent*

finance *verb* **1** to provide the money for something: *financed by the government*

back: *a fund backed by local businesses*

fund: *The scheme is funded by the banks*

pay for: *He paid for his trip out of his savings*

support: *She supported herself through university*

▷ *noun* **2** the managing of money and investments: *the world of high finance*

banking: *the international banking system*

budgeting: *We must exercise caution in our budgeting this year*

commerce: *industry and commerce*

economics: *the economics of the third world*

investment: *tax incentives to encourage investment*

see also **fund**

financial *adjective* relating to money: *financial difficulties*

economic: *an economic crisis*

fiscal: *the long-term fiscal policy of this country*

money: *on the money markets*

see also **economic**

find *verb* **1** to discover something: *I can't find my notes*

come across: *He came across the book by chance*

discover: *They discovered the body in the bushes*

locate: *locating the position of the gene*

track down: *to track down her parents*

turn up: *They failed to turn up any evidence*

unearth: *to unearth the missing copy*

2 to realize or learn something: *We found that we got on well*

become aware: *I became aware of his work last year*

detect: *I detected a note of envy in her voice*

discover: *It was discovered that the goods were missing*

learn: *I flew from New York on*

learning of his death
realize: They realized too late that it
was wrong
see also **discover, locate**
find a solution to see **resolve**
find fault see **complain, put down**
find fault with see **criticize**
find out see **determine, discover,
hear, learn, see**
find unacceptable see **disapprove**
finding see **decision, verdict**
fine adjective **1** very good and
admirable: fine clothes
  admirable: with many admirable
qualities
  beautiful: a beautiful view of the river
  excellent: inns with excellent cuisine
  magnificent: his magnificent
country house
  outstanding: an area of outstanding
natural beauty
  splendid: a splendid collection of
cartoons
  2 small in size or thickness: powder
with very fine particles
  delicate: delicate curtains to let in
the light
  lightweight: certain lightweight
fabrics
  powdery: soft powdery dust
  sheer: a sheer chiffon shirt
  small: netting with a small mesh
  3 subtle and precise: the fine details
  fastidious: fastidious attention
to detail
  keen: a keen eye for a bargain
  precise: a gauge with precise
adjustment
  refined: a woman of refined tastes
  sensitive: The radio had very sensitive
tuning
  subtle: a very subtle distinction
see also **beautiful, excellent,
narrow, sheer, sound, splendid,
thin**
finesse see **polish**

finger see **feel, handle, touch**
finish verb **1** to complete something:
to finish a report
  close: They have closed the deal
  complete: She completed her first
novel
  conclude: He concluded his speech
  end: That ended our discussion
  finalize: to finalize an agreement
  ▷ noun **2** the last part of something:
to see it through to the finish
  close: to bring to a close
  completion: The project is nearing
completion
  conclusion: at the conclusion of the
programme
  end: the end of the race
  ending: The film had an unexpected
ending
  finale: the grand finale of the evening
  3 the surface appearance of
something: a glossy finish
  grain: the smooth grain of the wood
  lustre: a similar lustre to silk
  polish: The bodywork had a high
polish
  shine: It gives a beautiful shine to
the hair
  surface: a polished surface
  texture: paper with a linen-like
texture
see also **cease, complete, conclude,
conclusion, end, stop**
finished see **over**
fire noun **1** the flames produced when
something burns: a ball of fire
  blaze: The firemen were hurt in
the blaze
  combustion: Energy is released by
combustion
  flames: rescued from the flames
  inferno: The building was an inferno
  ▷ verb **2** to shoot or detonate
something: to fire a cannon
  detonate: to detonate an explosive
device

explode: They exploded a bomb

launch: The protesters launched the missile from a boat

set off: the largest nuclear explosion ever set off on Earth

shoot: people shooting guns in all directions

3 informal to dismiss someone from a job: She was fired yesterday

discharge: A trooper has been discharged from the army

dismiss: He was dismissed by the bank

make redundant: Many people were made redundant

sack informal: Jones was sacked for disciplinary reasons

see also **discharge, passion, sack, spirit**

firm adjective **1** solid and not soft: Leave the ice cream until it is firm

compressed: compressed wood pulp made into cardboard

congealed: a bowl of congealed grease

hard: The snow was hard and slippery

rigid: Pour the mixture into a rigid plastic container

set: The glue wasn't completely set

solid: a block of solid wax

stiff: egg whites beaten until stiff

2 resolute and determined: The department needs a firm manager

adamant: He was adamant that he would not resign

determined: She was determined to finish the game

inflexible: his inflexible routine

resolute: a willingness to take resolute action

staunch: many staunch supporters

unshakable: an unshakable belief in democracy

▷ noun **3** a commercial organization: a firm of builders

business: a stockbroking business

company: his software development company

corporation: one of the leading banking corporations

enterprise: small business enterprises

organization: a multinational organization

see also **business, company, enterprise, hard, positive, rigid, secure, set, solid, steadfast, steady, stiff, strict, tight, trusty**

firmly see **fast**

first adjective **1** done or in existence before anything else: the first moon landing

earliest: The earliest settlers lived there

initial: our initial meeting

opening: There was a standing ovation on opening night

original: She was one of the original cast

primeval: the primeval forests of Europe

▷ adverb **2** done or occurring before anything else: You must do that first

beforehand: Bill had prepared beforehand

earlier: I did that one earlier

firstly: Firstly, I'd like to thank you all for coming

initially: not as bad as they initially predicted

to begin with: To begin with, we must prepare the soil

3 more important than anything else: our first responsibility

chief: the chief pilot

foremost: one of our foremost thinkers

leading: the team's leading scorer

prime: He was the prime suspect

principal: the principal reason

see also **foremost, opening, original, principal**

first-class see **brilliant, excellent, first-rate, outstanding, select**

first-hand see **direct**

firstly see **first**

first-rate *adjective* excellent: *They were dealing with a first-rate professional*
  excellent: *She does an excellent job as Fred's personal assistant*
  exceptional: *His piano playing is exceptional*
  first-class: *The food was first-class*
  marvellous: *He certainly is a marvellous actor*
  outstanding: *an outstanding athlete*
  splendid: *We had a splendid meal*
  superb: *a superb 18-hole golf course*
  see also **able, marvellous, outstanding, prime, prize, select, superior**

fiscal see **financial**

fishy see **suspect, suspicious**

fissure *noun* a deep crack in rock or the ground: *There was a rumbling, and a fissure opened up*
  cleft: *a narrow cleft in the rocks*
  crack: *The building developed large cracks in walls and ceilings*
  crevice: *a huge boulder with ferns growing in every crevice*
  fault: *the San Andreas Fault*
  rift: *In the open bog are many rifts and potholes*
  split: *The slate has a few small splits around the edges*
  see also **abyss, leak, split**

fit *verb* **1** to be the right shape or size: *made to fit a child*
  belong: *I just didn't belong there*
  correspond: *The two angles didn't correspond exactly*
  dovetail: *The movement's interests dovetailed with her own*
  go: *small enough to go in your pocket*
  match: *Match the pegs with the holes*
  2 to place something in position: *a*

fitted carpet
  adapt: *shelves adapted to suit the smaller books*
  arrange: *Arrange the pieces to form a picture*
  place: *Place the card in the slots*
  position: *plants which are carefully positioned in the alcove*
  ▷ *adjective* **3** in good physical condition: *a reasonably fit person*
  healthy: *a healthy mind in a healthy body*
  in good condition: *in good condition for his age*
  robust: *a strong, robust man*
  trim: *a trim figure*
  well: *Alison was looking well*
  see also **burst, correspond, healthy, match, right, sound, suitable, well**

fit out see **equip**

fitness see **health**

fitting *adjective* **1** appropriate and suitable for something: *a fitting end*
  appropriate: *an appropriate outfit for the occasion*
  correct: *the correct thing to say*
  proper: *It isn't proper that she should be here*
  right: *He always said just the right thing*
  suitable: *some hymns suitable for a wedding*
  ▷ *noun* **2** a part attached to something else: *fixtures and fittings*
  accessory: *bathroom accessories*
  attachment: *a wide range of attachments*
  component: *special components*
  part: *Extra parts can be added later*
  unit: *The unit plugs into any TV set*
  see also **appropriate, attachment, correct, proper, right, suitable**

fix *verb* **1** to attach or secure something: *fixed to the wall*
  attach: *The label was attached with glue*

bind: sticks bound together with string
fasten: Fasten the two parts securely
secure: firmly secured by strong nails
stick: She stuck the pictures into the book

2 to repair something broken: The bike is fixed now
correct: to correct our mistakes
mend: They finally got round to mending the roof
patch up: Patch up those holes
repair: I had my shoes repaired
▷ noun **3** informal a difficult situation: in a bit of a fix
difficulty: He was in real difficulties with money
mess: Their economy was in a mess
predicament: a tricky predicament
quandary: in a quandary about what to do
see also **confirm, corrupt, determine, fasten, focus, glue, hang, hole, jam, limit, mend, mess, predicament, repair, secure, settle, stick**

fix up see **arrange, restore**
fixation see **complex, obsession**
fixed see **constant, definite, rigid, secure, set**
fixture see **attachment**
fizz see **boil, foam**
flabby adjective fat and with loose flesh: a flabby stomach
floppy: The floppy bodies in tracksuits
sagging: a sagging double chin
slack: The skin around her eyelids is now slack and baggy
see also **limp**
flag see **label, weaken**
flagrant see **shameless**
flair see **gift, style, talent**
flak see **criticism**
flamboyant see **flashy, loud, ostentatious**
flame see **burn**

flames see **fire**
flap see **wave**
flare see **burn, flash**
flash noun **1** a sudden short burst of light: a flash of lightning
burst: a burst of fire
flare: the sudden flare of a match
sparkle: sparkles from her sequinned dress
▷ verb **2** to shine briefly and often repeatedly: They signalled by flashing a light
flare: matches flaring in the darkness
glint: the low sun glinting off the windscreens
glitter: the glittering crown on his head
sparkle: Diamonds sparkled on her wrists
twinkle: stars twinkling in the night sky
see also **instant, minute, speed**

flashy adjective showy in a vulgar way: flashy clothes
flamboyant: an unsuitably flamboyant outfit
garish: curtains in garish colours
showy: an expensive and showy watch
tacky informal: tacky red sunglasses
tasteless: a house with tasteless decor
see also **bold, gaudy, loud, ostentatious, tasteless, vulgar**

flat noun **1** a set of rooms for living in: a two-bedroomed flat
apartment: a huge apartment overlooking the park
rooms: We shared rooms while we were students
▷ adjective **2** level and smooth: a flat surface
horizontal: horizontal with the ground
level: a completely level base
levelled: The floor must be levelled

before you start

smooth: *a smooth marble top*

unbroken: *the unbroken surface of the sea*

3 without emotion or interest: *a dreadfully flat speech*

boring: *a boring menu*

dull: *He told some really dull stories*

insipid: *an insipid performance*

monotonous: *an interesting story expressed in a monotonous voice*

weak: *A weak ending spoiled the story*

see also **boring, even, level, stale**

flatness *see* **boredom**

flatten *see* **level**

flatter verb **1** to praise someone insincerely: *flattering remarks*

compliment: *She was often complimented for her looks*

fawn: *surrounded by fawning attendants*

2 to make more attractive: *clothes that flatter your figure*

enhance: *an enhancing neckline*

set off: *Blue sets off the colour of your eyes*

suit: *That shade really suits your skin tone*

see also **humour**

flattery noun flattering words and behaviour: *susceptible to flattery*

adulation: *received with adulation by the critics*

fawning: *the constant fawning of her courtiers*

flavour *see* **taste**

flaw noun an imperfection in something: *The program contained serious flaws*

blemish: *A small blemish spoiled the surface*

defect: *a manufacturing defect*

fault: *a fault in the engine*

imperfection: *slight imperfections in the weave*

see also **defect, fault, hole,**

weakness

flawed *see* **faulty, imperfect**

flawless *see* **correct, perfect**

flee verb to run away from something: *to flee the country*

bolt: *He bolted for the exit*

escape: *They escaped across the frontier*

fly: *to fly from war*

leave: *to leave the scene of the crime*

run away: *to run away from the police*

take flight: *250,000 took flight from the floods*

see also **bolt**

fleece *see* **cheat, coat**

fleeting *see* **brief, short, temporary**

flexible adjective **1** able to bend or be bent easily: *long flexible bristles*

elastic: *an elastic rope*

lithe: *lithe and graceful movements*

pliable: *baskets made from pliable cane*

supple: *exercises to keep you supple*

2 able to adapt or change: *flexible working hours*

adaptable: *an adaptable attitude to work*

discretionary: *the discretionary powers of the courts*

open: *an open mind*

see also **soft**

flick *see* **flourish**

flicker *see* **burn**

flight *see* **retreat**

flimsy *see* **fragile, lame, light**

flinch verb to move suddenly with fear or pain: *The sharp pain made her flinch*

cringe: *to cringe in terror*

shrink: *She shrank from the flames*

start: *They started at the sudden noise*

wince: *I could see him wincing with pain*

fling *see* **affair, throw**

flippant *see* **frivolous**

flit see **fly**

float verb **1** to be supported by water: *leaves floating on the river*

be on the surface: *The oil is on the surface of the sea*

bob: *toys bobbing in the bath*

drift: *to drift in on the tide*

lie on the surface: *The boat lay on the surface of the lake*

stay afloat: *They could stay afloat without swimming*

2 to be carried on the air: *floating on the breeze*

drift: *The music drifted in through the window*

glide: *eagles gliding above us*

hang: *A haze of perfume hung in the room*

hover: *Butterflies hovered above the flowers*

flock see **gather**

flood noun **1** a large amount of water coming suddenly: *Many people were drowned in the floods*

deluge: *houses overwhelmed by the deluge*

downpour: *a downpour of torrential rain*

spate: *The river was in spate*

torrent: *Torrents of water gushed into the reservoir*

2 a sudden surge of something: *a flood of angry letters*

rush: *a sudden rush of panic*

stream: *a stream of bad language*

torrent: *He replied with a torrent of abuse*

▷ verb **3** to overflow with water: *The river flooded its banks*

deluge: *Heavy rain deluged the capital*

drown: *a drowned village*

overflow: *an overflowing bath*

submerge: *to prevent water submerging the cobbled streets*

swamp: *His small boat was swamped*

by the waves

see also **flow, rash, wave**

floor see **bottom**

flop see **failure**

floppy see **flabby, limp**

flourish verb **1** to develop or function successfully or healthily: *Business was flourishing*

bloom: *Not many economies bloomed during that period*

boom: *Sales are booming*

come on: *He is coming on very well at his new school*

do well: *Out-of-town superstores are doing well*

prosper: *The high street banks continue to prosper*

succeed: *the qualities needed to succeed in small businesses*

thrive: *Today the company continues to thrive*

2 to wave or display something: *He flourished his glass*

brandish literary: *He appeared brandishing a sword*

display: *She proudly displayed the letter and began to read*

hold aloft: *He held the cup aloft*

wave: *Crowds were waving flags and applauding*

▷ noun **3** a bold sweeping or waving movement: *with a flourish of his hand*

flick: *a flick of the whip*

sweep: *With one sweep of her hand she threw back the sheets*

wave: *Steve stopped him with a wave of the hand*

see also **grow, shake, succeed, thrive, wave**

flourishing see **successful**

flout see **disobey**

flow verb **1** to move or happen in a continuous stream: *a river flowing gently down into the valley*

circulate: *to circulate round the entire house*

glide: *models gliding down the catwalk*
roll: *rolling gently to the sea*
run: *A stream ran beside the road*
slide: *Tears slid down her cheeks*
▷ *noun* **2** a continuous movement of something: *traffic flow*
current: *currents of air*
drift: *the drift towards the cities*
flood: *a flood of complaints*
stream: *a constant stream of visitors*
tide: *to slow the tide of change*
see also **current, drain, gush, movement, pour**

flower see **pick**
flowing see **fluent**
fluctuate see **vary**
fluctuating see **uneven**
fluent *adjective* expressing yourself easily and without hesitation: *a fluent speaker of French*
articulate: *an articulate young woman*
easy: *the easy flow of his argument*
effortless: *He spoke with effortless ease*
flowing: *a smooth, flowing presentation*
ready: *a ready answer*
fluid see **liquid**
flunk see **fail**
flurry see **bustle**
flush see **blush, discharge**
fluster see **embarrass**
flutter see **blow, fly, wave**
fly *verb* **1** to move through the air: *to fly to Paris*
flit: *butterflies flitting among the flowers*
flutter: *The birds fluttered on to the feeder*
sail: *a kite sailing above the trees*
soar: *eagles soaring in the sky*
2 to move very quickly: *She flew down the stairs*
dart: *She darted to the window*

dash: *We had to dash*
hurry: *They hurried to catch the train*
race: *I had to race round the shops*
rush: *rushing off to work*
speed: *The car sped off*
tear: *He tore off down the road*
see also **bolt, dash, flee, go, hurry, race, rush, tear**

foam *noun* **1** a mass of tiny bubbles: *waves tipped with foam*
bubbles: *She loved to have bubbles in the bath*
froth: *Yeast swells up to form a froth*
head: *the foamy head on beer*
lather: *It took a lot of shampoo to get a good lather*
▷ *verb* **2** to swell and form bubbles: *a foaming river*
bubble: *The boiling liquid bubbled up*
fizz: *a drink fizzing in the glass*
froth: *It frothed up over the top*
see also **boil**

focal point see **focus**
focus *verb* **1** to concentrate your vision on something: *His eyes began to focus*
aim: *Astronomers aimed optical telescopes in their direction*
concentrate: *concentrating his gaze on a line of ants*
direct: *He directed the light on to the roof*
fix: *Their radar was fixed on the enemy ship*
▷ *noun* **2** the centre of attention: *the focus of the conversation*
centre: *She was the centre of an admiring crowd*
focal point: *the focal point of the whole room*
hub: *the hub of the financial world*
target: *a target group*
see also **centre**
focus your attention on see **concentrate**
foe see **enemy**

fog *see* **cloud**

foil *verb* **1** to prevent something from happening: *The police foiled an armed robbery*
  check: *to check the rise in crime*
  counter: *countering the threat of strike action*
  defeat: *an important role in defeating the rebellion*
  frustrate: *a frustrated attempt*
  thwart: *to thwart someone's plans*
  ▷ *noun* **2** a contrast to something: *a perfect foil for his temperament*
  antithesis: *the antithesis of his crooked brother*
  background: *a fitting background for her beauty*
  complement: *the perfect complement to the antique furniture*
  contrast: *The green woodwork is a stunning contrast to the black walls*
  see also **dash, frustrate, prevent**

fold *verb* **1** to bend something: *He folded the paper carefully*
  bend: *Bend the top towards you*
  crease: *Crease along the dotted line*
  crumple: *He crumpled the note and put it in his pocket*
  tuck: *Tuck in the top and bottom*
  turn under: *The bottom was turned under*
  ▷ *noun* **2** a crease in something: *hanging in folds*
  bend: *There was a bend in the photograph*
  crease: *sharp creases in his shirt*
  pleat: *a skirt with pleats*
  wrinkle: *all the little wrinkles on Paul's face*
  see also **collapse**

follow *verb* **1** to pursue someone: *We were being followed*
  hound: *constantly hounded by photographers*
  pursue: *He was pursued across several countries*
  stalk: *Her former husband was stalking her*
  track: *They tracked him to his home*
  2 to come after someone or something: *Night follows day*
  come after: *Summer comes after spring*
  succeed: *He was succeeded by his son*
  supersede: *Horses were superseded by cars*
  3 to act in accordance with something: *Follow the instructions carefully*
  comply: *in order to comply with EC regulations*
  conform: *conforming to the new safety requirements*
  obey: *You must obey the law*
  observe: *The army was observing a ceasefire*
  see also **copy, happen, heed, obey, practise, result, see, understand**

follower *noun* a supporter of a person or belief: *a loyal follower of the movement*
  believer: *many devout believers in the faith*
  disciple: *one of his disciples*
  fan: *football fans*
  henchman: *always surrounded by his henchmen*
  supporter: *He was a major supporter of the plan*
  see also **supporter**

following *see* **after, next**

folly *see* **stupidity**

fond *adjective* **1** feeling affection or liking: *a fond father*
  adoring: *an adoring husband*
  affectionate: *an affectionate smile*
  devoted: *a devoted couple*
  doting: *doting grandparents*
  having a liking for: *She had a great liking for chocolate*
  loving: *a loving son*
  2 unlikely to happen or be fulfilled:

fond wishes for a better life
deluded: a deluded belief in future improvement
empty: empty promises of full employment
foolish: What foolish dreams we have!
naive: her naive belief in others' goodness
vain: the vain hope that he might lose weight
see also **affectionate, loving**

fond of see **keen**

fondle see **feel**

fondness see **affection, attachment, love, taste, weakness**

food noun things eaten to provide nourishment: our favourite food
diet: a healthy balanced diet
fare: traditional regional fare
foodstuffs: basic foodstuffs
kai Australian, New Zealand informal: There's no kai in the house
nourishment: unable to take nourishment
provisions: provisions for two weeks
refreshment: Refreshments will be provided
tucker Australian, New Zealand informal: some of the cheapest pub tucker in town
see also **kai**

foodstuffs see **food**

fool noun **1** an unintelligent person: What a stupid fool he is!
dope informal: He felt such a dope
dunce: I was a complete dunce at chemistry
idiot: acting like an idiot
ignoramus: the ignoramus of the group
moron: They treated him like a moron
▷ verb **2** to trick someone: Don't let him fool you
con informal: conned out of all his money

deceive: deceiving the audience
dupe: in order to dupe the medical staff
mislead: a deliberately misleading statement
trick: They tricked him into believing it
see also **deceive, dupe, idiot, take in, trick**

foolhardy see **mad, rash**

foolish adjective silly and unwise: feeling foolish
inane: an inane remark
nonsensical: a nonsensical thing to say
senseless: It would be senseless to stop her
silly: a silly thing to say
unintelligent: a weak and unintelligent man
unwise: He had made some unwise investments
see also **crazy, daft, fond, frivolous, idiotic, mad, silly, stupid, unwise**

foolishness see **stupidity**

foolproof see **sure**

foot see **base, bottom**

footpath see **path**

for that reason see **therefore**

forage see **fossick, look for, search**

foray see **raid**

forbid verb to order someone not to do something: forbidden to go out
ban: banned from driving
exclude: Women were excluded from the classes
outlaw: the outlawed political parties
prohibit: Fishing is prohibited
veto: Their application was vetoed
see also **ban, exclude, prohibit, veto**

forbidding see **sinister**

force verb **1** to compel someone to do something: We were forced to turn right
compel: I felt compelled to act
drive: They are driving the company into bankruptcy

make: They made me do it

oblige: We were obliged to abandon the car

pressurize: trying to pressurize them ▷ noun **2** a pressure to do something: They made him agree by force

compulsion: a compulsion to write

duress: carried out under duress

pressure: under pressure to resign **3** the strength of something: the force of the explosion

impact: the impact of the blast

might: the full might of the army

power: massive computing power

pressure: the pressure of work

strength: The storm was gaining strength

see also **bully, drive, jam, make, reduce, spirit, strength, stuff, violence**

forced see **stiff**

forceful see **powerful, pushy**

ford see **cross**

forebear see **ancestor**

foreboding see **premonition**

forecast see **predict, prediction**

forefather see **ancestor**

forego see **sacrifice**

foreign adjective relating to other countries: foreign travel

distant: in that distant land

exotic: filmed in an exotic location

overseas: a long overseas trip

see also **strange, unfamiliar**

foremost adjective most important or best: one of the world's foremost scholars

best: He was the best player in the world throughout the 1950s

chief: my chief reason for objecting to the plan

first: The first priority is to defeat inflation

greatest: one of the West Indies' greatest cricketers

leading: the leading researchers in this area

most important: the country's most important politicians and philosophers

prime: I regard this as my prime duty

principal: one of the country's principal publishing houses

top: The President met with his top military advisers

see also **chief, first, important, main, principal, supreme, top**

forensic see **legal**

foresee see **predict**

foresight see **vision**

forest noun

foretell see **predict**

forever see **always**

forewarn see **alert, warn**

foreword see **introduction**

forfeit see **sacrifice**

forged see **false, phoney**

forgery see **copy, fake, fraud**

forget verb to fail to remember something: I forgot to lock the door

fail to remember: He failed to remember my name

omit: omitting to mention the details

overlook: to overlook an important fact

see also **neglect, overlook**

forgetful see **absent-minded**

forgive verb to stop blaming someone for something: Can you ever forgive me?

absolve: The verdict absolved him from blame

condone: We cannot condone violence

excuse: Please excuse our bad behaviour

pardon: Relatives had begged authorities to pardon him

see also **excuse**

forgiveness noun the act of forgiving: I ask for your forgiveness

acquittal: The jury voted for acquittal

mercy: to beg for mercy
pardon: a presidential pardon
remission: with remission for good behaviour
see also **mercy**

forgiving see **merciful**

forgo see **abstain**

fork see **split**

forlorn see **futile, hopeless, lonely**

form noun **1** a type or kind: He contracted a rare form of cancer
class: a new class of nuclear-powered submarine
kind: a new kind of leadership
sort: Try to do some sort of exercise every day
type: There are various types of this disease
variant: The quagga was a beautiful variant of the zebra
variety: an unusual variety of this common garden flower

2 the shape or pattern of something:
Valleys often take the form of deep canyons
contours: the contours of the body
layout: He tried to recall the layout of the farmhouse
outline: I could just see the outline of a building in the mist
shape: little pens in the shape of baseball bats
structure: the chemical structure of this molecule

▷ verb **3** to be the elements that something consists of: the articles that formed the basis of his book
compose: The force would be composed of troops from NATO countries
constitute: The country's ethnic minorities constitute about 7% of its total population
make up: Women officers make up 13 per cent of the police force
serve as: an arrangement of bricks

and planks that served as a bookshelf
4 to organize, create, or come into existence: The bowl was formed out of clay
assemble: a model assembled entirely from matchsticks
create: These patterns were created by the action of water
develop: We must develop closer ties with Germany
draw up: We've drawn up a plan of action
establish: The school was established in 1989 by an Italian professor
fashion: Stone Age settlers fashioned necklaces from animals' teeth
make: The organic waste decomposes to make compost
see also **body, build, condition, design, figure, make, make up, model, outline, shape**

formal adjective **1** in accordance with convention: a formal dinner
conventional: a conventional style of dress
correct: polite and correct behaviour
precise: They spoke very precise English
stiff: his stiff manner and lack of humour

2 official and publicly recognized:
No formal announcement has been made
approved: a legally approved method of dealing with these
legal: They have a legal responsibility
official: according to the official figures
prescribed: There is a prescribed procedure for situations like this
regular: through the regular channels
see also **impersonal, official, stiff, stuffy**

formality see **ceremony**

format see **layout**

former adjective existing in the past:

a former tennis champion
ancient: *the ancient civilizations*
bygone: *memories of a bygone age*
old: *our old school*
past: *a long list of past winners*
see also **past, previous**
former times *see* **the past**
formerly *see* **before**
formidable *adjective* difficult to
overcome: *They faced formidable
obstacles*
  challenging: *a more challenging job*
  daunting: *a daunting prospect*
  difficult: *A difficult task lay ahead*
  intimidating: *She was an
intimidating opponent*
  mammoth: *a mammoth undertaking*
  onerous: *onerous responsibilities*
  see also **stiff**
formulate *see* **create, invent, plan**
forsake *see* **leave**
forsaken *see* **lonely**
fort *noun* a building for defence and
shelter: *They had to abandon the fort*
  castle: *a heavily-guarded castle*
  citadel: *The citadel towered above
the river*
  fortification: *fortifications along
the border*
  fortress: *an ancient fortress*
forthcoming *see* **future, imminent,
near**
forthright *see* **blunt, direct,
straight, straightforward**
fortification *see* **fort**
fortified *see* **secure**
fortify *see* **secure, strengthen**
fortitude *see* **bravery**
fortress *see* **fort**
fortuitous *see* **lucky**
fortunate *see* **lucky**
fortune *see* **chance, fate, luck,
wealth**
forum *see* **conference**
forward *see* **bold, send**
fossick *verb* Australian, New

Zealand to search for something: *If
you fossick around in some specialist
music stores, you may find a copy*
  forage: *They were forced to forage for
clothing and fuel*
  hunt: *A forensic team was hunting
for clues*
  look: *I've looked through all my
drawers and I can't find it anywhere*
  rummage: *He rummaged around the
post room and found the document*
  search: *We've searched through the
whole house for the keys*
  see also **search**
foul *see* **disgusting, nasty, scungy,
smelly, soil**
found *see* **base, start**
foundation *see* **base, fund, start,
support**
founder *see* **collapse**
fraction *see* **part**
fractious *see* **cross**
fracture *see* **crack**
fractured *see* **broken**
fragile *adjective* easily broken or
damaged: *fragile china*
  breakable: *Anything breakable or
sharp had to be removed*
  dainty: *a dainty Japanese tea service*
  delicate: *a delicate instrument*
  flimsy: *packed in a flimsy box*
  frail: *a frail shell*
fragility *see* **weakness**
fragment *see* **bit, disintegrate,
part, piece**
fragmented *see* **broken**
fragrance *noun* a pleasant smell: *the
fragrance of the roses*
  aroma: *the aroma of fresh bread*
  bouquet: *a wine with a lively fruit
bouquet*
  perfume: *enjoying the perfume of the
lemon trees*
  scent: *flowers chosen for their scent*
  smell: *a sweet smell of pine*
  see also **smell**

fragrant adjective having a pleasant smell: *fragrant oils*
  aromatic: *a plant with aromatic leaves*
  perfumed: *perfumed body cream*
  sweet-smelling: *posies of sweet-smelling flowers*
  see also **sweet**
frail see **fragile, puny, weak**
frailty see **weakness**
frame see **body, build**
frame of mind see **humour, mood**
frank adjective open and straightforward: *a frank discussion*
  blunt: *his blunt approach*
  candid: *She was completely candid with me*
  honest: *my honest opinion*
  open: *an open, trusting nature*
  plain: *plain talking*
  straightforward: *spoken in a straightforward manner*
  see also **blunt, candid, direct, natural, open, straight, straightforward**
frantic see **furious, hysterical, upset**
fraud noun **1** the act of deceiving someone: *electoral fraud*
  deceit: *deliberate deceit*
  deception: *obtaining money by deception*
  guile: *children's lack of guile*
  hoax: *a bomb hoax*
  trickery: *They had to resort to trickery*
  2 someone or something that deceives you: *Many psychics are frauds*
  charlatan: *exposed as a charlatan*
  cheat: *Cheats will be disqualified*
  fake: *The painting was a fake*
  forgery: *just a clever forgery*
  imposter: *an imposter with false documents*
  quack: *He tried all sorts of quacks*
  see also **con, corruption, fake, racket**

fraudulent see **corrupt, crooked, deceptive, dishonest**
fray see **wear**
freak see **curiosity, weirdo**
free adjective **1** not being held prisoner: *a free man*
  at large: *Three prisoners are at large*
  at liberty: *the last top Nazi still at liberty*
  liberated: *newly liberated slaves*
  loose: *He broke loose from his bonds*
  2 available without payment: *a free brochure*
  complimentary: *complimentary tickets*
  gratis: *The meal was gratis*
  unpaid: *unpaid voluntary work*
  without charge: *They mended it without charge*
  ▷ verb **3** to release from captivity: *to free the slaves*
  discharge: *discharged from prison*
  liberate: *liberated under the terms of the amnesty*
  release: *The hostages were soon released*
  set at liberty: *He was set at liberty after ten years*
  set loose: *The animals were set loose after treatment*
  see also **available, discharge, immune, independent, loose, release, spare, wild**
free time see **leisure**
freedom noun **1** the ability to choose: *freedom of action*
  discretion: *Use your own discretion*
  latitude: *There is more latitude for personal opinions*
  leeway: *granted more leeway to pass reforms*
  licence: *a licence to kill*
  scope: *plenty of scope for improvement*
  2 the state of being free or being set free: *gaining their freedom after*

months of captivity

emancipation: *the emancipation of the slaves*

liberty: *three months' loss of liberty*

release: *the immediate release of the captives*

3 the absence of something unpleasant: *freedom from pain*

exemption: *granted exemption from all taxes*

immunity: *information in exchange for immunity from prosecution*

see also **release**

freeze *see* **cool, harden, numb**

freezing *see* **cold**

freight *see* **load**

frenzied *see* **furious, hysterical**

frenzy *noun* wild and uncontrolled behaviour: *gripped by a frenzy of nationalism*

agitation: *in a state of intense agitation*

fury: *She stalked out in a fury*

hysteria: *mass hysteria*

madness: *a moment of madness*

rage: *She flew into a rage*

see also **rage**

frequency *see* **rate**

frequent *adjective* **1** happening often: *his frequent visits*

common: *a common occurrence*

continual: *continual demands for money*

everyday: *an everyday event*

habitual: *a habitual daydreamer*

recurrent: *a recurrent theme in her work*

repeated: *His parents made repeated attempts to visit*

▷ *verb* **2** to go somewhere often: *a restaurant which he frequents*

attend: *He often attends their meetings*

haunt: *She haunted their house*

patronize: *to patronize a hotel*

visit: *a place we often visit*

see also **continual**

frequently *see* **often**

fresh *see* **original, recent**

fret *see* **fuss, worry**

fretful *see* **cross, restless**

friction *see* **conflict**

friend *noun* a person you know and like: *lifelong friends*

china *South African informal*: *a drinking session with his chinas*

companion: *my constant companion*

confidant or **confidante**: *her only confidant*

crony: *surrounded by her cronies*

mate *informal*: *going out with his mates*

pal: *We are great pals*

see also **china, companion**

friendliness *see* **goodwill**

friendly *adjective* kind and pleasant: *a very friendly crowd*

affectionate: *on affectionate terms*

amiable: *He was very amiable company*

close: *The two were very close*

cordial: *a most cordial welcome*

genial: *a genial host*

welcoming: *a welcoming house*

see also **cosy, favourable, pleasant, sociable, warm**

friendship *noun* a state of being friendly with someone: *I value our friendship*

affection: *to win their affection*

attachment: *the deep attachment between them*

closeness: *her closeness to her sister*

goodwill: *as a gesture of goodwill*

see also **goodwill**

fright *see* **alarm, fear, horror, panic, scare**

frighten *verb* to make someone afraid: *trying to frighten us*

alarm: *alarmed by the noise*

intimidate: *She is intimidated by her boss*

scare: You aren't scared of mice, are you?
startle: I didn't mean to startle you
terrify: Heights terrified her
terrorize: The gunmen terrorized the villagers
unnerve: an unnerving silence
see also **alarm, scare**

frightened adjective having feelings of fear about something: frightened of thunder
afraid: Jane was afraid of the other children
alarmed: Don't be alarmed
petrified: petrified of wasps
scared: scared of being alone in the house
startled: a startled animal
terrified: a terrified look
see also **afraid**

frightening adjective causing someone to feel fear: a frightening experience
alarming: an alarming increase
hair-raising: at hair-raising speed
intimidating: threatening and intimidating behaviour
menacing: a menacing glance
terrifying: one of the most terrifying diseases
see also **scary, spooky**

frightful see **awful, dreadful, terrible**
frigid see **cold, frozen**
fringe see **border, edge**
fritter away see **waste**
frivolous adjective not serious or sensible: a frivolous new dress
flippant: a flippant comment
foolish: saying foolish and inappropriate things
juvenile: juvenile behaviour
puerile: your puerile schoolboy humour
silly: making silly jokes
frock see **dress**

frolic see **play**
from time to time see **sometimes**
front noun 1 the part that faces forward: the front wall of the house
face: the face of the building
frontage: a restaurant with a river frontage
2 the outward appearance of something: a respectable front
appearance: the appearance of fair treatment
exterior: his tough exterior
face: a brave face
show: a convincing show of affection
in front preposition further forward: too close to the car in front
ahead: ahead of the rest of the field
before: I'm before you
leading: the leading rider
see also **face, head**

frontage see **front**
frontier see **border**
froth see **boil, foam**
frown verb to draw the eyebrows together: She frowned in concentration
glare: The woman glared angrily at him
glower: She glowered but said nothing
knit your brows: He knitted his brows in concentration
scowl: He scowled at the waiter
see also **glare**

frozen adjective extremely cold: frozen to the bone
arctic: arctic weather conditions
chilled: chilled to the marrow
frigid: frigid temperatures
icy: an icy wind
numb: numb with cold
see also **numb**

frugal see **economical, thrifty**
frugality see **economy**
fruit see **effect**
fruitful see **fertile, productive**

fruitless see **in vain, vain**

frustrate verb to prevent something from happening: *His efforts were frustrated*

block: *They are blocking the peace process*

check: *to check the spread of the virus*

foil: *They foiled all my plans*

thwart: *his way to thwart your club's ambitions*

see also **dash, foil, hamper, hinder**

fry see **cook**

fulfil verb to carry out or achieve something: *He decided to fulfil his dream and go to college*

accomplish: *If they all work together they can accomplish their goal*

achieve: *We will strive to achieve these goals*

carry out: *They have no intention of carrying out their commitments*

perform: *Each component performs a different function*

realize: *The question is, will our hopes ever be realized?*

satisfy: *The procedures should satisfy certain basic requirements*

see also **accomplish, achieve, carry out, keep, meet, perform, satisfy**

full adjective **1** filled with something: *full of books*

filled: *filled up to the top*

loaded: *The van was loaded with furniture*

packed: *The train was packed*

saturated: *completely saturated with liquid*

2 missing nothing out: *I want a full account of what happened*

comprehensive: *a comprehensive guide to the area*

detailed: *a detailed description*

exhaustive: *an exhaustive treatment of the subject*

extensive: *extensive coverage of the earthquake*

maximum: *the way to take maximum advantage of pay TV*

thorough: *a thorough search*

3 loose-fitting: *a full skirt*

baggy: *a baggy sweater*

loose: *hidden under his loose shirt*

voluminous: *voluminous sleeves*

see also **abundant, busy, complete, crowded, thorough, whole**

full of life see **alive**

full-grown see **mature**

fully see **quite, well**

fully-fledged see **mature**

fume see **rage**

fuming see **furious, mad**

fun noun **1** an enjoyable activity: *It was great fun*

amusement: *There is no amusement for teenagers in this village*

enjoyment: *It gave us much enjoyment*

entertainment: *little opportunity for entertainment*

pleasure: *to mix business and pleasure*

recreation: *time for recreation*

make fun of verb to tease someone: *Don't make fun of him*

deride: *This theory is widely derided*

laugh at: *They laughed at his hat*

mock: *He was often mocked by his classmates*

ridicule: *She allowed them to ridicule her*

taunt: *a fellow pupil who had taunted him about his height*

see also **entertainment**

function noun **1** the useful thing that something or someone does: *The main function of merchant banks is to raise capital*

duty: *My duty is to look after the animals*

job: *Their main job is to keep us healthy*

purpose: *The purpose of the occasion was to raise money for charity*

---

remit: The centre's remit is to advise businesses

responsibility: He handled his responsibilities as a counsellor in an intelligent fashion

role: information about the drug's role in preventing infection

2 a large formal dinner, reception, or party: We were going down to a function in London

dinner: a series of official dinners

gathering: I'm always shy at formal gatherings like that

party: They met at a party

reception: At the reception they served smoked salmon

▷ verb **3** was not functioning properly

go: My car won't go in fog

operate: Ceiling and wall lights can operate independently

perform: When there's snow, how is this car going to perform?

run: The system is now running smoothly

work: Is the telephone working today?

see also **act, behave, go, job, part, party, purpose**

functional see **practical**

fund noun **1** an amount of money: the pension fund

capital: difficulty in raising capital

foundation: money from a research foundation

pool: a reserve pool of cash

reserve: a drain on the cash reserves

supply: to curb money supply and inflation

2 a large amount of something: an extraordinary fund of energy

hoard: his hoard of supplies

mine: a mine of information

reserve: oil reserves

reservoir: the body's short-term reservoir of energy

store: a store of fuel

▷ verb **3** to provide the money for something: to raise money to fund research into breast cancer

finance: big projects financed by foreign aid

pay for: His parents paid for his holiday

subsidize: heavily subsidized by the government

support: He is supporting himself through college

see also **bank, finance, hoard, reserve, store, supply**

fundamental see **basic, basis, essential, principle**

fundamentals see **essentials**

fundi noun South African an expert: The local fundis are wonderfully adept and have created a car for hunting

expert: our team of experts

guru: Fashion gurus dictate some crazy ideas

master: a master of the English language

specialist: a specialist in diseases of the nervous system

virtuoso: He was gaining a reputation as a piano virtuoso

funds see **money**

funny adjective **1** being strange or odd: They heard a funny noise

mysterious: in mysterious circumstances

odd: There was something odd about her

peculiar: It tasted very peculiar

puzzling: a puzzling development

strange: A strange thing happened

unusual: a most unusual man

2 causing amusement: a funny story

amusing: a most amusing lecturer

comic: comic moments

comical: the comical expression on his face

hilarious: We thought it was hilarious

humorous: a humorous magazine

witty: a very witty speech

see also **odd, peculiar, strange,**

suspicious, weird, witty

funny feeling see premonition

fur see coat, pile

furious adjective **1** extremely angry: He is furious at the way his wife has been treated

enraged: I got more and more enraged at my father

fuming: He was still fuming over the remark

infuriated: He knew how infuriated the conversation had made me

livid: She was absolutely livid about it

mad: I'm pretty mad about this, I can tell you

raging: Inside, Sally was raging

2 involving great energy, effort, or speed: a furious gunbattle

breakneck: Jack drove to Mayfair at breakneck speed

fierce: Competition has been fierce between the rival groups

frantic: There was frantic activity behind the scenes

frenzied: the frenzied activity of the general election

intense: The military on both sides are involved in intense activity

manic: Preparations continued at a manic pace

see also **angry, mad, violent**

furnish see issue, provide, supply

further see benefit, extra, more

furthermore see also

furtive see mysterious, secret

fury see anger, frenzy, rage

fuse see bond, combine, stick

fusion see blend, mixture, union

fuss noun **1** anxious or excited behaviour: What's all the fuss about?

agitation: in a state of nervous agitation

bother: I don't want any bother

commotion: a commotion in the market

confusion: in the confusion after an ammunition dump blew up

stir: The play caused a stir here

to-do informal: a big to-do

▷ verb **2** to behave in a nervous or restless way: Waiters fussed around the table

bustle: shoppers bustling around the store

fidget: He was fidgeting with his tie

fret: Stop fretting about the details

see also **bustle**

fussy adjective difficult to please: fussy about his food

choosy informal: Cats can be choosy about what they eat

discriminating: a discriminating visitor

exacting: She failed to meet his exacting standards

fastidious: Disney was also fastidious about cleanliness

particular: very particular about the colours he used

see also **elaborate, particular**

futile adjective having no chance of success: a futile effort to run away

abortive: the abortive coup attempt

forlorn: forlorn hopes of future improvement

unsuccessful: an unsuccessful bid for independence

useless: It was useless to even try

vain: in the vain hope of success

see also **hopeless, useless, vain**

future adjective **1** relating to a time after the present: to predict future growth

approaching: concerned about the approaching winter

coming: in the coming months

forthcoming: candidates for the forthcoming elections

impending: her impending marriage

later: We'll discuss it at a later date

prospective: my prospective employers

see also **outlook**

g

gabble *see* **babble**

gadget *noun* a small machine or tool: *kitchen gadgets such as toasters and kettles*
appliance: *Switch off all electrical appliances when they're not in use*
device: *a device that warns you when the batteries need changing*
machine: *a machine for slicing vegetables*
tool: *a tool for cutting wood, metal or plastic*

gaffe *see* **mistake**

gaffer *see* **employer**

gag *see* **joke**, **silence**

gaggle *see* **bunch**

gain *verb* **1** to get something gradually: *Students can gain valuable experience by working*
achieve: *Achieving our goals makes us feel good*
acquire: *Companies should reward workers for acquiring more skills*
earn: *She has earned the respect of the world's top women cyclists*
obtain: *You would need to obtain permission to copy the design*
secure: *He failed to secure enough votes for outright victory*
win: *The long-term aim is to win promotion*
2 to get an advantage: *Areas of the world would actually gain from global warming*
benefit: *Both sides have benefited from the talks*
profit: *Frankie is now profiting from his crimes*
▷ *noun* **3** an increase or improvement in something: *The Party has made substantial gains in local elections*
advance: *advances in computer technology*
growth: *The area has seen a rapid population growth*
improvement: *a major improvement in standards*
increase: *an increase of 7% in visitors to the UK*
rise: *a 3% rise in electricity prices*
see also **acquire**, **advance**, **benefit**, **increase**, **secure**, **win**

gait *see* **walk**

gala *see* **celebration**, **festival**

galah *see* **idiot**

gall *see* **cheek**, **impudence**

gallantry *see* **courtesy**

gallop *see* **run**, **speed**

gamble *verb* **1** to bet money on something: *John gambled heavily on the horses*
back: *I backed Germany to win 1-0*
bet: *He bet them 500 pounds they would lose*
2 to take a risk: *Few firms will be willing to gamble on new products*
chance: *Armstrong chanced a gallop to the water*
risk: *One of his daughters risked everything to join him in exile*
stake: *He has staked his reputation on the outcome*
▷ *noun* **3** a risk that someone takes: *We are taking a gamble on a young player*

chance: You take a chance on the weather when you holiday in the UK
lottery: Robinson described the final as a bit of a lottery
risk: How much risk are you prepared to take?
see also **risk**

game noun an occasion on which people compete: South Africa's first game of the season
clash: the clash between Australia and the West Indies
contest: The rain spoiled a good contest
match: a football match
see also **agreeable, contest, match, willing**

gamut see **range**

gang see **band, bunch, group, party, team**

gap noun 1 a space or a hole in something: They squeezed through a gap in the fence
break: stars twinkling between the breaks in the clouds
chink: All the walls have wide chinks in them
crack: a crack in the curtains
hole: a hole in the wall
opening: an opening in the trees
space: the space between their car and the one in front
2 a period of time: After a gap of nearly a decade, Manley was back
hiatus formal: The shop is open again after a two year hiatus
interlude: a happy interlude in the Kents' life
interval: There was a long interval of silence
lull: a lull in the conversation
pause: Then, after a pause, he goes on
3 a difference between people or things: the gap between rich and poor
difference: He denied there were any major differences between them

disparity formal: disparities between poor and wealthy school districts
inconsistency: There were major inconsistencies in his evidence
see also **breach, hole, interval, opening, space**

garb see **dress**

garbage noun 1 things that people do not want: piles of garbage
debris: screws, bolts and other debris from a scrapyard
junk informal: What are you going to do with all that junk?
litter: If you see litter in the corridor, pick it up
refuse formal: refuse collection and street cleaning
rubbish: household rubbish
trash: I forgot to take out the trash
waste: industrial waste
2 informal ideas and opinions that are untrue or unimportant: I personally think this is complete garbage
drivel: What absolute drivel!
gibberish: a politician talking gibberish
nonsense: all that poetic nonsense about love
rubbish: He's talking rubbish
see also **nonsense, refuse, rubbish, trash**

garbled adjective confused or incorrect: A garbled message awaited us at the desk
confused: the latest twist in a murky and confused story
distorted: a distorted version of what was said
incomprehensible: Her speech was incomprehensible
jumbled: his jumbled account of how Jack had been hired
unintelligible: He muttered something unintelligible

gardens see **grounds**

garish see **flashy, gaudy, loud, tasteless**

garments see **clothes**

gash see **cut**

gasp verb **1** to breathe in quickly through your mouth: *She gasped for air*

choke: *People began to choke as smoke filled the air*

gulp: *She gulped air into her lungs*

pant: *Amy climbed rapidly until she was panting with the effort*

puff: *I could see he was unfit because he was puffing*

▷ noun **2** a short quick breath of air: *An audible gasp went round the court*

gulp: *I took in a large gulp of air*

pant: *Her breath came in pants*

puff: *He blew out a little puff of air*

gate see **entrance, entry**

gather verb **1** to come together in a group: *We gathered around the fireplace*

assemble: *a place for students to assemble between classes*

congregate: *Youngsters love to congregate here in the evenings*

flock: *The criticisms will not stop people flocking to see the film*

mass: *The General was massing his troops for a counterattack*

round up: *The police rounded up a number of suspects*

2 to bring things together: *I suggest we gather enough firewood to last the night*

accumulate: *In five years it has accumulated a huge debt*

amass: *She has amassed a personal fortune of $38 million*

collect: *1.5 million signatures have been collected*

hoard: *They've begun to hoard food and gasoline*

stockpile: *People are stockpiling food for the coming winter*

3 to learn or believe something: *"He speaks English." "I gathered that."*

assume: *I assume the eggs are fresh*

conclude: *He concluded that Oswald was somewhat abnormal*

hear: *I heard that he was forced to resign*

learn: *She wasn't surprised to learn that he was involved*

understand: *I understand that he's just taken early retirement*

see also **assemble, collect, concentrate, crowd, hear, imagine, learn, mass, meet, pick, stockpile, understand**

gathering noun a meeting with a purpose: *polite social gatherings*

assembly: *an assembly of party members*

congregation: *The congregation sang hymns and said prayers*

get-together informal: *family get-togethers*

meeting: *Can we have a meeting to discuss that?*

rally: *a pre-election rally*

see also **function, hui, meeting, party**

gauche see **clumsy**

gaudy adjective colourful in a vulgar way: *gaudy fake jewellery*

bright: *fake fur, dyed in bright colours*

flashy: *women in flashy satin suits*

garish: *They climbed the garish purple-carpeted stairs*

loud: *a loud checked shirt*

showy: *He favoured large showy flowers*

tacky informal: *tacky red sunglasses*

vulgar: *I think it's a very vulgar house*

see also **loud, tasteless, vulgar**

gauge see **measure**

gaze see **look, regard, stare**

gaze at see **watch**

gear see **clothes, equipment, stuff, things**

general adjective **1** relating to the whole of something: *a general decline in employment*

broad: *a broad outline of the Society's development*

comprehensive: *a comprehensive guide to the region*

overall: *The overall quality of pupils' work had shown a marked improvement*

2 widely true, suitable or relevant: *The project should raise general awareness about bullying*

accepted: *the accepted version of events*

broad: *a film with broad appeal*

common: *Such behaviour is common to all young people*

universal: *Music and sports programmes have a universal appeal*

widespread: *The proposals have attracted widespread support*

see also **broad, common, mass, popular, public, universal**

generally *see* **as a rule, mainly, on average**

generate *see* **bring about, cause**

generosity noun willingness to give money, time or help: *She is well known for her generosity*

benevolence: *Banks are not known for their benevolence*

charity: *private acts of charity*

kindness: *We have been treated with such kindness by everyone*

generous adjective **1** willing to give money, time or help: *The gift is generous by any standards*

charitable: *Individuals can be charitable and help their neighbours*

hospitable: *He was very hospitable to me when I came to New York*

kind: *She is warm-hearted and kind to everyone*

lavish: *The Princess received a number of lavish gifts from her hosts*

liberal: *Don't be too liberal with your spending*

2 very large: *a generous portion of spaghetti*

abundant: *an abundant supply of hot food*

ample: *There is ample space for a good-sized kitchen*

plentiful: *a plentiful supply of beer*

see also **handsome, noble**

genial *see* **friendly, warm**

genius noun **1** a very clever or talented person: *a mathematical genius*

brain: *the financial brain behind the company*

master: *Spiro Rosakis is a master of his craft*

mastermind: *the mastermind of the plot to kill the ex-prime minister*

virtuoso: *The man is a virtuoso of pop music*

2 extraordinary ability or talent: *a poet of genius*

brains: *She has brains as well as beauty*

brilliance: *his brilliance as a director*

intellect: *people of great intellect*

see also **talent**

genre *see* **class, kind**

genteel *see* **polite, posh, refined**

gentle adjective not violent or rough: *a quiet and gentle man*

benign: *a good-natured chap with a benign expression*

kind: *I fell in love with him because of his kind nature*

kindly: *a kindly old gentleman*

meek: *He was a meek, mild-mannered fellow*

mild: *Alexis was quiet, mild and happy-go-lucky*

placid: *a look of impatience on her normally placid face*

soft: *She had a very soft heart*

tender: *Her voice was tender*

see also **leisurely, mild, soft, tender, win**

gentleman *see* **man**

gentlemanly *see* **refined**

gentleness *see* **kindness**

genuine *adjective* not false or pretend: *They're convinced the picture is genuine*
  authentic: *an authentic French recipe*
  bona fide: *We are happy to donate to bona fide charities*
  dinkum *Australian, New Zealand informal*: *They are all dinkum stolen bank notes*
  real: *a real Rembrandt*
see also **actual, authentic, dinkum, natural, real, right, serious, sincere, true**

germ-free *see* **pure, sterile**

germinate *see* **grow**

gesticulate *see* **signal**

gesture *see* **signal**

get *verb* **1** to fetch or receive something: *I'll get us all a cup of coffee*
  acquire: *I have recently acquired a new camera*
  fetch: *Sylvia fetched a towel from the bathroom*
  obtain: *Evans was trying to obtain a false passport*
  procure *formal*: *It remained very difficult to procure food*
  receive: *I received your letter of November 7*
  secure *formal*: *He failed to secure enough votes for outright victory*
  2 to change from one state to another: *People draw the curtains once it gets dark*
  become: *The wind became stronger*
  grow: *He grew to love his work*
  turn: *The leaves have turned golden-brown*
see also **acquire, develop, earn, extract, grow, obtain, receive, secure, see, take in, understand,**

get across *see* **convey**

get away *see* **escape**

get back *see* **recover**

get back at *see* **retaliate**

get better *see* **recover**

get even *see* **revenge**

get even with *see* **retaliate**

get going *see* **start**

get hold of *see* **contact, obtain**

get in the way *see* **impede**

get in touch with *see* **contact**

get off your chest *see* **reveal**

get on someone's nerves *see* **annoy, bother, pester**

get out of *see* **dodge**

get rid of *see* **dispose of, dump, eliminate, remove**

get through *see* **pass**

get to *see* **reach**

get together *see* **meet**

get well *see* **recover**

get your own back *see* **retaliate, revenge**

get on *verb* to enjoy someone's company: *I get on very well with his wife*
  be compatible: *Mary and I are very compatible*
  hit it off *informal*: *They hit it off straight away*
see also **do**

get-together *see* **gathering, meeting, party**

ghastly *see* **awful, dreadful**

ghost *noun* the spirit of a dead person: *the ghost of the drowned girl*
  apparition: *She felt as if she were seeing a ghostly apparition*
  phantom: *She was relentlessly pursued by a grossly disfigured phantom*
  spectre: *The Tower is said to be haunted by the spectre of Anne Boleyn*
  spirit: *the spirits of our dead ancestors*
see also **spirit**

ghostly see **spooky**

giant see **huge, immense, large, vast**

gibberish see **garbage**

gidday interjection Australian, New Zealand hello: Gidday, mate!
hello: Hello, Trish. Glad you could make it
hi informal: Hi, how are you doing?
good morning formal: Good morning, class
good afternoon formal: Good afternoon, Miss Bates
good evening formal: Good evening, ladies and gentlemen!
see also **hello**

giddy see **dizzy, faint**

gift noun **1** something you give someone: He showered her with gifts
bequest formal: They received a bequest of $310,000
bonsela South African: a generous bonsela
contribution: companies that make charitable contributions
donation: donations of food and clothing for victims of the hurricane
legacy: What about the legacy from your uncle?
present: This book would make a great Christmas present
2 a natural skill or ability: a gift for comedy
ability: It's obvious he has an exceptional ability
aptitude: She realised she had an aptitude for writing
flair: Tony found he had a real flair for design
talent: Both her children have a talent for music
see also **blessing, capacity, present, talent**

gigantic see **colossal, enormous, immense, large, vast**

giggle see **laugh**

girl see **female, woman**

girlish see **female**

gist see **meaning**

give verb **1** to provide someone with something: I gave her a CD
award: The Mayor awarded him a medal
deliver: The Canadians plan to deliver more food to southern Somalia
donate: Others donated second-hand clothes
grant: Permission was granted a few weeks ago
hand: Isabel handed me a glass of orange juice
present: The Queen presented the prizes
provide: The government was not in a position to provide them with food
supply: a contract to supply radar equipment to the Philippines
2 to collapse or break under pressure: My knees gave under me
buckle: His left wrist buckled under the strain
cave in: Half the ceiling caved in
collapse: The roof supports had collapsed
give way: He fell when a ledge gave way beneath him
yield: The handle yielded to her grasp
see also **grant, hand down, issue, present, spare, supply**

give a kick see **thrill**

give a talk see **lecture**

give back see **return**

give off see **discharge, emit**

give out see **emit, fail, issue**

give up see **abstain, cease, quit, renounce, sacrifice, surrender**

give way see **collapse, give**

give in verb to admit that you are defeated: Juppe should not give in to the strikers
capitulate: Cohen capitulated to virtually every demand

concede: Mr Pyke is not prepared to concede defeat
submit: Mrs Jones submitted to an operation on her right knee
succumb: The Minister said his country would never succumb to pressure
surrender: He surrendered to American troops
yield: an enemy who had shown no desire to yield
see also **submit, surrender**
given see **prone**
glad adjective happy about something: They'll be glad to get away from it all
delighted: Frank will be delighted to see you
happy: Jacques is very happy that you are here
joyful: a joyful reunion with his mother
overjoyed: Shelley was overjoyed to see me
pleased: They're pleased to be going home
see also **pleased**
glance noun 1 a brief look at something: The boys exchanged glances
glimpse: They caught a glimpse of their hero
look: Lucille took a last look in the mirror
peek: Could I just have another quick peek at the bedroom?
peep: Would you take a peep out of the window?
▷ verb 2 to look at something quickly: He glanced at his watch
glimpse: I soon glimpsed the doctor in his garden
look: Bethan looked quickly at the elegant people around her
peek: She had peeked at him through a crack in the wall

peep: Now and then she peeped to see if he was noticing her
scan: She scanned the advertisement pages of the newspaper
3 to hit something quickly and bounce away: My fist glanced off his jaw
bounce: The ball bounced off the opposite post
brush: She brushed her lips across Michael's cheek
skim: pebbles skimming across the water
see also **look, peek**
glance at see **read**
glare verb 1 to look angrily at someone: Joe glared at his brother
frown: She looked up to see Vic frowning at her
glower: He glowered at me but said nothing
scowl: Robert scowled, and slammed the door behind him
▷ noun 2 an angry look: The waiter lowered his eyes to avoid Harold's furious glare
frown: There was a deep frown on the boy's face
scowl: Chris met the remark with a scowl
3 very bright light: the glare of the headlights
blaze: There was a sudden blaze of light
glow: the glow of the fire
see also **frown, light**
glaring see **manifest**
glassy see **clear, smooth**
gleam see **gloss, glow, shine, sparkle**
gleaming see **brilliant, shining**
glean see **extract**
glee see **delight**
glide see **float, flow**
glimmer see **glow**
glimpse see **glance, look, peek, see**

glint see **flash**

glisten see **sparkle**

glitter see **flash**, **sparkle**

gloat see **glory**

globe see **ball**, **earth**

gloom see **dark**, **despair**

gloomy adjective **1** feeling very sad: *They are gloomy about their chances of success*

dejected: *Everyone has days when they feel dejected*

down: *The old man sounded really down*

glum: *What on earth are you looking so glum about?*

miserable: *She went to bed, miserable and depressed*

sad: *You must feel sad about what's happened*

2 dark and depressing: *a gloomy house on the edge of Phoenix Park*

dark: *The house looked dark and gloomy*

dismal: *damp and dismal weather*

dreary: *the dreary, industrial city of Ludwigshafen*

dull: *It's always dull and raining*
see also **cloudy**, **drab**, **dull**, **miserable**, **pessimistic**, **sad**

glorify see **honour**, **worship**

glorious see **splendid**

glory noun **1** fame and admiration that someone gets: *It was her moment of glory*

fame: *The film earned him international fame*

honour: *the honour of captaining one's country*

immortality: *Some people want to achieve immortality through their work*

praise: *Holbroke deserves full praise for his efforts*

prestige: *I'm not in this job for the prestige*

2 something impressive or beautiful: *Spring arrived in all its glory*

grandeur: *the grandeur of the country mansion*

magnificence: *the magnificence of the sunset*

majesty: *the majesty of Niagara Falls*

splendour: *the splendour of the palace of Versailles*

▷ verb **3** to enjoy something very much: *The workers were glorying in their new-found freedom*

gloat: *Their rivals were gloating over their triumph*

relish: *He relished the idea of getting some cash*

revel: *a ruthless killer who revels in his job*
see also **credit**, **fame**, **rejoice**

gloss noun a bright shine on a surface: *aluminium foil with a high gloss surface*

brilliance: *ceramic tiles of great brilliance*

gleam: *the gleam of brass*

polish: *His boots had a high polish*

sheen: *The carpet had a silvery sheen to it*

shine: *This gel gives a beautiful shine to the hair*

glossy adjective smooth and shiny: *The leaves were dark and glossy*

bright: *Her eyes were bright with excitement*

brilliant: *The woman had brilliant green eyes*

polished: *a highly polished floor*

shiny: *a shiny new sports car*

sleek: *sleek black hair*
see also **smooth**

glow noun **1** a dull steady light: *the glow of the fire*

gleam: *the first gleam of dawn*

glimmer: *In the east there was the slightest glimmer of light*

light: *the light of the evening sun*

▷ verb **2** to shine with a dull steady light: *A light glowed behind the* curtains

gleam: Lights gleamed in the deepening mist

glimmer: A few stars still glimmered

shine: Scattered lights shone on the horizon

smoulder: A very small fire was smouldering in the grate

see also **blush, glare, light, shine**

glower see **frown, glare**

glowing see **bright, brilliant**

glue verb to stick things together: Glue the two halves together

fix: Fix the fabric to the roller

paste: The children were busy pasting gold stars on a chart

seal: He sealed the envelope and put on a stamp

stick: I stuck the notice on the board

see also **bond, stick**

glum see **down, gloomy, pessimistic, sad**

glut see **excess**

gnaw see **bite, chew**

go verb 1 to move or travel somewhere: I went home at the weekend

advance: Rebel forces are advancing on the capital

drive: My husband and I drove to Liverpool to see my mum

fly: He flew to Los Angeles

journey formal: They intended to journey up the Amazon

leave: What time are you leaving?

proceed formal: The taxi proceeded along a lonely road

set off: He set off for the station

travel: Students often travel hundreds of miles to get here

2 to work properly: stuck on the motorway with a car that won't go

function: All the instruments functioned properly

work: The pump doesn't work and we have no running water

▷ noun 3 an attempt to do something: I always wanted to have a go at waterskiing

attempt: one of his rare attempts at humour

shot informal: a shot at winning a brand new car

stab informal: Several sports stars have had a stab at acting and singing

try: After a few tries, Patrick had given up

see also **attempt, fit, function, journey, range, travel, try, turn, work out**

go across see **cross**

go against see **clash**

go as far as see **reach**

go away see **disappear, vanish**

go back see **return**

go beyond see **pass, top**

go down see **decline, descend**

go down with see **develop**

go for see **like, prefer**

go into see **discuss**

go off see **explode**

go on see **continue, proceed, remain, stretch, take place**

go on at see **hassle**

go over see **examine**

go together with see **accompany**

go up see **rise**

go well see **blend**

go with see **accompany, match, suit**

go wrong see **err**

goad see **incite, provoke**

go-ahead see **permission**

goal noun something that a person hopes to achieve: The goal is to make as much money as possible

aim: The aim of the festival is to raise awareness of this issue

end: This is another policy designed to achieve the same end

intention: He announced his intention of standing for parliament

object: The object of the exercise is to

raise money for charity

objective: His objective was to play golf and win

purpose: His purpose was to make a profit

target: She failed to achieve her target of losing 20 pounds

see also **aim, intention, object, point**

gobble verb to eat food very quickly: Pete gobbled all the beef stew

bolt: Being under stress can cause you to bolt your food

devour: She devoured two bars of chocolate

wolf: Pitt wolfed down a peanut butter sandwich

God-fearing see **religious**

godly see **religious**

godsend see **blessing**

gone see **absent, over**

good adjective **1** pleasant, acceptable or satisfactory: We had a really good time

2 skilful or successful: I'm not very good at art

3 kind, thoughtful and loving: You are so good to me

see **word studies good**

see also **benefit, favourable, kind, respectable, sound**

good afternoon see **gidday, hello**

good evening see **gidday, hello**

good morning see **gidday, hello**

good-looking see **cute, handsome**

goodness see **honour, virtue**

goods see **product, stock**

goodwill noun kindness and helpfulness towards other people: I invited them to dinner as a gesture of goodwill

benevolence: He chuckles often and radiates benevolence

favour: in order to gain the favour of whoever is in power

friendliness: Visitors remarked on the friendliness of the people

friendship: The two countries signed treaties of friendship

see also **friendship**

gorge see **abyss, fill**

gorgeous see **beautiful, cute, splendid**

gossip noun informal conversation about other people: Don't you like a good gossip?

dirt: the latest dirt on the other candidates

hearsay: They have had only hearsay and rumour to go on

see also **chat, rumour**

go through verb to experience an unpleasant event: I was going through a very difficult time

endure: He'd endured years of pain and sleepless nights

experience: British business was experiencing a severe recession

undergo: Magee underwent emergency surgery

see also **endure, examine, suffer, undergo**

gouge see **dig**

govern see **control, determine, guide, lead, rule**

government see **control**

governor see **chief, ruler**

gown see **dress**

grab verb to take hold of something roughly: I grabbed him by the neck

clutch: Michelle clutched my arm

grasp: He grasped both my hands

seize: She seized a carving fork and advanced in my direction

snatch: Mick snatched the cards from Archie's hand

see also **grasp, seize**

grace noun an elegant way of moving: He moved with the grace of a trained boxer

elegance: She is elegance personified

poise: Ballet classes are important for

poise and grace
see also **courtesy, favour, polish**

graciousness see **courtesy**

grade verb to arrange things
according to quality: *The oil is tasted
and graded according to quality*
  class: *They are officially classed as
  visitors*
  classify: *Rocks can be classified
  according to their origin*
  group: *The fact sheets are grouped
  into seven sections*
  rate: *He was rated as one of the
  country's top young players*
  sort: *The students are sorted into
  three ability groups*
see also **class, classify, kind, level,
quality, rank, sort**

gradient see **slope, tilt**

gradual adjective happening
or changing slowly: *the gradual
improvement in communications*
  continuous: *Our policy is one of
  continuous improvement*
  progressive: *One symptom of the
  disease is progressive loss of memory*
  slow: *The distribution of passports
  has been a slow process*
  steady: *a steady rise in sales*
see also **slow**

gradually see **slowly**

graduate see **pass, qualify**

grain see **bit, finish**

grammar noun

grand adjective **1** very impressive in
size or appearance: *a grand building
in the centre of town*
  imposing: *the imposing gates at the
  entrance to the estate*
  impressive: *The old boat presented
  an impressive sight*
  magnificent: *magnificent views over
  the San Fernando valley*
  majestic: *a stupendous vista of
  majestic peaks*
  monumental: *a monumental

sculpture of a human face
  splendid: *a splendid Victorian
  mansion*
2 informal pleasant or enjoyable: *It
was a grand day*
  brilliant informal: *I've had a brilliant
  time*
  great informal: *I had a great time at
  university*
  marvellous informal: *It was a
  marvellous day and we were all so
  happy*
  terrific informal: *Everybody there was
  having a terrific time*
  wonderful: *It was a wonderful
  experience*
see also **impressive, splendid**

grandeur see **glory**

grandiose see **ostentatious,
pompous**

grant noun **1** a money award
given for a particular purpose:
*My application for a grant has been
accepted*
  allocation: *The aid allocation for that
  country is under review*
  allowance: *She gets an allowance for
  looking after Lillian*
  award: *a study award worth £2,000*
  handout: *a cash handout of six
  thousand rupees*
  subsidy: *state subsidies to public
  transport companies*
▷ verb **2** to allow someone to have
something: *France has agreed to
grant him political asylum*
  allocate: *The budget allocated $7
  billion for development programmes*
  allow: *Children should be allowed the
  occasional treat*
  award: *A High Court judge awarded
  him £6 million damages*
  give: *We have been given permission
  to attend the meeting*
  permit: *The doorman said he could
  not permit them entry to the film

3 to admit that something is true: *I grant you had some justification for your actions*

accept: *I do not accept that there is a crisis in British science*

acknowledge: *He acknowledged that he had been partly to blame*

admit: *I admit that I do make mistakes*

allow: *He allows that capitalist development may result in social inequality*

concede: *Bess finally conceded that Nancy was right*

see also **admit, allow, give, permit, present**

graphic see colourful

grapple see fight

grasp verb **1** to hold something firmly: *He grasped both my hands*

clutch: *I staggered and had to clutch at a chair for support*

grab: *I grabbed him by the neck*

grip: *She gripped the rope*

hold: *He held the pistol tightly in his right hand*

seize: *He seized my arm to hold me back*

snatch: *I snatched at a hanging branch and pulled myself up*

2 to understand an idea: *The Government has not yet grasped the seriousness of the crisis*

absorb: *He only absorbed about half the information we gave him*

appreciate: *She never really appreciated the bitterness of the conflict*

assimilate: *My mind could only assimilate one concept at a time*

realize: *People don't realize how serious this recession is*

take in: *She listens to the explanation, but you can see she's not taking it in*

understand: *They are too young to understand what is going on*

▷ noun **3** a firm hold: *She slipped her hand from his grasp*

clasp: *He gripped my hand in a strong clasp*

embrace: *He held her in a passionate embrace*

grip: *His strong hand eased the bag from her grip*

hold: *He released his hold on the camera*

4 a person's understanding of something: *They have a good grasp of foreign languages*

awareness: *The children demonstrated their awareness of green issues*

comprehension formal: *This was utterly beyond her comprehension*

grip: *He has lost his grip on reality*

knowledge: *She has a good knowledge of these processes*

understanding: *a basic understanding of computers*

see also **command, comprehend, grab, grip, handle, hold, learn, master, realize, see, seize, take in, understand, understanding**

grass on see inform on

grate see scrape

grateful adjective pleased and wanting to thank someone: *I am grateful to you for your help*

appreciative: *We have been very appreciative of their support*

indebted: *I am deeply indebted to him for his help*

thankful: *I'm just thankful that I've got a job*

gratified see proud

gratify see satisfy

gratis see free

gratitude noun the feeling of being grateful: *I wish to express my gratitude to Kathy Davis for her help*

appreciation: *their appreciation of his efforts*

recognition: *an honour given in recognition of his help to the college*
thanks: *They accepted their certificates with words of thanks*

grave *noun* **1** *a place where a corpse is buried: They visited her grave twice a year*
mausoleum: *the great mausoleum at the top of the hill*
pit: *The bodies were buried in a shallow pit*
sepulchre: *Death holds him in his sepulchre*
tomb: *the tomb of the Unknown Soldier*
▷ *adjective* **2** *formal* very serious: *The situation in his country is very grave*
acute: *The report has caused acute embarrassment to the government*
critical: *Its finances are in a critical state*
heavy: *Things were just starting to get heavy when the police arrived*
serious: *The government faces very serious difficulties*
sober: *a room filled with sad, sober faces*
solemn: *His solemn little face broke into smiles*
sombre: *His expression became increasingly sombre*
see also **acute, critical, deep, grim, heavy, serious, severe, solemn, tomb**

graze *verb* **1** to slightly injure your skin: *He fell heavily and grazed his left arm*
scrape: *She stumbled and fell, scraping her hands and knees*
scratch: *The branches scratched my hands and face*
skin: *He fell and skinned both his knees*
▷ *noun* **2** a slight injury to your skin: *He just has a slight graze*
abrasion *formal*: *He had severe abrasions to his right cheek*
scratch: *She had scratches to her face*
see also **scrape, touch**

great *adjective* **1** very large in size: *great columns of ice*
2 important or famous: *the great novels of the nineteenth century*
3 *informal* very good: *I thought it was a great idea*
see **word studies great**
see also **acute, brilliant, deep, excellent, extensive, extreme, grand, intense, large, outstanding, splendid, uncommon, vast, wonderful**

great deal see **plenty**

greatest see **foremost, supreme, ultimate**

greatly see **very**

greedy *adjective* wanting more than you need: *greedy bosses who award themselves huge pay rises*
materialistic: *During the 1980s Britain became a very materialistic society*
snoep *South African informal*: *a bunch of snoep businessmen*
see also **selfish**

green *adjective* concerned with environmental issues: *Children and adolescents are now aware of green issues*
conservationist: *a chorus of protest from conservationist groups*
ecological: *shared interest in ecological issues*
see also **field, ignorant, inexperienced**

greet *verb* to say hello to someone when they arrive: *The president was greeted by local political leaders*
meet: *A nurse met me at the entrance*
receive *formal*: *250 guests were received by the bride and bridegroom*
welcome: *She was there to welcome him home*

see also **receive**

gregarious see **sociable**

grey noun or adjective
see also **dim, drab**

grief noun a feeling of extreme sadness: *a huge outpouring of national grief*

    distress: *The intense distress they were causing my family*

    heartache: *She has suffered more heartache than anyone deserves*

    misery: *All that money brought nothing but misery*

    sadness: *It is with a mixture of sadness and joy that I say farewell*

    sorrow: *a time of great sorrow*

    unhappiness: *There was a lot of unhappiness in my adolescence*
see also **misery, pain, regret, sorrow**

grief-stricken see **sad**

grievance see **complaint, wrong**

grieve verb **1** to feel extremely sad: *He still grieves for his wife*

    lament: *All who knew Spender will lament his death*

    mourn: *The whole nation mourns the death of their great leader*

    2 to make someone feel extremely sad: *It grieved Elaine to be separated from her son*

    distress: *It distresses me that the President has not tackled crime*

    pain: *It pains me to think of you struggling all alone*

    sadden: *The cruelty in the world saddens me*

    upset: *The news upset me*
see also **distress, lament, regret, upset**

grievous see **painful, serious**

grill see **cook, interrogate**

grim adjective looking very serious: *Her face was grim*

    grave: *Mrs Williams was looking very grave*

    severe: *He leaned towards me, a*
severe expression on his face

    solemn: *What a solemn-faced kid he had been*

    stern: *Michael gave the dog a stern look*
see also **horrible, serious, severe**

grime see **dirt**

grimy see **dirty**

grin see **smile**

grind see **scrape**

grip noun **1** a firm hold on something: *His strong hand eased the bag from her grip*

    clasp: *With one last clasp of his hand, she left him*

    grasp: *The spade slipped from her grasp and fell to the ground*

    hold: *He released his hold on the camera*

    2 someone's control over something: *The president maintains an iron grip on his country*

    clutches: *She fell into the clutches of the wrong sort of person*

    control: *The port area is under the control of rebel forces*

    influence: *Alexandra fell under the influence of Grigori Rasputin*

    power: *I was really in the power of my mother*

   ▷ verb **3** to hold something firmly: *Alison gripped the steering wheel and stared straight ahead*

    clutch: *Michelle clutched my arm*

    grasp: *He grasped both my hands*

    hold: *He was struggling to hold on to the rope*
see also **clasp, grasp, handle, hold**

gripping see **interesting**

groan see **grumble, moan**

grog see **alcohol**

gross see **disgusting**

ground noun the surface of the earth: *We slid down the roof and dropped to the ground*

    dirt: *They sat on the dirt in the shade*

of a tree

earth: *The road winds for miles through parched earth*

land: *800 acres of agricultural land*

soil: *In Southern India the soil is fertile*

terrain: *Farms give way to hilly terrain*

see also **base**, **bottom**, **earth**, **soil**

grounds plural noun **1** the land surrounding a building: *the grounds of the university*

estate: *Lord Wyville's estate in Yorkshire*

gardens: *an elegant Regency house set in beautiful gardens*

land: *Their home is on his father's land* **2** the reason for doing or thinking something: *Owen was against it on the grounds of expense*

basis: *Could you tell me on what basis the fee is calculated?*

cause: *No one had cause to get angry or unpleasant*

excuse: *There's no excuse for behaviour like that*

justification: *There was no justification for what I was doing*

reason: *Who would have a reason to want to kill her?*

see also **argument**, **cause**, **land**, **reason**

group noun **1** a number of people or things: *a group of football supporters*

band: *a band of rebels*

bunch: *They're a nice bunch of lads*

collection: *a collection of essays from foreign affairs experts*

crowd: *A small crowd of onlookers has gathered*

gang: *Gangs of teenagers hang out in shop doorways*

pack: *a pack of journalists eager to question him*

party: *a party of sightseers*

set: *Different sets of people often use the same buildings*

▷ verb **2** to link people or things together: *Their responses are grouped into 11 categories*

arrange: *He started to arrange the books in piles*

class: *They are officially classed as visitors*

classify: *Rocks can be classified according to their origin*

organize: *I was organizing the vast array of junk we had collected*

sort: *The students are sorted into three ability groups*

see also **arrange**, **association**, **band**, **bunch**, **category**, **class**, **club**, **collection**, **company**, **grade**, **lot**, **mass**, **movement**, **organization**, **society**, **sort**, **team**, **type**

grouping see **party**

grouse see **complain**

grow verb **1** to increase in size or amount: *Bacteria grow more quickly once food is contaminated*

develop: *These clashes could develop into open warfare*

expand: *Will the universe continue to expand forever?*

increase: *Industrial output increased by 2%*

multiply: *Her husband multiplied his demands on her time*

2 to be alive or exist: *Trees and bushes grew down to the water's edge*

flourish: *The plant flourishes in slightly harsher climates*

germinate: *Heat will encourage seeds to germinate*

sprout: *It only takes a few days for beans to sprout*

3 to change gradually: *I grew a little afraid of the guy next door*

become: *The wind became stronger*

get: *The boys were getting bored*

turn: *In October it turned cold*

see also **develop**, **expand**, **get**, **increase**, **rise**, **spread**

grow up see **mature**

grown see **mature**

grown-up see **adult, mature**

growth noun the act of getting bigger: *the growth of the fishing industry*

development: *What are your plans for the development of your company?*

enlargement: *the enlargement of the European Union*

expansion: *a new period of economic expansion*

increase: *a sharp increase in the number of homeless people*
see also **gain, increase, spread**

grub see **kai**

grubby see **dirty**

grudge see **resentment**

grudging see **unwilling**

gruesome see **horrible**

gruff see **hoarse**

grumble verb **1** to complain in a bad-tempered way: *"This is very inconvenient,"* he grumbled

carp: *the man whom other actors love to carp about*

complain: *They complained about the high cost of visiting Europe*

groan: *parents groaning about the price of college tuition*

moan: *moaning about the weather*

mutter: *She could hear the old woman muttering about young people*

whine: *children who whine that they are bored*

whinge: *All she ever does is whinge*

▷ noun **2** a bad-tempered complaint: *I didn't hear any grumbles from anyone at the time*

complaint: *I get nothing but complaints about my cooking*

moan: *Sometimes it helps to have a good old moan*

murmur: *She paid without a murmur*

objection: *If you have any objections, please raise them now*

protest: *Despite our protests, they went ahead with the plan*

whinge: *It's depressing listening to everybody's whinges*
see also **complain, complaint, moan**

grumpy adjective bad-tempered and annoyed: *a grumpy old man*

irritable: *He had missed his dinner and grew irritable*

sulky: *She still looked like a sulky teenager*

sullen: *Several leading players have maintained a sullen silence*

surly: *They were surly, sometimes downright rude to me*
see also **cross**

grunt see **moan**

guarantee noun **1** something that makes another thing certain: *The package offered a guarantee of job security*

assurance: *a written assurance that he would start work at once*

pledge: *a pledge of support from the Ministry of Culture*

promise: *I'd made him a promise that I'd write a book for him*

undertaking: *She gave an undertaking not to repeat the allegations*

word: *He simply cannot be trusted to keep his word*

▷ verb **2** to make it certain that something will happen: *Reports of this kind are guaranteed to cause anxiety*

ensure: *We need to ensure that every student has basic literacy skills*

pledge: *Both sides pledged that a nuclear war would never be fought*

promise: *He promised that the rich would not get preferential treatment*
see also **ensure, promise**

guaranteed see **certain, definite**

guard verb **1** to protect someone: *Police were guarding his home* yesterday

defend: He and his friends defended themselves against racist thugs

protect: What can women do to protect themselves from heart disease?

safeguard: measures to safeguard their forces from chemical weapons

shelter: A neighbour sheltered the boy for seven days

shield: She had shielded him from the terrible truth

watch over: two policewomen to watch over him

2 to stop someone making trouble or escaping: The soldiers had been guarding paramilitary prisoners

patrol: Prison officers continued to patrol the grounds

police: It is extremely difficult to police the border

supervise: Only two staff were supervising over 100 prisoners

▷ noun **3** someone who guards people or places: The prisoners overpowered their guards and locked them in a cell

sentry: We can sneak past the sentries

warden: The siege began when the prisoners seized three wardens

see also **defend, protect, safeguard, watch**

guard against see **beware**

guarded see **cautious, wary**

guardian see **champion**

guess verb **1** to form an idea or opinion about something: Wood guessed that he was a very successful banker

estimate: It's difficult to estimate how much money is involved

imagine: "Was he meeting someone?" "I imagine so."

reckon: Toni reckoned that it must be about three o'clock

speculate: The reader can speculate what will happen next

suppose: I supposed you would have a meal somewhere

suspect: I suspect they were right

think: Nora thought he was seventeen years old

▷ noun **2** an attempt to give the right answer: My guess is that the answer will be negative

feeling: My feeling is that everything will come right for us

reckoning: By my reckoning, 50% of the team will be available

speculation: speculations about the future of the universe

see also **assume, estimate, figure, idea, imagine, suppose, suspect**

guffaw see **laugh**

guidance see **advice, direction, help**

guide verb **1** to lead someone somewhere: He took Elliott by the arm and guided him out

accompany: We accompanied Joe to the magazine's midtown offices

direct: Officials directed him to the wrong airport

escort: I escorted him to the door

lead: The nurse led me to a large room

2 to influence someone: He should have let his instinct guide him

counsel formal: Green was counselled not to talk to reporters

govern: Our thinking is as much governed by habit as by behaviour

influence: My dad influenced me to do electronics

see also **direct, ease, influence, lead, manoeuvre, take**

guideline see **rule, standard**

guild see **club, society**

guile see **cunning, fraud**

guileless see **dinkum, innocent**

guilt see **blame, responsibility**

guilty adjective **1** having done something wrong: They were found guilty of murder

convicted: a convicted drug dealer

criminal: *He had a criminal record for petty theft*
2 unhappy because you have done something bad: *When she saw me she looked guilty*
ashamed: *Zumel said he was not ashamed of what he had done*
regretful: *Surprisingly, she didn't feel regretful about her actions*
remorseful *formal*: *He felt remorseful for what he had done*
sorry: *She was very sorry about all the trouble she'd caused*
see also **ashamed, responsible**

gulf *see* **bay**
gullibility *see* **innocence**
gullible *adjective* easily tricked: *I'm so gullible I would have believed him*
naive: *It would be naive to believe Mr Gonzalez's statement*
trusting: *She has an open, trusting nature*
see also **impressionable**

gulp *see* **drink, gasp**
guru *see* **adviser, expert, fundi, teacher**
gush *verb* to flow in large quantities: *Piping-hot water gushed out*
flow: *Tears flowed down his cheeks*
pour: *Blood was pouring from his broken nose*
spurt: *a fountain that spurts water nine stories high*
stream: *water streaming from the pipes*
see also **pour, rave, rush**

gutless *see* **cowardly**
guts *see* **courage, daring, insides**
guy *see* **man**
guzzle *see* **drink**

habit *noun* **1** something that is done regularly: *his habit of smiling at everyone he saw*
convention: *It's just a social convention that men don't wear skirts*
custom: *an ancient Japanese custom*
practice: *the practice of clocking in at work*
routine: *my daily routine*
tradition: *a family tradition at Christmas*
2 an addiction to something: *her cocaine habit*
addiction: *his addiction to gambling*
dependence: *the effects of drug dependence*
see also **custom, practice**

habitat *noun* the natural home of a plant or animal: *the habitat of the spotted owl*
environment: *a safe environment for marine mammals*
territory: *a bird's territory*

habitual *see* **frequent, normal, regular, usual**
hack *see* **chop**
hack off *see* **annoy**
hackneyed *adjective* used too often to be meaningful: *hackneyed postcard snaps of lochs and glens*

banal: banal lyrics
clichéd: clichéd slogans
stale: Her relationship with Mark has become stale
tired: a tired excuse
trite: The film is teeming with trite ideas
see also **corny, stock**

hail noun **1** a lot of things falling together: a hail of bullets
barrage: a barrage of angry questions
bombardment: the sound of heavy aerial bombardment
shower: a shower of rose petals
storm: The announcement provoked a storm of protest
volley: A volley of shots rang out
▷ verb **2** to attract someone's attention: He hailed me from across the street
call: He called me over the Tannoy
signal to: The lollipop lady signalled to me to stop
wave down: I ran on to the road and waved down a taxi

hair see **coat, pile**
hair-raising see **frightening, scary**
half-pie see **incomplete**
halfway see **middle**
halfway point see **middle**
hall see **passage**
hallmark see **property**
hallow see **bless**
hallowed see **holy**
hallucination see **dream, illusion, vision**

halt verb **1** to come or bring to a stop: She held her hand out to halt him
draw up: The car drew up outside the house
pull up: The cab pulled up, and the driver jumped out
stop: The event literally stopped the traffic
2 to bring something to an end: Production was halted

cease: A small number of firms have ceased trading
check: We have managed to check the spread of terrorism
curb: efforts to curb the spread of nuclear weapons
cut short: They had to cut short a holiday abroad
end: They decided to end the ceasefire
terminate: His contract has been terminated
▷ noun **3** an interruption or end to something: He brought the car to a halt
close: Their 18-month marriage was brought to a close
end: The war came to an end
pause: There was a pause before he replied
standstill: The country was brought to a standstill by strikes
stop: He slowed the car almost to a stop
stoppage: Air and ground crew are staging a 24-hour stoppage today
see also **block, check, pause, stop**

hammer see **bang, drive**
hamper verb to make movement or progress difficult for someone: I was hampered by a lack of information
frustrate: His attempt was frustrated by the weather
hinder: A thigh injury hindered her mobility
impede: Their work was being impeded by shortages of supplies
obstruct: charged with obstructing the course of justice
restrict: Her life is restricted by asthma
see also **handicap, hinder, impede, restrain, restrict**

hand see **employee, give**
hand down verb to pass from one generation to another: Recipes are handed down from mother to daughter

bequeath: *He bequeathed all his silver to his children*

give: *a typewriter given to me by my father*

pass down: *an heirloom passed down from generation to generation*

pass on: *My parents passed on their love of classical music to me*

handicap noun **1** a physical or mental disability: *He learnt to overcome his handicap*

defect: *a rare birth defect*

disability: *children with learning disabilities*

2 something that makes progress difficult: *Being a foreigner was not a handicap*

barrier: *Taxes are the most obvious barrier to free trade*

disadvantage: *the disadvantage of unemployment*

drawback: *The flat's only drawback was that it was too small*

hindrance: *She was a help rather than a hindrance to my work*

impediment: *an impediment to economic development*

obstacle: *the main obstacle to the deal*

▷ verb **3** to make something difficult for someone: *Greater levels of stress may seriously handicap some students*

burden: *We decided not to burden him with the news*

hamper: *I was hampered by a lack of information*

hinder: *A thigh injury hindered her mobility*

impede: *Fallen rocks impeded the progress of the rescue workers*

restrict: *laws to restrict foreign imports*

see also **barrier, disadvantage, restrict**

handle noun **1** the part of an object by which it is held: *a broom handle*

grip: *He fitted new grips to his golf clubs*

hilt: *the hilt of the small, sharp knife*

▷ verb **2** to hold or move with the hands: *Wear rubber gloves when handling cat litter*

feel: *The doctor felt his arm*

finger: *He fingered the few coins in his pocket*

grasp: *Grasp the end firmly*

hold: *Hold it by the edge*

touch: *She touched his hand reassuringly*

3 to deal or control with something: *She handled the travel arrangements*

administer: *The project is administered by the World Bank*

conduct: *This is no way to conduct a business*

deal with: *The matter has been dealt with by the school*

manage: *Within two years he was managing the store*

supervise: *I supervise the packing of all mail orders*

take care of: *He took care of the catering arrangements*

see also **deal, process, take care of, touch**

hand in see **submit, tender**

hand out see **distribute, present**

handout see **grant**

hand-pick see **pick**

hand-picked see **select**

handsome adjective **1** very attractive in appearance: *a handsome man*

attractive: *an attractive young woman*

good-looking: *good-looking actors*

2 large and generous: *a handsome profit*

ample: *ample space for a good-sized kitchen*

considerable: *his considerable wealth*

generous: *a generous gift*

liberal: *a liberal donation*

plentiful: *a plentiful supply of vegetables*

sizable or **sizeable**: *He inherited the house and a sizeable chunk of land*
see also **attractive**

handy *adjective* **1** conveniently near: *Keep a pencil and paper handy*

at hand: *Having the right equipment at hand will be enormously useful*

at your fingertips: *Firms need information at their fingertips*

close: *a secluded area close to her home*

convenient: *Martin drove along until he found a convenient parking space*

nearby: *He tossed the match into a nearby wastepaper bin*

on hand: *Experts are on hand to offer advice*

2 easy to handle or use: *handy hints on looking after indoor plants*

convenient: *a convenient way of paying*

easy to use: *This ice cream maker is cheap and easy to use*

helpful: *helpful instructions*

neat: *It had been such a neat, clever plan*

practical: *the most practical way of preventing crime*

useful: *useful information*
see also **available**, **convenient**, **ready**

hang *verb* **1** to be attached at the top with the lower part free: *His jacket hung from a hook behind the door*

dangle: *A gold bracelet dangled from his left wrist*

droop: *Pale wilting roses drooped from a vase*

2 to fasten something to another thing by its top: *She came out of the house to hang clothes on the line*

attach: *He attached the picture to the wall with a nail*

drape: *He draped the coat round his shoulders*

fasten: *stirrups fastened to the saddle*

fix: *He fixed a pirate flag to the mast*

suspend: *The TV is suspended from the ceiling on brackets*
see also **extend**, **float**, **stretch**

hang around see **stay**

hang out see **associate**

hanker after see **fancy**

hankering see **desire**, **longing**, **wish**

haphazard see **irregular**, **random**

haphazardly see **at random**

hapless see **unlucky**

happen *verb* to take place: *The accident happened on Wednesday*

come about: *It came about almost by accident*

follow: *He was arrested in the confusion which followed*

occur: *The crash occurred on a sharp bend*

result: *Ignore the early warnings and illness could result*

take place: *The festival took place last September*
see also **come**, **occur**, **result**, **take place**, **work out**

happening see **incident**

happiness *noun* a feeling of great pleasure: *Money can't buy happiness*

delight: *To my delight, it worked perfectly*

ecstasy: *a state of almost religious ecstasy*

elation: *His supporters reacted to the news with elation*

joy: *tears of joy*

pleasure: *Everybody takes pleasure in eating*

satisfaction: *job satisfaction*
see also **delight**, **pleasure**

happy *adjective* **1** feeling or causing joy: *a happy atmosphere*

2 fortunate or lucky: *a happy coincidence*

see word studies **happy**
see also **agreeable, bright, cheerful, cheery, comfortable, glad, pleased, ready, satisfied, willing**

harass see **hassle**

harbour see **bear, refuge, shelter**

hard adjective **1** firm, solid, or rigid: a hard piece of cheese
firm: a firm mattress
rigid: rigid plastic containers
solid: solid rock
stiff: stiff metal wires
strong: It has a strong casing which won't crack or chip
tough: dark brown beans with a rather tough outer skin
2 requiring a lot of effort: hard work
arduous: a long, arduous journey
exhausting: It's a pretty exhausting job
laborious: Keeping the garden tidy can be a laborious task
rigorous: rigorous military training
strenuous: Avoid strenuous exercise in the evening
tough: Change is often tough to deal with
3 difficult to understand: That's a very hard question
baffling: a baffling remark
complex: a complex problem
complicated: a complicated system of voting
difficult: It was a very difficult decision to make
puzzling: Some of this book is rather puzzling
see also **difficult, firm, harsh, rigid, rough, severe, solid, stiff, tough, tricky**

hard up see **poor**

harden verb to make or become stiff or firm: Give the cardboard two coats of varnish to harden it
bake: The soil had been baked solid by the heatwave

cake: The blood had begun to cake and turn brown
freeze: The lake freezes in winter
set: Lower the heat and allow the omelette to set
stiffen: paper that had been stiffened with paste
see also **strengthen**

hardened see **tough**

hardly adverb almost not or not quite: I could hardly believe what I was seeing
barely: His voice was barely audible
just: Her hand was just visible under her coat
only just: For centuries farmers there have only just managed to survive
scarcely: He could scarcely breathe
see also **barely**

hardship noun difficult circumstances: Many people are suffering economic hardship
adversity: They manage to enjoy life despite adversity
destitution: a life of poverty and destitution
difficulty: Many new golf clubs are in serious financial difficulty
misfortune: She seemed to enjoy the misfortunes of others
want: They were fighting for freedom of speech and freedom from want
see also **difficulty, ordeal, poverty, sorrow**

hard-wearing see **tough**

hard-working see **active, industrious**

hardy see **sturdy, tough**

hark see **listen**

harm verb **1** to injure someone or damage something: The hijackers seemed anxious not to harm anyone
abuse: Animals are still being exploited and abused
damage: He damaged his knee during training

hurt: He fell and hurt his back
ill-treat: They thought he had been ill-treating is wife
ruin: My wife was ruining her health through worry
wound: The bomb killed six people and wounded another five
▷ noun **2** injury or damage: All dogs are capable of doing harm to human beings
abuse: The abuse of animals is inexcusable
damage: The bomb caused extensive damage
hurt: an evil desire to cause hurt and damage
injury: The two other passengers escaped serious injury
see also **abuse, damage, hurt, injure, injury, spoil**

harmful adjective having a bad effect on something: Whilst most stress is harmful, some is beneficial
damaging: damaging allegations about his personal life
destructive: the awesome destructive power of nuclear weapons
detrimental: levels of radioactivity which are detrimental to public health
hurtful: Her comments can only be hurtful to the family
pernicious: The pernicious influence of secret societies
see also **unhealthy**

harmless adjective safe to use or be near: This experiment was harmless to the animals
innocuous: Both mushrooms look innocuous but are in fact deadly
nontoxic: a cheap and nontoxic method of cleaning up our water
not dangerous: The tests are not dangerous to the environment
safe: The doll is safe for children
see also **safe**

harmonious see **compatible, sweet**

harmonize see **blend**
harmony see **order**
harrowing see **sad**
harsh adjective severe, difficult, and unpleasant: harsh weather conditions
austere: The life of the troops was still comparatively austere
cruel: an unusually cruel winter
hard: He had a hard life
ruthless: the ruthless treatment of staff
severe: My boss gave me a severe reprimand
stern: a stern warning
see also **drastic, severe**

harshness see **violence**
harvest see **pick**

hassle noun **1** informal something that is difficult or causes trouble: It's not worth the hassle
bother: I buy sliced bread – it's less bother
effort: This chore is well worth the effort
inconvenience: the expense and inconvenience of having central heating installed
trouble: You've caused us a lot of trouble
upheaval: Moving house is always a big upheaval
▷ verb **2** informal to annoy someone by nagging or making demands: My husband started hassling me
badger: They kept badgering me to go back
bother: Go away and don't bother me about all that just now
go on at: She's always going on at me to have a baby
harass: We are routinely harassed by the police
nag: She had stopped nagging him about his drinking
pester: the creep who's been pestering you to go out with him

see also **annoy, difficulty, nuisance, stress, trouble, worry**

haste see **speed**

hasten see **hurry, rush**

hastily see **fast, quickly**

hasty adjective done or happening suddenly and quickly: The signs of their hasty departure could be seen everywhere
brisk: a brisk walk
hurried: a hurried breakfast
prompt: It is not too late, but prompt action is needed
rapid: a rapid retreat
swift: my swift departure
see also **quick, rash, sudden**

hatch see **plot**

hate verb 1 to have a strong dislike for something or someone: Most people hate him, but they don't care to say so
abhor: He abhorred violence
be sick of: We're sick of being ripped off
despise: A lot of people despise and loathe what I do
detest: Jean detested being photographed
dislike: those who dislike change
loathe: a play universally loathed by the critics
▷ noun 2 a strong dislike: a violent bully, destructive and full of hate
animosity: The animosity between the two men grew
aversion: I've always had an aversion to being part of a group
dislike: Consider what your likes and dislikes are about your job
hatred: her hatred of authority
hostility: He looked at her with open hostility
loathing: Critics are united in their unmitigated loathing of the band
see also **dislike, hatred**

hateful adjective extremely

unpleasant: It was a hateful thing to say
abhorrent: Discrimination is abhorrent to my council and our staff
despicable: a despicable crime
horrible: a horrible little boy
loathsome: the loathsome spectacle we were obliged to witness
obnoxious: He was a most obnoxious character. No-one liked him
offensive: an offensive remark

hatred noun an extremely strong feeling of dislike: He has been accused of inciting racial hatred
animosity: The animosity between the two men grew
antipathy: public antipathy towards scientists
aversion: my aversion to housework
dislike: his dislike of modern buildings
hate: These people are so full of hate
revulsion: They expressed their revulsion at his violent death
see also **animosity, dislike, hate, horror, hostility**

haughty adjective showing excessive pride: He spoke in a haughty tone
arrogant: an air of arrogant indifference
conceited: They had grown too conceited and pleased with themselves
disdainful: She cast a disdainful glance at me
proud: She was said to be proud and arrogant
snobbish: They had a snobbish dislike for their intellectual inferiors
stuck-up informal: She was a famous actress, but she wasn't a bit stuck-up
see also **stuck-up, superior**

haul see **drag, draw, loot, pull, tug**

haunt see **frequent**

haunted see **spooky**

have verb 1 to own something: We have two tickets for the concert

hold: He does not hold a firearm certificate
keep: We keep chickens
own: His father owns a local pub
possess: He is said to possess a fortune
2 to experience something: He had a marvellous time
endure: The company endured heavy losses
enjoy: The average German will enjoy 40 days' paid holiday this year
experience: Widows seem to experience more distress than do widowers
feel: I felt a sharp pain in my shoulder
sustain: He had sustained a cut on his left eyebrow
undergo: He recently underwent brain surgery
see also **bear, experience, own, possess**

have fun see **play**
have on see **wear**
haven see **refuge, retreat, shelter**
hawk see **sell**
hazard see **danger, threat**
hazardous see **dangerous, treacherous**
haze see **cloud**
hazy see **dim, vague**
head noun **1** a person's mind and mental abilities: I don't have a head for business
aptitude: an aptitude for accountancy
brain: If you stop using your brain you'll go stale
common sense: Use your common sense
intelligence: Try to use your intelligence to solve the puzzle – don't just guess
mind: I'm trying to clear my mind of all this
wits: She has used her wits to get

where she is today
2 the top, front, or start of something: the head of the queue
beginning: the beginning of this chapter
front: Stand at the front of the line
source: the source of this great river
start: Go back to the start of this section
top: the top of the stairs
3 the person in charge of something: heads of government
boss: the boss of the new company
chief: the President's chief of security
director: the director of the intensive care unit
leader: the leader of the Conservative Party
manager: the manager of our division
president: the president of the medical commission
principal: the principal of the school
▷ verb **4** to be in charge of something: He heads the department
be in charge of: She's in charge of the overseas division
control: He controls the largest fast food empire in the world
direct: Christopher will direct day-to-day operations
lead: leading a campaign to save the rainforest
manage: Within two years he was managing the store
run: Each teacher will run a different workshop
see also **boss, chief, command, foam, lead, leader, mind, top**
head of state see **ruler**
headquarters see **base**
headstrong see **obstinate**
headway see **progress**
heal see **cure**
healing see **recovery**
health noun **1** the condition of your body: Smoking is bad for your health

condition: He remains in a critical condition in hospital

constitution: He must have an extremely strong constitution

shape: He was still in better shape than many younger men

2 a state in which a person is feeling well: In hospital they nursed me back to health

fitness: He has fitness problems

good condition: He is in great condition for a man of 56

wellbeing: Singing can create a sense of wellbeing

healthy adjective **1** having good health: She was a very healthy child

active: an active lifestyle

fit: A short, physically fit man of 61

in good shape informal: I kept myself in good shape by swimming

robust: a robust and vibrant young man

strong: a strong constitution

well: I'm not very well today

2 producing good health: a healthy diet

beneficial: Wine in moderation is beneficial to health

bracing: a bracing walk

good for you: Regular, moderate exercise is good for you

nourishing: sensible, nourishing food

nutritious: a hot, nutritious meal

wholesome: fresh, wholesome ingredients

see also **beneficial, fit, sound, well**

heap noun **1** a pile of things: a heap of rubble

hoard: a hoard of silver and jewels

mass: a mass of flowers

mound: The bulldozers piled up huge mounds of dirt

pile: a pile of betting slips

stack: stacks of books on the bedside table

▷ verb **2** to pile things up: She heaped

vegetables onto his plate

pile: He was piling clothes into the suitcase

stack: They stacked up pillows behind his back

see also **bunch, mass, pile**

heaps plural noun informal plenty of something: heaps of cash

loads informal: I've got loads of money

lots informal: lots of fun

plenty: We've got plenty of time for a drink

stacks: stacks of magazines

tons informal: I've got tons of work to do

see also **plenty**

hear verb **1** to listen to something: I heard the sound of gunfire

catch: I don't believe I caught your name

eavesdrop: The government illegally eavesdropped on his phone conversations

heed: Few at the conference heeded his warning

listen in: Secret agents listened in on his phone calls

listen to: He spent his time listening to the radio

overhear: I overheard two doctors discussing my case

2 to learn about something: I heard that he was forced to resign

ascertain: They had ascertained that he was not a spy

discover: She discovered that they'd escaped

find out: As soon as we found this out, we closed the ward

gather: I gather the report is critical of the judge

learn: She wasn't surprised to learn that he was involved

understand: I understand that she's just taken early retirement

see also **gather, learn, listen,**

understand

hearsay see **gossip, rumour**

heart see **basis, centre, essence**

heartache see **distress, grief, sorrow**

heartbreaking see **pathetic, tragic**

hearten see **encourage**

heartfelt see **passionate, serious, sincere**

heartless see **callous, cruel, merciless**

heart-rending see **sad, tragic**

heat noun **1** the quality of being warm or hot: *the heat of the sun*

  warmth: *the warmth of the sand between her toes*

  2 a state of strong emotion: *in the heat of the election campaign*

  excitement: *in a state of great excitement*

  fervour: *religious fervour*

  intensity: *the intensity of feeling about this issue*

  passion: *He spoke with great passion*

  vehemence: *I was surprised by the vehemence of his criticism*

  ▷ verb **3** to raise the temperature of something: *Heat the oil in a frying pan*

  reheat: *Reheat the soup to a gentle simmer*

  warm up: *Just before serving, warm up the tomato sauce*

  see also **feeling, warm**

heat up see **warm**

heated see **hot, warm**

heathen noun old-fashioned someone who does not believe in an established religion: *She called us all heathens and hypocrites*

  pagan: *the sky-god of the ancient pagans*

  unbeliever: *punishing unbelievers and traitors*

heave see **raise, tug, vomit**

heaven noun **1** the place where good people are believed to go when they die: *She told them their mother was now in heaven*

  next world: *He said, "We will see each other again in the next world."*

  paradise: *They believed they would go to paradise if they died in battle*

  2 a place or situation liked very much: *I was in cinematic heaven*

  bliss: *a scene of domestic bliss*

  ecstasy: *the ecstasy of being in love*

  paradise: *The Algarve is a golfer's paradise*

  rapture: *the sheer rapture of listening to Bach's music*

heavy adjective **1** great in weight or force: *a heavy frying pan*

  bulky: *a bulky grey sweater*

  massive: *a massive blue whale*

  2 serious or important: *a heavy speech*

  deep: *a period of deep personal crisis*

  grave: *the grave crisis facing the country*

  profound: *Anna's patriotism was profound*

  serious: *It was a question which deserved serious consideration*

  solemn: *a simple, solemn ceremony*

  weighty: *Surely such weighty matters merit a higher level of debate*

  see also **grave, stuffy**

heckle see **interrupt**

hectic see **busy**

heed verb **1** to pay attention to someone's advice: *Few at the conference heeded his warning*

  follow: *If you are not going to follow my advice, we are both wasting our time*

  listen to: *They won't listen to my advice*

pay attention to: *The food industry is now paying attention to young consumers*

take notice of: *We want the government to take notice of what we think*

▷ *noun* **2** careful attention: *He pays too much heed to her*

attention: *He never paid much attention to his audience*

notice: *So do they take any notice of public opinion?*

see also **hear**

hefty *see* **overweight**

height *see* **extreme, maximum, top, ultimate**

heirloom *see* **legacy**

heirlooms *see* **valuables**

hell *noun* **1** the place where souls of evil people are believed to go after death: *Milton's Satan would rather "reign in Hell, than serve in Heaven"*

abyss: *Satan rules over the dark abyss*

inferno: *an inferno described in loving detail by Dante*

2 *informal* an unpleasant situation or place: *Bullies can make your life hell*

agony: *the agony of divorce*

anguish: *the anguish of families unable to trace relatives who've disappeared*

misery: *All that money brought nothing but sadness and misery*

nightmare: *The years in prison were a nightmare*

ordeal: *the painful ordeal of the last year*

hello *interjection* a greeting: *I popped my head in to say hello*

gidday *Australian, New Zealand*: *Gidday, mate! How you doing?*

hi *informal*: *She smiled and said, "Hi"*

how do you do? *formal*: *"How do you do, Mrs Brown?" Sam said, holding out his hand*

good afternoon *formal*: *Good afternoon. Won't you sit down?*

good evening *formal*: *Good evening, and welcome!*

good morning *formal*: *Good morning, everyone*

see also **gidday**

help *verb* **1** to make something easier or better for someone: *He began to help with the chores*

aid: *a software system to aid managers*

assist: *information to assist you*

lend a hand: *I'd be glad to lend a hand*

support: *He thanked everyone who had supported the strike*

▷ *noun* **2** assistance or support: *The books were not much help*

advice: *He has given me lots of good advice in my time here*

aid: *millions of dollars of aid*

assistance: *I would be grateful for any assistance*

guidance: *the reports which were produced under his guidance*

helping hand: *Most mums would be grateful for a helping hand*

support: *Only 60 clubs pledged their support for the scheme*

see also **benefit, blessing, comfort, encourage, support**

helper *noun* a person who gives assistance: *There is an adult helper for every two children*

aide: *a presidential aide*

assistant: *a research assistant*

deputy: *I can't make it so I'll send my deputy*

henchman: *Adolf Eichmann, Hitler's notorious henchman*

right-hand man: *He was the perfect right-hand man for the president*

supporter: *He is a strong supporter of the plan*

see also **assistant**

helpful *adjective* **1** giving assistance

or advice: *The staff in the office are very helpful*

accommodating: *Lindi seemed a nice, accommodating girl*

cooperative: *I made every effort to be cooperative*

kind: *I must thank you for being so kind to me*

supportive: *Her boss was very supportive*

2 making a situation better: *Having the right equipment will be enormously helpful*

advantageous: *an advantageous arrangement*

beneficial: *beneficial changes in the tax system*

constructive: *constructive criticism*

profitable: *a profitable exchange of ideas*

useful: *useful information*

see also **accommodating, beneficial, convenient, handy, positive, useful, valuable**

helping *see* **portion**

helping hand *see* **help**

helpless *adjective* weak or unable to cope: *a helpless baby*

defenceless: *a savage attack on a defenceless girl*

powerless: *He was powerless to help*

unprotected: *She felt unprotected and defenseless*

vulnerable: *the most vulnerable members of society*

weak: *taking ruthless advantage of a weak old man*

see also **powerless**

hem *see* **border**

hem in *see* **confine, enclose, surround**

hence *see* **therefore**

henchman *see* **follower, helper**

here *see* **present**

heritage *see* **inheritance**

hero *see* **champion**

heroic *see* **brave**

heroism *see* **bravery, courage**

hesitant *adjective* uncertain about something: *At first he was hesitant to accept the role*

diffident: *John was as outgoing as Helen was diffident*

doubtful: *I was very doubtful about the chances for success*

reluctant: *She was reluctant to get involved*

unsure: *He made her feel awkward and unsure of herself*

wavering: *wavering voters*

see also **reluctant**

hesitate *verb* to pause or show uncertainty: *She hesitated before replying*

dither: *We're still dithering over whether to marry*

pause: *The crowd paused for a minute, wondering what to do next*

waver: *Louise never wavered in her determination to take up the post*

hi *see* **gidday, hello**

hiatus *see* **gap, interval**

hibernate *see* **sleep**

hibernation *see* **sleep**

hidden *see* **invisible, secret**

hide *verb* **1** to put something where it cannot be seen: *She hid her face in her hands*

cache: *He has £289 million cached away*

conceal: *The hat concealed her hair*

secrete: *She secreted the gun in the kitchen cabinet*

stash *informal*: *He had stashed money away in a secret offshore account*

▷ *noun* **2** the skin of a large animal: *the process of tanning hides*

pelt: *a bed covered with beaver pelts*

skin: *a leopard skin coat*

see also **coat, cover, obscure, shelter**

high *adjective* **1** tall or a long way above the ground: *a high tower* **2** great in degree, quantity, or intensity: *There is a high risk of heart disease*

see **word studies high**

see also **excited, steep, tall, thrill**

high point see **peak, top**

high temperature see **heat**

higher than see **above**

highest see **supreme, top**

highlight see **emphasize**

highly see **very, well**

high-ranking see **senior**

high-speed see **express**

hijack see **seize**

hike see **ramble, walk**

hilarious see **funny, hysterical**

hilt see **handle**

hinder *verb* to get in the way of someone or something: *A thigh injury hindered her mobility*

block: *The President is blocking the release of the two men*

check: *We have managed to check the spread of terrorism*

delay: *Various problems have delayed production*

frustrate: *They have frustrated his efforts to gain a work permit*

hamper: *I was hampered by a lack of information*

impede: *Fallen rocks are impeding the progress of rescue workers*

see also **delay, hamper, handicap, impede, interfere, prevent, restrain**

hindrance see **barrier, handicap, obstacle**

hinge see **base**

hinge on see **depend**

hint *noun* **1** an indirect suggestion: *He gave a strong hint that there would be a referendum sooner rather than later*

clue: *How a man shaves may be a telling clue to his age*

indication: *He gave no indication that he was ready to compromise*

intimation: *I did not have any intimation that he was going to resign*

suggestion: *We reject any suggestion that the law needs amending*

2 a helpful piece of advice: *I hope to get some fashion hints*

advice: *Don't be afraid to ask for advice*

pointer: *Here are a few pointers to help you make your choice*

suggestion: *Can I give you a few suggestions?*

tip: *tips for busy managers*

▷ *verb* **3** to suggest something indirectly: *Criticism is hinted at but never made explicit*

imply: *The report implied that his death was inevitable*

indicate: *She has indicated that she may resign*

insinuate: *an article which insinuated that he was lying*

intimate: *He intimated that he was contemplating a shake-up of the company*

suggest: *Are you suggesting that I need to lose some weight?*

see also **idea, indication, mention, note, sign, suggest, suggestion, trace**

hint at see **promise**

hire *verb* **1** to pay money to use something: *She hired the car for three days*

charter: *They chartered a jet to fly her home*

lease: *He went to Toronto, where he leased an apartment*

rent: *She rents a house with three other girls*

2 to employ the services of someone: *The staff have been hired on short-term contracts*

appoint: *The Prime Minister has appointed a civilian as defence minister*
commission: *You can commission her to paint something especially for you*
employ: *They employed me as a nanny*
engage: *We engaged the services of a recognized engineer*
sign up: *He persuaded the company to sign her up*
see also **employ**
hire out see **let**
hiring see **employment**
historic see **memorable**
history see **background**
histrionic see **melodramatic**
hit verb **1** to strike someone or something forcefully: *Both men had been hit with baseball bats*
see **word studies hit**
2 to collide with something: *The car had apparently hit a traffic sign*
bang into: *She fell after another skier banged into her*
bump: *The boat bumped against something*
collide with: *He almost collided with Daisy*
meet head-on: *Their cars met head-on down a narrow alleyway*
run into: *The mail train ran into a derailed goods train at 75mph*
smash into: *The car plunged down a cliff and smashed into a tree*
▷ noun **3** the action of hitting something: *Give it a good hard hit with the hammer*
blow: *He went to hospital after a blow to the face*
knock: *a painful knock on the knee*
rap: *There was a rap on the door*
slap: *She reached forward and gave him a slap*
smack: *a smack with a ruler*
stroke: *six strokes of the cane*

see also **bang, beat, bump, success**
hit and miss see **unpredictable**
hit back see **retaliate, revenge**
hit it off see **get on**
hitch see **drawback**
hoard verb **1** to store for future use: *People have begun to hoard food and petrol*
save: *Save some fuel in case of emergencies*
stockpile: *People are stockpiling food for the coming winter*
store: *It's perfect for storing eggs or vegetables*
▷ noun **2** a store of things: *a hoard of silver and jewels*
cache: *a cache of weapons and explosives*
fund: *a scholarship fund for engineering students*
reserve: *the world's oil reserves*
stockpile: *stockpiles of nuclear warheads*
store: *I have a store of food and water here*
supply: *food supplies*
see also **bank, fund, gather, heap, pile, reserve, save, stockpile, store, supply**
hoarse adjective rough and unclear: *Nick's voice was hoarse with screaming*
croaky: *He sounds a bit croaky today*
gruff: *his gruff Scottish growl*
husky: *Her deep husky voice was her trademark*
rasping: *Both men sang in a deep rasping tone*
hoax see **fraud, trick**
hobbling see **lame**
hobby noun an enjoyable activity pursued in your spare time: *My hobbies are music and photography*
diversion: *Finger painting is very messy but an excellent diversion*
leisure activity: *America's top leisure activity is watching television*

leisure pursuit: *His main leisure pursuit is hill walking*
pastime: *His favourite pastime is golf*
see also **activity, interest, pastime**

hog *see* **pig**

hoist *see* **lift, raise**

hold *verb* **1** to carry or support something: *Hold the baby while I load the car*
carry: *He was carrying a briefcase*
clasp: *She clasped the children to her*
clutch: *He was clutching a photograph*
embrace: *The couple in the corridor were embracing each other*
grasp: *He grasped both my hands*
grip: *They gripped the rope tightly*
▷ *noun* **2** power or control over someone or something: *The party has a considerable hold over its own leader*
control: *He will have to give up his control of the company*
dominance: *the gang's dominance of the London underworld*
sway: *ideas that held sway for centuries*
3 the act or a way of holding something: *He grabbed the rope and got a hold on it*
grasp: *His hand was taken in a warm, firm grasp*
grip: *His strong hand eased the bag from her grip*
see also **claim, clasp, grasp, grip, handle, have, influence, keep, possess, reserve, think**

hold back *see* **restrain**

hold out *see* **offer**

hold up *see* **support**

holder *see* **container**

hole *noun* **1** an opening or hollow in something: *The builders had cut holes into the stone*
gap: *The wind was tearing through gaps in the window frames*
hollow: *Water gathers in a hollow and*

forms a pond
opening: *He squeezed through a narrow opening in the fence*
pit: *He lost his footing and began to slide into the pit*
split: *The seat has a few small splits around the corners*
tear: *I peered through a tear in the van's curtains*
2 a weakness in a theory or argument: *There are some holes in that theory*
defect: *A defect in the aircraft caused the crash*
error: *NASA discovered an error in its calculations*
fault: *There is a fault in the computer program*
flaw: *Almost all of these studies have serious flaws*
loophole: *They exploited a loophole in the law*
3 *informal* a difficult situation: *He admitted that the government was in a hole*
fix *informal*: *This will put homeowners in a fix*
hot water *informal*: *They have already been in hot water over high prices this year*
mess: *the many reasons why the economy is in such a mess*
predicament: *the once great club's current predicament*
tight spot: *This was one tight spot he couldn't get out of*
see also **breach, gap, jam, leak, opening, pit, tear**

holiday *noun* time spent away from home for enjoyment: *I'm exhausted – I really need a holiday*
break: *They are currently taking a short break in Spain*
leave: *Why don't you take a few days' leave?*
recess: *Parliament returns today after*

its summer recess

time off: He took time off to go sailing with wife

vacation: We went on vacation to Puerto Rico

see also **festival, leave, rest**

hollow *see* **hole**

hollow out *see* **dig**

holy adjective **1** relating to God or a particular religion: All Christian holy places were closed for a day in protest

blessed: Blessed are the peacemakers, for they shall be called the children of God

consecrated: the consecrated bread from the Eucharist

hallowed: hallowed ground

sacred: sacred music

sacrosanct: For him the Sabbath was sacrosanct

venerated: Jerusalem is Christianity's most venerated place

2 religious and leading a good life: In the East, holy men have always had long hair

devout: She is a devout Catholic

pious: He was brought up by pious female relatives

religious: They are both very religious

saintly: his saintly mother

virtuous: a virtuous family man

see also **religious**

homage *see* **honour, worship**

home noun **1** the building in which someone lives: They stayed at home and watched TV

abode: a luxurious abode

dwelling: One thousand new dwellings are planned for the area

house: our new house

residence: the Royal Family's private residence

▷ adjective **2** involving your own country: the home news pages of this newspaper

domestic: over 100 domestic flights a

day to 15 UK destinations

internal: The government stepped up internal security

national: major national and international issues

native: He was glad to be back on his native soil

see also **house**

homely adjective simple, ordinary and comfortable: The room was small and homely

comfortable: A home should be warm and comfortable

cosy: Guests can relax in the cosy bar

modest: the modest home of a family who lived off the land

simple: They celebrated mass in a simple chapel

welcoming: The restaurant is small and very welcoming

see also **comfortable**

homicide *see* **murder**

hone *see* **perfect**

honest adjective truthful and trustworthy: He is a very honest, decent man

law-abiding: law-abiding citizens

reputable: a reputable car dealer

trustworthy: He is a trustworthy and level-headed leader

truthful: She could not give him a truthful answer

virtuous: a virtuous family man

see also **candid, dinkum, frank, open, real, serious, straight, straightforward**

honesty *see* **honour**

honour noun **1** personal integrity: I can no longer serve with honour in your government

decency: No-one had the decency to tell me to my face

goodness: He retains a faith in human goodness

honesty: His reputation for honesty and integrity is second to none

integrity: He was praised for his fairness and high integrity

2 an award or mark of respect: He was showered with honours – among them an Oscar

accolade: the ultimate international accolade, the Nobel Peace prize

commendation: The officer received a commendation for brave conduct

homage: films that pay homage to our literary heritage

praise: He had won consistently high praise for his theatre work

recognition: At last, her father's work has received popular recognition

tribute: He paid tribute to the organizing committee

▷ verb **3** to give someone special praise: He was honoured by the French government with the Legion d'Honneur

commemorate: a plaque commemorating the servicemen who died

commend: I commended her for that action

decorate: He was decorated for his gallantry by the General

glorify: My philosophy of life is to glorify God in all I do

praise: He praised their excellent work
see also **character, commemorate, glory, keep, pay, prize, recognize, respect, right, tribute, worship**

honourable see **noble, respectable**

honoured see **proud**

hooley see **party**

hoolie see **party**

hooligan noun a destructive and violent young person: English football hooligans

delinquent: a nine-year-old delinquent

hoon Australian, New Zealand informal: the rocks hurled by hoons

lout: He was attacked by stone-throwing louts

tough: Residents may be too terrified of local toughs to protest

vandal: The Scout hut was burnt down by vandals

yob British, Australian slang: drunken yobs chanting football songs
see also **thug**

hoon see **hooligan**

hoop see **ring**

hope noun a wish or feeling of desire and expectation: There was little hope of recovery

ambition: His ambition is to sail around the world

dream: his dream of becoming a pilot

expectation: The hotel was being renovated in expectation of a tourist boom
see also **possibility, prospect**

hopeful see **optimistic**

hopeless adjective **1** certain to fail or be unsuccessful: Our situation is hopeless

forlorn: the forlorn hope of finding a better life

futile: their futile attempts to avoid publicity

impossible: The tax is impossible to administer

pointless: a pointless exercise that would only waste more time

useless: She knew it was useless to protest

vain: a vain attempt to sign a goalkeeper

2 bad or inadequate: I don't drive and the buses are hopeless

inadequate: The problem lies with inadequate staffing

pathetic: the pathetic state of the rail network

poor: The flat was in a poor state of repair

useless informal: My husband is useless around the house see also **doomed, impossible, pessimistic**

hopelessness see **despair**

horde see **crowd, number**

horizontal see **even, flat, level, straight**

horrendous see **awful, dreadful, terrible**

horrible adjective **1** disagreeable or unpleasant: *a horrible little boy*
  awful: *I had an awful time*
  disagreeable: *a disagreeable odour*
  horrid: *My parents are horrid to each other*
  mean: *Why are you always so mean to me?*
  nasty: *This divorce could turn nasty*
  unpleasant: *He's a very unpleasant little man*
  2 causing shock, fear, or disgust: *horrible crimes*
  appalling: *They have been living under the most appalling conditions*
  dreadful: *She told me the dreadful news*
  grim: *a grim discovery*
  gruesome: *gruesome murders*
  terrifying: *a terrifying experience*
  see also **disagreeable, hateful, nasty, terrible**

horrid see **disagreeable, horrible, terrible, unpleasant**

horrify verb to cause to feel horror or shock: *a crime trend that will horrify parents*
  appal: *I was appalled by her behaviour*
  disgust: *He disgusted everyone with his boorish behaviour*
  dismay: *He was deeply dismayed by the decision*
  outrage: *Human rights campaigners were outraged by the execution*
  shock: *Pictures of emaciated prisoners shocked the world*
  sicken: *What he saw at the accident sickened him*

horror noun **1** a strong feeling of alarm or disgust: *He gazed in horror at the knife*
  alarm: *She sat up in alarm*
  dread: *She thought with dread of the cold winter to come*
  fear: *I stood there crying and shaking with fear*
  fright: *He uttered a shriek and jumped with fright*
  panic: *He felt a sudden rush of panic at the thought*
  terror: *She shook with terror*
  2 a strong fear of something: *his horror of death*
  abhorrence: *their abhorrence of racism*
  aversion: *Many people have a natural aversion to insects*
  disgust: *I threw the book aside in disgust*
  hatred: *My hatred for him is intense*
  loathing: *She looked at him with loathing*
  revulsion: *They expressed their revulsion at his violent death*

horse noun an animal kept for riding: *a fall from a horse*
  brumby *Australian, New Zealand*: *There's a mob of about 30 brumbies up there*
  equine: *the history and uses of equines*
  moke *Australian, New Zealand slang*: *a tired old moke*
  nag *informal*: *He unhitched his sorry-looking nag from a nearby post*
  pony: *Peter trotted about on the fat pony he had been given*

hospitable see **accommodating, generous**

host see **crowd**

hostage see **prisoner**

hostel see **shelter**

hostile adjective unfriendly, aggressive, and unpleasant: *The*

Governor faced hostile crowds

antagonistic: They were nearly all antagonistic to the idea

belligerent: a belligerent war of words between India and Pakistan

malevolent: He fixed our photographer with a malevolent stare

unkind: All last summer he'd been unkind to her

see also **aggressive, unfriendly**

hostile to see **against**

hostilities see **war**

hostility noun aggressive or unfriendly behaviour towards someone or something: hostility to Black and ethnic groups

animosity: The animosity between the two men grew

antagonism: a history of antagonism between the two sides

hatred: her lifelong hatred of authority

ill will: He didn't bear anyone any ill will

malice: There was no malice in her voice

resentment: There is growing resentment against newcomers

see also **animosity, conflict, dislike, hate, opposition**

hot adjective **1** having a high temperature: a hot climate

boiling: It's boiling in here

heated: a heated swimming pool

scalding: Her son was burned by scalding tea

scorching: It was a scorching hot day

warm: a warm, dry summer

2 very spicy: a hot, aromatic Thai red curry

peppery: a rich, peppery extra virgin olive oil

spicy: a spicy Cajun sauce

hot air see **rubbish**

hot water see **hole, predicament**

hound see **chase, follow, persecute**

house noun a building where a person or family lives: They live in a large house with eight rooms

abode: I went round the streets and found his new abode

building: Their flat was on the first floor of the building

dwelling: One thousand new dwellings are planned for the area

home: One in four people are without adequate homes

residence: the Royal Family's private residence

see also **accommodate, accommodation, company, home**

household name see **personality**

housing see **accommodation**

hover see **float**

how do you do? see **hello**

howl see **bay, scream**

howling see **wild**

hub see **centre, focus**

hubbub see **noise, racket, sound**

huddle see **shelter**

hue see **colour**

huff see **resentment**

huffy see **resentful, sulky**

hug verb **1** to hold someone close to you: Lynn and I hugged each other

clasp: She clasped the children to her

cuddle: They used to kiss and cuddle in front of everyone

embrace: The couple in the corridor were embracing each other

squeeze: I le kissed her on the cheek and squeezed her tight

▷ noun **2** the act of holding someone close to you: She gave him a hug

clinch slang: They were caught in a clinch when her parents returned home

embrace: a young couple locked in an embrace

see also **clasp**

huge adjective extremely large in amount, size, or degree: a huge crowd

colossal: a colossal waste of money

enormous: *The main bedroom is enormous*
giant: *a giant statue*
immense: *He wielded immense power*
massive: *a massive surge in popularity*
vast: *this vast area of northern Canada*
see also **colossal, enormous, immense, large, spacious, vast**

hui noun *New Zealand* a meeting: *He arranged a hui which called together a broad span of Maori tribes*
assembly: *an assembly of prizewinning journalists*
conference: *a conference attended by 280 delegates*
congress: *a congress of coal miners*
convention: *the annual convention of the Society of Professional Journalists*
gathering: *the annual gathering of the South Pacific Forum*
meeting: *Can we have a meeting to discuss that?*
rally: *They held a rally to mark International Human Rights Day*

human see **person**
human being see **individual, person**
human beings see **people**
human race see **man**
humane adjective showing kindness and sympathy towards others: *a more just and humane society*
benevolent: *A most benevolent employer*
caring: *a very caring boy*
charitable: *charitable work*
compassionate: *a deeply compassionate man*
kind: *She is warmhearted and kind*
merciful: *a merciful God*
thoughtful: *a very thoughtful gesture*
see also **benevolent, compassionate, kind, merciful**

humanely see **well**
humanity see **kindness, man, people**
humans see **people**
humble adjective **1** not vain or boastful: *He gave a great performance, but he was very humble*
meek: *He was a meek, mild-mannered fellow*
modest: *He's modest, as well as being a great player*
unassuming: *She has a gentle, unassuming manner*
2 ordinary or unimportant: *A splash of wine will transform a humble casserole*
lowly: *He was irked by his lowly status*
modest: *his modest beginnings*
ordinary: *It was just an ordinary weekend*
simple: *a simple dinner of rice and beans*
▷ verb **3** to make someone feel humiliated: *the little car company that humbled the industry giants*
disgrace: *I have disgraced the family's name*
humiliate: *His teacher continually humiliates him in maths lessons*
see also **humiliate, modest, unknown**

humdrum see **boring, dreary, dull**
humid adjective damp and hot: *a hot, humid Italian summer*
clammy: *My shirt was clammy with sweat*
muggy: *The weather was muggy and overcast*
steamy: *The air was hot and steamy from the heat of a hundred bodies*
sticky: *four hot, sticky days in the middle of August*
see also **damp, wet**
humidity see **damp**
humiliate verb to hurt someone's

pride: *He enjoyed humiliating me*
disgrace: *I have disgraced my family*
embarrass: *It embarrassed him that he had no idea of what was going on*
humble: *The champion was humbled by the unseeded qualifier*
put down: *I know that I do put people down occasionally*
shame: *I ler son's affair had shamed her*
see also **degrade, embarrass, humble, put down, shame**
humiliated *see* **ashamed, embarrassed**
humiliation *see* **embarrassment, shame**
humorous *see* **funny, witty**
humour noun **1** something which is thought to be funny: *The film's humour contains a serious message*
comedy: *his career in comedy*
wit: *She was known for her biting wit*
2 the mood someone is in: *He hasn't been in a good humour lately*
frame of mind: *Clearly, she was not in the right frame of mind to continue*
mood: *Lily was in one of her aggressive moods*
spirits: *He was in very low spirits*
temper: *Lee stormed off the field in a furious temper*
▷ verb **3** to please someone so that they will not become upset: *I nodded, partly to humour him*
flatter: *I knew she was just flattering me*
indulge: *He did not agree with indulging children*
mollify: *The investigation was undertaken primarily to mollify pressure groups*
pander to: *politicians who pander to big business*
see also **mood**
humourless *see* **serious**
hump *see* **bulge, bump, lump**

hunch *see* **impression, suspicion**
hunger *see* **long, longing, wish**
hunger for *see* **be dying for**
hungry adjective wanting to eat: *I didn't have any lunch, so I'm really hungry*
famished: *Isn't dinner ready? I'm famished*
ravenous: *a pack of ravenous animals*
starving: *starving refugees*
hunk *see* **beauty, lump**
hunt *see* **chase, fossick, look for, search, seek**
hurdle *see* **barrier, difficulty, jump, obstacle**
hurl *see* **dash, throw**
hurried *see* **fast, hasty, quick, swift**
hurriedly *see* **fast, quickly**
hurry *see* **rush**
hurry verb **1** to move or do something as quickly as possible: *She hurried through the empty streets*
dash: *He dashed upstairs*
fly: *I must fly or I'll miss my train*
get a move on informal: *Get a move on because my car's on a double yellow line*
rush: *I've got to rush. I've got a meeting in a few minutes*
scurry: *Reporters scurried to find telephones*
2 to make something happen more quickly: *his attempt to hurry the process of independence*
accelerate: *They must now accelerate the development of their new car*
hasten: *This will hasten the closure of small pubs*
quicken: *He quickened his pace a little*
speed up: *an effort to speed up the negotiations*
see also **accelerate, bustle, fly, race, rush, speed**
hurt verb **1** to cause someone to feel

pain: *I didn't mean to hurt her*
harm: *The hijackers seemed anxious not to harm anyone*
injure: *motorists who kill, maim, and injure*
wound: *The bomb killed six people and wounded another five*
2 to upset someone or something: *What you said really hurt me*
distress: *I did not want to frighten or distress the horse*
sadden: *He is saddened that they did not win anything*
upset: *I'm sorry if I've upset you*
wound: *My relatives have wounded me in the past*
▷ *adjective* **3** upset or offended: *He felt hurt by all the lies*
aggrieved: *He is still aggrieved at the size of the fine*
offended: *He was offended at being left out*
upset: *I'm upset by your attitude*
wounded: *I think she feels desperately wounded and unloved*
see also **abuse, damage, harm, injure, upset**
hurtful *see* **harmful**
hurtle into *see* **crash**
husband *see* **partner**
hush *see* **silence**
hushed *see* **quiet, silent**
husky *see* **hoarse**
hustle *see* **rush**
hygiene *noun* the principles and practice of health and cleanliness: *Be extra careful about personal hygiene*
cleanliness: *Many of the beaches fail to meet minimum standards of cleanliness*
sanitation: *the hazards of contaminated water and poor sanitation*
hygienic *see* **clean**
hypnotize *verb* to put someone into a state in which they seem

to be asleep but can respond to suggestions: *She will hypnotize you and will stop you from smoking*
put in a trance: *A stage hypnotist put her in a trance*
put to sleep: *First the hypnotist will put you to sleep*
hypocritical *see* **two-faced**
hypothesis *see* **theory**
hypothetical *see* **imaginary**
hysteria *see* **frenzy, panic, scare**
hysterical *adjective* **1** in a state of uncontrolled excitement or panic: *Calm down. Don't get hysterical.*
frantic: *A bird had been locked in and was by now quite frantic*
frenzied: *her frenzied attempts to get free*
overwrought: *One overwrought man had to be restrained by friends*
raving: *He looked at her as if she were a raving lunatic*
2 *informal* extremely funny: *His stand-up routine was hysterical*
comical: *Her expression is almost comical*
hilarious: *He had a fund of hilarious jokes on the subject*

i

icy *see* **cold, frozen**

idea *noun* **1** a plan or suggestion for something: *She said she'd had a brilliant idea*

plan: *I have a cunning plan*

recommendation: *a range of recommendations for change*

scheme: *a proposed scheme*

solution: *He came up with a solution to the problem*

suggestion: *Do you have a better suggestion?*

2 an opinion or belief about something: *old-fashioned ideas about women*

belief: *my religious beliefs*

conviction: *a firm conviction that things have improved*

impression: *your first impressions of college*

notion: *I have a notion of what he is like*

opinion: *a favourable opinion of our neighbours*

view: *Make your views known to local politicians*

3 what you know about something: *They had no idea where they were*

clue: *I don't have a clue what you mean*

guess: *My guess is he went east*

hint: *He gave no hint about where he was*

inkling: *We had an inkling that something was happening*

notion: *I have a notion how it is done*

suspicion: *I have a strong suspicion they are lying*

see also **impression, intention, object, suspicion, thought**

ideal *noun* **1** a principle or idea you try to achieve: *I don't live up to my ideal of myself*

principle: *acts that go against your principles*

standard: *My father has high moral standards*

value: *the values of liberty and equality*

2 the best example of something: *She remains his feminine ideal*

epitome: *The hotel was the epitome of luxury*

example: *He was held up as an example of courage*

model: *a model of good manners*

paragon: *You are not a paragon of virtue*

prototype: *He was the prototype of a strong leader*

standard: *the standard by which we are compared*

▷ *adjective* **3** being the best example of something: *the ideal person for the job*

classic: *a classic example of hypocrisy*

complete: *She is the complete athlete*

consummate: *a consummate politician*

model: *She is a model pupil*

perfect: *He is the perfect husband for her*

supreme: *a supreme method of cooking vegetables*

see also **cause, example, imaginary, model, vision**

ideals see **standards**

identical see **alike, equal, even, like, same**

identification see **pass**

identify verb **1** to recognize or name someone or something: *I tried to identify her perfume*
 diagnose: *This illness is easily diagnosed*
 label: *Poisonous substances should be labelled as such*
 name: *The victims of the fire have been named*
 pinpoint: *They could not pinpoint the cause of death*
 place: *The man was familiar, but I couldn't place him*
 recognize: *a man I recognized as Luke's father*

identify with verb to understand someone's feelings: *I can't identify with the characters*
 associate with: *I associate myself with the green movement*
 empathize with: *I empathize with the people who live here*
 feel for: *I pitied and felt for him*
 relate to: *We have difficulty relating to each other*
 respond to: *She responded to his pain*
 see also **associate, recognize**

identity see **personality**

ideology see **belief**

idiom see **expression, language**

idiosyncratic see **individual**

idiot noun a stupid person: *You're an idiot!*
 fool: *He'd been a fool to get involved*
 galah *Australian informal*: *sounding like an illiterate galah*
 imbecile: *I don't want to deal with these imbeciles*
 moron: *I think that Gordon is a moron*
 oaf: *You clumsy oaf!*
 twit *informal*: *I feel such a twit*
 see also **fool**

idiotic adjective extremely foolish or silly: *an idiotic thing to do*
 crazy: *You were crazy to leave then*
 daft *informal*: *He's not so daft as to listen to them*
 dumb *informal*: *I've met a lot of dumb people*
 foolish: *It is foolish to risk injury*
 senseless: *acts of senseless violence*
 stupid: *stupid ideas*
 see also **silly, stupid, unwise**

idle adjective doing nothing: *a popular occupation for idle, wealthy young women*
 jobless: *One in four people are now jobless*
 redundant: *redundant workers*
 unemployed: *jobs for the unemployed*
 see also **laze, lazy, rest, unemployed**

idol see **favourite, star**

idolize see **worship**

ignite see **light**

ignominy see **shame**

ignoramus see **fool**

ignorant adjective **1** not knowing about something: *He was completely ignorant of the rules*
 inexperienced: *I am inexperienced at decorating*
 innocent: *He is innocent about the harm he is doing*
 oblivious: *John appeared oblivious to his surroundings*
 unaware: *She was unaware that she was being filmed*
 unconscious: *He was unconscious of his failure*
 2 not knowledgeable about things: *People are afraid to appear ignorant*
 green: *The new boy is very green and immature*
 naive: *a shy, naive man*
 unaware: *Young children are fairly unaware*
 see also **unaware**

ignore *verb* to take no notice of someone or something: *Her husband ignored her*

  blank *slang: The crowd blanked her for the first four numbers*
  discount *They simply discounted his feelings*
  disregard *He disregarded his father's advice*
  neglect *They never neglect their duties*
  overlook *a fact that we all tend to overlook*
  see also **exclude, neglect, overlook**

ill *adjective* unhealthy or sick: *Payne was seriously ill with pneumonia*

  ailing *The President is said to be ailing*
  poorly *British informal: Julie is still poorly*
  queasy *I feel queasy on boats*
  sick *He's very sick and he needs treatment*
  unhealthy *an unhealthy-looking fellow*
  unwell *She felt unwell back at the office*
  see also **crook, evil, queasy, sick, unhealthy, unwell**

ill at ease *see* uncomfortable
ill will *see* animosity, hostility, spite
illegal *adjective* forbidden by the law: *an illegal organization*

  banned *banned substances*
  criminal *a criminal offence*
  illicit *illicit drugs*
  outlawed *a place where hunting is outlawed*
  prohibited *a country where alcohol is prohibited*
  unlawful *unlawful acts*
  see also **criminal, crooked, wrong**

ill-fated *see* doomed
ill-fitting *see* uncomfortable
illicit *see* criminal, illegal
illness *noun* a particular disease: *a mystery illness*

  affliction *a severe mental affliction*
  ailment *common ailments*
  complaint *a skin complaint*
  disease *He has been cured of the disease*
  disorder *a rare nervous disorder*
  lurgy *British, Australian, New Zealand informal: It's only a matter of days before Joan gets the lurgy as well*
  sickness *radiation sickness*
  see also **disorder**

illogical *see* absurd, irrational
ill-treat *see* harm, mistreat, persecute
ill-treatment *see* abuse
illuminate *see* light
illumination *see* light
illusion *noun* **1** a thing that you think you can see: *Painters create the illusion of space*

  hallucination *Perhaps the footprint was a hallucination*
  mirage *I began to see mirages*
  semblance *A semblance of normality has been restored*

  2 a false belief: *Their hopes proved to be an illusion*

  delusion *I was under the delusion that I could win*
  fallacy *It's a fallacy that the rich are generous*
  fancy *childhood fancies*
  misconception *There are many misconceptions about school*
  see also **vision**

illusory *see* deceptive, imaginary
illustrate *see* explain
illustration *see* case, example, picture
illustrative *see* representative
illustrious *see* famous
image *see* appearance, vision
imaginable *see* believable, possible
imaginary *adjective* existing in your mind but not in real life: *an*

imaginary friend

fictional: *a fictional character*
fictitious: *a fictitious illness*
hypothetical: *a hypothetical situation*
ideal: *in an ideal world*
illusory: *Freedom is illusory*
invented: *distorted or invented stories*
mythological: *mythological creatures*

imagination noun the ability to form new ideas: *a girl who lacks imagination*

creativity: *She paints with great creativity*
ingenuity: *the ingenuity of engineers*
inventiveness: *the artistic inventiveness of Mozart*
originality: *a composer of great originality*
vision: *a leader with vision*
see also **mind, vision**

imaginative see **creative**

imagine verb 1 to have an idea of something: *He could not imagine a more peaceful scene*

conceive: *I can't even conceive that much money*
envisage: *I envisage them staying together*
fantasize: *I fantasized about writing music*
picture: *I tried to picture the place*
visualize: *He could not visualize her as old*

2 to believe that something is the case: *I imagine you're talking about my brother*

assume: *Don't assume we are similar*
believe: *I believe you have my pen*
gather: *I gather that his mother was Scottish*
guess informal: *I guess he's right*
suppose: *He supposed I would be back at school*

suspect: *Susan suspected that things would get worse*
see also **assume, expect, guess, picture, suppose, think**

imbecile see **idiot**

imitate verb to copy someone or something: *She imitated her parents*

ape: *She is aping her sister's style*
copy: *I used to copy everything my big brother did*
emulate: *Sons are expected to emulate their fathers*
impersonate: *He could impersonate all the other students*
mimic: *He mimicked her accent*
simulate: *a machine which simulates natural sounds*
see also **copy**

imitation see **copy, fake, mock, parody**

immaculate see **clean**

immature see **childish, young**

immediate adjective 1 happening or done without delay: *My immediate reaction was fear*

instant: *He took an instant dislike to Mark*
instantaneous: *The applause was instantaneous*

2 most closely connected to you: *my immediate family*

close: *I have a few close friends*
direct: *your direct descendants*
near: *near relatives*
see also **direct, instant, prompt, urgent**

immediately adverb 1 right away: *Ingrid answered Peter's letter immediately*

at once: *You must come at once*
directly: *He will be there directly*
instantly: *She'd been knocked down in the street and died almost instantly*
now: *Get out, now!*
promptly: *The telephone was answered promptly*

right away: You'd better tell them right away

straightaway: I'd like to see you straightaway

2 very near in time or position: immediately behind the house

closely: He rushed out, closely followed by Kemp

directly: James stopped directly under the window

right: He stood right behind me
see also **now**

immense adjective very large or huge: an immense cloud of smoke

colossal: a colossal waste of money

enormous: The main bedroom is enormous

giant: a giant oak table

gigantic: a gigantic task

huge: Several painters were working on a huge piece of canvas

massive: a massive cruise liner

vast: a vast expanse of water
see also **colossal, enormous, huge, large, vast**

immensity see **size**

immerse see **busy, steep**

immersed see **preoccupied**

imminent adjective going to happen very soon: my sister's imminent arrival

close: My birthday is quite close

coming: the coming dawn

forthcoming: their forthcoming marriage

impending: impending doom

looming: My exams are looming

near: in the near future
see also **near**

immoral see **perverted, wrong**

immorality see **evil**

immortal see **eternal**

immortality see **glory**

immovable see **steadfast**

immune adjective not subject to or affected by something: He seems immune to pressure

exempt: She is exempt from blame

free: He was not completely free of guilt

protected: He is protected from the law

resistant: crops that are resistant to disease

safe: I was safe from punishment

unaffected: She is unaffected by the sight of blood
see also **exempt**

immunity see **freedom, safety**

impact see **force**

impair see **cripple, ruin, spoil, undermine**

impart see **communicate, convey**

impartial see **fair, neutral**

impartiality see **justice**

impassioned see **fervent, intense, passionate**

impassive see **blank, calm, uninterested**

impatient adjective **1** easily annoyed: You are too impatient with others

brusque: a brusque manner

curt: He had spoken in a very curt tone of voice

irritable: Brian was nervous and irritable with her

2 eager to do something: He was impatient to leave

eager: Children are eager to learn

restless: The kids were bored and restless

impeccable see **clean**

impede verb to make someone's or something's progress difficult: Fallen rocks are impeding the progress of rescue workers

block: The country has been trying to block these imports

delay: Various set-backs delayed production

disrupt: The drought has severely disrupted agricultural production

get in the way: She had a job which never got in the way of her hobbies

hamper: The bad weather hampered rescue operations

hinder: The investigation was hindered by the loss of vital documents

obstruct: The authorities are obstructing the inquiry

see also **delay, hamper, handicap, hinder, interfere, prevent, restrict**

impediment see **barrier, handicap, obstacle**

impending see **future, imminent**

imperative see **necessary, urgent**

imperfect adjective having faults or problems: We live in an imperfect world

broken: broken toys

damaged: damaged cars

defective: defective eyesight

faulty: a car with faulty brakes

flawed: a flawed character

see also **faulty**

imperfection see **defect, fault, flaw, weakness**

imperial see **royal**

imperious see **bossy**

impersonal adjective not concerned with people and their feelings: I found him strangely distant and impersonal

aloof: His manner was aloof

cold: Sharon was very cold with me

detached: He felt emotionally detached from the victims

formal: Business relationships are usually formal

neutral: He told me the news in a neutral manner

remote: She was beautiful but remote

impersonate see **imitate, pose**

impertinence see **impudence**

impertinent see **cheeky, rude**

impetuous see **rash**

impinge on see **affect**

impish see **naughty, wicked**

implacable see **merciless**

implant see **insert**

implausible see **improbable, unbelievable, unlikely**

implement see **tool**

implore verb to beg someone to do something: "Tell me what to do!" she implored him

beg: I begged him to come with me

beseech literary: I beseech you to show him mercy

plead with: The lady pleaded with her daughter to come home

see also **ask, beg, plead, press, urge**

imply see **hint, suggest**

importance see **emphasis, influence, value**

important adjective **1** necessary or significant: Her sons are the most important thing to her

momentous: the momentous decision to go to war

serious: a serious matter

significant: a significant discovery

weighty: We discussed weighty matters

2 having great influence or power: the most important person in the country

eminent: an eminent scientist

foremost: a foremost expert in American history

influential: one of the most influential books ever written

leading: a leading nation in world politics

notable: notable celebrities

powerful: large, powerful countries

see also **prominent, serious, significant, special, valuable, vital**

impose verb **1** to force something on someone: Fines were imposed on the culprits

dictate: The policy is dictated from the top

enforce: It is a difficult law to enforce

inflict: Inflicting punishment to stop crime is not the answer

levy: a tax levied on imported goods

ordain: the task of trying to ordain parliamentary behaviour

impose on verb to take advantage of someone: I should stop imposing on your hospitality

abuse: They abused my hospitality by eating everything

take advantage of: He took advantage of her generosity

use: She's just using you
see also **administer**, **exact**

impose upon see **trouble**

imposing see **grand**, **splendid**

impossible adjective unable to happen or be believed: You shouldn't promise impossible things

absurd: absurd claims to have met big stars

hopeless: a hopeless task

inconceivable: It's inconceivable that people can still be living in those conditions

ludicrous: his ludicrous plan to build a house

out of the question: Is a pay increase out of the question?

unthinkable: The idea of splitting up is unthinkable
see also **hopeless**

imposter see **fraud**

impotence see **inability**

impotent see **powerless**

impound see **seize**

impoverished see **poor**

impractical see **useless**

impregnable see **invincible**, **secure**

impression noun 1 the way someone or something seems to you: your first impressions of college

feeling: the feeling that she was wasting her life

hunch: Was your hunch right or wrong?

idea: I had my own ideas about what had happened

notion: I have a notion of what he is like

sense: She has the sense that she was in trouble

make an impression verb to have a strong effect on people: He certainly made an impression on his teachers

cause a stir: News of her death caused a stir

influence: You can't do anything to influence him

make an impact: Events can make an impact on our lives
see also **idea**, **sense**, **suspicion**

impressionable adjective easy to influence: impressionable teenagers

gullible: I'm so gullible I'd have believed him

open: an open, trusting nature

receptive: moulding their young, receptive minds

sensitive: Ouija boards can be dangerous, especially to sensitive people

susceptible: Children can be susceptible to advertisements

vulnerable: vulnerable old people

impressive adjective tending to impress: an impressive achievement

awesome: awesome mountains, deserts and lakes

exciting: He tells the most exciting stories

grand: a grand old building

powerful: a powerful image

stirring: stirring music

striking: her striking personality
see also **grand**, **significant**, **splendid**

imprison verb to lock someone up: He was imprisoned for murder

confine: Keep your dog confined to the house

detain: They'll be detained and charged

incarcerate: Prisoners were incarcerated in terrible conditions
jail: An innocent man was jailed
lock up: You people should be locked up!
send to prison: The judge sent him to prison for life
see also **confine, jail**
improbable adjective unlikely or unbelievable: improbable stories
doubtful: It was doubtful if they would arrive on time
dubious: dubious evidence
far-fetched: This all sounds a bit far-fetched
implausible: a film with an implausible ending
unbelievable: an unbelievable storyline
unlikely: It is unlikely that he is alive
see also **incredible, unbelievable**
improper see **inappropriate, indecent, unsuitable**
improve verb to get or make better: He improved their house
advance: Medical technology has advanced
better: They tried to better their working conditions
enhance: Good jewellery enhances your outfits
look up informal: Things are looking up for me now
progress: Jack's condition is progressing well
upgrade: You'll have to upgrade your image
see also **correct, perfect, polish, progress, recover**
improve on see **top**
improvement noun the fact or process of getting better: dramatic improvements in conditions
advance: the advances in air safety since the 1970s
development: monitoring her language development
enhancement: the enhancement of the human condition
progress: The doctors are pleased with her progress
upturn: an upturn in the economy
see also **gain, progress, recovery, reform, rise**
impudence noun disrespectful talk or behaviour towards someone: Have you ever heard such impudence?
audacity: He had the audacity to speak up
boldness: I was amazed at her boldness towards him
cheek informal: I can't believe he had the cheek to complain
chutzpah American informal: He had the chutzpah to ask us to leave
gall: the most presumptuous question any interviewer has ever had the gall to ask
impertinence: His words sounded like impertinence
insolence: I got punished for insolence
nerve: You've got a nerve coming round here after what you've done
see also **cheek**
impudent see **bold, cheeky, rude**
impulse see **instinct, urge, whim**
impulsive see **rash**
in see **fashionable, trendy**
in addition see **too**
in advance see **before, early**
in charge see **responsible**
in fact see **really**
in favour see **popular**
in keeping see **compatible**
in part see **partly**
in sight see **visible**
in spite of see **despite**
in the end see **finally**
in the middle of see **among**
inability noun a lack of ability to do something: an inability to

concentrate
impotence: *a sense of impotence in the situation*
inadequacy: *my inadequacy as a gardener*
incompetence: *the incompetence of government officials*
ineptitude: *political ineptitude*
inaccessible *see* **remote**
inaccurate *see* **untrue**
inadequacy *see* **deficiency, inability**
inadequate *adjective* **1** not enough in quantity: *Supplies of medicine are inadequate*
insufficient: *insufficient evidence to justify criminal proceedings*
lacking: *Why was military intelligence so lacking?*
poor: *poor wages*
scarce: *the region's scarce supplies of water*
short: *Deliveries are unreliable and food is short*
2 not good enough: *She felt painfully inadequate in the crisis*
deficient: *He made me feel deficient as a mother*
incapable: *He lost his job for being incapable*
incompetent: *the power to sack incompetent teachers*
inept: *He was inept and lacked the intelligence to govern*
pathetic: *She made some pathetic excuse*
useless: *I'm useless around the house*
see also **deficient, hopeless, insufficient, meagre, unsatisfactory, weak**
inadvertent *see* **accidental**
inane *see* **empty, foolish, silly, stupid**
inanity *see* **nonsense, stupidity**
inappropriate *noun* not suitable for a purpose or occasion: *This behaviour is inappropriate*

improper: *the improper use of resources*
incongruous: *an incongruous assortment of clothes*
unfit: *houses that are unfit for living in*
unseemly: *He thought crying was unseemly*
unsuitable: *food that is unsuitable for children*
untimely: *their unjustified and untimely interference*
see also **unsuitable**
inaudible *see* **quiet**
inaugural *see* **opening**
inaugurate *see* **begin, start**
inauguration *see* **introduction, start**
inborn *see* **natural**
incapable *see* **inadequate, incompetent, inefficient, powerless**
incarcerate *see* **imprison, jail**
incensed *see* **mad**
incentive *noun* something that encourages you to do something: *the incentive to work*
bait: *He added some bait to make the agreement sweeter*
encouragement: *She didn't get much encouragement to do anything*
inducement: *Are gangster films an inducement to crime?*
motivation: *Money is my motivation*
stimulus: *He needed all the stimulus he could get*
see also **reason**
inception *see* **start**
incessant *see* **relentless**
inch *see* **ease, edge**
incident *noun* an event: *Little incidents can shape our lives*
circumstance: *This is a fortunate circumstance*
episode: *I'm glad this episode is over*
event: *recent events in Europe*

happening: the latest happenings in sport

occasion: I remember that occasion fondly

occurrence: Nancy wondered about the strange occurrence

see also **event, experience**

incidental see **casual**

incinerate see **burn**

incision see **cut**

incite verb to excite someone into doing something: The campaigners incited a riot

agitate for: Workers agitated for better conditions

goad: He tried to goad me into a response

instigate: The violence was instigated by a few people

provoke: I provoked him into doing something stupid

whip up: an attempt to whip up public hostility to the president

see also **encourage, excite**

inclination see **feeling, tendency, will**

incline see **bend, slope, tilt**

incline towards see **prefer**

inclined see **prone**

include verb to have as a part: A British breakfast always includes sausages

contain: This sheet contains a list of names

cover: The books covers many topics

embrace: a small county embracing two cities

encompass: classes which encompass a wide range of activities

incorporate: The new cars incorporate many improvements

involve: a high-energy workout which involves nearly every muscle

see also **contain**

income noun the money someone or something earns: families on low incomes

earnings: his earnings as an accountant

pay: We complained about our pay

profits: The bank made profits of millions of dollars

salary: The lawyer was paid a good salary

takings: The shop had huge takings that week

wages: His wages have gone up

see also **pay**

incomparable adjective too good to be compared with anything else: an area of incomparable beauty

inimitable: his inimitable style

peerless literary: He gave a peerless performance

superlative: The hotel has superlative views

supreme: the supreme piece of writing about the war

unparalleled: unparalleled happiness

unrivalled: an unrivalled knowledge of music

incomparably see **far**

incompetence see **inability**

incompetent adjective lacking the ability to do something properly: You are incompetent, and you know it

bungling: a bungling amateur

cowboy British informal: cowboy builders

incapable: an incapable leader

inept: an inept performance

unable: He felt unable to handle the situation

useless: I felt useless and a failure

see also **inadequate, inefficient**

incomplete adjective not finished or whole: an incomplete book

deficient: a deficient diet

half-pie New Zealand informal: His report was half-pie

insufficient: insufficient information

partial: The concert was a partial

success

incomprehensible *see* garbled

inconceivable *see* impossible, unbelievable

incongruous *see* inappropriate

inconsistency *see* gap

inconsistent *see* uneven

inconspicuous *see* invisible

inconvenience *see* bother, hassle, nuisance, trouble

incorporate *see* include, involve

incorrect *see* false, untrue, wrong

increase *verb* **1** to make or become larger in amount: *The population continues to increase*

   enlarge: *They are trying to enlarge their customer base*

   expand: *We will expand the size of the picture*

   extend: *She plans to extend her stay*

   grow: *The sound grew in volume*

   multiply: *viruses which can multiply rapidly in the human body*

   swell: *His anger swelled within him*

   ▷ *noun* **2** a rise in the amount of something: *a pay increase*

   gain: *a gain in speed*

   growth: *the growth of unemployment*

   increment: *tiny increments of movement*

   rise: *a rise in prices*

   upsurge: *an upsurge of interest in books*

   see also addition, augment, build, enlarge, expand, gain, grow, growth, jump, multiply, rise, spread

incredible *adjective* **1** totally amazing: *a champion with incredible skill*

   amazing: *an amazing success*

   astonishing: *an astonishing piece of good luck*

   astounding: *an astounding discovery*

   extraordinary: *extraordinary beauty*

   marvellous: *a marvellous thing to do*

sensational *informal: a sensational performance*

   2 impossible to believe: *the incredible stories of some children*

   absurd: *absurd ideas*

   far-fetched: *This all sounds very far-fetched to me*

   improbable: *highly improbable claims*

   unbelievable: *The film has an unbelievable plot*

   unimaginable: *unimaginable wealth*

   unthinkable: *It's unthinkable that Tom forgot your birthday*

   see also unbelievable, unlikely, wonderful

incredulity *see* surprise

increment *see* increase

incurable *see* fatal

indebted *see* grateful

indecent *adjective* shocking or rude: *indecent lyrics*

   crude: *crude pictures*

   dirty: *dirty jokes*

   improper: *improper behaviour*

   lewd: *lewd comments*

   rude: *a rude gesture*

   vulgar: *vulgar language*

   see also crude, obscene, vulgar

indeed *see* exactly

indefatigable *see* energetic

indefinite *see* uncertain, vague

independent *adjective* **1** separate from other people or things: *an independent political party*

   autonomous: *an autonomous country*

   free: *Do we have a free press?*

   liberated: *liberated views*

   separate: *We live separate lives*

   unrelated: *two unrelated incidents*

   2 not needing other people's help: *a fiercely independent woman*

   individualistic: *individualistic behaviour*

   liberated: *a genuinely liberated*

woman
self-sufficient: I am quite self-sufficient
unaided: She raised her children unaided
see also **individual**
independently see **on your own**
indeterminate see **uncertain**
index see **list**
indicate verb to show that something is true: a gesture which indicates his relief
denote: Messy writing denotes a messy mind
reveal: His diary revealed his disturbed state of mind
show: I would like to show my appreciation
signal: Ted signalled that everything was all right
signify: A white flag signifies surrender
see also **hint, mean, promise, show, specify, suggest**
indication noun a sign of something: He gave no indication that he had heard me
clue: Did she give any clue as to how she was feeling?
hint: The Minister gave a strong hint that he intended to resign
sign: Your blood will be checked for any sign of kidney failure
signal: They saw the visit as an important signal of support
suggestion: There is no suggestion that the two sides are any closer to agreeing
warning: a warning of impending doom
see also **hint, lead, sign, suggestion, trace**
indifference see **neglect**
indifferent see **apathetic, callous, uninterested**
indignant see **resentful**

indignation see **resentment**
indirect adjective not done or going directly but by another way: the indirect effects of smoking
meandering: the meandering course of the river
oblique: oblique threats
rambling: In a rambling answer, he denied the charge
roundabout: a roundabout way of getting information
tortuous: a tortuous path
wandering: a wandering route through the woods
indiscriminate see **random**
indiscriminately see **at random**
indispensable see **essential, necessary, vital**
indistinct see **dim, faint, vague**
indistinguishable see **same**
individual adjective 1 relating to separate people or things: individual dishes of trifle
discrete formal: breaking down the job into discrete steps
independent: two independent studies
separate: Use separate chopping boards for different foods
single: every single house in the street
2 different and unusual: Develop your own individual writing style
characteristic: a characteristic feature
distinctive: His voice was very distinctive
idiosyncratic: a highly idiosyncratic personality
original: a chef with an original touch
personal: his own personal method of playing
special: her own special way of doing things
unique: Each person's signature is unique
▷ noun 3 a person, different from

any other person: *the rights of the individual*

character: *a remarkable character*

human being: *a fellow human being*

party: *Who is the guilty party?*

person: *One person died and several others were injured*

soul: *He's a jolly soul*

see also **different, peculiar, person, personal, private, single, special**

individualistic *see* **independent**

individuality *see* **personality**

indomitable *see* **invincible**

induce *see* **occasion, persuade, prompt**

inducement *see* **bait, incentive**

indulge *see* **humour, satisfy, spoil**

indulgence *see* **excess, luxury**

industrious *adjective* tending to work hard: *industrious groups of students*

busy: *an exceptionally busy man*

conscientious: *Sherry was slow but conscientious*

diligent: *Williams was diligent in the writing of letters*

hard-working: *an exceptionally disciplined and hard-working young man*

tireless: *a tireless and willing worker*

see also **active**

industry *see* **business, labour**

inefficient *adjective* badly organized and slow: *an inefficient government*

disorganized: *My boss is completely disorganized*

incapable: *If he fails he will be considered incapable*

incompetent: *an incompetent officer*

inept: *an inept use of power*

sloppy: *sloppy management*

inept *see* **inadequate, incompetent, inefficient**

ineptitude *see* **inability**

inequality *see* **injustice**

inert *see* **still**

inevitable *see* **certain, necessary**

inexact *see* **approximate**

inexhaustible *see* **infinite**

inexorable *see* **necessary**

inexpensive *see* **cheap, economical, reasonable**

inexperience *see* **innocence**

inexperienced *adjective* lacking experience of a situation or activity: *inexperienced drivers*

green *informal*: *He was a young lad, and very green*

new: *a new mother*

raw: *raw talent*

unaccustomed: *Kate is unaccustomed to being on TV*

see also **ignorant**

infallible *see* **sure**

infamous *see* **notorious**

infant *see* **baby, child, young**

infantile *see* **childish**

infatuation *see* **love, passion**

infect *verb* to cause disease in something: *One mosquito can infect many people*

affect: *Neil has been affected by the virus*

blight: *trees blighted by pollution*

contaminate: *These substances can contaminate fish*

taint: *blood that had been tainted with HIV*

see also **pollute**

infectious *adjective* spreading from one person to another: *infectious diseases*

catching: *There is no suggestion that multiple sclerosis is catching*

contagious: *a highly contagious disease of the lungs*

spreading: *The spreading virus is threatening the population*

infer *see* **conclude**

inference *see* **conclusion**

inferior *adjective* **1** having a lower position than something or

someone else: *Women were given inferior status*
lesser: *the work of lesser writers*
lower: *lower animals*
minor: *a minor celebrity*
secondary: *He was relegated to a secondary position*
second-class: *second-class citizens*
subordinate: *His subordinate officers followed his example*
2 of low quality: *inferior quality cassette tapes*
mediocre: *mediocre music*
poor: *a poor standard of service*
second-class: *a second-class education*
second-rate: *second-rate restaurants*
shoddy: *Customers no longer tolerate shoddy goods*
▷ noun **3** a person in a lower position than another: *You must still be polite to your inferiors*
junior: *the office junior*
menial: *menials in poorly paid jobs*
subordinate: *All her subordinates adored her*
underling: *Every underling feared him*
see also **cheap, junior, poor, rotten**
inferno see **fire, hell**
infertile see **barren**
infinite *adjective* without any limit or end: *an infinite number of possibilities*
boundless: *boundless energy*
eternal: *the secret of eternal youth*
everlasting: *our everlasting friendship*
inexhaustible: *an inexhaustible supply of ideas*
perpetual: *a perpetual source of worry*
untold: *untold wealth*
see also **countless, plentiful**
inflamed see **sore, tender**
inflexible see **firm, obstinate, rigid,**

stubborn
inflict see **administer, bring, impose**
influence *noun* **1** power over other people: *He has quite a lot of influence*
authority: *You have no authority over me*
control: *Teachers have a lot of control over students*
importance: *a politician of great importance*
power: *a position of power*
sway: *My mother holds sway at home*
2 an effect that someone or something has: *under the influence of alcohol*
effect: *Your age has an effect on your views*
hold: *He is losing his hold on the public*
magnetism: *a man of great personal magnetism*
spell: *under the spell of one of his teachers*
weight: *the weight of the law*
▷ verb **3** to have an effect on someone or something: *I never try to influence my children*
affect: *He will not let personal preference affect his choice*
control: *I can't control him*
direct: *I don't need you directing my life*
guide: *Let your instinct guide you*
manipulate: *I hate the way he manipulates people*
sway: *efforts to sway voters*
see also **factor, grip, guide, make an impression, mana**
influential see **important, powerful**
inform *verb* to tell someone about something: *Please inform me of your progress*
advise *formal*: *I can advise you of his whereabouts*
enlighten: *a history lesson which enlightens you*

notify: Ann was notified of her sister's illness

tell: Tell me what is going on

see also **advise, alert, brief, communicate, notify, tell**

inform of see **report**

inform on verb to tell the police about someone who has committed a crime: Somebody must have informed on the thieves

betray: They betrayed their associates to the police

denounce: He was denounced as a dangerous rebel

grass on British slang: He grassed on the members of his own gang

tell on informal: It's all right, I won't tell on you

see also **betray**

informal adjective relaxed and casual: His manner was informal and relaxed

casual: a casual attitude towards money

colloquial: colloquial language

easy: easy conversation

familiar: John was too familiar towards his teacher

natural: Beth was friendly and natural with us

relaxed: a relaxed atmosphere in class

see also **colloquial, cosy, relaxed**

information noun the details you know about something: Pat would not give any information about Sarah

data: The survey provided valuable data

drum Australian informal: I don't have the drum on this yet

facts: Pass on all the facts to the police

material: highly secret material

news: We have news of your brother

notice: advance notice of the event

word: I received word that the guests had arrived

see also **news, word**

informed see **aware, wise**

infrequent see **few, uncommon**

infringe see **break, disobey, intrude**

infringed see **broken**

infringement see **breach**

infuriate see **anger**

infuriated see **furious, mad**

ingenious see **bright, smart**

ingenuity see **imagination**

ingot see **block**

ingredient noun a thing that something is made from: Place all the ingredients in a pan

component: the components of hamburgers

constituent: the main constituent of fish oil

element: the various elements in a picture

inhabit verb to live in a place: the people who inhabit these islands

dwell: the people who dwell in the forest

live: She has lived here for ten years

lodge: Some people lodged permanently in the hallway

occupy: Forty tenants occupy the block

populate: a swamp populated by huge birds

reside formal: He resides in the country

see also **live**

inhabitant noun someone who lives in a place: an inhabitant of Norway

citizen: American citizens

inmate: prison inmates

native: Dr Brown is a native of New Zealand

occupant: the previous occupant of the house

resident: the residents of the retirement home

see also **local**

inhabitants see **people**

inherent see **natural**

inheritance noun something that is passed on: *The house would be his son's inheritance*

bequest: *His aunt left a bequest for him in her will*

heritage: *This building is part of our heritage*

legacy: *His politeness was the legacy of his upbringing*
see also **legacy**

inhibit see **check, interfere, restrain, restrict**

inhibited see **pent-up**

inhuman see **savage**

inhumane see **cruel**

inhumanity see **cruelty**

inimitable see **incomparable**

initial see **first, opening, original**

initially see **first**

initiate see **begin, start**

initiation see **introduction, start**

initiative see **drive**

injunction see **command**

injure verb to damage part of someone's body: *A bomb exploded, injuring five people*

harm: *The hijackers did not harm anyone*

hurt: *He hurt his back in an accident*

maim: *Mines in rice paddies maim and kill civilians*

wound: *wounded by shrapnel*
see also **damage, hurt**

injury noun damage to part of the body: *He sustained serious injuries in the accident*

damage: *brain damage*

harm: *Dogs can do harm to human beings*

wound: *a head wound*
see also **damage, harm**

injustice noun unfairness and lack of justice: *the injustice of the system*

bias: *He shows bias against women*

discrimination: *racial discrimination*

inequality: *people concerned about social inequality*

prejudice: *prejudice against workers over 45*

unfairness: *the unfairness of the decision*

wrong: *I intend to right past wrongs*
see also **wrong**

inkling see **idea**

inlet see **bay**

inmate see **inhabitant**

inn see **pub**

innards see **insides**

innate see **natural**

inner see **inside**

innermost see **inside**

innocence noun inexperience of evil or unpleasant things: *the innocence of babies*

gullibility: *I'm paying for my gullibility back then*

inexperience: *their inexperience of the real world*

naivety: *There was a youthful naivety to his honesty*

simplicity: *She prayed with childlike simplicity*

innocent adjective **1** not guilty of a crime: *the arrest of innocent suspects*

blameless: *I have led a blameless life*

clear: *He was clear of blame for the accident*

not guilty: *Both men were found not guilty*

2 without experience of evil or unpleasant things: *They seem so young and innocent*

childlike: *childlike trust*

guileless: *Her eyes were as guileless as a doll's*

naive: *I was young and naive when I left home*

pure: *She had led a pure life*

spotless: *a spotless, pure child*

virginal: *a shy, virginal princess*
see also **ignorant**

innocuous see **harmless, safe**
innumerable see **countless, many**
inquire see **ask**
inquiring see **curious**
inquiry see **query**
inquisitive see **curious, nosy**
inquisitiveness see **curiosity**
insane adjective mad: Some people can't take the pressure and go insane
  crazy: If I sat home and worried, I'd go crazy
  deranged: a deranged man who shot 14 people in the main square
  mad: She was afraid of going mad
  mentally ill: a patient who is mentally ill
  out of your mind: I wonder if I'm going out of my mind
  unhinged: an experience which left her completely unhinged
  see also **crazy, mad**
insanitary see **unhealthy**
inscribe see **carve, write**
insensitive see **callous, numb, thoughtless**
insert verb to put something into something else: He inserted the key into the lock
  enter: Enter your name in the box
  implant: a device implanted in the arm
  introduce: Scientists introduced new genes into mice
  place: Cover the casserole tightly and place in the oven
  put: She put a coin in the slot
  set: diamonds set in gold
  see also **stick**
inside adjective surrounded by the main part and often hidden: We booked an inside cabin
  inner: the inner ear
  innermost: the innermost parts of the galaxy
  interior: a car with plenty of interior space

internal: your internal organs
insides plural noun informal the parts inside your body: My insides ached from eating too much
  entrails: chicken entrails
  guts: fish guts
  innards: the innards of a human body
  internal organs: damage to internal organs
insight see **vision, wisdom**
insignificant adjective small and unimportant: a small, insignificant village
  irrelevant: irrelevant details
  little: It seems such a little thing to get upset over
  minor: Western officials say the problem is minor
  petty: Rows can start over petty things
  trifling: These difficulties may seem trifling to you
  trivial: He tried to wave aside these issues as trivial matters
  unimportant: The age difference seemed unimportant
  see also **petty, slight, trivial, unimportant**
insincere adjective saying things you do not mean: A lot of actors are insincere
  deceitful: deceitful and misleading remarks
  dishonest: dishonest salespeople
  false: a false confession
  two-faced: the most two-faced politicians in the world
  see also **false, two-faced**
insinuate see **hint, suggest**
insinuation see **suggestion**
insipid see **flat, mild, tasteless**
insist verb to demand something forcefully: My family insisted I should not give in
  demand: The teacher demanded an explanation

press: *She is pressing for improvements to education*
urge: *We urge vigorous action be taken immediately*
see also **claim**
insist on *see* **exact**
insist upon *see* **exact**
insolence *see* **cheek, impudence**
insolent *see* **cheeky, rude**
insolvency *see* **poverty**
inspect *verb* to examine something carefully: *the right to inspect company files*
check: *Check each item for obvious flaws*
examine: *He examined her passport and stamped it*
eye: *We eyed each other thoughtfully*
investigate: *Police are investigating the scene of the crime*
scan: *The officer scanned the room*
survey: *He surveyed the ruins of the building*
see also **check, examine, scrutinize**
inspection *see* **check, examination**
inspire *see* **excite, motivate, prompt**
inspired *see* **creative**
install *see* **set up**
instalment *see* **issue, payment, section**
instance *see* **case**
instant *noun* **1** a short period of time: *The pain disappeared in an instant*
flash: *It was all over in a flash*
minute: *I'll see you in a minute*
moment: *In a moment he was gone*
second: *Seconds later, firemen reached her door*
split second: *Her gaze met Michael's for a split second*
trice: *She was back in a trice*
▷ *adjective* **2** immediate and without delay: *He had taken an instant dislike to her*

immediate: *We need an immediate reply*
instantaneous: *an explosion resulting in the instantaneous deaths of all crew members*
prompt: *Prompt action is needed*
see also **immediate, minute, moment, prompt**
instantaneous *see* **immediate, instant, prompt**
instantly *see* **immediately**
instigate *see* **incite, start**
instinct *noun* a natural tendency to do something: *My first instinct was to protect myself*
feeling: *You seem to have a feeling for drawing*
impulse: *Peter resisted an impulse to smile*
intuition: *You should trust your intuition*
sixth sense: *Some sixth sense told him to keep going*
urge: *He fought the urge to panic*
instinctive *see* **automatic, natural**
institute *see* **set up, society, start**
institution *see* **association, introduction, organization**
instruct *verb* **1** to tell someone to do something: *They have instructed solicitors to sue*
command: *He commanded his troops to attack*
direct: *They have been directed to give attention to this problem*
order: *Williams ordered him to leave*
tell: *A passer-by told him to move his car*
2 to teach someone about a subject or skill: *He instructs therapists in relaxation techniques*
coach: *He coached me in French*
educate: *We need to educate people about the destructive effects of alcohol*
school: *She's been schooling her kids herself*

teach: She taught children French
train: We train them in a range of building techniques
tutor: He was tutoring her in the stringed instruments
see also **brief, order, require, show, teach, tell, train**

instruction see **command, education, order**

instructor see **master, teacher**

instrument see **machine, tool**

insufficient adjective not enough for a particular purpose: insufficient information
deficient: a deficient diet
inadequate: The problem lies with inadequate staffing
lacking: My confidence is lacking
scant: Gareth paid scant attention to what was going on
short: He was short of breath
see also **inadequate, incomplete**

insular see **narrow-minded**

insult verb 1 to offend someone by being rude to them: I did not mean to insult you
abuse: footballers abusing referees
affront: He pretended to be affronted by what I said
offend: I had no intention of offending the community
put down: They seemed to delight in putting me down
slag British informal: He's always slagging me in front of his mates
slight: They felt slighted by not being consulted
snub: He snubbed her in public and made her feel foolish
▷ noun 2 a rude remark that offends someone: The two men exchanged insults
abuse: Raft hurled verbal abuse at his co-star
affront: She took my words as a personal affront

offence: I meant no offence to Mr Hardy
slight: She is very sensitive to slights
snub: This was a deliberate snub to me
see also **abuse, offend, provoke**

insulting see **abusive, offensive**

insults see **abuse**

insurance see **precaution**

insurrection see **rebellion**

intact see **complete, sound**

integrate see **combine**

integrity see **character, honour, principle, right, virtue**

intellect see **genius, intelligence, mind, reason**

intellectual see **educated, learned**

intelligence noun the ability to understand and learn things: students of high intelligence
cleverness: Her cleverness gets in the way of her emotions
comprehension: an idea beyond human comprehension
intellect: Lucy's lack of intellect disappointed her father
perception: You have brilliant perception and insight
sense: They have the sense to seek help
understanding: I've got no sense, no understanding
wit: He had the wit to see this was a good idea
see also **head, news, sense, word**

intelligent adjective able to understand and learn things: Dolphins are an intelligent species
acute: His relaxed exterior hides a very acute mind
brainy informal: I don't consider myself brainy
bright: an exceptionally bright child
clever: a clever girl
quick: His quick mind soon grasped the situation
sharp: a very sharp intellect

smart: He thinks he's as smart as Sarah

see also **bright, brilliant, clever, smart**

intend verb **1** to decide or plan to do something: She intended to move back to Cape Town

aim: We aim to raise funds for charity

be determined: Kate was determined to enjoy the day

mean: I didn't mean any harm

plan: He planned to leave Adelaide on Monday

propose: Where do you propose building such a huge thing?

resolve: She resolved to report the matter

2 to mean for a certain use: a book intended for serious students

aim: children's games aimed at developing quickness

design: The house had been designed for a large family

earmark: That money was earmarked for house repairs

mean: I was not meant for domestic life

see also **aim, mean, resolve**

intended see **calculated**

intense adjective **1** very great in strength or amount: intense heat

acute: an acute shortage of accommodation

deep: He felt a deep sense of relief

extreme: Proceed with extreme caution

fierce: There was fierce competition for the job

great: Dawes felt a great pain and weakness

powerful: I had a powerful urge to scream at him

profound: The book had a profound effect in the USA

severe: I had severe problems

2 tending to have strong feelings: He was dark-haired and intense

ardent: one of his most ardent supporters

earnest: Ella was a pious, earnest woman

fervent: a fervent admirer of Beethoven's music

fierce: fierce loyalty to his friends

impassioned: He made an impassioned appeal for peace

passionate: He is very passionate about the project

vehement: a vehement critic of the plan

see also **acute, ardent, colourful, deep, extreme, fierce, furious, passionate, serious, severe, uncommon, violent**

intensify see **build, rise**

intensity see **heat, passion, strength, violence**

intensive see **thorough**

intent see **set on**

intent on see **determined**

intention noun a plan to do something: He announced his intention of retiring

aim: The aim of this book is to inform you

goal: The goal is to raise a lot of money

idea: I bought books with the idea of reading them

object: It was his object in life to find the island

objective: His objective was to play golf and win

purpose: He did not know the purpose of Vincent's visit

see also **aim, goal, object, point, purpose**

intentional see **deliberate**

intentionally see **on purpose**

interchange see **change, exchange, substitute, swap**

interest noun **1** a feeling of wanting to know about something: I have a great interest in that period of history

attention: The book attracted considerable attention

fascination: a lifelong fascination with the sea

concern: How it happened is of little concern to me

curiosity: His reply satisfied our curiosity

2 a hobby: He has a wide range of sporting interests

activity: I enjoy outdoor activities like canoeing and climbing

hobby: My hobbies are football, photography and tennis

pastime: His favourite pastime is golf

pursuit: his favourite childhood pursuits

▷ verb **3** to attract someone's attention and curiosity: This part of the book interests me most

appeal: The bright colours seem to appeal to children

captivate: this author's ability to captivate young minds

fascinate: Politics fascinated my father

intrigue: The situation intrigued him

stimulate: Bill was stimulated by the challenge

see also **activity, appeal, curiosity, enthusiasm**

interested see **curious**

interesting adjective making you want to know, learn or hear more: an interesting hobby

absorbing: an absorbing conversation

compelling: compelling drama

entertaining: a cheerful and entertaining companion

gripping: a gripping story

intriguing: the intriguing character of the author

stimulating: My trip to India had been stimulating

see also **colourful**

interfere verb **1** to try to influence a situation: Stop interfering and leave me alone

butt in: I butted in where I didn't belong

intervene: Soldiers don't like civilians intervening in their affairs

intrude: I don't want to intrude on your meeting

meddle: Scientists should not meddle in such matters

tamper: the price we pay for tampering with the environment

2 to have a damaging effect on a situation: His problems interfered with his work

conflict: an evening that conflicted with my work schedule

disrupt: Strikes disrupted air traffic in Italy

hinder: A thigh injury hindered her movement

impede: Fallen rocks impeded the progress of the rescue workers

inhibit: factors which inhibit growth

obstruct: Lack of funds obstructed our progress

see also **pry**

interim see **temporary**

interior see **inside**

interlude see **break, gap, interval**

intermission see **interval**

intermittent see **occasional**

internal see **home, inside**

internal organs see **insides**

interpret see **read**

interrogate verb to question someone thoroughly: I interrogated everyone even slightly involved

examine: Lawyers examined the witnesses

grill informal: Jenkins kept telling police who grilled him: "I didn't kill her."

question: He was questioned by police

quiz: *She quizzed me quite closely for a while*
see also **ask, question**

interrupt *verb* **1** to start talking when someone else is talking: *He tried to speak, but she interrupted him*

butt in: *Mirella butted in without a greeting*

heckle: *It is easy to heckle from the safety of the audience*

2 to stop a process or activity for a time: *The match was interrupted by rain*

break: *allowing passengers to break their journey with a stay in Fiji*

discontinue: *Do not discontinue the treatment without seeing your doctor*

suspend: *Relief convoys will be suspended until the fighting stops*
see also **intrude**

interruption *see* **delay, pause**

intersect *see* **cross**

interval *noun* a period of time between two moments or dates: *There was a long interval of silence*

break: *a short break from work*

gap: *the gap between school terms*

hiatus: *There was a momentary hiatus in the sounds*

interlude: *It was a happy interlude in the Kents' life*

intermission: *There will be a short intermission between acts*

pause: *a pause between two periods of intense activity*
see also **break, gap, pause, period, space, time, wait**

intervene *verb* to step in to prevent conflict: *I relied on them to intervene if anything happened*

arbitrate: *A committee was set up to arbitrate in the dispute*

mediate: *efforts to mediate between the two communities*
see also **interfere**

interview *see* **appointment**

intimate *see* **cosy, hint, mention, suggest**

intimation *see* **hint, notice, suggestion**

intimidate *see* **bully, frighten, scare**

intimidating *see* **formidable, frightening**

into *see* **keen**

into the bargain *see also*, **too**

intolerable *see* **unbearable**

intoxicated *see* **drunk**

intractable *see* **difficult, obstinate**

intrepid *see* **bold**

intricate *see* **complex, complicated, elaborate, fancy, sophisticated**

intrigue *see* **fascinate, interest, plot**

intriguing *see* **interesting**

introduce *see* **insert, raise, start**

introduction *noun* **1** the act of presenting someone or something new: *the introduction of a single European currency*

establishment: *the establishment of a democratic system*

inauguration: *the inauguration of the President*

initiation: *your initiation into adulthood*

institution: *the institution of new laws*

launch: *the launch of this popular author's new book*

2 a piece of writing at the beginning of a book: *The book contains a new introduction by the author*

foreword: *I am happy to write the foreword to this collection*

preface: *I read through the preface quickly*

prologue: *the General Prologue to The Canterbury Tales*
see also **appearance**

introductory *see* **opening**

intrude *verb* to disturb someone or something: *I don't want to intrude on your parents*

butt in: I butted in where I didn't belong

encroach: Does your work encroach on your private life?

infringe: She promised not to infringe on his space

interrupt: Georgina interrupted his thoughts

trespass: I don't like to trespass on your time

violate: These men were violating her family's privacy

see also **interfere, pry**

intrude on see **disturb**

intuition see **instinct, vision**

intuitive see **natural**

invade verb to enter a country by force: The allies invaded the Italian mainland at Anzio

attack: Government planes attacked the town

enter: The Taleban entered western Kabul

occupy: Soldiers occupied the town within a few minutes

violate: A helicopter violated Greek territory yesterday

see also **attack, raid**

invalid see **faulty, patient**

invalidate see **disprove, reverse**

invaluable see **precious**

invariably see **always**

invasion see **attack**

invective see **abuse**

invent verb 1 to be the first person to think of a device: He invented the first electric clock

coin: Lanier coined the term 'virtual reality'

come up with informal: He came up with a gadget to relieve hayfever

conceive: He conceived the first portable computer

create: The company decided to create a new perfume

formulate: He formulated his plan for escape

originate: the designer who originated platform shoes

2 to make up a story or excuse: I tried to invent a plausible excuse

concoct: A newspaper concocted an imaginary interview

fabricate: The evidence against them was fabricated

make up: Donna was known for making up stories about herself

manufacture: The children manufactured an elaborate tale

see also **compose, create, make up, produce**

invented see **imaginary**

inventive see **creative**

inventiveness see **imagination**

inventory see **list**

invest in see **buy**

investigate verb to find out all the facts about something: Police are still investigating the incidents

examine: I have examined all the possible alternatives

explore: a book which explores the history of technology

probe: He probed into her private life

research: I'm researching for an article on New England

sift: I sifted the evidence for conclusions

study: Experts are studying the security in the building

see also **inspect, research**

investigation see **research**

investment see **finance**

investments see **stock**

invincible adjective unable to be defeated: When Woods is on form he is invincible

impregnable: an impregnable fortress

indomitable: the indomitable spirit of the Polish people

unbeatable: a performance record

that is unbeatable

invisible *adjective* unable to be seen: *His face was invisible beneath his hat*
  concealed: *a concealed weapon*
  disguised: *a disguised panel in the wall*
  hidden: *a hidden camera*
  inconspicuous: *She tried to make herself inconspicuous*
  unseen: *His work was guided by an unseen hand*

invite *see* **ask, challenge**

invoice *see* **bill**

involuntary *see* **automatic**

involve *verb* to have as a necessary part: *Running a kitchen involves a great deal of discipline*
  incorporate: *The program incorporates a range of activities*
  require: *Caring for a baby requires special skills*
  take in: *This study takes in a number of areas*
  see also **concern, demand, include**

involved *see* **active, complex, complicated, elaborate**

involvement *see* **part**

irate *see* **mad**

ironic *see* **sarcastic**

irrational *adjective* not based on logical reasons: *irrational fears*
  absurd: *It was an absurd over-reaction*
  crazy: *crazy ideas*
  illogical: *his completely illogical arguments*
  nonsensical: *Such an idea sounds paradoxical, if not downright nonsensical*
  unsound: *The thinking is good-hearted, but muddled and unsound*

irregular *adjective* **1** not smooth or even: *an irregular surface*
  asymmetrical: *She has asymmetrical features*
  bumpy: *bumpy roads*

jagged: *jagged fragments of stained glass*
  lopsided: *his lopsided smile*
  ragged: *the ragged edges of a tear*
  uneven: *uneven teeth*
  2 not forming a regular pattern: *He worked irregular hours*
  erratic: *a planet with an erratic orbit*
  haphazard: *a haphazard system*
  occasional: *occasional rain showers*
  patchy: *Her career has been patchy*
  random: *The stock market is random and unpredictable*
  variable: *a variable rate of interest*
  see also **changeable, crooked, uneven**

irrelevant *see* **insignificant**

irresponsible *adjective* not concerned with the consequences of your actions: *an irresponsible attitude*
  careless: *a careless driver*
  reckless: *reckless spending*
  thoughtless: *a thoughtless remark*
  wild: *a night of wild abandon*
  see also **careless, unwise**

irrigate *see* **wet**

irritable *adjective* easily annoyed: *Nicol was unusually tense and irritable*
  bad-tempered: *You're very bad-tempered today*
  cantankerous: *a cantankerous old man*
  petulant: *He was like a petulant child*
  ratty *British, New Zealand informal*: *There's no need to get ratty*
  see also **cross, grumpy, impatient, moody**

irritate *verb* to annoy someone: *Their attitude irritates me*
  anger: *This article angered me*
  annoy: *It just annoyed me to hear him going on*
  bother: *Nothing bothers me*
  exasperate: *Bertha was exasperated by the delay*
  needle *informal*: *If her remark needled*

him, he didn't show it
ruffle: He doesn't get ruffled by anything
see also **annoy, provoke**

irritation see **annoyance, bother, nuisance, pain**

isolated see **alone, exceptional, lonely, remote, separate**

isolation see **solitude**

issue noun **1** a subject that people are talking about: *important issues of the day*
concern: *Political concerns continue to dominate the news*
matter: *He touched on many matters in his speech*
problem: *the energy problem*
question: *The whole question of aid is a tricky one*
subject: *the president's views on the subject*
topic: *the main topic for discussion*
2 a particular edition of a newspaper or magazine: *the latest issue of the Lancet*
copy: *a copy of "USA Today"*
edition: *There's an article about the film in next month's edition*
instalment: *a magazine published in monthly instalments*
▷ verb **3** to make a formal statement: *They have issued a statement denying the allegations*
deliver: *He delivered a speech to his fellow union members*
give: *The minister gave a warning that war should be avoided at all costs*
make: *He says he was depressed when he made the statement*
pronounce: *The authorities took time to pronounce their verdicts*
read out: *She read out an announcement outside the court*
release: *The police are not releasing any more details about the attack*
4 to give something officially: *Staff*

will be issued with badges
equip: *plans to equip the reserve army with guns*
furnish formal: *They will furnish you with the necessary items*
give out: *The prizes were given out by a local dignitary*
provide: *The government was unable to provide them with food*
supply: *an agreement not to supply these countries with chemical weapons*
see also **affair, business, consideration, matter, question, release, subject**

it could be see **maybe, perhaps**

item noun **1** one of a collection or list of things: *an item on the agenda*
article: *articles of clothing*
matter: *He dealt with a variety of matters*
point: *Many of the points in the report are correct*
thing: *Big things are paid for by the government*
2 a newspaper or magazine article: *There was an item in the paper about him*
article: *a short article in one of the papers*
feature: *The magazine contained a special feature on the project*
notice: *notices in today's national newspapers*
piece: *I disagree with your recent piece about Australia*
report: *a film report on the scandal*
see also **article, entry, feature**

itinerary see **route**

j

jab see **dig, poke, stick**
jack up see **organize**
jacket see **cover**
jagged adjective sharp and spiky: *jagged black cliffs*
  barbed: *barbed wire*
  craggy: *craggy mountains*
  rough: *the rough surface of the rock*
  serrated: *a serrated knife*
  see also **irregular, sharp**
jail noun **1** a place where prisoners are held: *sentenced to 18 months in jail*
  nick British, Australian, New Zealand slang: *He spent seven years in the nick*
  prison: *his release from prison*
  ▷ verb **2** to put in prison: *He was jailed for twenty years*
  detain: *Police can detain a suspect for 48 hours*
  imprison: *imprisoned for 18 months on charges of theft*
  incarcerate: *They have been incarcerated as political prisoners*
  see also **imprison, prison**
jam noun **1** a crowded mass of people or things: *stuck in a jam on the motorway*
  crowd: *elbowing his way through the crowd*
  crush: *We got separated in the crush*
  mass: *a mass of excited fans*
  mob: *a growing mob of demonstrators*
  multitude: *surrounded by a noisy multitude*
  throng: *An official pushed through the throng*
  2 a difficult situation: *We're in a real jam now*
  dilemma: *faced with a dilemma*
  fix informal: *a difficult economic fix*
  hole slang: *He admitted that the government was in a hole*
  plight: *the plight of the Third World countries*
  predicament: *a way out of our predicament*
  quandary: *We're in a quandary over our holiday plans*
  trouble: *You are in serious trouble*
  ▷ verb **3** to push something somewhere roughly: *He jammed his hat on to his head*
  cram: *He crammed the bank notes into his pocket*
  force: *I forced the key into the ignition*
  ram: *He rammed the muzzle of the gun against my forehead*
  stuff: *She stuffed the newspaper into a litter bin*
  4 to become stuck: *The second time he fired, his gun jammed*
  stall: *The engine stalled*
  stick: *She tried to open the window but it was stuck*
  see also **cram, mess, predicament, stick, stuff**
jar see **clash**
jargon see **language**
jaundiced see **sour**
jaunt see **drive, trip**
jaunty see **cheerful**
jazzy see **colourful**

jealous adjective wanting to have something which someone else has: *She was jealous of his success*

envious: *envious of the attention his brother was getting*

resentful: *resentful of her husband's hobby*

jealousy see **envy**

jeering see **mockery**

jeopardize see **endanger, risk, threaten**

jeopardy see **danger**

jerk see **tug**

jest see **joke**

jettison see **discard, dispose of, dump, get rid of**

jiggle see **fidget**

jilt see **abandon**

jingle see **slogan**

jittery see **nervous, tense**

job noun 1 the work someone does to earn money: *I'm still looking for a job*

employment: *unable to find employment*

occupation: *his occupation as a carpenter*

position: *He's leaving to take up a position abroad*

post: *She has resigned her post as his assistant*

profession: *She chose nursing as her profession*

trade: *her trade as a jeweller*

2 a duty or responsibility: *It's your job to find out what's going on*

concern: *The technical aspects are the concern of the engineers*

duty: *I consider it my duty to write and thank you*

function: *an important function to fill*

responsibility: *It's not my responsibility to look after your mother*

role: *Our role is to keep the peace*

task: *She had the task of breaking the bad news*

see also **appointment, duty,**

function, task, undertaking, work

jobless see **idle, unemployed**

jog see **run**

jog someone's memory see **remind**

join verb 1 to become a member of something: *He joined the Army five years ago*

enlist: *He was 18 when he enlisted in the US Navy*

enrol: *She has enrolled in an acting class*

sign up: *I've signed up as a member*

2 to fasten two things together: *two sticks joined together by a chain*

attach: *The gadget can be attached to any surface*

connect: *two rooms connected by a passage*

couple: *an engine coupled to a gearbox*

fasten: *a wooden bench fastened to the floor*

link: *tree houses linked by ropes*

tie: *He tied the dog to a post by its leash*

see also **attach, connect, fasten, link, piece together, unite**

join forces see **cooperate, team, unite**

join in see **participate, take part in**

jointly see **together**

joke noun 1 something that makes people laugh: *I heard a great joke today*

gag informal: *a gag about unscrupulous lawyers*

jest: *It was only intended as a jest*

lark: *They just did it for a lark*

prank: *an end-of-term prank*

quip: *a famous quip by Groucho Marx*

wisecrack informal: *She was tempted to make a wisecrack*

witticism: *laughing at each other's witticisms*

▷ verb 2 to say something funny:

She was always joking about her appearance

banter: He played trick shots and bantered with the crowd

chaff: They chaffed us about our chances of winning

jest: drinking and jesting with his cronies

kid informal: Don't worry, I'm only kidding

quip: "You'll have to go on a diet," he quipped

tease: "You must be in love," she teased

jolly see **bright, cheerful, cheery**

jolt see **bump, shake, surprise**

jotting see **note**

journal see **record**

journey noun 1 the act of travelling from one place to another: the journey from Paris to Bordeaux

excursion: The trip includes an excursion to Zermatt

expedition: an expedition to the South Pole

passage: a 10-hour passage from Swansea

tour: a two-month tour of Europe

trek: a trek through the Gobi desert

trip: a business trip

voyage: the first space shuttle voyage

▷ verb 2 to travel from one place to another: In 1935, she journeyed through Turkey and Africa

go: We went from Glasgow to London in six hours

proceed: proceeding along the road in the wrong direction

tour: He toured China in 1993

travel: Gran travelled down by train

trek: trekking through the jungle

voyage: They voyaged as far as Spain

see also **drive, go, travel, trip**

joy noun great happiness: Her face shone with joy

bliss: an expression of pure bliss

delight: He let out a yell of delight

ecstasy: Her eyes closed in ecstasy

elation: He felt a surge of elation at the news

rapture: His speech was received with rapture

see also **delight, ecstasy, happiness, pleasure**

joyful adjective extremely happy: a joyful smile

delighted: I'm delighted to be here

elated: the elated faces of the freed hostages

jubilant: the jubilant crowds

over the moon informal: I was over the moon to hear about your promotion

see also **glad**

jubilant see **joyful**

judge noun 1 the person in charge of a law court: The judge awarded him £2000 in damages

beak British slang: a third appearance before the beak

justice: his appointment as a Justice of the High Court

magistrate: defendants appearing before a magistrate

2 someone who picks the winner or keeps control of a competition: A panel of judges are selecting the finalists

referee: The referee awarded a free kick against Rourke

umpire: The umpire's decision is final

▷ verb 3 to form an opinion about someone or something: Don't judge people by their looks

appraise: The teachers are appraised by an official

assess: It is too early to assess the impact of the change

consider: We consider him to be dangerous

estimate: The cost of the damage is estimated at over a million dollars

evaluate: a test to evaluate a

candidate's potential
rate: *The film was rated a hit*
4 to pick the winner or keep control
in a competition: *Entrants will be
judged in two age categories*
referee: *He has refereed in two
World Cups*
umpire: *He umpired baseball games*
see also **conclude, consider, feel,
justice, reckon, regard, think, view**

judgment *noun* an opinion or
decision based on evidence: *It's
hard to form a judgment without all
the facts*
appraisal: *a calm appraisal of the
situation*
assessment: *my own personal
assessment of our position*
conclusion: *I've come to the
conclusion that she knows what she's
talking about*
opinion: *Seek a medical opinion
before you travel*
ruling: *a High Court ruling*
verdict: *The doctor's verdict was that
he was entirely healthy*
view: *In my view, things aren't going
to get any better*
see also **belief, common sense,
conclusion, decision, opinion,
reason, sense, verdict, wisdom**

judicial see **legal**
judiciary see **legal**
judicious see **logical, sane, sensible,
wise**

jumble see **muddle, tangle**
jumbled see **garbled, untidy**

jump *verb* **1** to leap up or over
something: *I jumped over the fence*
bound: *He bounded up the steps*
clear: *The horse cleared the gate
by inches*
hurdle: *He crossed the lawn and
hurdled the fence*
leap: *He had leapt from a window
and escaped*

spring: *The lion roared once and
sprang*
vault: *Ned vaulted over a fallen tree*
2 to increase suddenly: *Sales jumped
by 25% last year*
escalate: *Costs escalated
dramatically*
increase: *Trading has increased by
20% this month*
rise: *Unemployment is rising rapidly*
surge: *The party's share of the vote
surged from 10% to 17%*
▷ *noun* **3** a leap into the air: *the
longest ever jump by a man*
bound: *With one bound Jack was free*
leap: *Smith took the gold medal with a
leap of 2.37 metres*
vault: *She regained the record with a
vault of 3.80 metres*
see also **bounce, dive, leap**

jumpy see **nervous, restless, tense**

junction see **connection**

junior *adjective* having a relatively
low position compared to others: *a
junior minister*
inferior: *inferior status*
lesser: *He resigned to take a lesser
position and a cut in wages*
lower: *the lower ranks of council
officers*
subordinate: *sixty of his subordinate
officers*
see also **inferior, young**

junk *noun* old articles that people
usually throw away: *What are you
going to do with all that junk?*
clutter: *She likes her worktops to be
clear of clutter*
odds and ends: *My handbag's full of
useless odds and ends*
refuse: *a weekly collection of refuse*
rubbish: *They piled most of their
rubbish into skips*
scrap: *a small yard containing a
heap of scrap*
trash: *cluttered with trash*

see also **garbage, refuse**
just see **barely, exactly, hardly, only**
just about see **nearly**
justice noun **1** fairness in the way
that people are treated: *He wants
freedom, justice and equality*
  equity: *Income should be distributed
  with some sense of equity*
  fairness: *concern about the fairness
  of the election campaign*
  impartiality: *a system lacking
  impartiality*
  2 the person in charge of a law
  court: *his appointment as a Justice of
  the High Court*
  judge: *The judge awarded him £2000
  in damages*
  magistrate: *defendants appearing
  before a magistrate*
  see also **judge, right**
justifiable see **reasonable**
justification see **cause, defence,
excuse, grounds**
justify verb to show that something
is reasonable or necessary: *How can
you justify what you've done?*
  defend: *Her conduct is hard to defend*
  excuse: *That still doesn't excuse his
  behaviour*
  explain: *She left a note explaining
  her actions*
  vindicate: *Ministers are confident
  their decision will be vindicated*
  warrant: *These allegations warrant
  an investigation*
  see also **defend, deserve**
jut out see **extend**
jutting see **prominent**
juvenile see **child, childish,
frivolous, young**
juxtapose see **compare**

K

kai noun *New Zealand informal* food:
I'm starving – let's have some kai
  food: *Enjoy your food*
  grub *informal*: *Get yourself some grub*
  provisions: *enough provisions for
  two weeks*
  rations: *The soldiers sampled the
  officers' rations*
  tucker *Australian, New
  Zealand informal*: *I haven't had any
  decent tucker for days formal*
  see also **food, meal**
keen adjective **1** showing eagerness
and enthusiasm for something: *a
keen amateur photographer*
  ardent: *one of his most ardent
  supporters*
  avid: *an avid reader*
  eager: *We're eager to have another
  baby*
  enthusiastic: *Tom was very
  enthusiastic about the place*
  fond of: *Are you fond of Chinese
  cuisine?*
  into *informal*: *I'm really into football*
  2 quick to notice or understand
  things: *a keen intellect*
  astute: *an astute judge of character*
  brilliant: *She had a brilliant mind*
  perceptive: *a perceptive gaze*

quick: His quick mind soon grasped the situation

shrewd: Her questions showed a shrewd perception

see also **acute, ardent, astute, eager, enthusiastic, fierce, fine, ready, sharp**

keenness see **enthusiasm**

keep verb **1** to have and look after something: His father keeps a small shop

care for: vintage cars lovingly cared for by their owners

maintain: The house costs a fortune to maintain

preserve: the need to preserve the rainforests

2 to store something: She kept her money under the mattress

deposit: You are advised to deposit your valuables in the hotel safe

hold: Our stock is held in a warehouse

store: Store the cookies in an airtight tin

3 to do what you said you would do: I always keep my promises

carry out: He carried out his threat

fulfil: He fulfilled all his responsibilities

honour: The two sides have agreed to honour a new ceasefire

see also **breed, have, own, reserve, save, store, upkeep**

keep an eye on see **mind, supervise**

keep on see **continue**

keep out see **exclude**

keep safe see **save**

keep your eyes open see **watch out**

keepsake see **souvenir**

key see **basic, chief, essential, leading**

kick see **thrill**

kick up a fuss see **complain**

kid see **child, joke**

kidnap verb to take someone away by force: Four tourists have been kidnapped by rebels

abduct: people claiming to have been abducted by aliens

capture: The guerrillas shot down one plane and captured the pilot

seize: hostages seized by terrorists

kill verb to make someone or something die: The earthquake killed 62 people

assassinate: the plot to assassinate Martin Luther King

butcher: The guards butchered hundreds of prisoners

destroy: The jockey was unhurt but his horse had to be destroyed

execute: He was executed for treason

exterminate: an effort to exterminate all the rats

massacre: 300 civilians have been massacred by the rebels

murder: the widow of the murdered leader

slaughter: Whales are being slaughtered for commercial gain

slay: a painting of Saint George slaying the dragon

see also **murder, put down**

killing see **murder**

kin noun the people who are related to you: She has gone to live with her husband's kin

family: There's a history of heart disease in our family

kindred: his loyalty to his friends and kindred

people: She was reunited with her people

relations: I was staying with relations in Atlanta

relatives: On Sundays his relatives come to visit

see also **relation**

kind noun **1** a particular type of person or thing: I don't like that kind of film

brand: his favourite brand of whisky

breed: *a rare breed of cattle*
category: *Cereal bars are the fastest-growing category of breakfast products*
class: *a better class of restaurant*
classification: *the cost of coverage for different classifications of motorcycle*
genre: *a writer who does not confine himself to one particular genre*
grade: *an improved grade of fertilizer*
sort: *a dozen trees of various sorts*
species: *a rare species of moth*
type: *What type of guns were they?*
variety: *a new variety of rose*
▷ *adjective* **2** considerate towards other people: *Thank you for being so kind to me*
benevolent: *a very benevolent employer*
benign: *a benign ruler*
charitable: *a charitable nature*
compassionate: *My father was a deeply compassionate man*
considerate: *a caring and considerate husband*
good: *a good man driven to a desperate act*
humane: *the humane treatment of prisoners*
kind-hearted: *Mark was kind-hearted, generous, and loved life*
kindly: *a kindly old man*
thoughtful: *a thoughtful gesture*
unselfish: *his generous and unselfish attitude towards others*
see also **accommodating, benevolent, breed, class, compassionate, family, form, generous, gentle, helpful, humane, merciful, sort, tender, thoughtful, type, variety**
kind of see **pretty**
kind-hearted see **compassionate, kind**
kindle see **light**
kindly see **gentle, kind, well**

kindness *noun* the quality of being considerate towards other people: *Everyone has treated me with great kindness*
benevolence: *an act of selfless benevolence*
charity: *Ms Rubens writes with warmth and charity*
compassion: *He showed no compassion to his victim*
gentleness: *the gentleness with which she treated her mother*
humanity: *Her speech showed great maturity and humanity*
see also **consideration, favour, generosity, mercy, pity**
kindred see **kin**
king *noun* a man who is the head of a royal family: *the king and queen of Spain*
monarch: *the coronation of the new monarch*
sovereign: *the first British sovereign to visit the country*
kingdom see **country, state**
kinsman see **relation**
kinswoman see **relation**
kip see **sleep**
kit see **set, stuff**
kitty see **cat**
knack see **skill, talent**
knick-knack see **ornament**
knit your brows see **frown**
knob see **bump**
knock see **bang, blow, bump, criticize, drive, hit**
knock down see **overturn**
knock out see **eliminate**
knock over see **overturn, upset**
knot see **tangle, tie**
know *verb* **1** to understand or be aware of something: *I don't know anything about cars*
apprehend: *It is impossible to apprehend the whole painting at once*
be aware of: *Smokers are aware of*

the risks they run
comprehend: *They do not comprehend the nature of the problem*
perceive: *the world as we perceive it*
see: *Don't you see what he's up to?*
understand: *too young to understand what was happening*
2 to be familiar with a person or thing: *I believe you two already know each other*
be acquainted with: *Are you acquainted with my husband?*
be familiar with: *I am familiar with his work*
recognize: *She recognized him at once*
see also **recognize**
know-how *see* **experience**
knowingly *see* **on purpose**
knowledge *noun* all you know about something: *She had no knowledge of French*
education: *a man with little education*
learning: *people of great learning*
scholarship: *a lifetime of scholarship*
wisdom: *a source of wisdom and knowledge*
see also **command, experience, grasp, understanding, wisdom**
knowledgeable *see* **aware, experienced, expert**
knowledgeable about *see* **familiar**
known *see* **certain**

label *noun* **1** a piece of paper or plastic attached to something for information: *He peered at the label on the bottle*
sticker: *She's got a disabled sticker on her car*
tag: *a name tag*
ticket: *a price ticket*
▷ *verb* **2** to put a label on something: *The produce was labelled "Made in China"*
flag: *Flag the pages which need corrections*
sticker: *products stickered at a special price*
tag: *The pigeon was tagged with a numbered band*
see also **identify**
laborious *see* **difficult, hard**
labour *noun* **1** very hard work: *the labour of weeding and digging*
effort: *legs aching with the effort of the climb*
exertion: *She felt dizzy with the exertion of walking*
industry: *At last his industry was rewarded*
toil: *their day's toil in the fields*
work: *All our work is starting to pay off*

2 the workforce of a country or industry: *unskilled labour*

employees: *Only a third of all employees are union members*

workers: *Thousands of workers have been laid off*

workforce: *a country where half the workforce is unemployed*

▷ verb **3** to work very hard: *peasants labouring in the fields*

slave: *We've been slaving half the night to finish this*

toil: *workers toiling in wretched conditions*

work: *He works twelve hours a day*

see also **struggle, work**

labourer see **worker**

lack noun **1** the shortage or absence of something which is needed: *a lack of funds*

absence: *an absence of evidence*

deficiency: *tests for vitamin deficiency*

scarcity: *a scarcity of water*

shortage: *a food shortage*

want: *becoming weak from want of rest*

▷ verb **2** to be without something that is needed: *She lacks confidence*

be deficient in: *Your diet is deficient in vitamins*

be short of: *I'm short of cash*

miss: *Your jacket is missing a button*

see also **deficiency, shortage, want**

lacking see **deficient, inadequate, insufficient**

lad see **boy**

ladder see **tear**

lady see **female, woman**

ladylike see **refined**

lag verb to make slower progress than other people or things: *He is now lagging 10 points behind the champion*

fall behind: *The city is falling behind in attracting tourists*

trail: *The Communist party is trailing badly in the opinion polls*

lame adjective **1** unable to walk properly because of an injured leg: *She was lame in one leg*

crippled: *a woman crippled by arthritis*

hobbling: *a hobbling old man*

limping: *limping from a hamstring injury*

2 weak or unconvincing: *a lame excuse*

feeble: *his feeble attempt at humour*

flimsy: *MPs condemned his evidence as flimsy*

pathetic: *a pathetic attempt at humour*

poor: *a poor effort*

unconvincing: *an unconvincing argument*

weak: *a weak performance*

see also **cripple**

lament verb **1** to express sorrow or regret over something: *She lamented the death of her brother*

grieve: *grieving over his dead wife and son*

mourn: *We mourned the loss of our home*

wail: *a mother wailing for her lost child*

weep: *She wept for her lost love*

▷ noun **2** something you say to express sorrow or regret: *a lament for a vanished age*

moan: *a moan of sorrow*

wail: *wails of grief*

see also **grieve, regret**

lamentable see **pathetic**

lance see **pierce**

land noun **1** an area of ground which someone owns: *a dispute over land*

estate: *a shooting party on his estate in Yorkshire*

grounds: *the palace grounds*

property: *travellers who camped on*

his property

2 a region or country: *America is the land of opportunity*

country: *the boundary between the two countries*

nation: *the nation's financial crisis*

province: *The Algarve is Portugal's southernmost province*

region: *the region of Tuscany*

territory: *the disputed territory of Kashmir*

▷ *verb* **3** to arrive on the ground after flying or sailing: *We landed in New York around noon*

alight: *A thrush alighted on a nearby branch*

dock: *The ship docked in Le Havre*

touch down: *The plane touched down in Barbados*

see also **country, ground, grounds, region, state, territory**

landscape see **scene, scenery, view**

lane see **way**

language *noun* **1** the system of words people use to communicate: *She speaks four languages*

dialect: *the Cantonese dialect*

idiom: *the Gaelic folk idiom*

jargon: *scientific jargon*

lingo *informal*: *I don't speak the lingo*

tongue: *The French feel passionately about their native tongue*

vernacular: *an Indian vernacular derived from Sanskrit*

vocabulary: *a new word in the German vocabulary*

2 the style in which you speak or write: *He explained the process in plain language*

phrasing: *The phrasing of this report is confusing*

style: *a simple writing style*

wording: *The wording of the contract was ambiguous*

lanky see **tall**

lap see **round, stage**

lapse see **error**

large *adjective* of a greater size or amount than usual: *a large room*

big: *Her husband was a big man*

colossal: *a colossal task*

enormous: *an enormous house*

giant: *a giant bird*

gigantic: *a gigantic spider*

great: *a great hall as long as a church*

huge: *huge profits*

immense: *an immense chamber*

massive: *a massive ship*

vast: *a vast desert*

see also **broad, extensive, spacious**

large numbers see **many**

largely see **mainly**

lark see **joke**

lash see **tie**

lass see **woman**

last *adjective* **1** the most recent: *last year*

latest: *his latest thriller*

most recent: *her most recent film*

preceding: *The bank's turnover had risen during the preceding year*

previous: *his previous marriage*

2 happening or remaining after all the others of its kind: *the last three chapters of the book*

closing: *the closing years of this century*

concluding: *the concluding scene of the film*

final: *This is your final chance*

ultimate: *the ultimate result of the move*

▷ *verb* **3** to continue to exist or happen: *The film lasted for two and a half hours*

carry on: *Our marriage can't carry on like this*

continue: *The exhibition continues till 25 November*

endure: *Somehow their friendship endures*

persist: *The problem persists*

remain: The building remains to this day
survive: companies which survived after the recession
see also **continue, endure, final, remain, remainder, stretch, survive, ultimate**

lasting see **permanent**
lastly see **finally**
last-minute see **late**
latch see **catch, lock**
late adjective **1** after the expected time: The train was late
behind: I've got behind with my payments
behind time: Hurry up. We're behind time already
belated: a belated birthday card
delayed: The kick-off was delayed by 10 minutes
last-minute: buying some last-minute Christmas presents
overdue: The birth is two weeks overdue
2 dead, especially recently: my late husband
dead: He has been dead for a year now
deceased: his recently deceased mother
departed: memories of departed friends
see also **dead**
later see **after, future**
latest see **fashionable, last, modern, news, trendy**
lather see **foam**
latitude see **freedom**
laugh verb **1** to make a noise which shows you are amused or happy: You never laugh at my jokes
chortle: He began chortling to himself
chuckle: He chuckled with pleasure
giggle: Both girls began to giggle
guffaw: Everyone guffawed loudly
snigger: People were sniggering behind my back

titter: The audience tittered nervously
▷ noun **2** the noise you make when amused or happy: She has a very infectious laugh
chortle: "That's what you think," he said with a chortle
chuckle: We had a quiet chuckle at his mistake
giggle: She gave a nervous giggle
guffaw: He let out a huge guffaw of amusement
snigger: barely able to stifle a snigger
titter: A titter went round the room
laugh at see **make fun of, mock**
laughable see **ridiculous**
launch see **fire, introduction, release, start**
launder see **wash**
laundered see **clean**
laurels see **victory**
lavish see **generous, luxurious**
law noun **1** a country's system of rules: The use of this drug is against the law
charter: a citizen's charter for France
code: a code of conduct
constitution: proposed changes to the constitution
2 one of the rules of a country: The anti-stalking law was introduced in 1990
act: A new act has been passed by Parliament
code: a code designed to protect the rights of children
decree: a decree lifting sanctions against China
regulation: regulations outlawing child labour
rule: a rule that was imposed in 1962
statute: A practice regulated by statute
see also **principle, rule**
law court see **court**
law-abiding see **honest, obedient**
lawful see **legal**

lawsuit see **case**

lawyer noun someone who advises people about the law: *I'm discussing the matter with my lawyers*

advocate: *A public advocate will be appointed to represent you*

attorney: *a prosecuting attorney*

barrister: *The author is a practising barrister*

counsel: *His counsel advised him to appeal against the verdict*

solicitor: *She took advice from a solicitor*

lay verb **1** to put something somewhere: *Lay a sheet of newspaper on the floor*

place: *She placed a mug of coffee in front of him*

put: *He put the photograph on the desk*

set: *He set his briefcase on the floor*

set down: *I set the glasses down on the table*

settle: *He settled his coat over my shoulders*

spread: *She spread a towel over the sand and lay down*

2 to arrange or set something out: *A man came to lay the carpet*

arrange: *He started to arrange the books in piles*

set out: *The flower garden was set out with large beds of roses*

see also **deposit**, **put**, **set**

lay out see **position**

layer noun something that covers a surface or comes between two other things: *A fresh layer of snow covered the street*

blanket: *a blanket of fog*

coat: *a coat of paint*

coating: *a crisp chocolate coating*

covering: *a thin covering of dust*

film: *a film of plastic*

sheet: *a sheet of ice*

stratum: *the correct geological stratum*

see also **coating**

layout noun the way in which something is arranged: *the layout of the garden*

arrangement: *the arrangement of a room*

design: *the design of the museum*

format: *the format of the book*

plan: *a detailed plan of the house*

see also **form**, **plan**

laze verb to relax and do no work: *We spent a few days lazing around by the pool*

idle: *We spent hours idling in one of the cafés*

loaf: *loafing around the house all day*

lounge: *They lounged in the shade*

see also **outspan**, **relax**, **rest**

lazy adjective not willing to work: *a lazy and incompetent employee*

idle: *an idle young layabout*

slack: *Many workers have simply become too slack*

lead verb **1** to guide or take someone somewhere: *She led him into the house*

conduct: *He asked if he might conduct us to the ball*

escort: *They were escorted by police to their plane*

guide: *He took me by the arm and guided me out*

steer: *Nick steered them towards the door*

usher: *I ushered him into the office*

2 to be in charge of: *He led the country between 1949 and 1984*

command: *the general who commanded the troops*

direct: *He will direct day-to-day operations*

govern: *his ability to govern the country*

head: *Who heads the firm?*

manage: *I manage a small team*

of workers

supervise: *He supervised more than 400 volunteers*

▷ noun **3** a clue which may help solve a crime: *The police are following up several leads*

clue: *a vital clue to the killer's identity*

indication: *All the indications suggest that he is the murderer*

trace: *No traces of violence were found on the body*

see also **bring, command, direct, drive, guide, head, motivate, rule, take, top**

leaden see **cloudy, dull**

leader noun the person in charge of something: *the leader of the Republican Party*

boss informal: *Who's the boss around here?*

captain: *the captain of the team*

chief: *the chief of police*

commander: *a commander in the Royal Navy*

director: *the director of the film*

head: *Heads of government met in New York*

principal: *the principal of the school*

ringleader: *the ringleader of the gang*

see also **boss, chief, head, ruler**

leadership see **direction**

leading adjective particularly important, respected, or advanced: *a leading industrial nation*

chief: *one of his chief rivals*

eminent: *an eminent surgeon*

key: *the key witness at the trial*

major: *Exercise has a major part to play in preventing disease*

main: *one of the main tourist areas of Amsterdam*

principal: *one of the principal figures in politics today*

prominent: *a prominent member of the Law Society*

top: *a top model*

see also **first, foremost, important, in front, main, major, prime, supreme, top**

lead to verb to cause something to happen: *Smoking leads to heart disease and cancer*

cause: *Knocks can cause damage to the spine*

contribute to: *injuries which contributed to his death*

produce: *The drug produces side effects*

see also **create, result in**

leaflet noun a piece of paper with information about a subject: *Protesters were handing out leaflets in the street*

booklet: *a booklet about mortgage rates*

brochure: *a travel brochure*

circular: *A circular was sent out to shareholders*

pamphlet: *an anti-vivisection pamphlet*

league see **association, fellowship, society, union**

leak verb **1** to escape from a container or other object: *The gas had leaked from a cylinder*

escape: *A vent was opened to let some air escape*

ooze: *Blood was oozing from the wound*

seep: *Radioactive water has seeped into underground reservoirs*

spill: *70,000 tonnes of oil spilled from the tanker*

▷ noun **2** a hole which lets gas or liquid escape: *Have you plugged the leaks?*

chink: *A mist rose from the chinks in the pavement*

crack: *The lava oozed through cracks in the rock*

fissure: *Water trickled out of fissures in the limestone*

hole: *The sea was flowing in through the hole in the ship's hull*
puncture: *My tyre has a slow puncture*

lean *see* **bend, skinny, slender, tilt**

leaning *see* **tendency**

leap *verb* **1** to jump a great distance or height: *The deer leapt into the air*
bounce: *She bounced up and down on the spot, looking for attention*
bound: *The dog came bounding up the stairs*
jump: *I jumped over the fence*
spring: *He sprang to his feet*
vault: *He could easily vault the wall*
▷ *noun* **2** a jump of great distance or height: *a leap of 2.37 metres*
jump: *the longest jumps by a man and a woman*
bound: *With one bound, Jack was free*
spring: *The cheetah gave a great spring into the air*
see also **dive, jump**

learn *verb* **1** to gain knowledge by studying or training: *I am trying to learn French*
grasp: *The basics of the language are easy to grasp*
master: *He's having trouble mastering the piano*
pick up: *You'll soon pick up enough German to get by*
2 to find out about something: *On learning who she was, I asked to meet her*
ascertain: *They had ascertained that he was not a spy*
determine: *calculations to determine the rate of tax*
discover: *She discovered that they'd escaped*
find out: *As soon as we found this out, we closed the ward*
gather: *I gather the report is critical of the judge*
hear: *I heard he had moved away*

understand: *I understand that she's just taken early retirement*
see also **discover, find, gather, hear, master, study, understand**

learned *adjective* having gained a lot of knowledge by studying: *a very learned man*
academic: *I feel intimidated by academic people*
erudite: *a witty and erudite leader*
intellectual: *an artistic and intellectual couple*
literate: *a literate and educated readership*
scholarly: *a scholarly researcher*
see also **educated**

learner *see* **beginner**

learning *see* **knowledge**

lease *see* **hire, let**

least *adjective* as small or few as possible: *Stick to foods with the least fat*
fewest: *Which product has the fewest calories?*
lowest: *the lowest temperatures on record for this time of year*
minimum: *the minimum height for a policeman*
slightest: *He showed only the slightest hint of emotion*
smallest: *the smallest measurable unit of light*

least possible *see* **minimum**

leathery *see* **tough**

leave *verb* **1** to go away from a person or place: *He is not allowed to leave the country*
abandon: *He claimed that his parents had abandoned him*
depart: *A number of staff departed during his time as director*
desert: *Medical staff have deserted the city's main hospital*
forsake: *I would never forsake my children*
go: *Let me know when you're ready*

to go

quit: He quit his job as an office boy

withdraw: Troops withdrew from the country last month

▷ noun **2** a period of time off work: Why don't you take a few days' leave?

holiday: I still have several days' holiday to take

time off: He took time off to go sailing with his wife

vacation: We went on vacation to Puerto Rico

see also **abandon, blessing, deposit, flee, go, holiday, quit, resign, will, withdraw**

leave behind see **abandon**

leave out see **exclude, omit**

lecherous see **lustful**

lecture noun **1** a formal talk about a particular subject: In his lecture he covered several topics

address: an address to the American people

discourse: a lengthy discourse on market strategy

presentation: a business presentation

sermon: his first sermon as a bishop

speech: He delivered his speech in French

talk: a brief talk on the history of the site

2 a talk intended to tell someone off: The police gave us a stern lecture on safety

reprimand: He has been given a severe reprimand

scolding: given a scolding for offending his opponents

ticking-off informal: We were given a ticking-off for running in the corridors

warning: He was given a severe warning from the referee

▷ verb **3** to teach by giving formal talks to audiences: She has lectured all over the world

give a talk: He set about campaigning, giving talks and fund-raising

speak: He's been invited to speak at the Democratic Convention

talk: Today, I plan to talk about the issues of education and nursery care

teach: She has taught at the university for 34 years

see also **lesson, scold, speech, talk**

lecturer see **teacher**

leeway see **freedom**

leftist see **left-wing**

leftover see **waste**

leftovers see **remains**

left-wing adjective believing in socialist policies: a left-wing demonstration

leftist: three leftist guerrilla groups

liberal: a politician with liberal views

radical: a radical feminist

socialist: Europe's last socialist state

legacy noun property someone leaves you when they die: He left his sons a generous legacy

bequest: He made a bequest to his favourite charity

estate: documents concerning the estate

heirloom: a family heirloom

inheritance: She was worried she'd lose her inheritance to her stepmother

see also **gift, inheritance**

legal adjective **1** relating to the law: the Dutch legal system

forensic: the forensic skill of a good barrister

judicial: a judicial review

judiciary: various levels of the judiciary system

2 allowed by the law: The strike was perfectly legal

authorized: an authorized procedure

lawful: What I did was lawful and proper

legitimate: a legitimate business

permissible: the current permissible levels of pesticide in food
rightful: the rightful owner of the property
valid: a valid passport
see also **formal**

legality see **right**

legend see **story**

legendary see **famous**

legitimate see **fair, legal, real, reasonable**

leisure noun time when you can relax: There wasn't a lot of time for leisure
free time: He played piano in his free time
recreation: Saturday afternoons are for recreation
relaxation: Make time for a bit of relaxation
time off: I haven't had any time off all day
see also **ease, rest**

leisure activity see **hobby**

leisure pursuit see **hobby**

leisurely adjective unhurried or calm: a leisurely walk along the beach
comfortable: going at a comfortable speed
easy: an easy pace
gentle: His movements were gentle and deliberate
relaxed: a relaxed meal
unhurried: an unhurried way of life
see also **easy, slow**

lekker adjective South African slang pleasant or tasty: We had a really lekker meal
delectable: delectable chocolates
delicious: a wide selection of delicious desserts
luscious: luscious fruit
pleasant: a pleasant dinner
tasty: Try this tasty dish for supper
see also **pleasant, tasty**

lend see **loan**

lend a hand see **help**

length noun **1** the distance from one end of something to the other: The fish was about a metre in length
distance: Work out the distance of the journey
extent: the extent of the rain forest
span: a butterfly with a two-inch wing span
2 the amount of time something lasts for: The film is over two hours in length
duration: The duration of the course is one year
period: for a limited period only
space: A dramatic change takes place in the space of a few minutes
span: The batteries have a life span of six hours
term: a 12-month term of service

lengthen verb to make something longer: The runway had to be lengthened
extend: They have extended the deadline
make longer: You can make your hair longer by using extensions
prolong: a move which will prolong the strike
stretch: Take care not to stretch the fabric

leniency see **mercy**

lenient see **merciful**

lessen verb to decrease in size or amount: changes to their diet that would lessen the risk of disease
abate: The storm gradually abated
decrease: Population growth is decreasing by 1.4% each year
diminish: The threat of war has diminished
dwindle: his dwindling authority
lower: The Central Bank has lowered interest rates
minimize: attempts to minimize the risk of developing cancer

reduce: Gradually reduce the dosage
shrink: The forests have shrunk to half their size
see also **abate, decrease, diminish, lower, reduce, weaken**
lessening see **decrease**
lesser see **inferior, junior, minor**
lesson noun a period of time for being taught: Johanna took piano lessons
class: I go to dance classes
coaching: He needs extra coaching in maths
lecture: a series of lectures on art
period: We get six periods of French a week
tutoring: a growing demand for private tutoring
lessons see **study**
let verb 1 to allow someone to do something: The authorities won't let her leave the country
allow: I pleaded to be allowed to go
give permission: Who gave you permission to come here?
permit: Permit me to express my opinion
sanction: He may now be ready to sanction the use of force
2 to let someone use your property for money: She always lets her house for the summer
hire out: The machines are hired out to farmers
lease: She plans to lease the building to students
rent: He rents rooms to backpackers
see also **allow**
let down see **lower**
let go see **discharge, release**
let in see **admit**
let off see **spare**
let on see **reveal**
lethal see **deadly, fatal**
lethargic see **sleepy**
letter see **note**

level adjective 1 completely flat: a plateau of level ground
flat: Cricket should be played on a totally flat field
horizontal: Every horizontal surface was covered with plants
▷ verb 2 to make something flat: We levelled the ground
flatten: Flatten the dough and cut it into four pieces
plane: planing the surface of the wood
smooth: He smoothed his hair
▷ noun 3 a point on a scale which measures something: Crime levels have started to decline
grade: the lowest grade of staff
rank: He rose to the rank of captain
stage: an early stage of development
standard: a decent standard of living
status: We were reduced to the status of animals
see also **balance, even, extent, flat, rank, standard, straight**
level-headed see **cool, realistic, responsible, sane**
level-headedness see **common sense**
levelled see **flat**
levy see **charge, duty, impose, tax**
lewd see **indecent, lustful, naughty, obscene**
liability see **blame, fault, responsibility**
liable see **likely, prone**
liaison see **affair, relationship**
libel see **slander**
liberal see **generous, handsome, left-wing**
liberate see **discharge, free, release**
liberated see **free, independent**
liberation see **release**
liberty see **freedom, release**
licence see **freedom, permission, permit, power**
licensed see **official**
lid see **top**

lie verb **1** to rest somewhere horizontally: The injured man was lying on his back

loll: He was lolling on the sofa

lounge: We lounged on the beach all day

recline: She reclined on the couch

sprawl: They sprawled in a lawn chair, snoozing

2 to say something that is not true: She always lies about her age

fib: He fibbed when she asked him where he'd been

perjure oneself: All of the witnesses perjured themselves

tell a lie: He could never tell a lie or do anything devious

▷ noun **3** something you say which is not true: His whole story was a lie

deceit: the deceits of political leaders

fabrication: She described the magazine interview as "a complete fabrication"

falsehood: He accused them of spreading falsehoods about him

fib: I caught him out in another fib

fiction: His account of events is a complete fiction

life noun the time during which you are alive: a long and active life

existence: a very miserable existence

life span: This species of snake has a life span of up to 25 years

lifetime: a lifetime devoted to service for others

time: If I had my time again, I would do things differently

see also **energy**

life force see **spirit**

life span see **life**

lifelike see **realistic**

lifetime see **life**

lift verb **1** to move something to a higher position: straining to lift heavy weights

elevate: a mechanism to elevate the platform

hoist: I hoisted my rucksack on to my shoulder

pick up: Anthony picked up his case from the floor

raise: He raised his hand to wave

2 to remove something such as a ban or law: the decision to lift sanctions against Iran

cancel: The government has cancelled the state of emergency

end: pressure to end the embargo

relax: an attempt to persuade the US Congress to relax the law

remove: an amendment to remove the ban on divorce

see also **raise**

light noun **1** brightness that enables you to see things: Cracks of light filtered through the shutters

brightness: the brightness of the full moon

brilliance: the brilliance of the noonday sun

glare: shading his eyes from the glare

glow: the red glow of the dying fire

illumination: The only illumination came from a small window

radiance: The bedside lamp cast a soft radiance over her face

▷ adjective **2** pale in colour: a light blue shirt

bleached: bleached pine tables

blonde or **blond**: blonde hair

fair: to protect my fair skin

pale: dressed in pale pink

pastel: delicate pastel shades

3 not weighing much: working out with light weights

flimsy: a flimsy cardboard box

lightweight: They will carry lightweight skis on their backs

portable: a portable television

slight: She is small and slight

▷ verb **4** to make a place bright: The room was lit by a single candle

brighten: The late afternoon sun brightened the room
illuminate: No streetlights illuminated the road
light up: Fireworks lit up the sky
5 to make a fire start burning: It's time to light the barbecue
ignite: A stray spark ignited the fireworks
kindle: I kindled a fire in the stove
see also **easy, fair, glow, soft**

light up see **light**
light-headed see **dazed, dizzy, faint**
light-hearted see **bright, cheerful**
lightweight see **fine, light, sheer**
likable see **pleasant**

like adjective **1** similar to another thing: He looks just like my father
akin: She looked at me with something akin to hatred
alike: They are very alike in temperament
analogous: a process analogous to the curing of tobacco
identical: Nearly all the houses were identical
parallel: Our situation is parallel to yours
same: His uniform was exactly the same colour as the car
similar: a taste similar to that of celery
▷ verb **2** to find someone or something pleasant: I really like this music
adore informal: All her employees adored her
appreciate: I know you appreciate good food
be fond of: Are you fond of Chinese cuisine?
be keen on: I'm not very keen on sport
be partial to: I'm partial to men with dark hair
enjoy: Most children enjoy cartoons
go for: What kind of man do you

go for?
have a soft spot for: I've always had a soft spot for him
have a weakness for: I have a weakness for slushy romantic novels
love: She loves reading
relish: He relished the idea of proving me wrong
revel in: She appears to revel in being unpopular
see also **enjoy, love, similar**

like better see **prefer**
likeable see **pleasant**
likelihood see **chance, possibility, probability**

likely adjective having a good chance of happening: It seems likely that he will come back
anticipated: the anticipated result
expected: the expected response
liable: He is liable to be a nuisance
possible: It's quite possible that I'm wrong
probable: the probable outcome
see also **believable, possible, potential, probable, probably**

likeness see **resemblance, similarity**
likewise see **too**
liking see **affection, attachment, love, taste, weakness**

limit noun **1** a point beyond which something cannot go: the speed limit
bounds: the bounds of good taste
deadline: We finished the job within the deadline
maximum: He was given two years in prison, the maximum allowed for the charges
ultimate: This hotel is the ultimate in luxury
utmost: His skills were tested to the utmost
▷ verb **2** to prevent something from going any further: Limit yourself to six units of alcohol a week
confine: Damage was confined to a

small portion of the building
curb: measures to curb inflation
fix: The mortgage rate is fixed at 8.5%
ration: I'm rationing myself to ten cigarettes a day
restrict: The patient was restricted to a meagre diet
see also **confine**, **curb**, **extreme**, **restrict**

limitation see **curb**, **restriction**

limited see **modest**

limits see **border**, **range**

limp adjective not stiff or firm: a limp lettuce leaf
drooping: the drooping branches of a birch
flabby: a flabby stomach
floppy: She fondled the dog's floppy ears
slack: his slack belly
soft: a soft dough

limping see **lame**

line noun 1 a long thin mark on something: Draw a line down the centre of the page
rule: He drew a rule under the last name
score: There was a long score on the car's bonnet
streak: dark streaks on the surface of the moon
stripe: a green jogging suit with white stripes down the sides
2 a row of people or things: a line of spectators
column: a column of figures
file: A file of mourners walked behind the coffin
queue: a long queue of angry motorists
rank: ranks of police in riot gear
row: a row of pretty little cottages
3 the route along which something moves: the line of flight
course: the course of the river
path: The lava annihilates everything

in its path
route: the most direct route
track: a railway track
trajectory: the trajectory of the missile
see also **border**, **course**, **rank**, **row**, **trade**

lineage see **origin**, **stock**

lines see **shape**

linger see **remain**, **stay**, **wait**

lingering see **slow**

lingo see **language**

link noun 1 a connection between two things: the link between sunbathing and skin cancer
affiliation: He has no affiliation with any political party
association: the association between the two companies
attachment: Mother and child form a close attachment
bond: The experience created a bond between us
connection: He has denied any connection to the bombing
relationship: the relationship between humans and their environment
tie: She has ties with this town
▷ verb 2 to connect two things: tree houses linked by ropes
attach: Attach the curtains to the rods with hooks
connect: two rooms connected by a passage
couple: The engine is coupled to a gearbox
fasten: a wooden bench fastened to the floor
join: the skin which joins the eye to the eyelid
tie: He tied the dog to the tree by its lead
see also **associate**, **attach**, **bond**, **connect**, **connection**, **join**, **relation**, **relationship**

link up see team, unite
lip see edge
liquid noun **1** a substance which is not solid and can be poured: *Drink plenty of liquids for the next few days*
fluid: *The fluid can be removed with a syringe*
liquor: *Pour the liquor off into the pan*
solution: *a solution of honey and vinegar*
▷ adjective **2** in the form of a liquid: *wash in warm water with liquid detergent*
fluid: *a fluid fertiliser*
molten: *molten metal*
runny: *a dessertspoon of runny honey*
liquor see alcohol, liquid
list noun **1** a set of things written down one below the other: *There were six names on the list*
catalogue: *a chronological catalogue of the Beatles' songs*
directory: *a telephone directory*
index: *The book includes a comprehensive subject index*
inventory: *an inventory of stolen goods*
listing: *a listing of all the schools in the area*
record: *Keep a record of everything you eat and drink*
register: *a register of births, deaths and marriages*
▷ verb **2** to set things down in a list: *All the ingredients are listed on the label*
catalogue: *I was cataloguing my video collection*
index: *Most of the archive has been indexed*
record: *400 species of fungi have been recorded*
register: *a registered charity*
listen verb to hear and pay attention to something: *I'll repeat that for those of you who weren't listening*

attend: *Close your books and attend to me*
hark: *Hark! I hear the sound of footsteps*
hear: *Will you hear me saying my lines?*
pay attention: *Pay attention or you won't know what to do*
listen in see hear
listen to see hear, heed
listing see list
literate see learned
lithe see agile, flexible
litter see garbage, refuse, rubbish, young
little adjective **1** small in size or amount: *a little old lady*
▷ noun **2** a small amount or degree: *Would you like a little fruit juice?*
see word studies **little**
see also **insignificant, low, young**
little ones see young
little-known see obscure
live verb **1** to have your home somewhere: *She has lived here for 20 years*
dwell: *the people who dwell in the forest*
inhabit: *the fish that inhabit the coral reefs*
reside: *He used to reside in England*
stay *Scottish, South African*: *We've stayed in this house since we got married*
2 to be alive: *He will not live much longer*
be alive: *You are lucky to be alive*
exist: *the chances of finding life existing on Mars*
▷ adjective **3** not dead or artificial: *a live spider*
alive: *It is unlikely that he is still alive*
animate: *an animate object*
living: *living tissue*
see also **inhabit, survive**
live on see endure

livelihood see **work**
liveliness see **activity**
lively *adjective* full of life and
enthusiasm: *a lively personality*
active: *an active youngster*
animated: *an animated discussion*
energetic: *She gave an energetic
performance*
perky: *He wasn't quite as perky
as usual*
sparkling: *I was enjoying a sparkling
conversation*
sprightly: *a sprightly old man*
vivacious: *She is vivacious and
charming*
see also **active, alive, bright, busy,
colourful, vital**

livid see **furious, mad**
living see **alive, live**
living soul see **person**
load *noun* **1** something being
carried: *This truck can carry a load of
up to 10 tons*
cargo: *The boat was carrying its usual
cargo of bananas*
consignment: *The first consignment
of food has been sent*
freight: *Most of the freight was
carried by rail*
shipment: *a shipment of weapons*
▷ *verb* **2** to put a lot of things on
or into: *The trucks were loaded with
blankets and supplies*
fill: *The van was filled with crates*
pack: *helicopters packed with medical
supplies*
pile: *Her trolley was piled with
groceries*
stack: *stalls stacked with wares*
see also **bunch, burden, mass, stuff**

loaded see **full, rich**
loads see **heaps**
loaf see **laze**
loan *noun* **1** a sum of money that you
borrow: *a small business loan*
advance: *She was paid a $100,000

advance on her next novel*
credit: *He can't get credit to buy the
equipment*
mortgage: *I took out a second
mortgage on the house*
▷ *verb* **2** to lend something to
someone: *He loaned us the painting
for our exhibition*
advance: *I advanced him some money
till we got home*
lend: *Will you lend me your jacket?*

loath see **reluctant, unwilling**
loathe see **dislike, hate**
loathing see **dislike, hate, horror**
loathsome see **hateful**
lob see **throw**
lobby see **passage**
local *adjective* **1** belonging to the area
where you live: *This is a local shop for
local people*
community: *the revival of family and
community life*
district: *the district council*
neighbourhood: *a neighbourhood
watch scheme*
parish: *the parish priest*
regional: *the regional elections*
▷ *noun* **2** a person who lives in a
particular area: *That's what the locals
call the place*
inhabitant: *the inhabitants of
Glasgow*
native: *She is proud to be a native
of Sydney*
resident: *a protest by residents of
the village*
locality see **area, region**
locate *verb* to find out where
someone or something is: *We have
been unable to locate him*
find: *They can't find it on the map*
pinpoint: *Computers pinpointed
where the shells came from*
track down: *She has spent years
trying to track down her parents*
see also **find, place, position, set,**

trace

located adjective existing or
standing in a particular place: The
restaurant is located near the cathedral
placed: The hotel is wonderfully
placed right in the city centre
sited: a castle romantically sited on a
river estuary
situated: His hotel is situated in a
lovely place

location noun a place or position: a
house with a beautiful location
place: the place where the temple
used to stand
point: a popular meeting point for
tourists
position: The ship radioed its position
to the coastguard
site: the site of the murder
situation: The hotel has a superb
isolated situation
spot: Can you show me the spot where
it happened?
whereabouts: His exact
whereabouts are still not known
see also **place, position, scene,
spot, surroundings**

lock verb 1 to close and fasten
something with a key: Are you sure
you locked the door?
latch: He latched the gate
padlock: The box has been padlocked
shut
▷ noun 2 a device used to fasten
something: The lock had been burst
open
latch: A key clicked in the latch of the
front door
padlock: He put a padlock on the
door of his flat
see also **fasten, secure**

lock up see **imprison**
locked see **secure**
lodge see **inhabit, stick**
lodgings see **accommodation**
lofty see **superior, tall**

log see **record**
logic see **argument**
logical adjective 1 using logic to work
something out: a logical argument
consistent: a consistent and well-
presented theory
rational: a rational analysis
reasoned: a reasoned discussion
sound: His reasoning is sound, but he
has missed the point
valid: Both sides put forward valid
points
2 sensible in the circumstances: a
logical deduction
judicious: the judicious use of
military force
obvious: I jumped to the obvious
conclusion
plausible: a plausible explanation
reasonable: a reasonable course
of action
sensible: the sensible thing to do
wise: a wise decision
see also **rational, reasonable**

logo see **sign, symbol**
loiter see **stay**
loll see **lie**
lolly see **sweet**
lone see **single**
loneliness see **solitude**
lonely adjective 1 unhappy because
of being alone: She's lonely and just
wants to talk
alone: scared of being alone in the
house
forlorn: He looked a forlorn figure as
he left the pitch
forsaken: a forsaken and bitter man
lonesome: I'm lonesome without you
2 isolated and not visited by many
people: a lonely hillside
deserted: a deserted farmhouse
desolate: a desolate place
isolated: Many of the villages are in
isolated areas
remote: a remote outpost

secluded: *a secluded area close to her home*

uninhabited: *an uninhabited island*
see also **remote**

lonesome see **lonely**

long *adjective* **1** continuing for a great amount of time: *a long interval when no-one spoke*
see **word studies long**

2 great in length or distance: *a long line of people*
see **word studies long**

▷ *verb* **3** to want something very much: *He longed for a cigarette*

ache: *She still ached for her dead husband*

covet: *She coveted his job*

crave: *I crave her approval*

hunger: *Jules hungered for adventure*

lust: *She lusted after a designer kitchen*

pine: *I pine for the countryside*

yearn: *He yearned for freedom*
see also **far, wish**

long ago see **the past**

long for see **be dying for, desire, miss**

longing *noun* a strong wish for something: *her longing to return home*

craving: *a craving for sugar*

desire: *her desire for a child of her own*

hankering: *a hankering to be an actress*

hunger: *a hunger for success*

thirst: *a thirst for adventure*

yearning: *a yearning to be part of a normal family*
see also **desire, urge, wish**

long-suffering see **patient**

long-winded see **talkative**

look *verb* **1** to turn your eyes towards something and see it: *She looked at me with something like hatred*
see **word studies look**

2 to appear or seem to be: *the desire*

to look attractive

appear: *He appeared intoxicated*

look like: *You look like you need a good night's sleep*

seem: *She seemed tense*

seem to be: *They seem to be lacking in enthusiasm*

▷ *noun* **3** the action of turning your eyes towards something: *Lucy took a last look in the mirror*

gaze: *her concentrated gaze*

glance: *a cursory glance*

glimpse: *a fleeting glimpse*

peek: *Give me a peek at his letter*

4 the way someone or something appears: *He had the look of a desperate man*

air: *a nonchalant air*

appearance: *He was fastidious about his appearance*

bearing: *a man of military bearing*

expression: *I saw his puzzled expression*

face: *Why are you all wearing such long faces?*

semblance: *a semblance of normality*
see also **appearance, fossick, glance, peek, regard, search, see, seem, stare**

look at see **examine, face, read, watch**

look down on see **scorn**

look like see **look, resemble, seem**

look on see **regard**

look out see **beware, watch out**

look over see **examine**

look up see **improve, refer, visit**

look up to see **admire, respect**

look after *verb* to take care of someone or something: *Will you look after my cats when I go on holiday?*

care for: *vintage cars lovingly cared for by their owners*

mind: *Jim will mind the shop while I'm away*

nurse: *My mother nursed him while*

307 | **lose heart**

he was ill
take care of: *I'll take care of the
house for you*
tend: *He tended his flower beds*
watch: *My mother will watch the kids
while we're out*
see also **mind, run, safeguard, take
care of, tend, watch**

lookalike *noun* a person who looks
like someone else: *an Elvis lookalike*
dead ringer *informal*: *a dead ringer
for his brother*
double: *He's the exact double of his
father at that age*
spitting image *informal*: *She is the
spitting image of me*

look for *verb* to try to find a person or
thing: *I'm looking for my son*
forage: *foraging for food*
hunt: *Police are hunting for clues*
search: *Rescue teams are searching
for the missing crew members*
seek: *They have had to seek work as
labourers*
see also **seek**

looks *see* **appearance**

looming *see* **imminent, near**

loony *see* **mad, weirdo**

loop *see* **bend, coil, ring**

loophole *see* **hole**

loose *adjective* **1** not firmly held or
fixed: *a loose tooth*
free: *She broke her fall with her
free hand*
unsecured: *corridors blocked by
unsecured objects*
wobbly: *a wobbly bridge*
2 not fitting closely: *Wear loose
clothes for comfort*
baggy: *a baggy black jumper*
slack: *Those trousers are very slack
on you*
sloppy: *wearing a sloppy t-shirt,
jeans and trainers*
see also **approximate, free, full,
promiscuous, vague**

loosen *verb* to make something
looser: *He loosened his tie*
slacken: *We slackened the guy-ropes*
undo: *She began to undo the tiny
buttons*
untie: *He untied his shoes and slipped
them off*

loot *verb* **1** to steal from a place
during a riot or battle: *Gangs began
breaking windows and looting shops*
pillage: *The bandits pillaged the
church*
plunder: *They plundered and burned
the town*
raid: *Rustlers have raided a village
in the region*
ransack: *The three raiders ransacked
the house*
▷ *noun* **2** stolen or illegal money or
goods: *The loot was never recovered*
booty: *They divided the booty
between them*
haul: *the biggest haul of cannabis
ever seized*
plunder: *pirates in search of easy
plunder*
spoils: *the spoils of war*
swag *slang*: *The thieves carried the
swag off in a stolen car*
see also **rob**

lop *see* **chop**

lopsided *see* **irregular**

lord *see* **noble**

lose *verb* **1** to be unable to find: *I've
lost my keys*
drop: *She's dropped a contact lens*
mislay: *I seem to have mislaid my
glasses*
misplace: *Somehow my suitcase was
misplaced*
2 to be beaten: *We lost the match*
be beaten: *He was soundly beaten
in the election*
be defeated: *They were defeated
in the final*

lose heart *see* **despair**

lose hope see **despair**

lose your nerve see **panic**

lose your temper see **rage**

loser see **failure**

lost adjective **1** not knowing where you are: I think we're lost

adrift: two men adrift on a raft in the middle of the sea

astray: Our baggage went astray in transit

off-course: After a while I realized I was completely off-course

2 unable to be found: a mother wailing for her lost child

mislaid: searching for his mislaid keys

misplaced: I've found your misplaced glasses

missing: a missing person

vanished: unable to contact the vanished convoy

lot a lot or **lots** noun a large amount of something: Remember to drink lots of water

abundance: an abundance of food

a great deal: I've spent a great deal of time on this project

masses informal: There were masses of flowers at her funeral

piles informal: He's got piles of money

plenty: We've got plenty of time

quantities: She drank quantities of hot, sweet tea

scores: There were scores of witnesses

2 an amount or number: We've just sacked one lot of builders

batch: a batch of cookies

bunch informal: My neighbours are a noisy bunch

crowd: They're a real crowd of villains

group: a small group of football supporters

quantity: a small quantity of water

set: a set of photographs

see also **bunch**, **whole**

lots see **heaps**, **many**, **numerous**, **plenty**

lottery see **gamble**

loud adjective **1** having a high level of sound: a loud explosion

blaring: a blaring television

deafening: a deafening roar

noisy: a noisy old car

resounding: a resounding slap

strident: her strident voice

thunderous: thunderous applause from the crowd

2 too brightly coloured: a loud tie

flamboyant: a flamboyant outfit

flashy: flashy clothes

garish: a garish three-piece suite

gaudy: a gaudy purple-and-orange hat

lurid: She painted her toenails a lurid pink

see also **bold**, **gaudy**, **noisy**

lounge see **laze**, **lie**, **pub**

lousy see **rotten**

lout see **hooligan**, **oaf**, **savage**

lovable adjective easy to love: His vulnerability makes him very lovable

adorable: an adorable black kitten

charming: a charming young Frenchman

enchanting: He was an enchanting baby

endearing: one of his most endearing qualities

sweet: a sweet little girl

love verb **1** to feel strong affection for someone: I loved my husband very much

adore: She adored her parents

cherish: He genuinely loved and cherished her

worship: She had worshipped him from afar for years

2 to like something very much: We both love fishing

appreciate: I know you appreciate good food

enjoy: Do you enjoy opera?

like: I've always liked horror films

relish: I relish the challenge of
dangerous sports
▷ noun **3** a strong feeling of
affection: a mother's love for her
children
adoration: He had been used to
female adoration all his life
affection: She thought of him with
great affection
ardour: an attempt to rekindle their
lost ardour
devotion: At first she was flattered
by his devotion
infatuation: consumed with
infatuation for her
passion: the object of her passion
4 a strong liking for something: her
love of animals
devotion: his devotion to literature
fondness: a fondness for good wine
liking: my liking for classical music
weakness: He had a weakness
for cats
see also **affection, attachment,
enjoy, like, passion, worship**
loveliness see beauty
lovely adjective very attractive and
pleasant: You look lovely
attractive: Polperro is an attractive
harbour village
beautiful: She's a very beautiful
woman
delightful: a delightful garden
enjoyable: I've had a very enjoyable
time
pleasant: a pleasant little apartment
pretty: a pretty room overlooking a
beautiful garden
see also **agreeable, attractive,
beautiful, pleasant, pretty**
lover see fan
loving adjective feeling or showing
love: a loving husband and father
affectionate: openly affectionate
with each other
devoted: a devoted couple

doting: a doting father
fond: She gave him a fond smile
tender: Her voice was tender
warm: a warm and loving mother
see also **affectionate, devoted,
fond, romantic, tender, warm**

low adjective **1** short or not far above
the ground: The sun was low in the sky
little: a little table
short: a short flight of steps
small: a small stool
squat: squat stone houses
stunted: stunted trees
sunken: a sunken garden
2 small in degree or quantity: low
prices
minimal: minimal expenditure
modest: a modest rate of
unemployment
poor: working for poor wages
reduced: reduced customer demand
scant: scant stocks of fish
small: produced in small numbers
3 not considered respectable: a man
of low birth
common: She might be a little
common, but at least she wasn't boring
contemptible: He mixes with the
most contemptible people in society
despicable: a despicable wretch
disreputable: the company of
disreputable women
lowly: his lowly status
vulgar: She considers herself to be
above the vulgar rabble
see also **deep, faint, miserable,
quiet, reasonable, sad, soft**

lower verb **1** to move something
downwards: They lowered the coffin
into the grave
drop: He dropped his plate into
the sink
let down: They let the barrier down
take down: The pilot took the
helicopter down
2 to make something less in

amount: *a commitment to lower taxes*

cut: *The first priority is to cut costs*

decrease: *The government plans to decrease interest rates*

diminish: *to diminish the prestige of the monarchy*

lessen: *a diet that would lessen the risk of disease*

minimize: *attempts to minimize the risk of cancer*

reduce: *Gradually reduce the dosage*

slash: *We're slashing our prices*

see also **below, cut, decrease, diminish, ease, inferior, junior, lessen, reduce**

lowering see **cut**

lowest see **bottom, least**

lowly see **humble, low**

loyal *adjective* **1** having a lot of good luck: *He had always been lucky at cards*

constant: *I've lost my best friend and constant companion*

dependable: *a cheerful, dependable mate*

faithful: *She remained faithful to her husband*

staunch: *a staunch supporter*

true: *a true friend*

trusty: *a trusty ally*

see also **devoted, faithful**

lucid see **sane**

luck *noun* something that happens by chance: *It was just luck that we happened to meet*

accident: *It came about almost by accident*

chance: *We only met by chance*

destiny: *Is it destiny that brings people together?*

fate: *a simple twist of fate*

fortune: *smiled on by fortune*

see also **chance**

luckless see **unlucky**

lucky *adjective* **1** having a lot of good luck: *He had always been lucky at cards*

blessed: *being blessed with good looks*

charmed: *She seems to have a charmed life*

fortunate: *He was extremely fortunate to survive*

2 happening by chance with good consequences: *a lucky break*

fortuitous: *a fortuitous combination of circumstances*

fortunate: *a fortunate accident*

opportune: *I had arrived at an opportune moment*

timely: *his timely intervention*

lucrative see **successful**

ludicrous see **absurd, daft, impossible, ridiculous**

lug see **carry, drag**

lukewarm see **cold, warm**

lull see **gap, silence**

lumbering see **clumsy**

luminary see **star**

luminous see **bright, brilliant, shining**

lump *noun* **1** a solid piece of something: *a big lump of dough*

ball: *a ball of clay*

cake: *a cake of soap*

chunk: *a chunk of bread*

hunk: *a hunk of beef*

piece: *a piece of cake*

wedge: *a wedge of cheese*

2 a bump on the surface of something: *I've got a big lump on my head*

bulge: *My purse made a bulge in my pocket*

bump: *a bump in the road*

hump: *a hump on his back*

swelling: *a swelling over one eye*

see also **block, bulge, bump, mass**

lunch see **eat**

lure *verb* **1** to attract someone somewhere or into doing something: *We are being lured into a trap*

attract: *Warm weather attracts the fish close to the shore*
beckon: *The mermaids beckoned the sailors towards the rocks*
draw: *What drew him to the area was its proximity to London*
entice: *Retailers will do anything to entice shoppers through their doors*
tempt: *trying to tempt American tourists back to Britain*
▷ noun **2** something that you find very attractive: *the lure of rural life*
attraction: *The attraction of living on the waterfront*
bait: *using cheap bread and milk as a bait to get people into the shop*
magnet: *The park is a magnet for health freaks*
pull: *feel the pull of the past*
temptation: *the many temptations to which they will be exposed*
see also **attract, bait, pull, tempt**
lurgy see **illness**
lurid see **loud**
lurk see **sneak**
luscious see **delicious, lekker, tasty**
lush see **thick**
lust see **long, passion**
lustful adjective *feeling or showing strong sexual desire*: *lustful thoughts*
carnal: *carnal desires*
lecherous: *a lecherous old man*
lewd: *his arrest for lewd behaviour*
lustre see **finish**
luxuriant see **thick**
luxurious adjective *expensive and full of luxury*: *a luxurious lifestyle*
de luxe: *de luxe cars*
lavish: *a lavish party*
opulent: *an opulent office*
plush informal: *a plush hotel*
sumptuous: *a sumptuous feast*
luxury noun **1** *comfort in expensive surroundings*: *a life of luxury*
affluence: *the trappings of affluence*
opulence: *the sheer opulence of*

her new life
sumptuousness: *The hotel lobby was sumptuousness itself*
2 something enjoyable which you do not have often: *Telephones are still a luxury in poor countries*
extra: *The car is a basic model with no extras*
extravagance: *Eating out is an extravagance*
indulgence: *This car is one of my few indulgences*
treat: *I only eat cakes as a treat*
see also **comfort**

lying noun **1** *the action of telling lies*: *I've had enough of your lying*
deceit: *the deceits of political leaders*
dishonesty: *deliberate dishonesty*
fabrication: *His story is pure fabrication*
fibbing: *Her fibbing eventually got her into trouble*
perjury: *This witness has committed perjury*
▷ adjective **2** *telling lies*: *The man is just a lying cheat*
deceitful: *deceitful and misleading remarks*
dishonest: *a dishonest account of events*
false: *a false confession*
untruthful: *She unwittingly gave untruthful answers*
see also **dishonest**

m

macabre see **creepy**

mace see **stick**

machine noun a piece of equipment: *a machine to pump water out of mines*
  apparatus: *an apparatus for use in fires*
  appliance: *electrical appliances*
  contraption: *a strange contraption called the General Gordon Gas Bath*
  device: *a timer device for a bomb*
  instrument: *navigation instruments*
  mechanism: *the locking mechanism* see also **gadget**

mad adjective **1** mentally ill: *She was afraid of going mad*
  barmy slang: *Bill used to say I was barmy*
  batty slang: *some batty uncle of theirs*
  crazy informal: *If I worried about all this stuff, I'd go crazy*
  deranged: *after a deranged man shot 14 people*
  insane: *Some people can't take it and go insane*
  loony slang: *She's as loony as her brother!*
  2 very foolish or unwise: *He'd be mad to refuse*
  barmy slang: *a barmy idea*

  crazy informal: *People thought they were crazy to try it*
  daft informal: *That's a daft question*
  foolhardy: *Some described the act as foolhardy*
  foolish: *It would be foolish to raise hopes unnecessarily*
  stupid: *It would be stupid to pretend otherwise*
  3 informal angry about something: *They both got mad at me for interfering*
  angry: *She was angry at her husband*
  crazy informal: *This sitting around is driving me crazy*
  enraged: *I got more and more enraged at my father*
  fuming: *Mrs Vine was still fuming*
  furious: *He is furious at the way his wife has been treated*
  incensed: *Mum was incensed at his lack of compassion*
  infuriated: *He knew how infuriated this would make me*
  irate: *Bob was very irate, shouting and screaming about the flight delay*
  livid informal: *I am absolutely livid about it*
  see also **angry, crazy, furious, insane**

madness see **frenzy**

magic noun a special power: *They believe in magic*
  sorcery: *the use of sorcery to combat evil influences*
  witchcraft: *people who practise witchcraft*

magical adjective wonderful and exciting: *Paris is a magical city*
  bewitching: *bewitching brown eyes*
  enchanting: *an enchanting child*

magistrate see **judge, justice**

magnanimous see **noble**

magnet see **lure**

magnetism see **charm, influence, pull**

magnificence see **glory**

magnificent see **brilliant, fine, grand, marvellous, splendid, superb, wonderful**

magnify see **enlarge**

maim see **cripple, injure**

main adjective most important: the main reason

cardinal: one of the cardinal rules of movie reviewing

chief: one of his chief rivals

foremost: one of the foremost scholars on ancient Indian culture

leading: a leading industrial nation

major: one of the major causes of cancer

predominant: Her predominant emotion was confusion

primary: the primary source of water in the region

prime: the prime suspect

principal: the principal source of sodium in our diets

see also **chief, essential, leading, prime, principal**

mainly adverb true in most cases: The staff were mainly Russian

chiefly: He painted chiefly portraits

generally: It is generally true that the darker the fruit the higher its iron content

largely: The early studies were done on men, largely by male researchers

mostly: Cars are mostly metal

predominantly: Business is conducted predominantly by phone

primarily: The body is made up primarily of bone, muscle, and fat

principally: This is principally because the market is weak

see also **as a rule**

maintain see **argue, claim, keep**

maintenance see **upkeep**

majestic see **grand**

majesty see **glory**

major adjective very important or serious: a major problem

critical: a critical factor

crucial: He took the crucial decisions himself

leading: a leading industrial nation

outstanding: an outstanding contribution

significant: Her upbringing had a significant effect on her relationships

see also **leading, main, principal**

majority noun more than half: The majority of our cheeses are made with pasteurized milk

best part: for the best part of 24 hours

better part: I spent the better part of £100 on her

bulk: the bulk of the world's great poetry

mass: the mass of the population

most: Most of the book is completely true

make verb **1** to construct something: Sheila makes all her own clothes

assemble: Workers were assembling planes

build: Workers at the site build the F-16 jet fighter

construct: the campaign to construct a temple on the site

create: It's great for a radio producer to create a show like this

fabricate: All the tools are fabricated from high quality steel

fashion: Stone Age settlers fashioned necklaces from sheep's teeth

form: a figure formed from clay

manufacture: They manufacture plastics

produce: We try to produce items that are the basics of a stylish wardrobe

2 to force someone to do something: Mary made him clean up the plate

compel: legislation to compel cyclists to wear a helmet

drive: Jealousy drives people to murder

force: *A back injury forced her to withdraw from the competition*
oblige: *Finally I was obliged to abandon the car*
▷ **noun 3** *a particular type*: *a certain make of wristwatch*
brand: *a brand of cigarette*
model: *To keep the cost down, opt for a basic model*
see also **assemble, build, construct, earn, fashion, force, form, issue, manufacture, produce, reach, shape, sort, type**
make a difference see **matter**
make a mistake see **err**
make an attempt see **try**
make an effort see **strive, try**
make certain see **ensure**
make fun of see **mock, tease**
make it see **succeed**
make known see **advise, announce**
make out see **distinguish**
make sure see **ensure**
make up for see **compensate**
make up your mind see **decide, resolve**
make use of see **employ**
make up verb **1** to form the parts of something: *Women police officers make up 13% of the police force*
compose: *The force would be composed of troops from NATO countries*
comprise: *a crowd comprised of the wives and children of scientists*
constitute: *Hindus constitute 83% of India's population*
form: *Cereals form the staple diet*
2 *to invent a story*: *It's very unkind of you to make up stories about*
concoct: *The prisoner concocted the story to get a lighter sentence*
fabricate: *Officers fabricated evidence against them*
invent: *I must invent something I can tell my mother*

see also **form, invent**
make-up see **character, nature, personality, structure**
making noun **1** *the act of creating something*: *the making of this movie*
assembly: *the assembly of an explosive device*
building: *The building of the airport continues*
construction: *boat construction*
creation: *the creation of large parks and forests*
fabrication: *the design and fabrication of the space shuttle*
manufacture: *the manufacture of nuclear weapons*
production: *These proteins stimulate the production of blood cells*
in the making adjective *about to become something*: *a captain in the making*
budding: *a budding author*
emergent: *an emergent state*
potential: *a potential champion*
up-and-coming: *an up-and-coming golfer*
see also **manufacture**
male adjective *relating to men*: *a deep male voice*
manly: *He was the ideal of manly beauty*
masculine: *masculine characteristics like facial hair*
see also **man**
malevolence see **spite**
malevolent see **evil, hostile, malicious, spiteful**
malice see **animosity, hostility, spite**
malicious adjective *having the intention of hurting someone*: *She described the charges as malicious*
cruel: *Children can be so cruel*
malevolent formal: *She gave me a malevolent stare*
mean: *Someone's played a mean*

trick on you

spiteful: *spiteful telephone calls*

vicious: *a vicious attack on an innocent man's character*
see also **spiteful, unkind**

malign see **slander**

mammoth see **colossal, formidable**

man noun **1** an adult male human being: *a young man*

bloke *British, Australian, New Zealand informal*: *a really nice bloke*

chap *informal*: *I am a very lucky chap*

gentleman: *It seems this gentleman was waiting for the doctor*

guy *informal*: *a guy from Manchester*

male: *A high proportion of crime is perpetrated by young males*

2 people in general: *All men are equal*

humanity: *He has rendered a great service to humanity*

human race: *Can the human race carry on expanding?*

mankind: *the evolution of mankind*
see also **adult**

mana noun *New Zealand* the authority and influence of an important person: *a leader of great mana*

authority: *figures of authority*

influence: *He denies using any political influence*

power: *positions of great power*

standing: *The Prime Minister's standing was high in the US*

stature: *his stature as the world's greatest cellist*

status: *the status of a national hero literary*

manage verb **1** to succeed in doing something: *We managed to find somewhere to sit*

cope with: *how my mother coped with bringing up three children*

succeed in: *We have succeeded in persuading cinemas to show the video*

2 to be in charge of something:

Within two years he was managing the store

be in charge of: *Who's in charge of the canteen?*

command: *Who would command the troops in the event of war?*

control: *He now controls the largest retail development empire in southern California*

direct: *Christopher will direct day-to-day operations*

run: *Is this any way to run a country?*
see also **accomplish, administer, command, conduct, control, deal, direct, do, handle, head, lead, oversee, run, supervise, take care of**

management noun **1** the act of running an organization: *The zoo needed better management*

control: *The restructuring involves Mr Ronson giving up control of the company*

direction: *Organizations need clear direction*

running: *the day-to-day running of the clinic*

2 the people who run an organization: *The management is doing its best*

administration: *They would like the college administration to exert more control*

board: *a recommendation which he wants to put before the board*

bosses *informal*: *a dispute between workers and bosses*

directors: *the board of directors of a local bank*

employers: *Employers are said to be considering the demand*
see also **control, direction**

manager noun a person in charge of running an organization: *the manager of Daiwa's New York branch*

boss *informal*: *He cannot stand*

his boss

director: *the financial director of Braun UK*

executive: *an advertising executive*
see also **boss, chief, head, superior**

mandatory see **compulsory**

mangle see **twist**

mania see **obsession**

manic see **furious**

manifest adjective formal obvious or easily seen: *the manifest failure of the policy*

blatant: *a blatant attempt to spread the blame*

clear: *a clear case of homicide*

conspicuous: *Politics has changed in a conspicuous way*

glaring: *a glaring example of fraud*

obvious: *an obvious injustice*

patent: *This was patent nonsense*

plain: *He's made it plain that he wants to be involved*
see also **betray, naked, show, visible**

manipulate see **influence**

mankind see **man, people**

manly see **male**

manner noun 1 the way that you do something: *She smiled again in a friendly manner*

fashion: *another drug that works in a similar fashion*

mode: *He switched automatically into interview mode*

style: *Kenny's writing style*

way: *He had a strange way of talking* 2 the way that someone behaves: *his kind manner*

bearing: *his military bearing*

behaviour: *her anti-social behaviour*

conduct: *principles of civilized conduct*

demeanour: *a cheerful demeanour*
see also **fashion, style, way**

manners see **conduct**

manoeuvre verb 1 to move something skilfully: *It took expertise*

to manoeuvre the boat so close to the shore

guide: *He took Elliott by the arm and guided him out*

navigate: *He attempted to navigate his way through the crowds*

negotiate: *I negotiated my way out of the airport*

steer: *I steered him towards the door*
▷ noun 2 a clever action: *manoeuvres to block the electoral process*

dodge: *a tax dodge*

ploy: *a cynical marketing ploy*

ruse: *This was a ruse to divide them*

tactic: *The tactic paid off*
see also **ease, measure**

manslaughter see **murder**

manufacture verb 1 to make goods in a factory: *Several models are being manufactured here*

assemble: *a factory where they assemble tractors*

fabricate: *a plant which fabricates aeroplane components*

make: *making cars at two plants in Europe*

mass-produce: *the invention of machinery to mass-produce footwear*

process: *The material will be processed into plastic pellets*

produce: *The company produced computer parts*
▷ noun 2 the making of goods in a factory: *the manufacture of nuclear weapons*

assembly: *the assembly of cars by robots*

fabrication: *the design and fabrication of the shuttle*

making: *the steps that go into the making of a book*

mass production: *the mass production of baby food*

production: *We need to maintain the production of cars at last year's level*
see also **invent, make, making,**

produce

many adjective **1** a large number: *Among my many hobbies was the breeding of fine horses*
countless: *She brought joy to countless people*
innumerable: *He has invented innumerable excuses*
myriad: *the myriad other tasks we are trying to perform*
numerous: *Sex crimes were just as numerous as they are today*
umpteen informal: *He has produced umpteen books*
▷ noun **2** a large number of people or things: *in many of these neighbourhoods*
a lot: *A lot of people would agree with you*
a mass: *a mass of books and papers*
a multitude: *for a multitude of reasons*
large numbers: *Large numbers of people stayed away*
lots informal: *lots of strange new animals*
plenty: *plenty of vegetables*
scores: *Scores of people were injured*
see also **numerous**

mar see **botch, ruin, spoil**

march see **parade, walk**

margin see **border, edge**

marinate see **steep**

mark noun **1** a small stain: *I can't get this mark off the curtain*
see word studies **mark**
▷ verb **2** to stain something: *to stop the horses' hooves from marking the turf*
smudge: *Her face was smudged with dirt*
stain: *His clothing was stained with mud*
streak: *Rain had begun to streak the window-panes*
see also **feature, quality, sign, spot,**

stain, symbol

marked see **particular, sharp, significant**

market noun a place to buy or sell things: *the fish market at Billingsgate*
bazaar: *an Eastern bazaar*
fair: *a craft fair*
see also **shop**

market price see **value**

marriage noun the relationship between a husband and wife: *six years of marriage*
matrimony formal: *the bonds of matrimony*
wedlock formal: *a child conceived out of wedlock*

marsh see **marsh**

marvel see **curiosity, miracle, wonder**

marvellous adjective wonderful or excellent: *a marvellous actor*
brilliant: *a brilliant performance*
excellent: *He does an excellent job as Bill's secretary*
first-rate: *The meal was absolutely first-rate*
magnificent: *She was magnificent as Lady Macbeth*
remarkable: *a remarkable achievement*
splendid: *splendid photographs*
superb: *a superb novel*
wonderful: *It's wonderful to see you*
see also **brilliant, first-rate, grand, incredible, splendid, superb, wonderful**

masculine see **male**

mash see **crush, press**

mask see **cover, obscure**

masquerade as see **pose**

mass noun **1** a large number or amount: *a mass of papers*
crowd: *A huge crowd of people gathered in the square*
heap: *a heap of bricks*
load: *a load of kids*

throng: A shout went up from the throng of spectators
lump: a lump of clay
mob: a growing mob of demonstrators
pile: a pile of sand
▷ adjective **2** involving a large number of people: mass unemployment
general: We are trying to raise general awareness about this issue
popular: popular anger at the decision
universal: universal health care
widespread: widespread support for the proposals
▷ verb **3** to gather together in a large group: Police began to mass at the shipyard
assemble: Thousands of people assembled in the stadium
congregate: Youngsters congregate here in the evenings
gather: In the evenings, we gathered round the fireplace
group: The children grouped together under the trees
see also **assemble, crowd, gather, heap, jam, majority, tangle**
mass production see **manufacture**
massacre see **kill**
masses see **a lot or lots, public**
massive see **colossal, enormous, heavy, huge, immense, large, vast**
mass-produce see **manufacture**
master noun **1** a male schoolteacher: a retired maths master
instructor: a college instructor
teacher: her chemistry teacher
tutor: an adult education tutor in German
▷ verb **2** to learn how to do something: She found it easy to master the typewriter
become proficient in: He quickly became proficient in the language
get the hang of informal: It's a bit

tricky till you get the hang of it
grasp: It took him a while to grasp the basics of the process
learn: He enjoyed learning new skills
see also **expert, fundi, genius, learn, overcome, teacher**
masterly see **perfect, skilful, skilled**
mastermind see **genius**
mastery see **command**
mat see **tangle**
match noun **1** an organized game: a football match
competition: a surfing competition
contest: one of the best contests in recent boxing history
game: England's first game of the new season
▷ verb **2** to be similar to: The shoes matched her dress
agree: Their statements do not agree
correspond: The two maps correspond closely
fit: The punishment must always fit the crime
go with: The curtains didn't go with the carpet
suit: the best package to suit your needs
tally: The figures didn't seem to tally
see also **agree, blend, contest, correspond, equal, fit, game, rival, suit**
mate see **china, companion, friend, partner**
material noun **1** any type of cloth: the thick material of her skirt
cloth: a piece of cloth
fabric: silk and other delicate fabrics
2 a solid substance: the materials to make red dye
matter: waste matter from industries
stuff: the stuff from which the universe is made
substance: a crumbly black substance
see also **cloth, information, matter,**

stuff, substance
materialistic see **greedy**
materialize see **come**
matrimony see **marriage**
matter noun **1** something that you
have to deal with: *business matters*
  affair: *The funeral was a sad affair*
  business: *This whole business has
  upset me*
  issue: *a major political issue*
  question: *the difficult question of
  unemployment*
  situation: *The situation is now
  under control*
  subject: *a difficult subject on which
  to reach a compromise*
  2 any substance: *The atom is the
  smallest divisible particle of matter*
  material: *a conducting material
  such as metal*
  stuff: *a dress made from some
  flimsy stuff*
  substance: *a poisonous substance*
  ▷ verb **3** to be important: *It does not
  matter how long their hair is*
  be of consequence: *Their choice of
  partner is of no consequence to anyone
  but themselves*
  count: *It's as if my opinions just
  don't count*
  make a difference: *Exercise makes
  all the difference*
  see also **affair, business, count,
  event, issue, item, material,
  subject**
matter-of-fact see **realistic**
mature verb **1** to become fully
developed: *Children mature earlier
these days*
  come of age: *The money was held in
  trust until he came of age*
  grow up: *She grew up in Tokyo*
  reach adulthood: *She died before
  reaching adulthood*
  ▷ adjective **2** fully developed: *He's
  very mature for his age*

adult: *a pair of adult birds*
  full-grown: *a full-grown male
  orang-utan*
  fully-fledged: *He has developed into
  a fully-fledged adult*
  grown: *a grown man*
  grown-up: *They have two grown-up
  children*
  see also **develop**
maudlin see **corny, sentimental**
maul see **savage**
mausoleum see **grave, tomb**
maxim see **saying**
maximum noun **1** the most that is
possible: *a maximum of fifty men*
  ceiling: *an agreement to put a ceiling
  on salaries*
  height: *when emigration was at
  its height*
  most: *The most he'll make is a
  hundred pounds*
  upper limit: *the need to put an upper
  limit on spending*
  utmost: *He did his utmost to make
  her agree*
  ▷ adjective **2** being the most that is
  possible: *the maximum recommended
  intake*
  top: *a top speed of 200 mph*
  utmost: *a question of the utmost
  importance*
  see also **full, limit**
maybe adverb it is possible that:
Maybe I should have done a bit more
  conceivably: *The mission could
  conceivably be accomplished within
  a week*
  it could be: *It could be that's why
  he refused*
  perhaps: *Perhaps, in time, she'll
  understand*
  possibly: *Television is possibly to
  blame for this*
  see also **perhaps**
meadow see **field**
meagre adjective very small and

inadequate: *his meagre pension*

inadequate: *inadequate portions*

measly *informal*: *The average British bathroom requires a measly 3.5 square metres*

paltry: *a paltry fine of £150*

scant: *She berated the police for paying scant attention to the theft*

sparse: *sparse vegetation*

see also **few**

meal *noun* an occasion when people eat: *She sat next to him throughout the meal*

banquet: *a state banquet at Buckingham Palace*

dinner: *a series of official dinners*

feast: *the wedding feast*

kai *Australian, New Zealand informal*: *a cheap kai in a local restaurant*

mean *verb* **1** to convey a message: *The red signal means that you can shoot*

denote: *Red eyes denote strain and fatigue*

indicate: *Today's vote indicates a change in policy*

signify: *Becoming a father signified that he was now an adult*

2 to intend to do something: *I meant to phone you, but didn't have time*

aim: *I aim to arrive early*

intend: *She intended to move back to France*

plan: *They plan to marry in the summer*

▷ *adjective* **3** unwilling to spend money: *Don't be mean with the tip*

miserly: *He is miserly with both his time and his money*

snoep *South African informal*: *Have you ever met anyone as snoep as him?*

tight *informal*: *He was so tight that he wouldn't even spend three rupees*

see also **horrible, intend, malicious, petty, represent, shabby, sneaky, unkind**

meandering see **indirect**

meaning *noun* the idea expressed by something: *the meaning of this dream*

drift: *Grace was beginning to get his drift*

gist: *I could not get the gist of their conversation*

message: *the message of the film*

sense: *The word has two main senses*

significance: *The President's visit is loaded with symbolic significance*

see also **message**

meaningless see **empty, worthless**

means see **measure, process, way, wealth**

meant see **supposed**

measly see **meagre, petty**

measure *verb* **1** to check the size of something: *We measured how tall he was*

gauge: *He gauged the wind at over 30 knots*

survey: *geological experts who surveyed the cliffs*

▷ *noun* **2** an amount of something: *There has been a measure of agreement*

amount: *a certain amount of disappointment*

degree: *a degree of success*

portion: *I have spent a considerable portion of my life here*

proportion: *A large proportion of my time was spent abroad*

3 an action in order to achieve something: *Tough measures are needed to maintain order*

expedient: *I reduced my spending by the simple expedient of destroying my credit card*

manoeuvre: *manoeuvres to block the electoral process*

means: *The move is a means to fight crime*

procedure: *safety procedures*

step: *steps to discourage drink-driving*

see also **extent, quantity**

measured see **deliberate**

mechanical see **automatic**

mechanism see **machine**

meddle see **interfere**

meddler see **snooper**

mediate see **intervene**

medical see **examination**

medication see **drug, medicine**

medicine noun something you take to make you better: *They prevent the food and medicine from reaching Iraq*

drug: *Three new drugs recently became available*

medication: *some medication for her ulcers*

muti *South African informal*: *muti for treating a fever*

remedy: *At the moment we are trying a herbal remedy*

see also **cure, drug**

mediocre see **inferior, poor, unsatisfactory**

meditate see **consider, deliberate, think**

meditation see **thought**

medium adjective **1** average in size: *He was of medium height*

average: *a ginger tomcat of average size*

medium-sized: *a medium-sized saucepan*

middling: *Small and middling flats have increased in price much more than luxury ones*

▷ noun **2** a means of communication: *the medium of television*

channel: *through diplomatic channels*

vehicle: *The play seemed an ideal vehicle for his music*

see also **moderate**

medium-sized see **medium**

medley see **mixture, variety**

meek adjective quiet and timid: *a meek, mild-mannered fellow*

deferential: *the traditional requirement for Asian women to be deferential to men*

docile: *docile, obedient children*

mild: *a mild man*

submissive: *Most doctors want their patients to be submissive*

timid: *a timid child*

unassuming: *He's very polite and unassuming*

see also **gentle, humble, mild**

meet verb **1** to be in the same place as someone: *I met him quite by chance*

bump into *informal*: *I bumped into a friend of yours today*

come across: *where I came across a group of noisy children*

come upon: *We turned the corner and came upon a group of hikers*

encounter: *the most gifted child he had ever encountered*

run across: *We ran across some old friends*

run into: *You'll never guess who I ran into the other day*

2 to gather in a group: *We meet for lunch once a week*

assemble: *a convenient place for students to assemble between classes*

congregate: *Youngsters love to congregate here in the evening*

convene: *Senior officials convened in October*

gather: *We all gathered in the boardroom*

get together: *the last time we all got together*

3 to fulfil a need: *services intended to meet the needs of the elderly*

answer: *Would communism answer their needs?*

fulfil: *All the requirements were fulfilled*

satisfy: *Candidates must satisfy the general conditions for admission*

see also **experience, greet, receive,**

satisfy, touch

meeting noun **1** an event at which people come together for a purpose: *a business meeting*
  audience: *an audience with the Pope*
  conference: *a conference on education*
  congress: *a medical congress*
  convention: *the annual convention of the World Boxing Council*
  gathering: *a social gathering*
  get-together informal: *a get-together I had at my home*
  reunion: *a family reunion*
2 an occasion when you meet someone: *a chance meeting*
  assignation literary: *She had an assignation with her boyfriend*
  encounter: *a remarkable encounter with a group of soldiers*
  rendezvous: *Baxter arranged a six o'clock rendezvous*
  tryst: *a lovers' tryst*
  see also **appointment, conference, convention, gathering, hui**

melancholy see **down, miserable, misery, sad, sadness, sorrow**

mellow see **soft, sweet**

melodious see **sweet**

melodramatic adjective behaving in an exaggerated way: *Don't you think you're being rather melodramatic?*
  histrionic: *She let out a histrionic groan*
  sensational: *sensational tabloid newspaper reports*
  theatrical: *In a theatrical gesture Glass clamped his hand over his eyes*

melody see **tune**

melt verb **1** to become liquid: *The snow had melted*
  dissolve: *Heat gently until the sugar dissolves*
  thaw: *It's so cold the snow doesn't get a chance to thaw*
2 to disappear: *Her inhibitions melted*
  disappear: *The immediate threat has disappeared*
  disperse: *The crowd dispersed peacefully*
  dissolve: *His new-found optimism dissolved*
  evaporate: *My anger evaporated*
  vanish: *All her fears suddenly vanished*
  see also **warm**

melt away see **disappear, vanish**

memento see **souvenir**

memo see **message, note**

memorable adjective likely to be remembered: *a memorable victory*
  catchy: *a catchy tune*
  historic: *a historic meeting*
  notable: *with a few notable exceptions*
  striking: *the most striking feature of those statistics*
  unforgettable: *an unforgettable experience*

memorandum see **message, note**

memory noun the ability to remember: *Every detail is fresh in my memory*
  recall: *a man blessed with total recall*
  remembrance formal: *My remembrance of the incident is somewhat hazy*

menace see **danger, threat, threaten**

menacing see **frightening, sinister**

mend verb to repair something broken: *I should have had the catch mended*
  darn: *a woman darning socks*
  fix: *If something is broken, we get it fixed*
  patch: *They patched the barn roof*
  renovate: *The couple spent thousands renovating the house*
  repair: *to get her car repaired*
  restore: *experts who specialize in*

restoring ancient parchments
see also **fix, piece together, repair, restore**

menial see **inferior**

mentally ill see **insane**

mention verb **1** to talk about something briefly: *I may not have mentioned it to her*

allude to: *She alluded to his absence in vague terms*

bring up: *Why are you bringing it up now?*

broach: *I broached the subject of her early life*

hint: *The President hinted that he might make some changes*

intimate: *He did intimate that he is seeking legal action*

refer to: *In his speech, he referred to a recent trip to Canada*

touch on: *The film touches on these issues, but only superficially*

touch upon: *I'd like to touch upon a more serious question now*

▷ noun **2** a brief comment about something: *There was no mention of elections*

allusion: *She made an allusion to the events in Los Angeles*

reference: *He made no reference to any agreement*

see also **comment, note, observe, refer, remark**

mentor see **adviser**

merchandise see **product, stock**

merchant see **trader**

merciful adjective **1** showing kindness: *He is merciful and sympathetic to others*

compassionate: *a deeply compassionate man*

humane: *the desire for a more humane society*

kind: *She is warm-hearted and kind to everyone*

2 showing forgiveness: *We can only hope the court is merciful*

forgiving: *I don't think people are in a very forgiving mood*

lenient: *He believes the government is already lenient with drug traffickers*

see also **compassionate, humane**

merciless adjective showing no kindness or forgiveness: *the merciless efficiency of a modern police state*

callous: *his callous disregard for human life*

cruel: *Children can be so cruel*

heartless: *I couldn't believe they were so heartless*

implacable: *a powerful and implacable enemy*

ruthless: *his ruthless treatment of employees*

mercy noun **1** the quality of kindness: *He showed no mercy*

compassion: *his compassion for a helpless woman*

kindness: *He was treated with kindness by numerous officials*

pity: *She saw no pity in their faces*

2 the quality of forgiveness: *He threw himself upon the mercy of the court*

forgiveness: *He fell to his knees begging for forgiveness*

leniency: *He said he would show no leniency towards them*

see also **forgiveness, pity**

merely see **only**

merge see **blend, combine, mix, unite**

merit noun **1** worth or value: *Box-office success mattered more than artistic merit*

excellence: *the top US award for excellence in journalism*

value: *The value of this work experience should not be underestimated*

virtue: *There is little virtue in such an approach*

worth: people who had already proved their worth to their companies
2 a good quality that something has: Whatever its merits, their work would never be used
advantage: The great advantage of home-grown oranges is their flavour
asset: Her leadership qualities were her greatest asset
strength: The book's strength lay in its depiction of modern-day Tokyo
strong point: Science was never my strong point at school
virtue: Its other great virtue is its hard-wearing quality
▷ verb **3** to deserve something: Such ideas merit careful consideration
be entitled to: She is entitled to feel proud
be worthy of: The bank might think you're worthy of a loan
deserve: He deserves a rest
earn: Companies must earn a reputation for honesty
warrant: no evidence to warrant a murder investigation
see also **deserve, quality, value, virtue**

merry see **bright, cheerful**

mess noun **1** a state of untidiness: I'll clear up the mess later
chaos: Their concerts often ended in chaos
disarray: He found the room in disarray
disorder: Inside all was disorder
2 a situation that is full of problems: the reasons why the economy is in such a mess
fix informal: The government has really got itself into a fix
jam informal: They were in a real jam
muddle: Our finances are in a muddle
turmoil: Her marriage was in turmoil
▷ verb **3** to spoil something: He had messed up his career

botch up: I hate having builders botch up repairs on my house
bungle: Two prisoners bungled an escape bid
make a hash of informal: The government made a total hash of things
muck up slang: He always seemed to muck everything up
see also **confusion, fix, hole, muddle**
mess up see **botch, ruin, spoil**

message noun **1** a piece of information for someone: He left a message on her answerphone
bulletin: a news bulletin
communication: The ambassador brought a communication from the President
despatch or **dispatch**: this despatch from our West Africa correspondent
memo: office memos
memorandum: a memorandum from the Ministry of Defence
note: I'll have to leave a note for Karen
word: There is no word from the authorities on the reported attack
2 the idea conveyed by something: the story's anti-drugs message
meaning: while we discussed the meaning of the play
moral: the moral of the story
point: My point is that I'm not going to change
theme: The book's central theme is power
see also **meaning, note, word**

messenger noun someone who carries a message: There will be a messenger at the airport to collect the photographs
courier: a motorcycle courier
envoy: an envoy to the King
runner: a bookie's runner

messy see **untidy**

method noun a way of doing something: the traditional method of

making wine
approach: *different approaches to gathering information*
mode: *the capitalist mode of production*
procedure: *He did not follow the correct procedure*
technique: *the techniques of modern agriculture*
way: *a way of making new friends*
see also **fashion, plan, practice, procedure, process, style, system, way**

methodical *see* **deliberate**
meticulous *see* **careful, particular, strict, thorough**
meticulously *see* **well**
metre *see* **beat**
metropolis *see* **city**
microscopic *see* **minute, tiny**
microwave *see* **cook**
middle *noun* **1** *the part furthest from the edges: in the middle of the room*
centre: *the centre of the table*
halfway point: *Postle was third fastest at the halfway point*
midst: *a house in the midst of huge trees*
▷ *adjective* **2** *furthest from the edges: the middle house*
central: *central London*
halfway: *a point halfway between the two posts*
see also **centre**

middling *see* **medium, moderate, modest**
midst *see* **middle**
might *see* **force, power, strength**
mighty *see* **powerful**
migrate *see* **move**
mild *adjective* **1** *not strong or powerful: a mild shampoo*
insipid: *It tasted bland and insipid*
weak: *weak beer*
2 *gentle and good-tempered: a mild man*

gentle: *her gentle nature*
meek: *a meek, mild-mannered fellow*
placid: *a placid child who rarely cried*
3 *warmer than usual: The area is famous for its mild winter climate*
balmy: *balmy summer evenings*
temperate: *a temperate climate*
see also **calm, gentle, meek, quiet**

miles *see* **far**
militant *see* **fanatic**
mill *see* **factory**
mimic *see* **copy, imitate**
mind *noun* **1** *your ability to think: You have a very suspicious mind*
brain: *Once you stop using your brain you soon go stale*
head: *I can't get that song out of my head*
imagination: *Africa was alive in my imagination*
intellect: *good health and a lively intellect*
psyche: *disturbing elements of the human psyche*
▷ *verb* **2** *to be annoyed by something: I don't mind what you do*
be bothered: *I'm not bothered if he has another child*
care: *young men who did not care whether they lived or died*
object: *I don't object to his smoking*
3 *to look after something: My mother is minding the shop*
keep an eye on: *She asked me to keep an eye on the children*
look after: *I looked after the dogs while she was away*
take care of: *There was no one else to take care of the children*
watch: *She bought the tickets while I watched the cases*
see also **care, head, look after, take care of, watch, with**

mindful of *see* **aware of**
mine *see* **extract, fund**
mingle *see* **associate, blend, mix**

miniature see **tiny**
minimal see **low, minimum**
minimize see **lessen, lower**
minimum adjective being the least possible: *the minimum height for a policeman*
  least possible: *I try to cause the least amount of trouble possible*
  minimal: *The aim is to incur minimal expense*
  see also **least**
minor adjective less important: *a minor injury*
  lesser: *They pleaded guilty to lesser charges*
  petty: *petty crime*
  secondary: *matters of secondary importance*
  slight: *We have a slight problem*
  trifling: *Outside California these difficulties may seem trifling*
  trivial: *trivial details*
  see also **child, inferior, insignificant, slight, trivial, unimportant**
minus see **disadvantage**
minute noun **1** a short period of time: *I'll be with you in just a minute*
  flash: *It was all over in a flash*
  instant: *For an instant, Catherine was tempted to flee*
  moment: *Stop for one moment and think about what you're doing!*
  second: *Just a second. I'm coming*
  trice: *I'll be back in a trice*
  ▷ adjective **2** extremely small: *Only a minute amount is needed*
  microscopic: *microscopic fibres*
  negligible: *They are convinced the strike will have a negligible impact*
  slender: *We won the vote by a slender majority*
  small: *small particles of dust*
  tiny: *a tiny fraction of US production*
  see also **instant, moment, record, tiny**
miracle noun a surprising and

fortunate event: *the Italian economic miracle*
  marvel: *a marvel of high technology*
  wonder: *the wonders of science*
  see also **wonder**
mirage see **illusion, vision**
miscalculate see **err**
miscarriage see **failure**
miscellaneous see **various**
mischievous see **naughty, wicked**
misconception see **illusion**
misdemeanour see **crime**
miserable adjective **1** very unhappy: *a job which made me miserable*
  dejected: *Everyone has days when they feel dejected*
  depressed: *He seemed somewhat depressed*
  down: *Try to support each other when one of you is feeling down*
  downcast: *After his defeat Mr Rabin looked downcast*
  low: *"I didn't ask for this job," he tells friends when he is low*
  melancholy: *It was in these hours that he felt most melancholy*
  mournful: *He looked mournful, even near to tears*
  sad: *It left me feeling sad and empty*
  unhappy: *She is desperately unhappy*
  wretched: *I feel really confused and wretched*
  2 causing unhappiness: *a miserable little flat*
  gloomy: *Officials say the outlook for next year is gloomy*
  pathetic: *a pathetic sight*
  sorry: *The fires have left the industry in a sorry state*
  wretched: *He died in wretched poverty*
  see also **down, gloomy, sorry, unhappy**
miserly see **mean**
misery noun great unhappiness: *All that money brought nothing but*

misery

depression: He's been suffering from depression

despair: feelings of despair

grief: her grief at her husband's suicide

melancholy: with an air of melancholy

sadness: with a mixture of sadness and joy

sorrow: a time of great sorrow

unhappiness: There was a lot of unhappiness in my adolescence

woe: a tale of woe

see also **evil, grief, hell, pain, sorrow, spoilsport**

misfortune noun an unfortunate event: I had the misfortune to fall off my bike

adversity: times of adversity

bad luck: He has had his share of bad luck

see also **blow, disaster, hardship, sorrow**

misgiving see **anxiety, doubt, suspicion, worry**

misinterpret as see **mistake**

mislaid see **lost**

mislay see **lose**

mislead see **con, deceive, fool, take in**

misleading see **deceptive, untrue**

misplace see **lose**

misplaced see **lost**

misrepresent verb to give a false account of something: Keynes deliberately misrepresented the views of his opponents

distort: The minister said his remarks had been distorted by the press

falsify: falsifying personal details on his CV

twist: You're twisting my words

miss verb 1 to fail to notice: It's on the second floor. You can't miss it

fail to notice: He failed to notice that the lights had turned red

mistake: There's no mistaking her sincerity

overlook: a fact that we all tend to overlook

2 to feel the loss of: The boys miss their father

long for: Steve longed for the good old days

pine for: Make sure your pet won't pine for you while you're away

yearn for: He yearned for his freedom

see also **lack, overlook**

miss out see **omit**

missile see **bomb**

missing see **absent, lost**

mission see **task**

mist see **cloud**

mistake noun 1 something that is wrong: spelling mistakes

blunder: It had been a monumental blunder to give him the assignment

error: a mathematical error

gaffe: a social gaffe

oversight: By an unfortunate oversight, full instructions do not come with the product

slip: There must be no slips

▷ verb 2 to think one thing is another thing: I mistook him for the owner of the house

confuse with: I can't see how anyone could confuse you with your brother!

misinterpret as: She misinterpreted his remarks as a threat

mix up with: People often mix me up with other actors

take for: She had taken him for a journalist

see also **confuse, error, miss, mix-up, slip**

mistaken see **false, untrue, wrong**

mistreat verb to treat someone badly: She had been mistreated by men in the past

abuse: parents who abuse their children

ill-treat: They thought Mr Smith had been ill-treating his wife

mistress see **teacher**

mistrust see **suspect, suspicion**

misty see **wet**

misunderstanding see **mix-up**

misuse see **waste**

mix verb to combine things: Mix the ingredients together slowly

amalgamate: a need to amalgamate the two companies

blend: Blend the butter with the sugar

combine: Combine the flour with 3 tablespoons of water

merge: how to merge the graphic with text

mingle: the mingled smell of flowers and cigar smoke

see also **associate, blend, combination, combine**

mix up with see **mistake**

mixture noun a combination of things: a sticky mixture of flour and water

alloy: an alloy of copper and tin

amalgamation: an amalgamation of two organizations

blend: a blend of wine and sparkling water

combination: a fantastic combination of colours

compound: a compound of water, sugar, vitamins and enzymes

fusion: fusions of jazz and pop

medley: We communicated in a medley of foreign words and gestures

see also **blend, combination, cross, union, variety**

mix up verb to confuse two things: People often mix us up

confuse: Great care is taken to avoid confusing the two projects

muddle: Critics have begun to muddle the two names

see also **confuse, muddle**

mix-up noun a mistake in something

planned: a mix-up with the bookings

mistake: There must be some mistake

misunderstanding: Ensure that there is no misunderstanding about the instructions

muddle: There's been a muddle about whose responsibility it is

moan verb 1 to make a low sound: Laura moaned in her sleep

groan: He began to groan with pain

grunt: The driver grunted, convinced that Michael was crazy

2 to complain about something: Carol is always moaning about her husband

complain: People always complain that the big banks are unfriendly

groan: His parents were beginning to groan about the price of college tuition

grumble: A tourist grumbled that the waiter spoke too much Spanish

whine: They come to me to whine about their troubles

whinge informal: Stop whingeing and get on with it

▷ noun a low sound: She let out a faint moan

groan: a groan of disappointment

grunt: grunts of disapproval

see also **complain, grumble, lament**

mob see **crowd, jam, mass**

mob violence see **riot**

mock verb 1 to make fun of someone: Don't mock me

deride formal: Other countries are derided for selling arms to the enemy

laugh at: I thought they were laughing at me because I was ugly

make fun of: Don't make fun of me

poke fun at: She poked fun at people's shortcomings

ridicule: Mr Goss ridiculed that suggestion

scoff at: Some people may scoff at the idea that animals communicate

▷ adjective 2 not genuine: mock

surprise

artificial: *artificial limbs*

bogus: *their bogus insurance claim*

counterfeit: *counterfeit money*

dummy: *dummy weapons*

fake: *a fake fur*

false: *false teeth*

feigned: *with feigned indifference*

imitation: *imitation leather*

phoney or **phony** *informal*: *a phoney excuse*

pretended: *with pretended zeal*

sham: *sham marriages*

see also **make fun of, tease**

mockery noun the act of mocking someone: *Was there a glint of mockery in his eyes?*

derision: *shouts of derision*

jeering: *there was a chorus of jeering, whistles and laughter*

ridicule: *Davis was subjected to public ridicule*

see also **scorn**

mode *see* **fashion, manner, method, style**

model noun **1** a copy of something: *an architect's model of a wooden house*

dummy: *a tailor's dummy*

replica: *a replica of the Statue of Liberty*

representation: *a representation of a human figure*

2 a perfect example of something: *The essay is a model of clarity*

epitome: *the epitome of good taste*

example: *He is an example to the younger lads*

ideal: *the Japanese ideal of beauty*

paragon: *a paragon of virtue*

▷ verb **3** to make something into a shape: *clay modelled into the shape of a bear*

carve: *One of the prisoners had carved a wooden chess set*

fashion: *Stone Age settlers fashioned necklaces from sheep's teeth*

form: *figures formed from modelling clay*

mould: *We moulded a chair out of mud*

sculpt: *An artist sculpted a full-size replica of her head*

shape: *Shape each half into a loaf*

see also **design, example, ideal, make, shape**

moderate adjective **1** neither too much nor too little: *moderate exercise*

average: *I was only average academically*

fair: *Reimar had a fair command of English*

medium: *a medium size*

middling: *The Beatles enjoyed only middling success until 1963*

reasonable: *reasonable force*

▷ verb **2** to become or make less extreme: *They are hoping he can be persuaded to moderate his views*

abate: *The storm had abated*

curb: *You must curb your extravagant tastes*

ease: *Tensions had eased*

relax: *Rules have been relaxed recently*

soften: *to soften the blow of steep price rises*

temper: *He had to learn to temper his enthusiasm*

tone down: *He toned down his statements after the meeting*

see also **change, modest, reasonable**

moderately *see* **quite**

modern adjective **1** relating to the present time: *modern society*

contemporary: *contemporary music*

current: *the current situation*

present: *the government's present economic difficulties*

present-day: *Even by present-day standards these were large aircraft*

recent: *in recent years*

2 new and involving the latest ideas:

modern technology
latest: *the latest fashions*
new: *new methods of treating cancer*
up-to-date: *Germany's most up-to-date electric power station*
up-to-the-minute: *up-to-the-minute information*
modernize *see* **renovate**
modest *adjective* **1** small in size or amount: *a modest improvement*
limited: *They may only have a limited amount of time*
middling: *The Beatles enjoyed only middling success until 1963*
moderate: *moderate exercise*
small: *a relatively small problem*
2 not boastful: *Lord Carrington was modest about his achievements*
humble: *He gave a great performance, but he was very humble*
unassuming: *She has a gentle, unassuming manner*
see also **homely, humble, low, reasonable**
modification *see* **change, qualification**
modify *see* **adapt, change, vary**
moggie *see* **cat**
moggy *see* **cat**
moist *see* **damp, wet**
moisten *see* **wet**
moisture *see* **damp**
moke *see* **horse**
mollify *see* **humour, pacify**
molten *see* **liquid**
moment *noun* **1** a short period of time: *He paused for a moment*
instant: *The pain disappeared in an instant*
minute: *See you in a minute*
second: *Seconds later, firemen reached the door*
split second: *Her gaze met Michael's for a split second*
2 a point in time: *At that moment, the doorbell rang*

instant: *At that instant the museum was plunged into darkness*
point: *At this point Diana arrived*
time: *It seemed like a good time to tell her*
see also **instant, minute**
momentary *see* **brief, short, temporary**
momentous *see* **critical, crucial, important, serious**
momentum *see* **speed**
monarch *see* **king, ruler**
money *noun* coins or banknotes: *I needed to earn some money*
capital: *Companies are having difficulty in raising capital*
cash: *We were desperately short of cash*
dosh *British, Australian, New Zealand*: *They'll have the dosh to pay for a new sign*
dough *informal*: *He worked hard for his dough*
funds: *The concert will raise funds for research into AIDS*
see also **financial, wealth**
mongrel *see* **dog**
monitor *see* **observe**
monotonous *see* **boring, dreary, dull, flat**
monotony *see* **boredom**
monster *see* **savage**
monumental *see* **grand**
mood *noun* a state of mind: *She was in a really cheerful mood*
frame of mind: *Lewis was not in the right frame of mind to continue*
humour: *Could that have been the source of his good humour?*
spirits: *A bit of exercise will help lift his spirits*
state of mind: *I want you to get into a whole new state of mind*
temper: *I was in a bad temper last night*
see also **humour**

moody adjective **1** depressed or unhappy: Tony, despite his charm, could sulk and be moody

irritable: He had missed his dinner, and grew irritable

morose: She was morose and reticent

sulky: a sulky adolescent

sullen: a sullen and resentful workforce

2 liable to change your mood: David's mother was unstable and moody

temperamental: He is very temperamental

volatile: He has a volatile temper
see also **sulky**

moor see **secure**

moot see **raise**

moral see **message**

morality see **right, virtue**

morals see **principle, standards**

more adjective greater than something else: I've got more chips than you

added: For added protection choose lipsticks with a sun screen

additional: The US is sending additional troops to the region

extra: Extra staff have been taken on

further: There are likely to be further delays
see also **extra**

more than see **over**

moreover see **also, too**

moron see **fool, idiot**

morose see **moody**

mortal see **deadly, fatal**

mortgage see **loan**

most see **majority, maximum**

most important see **foremost**

most recent see **last**

mostly see **mainly**

mother see **parent**

motif see **pattern**

motion see **movement, question, signal**

motionless see **still**

motivate verb to cause a particular behaviour: What motivates athletes to take drugs?

drive: Jealousy drives people to murder

inspire: What inspired you to change your name?

lead: His abhorrence of racism led him to write the book

move: It was punk that first moved him to join a band

prompt: Japan's recession has prompted consumers to cut back on buying cars

provoke: The destruction of the mosque has provoked much anger
see also **drive, prompt**

motivation see **cause, drive, incentive**

motive see **cause, reason**

motor see **automobile, car**

motorway see **road**

motto see **slogan**

mould see **fashion, model, rot, shape**

mouldy see **rotten**

mound see **heap, pile**

mount see **climb, rise, stage**

mourn see **grieve, lament, regret**

mournful see **miserable, sad**

mourning see **sorrow**

mouthful see **taste**

move verb **1** to change position: The train began to move
see word studies **move**

2 to change residence: She had often considered moving to London

migrate: Peasants have migrated to the cities

move house: They move house fairly frequently

relocate: if the company was to relocate

3 to cause a deep emotion: Her story moved us to tears

affect: Her loss still clearly affects him

touch: Her enthusiasm touched me
see also **draw**, **motivate**, **touch**
move house see **move**
move to see **settle**
move up see **rise**
moved see **sorry**
movement noun 1 a change of
position: They monitor the movement
of the fish going up river
flow: the frantic flow of cars and buses
along the street
motion: the wind from the car's
motion
2 a group of people with similar
aims: the peace movement
campaign: the campaign against
public smoking
faction: the leaders of the country's
warring factions
group: members of an environmental
group
organization: the International
Labour Organization
see also **campaign**, **cause**, **wave**
moving adjective causing deep
emotion: It was a moving moment
affecting: one of the most affecting
scenes in the film
emotional: an emotional reunion
poignant: a poignant love story
stirring: a stirring speech
touching: the touching tale of a wife
who stood by husband she loved
see also **sad**, **touching**
much see **far**
muck see **dirt**
muck up see **mess**
mucky see **dirty**
mud see **dirt**
muddle noun 1 a state of disorder:
Our finances are in a muddle
chaos: Their concerts often ended
in chaos
confusion: There was confusion when
a man fired shots
disarray: He found the room in

disarray
disorder: Inside all was disorder
disorganization: a state of complete
disorganization
jumble: a meaningless jumble of
words
mess: the reasons why the economy is
in such a mess
tangle: a tangle of wires
▷ verb 2 to mix things up: One or
two critics have begun to muddle the
two names
confuse: Great care is taken to avoid
confusing the two projects
jumble: a number of animals whose
remains were jumbled together
mix up: People often mix us up
see also **cloud**, **disorder**, **mess**, **mix
up**, **mix-up**, **tangle**
muddle up see **confuse**
muddled see **confused**
muddy see **cloudy**, **dirty**
muffle see **silence**
mug see **face**
mugger see **thief**
muggy see **humid**, **stuffy**
mull over see **deliberate**, **ponder**,
think
multiply verb to increase in number:
The trip wore on and the hazards
multiplied
increase: The population continues
to increase
proliferate: Computerized databases
are proliferating fast
spread: Cholera is not spreading as
quickly as it did in the past
see also **breed**, **grow**, **increase**
multitude see **bunch**, **crowd**, **jam**,
number
mumble verb to speak quietly: He
mumbled a few words
murmur: He murmured something to
the professor
mutter: He sat there muttering to
himself

munch see **chew**

mundane see **everyday**

murder noun **1** the act of killing someone: *after being found guilty of murder*
assassination: *the assassination of John F. Kennedy*
homicide: *the scene of the homicide*
killing: *a brutal killing*
manslaughter: *She was found guilty of manslaughter*
slaughter: *the imperial army's slaughter of Chinese civilians*
slaying literary: *a trail of motiveless slayings*
▷ verb **2** to kill someone: *a thriller about two men who murder a third*
assassinate: *Robert Kennedy was assassinated in 1968*
kill: *a man who killed his wife*
slaughter: *Thirty four people were slaughtered while queueing up to cast their votes*
slay literary: *the field where Saint George is reputed to have slain the dragon*
take the life of: *He admitted to taking the lives of at least 35 more women*
see also **kill**

murderous see **fierce, violent**

murky see **cloudy, dark, dim, dull**

murmur see **grumble, mumble**

muscle see **strength**

muse see **consider, think**

muse on see **contemplate**

mushy see **sentimental**

musical see **sweet**

muster see **recruit**

mutate see **turn**

mute see **dumb, silent**

muted see **dull, faint, soft**

muteness see **silence**

muti see **medicine**

mutiny see **rebel, rebellion**

mutt see **dog**

mutter see **grumble, mumble**

myriad see **countless, many**

mysterious adjective **1** strange and not well understood: *He died in mysterious circumstances*
arcane formal: *the arcane world of high finance*
baffling: *a baffling array of wires*
cryptic: *My father's notes are more cryptic here*
enigmatic: *one of Orson Welles's most enigmatic films*
mystifying: *I find your attitude rather mystifying*
2 secretive about something: *Stop being so mysterious*
furtive: *with a furtive glance over her shoulder*
secretive: *the secretive world of spying*
see also **funny**

mystery noun something that is not understood: *the mystery surrounding his death*
conundrum: *this theological conundrum*
enigma: *Iran remains an enigma for the outside world*
puzzle: *"Women are a puzzle," he said*
riddle: *the answer to the riddle of why it was never finished*

mystify see **confuse, puzzle**

mystifying see **mysterious**

mythological see **imaginary**

n

nag see **hassle, horse**
nagging see **continual**
naive see **fond, gullible, ignorant, innocent**
naivety see **innocence**
naked adjective **1** not wearing any clothes: *a naked man diving into the sea*
bare: *her bare feet*
nude: *nude bathing*
stark-naked: *She didn't seem to notice I was stark-naked*
unclothed: *an unclothed male body*
undressed: *She couldn't remember getting undressed*
2 openly displayed or shown: *naked aggression*
blatant: *evidence of blatant discrimination*
evident: *the party's evident dislike of the president*
manifest: *his manifest enthusiasm*
open: *open opposition to the government*
unmistakable: *with unmistakable amusement in his eyes*
see also **bare**
name noun **1** a word that identifies a person or thing: *My name is Joe*
designation: *a level four alert, a designation reserved for very serious*

incidents
epithet: *the common epithet for the Buddha*
nickname: *He's heard your nickname is Codfish*
term: *I don't know the medical term for it*
title: *Your actual title would be business manager*
2 the opinion people have about someone: *to protect Janet's good name*
character: *a series of personal attacks on my character*
reputation: *I know Chris has a bad reputation*
▷ verb **3** to give a name to someone or something: *a little girl named Betsy*
baptize: *She could be baptized Margaret*
call: *in a town called Fishingport*
christen: *He wanted to christen his son Arthur Albert*
dub: *a girl cruelly dubbed "the Worm"*
style: *a character who styled himself the Memory Man*
term: *He had been termed a temporary employee*
see also **celebrity, identify, nominate, reputation, specify, term**
naming see **appointment**
nap see **pile, sleep**
narcotic see **drug**
narrative see **plot, story**
narrow adjective having a small distance from side to side: *a narrow stream*
fine: *the fine hairs on her arms*
slender: *long slender legs*
slim: *a slim volume of Auden's poems*
thin: *a thin layer of clay*
see also **shrink, thin**
narrow-minded adjective unwilling to consider new ideas or other people's opinions: *their own narrow-*

minded view of the world
biased: *a biased view*
bigoted: *bigoted opinions*
insular: *those insular British travellers*
opinionated: *the most opinionated rubbish I have read*
prejudiced: *a whole host of prejudiced and xenophobic ideas*

nasty adjective very unpleasant: *a nasty taste*
disagreeable: *a disagreeable experience*
disgusting: *the most disgusting behaviour*
foul: *They produce a foul smell of rotten eggs*
horrible: *I've got a horrible feeling about this one*
repellent: *the most repellent human being I have ever met*
unpleasant: *some unpleasant surprises*
vile: *All the food is vile*
see also **disagreeable, horrible, spiteful, unkind, unpleasant**

nation see **land, public, race, state**
national see **home**
native see **home, inhabitant, local, natural**
natter see **chat**

natural adjective **1** normal and to be expected: *the natural reaction to a failed marriage*
common: *It is a common response*
everyday: *the everyday drudgery of work*
normal: *Biting is normal for puppies when they are teething*
ordinary: *The cottage looks quite ordinary from the road*
typical: *typical symptoms of stress*
usual: *It was not usual for the women to accompany them*
2 not trying to pretend: *He was so natural with the children*
candid: *rather candid about her marriage*

frank: *an unusually frank interview*
genuine: *He always seems so genuine*
real: *She came across as a real person*
unaffected: *She sang with unaffected simplicity*
3 existing from birth and not learned: *I never had much natural rhythm*
inborn: *an inborn sense of optimism*
inherent: *the inherent goodness of people*
innate: *the innate conservatism of his predecessor*
instinctive: *an instinctive distrust of authority*
intuitive: *an intuitive understanding of the market*
native: *He relies on his native wit to get him through*
see also **automatic, informal, wild**

nature noun someone's character: *It's not in my nature to sit still*
character: *the funny side of his character*
make-up: *Compromise was never part of his make-up*
personality: *his dominating personality*
see also **character, essence, personality**

naughty adjective **1** tending to behave badly: *a naughty little boy*
bad: *the bad behaviour of their teenage children*
disobedient: *Lucy was similarly disobedient*
impish: *an impish sense of humour*
mischievous: *a mischievous child*
wayward: *He tried to control his wayward son*
2 rude or indecent: *a programme all about naughty words*
bawdy: *a series of bawdy jokes*
lewd: *his arrest for lewd behaviour*
obscene: *making obscene gestures*

to the crowd
vulgar: The lyrics were vulgar
see also **wicked**

nausea see **disgust**
nauseous see **crook, queasy, sick**
navigate see **manoeuvre**

near adjective **1** not far away in
distance: A beautiful woman is near
adjacent: an adjacent room
adjoining: A phone rang in an
adjoining office
close: a close neighbour
nearby: the nearby village
2 not far away in time: The time of
judgment is near
approaching: The deadline was
approaching
forthcoming: the forthcoming
football season
imminent: The day of our departure
was imminent
looming: Exams are looming and the
students are panicking
near at hand: His death is near
at hand
nigh: The end of the world is nigh
upcoming: the upcoming elections
▷ preposition **3** near from: He drew
his chair nearer the fire
adjacent to: a garden and maze
adjacent to the castle
alongside: the huts set up alongside
the river
close to: We parked close to the
pavement
next to: I realised someone was
standing next to me
not far from: a car park not far from
the entrance
see also **beside, immediate,
imminent**

near at hand see **near**
nearby see **handy, near**
nearest see **next**

nearly adverb not completely but
almost: The beach was nearly empty

almost: Over the past decade their
wages have almost doubled
as good as: The World Championship
is as good as over
just about: We are just about finished
with this section
practically: The house was
practically a wreck
virtually: Their country is virtually
bankrupt
see also **about, almost**

neat adjective **1** having everything
arranged in a tidy way: The house was
clean and neat
orderly: an orderly office
smart: a smart navy blue suit
spruce: Mundo was looking spruce
in a suit
tidy: He always kept his bedroom tidy
trim: a street of trim little villas
2 not mixed with anything else: a
small glass of neat vodka
pure: a carton of pure orange juice
straight: calling for a straight whisky
see also **handy, orderly, smart, tidy**

necessary adjective **1** needed so that
something can happen: Make the
necessary arrangements
essential: It is essential that you
visit a dentist
imperative: It is imperative we end
up with a win
indispensable: Jordan is an
indispensable part of the peace process
required: That book is required
reading
vital: Bone marrow is vital for
producing blood cells
2 formal certain to happen or exist:
a necessary consequence of war
certain: one certain outcome of the
conference
inevitable: She now accepts that a
divorce is inevitable
inexorable: The growth in travel has
been inexorable

unavoidable: *The union knows that job losses are unavoidable*
see also **basic, vital**

necessities see **essentials**

necessity see **requirement**

neck and neck see **even**

need verb to believe you must have or do something: *You need some fresh air*

demand: *The children demand her attention*

require: *If you require further information, please telephone*

want: *I want a drink*
see also **demand, distress, require, requirement, want**

needle see **irritate, tease**

needless see **excessive, unnecessary**

neglect verb **1** to fail to look after someone or something: *unhappy and neglected children*

ignore: *They see the government ignoring poor people*

overlook: *Pensioners feel they are being overlooked*

turn your back on: *Do not turn your back on the unemployed*

2 formal to fail to do something: *He had neglected to give her his address*

fail: *I was shattered and I failed to tell her about the good bits*

forget: *She forgot to lock her door*

omit: *He omitted to mention his connection with the company*

▷ noun **3** lack of care: *Most of her plants died from neglect*

disregard: *a callous disregard for his victims*

indifference: *Indifference to patients is rare in America*

unconcern: *the government's unconcern for the environment*
see also **fail, ignore, overlook**

neglected see **derelict**

neglectful see **careless**

negligible see **minute, slight, tiny, trivial**

negotiate see **manoeuvre**

neighbourhood see **area, local, surroundings**

neighbouring see **next**

nerve see **cheek, courage, daring, impudence**

nerve-racking see **tense**

nervous adjective worried about something: *She had been nervous before the match*

anxious: *I was very anxious about her safety*

apprehensive: *Their families are apprehensive about the trip*

edgy: *I was edgy and tired*

jittery informal: *She still feels jittery when she visits her sister*

jumpy: *The Italians are getting jumpy after drawing against the Swiss*

tense: *too tense to sleep*

toey Australian, New Zealand slang: *Dad's getting a bit toey*

uptight informal: *an uptight British couple*

worried: *You had me worried for a moment*
see also **afraid, anxious, dubious, tense, timid, uneasy, worried**

nervousness see **alarm, anxiety**

net see **trap**

neutral adjective not supporting either side: *We stayed neutral during the war*

disinterested: *a disinterested observer*

dispassionate: *a full and dispassionate account*

impartial: *How can he give impartial advice?*

nonaligned: *the Arab and nonaligned countries*
see also **impersonal**

never adverb at no time at all: *I never said I was leaving*

at no time: *At no time did he see the*

helicopter

not ever: The problem won't ever go away

new adjective recently created or discovered: a new hotel
see **word studies new**
see also **extra, inexperienced, modern, original, recent, strange, unfamiliar**

news noun information about things that have happened: news about the civil war

bulletin: the main evening bulletin

disclosure: disclosures about his private life

dispatch: the latest dispatches from the war zone

information: up-to-date information on weather

intelligence: military intelligence from behind Iraqi lines

latest informal: the latest on the bomb explosion

tidings formal: the bearer of bad tidings

word: There is no word about casualties
see also **information, word**

next adjective **1** coming immediately after something else: Their next child was a girl

ensuing: the ensuing years of violence

following: The following day I went to work as usual

subsequent: As subsequent events showed, he was wrong

succeeding: succeeding generations of students

▷ adverb **2** coming immediately after something else: Steve arrived next

afterwards: I felt dizzy afterwards and had to sit down

subsequently: She was subsequently married to his cousin

3 in a position nearest to

something: in the next room

adjacent: I pulled into the adjacent driveway

adjoining: in adjoining streets

closest: Britain's closest neighbours

nearest: the nearest Italian restaurant

neighbouring: Liberians fleeing to neighbouring countries

next to see **beside, near**

next world see **heaven**

nib see **point**

nibble see **bite**

nice adjective attractive or enjoyable: Did you have a nice time, dear?
see **word studies nice**
see also **agreeable, pleasant**

niceties see **ceremony**

nick see **arrest, jail, prison, steal**

nickname see **name**

nigh see **near**

nightmare see **hell, ordeal**

nil see **zero**

nimble see **agile**

nip see **bite**

no interjection not at all: "Any problems?" – "No, everything's fine."

absolutely not: "Did they consult you?" – "Absolutely not."

certainly not: "Perhaps it would be better if I withdrew." – "Certainly not!"

definitely not: "Are you going to the party?" – "Definitely not."

not at all: "You're not upset, are you?" – "Not at all."

of course not: "I'd like to talk to the lads, if you don't mind." – "Of course not, Chief."

noble adjective **1** deserving admiration because of honesty, bravery and unselfishness: a good and noble thing to do

generous: It reflects his generous nature

honourable: His colleagues were honourable people

magnanimous: Miss Balding is magnanimous in victory
upright: a very upright, trustworthy man
virtuous: the virtuous Mrs Friendall
worthy: less worthy members of our profession
▷ noun **2** someone from the highest social rank: The Scottish nobles were united
aristocrat: All his sisters had married German aristocrats
lord: They assumed that Amy was a snob because her father was a lord
nobleman: a Spanish nobleman
peer: He was made a life peer in 1981
nobleman see **noble**
nod see **signal**
no-hoper see **failure**
noise noun a loud or unpleasant sound: He is making an awful noise
commotion: There was a commotion in the corridor
din: He'd never heard a din like it
hubbub: the hubbub of Paris in the 1880s
pandemonium: There was pandemonium in the classroom
racket: There was a terrible racket going on
row: Whatever is that row?
uproar: The courtroom was in an uproar see also **racket, sound**
noisy adjective making a lot of noise: a noisy audience of schoolchildren
deafening: a deafening roar
loud: The disco music was a little too loud
piercing: her piercing laugh
strident: the strident vocals of Joy Malcolm
tumultuous: He took the field to tumultuous applause
vociferous: vociferous support from the Scottish fans
see also **loud, rowdy**

nominate verb to suggest someone for a position: The party refused to nominate him as its candidate
name: He'll be naming a new captain
propose: Cliff was proposed as chairman
recommend: He recommended him as his successor at Boston
select: no prospect of being selected to stand for Parliament
submit: Mr Heath submitted a list of 200 names
suggest: Some commentators have suggested Clark for the job
nomination see **appointment**
nonaligned see **neutral**
nonchalant see **careless, casual, uninterested**
nonsense noun foolish words or behaviour: I say the allegations are complete nonsense
bull slang: They're teaching our kids a load of bull
drivel: mindless drivel aimed at Middle America
garbage informal: One source claimed the rumours were complete garbage
inanity: the burbling inanities of the tabloids
rot: She is talking complete rot
rubbish: complete and utter rubbish
waffle British informal: He writes smug, sanctimonious waffle
see also **garbage, rubbish**
nonsensical see **absurd, foolish, irrational**
non-specific see **broad**
nonstop see **constant, express, relentless, steady**
nontoxic see **harmless**
norm see **standard**
normal adjective usual and ordinary: my normal routine
average: What's your average day like?
conventional: conventional tastes

habitual: *their country of habitual residence*
ordinary: *It was just an ordinary weekend*
regular: *It looks like a regular cigarette*
routine: *a routine medical check*
standard: *standard practice*
typical: *A typical day begins at 8.30*
usual: *She did not collect him at the usual time*
see also **average, natural, ordinary, regular, routine, sane, standard, typical, usual**

normally see **as a rule, on average**

nostalgic see **sentimental**

nosy *adjective* trying to find out about other people's business: *nosy neighbours watching us through the curtains*
curious: *surrounded by a group of curious villagers*
eavesdropping: *We don't want to be overheard by eavesdropping servants*
inquisitive: *Bears are naturally inquisitive creatures*
prying: *I hid it away, safe from prying eyes*
see also **curious**

not at all see **no**
not be able to abide see **dislike**
not be able to bear see **dislike**
not be able to stand see **dislike**
not dangerous see **harmless**
not ever see **never**
not far from see **near**
not guilty see **innocent**
not level see **uneven**
not liable see **exempt**
not many see **few**
not quite see **almost**
not smooth see **uneven**
not well see **unhealthy**
not working see **dead**

notable see **important, memorable, particular, prominent, significant**

note *noun* **1** a short letter: *I wrote him*

a note asking him to come round
communication *formal*: *a communication from the President*
letter: *I have received a letter from a friend*
memo: *a leaked memo to managers*
memorandum: *A memorandum has been sent to the members of the board*
message: *He sent his mate round with a message for me*
reminder: *We keep getting reminders from the garage to pay our bill old-fashioned*

2 a written record that helps you remember something: *I made a note of his address*
account: *Keep an account of all your outgoings*
jotting: *Carry a notebook with you for your jottings*
record: *Keep a record of all payments*
register: *She kept a register of each child's progress*

3 an atmosphere, feeling, or quality: *I detected a note of bitterness in his voice*
hint: *Was there was a hint of irony in that remark?*
tone: *He laughed again, this time with a cold, sharp tone*
touch: *There is an unmistakable touch of pathos in his last film*
trace: *He wrote on the subject without a trace of sensationalism*

▷ *verb* **4** to become aware of or mention a fact: *I noted that the rain had stopped*
mention: *I mentioned in passing that I liked her dress*
notice: *Contact the police if you notice anything suspicious*
observe *formal*: *Hooke observed a reddish spot on the surface of the planet*
perceive: *He perceived a certain tension between them*

register: The sound was so familiar that she didn't register it
remark: Everyone has remarked what a lovely lady she is
see: A lot of people saw what was happening but did nothing
see also **comment, entry, message, notice, observe, record**
noted see **famous, prominent**
nothing see **zero**
notice verb **1** to become aware of something: Then I noticed Billy wasn't laughing
detect: He detects signs of growing support for his plan
discern: I did not discern any change in attitudes
note: I noted that the rain had stopped
observe: I've observed how hard he had to work
perceive: gradually perceiving the possibilities
see: I saw that the lobby was swarming with police
spot: Allen spotted me on the other side of the dance floor
▷ noun **2** a written announcement: a handwritten notice in the window
advertisement: one advertisement in a local paper
bill: students posting bills near the campus for a demo
poster: a poster advertising a charity concert
sign: a hand-written cardboard sign hung round his neck
3 warning that something is going to happen: She was transferred without warning
advance warning: advance warning of the attack
intimation: He has given no intimation of an intention to resign
notification: Official notification is expected to arrive today
warning: I was sacked without

warning
see also **advertisement, discern, heed, information, item, note, observe, review, see, sign, warning**
noticeable adjective obvious and easy to see: a noticeable improvement
conspicuous: a conspicuous lack of sympathy
evident: He ate with evident enjoyment
obvious: There are obvious dangers
perceptible: Germany is showing a perceptible improvement
unmistakable: a growing but unmistakable impatience
see also **conspicuous, evident, prominent, visible**
notification see **notice**
notify verb to officially inform someone of something: The skipper notified the coastguard of the tragedy
advise formal: I think it best that I advise you of my decision first
inform: They would inform him of any progress they made
tell: He told me I was on a final warning
warn: They warned him of the dangers
see also **advise, alert, inform, report, tell, warn**
notion see **idea, impression, thought**
notorious adjective well-known for something bad: The district was notorious for violent crime
disreputable: a low and disreputable character
infamous: an industry infamous for late payment of debts
scandalous: her scandalous affair with the president
notwithstanding see **despite, in spite of**
nought see **zero**
nourishing see **healthy**
nourishment see **food**

novel see **original, strange, unfamiliar**

novelty see **curiosity**

novice see **beginner, recruit**

now adverb at the present time or moment: *I need to talk to him now*

at once: *I really must go at once*

currently: *The vaccines are currently being tested*

immediately: *Please come immediately*

nowadays: *I don't see much of Tony nowadays*

right now: *Stop that noise right now!*

straightaway: *I think you should see a doctor straightaway*

without delay: *We'll come round without delay*

see also **immediately**

now again see **sometimes**

now and then see **sometimes**

nowadays see **now**

noxious see **poisonous, unhealthy**

nude see **bare, naked**

nudge see **poke**

nuisance noun someone or something that is annoying: *Sorry to be a nuisance*

annoyance: *Snoring can be an annoyance*

bother: *Most men hate the bother of shaving*

hassle informal: *Writing out a cheque is a hassle*

inconvenience: *The inconvenience of a rail strike*

irritation: *He describes the tourists as "an irritation"*

pain informal: *She found dressing up for the occasion a real pain*

pest: *I didn't want to be a cry baby or a pest*

see also **annoyance, pest**

numb adjective 1 unable to feel anything: *Your right arm goes numb*

dead: *Hillier suffered a dead leg playing for the reserves*

frozen: *a frozen shoulder*

insensitive: *The brain itself is insensitive to pain*

paralysed: *He has been left with a paralysed arm*

▷ verb 2 to make you unable to feel anything: *The cold numbed my fingers*

dull: *morphine to dull the pain*

freeze: *an epidural to freeze the hip area*

paralyse: *people paralysed by illness or injury*

stun: *the gun used to stun the animals*

see also **frozen, shock**

numbed see **dazed**

number noun 1 a word or symbol used for counting: *Pick a number between one and ten*

digit: *a six-digit password*

figure: *a figure between a hundred and a thousand*

numeral: *Roman numerals*

2 a quantity of things or people: *Adrian has introduced me to a large number of people*

collection: *a huge collection of books about Keats*

crowd: *a huge crowd of supporters*

horde: *a horde of drunken villagers*

multitude: *Bands can play to multitudes of fans*

see also **figure, quantity**

numeral see **figure, number**

numerous adjective existing or happening in large numbers: *on numerous occasions*

lots: *I've got lots of photos of the kids*

many: *I have met Imran many times*

several: *He is fluent in several languages*

see also **many**

nurse see **look after, take care of, tend, treat**

nurture see **breed, raise**

nut see **weirdo**

nutritious see **healthy**

nutter see **weirdo**

O

oaf noun a clumsy or aggressive person: *You drunken oaf!*
brute: *Custer was an idiot and a brute*
lout: *a drunken lout*
see also **idiot**

oath noun a formal promise: *He took an oath of loyalty to the government*
pledge: *The meeting ended with a pledge to step up cooperation*
promise: *If you make a promise, you should keep it*
vow: *I made a silent vow to be more careful*
see also **word**

obedient adjective tending to do what you are told: *He was always very obedient to his parents*
law-abiding: *law-abiding citizens*
submissive: *Most doctors want their patients to be submissive*
subservient: *her willingness to be subservient to her children*

obese see **overweight**

obey verb to do what you are told: *Most people obey the law*
abide by: *They have got to abide by the rules*
adhere to: *All members adhere to a strict code of practice*
comply with: *The army will comply*

with the ceasefire
follow: *Take care to follow the instructions carefully*
observe: *forcing motorists to observe speed restrictions*
see also **follow**

object noun **1** anything solid and non-living: *everyday objects such as wooden spoons*
article: *household articles*
thing: *What's that thing in the middle of the fountain?*
2 an aim or purpose: *The object of the exercise is to raise money for the charity*
aim: *The aim of the festival is to increase awareness of Hindu culture*
goal: *The goal is to raise as much money as possible*
idea: *The idea is to give children the freedom to explore*
intention: *It is my intention to remain in my position*
objective: *His objective was to win*
purpose: *What is the purpose of your visit?*
▷ verb **3** to express disapproval: *A lot of people will object to the book*
oppose: *Many parents oppose bilingual education in schools*
protest: *He picked up the cat before Rosa could protest*
see also **article, disagree, goal, intention, mind, point, protest, purpose, subject, thing, use**

object to see **query, resent**

objection noun disapproval of something: *despite objections by the White House*
opposition: *Opposition to this plan has come from the media*
protest: *protests against the government*
see also **complaint, disagreement, grumble, protest**

objectionable see **disagreeable,**

offensive, unpleasant

objective see **aim, goal, intention, object**

obligation see **bond, duty, responsibility**

obligatory see **compulsory**

oblige see **force, make, require**

obliged see **supposed**

obliging see **accommodating**

oblique see **indirect**

obliterate see **blot out, destroy**

obliteration see **destruction**

oblivious see **ignorant, preoccupied, unaware, unconscious**

obnoxious see **disagreeable, disgusting, hateful, unpleasant**

obscene adjective indecent and likely to upset people: obscene pictures
bawdy: a bawdy song
blue: a blue movie
dirty: a dirty book
filthy: a filthy joke
indecent: an indecent suggestion
lewd: lewd comments
pornographic: a pornographic magazine
see also **crude, naughty**

obscure adjective 1 known by only a few people: an obscure Mongolian dialect
little-known: a little-known Austrian composer
unknown: an unknown writer
2 difficult to understand: The news was shrouded in obscure language
arcane: the arcane world of contemporary classical music
cryptic: cryptic comments
opaque: the opaque language of the inspector's reports
▷ verb 3 to make something difficult to see: His view was obscured by trees
cloak: a land permanently cloaked in mist
cloud: Perhaps anger had clouded

his vision
conceal: The hat concealed her hair
hide: The compound was hidden by trees and shrubs
mask: A thick grey cloud masked the sun
screen: Most of the road was screened by a block of flats
shroud: Mist shrouded the outline of Buckingham Palace
see also **blot out, cover, dim, unknown**

observable see **visible**

observance see **ceremony**

observant adjective good at noticing things: Painting makes you really observant of things
attentive: the attentive audience
perceptive: a perceptive remark
vigilant: He warned the public to be vigilant
watchful: Keep a watchful eye on babies and toddlers
see also **alert, sharp**

observation see **comment, remark, watch**

observe verb 1 to watch something carefully: He has spent years observing their behaviour
monitor: I have been monitoring his progress carefully
scrutinize: She scrutinized his features to see if he was telling the truth
study: Debbie studied her friend's face for a moment
survey: He surveys American politics from an interesting standpoint
view: You can view the lesson from the gallery
watch: A man was watching him from across the square
2 to notice something: I observed a number of strange phenomena
discover: They discovered that they were being watched

note: People noted how much care she took over her work

notice: Contact the police if you notice anything unusual

see: I saw a man coming towards me

spot: Moments later, smoke was spotted coming out of the kitchen

witness: Anyone who witnessed the attack should call the police

3 to make a comment about something: "You've had your hair cut," he observed

comment: Stuart commented that this was true

mention: I mentioned that I didn't like contemporary music

remark: "Some people have more money than sense," he remarked

say: She said that I looked tired

state: He stated that this was, indeed, the case

see also **comment, discern, follow, note, notice, obey, practise, remark, see, spot, watch, witness**

observer see **spectator, witness**

obsessed see **crazy**

obsession noun a compulsion to think about something: her obsession with Christopher

complex: I have never had a complex about my height

fixation: the country's fixation on the war

mania: a mania for horror films

preoccupation: today's preoccupation with royal misdeeds

thing informal: He's got this thing about ties

see also **complex**

obsessive see **fanatical**

obsolete see **old-fashioned, out of date**

obstacle noun something which makes it difficult to go forward: a large obstacle to improving housing conditions

barrier: Taxes are the most obvious barrier to free trade

difficulty: the difficulties ahead

hindrance: The higher rates have been a hindrance to economic recovery

hurdle: the first hurdle for many women returning to work

impediment: There was no legal impediment to the marriage

obstruction: an obstruction in the road

see also **barrier, difficulty, handicap**

obstinate adjective unwilling to change your mind: He is obstinate and will not give up

dogged: his dogged insistence on their rights

headstrong: He's young and very headstrong

inflexible: His opponents viewed him as dogmatic and inflexible

intractable: He protested but Wright was intractable

stubborn: a stubborn character who is used to getting his own way

wilful: a wilful child

see also **stubborn**

obstruct verb to block a road or path: Lorries obstructed the road

bar: He stood there, barring her way

block: Some students blocked the highway

choke: The roads are choked with cars

clog: The traffic clogged the Thames bridges

see also **bar, block, close, delay, hamper, impede, interfere**

obstruction see **barrier, blockage, delay, obstacle**

obtain verb to get something: He tried to obtain a false passport

acquire: I recently acquired a beautiful old lamp

get: trying to get enough food to live

get hold of: It's hard to get hold of guns

get your hands on informal: reading everything she could get her hands on

procure formal: It became hard to procure fuel

secure formal: continuing their efforts to secure a ceasefire

see also **acquire, buy, earn, extract, gain, get, secure**

obtrusive see **pushy**

obtuse see **dim, dumb, slow, stupid**

obvious adjective easy to see or understand: an obvious injustice

apparent: It was apparent that he had lost interest

blatant: a blatant foul

clear: a clear breach of the rules

evident: His love of nature is evident in his paintings

overt: parents who showed us no overt affection

palpable: The tension between them is palpable

plain: It was plain to him that I was having a nervous breakdown

self-evident: The implications for this country are self-evident

see also **clear, conspicuous, evident, logical, manifest, noticeable, plain, prominent, visible**

occasion noun 1 an important event: The launch of a ship was a big occasion

affair: The visit was to be a purely private affair

event: A new book by Grass is always an event

2 an opportunity to do something: an important occasion for setting out government policy

chance: the chance to practise medicine in British hospitals

opportunity: I had an opportunity to go to New York

time: This was no time to make a speech

▷ verb 3 formal to cause something: damage occasioned by fire

bring about: the only way to bring about peace

give rise to: The judge's decision gave rise to practical problems

induce: an economic crisis induced by high oil prices

produce: The drug is known to produce side-effects in women

prompt: The demonstration prompted fears of more violence

provoke: The incident has provoked outrage in Okinawa

see also **case, chance, create, incident**

occasional adjective happening sometimes: an occasional outing

intermittent: after three hours of intermittent rain

odd: at odd moments

periodic: periodic bouts of illness

sporadic: a year of sporadic fighting

see also **irregular**

occasionally see **sometimes**

occupant see **inhabitant**

occupation see **job, profession, trade, work**

occupied see **active, busy**

occupy see **busy, inhabit, invade, possess**

occur verb 1 to happen or exist: The disease occurs throughout Africa

appear: a test to reveal infection before symptoms appear

arise: A problem may arise later in pregnancy

be present: This vitamin is present in breast milk

exist: A conflict of interest may exist in such situations

happen: The accident happened close to Martha's Vineyard

take place: Elections will take place on the second of November

2 to come into your mind: *It didn't occur to me to check*

cross your mind: *The possibility of failure did cross my mind*

dawn on: *It dawned on me that I shouldn't give up without a fight*

strike: *A thought struck her*

see also **come**, **happen**, **take place**

occurrence see **case**, **incident**

odd *adjective* strange or unusual: *an odd coincidence*

bizarre: *his bizarre behaviour*

curious: *a curious mixture of the ancient and modern*

funny: *There's something funny about him*

peculiar: *Rachel thought it tasted peculiar*

queer old-fashioned: *There's something a bit queer going on*

singular formal: *Where he got that singular notion I just can't think*

strange: *Then a strange thing happened*

weird: *That first day was weird*

see also **bizarre**, **curious**, **extraordinary**, **funny**, **occasional**, **peculiar**, **strange**, **weird**

oddity see **curiosity**

odds see **chance**, **possibility**, **probability**

odds and ends see **junk**

odour see **smell**

of course not see **no**

off see **sour**

off-course see **lost**

offence see **breach**, **crime**, **insult**, **sin**

offend *verb* to upset or embarrass someone: *He says he had no intention of offending the community*

affront: *He pretended to be affronted, but inwardly he was pleased*

insult: *Buchanan says he was insulted by the judge's remarks*

outrage: *Many people have been*

outraged by what was said

see also **insult**, **repel**, **shock**

offended see **hurt**, **resentful**

offender see **criminal**

offensive *adjective* rude and upsetting: *offensive behaviour*

abusive: *abusive language*

insulting: *an insulting remark*

objectionable: *I find your tone highly objectionable*

see also **abusive**, **attack**, **hateful**

offer *verb* **1** to ask if someone wants something: *Rhys offered him an apple*

hold out: *I held out my ticket for him to check*

tender: *She has tendered her resignation*

▷ *noun* **2** something that someone offers you: *He had refused several excellent job offers*

proposition: *I made her a proposition*

tender: *a tender for a public contract*

see also **tender**

offering see **present**

offhand see **careless**, **casual**

office see **department**, **room**

officer see **official**

official *adjective* **1** approved by someone in authority: *the official figures*

authorized: *the authorized biography*

certified: *a certified accountant*

formal: *No formal announcement has been made*

licensed: *a licensed doctor*

▷ *noun* **2** someone in authority: *a senior UN official*

executive: *a senior bank executive*

officer: *a local authority education officer*

representative: *trade union representatives*

see also **formal**

officialdom see **bureaucracy**

offset see **compensate**, **counteract**

offspring see child, young

often adverb happening many times: They often spent Christmas at Prescott Hill
  frequently: He was frequently depressed
  repeatedly: Both men have repeatedly denied the allegations

ogle see stare

OK see all right, correct, safe, tolerable
see right

okay see all right, correct, right, safe, tolerable, yes

okay or **OK** adjective informal acceptable or satisfactory: Is it okay if I come by myself?
  acceptable: It is becoming more acceptable for women to drink
  all right: if it's all right with you
see also all right, correct, right

old adjective **1** having lived for a long time: an old lady
  2 in the past: my old art teacher
see word studies **old**
see also former, parent, stale

olden see past

old-fashioned adjective no longer fashionable: old-fashioned shoes
  antiquated: An antiquated system
  archaic: archaic practices such as these
  dated: Some of the language sounds quite dated
  obsolete: So much equipment becomes obsolete almost as soon as it's made
  outdated: outdated attitudes
  outmoded: toiling in outmoded factories
  out of date: a make of car that is now out of date
  passé: Punk is passé
see also out of date, stuffy

omen noun a sign of what will happen: Her appearance at this moment is an omen of disaster
  sign: people who look to the skies for signs
  warning: a warning of trouble to come
see also premonition

ominous adjective suggesting that something bad will happen: an ominous silence
  sinister: a sinister message
  threatening: a threatening sky
see also sinister

omit verb to not include something: Omit the salt in this recipe
  exclude: Women felt excluded form the workplace
  leave out: The Spaniard has been left out of the team
  miss out: What about Sally? You've missed her out!
  skip: It is all too easy to skip meals
see also exclude, fail, forget, neglect

on see about

on account of see by virtue of

on edge see restless

on guard see alert

on hand see handy

on the cards see probable

on the dot see exactly, prompt

on the whole see as a rule

on time see punctual

once in a while see sometimes

once more see again

one see only, single

onerous see formidable

one-sided see biased

one-sidedness see favouritism

one-time see previous

ongoing see current

onlooker see spectator, witness

only adverb **1** involving one person or thing: Only Keith knows whether he will continue
  just: It's not just a financial matter
  merely: Watson was far from being

merely a furniture expert
purely: a racing machine, designed purely for speed
simply: Most of the damage was simply because of fallen trees
solely: decisions based solely upon what we see in magazines
▷ adjective **2** having no other examples: their only hit single
one: My one aim is to look after the horses well
sole: Our sole intention is to reunite her with her baby
see also **single**

only just see **hardly**

onset see **start**

onslaught see **attack**

onus see **responsibility**

ooze see **leak**

opaque see **cloudy, obscure**

open verb **1** to cause something not to be closed: She opened the door
uncover: When the seedlings sprout, uncover the tray
undo: I managed secretly to undo a corner of the parcel
unlock: She unlocked the case
▷ adjective **2** not closed: an open box of chocolates
ajar: He left the door ajar
uncovered: The uncovered bucket in the corner stank
undone: pictures of him with his shirt undone
unlocked: an unlocked room
3 not trying to deceive someone: He had always been open with her
candid: I haven't been completely candid with him
frank: My client has been less than frank with me
honest: He had been honest with her and she had tricked him!
see also **bare, candid, flexible, frank, impressionable, naked, spread, start, straightforward,**
uncover

opening adjective **1** coming first: the opening day of the season
first: the first night of the play
inaugural: his inaugural address
initial: the aim of this initial meeting
introductory: an introductory offer
▷ noun **2** the first part of something: the opening of the film
beginning: the beginning of the book
commencement formal: at the commencement of the course
start: four years after the start of the Great War
3 a hole or gap: a narrow opening in the fence
chink: a chink in the wall
cleft: a narrow cleft in the rocks
crack: Kathryn had seen him through a crack in the curtains
gap: the wind tearing through gaps in the window frames
hole: a hole in the wall
slot: a slot in which to insert a coin
space: a half-inch space between the curtains
vent: Steam escaped from the vent at the front of the machine
see also **beginning, breach, chance, first, gap, hole, start**

open-minded see **tolerant**

operate see **act, behave, drive, function, use**

operation see **action, campaign, enterprise, undertaking, use**

opinion noun a belief or view: I wasn't asking for your opinion
assessment: What is your assessment of the situation?
belief: his religious beliefs
estimation: He has gone down considerably in my estimation
judgment: In your judgment, what has changed?
point of view: Thanks for your point of view, John

view: Make your views known to your local MP

viewpoint: to include as many viewpoints as possible
see also **advice, belief, feeling, idea, judgment, thought, verdict, view, viewpoint**

opinionated see **narrow-minded**

opponent see **competitor, enemy, rival**

opportune see **favourable, lucky**

opportunity see **chance, occasion, turn**

oppose verb to disagree with something: protesters opposing planned nuclear tests
fight against: a lifetime fighting against racism
resist: They resisted our attempts to modernize
speak out against: He spoke out strongly against some of the radical ideas
see also **contest, disagree, object, protest, resist**

opposed see **different, opposite**

opposite adjective **1** completely different to something: I take the opposite view to you
conflicting: three powers with conflicting interests
contrary: He has a contrary opinion to mine
contrasting: two men with completely contrasting backgrounds
opposed: This was a straight conflict of directly opposed aims
reverse: The wrong attitude will have exactly the reverse effect
▷ noun **2** a completely different person or thing: He was the complete opposite of Raymond
antithesis formal: The antithesis of the Middle Eastern buyer is the Japanese
contrary: I'm not a feminist, quite the contrary

converse: Don't you think that the converse might also be possible?
reverse: This didn't upset him at all, in fact quite the reverse
see also **reverse**

opposition noun disagreement about something: Much of the opposition to this plan has come from the media
disapproval: His action had been greeted with almost universal disapproval
hostility: There is hostility to this method among traditionalists
resistance: Initially I met resistance from my own family
see also **competition, competitor, conflict, disagreement, objection**

oppress see **bully, persecute**

oppressed adjective treated cruelly or unfairly: a member of an oppressed minority
abused: those who work with abused children
downtrodden: the downtrodden, bored housewife

oppression noun cruel or unfair treatment: the oppression of black people throughout history
persecution: the persecution of minorities
tyranny: The 1930s was a decade of tyranny in Europe
see also **abuse**

oppressive see **stuffy, unbearable**

oppressor see **bully**

opt see **vote**

opt for see **choose, pick, select**

optimistic adjective hopeful about the future: an optimistic mood
buoyant: She was in a buoyant mood
confident: I am confident that everything will come out right in time
hopeful: I am hopeful this misunderstanding will be rectified
positive: a positive frame of mind

sanguine: *They have begun to take a more sanguine view*

option *see* **choice**

opulence *see* **luxury**

opulent *see* **luxurious, rich, wealthy**

oral *adjective* spoken rather than written: *oral history*
  spoken: *the spoken word*
  verbal: *a verbal agreement*
  see also **exam**

orange *noun or adjective*

orchestra *see* **band**

orchestrate *see* **stage**

ordain *see* **impose, order**

ordeal *noun* a difficult and unpleasant experience: *the ordeal of being arrested*
  hardship: *One of the worst hardships is having so little time*
  nightmare: *Taking my son Peter to a restaurant was a nightmare*
  torture: *Waiting for the result was torture*
  trial: *the trials of adolescence*
  tribulation *formal*: *the trials and tribulations of everyday life*
  see also **experience, hell**

order *noun* **1** a command by someone in authority: *I don't take orders from him any more*
  command: *The tanker failed to respond to a command to stop*
  decree: *He issued a decree ordering all armed groups to disband*
  dictate: *to ensure that the dictates of the Party are followed*
  directive: *a new EU directive*
  instruction: *MPs defied a party instruction to vote against the Bill*
  2 a well-organized situation: *the wish to impose order upon confusion*
  harmony: *the ordered harmony of the universe*
  regularity: *the chessboard regularity of their fields*
  symmetry: *the beauty and symmetry of a snowflake*
  ▷ *verb* **3** to tell someone to do something: *He ordered his men to stop firing*
  command: *He commanded his troops to attack*
  decree: *the rule that decreed no alcohol on the premises*
  direct: *a court order directing the group to leave the land*
  instruct: *The family has instructed solicitors to sue Thomson*
  ordain: *Nehru ordained that socialism should rule*
  see also **arrange, command, instruct, require, routine, rule, sequence, tell**

orderly *adjective* well-organized or well-arranged: *Their vehicles were parked in orderly rows*
  neat: *She put her wet clothes in a neat pile in the corner*
  regular: *regular rows of wooden huts*
  tidy: *a tidy desk*
  see also **neat, tidy**

ordinary *adjective* not special or different: *an ordinary day*
  conventional: *a respectable married woman with conventional opinions*
  normal: *He lives a normal life*
  regular: *the regular barman*
  routine: *a routine procedure*
  standard: *It was standard practice*
  usual: *all the usual inner-city problems*
  see also **common, conventional, everyday, humble, natural, normal, regular, routine**

organization *noun* **1** a group or business: *charitable organizations*
  association: *research associations*
  body: *the Chairman of the policemen's representative body*
  company: *the Ford Motor Company*
  confederation: *the Confederation of Indian Industry*

group: an environmental group
institution: financial institutions
outfit informal: We are a professional outfit
2 the planning and arranging of something: He was involved in the organization of conferences and seminars

organizing: His duties involved the organizing of transport
planning: The trip needs careful planning
structuring: improvements in the structuring of courses
see also **body, business, firm, movement, society, structure**

organize verb to plan and arrange something: Organizing a wedding takes time

arrange: The bank can arrange a loan for students
establish: How do you establish a workable system?
jack up New Zealand informal: to jack up a demonstration
plan: A team meeting was planned for last night
set up: This tribunal was set up by the government
see also **arrange, book, conduct, group, set up, stage**

organized see **efficient, ready**

organizing see **organization**

origin noun **1** the beginning or cause of something: the origins of the custom

derivation: The derivation of its name is obscure
root: His sense of guilt had its roots in his childhood
source: the source of the problem
2 someone's family background: She was of Swedish origin
ancestry: Noel can trace her ancestry to the 11th century
descent: All the contributors were of African descent
extraction: a Malaysian citizen of Australian extraction
lineage: a respectable family of ancient lineage
stock: people of Mediterranean stock
see also **beginning, cause, source, stock**

original adjective **1** being the first example of something: the original owner of the cottage

first: Her first reaction was disgust
initial: His initial response was to disbelieve her
2 imaginative and clever: a stunningly original idea
fresh: These designers are full of fresh ideas
new: These proposals aren't new
novel: a novel way of losing weight
see also **first, individual**

originality see **imagination**

originate see **begin, create, invent, start**

originator see **source**

ornament noun an object that you display: a shelf containing ornaments
adornment: a building without any adornments
bauble: a Christmas tree decorated with coloured baubles
decoration: The only wall decorations are candles
knick-knack: Her flat is spilling over with knick-knacks
trinket: She sold trinkets to tourists
see also **decorate**

ornate see **elaborate, fancy**

orthodox see **conventional, proper, standard**

ostentatious adjective intended to impress people with appearances: an ostentatious lifestyle
extravagant: They make extravagant shows of generosity
flamboyant: flamboyant clothes

flashy: *a flashy sports car*
grandiose: *the grandiose building which housed the mayor's offices*
pretentious: *This pub was smaller and less pretentious*
showy: *large, showy flowers*
see also **pompous, pretentious, vain**

others see **remainder, rest**

oust see **overthrow**

out loud see **aloud**

out of danger see **safe**

out of shape see **crooked**

out of the ordinary see **exceptional, uncommon**

out of the question see **impossible**

out of your mind see **insane**

out-and-out see **total, utter**

outback see **country**

outbreak *noun* a sudden occurrence of something: *the outbreak of war*
eruption: *this sudden eruption of violence*
explosion: *the global explosion of interest in rugby*
see also **burst, rash**

outcome see **result**

outcry see **protest**

outdated see **old-fashioned, out of date**

outdo *verb* to do something better than another person: *She would love to outdo her sister Manuela*
go one better than: *You always have to go one better than anyone else*
outshine: *Jesse has begun to outshine me in sports*
surpass: *determined to surpass the achievements of his older brothers*
top: *How are you going to top that?*
see also **beat, pass, top**

outdoor see **outside**

outdoors see **country**

outer see **outside**

outfit see **clothes, organization, provide, set**

outgoing see **sociable**

outing see **trip**

outlandish see **bizarre, eccentric**

outlaw see **ban, forbid, prohibit**

outlawed see **illegal**

outlay see **cost**

outline *verb* 1 to describe something in a general way: *The mayor outlined his plan to clean up the town's image*
sketch: *Tudjman sketched his vision of a future Bosnia*
summarize: *The article can be summarized in three sentences*
▷ *noun* 2 a general description of something: *an outline of the survey's findings*
rundown informal: *Here's a rundown of the options*
summary: *a summary of the report*
synopsis: *a brief synopsis of the book*
3 the shape of something: *the hazy outline of the goalposts*
contours: *the contours of her body*
figure: *Alistair saw the dim figure of Rose in the chair*
form: *She'd never been so glad to see his bulky form*
shape: *dark shapes of herons silhouetted against the moon*
silhouette: *the dark silhouette of the castle ruins*
see also **form, shape, summary**

outlive see **survive**

outlook *noun* 1 your general attitude towards life: *I adopted a positive outlook on life*
attitude: *Being unemployed produces negative attitudes to work*
perspective: *It gave him a new perspective on life*
view: *an optimistic view of the future*
2 the future prospects of something: *The economic outlook is one of rising unemployment*
future: *a conference on the country's political future*
prospects: *a detailed review of the*

company's prospects
see also **attitude, prospect**

outlying see **distant, far, remote**

outmoded see **old-fashioned, out of date**

out of date *adjective* no longer useful: *The information is already out of date*
   antiquated: *an antiquated system*
   archaic: *archaic practices such as these*
   obsolete: *So much equipment becomes obsolete almost as soon as it's made*
   old-fashioned: *old-fashioned shoes*
   outdated: *outdated attitudes*
   outmoded: *toiling in outmoded factories*
   see also **old-fashioned**

out-of-the-way see **distant**

outpost see **colony**

outrage see **anger, horrify, offend, shock**

outright see **complete, pure, straight, total, utter**

outset see **beginning, start**

outshine see **outdo**

outside *noun* **1** the outer part of something: *The moth was on the outside of the glass*
   exterior: *the exterior of the building*
   facade: *the refurbishing of the cathedral's facade*
   face: *the face of the watch*
   surface: *the surface of the road*
   ▷ *adjective* **2** not inside: *an outside toilet*
   exterior: *the oven's exterior surfaces*
   external: *the external walls*
   outdoor: *outdoor activities*
   outer: *the outer suburbs of the city*
   outward: *with no outward sign of injury*
   surface: *Its total surface area was seven thousand square feet*

outskirts *plural noun* the edges of an

area: *the outskirts of New York*
   edge: *We were on a hill, right on the edge of town*
   perimeter: *the perimeter of the airport*
   periphery: *countries on the periphery of Europe*

outspan *verb* South African to relax: *Let's take a break and just outspan for a while*
   laze: *Fred lazed in an easy chair*
   relax: *I ought to relax and stop worrying*
   rest: *He rested for a while before starting work again*
   take it easy: *Try to take it easy for a week or two*

outspoken see **blunt**

outstanding *adjective* **1** extremely good: *an outstanding tennis player*
   brilliant: *a brilliant performance*
   excellent: *the recording quality is excellent*
   exceptional: *children with exceptional ability*
   first-class: *first-class service*
   first-rate: *The show was first-rate*
   great: *great cultural achievements*
   superb: *a superb 18-hole golf course*
   2 still owed: *The total debt outstanding is $70 billion*
   due: *They sent me £100 and advised me that no further payment was due*
   overdue: *pay overdue salaries*
   owing: *There is still some money owing for the rent*
   payable: *The amount payable is £175*
   unpaid: *The bills remained unpaid*
   see also **brilliant, excellent, exceptional, fine, first-rate, major, prize, superb**

outstrip see **beat, pass, top**

outward see **outside**

over *preposition* **1** more than a particular amount: *It cost over a million dollars*
   above: *speeds above 50 mph*

exceeding: *a budget exceeding $700 million a year*

in excess of: *a fortune in excess of 150 million pounds*

more than: *The airport had been closed for more than a year*

▷ adjective **2** completely finished: *I am glad it's all over*

at an end: *The matter is now at an end*

complete: *The work of restoring the farmhouse is complete*

done: *When her deal is done, the client emerges with her purchase*

finished: *once the season's finished*

gone: *Any chance of winning was now gone*

past: *The time for loyalty is past*

up: *when the six weeks were up*
see also **above, past**

over- see **too**

over the moon see **joyful**

overall see **general**

overbearing see **bossy**

overcast see **cloudy, dark, dull**

overcome verb to manage to deal with something: *Molly had overcome her fear of flying*

conquer: *He has never conquered his addiction to smoking*

get the better of: *She didn't allow her emotions to get the better of her*

master: *His genius alone has mastered every crisis*

surmount: *I realized I had to surmount the language barrier*

triumph over: *a symbol of good triumphing over evil*

vanquish *literary: the man who helped vanquish Napoleon*
see also **beat, crush, resolve, subdue, vanquish**

overconfident see **cocky**

overdo see **exaggerate**

overdose see **excess**

overdue see **late, outstanding**

overestimate see **exaggerate**

overflow see **flood**

overflowing see **crowded**

overheads see **upkeep**

overhear see **hear**

overjoyed see **glad**

overlay see **cover, spread**

overlook verb to ignore or fail to notice something: *We tend to overlook warning signals about our health*

disregard: *The police must not be allowed to disregard human rights*

forget: *She never forgets his birthday*

ignore: *For years her talents were ignored by the film industry*

miss: *His searching eye never missed a detail*

neglect: *She never neglects her duties*

turn a blind eye to: *Are teachers turning a blind eye to these issues?*
see also **excuse, face, forget, ignore, miss, neglect**

overly see **too**

overpower see **subdue**

overrule verb to reject a decision officially: *The Court of Appeal overruled this decision*

overturn: *when the Russian parliament overturned his decision*

reverse: *They will not reverse the decision to increase prices*
see also **overturn, reverse**

overseas see **foreign**

oversee verb to make sure a job is done properly: *Get a supervisor to oversee the work*

be in charge of: *She is in charge of day-to-day operations*

coordinate: *Government officials have been sent to coordinate the relief effort*

direct: *his coolness in directing the rescue of the hostages*

manage: *Within two years, he was managing the project*

preside: Mr Brown will be presiding over the day's events

supervise: He supervises the vineyards
see also **direct, supervise**

oversight see **mistake**

overstate see **exaggerate**

overt see **obvious**

overtake see **pass**

overthrow verb to remove someone from power by force: The government was overthrown in a military coup

bring down: They brought down the government by withdrawing their support

depose: He fled to Hawaii after being deposed as president

oust: His opponents tried to oust him with a vote of no confidence

topple: the revolution which toppled the regime

overturn verb **1** to knock something over: Alex jumped up so violently that he overturned his glass

capsize: I didn't count on his capsizing the raft

knock down: Isabel rose so abruptly that she knocked down her chair

knock over: Emma knocked over the box of cornflakes

tip over: He tipped the table over in front of him

topple: Winds and rain toppled trees and electricity lines

upset: Don't upset the piles of sheets under the box

2 to reject a decision officially: when the Russian parliament overturned his decision

overrule: The Court of Appeal overruled this decision

reverse: They will not reverse the decision to increase prices
see also **abolish, overrule, reverse, upset**

overused see **stock**

overweight adjective too fat, and therefore unhealthy: Being overweight increases your risk of heart problems

fat: I could eat what I liked without getting fat

hefty: She was quite a hefty woman

obese: Obese people tend to have higher blood pressure than lean people

stout: a stout man with grey hair
see also **tubby**

overwhelm see **beat**

overwork see **strain**

overwrought see **hysterical**

owing see **outstanding**

own adjective **1** belonging to a particular person or thing: She stayed in her own house

personal: That's my personal opinion

private: 76 bedrooms, all with private bathrooms

▷ verb **2** to have something that belongs to you: His father owns a local pub

have: They have a house in France

keep: His father kept a village shop

possess: I would give her everything I possess

on your own adverb without other people: I work best on my own

alone: She lives alone

by oneself: I didn't know if I could raise a child by myself

independently: several people working independently

unaided: She brought us up completely unaided
see also **have, personal**

own up see **confess**

owner noun the person to whom something belongs: the owner of the store

possessor: the proud possessor of a truly incredible voice

proprietor: the proprietor of a local restaurant

ownership see **possession**

p

pace see **rate, speed, walk**

pacify verb to calm down someone who is angry: *She shrieked again, refusing to be pacified*
appease: *The offer has not appeased separatists*
calm: *A business lunch helped calm her nerves*
mollify: *The investigation was undertaken to mollify pressure groups*
placate: *He went aboard to placate the angry passengers*
soothe: *She took him in his arms and soothed him*

pack see **cram, fill, group, load, stuff**

package see **tender**

packed see **crowded, full**

pact see **agreement, understanding**

padlock see **lock**

pagan see **heathen**

pageant see **parade**

pain noun 1 an unpleasant feeling of physical hurt: *I felt a sharp pain in my lower back*
ache: *Poor posture can cause neck aches*
discomfort: *Steve had some discomfort but no real pain*
irritation: *These oils may cause irritation to sensitive skin*
soreness: *The soreness lasted for about six weeks*
trouble: *back trouble*
twinge: *He felt a slight twinge in his hamstring*
2 a feeling of deep unhappiness: *the pain of rejection*
agony: *the agony of divorce*
anguish: *Mark looked at him in anguish*
distress: *Jealousy causes distress and painful emotions*
grief: *The grief soon gave way to anger*
misery: *All that money brought nothing but sadness and misery*
see also **annoyance, distress, grieve, nuisance, pest, sorrow**

pain in the neck see **annoyance, pest**

painful adjective 1 causing emotional pain: *painful memories*
distressing: *one of the most distressing episodes in his life*
grievous: *Their loss would be a grievous blow to our industry*
saddening: *a saddening experience*
unpleasant: *an unpleasant truth*
2 causing physical pain: *a painful knock on the knee*
aching: *his aching joints*
excruciating: *an excruciating headache*
sore: *a sore throat*
tender: *My leg is very tender and sore*
see also **sore, tender, uncomfortable**

painless see **easy**

pains see **care**

painstaking see **careful, thorough**

paint see **colour, draw**

painting see **picture**

pair up see **team**

pal see **china, companion, friend**

palatable see **tasty**

pale adjective rather white or without much colour: *Migrating*

birds filled the pale sky
ashen: *He fell back, shocked, his face ashen*
colourless: *a colourless liquid*
faded: *a girl in faded jeans*
sallow: *His face was sallow and shiny with sweat*
wan: *He looked wan and tired*
white: *He turned white and began to stammer*
see also **light, soft**
palpable *see* **evident, obvious**
paltry *see* **meagre, trivial, unimportant, worthless**
pamper *see* **spoil**
pamphlet *see* **leaflet**
pan *see* **criticize**
pandemonium *see* **noise**
pander to *see* **humour**
panel *see* **council**
pang of conscience *see* **regret**
panic *noun* **1** a very strong feeling of fear or anxiety: *The earthquake caused panic among the population*
alarm: *She sat up in alarm*
dismay: *She discovered to her dismay that she was pregnant*
fear: *my fear of the dark*
fright: *To hide my fright I asked a question*
hysteria: *mass hysteria*
terror: *She shook with terror*
▷ *verb* **2** to become afraid or anxious: *Guests panicked when the bomb exploded*
become hysterical: *Miss Brady became hysterical when he produced the gun*
go to pieces: *England went to pieces when they conceded a goal*
lose your nerve: *They lost their nerve and pulled out of the deal*
see also **alarm, fear, horror, scare**
panning *see* **criticism**
panorama *see* **scene, scenery, view**
pant *see* **gasp**

pantomime *see* **play**
parade *noun* a line of people moving as a display: *A military parade marched through the streets*
cavalcade: *a cavalcade of limousines and police motorcycles*
march: *Organizers expect 300,000 protesters to join the march*
pageant: *a traditional Christmas pageant*
procession: *religious processions*
tattoo: *the world-famous Edinburgh military tattoo*
paradise *see* **heaven**
paragon *see* **example, ideal, model**
paragraph *noun*
parallel *see* **like, relationship, resemblance, resemble**
paralyse *verb* to make someone lose feeling and movement: *Her sister had been paralysed in a road accident*
cripple: *He heaved his crippled leg into an easier position*
disable: *He was disabled by polio*
see also **cripple, numb, shock**
paralysed *see* **numb**
paramount *see* **supreme, ultimate**
paraphernalia *see* **equipment**
parched *see* **dry**
pardon *see* **excuse, forgive, forgiveness, spare**
parent *noun* your father or your mother: *I told my parents I was moving out*
father: *Her father was furious*
mother: *the mother of two girls*
old *Australian, New Zealand informal*: *a visit to the olds*
patriarch: *a domineering patriarch*
parentage *see* **stock**
parish *see* **local**
parity *see* **balance**
parody *noun* an amusing imitation of someone else's style: *a parody of an American sitcom*
imitation: *I can do a pretty good*

imitation of him

satire: a sharp satire on the American political process

spoof informal: a spoof on Hollywood life

takeoff informal: She did a brilliant takeoff of the Queen

part noun **1** a piece or section of something: I like that part of Edinburgh

bit: a bit of paper

fraction: a fraction of a second

fragment: fragments of glass

piece: a piece of cheese

portion: Damage was confined to a small portion of the castle

section: a large orchestra, with a vast percussion section

2 a person's involvement in something: He tried to conceal his part in the accident

capacity: He has served the club in many capacities

duty: My duty is to look after the animals

function: Their main function is to raise capital for industry

involvement: You have no proof of my involvement in anything

role: the drug's role in preventing infection

take part in verb to do an activity with other people: Thousands took part in the demonstrations

be instrumental in: He was instrumental in tracking down the killers

be involved in: My grandparents were involved in the Methodist church

have a hand in: He had a hand in three of the goals

join in: I hope that everyone will be able to join in the fun

participate in: They expected him to participate in the ceremony

play a part in: He continued to play a part in drug operations from prison

see also **aspect, attachment, bit, factor, fitting, piece, portion, quantity, section, separate, split**

partial see biased, incomplete

partiality see prejudice

partially see partly

participate verb to take part in an activity: Over half the population participate in sport

be involved in: HMS Cardiff was also involved in the exercise

engage in: They have refused to engage in all-party talks

enter into: We entered into discussions with them weeks ago

join in: Their rivals refused to join in any price war

take part: The oldest car taking part was built in 1907

see also **play**

participate in see take part in

particular adjective **1** relating to only one thing or person: That particular place is dangerous

distinct: The book is divided into two distinct parts

exact: Do you think I could get the exact thing I want?

express: I bought the camera for the express purpose of taking railway photographs

peculiar: This is not a problem peculiar to London

precise: the precise location of the ship

specific: There are several specific problems to be dealt with

2 especially great or intense: Pay particular attention to the forehead

exceptional: children with exceptional ability

marked: a marked increase in crime in the area

notable: Two other notable events took place last week

singular: It was a goal of singular brilliance
special: a special occasion
uncommon: Both are blessed with an uncommon ability to fix things
3 not easily satisfied: Ted was very particular about the colours he used
choosy informal: Skiers should be choosy about the insurance policy they buy
exacting: exacting standards of craftsmanship
fastidious: He was fastidious about his appearance
fussy: She is very fussy about her food
meticulous: meticulous attention to detail
see also **detail, fussy, personal, precise, special, strict**
partition see **divide, division**
partly adverb to some extent but not completely: This is partly my fault
in part formal: The levels of blood glucose depend in part on what you eat
in some measure formal: Power is in some measure an act of will
partially: Jo is partially sighted
to some degree: These statements are, to some degree, correct
to some extent: Her concern is, to some extent, understandable
partner noun **1** either member of a couple in a relationship: My partner moved in with me last year
husband or **wife**: Are husbands and wives included in the invitation?
mate: She has found her ideal mate
spouse: Anything left to your spouse is free from inheritance tax
2 the person someone is doing something with: my tennis partner
companion: her travelling companion
team-mate: his team-mate at Ferrari
see also **colleague, companion**
party noun **1** a social event where

people enjoy themselves: Most teenagers like to go to parties
celebration: a New Year's Eve celebration
function: a charity function at the hotel
gathering: a gathering of friends and relatives
get-together informal: a family get-together
hooley or **hoolie** New Zealand: a hooley down on the beach
reception: a wedding reception
2 an organization for people with the same political beliefs: his resignation as party leader
alliance: The two parties have agreed to form an electoral alliance
clique: the clique attached to Prime Minister
coalition: a coalition of right-wing and religious factions
faction: the party's small pro-European faction
grouping: two main political groupings pressing for independence
3 a group who are doing something together: a research party of scientists
band: a small but dedicated band of supporters
crew: a ship's crew
gang: a gang of criminals
squad: the West Indies squad to tour Australia
team: Each consultant has a team of doctors under him
unit: the health services research unit
see also **band, celebrate, celebration, company, function, group, individual, side**
pass verb **1** to exceed or go past something: He gave a triumphant wave as he passed the winning post
exceed: The demand for places at some schools exceeds the supply
go beyond: Did your relationship go

beyond a close friendship?

outdo: The Colombian fans outdid the home supporters in fervour

outstrip: Demand continues to outstrip supply

overtake: Britain's lottery will this year overtake Japan's as the world's biggest

surpass: He was determined to surpass the achievements of his brothers

2 to be successful in a test: Wendy has just passed her driving test

get through: I got through my banking exams last year

graduate: He graduated in engineering

qualify: I qualified as a doctor

succeed: the skills and qualities needed to succeed

▷ noun **3** a document that allows you to go somewhere: Don't let any cars onto the land unless they've got a pass

identification: Passport control asked me if I had any further identification

passport: You should take your passport with you when changing money

ticket: I'm not going to renew my season ticket

see also **disappear, permit, vanish**

pass around see **distribute**

pass away see **die**

pass down see **hand down**

pass on see **communicate, die, hand down, will**

pass out see **faint**

pass round see **distribute**

passable see **acceptable, decent, satisfactory, tolerable**

passage noun **1** a space that connects two places: He cleared a passage for himself through the crammed streets

channel: a drainage channel

course: the river's twisting course

path: A group of reporters blocked the path

road: the road between Jerusalem and Bethlehem

route: the most direct route to the town centre

way: This is the way in

2 a narrow space that connects one place with another: up some stairs and along a narrow passage towards a door

aisle: the frozen food aisle

corridor: They sat crowded together in the hospital corridor

hall: The lights were on in the hall and in the bedroom

lobby: the cramped pitch-dark lobby

3 a section of a book or piece of music: a passage from the Bible

excerpt: an excerpt from her speech

extract: an extract from his new book

quotation: a favourite quotation from St Augustine

section: a section from the first movement of Beethoven's Eroica symphony

see also **extract, journey, path**

passé see **old-fashioned**

passing see **temporary**

passion noun **1** a strong feeling of physical attraction: the passion had gone from their relationship

desire: sexual desire

infatuation: Daisy's infatuation for the doctor

love: our love for each other

lust: He is obsessed by his lust for her

2 any strong emotion: He spoke with great passion

emotion: Her voice trembled with emotion

excitement: I was in a state of great excitement

fire: His speeches were full of fire

intensity: His intensity alarmed me
warmth: He greeted us both with warmth and affection
zeal: his zeal for teaching
see also **feeling, heat, love, weakness**

passionate adjective expressing very strong feelings about something: I'm a passionate believer in public art
ardent: ardent supporters of capital punishment
emotional: an emotional farewell
heartfelt: My heartfelt sympathy goes out to all the relatives
impassioned: He made an impassioned appeal for peace
intense: intense hatred
strong: Many viewers have strong opinions about violence on TV
see also **ardent, crazy, enthusiastic, fanatical, fervent, intense, romantic**

passive adjective submissive or not playing an active part: His passive attitude made things easier for me
docile: docile, obedient children
receptive: The voters had seemed receptive to his ideas
resigned: She was already resigned to losing her home
submissive: Most doctors want their patients to be submissive
see also **apathetic, uninterested**

passport see **pass, permit**

past the past noun **1** the period of time before the present: We would like to put the past behind us
antiquity: famous monuments of classical antiquity
days gone by: This brings back memories of days gone by
former times: In former times he would have been clapped in irons
long ago: The old men told stories of long ago
▷ adjective **2** happening or existing

before the present: details of his past activities
ancient: ancient history
bygone: a bygone era
former: Remember him as he was in his former years
olden: We were talking about the olden days on his farm
previous: She has a teenage daughter from a previous marriage
▷ preposition **3** situated on the other side of somewhere: It's just past the church there
beyond: Beyond the garden was a small orchard
by: She was sitting in a chair by the window
over: He lived in the house over the road
see also **former, over, previous**

paste see **bond, glue, stick**

pastel see **light, soft**

pasteurized see **pure**

pastime noun a hobby or something done for pleasure: His favourite pastime is snooker
activity: activities range from canoeing to birdwatching
diversion: Finger painting is very messy but an excellent diversion
hobby: My hobbies are squash and swimming
recreation: Saturday afternoon is for recreation and outings
see also **activity, hobby, interest**

pasture see **field**

patch see **mend, repair**

patch together see **piece together**

patch up see **fix, repair**

patchy see **irregular, uneven**

patent see **manifest**

path noun **1** a strip of ground for people to walk on: We followed the paths along the clifftops
footpath: It is accessible only by footpath

pathway: *a pathway leading towards the nearby river*

towpath: *He took a cycle trip along a canal towpath*

track: *We set off over a rough mountain track*

trail: *He was following a broad trail through the trees*

way: *the Pennine Way*

2 the space ahead of someone as they move along: *A group of reporters stood in his path*

course: *obstacles blocking our course*

direction: *St Andrews is 10 miles in the opposite direction*

passage: *Two men elbowed a passage through the shoppers*

route: *All escape routes were blocked by armed police*

way: *Get out of my way!*

see also **course, direction, line, passage, route, way**

pathetic *adjective* **1** causing someone to feel pity: *She now looked small, shrunken, and pathetic*

heartbreaking: *a heartbreaking succession of miscarriages*

sad: *He seemed a rather sad figure*

2 very poor or unsuccessful: *pathetic excuses*

feeble: *This is a particularly feeble argument*

lamentable: *a lamentable display by the league leaders*

pitiful: *They are paid pitiful wages*

poor: *The flat was in a poor state of repair*

sorry: *Their oil industry is in a sorry state*

see also **hopeless, inadequate, lame, miserable, sad, sorry**

pathway *see* **path**

patience *noun* the ability to stay calm in a difficult situation: *It was exacting work and required all his patience*

calmness: *calmness under pressure*

composure: *He regained his composure and went on to win the match*

cool *slang*: *The big Irishman was on the verge of losing his cool*

restraint: *They behaved with more restraint than I'd expected*

tolerance: *a low tolerance of errors*

patient *adjective* **1** staying calm in a difficult situation: *Please be patient – your cheque will arrive*

calm: *She is usually a calm and diplomatic woman*

composed: *a composed and charming manner*

long-suffering: *long-suffering train commuters*

philosophical: *He is philosophical about the defeat*

serene: *She looks dreamily into the distance, serene, calm and happy*

▷ *noun* **2** a person receiving medical treatment: *patients who wish to change their doctor*

case: *He is a suitable case for treatment*

invalid: *elderly invalids*

sick person: *a ward full of very sick people*

sufferer: *asthma sufferers*

patriarch *see* **parent**

patrol *see* **guard**

patron *see* **customer**

patronize *see* **frequent**

patronizing *see* **superior**

pattern *noun* **1** a decorative design of repeated shapes: *red and purple thread stitched into a pattern of flames*

design: *tableware decorated with a blackberry design*

motif: *a rose motif*

2 a diagram or shape used as a guide for making something: *sewing patterns*

design: *They drew up the design for*

the house in a week
diagram: Follow the diagram on page 20
plan: a plan of the garden
stencil: flower stencils
template: Make a paper template of the seat of the chair
see also **design, routine, sequence**

paunch see **stomach**

pause verb **1** to stop doing something for a short time: On leaving, she paused for a moment at the door
break: They broke for lunch
delay: Various problems delayed the launch
halt: Striking workers halted production at the plant
rest: He rested briefly before pressing on
take a break: He needs to take a break from work
wait: I waited to see how she responded
▷ noun **2** a short period when activity stops: There was a pause while the barmaid set down two plates
break: Do you want to have a little break?
halt: Agricultural production was brought to a halt
interruption: The sudden interruption stopped her in mid-flow
interval: I had a drink during the interval
rest: I think he's due for a rest now
stoppage: Miners have voted for a one-day stoppage next month
see also **break, gap, halt, hesitate, interval, wait**

pay verb **1** to give money to someone to settle a debt: You can pay by credit card
compensate: Farmers could be compensated for their loss of subsidies
honour: The bank refused to honour

the cheque
settle: I settled the bill for our drinks
2 to give someone a benefit: It pays to be honest
be advantageous: It is easy to imagine cases where cheating is advantageous
be worthwhile: He believed the operation had been worthwhile
▷ noun **3** money paid to someone for work done: their complaints about pay and conditions
earnings: his earnings as an accountant
fee: solicitors' fees
income: a modest income
payment: a redundancy payment
salary: The lawyer was paid a good salary
wages: His wages have gone up
see also **income**

pay attention see **listen, watch**
pay attention to see **heed**
pay back see **repay, return**
pay for see **buy, finance, fund**
pay someone back see **retaliate, revenge**
pay tribute to see **praise**
payable see **outstanding**
payment noun an amount of money that is paid to someone: mortgage payments
advance: She was paid a £100,000 advance for her next two novels
deposit: A $50 deposit is required when ordering
instalment: The first instalment is payable on application
premium: higher insurance premiums
remittance: Please make your remittance payable in sterling
see also **charge, compensation, cost, pay, reward**

peace noun **1** a state of undisturbed calm and quiet: They left me in peace to recover from the funeral

calm: *the rural calm of Grand Rapids, Michigan*

quiet: *He wants some peace and quiet before his match*

silence: *They stood in silence*

stillness: *An explosion shattered the stillness of the night air*

tranquillity: *The hotel is a haven of tranquillity*

2 freedom from war: *The people do not believe that the leaders want peace*

armistice: *the armistice between North Korea and the United Nations*

cessation of hostilities: *a resolution calling for an immediate cessation of hostilities*

truce: *an uneasy truce between the two sides*

see also **calm, quiet, silence**

peaceful *adjective* quiet and calm: *a peaceful house in the heart of the countryside*

calm: *a calm spot amid the bustle of the city*

placid: *the placid waters of Lake Erie*

quiet: *The street was unnaturally quiet*

serene: *a beautiful, serene park*

still: *In the room it was very still*

tranquil: *the tranquil paradise of his native Antigua*

see also **quiet, relaxed**

peacefulness *see* **calm**

peak *noun* **1** the point at which something is at its greatest or best: *the peak of the morning rush hour*

climax: *The tournament is building up to a dramatic climax*

culmination: *The marriage was the culmination of an eight-month romance*

high point: *The high point of this trip was a day at the races*

zenith: *His career is now at its zenith*

2 the pointed top of a mountain: *snow-covered peaks*

brow: *He overtook a car as he approached the brow of a hill*

crest: *Burns was clear over the crest of the hill*

pinnacle: *He plunged 25 metres from a rocky pinnacle*

summit: *the first man to reach the summit of Mount Everest*

top: *the top of Mount Sinai*

▷ *verb* **3** to reach the highest point or greatest level: *His career peaked during the 1970s*

be at its height: *when trade union power was at its height*

climax: *a tour that climaxed with a three-night stint at Wembley Arena*

come to a head: *The siege came to a head with the death of a marshal*

culminate: *The celebration of the centenary will culminate with a dinner*

reach its highest point: *The stockmarket reached its highest point since the 1987 crash*

see also **top, ultimate**

peal *see* **ring, sound**

peasant *see* **yokel**

peculiar *adjective* **1** strange and perhaps unpleasant: *a very peculiar sense of humour*

bizarre: *bizarre behaviour*

curious: *a curious mixture of the ancient and modern*

funny: *Children get some funny ideas sometimes*

odd: *Something odd began to happen*

queer: *There's something queer going on*

strange: *There was something strange about the flickering blue light*

weird: *It must be weird to be so rich*

2 associated with one particular person or thing: *He has his own peculiar way of doing things*

distinctive: *She has a very distinctive laugh*

distinguishing: *Does he have any*

distinguishing features?
individual: *all part of her very individual personality*
personal: *cultivating their own personal style*
special: *Everyone has their own special problems or fears*
unique: *a feature unique to humans*
see also **bizarre, curious, funny, odd, particular, personal, special, strange, weird**

peddle see **sell**

pedestal see **base**

peek verb **1** to have a quick look at something: *She peeked at him through a crack in the wall*
glance: *He glanced at his watch*
peep: *Children came to peep at him round the doorway*
snatch a glimpse: *Spectators lined the route to snatch a glimpse of the Queen*
sneak a look: *We sneaked a look at his diary*
▷ noun **2** a quick look at something: *He took his first peek at the new course yesterday*
glance: *Trevor and I exchanged a glance*
glimpse: *Some people had waited all day to catch a glimpse of her*
look: *She took a last look in the mirror*
peep: *He took a peep at his watch*
see also **glance, look**

peep see **glance, peek**

peer see **noble**

peerless see **incomparable**

pellet see **ball**

pelt see **coat, hide**

penal institution see **prison**

penalize see **punish**

penalties see **sanctions**

penalty see **cost, punishment**

penchant see **taste, weakness**

penetrate see **pierce**

penetrating see **perceptive, shrill**

penitence see **regret**

penitent see **sorry**

penniless see **poor**

pensive see **serious, thoughtful**

pent-up adjective held back for a long time without release: *She had a lot of pent-up anger to release*
inhibited: *inhibited sexuality*
repressed: *repressed hostility*
suppressed: *Deep sleep allowed suppressed anxieties to surface*

people plural noun **1** men, women, and children: *Millions of people have lost their homes*
human beings: *The disease can be trapsmitted to human beings*
humanity: *crimes against humanity*
humans: *millions of years before humans appeared on earth*
mankind: *the evolution of mankind*
2 all the men, women, and children of a particular place: *It's a triumph for the American people*
citizens: *the citizens of New York City*
inhabitants: *the inhabitants of Hong Kong*
population: *Africa's rapidly rising population*
public: *the British public*
see also **kin, public, race, settle**

peppery see **hot**

perceive see **appreciate, discern, know, note, notice, see**

percentage see **proportion**

perceptible see **conspicuous, noticeable, visible**

perception see **intelligence, understanding**

perceptive adjective good at noticing or realizing things: *a perceptive account of the poet's life*
acute: *His relaxed exterior hides an extremely acute mind*
astute: *He made a series of astute business decisions*
aware: *They are politically very aware*

penetrating: He never stopped asking penetrating questions

sharp: He has a sharp eye and an excellent memory

see also **acute, astute, brilliant, keen, observant, sharp, shrewd, wise**

perfect adjective **1** of the highest standard and without fault: His English was perfect

expert: There is a great deal to learn from his expert approach

faultless: faultless technique

flawless: her flawless complexion

masterly: a masterly performance

polished: polished promotional skills

skilled: a skilled repair job

2 complete or absolute: They have a perfect right to say so

absolute: absolute nonsense

complete: The resignation came as a complete surprise

consummate: He acted the part with consummate skill

sheer: an act of sheer desperation

unmitigated: Last year's crop was an unmitigated disaster

utter: utter nonsense

▷ verb **3** to make something as good as it can be: The technique was perfected during the 1960s

hone: a chance to hone their skills

improve: Their French has improved enormously

polish: He spent time polishing the script

refine: Surgical techniques are constantly being refined

see also **complete, ideal, polish, utter**

perfectly see **quite**

perform verb **1** to carry out a task or action: people who have performed acts of bravery

carry out: Police believe the attacks were carried out by nationalists

complete: He completed the test in record time

do: He crashed trying to do a tricky manoeuvre

execute: The landing was skilfully executed

fulfil: Fulfil the tasks you have been allocated

2 to act, dance, or play music in public: students performing Shakespeare's Macbeth

act: acting in Tarantino's films

do: I've always wanted to do a one-man show on Broadway

play: His ambition is to play the part of Dracula

present: The company is presenting a new production of "Hamlet"

put on: The band are hoping to put on a UK show

stage: The group staged their first play in the late 1970s

see also **achieve, act, administer, appear, carry out, commit, conduct, do, fulfil, function**

perfume see **fragrance, smell**

perfumed see **fragrant, sweet**

perfunctory see **quick**

perhaps adverb maybe: Perhaps you're right

conceivably: The mission could conceivably be accomplished in a week

it could be: It could be he's upset at what you said

maybe: Maybe she is in love

possibly: Do you think that he could possibly be right?

see also **maybe**

peril see **danger, risk**

perilous see **dangerous, treacherous**

perimeter see **outskirts**

period noun a particular length of time: a period of a few months

interval: a long interval when no-one spoke

spell: *a long spell of dry weather*

stretch: *an 18-month stretch in the army*

term: *a 5-year prison term*

time: *At 15 he left home for a short time*

while: *I haven't seen him for a long while*

see also **length, lesson, round, space, stage, stretch, term, time**

periodic see **occasional, regular**

periphery see **outskirts**

perish see **die**

perjure oneself see **lie**

perjury see **lying**

perky see **lively**

permanent *adjective* lasting for ever or present all the time: *a permanent solution to the problem*

abiding: *one of his abiding interests*

constant: *Inflation is a constant threat*

enduring: *an enduring friendship*

eternal: *the quest for eternal youth*

lasting: *We are well on our way to a lasting peace*

perpetual: *a perpetual source of worry*

permeate see **soak**

permissible see **legal**

permission *noun* authorization to do something: *He asked permission to leave the room*

approval: *The plan will require official approval*

assent: *He requires the assent of parliament*

authorization: *his request for authorization to use military force*

consent: *Can she be examined without my consent?*

go-ahead: *The government gave the go-ahead for five major road schemes*

licence: *He has given me licence to do the job as I see fit*

see also **approval, blessing, permit,**

sanction

permit *verb* **1** to allow something or make it possible: *The guards permitted me to bring my camera*

allow: *Smoking will not be allowed*

authorize: *They are expected to authorize the use of military force*

enable: *The test should enable doctors to detect the disease early*

give the green light to: *He has been given the green light to resume training*

grant: *Permission was granted a few weeks ago*

sanction: *The chairman will not sanction a big-money signing*

▷ *noun* **2** an official document allowing someone to do something: *a work permit*

authorization: *We didn't have authorization to go*

licence: *a driving licence*

pass: *a rail pass*

passport: *My passport expires next year*

permission: *Permission for the march has not been granted*

warrant: *Police issued a warrant for his arrest*

see also **allow, approve, grant, let, sanction**

pernicious see **harmful**

perpendicular see **sheer, straight**

perpetrate see **commit**

perpetual see **constant, continual, infinite, permanent**

perpetually see **always**

perplexed see **confused**

persecute *verb* to treat someone with continual cruelty and unfairness: *The Communists began by brutally persecuting the Church*

hound: *He has been hounded by the press*

ill-treat: *They thought Mr Smith had been ill-treating his wife*

oppress: Minorities here have been oppressed for generations
pick on: She was repeatedly picked on by the manager
torment: They were tormented by other pupils
torture: He would not torture her further by trying to argue with her
see also **bully**
persecution *see* **oppression**
persecutor *see* **bully**
perseverance *see* **determination**
persist *see* **continue, last**
persistence *see* **determination**
persistent *see* **determined, relentless**
person noun a man, woman, or child: The amount of sleep we need varies from person to person
   human: the common ancestor of humans and the great apes
   human being: This protein occurs naturally in human beings
   individual: the rights and responsibilities of the individual
   living soul: The nearest living soul was 20 miles away
   soul: a tiny village of only 100 souls
   see also **figure, individual**
personal adjective belonging to a particular person or thing: personal belongings
   individual: Divide the vegetables among four individual dishes
   own: My wife decided I should have my own shop
   particular: his own particular style of preaching
   peculiar: her own peculiar talents
   private: my private life
   special: Every person will have his or her own special problems
   see also **direct, individual, own, peculiar, private**
personality noun 1 a person's character and nature: She has such a

kind, friendly personality
   character: a negative side to his character
   identity: our own sense of cultural identity
   individuality: People should be free to express their individuality
   make-up: There was some fundamental flaw in his make-up
   nature: She trusted people. That was her nature
   psyche: disturbing elements of the human psyche
2 a famous person in entertainment or sport: television personalities
   big name: the big names in French cinema
   celebrity: Hollywood celebrities
   famous name: a famous name from Inter Milan's past
   household name: The TV series that made him a household name
   star: film stars
   see also **celebrity, character, figure, nature**
personnel *see* **staff**
perspective *see* **attitude, outlook, view**
persuade verb to make someone do something by reason or charm: He persuaded the company to sign her up
   bring round informal: We will do what we can to bring them round to our point of view
   coax: She coaxed Bobby into talking about himself
   induce: I would do anything to induce them to stay
   sway: Don't ever be swayed by fashion
   talk into: He talked me into marrying him
   win over: By the end of the day he had won over the crowd
   see also **coax, convince, push, reason, satisfy**
persuasion *see* **faith**

persuasive see **convincing, powerful**

pertinent see **relevant**

perturbed see **uneasy**

pervasive see **extensive, widespread**

pervert see **corrupt**

perverted adjective practising abnormal and unacceptable behaviour: *She has been a victim of perverted phone calls and letters*
depraved: *the work of depraved and evil criminals*
deviant: *Not all drug abusers produce deviant offspring*
immoral: *those who think that birth control is immoral*
unhealthy: *His interest developed into an unhealthy obsession*

pessimistic adjective believing that bad things will happen: *a pessimistic view of life*
despondent: *despondent about their children's future*
gloomy: *a gloomy view of the future*
glum: *They are not entirely glum about the car industry's prospects*
hopeless: *Even able pupils feel hopeless about job prospects*

pest noun 1 an insect or animal that damages crops or livestock: *10% of the crop was lost to a pest called corn rootworm*
bane: *The bane of farmers across the country is the badger*
blight: *potato blight*
scourge: *This parasitic mite is the scourge of honey bees*
2 an annoying person: *I didn't want to be a cry baby or a pest*
bane: *Student journalists were the bane of my life*
bore: *I don't enjoy his company. He's a bore and a fool*
nuisance: *He could be a bit of a nuisance when he was drunk*

pain informal: *She's been a real pain recently*
pain in the neck informal: *I've always been a pain in the neck to publishers*
see also **annoyance, nuisance**

pester verb to bother someone continually: *He gets fed up with people pestering him for money*
annoy: *She kept on annoying me*
badger: *She badgered her doctor time and again*
bother: *We are playing a trick on a man who keeps bothering me*
bug informal: *Stop bugging me*
drive someone up the wall slang: *I sang in the bath and drove my sister up the wall*
get on someone's nerves informal: *I was beginning to get on her nerves*
see also **hassle, worry**

pet see **favourite**

peter out see **die**

petition see **appeal, beg, press**

petrified see **frightened**

petty adjective 1 small and unimportant: *endless rules and petty regulations*
insignificant: *In 1949, Bonn was a small, insignificant city*
measly informal: *The average bathroom measures a measly 3.5 square metres*
trifling: *The sums involved are trifling*
trivial: *trivial details*
unimportant: *It was an unimportant job, and paid very little*
2 selfish and small-minded: *I think that attitude is a bit petty*
cheap: *politicians making cheap political points*
mean: *I'd feel mean saying no*
small-minded: *their small-minded preoccupation with making money*
see also **insignificant, minor, trivial**

petulant see **irritable, sulky**

phantom see **ghost, spirit, vision**

phase see **stage**

phenomenal see **exceptional**

phenomenon see **wonder**

philosophical see **patient**

phobia see **complex**

phoney *adjective informal* false and intended to deceive: *a phoney accent*
bogus: *a bogus insurance claim*
counterfeit: *counterfeit currency*
fake: *fake certificates*
false: *a false name and address*
forged: *forged documents*
sham: *a sham marriage*
see also **fake, mock**

phony see **fake, mock**

photograph see **picture**

phrase see **express, expression, put**

phrasing see **language**

physique see **body, build, figure**

pick *verb* **1** to choose something: *He picked ten people to interview for six sales jobs*
choose: *There are several options to choose from*
decide upon: *He decided upon a career in publishing*
hand-pick: *He was hand-picked for his job by the Admiral*
opt for: *I think we should opt for a more cautious approach*
select: *the party's policy of selecting candidates*
settle on: *I finally settled on an Audi TT roadster*
2 to remove a flower or fruit with your fingers: *He helps his mother pick fruit*
gather: *We spent the afternoon gathering berries*
harvest: *Many farmers are refusing to harvest the cane*
pluck: *I plucked a lemon from the tree*
▷ *noun* **3** the best: *the pick of the country's young athletes*
elite: *the elite of women's tennis*

flower: *the flower of Polish manhood*
pride: *the hovercraft, once the pride of British maritime engineering*
see also **choose, favourite, select**

pick on *verb* to criticize someone unfairly or treat them unkindly: *Bullies pick on younger children*
bait: *He delighted in baiting his mother*
tease: *He teased me mercilessly about going to Hollywood*
torment: *They were tormented by other pupils*
see also **bully, persecute**

pick out see **distinguish**

pick up see **acquire, develop, learn, lift, receive**

pickpocket see **thief**

picnic see **eat**

picture *noun* **1** a drawing, painting, or photograph: *It's got a picture of me on the cover*
drawing: *She did a drawing of me*
illustration: *Tolkien's illustrations for The Hobbit*
painting: *his collection of Impressionist paintings*
photograph: *He wants to take some photographs of the house*
portrait: *Velazquez's portrait of Pope Innocent X*
sketch: *pencil sketches*
▷ *verb* **2** to imagine something clearly: *He pictured her with long black hair*
conceive of: *I can't conceive of doing work that doesn't interest me*
imagine: *It's difficult to imagine anything coming between them*
see: *A good idea, but can you see Taylor trying it?*
visualize: *He could not visualize her as old*
see also **imagine, represent**

piece *noun* **1** a portion or part of something: *a piece of cheese*

bit: *a bit of paper*

chunk: *He was accused of stealing a tin of pineapple chunks*

fragment: *There were fragments of cork in the wine*

part: *The engine has got only three moving parts*

portion: *Damage was confined to a small portion of the castle*

slice: *a slice of bread*

2 something that has been written, created, or composed: *his piece on fox hunting*

article: *a newspaper article*

composition: *Schubert's piano compositions*

creation: *the fashion designer's latest creations*

study: *Leonardo's studies of horsemen*

work: *In my opinion, this is Rembrandt's greatest work*

see also **article, bit, block, feature, item, lump, part, portion, section**

piece together *verb* to assemble things or parts to make something complete: *Doctors painstakingly pieced together the broken bones*

assemble: *He is assembling evidence concerning a murder*

join: *Join all the sections together*

mend: *I should have had it mended, but never got round to it*

patch together: *A hasty deal was patched together*

repair: *the cost of repairing earthquake damage*

restore: *The trust is playing a leading part in restoring old cinemas*

see also **reconstruct**

pierce *verb* to make a hole in something with a sharp instrument: *Pierce the potato with a fork*

bore: *tunnels bored into the foundations of the building*

drill: *I drilled five holes at equal distance*

lance: *It's a painful experience having the boil lanced*

penetrate: *The Earth's atmosphere was penetrated by a meteor*

puncture: *The bullet punctured the skull*

piercing *see* **noisy, shrill**

pig *noun* a farm animal kept for meat: *the number of pigs at the trough*

hog: *He's as fat as a hog*

piggy *informal*: *These two piggies are going to market!*

porker: *a 30kg Vietnamese potbellied porker*

swine: *herds of oxen, sheep and swine*

piggy *see* **pig**

pigment *see* **colour**

pigmentation *see* **colour**

pile *noun* **1** a quantity of things lying one on top of another: *a pile of books*

heap: *a compost heap*

hoard: *a hoard of jewels*

mound: *The bulldozers piled up hug mounds of dirt*

mountain: *They have mountains of coffee to sell*

stack: *a stack of magazines on the table*

2 the raised fibres of a soft surface: *the carpet's thick pile*

down: *The whole plant is covered with fine down*

fur: *This creature's fur is short and dense*

hair: *He has black hair*

nap: *The cotton is lightly brushed to heighten the nap*

▷ *verb* **3** to put things one on top of another: *A few newspapers were piled on the table*

heap: *She heaped more carrots onto his plate*

hoard: *They've begun to hoard petrol and food*

stack: *They are stacked neatly in piles of three*

see also **bunch, heap, load, mass**
piles see **a lot** or **lots**
pile-up see **crash**
pilfer see **steal**
pillage see **loot**
pillar see **support**
pilot see **drive**
pinch see **dash, emergency, steal**
pine see **long**
pine for see **be dying for, miss**
pinnacle see **peak, top**
pinpoint see **identify, locate**
pioneer see **start**
pious see **holy, religious**
pirouette see **spin**
pit noun a large hole in something:
He lost his footing and began to slide
into the pit
  chasm: The coach plunged down
  the chasm
  hole: The builders had cut holes into
  the soft stone
  pothole: She was seriously injured
  when she fell 90 feet down a pothole
  see also **abyss, grave, hole**
pitch see **throw**
pitfall see **difficulty, risk**
pitiful see **pathetic, sorry**
pity verb 1 to feel sorry for someone: I
don't know whether to hate or pity him
  feel for: She cried on the phone and I
  really felt for her
  feel sorry for: This is my biggest win
  but I don't feel sorry for the bookies
  sympathize with: I sympathize with
  you for your loss
  ▷ noun 2 sympathy for other
  people's suffering: She saw no pity
  in their faces
  charity: They showed a lack of charity
  and understanding to her
  compassion: his compassion for a
  helpless woman
  kindness: He was treated with
  kindness by numerous officials
  mercy: Neither side showed any

mercy
  sympathy: We expressed our
  sympathy for her loss
  understanding: We would like to
  thank them for their patience and
  understanding
3 a regrettable fact: It's a pity they
can't all have the same opportunities
  crime informal: It would be a crime
  to travel to Australia and not stop
  in Sydney
  crying shame: It would be a
  crying shame to split up a winning
  partnership
  shame: It's a shame it had to close
  see also **mercy, sympathy**
pivotal see **critical, crucial, vital**
placard see **sign**
placate see **pacify**
place noun any point or area: The pain
is always in the same place
  area: a picnic area
  location: The first thing he looked at
  was his office's location
  point: The pain originated from a
  point in his right thigh
  position: the ship's position
  site: a bat sanctuary with special
  nesting sites
  spot: the nation's top tourist spots
take place verb 1 to happen: The
meeting took place on Thursday
  come about: That came about when
  we went to Glastonbury last year
  go on: This has been going on for
  around a year
  happen: We cannot say for sure what
  will happen
  occur: The crash occurred when the
  crew shut down the wrong engine
  ▷ verb 2 to put something
  somewhere: Chairs were placed in
  rows for the parents
  deposit: Imagine if you were suddenly
  deposited on a desert island
  locate: the best city in which to locate

a business

plant: So far no one has admitted to planting the bomb

position: plants which are carefully positioned in the alcove

put: She put the photograph on her desk

situate: The hotel is situated next to the railway station

see also **appointment, deposit, fit, identify, insert, lay, location, position, put, recognize, scene, set, spot**

placed see **located**

placid see **gentle, mild, peaceful**

plague see **annoy, rash, worry**

plain adjective **1** very simple in style with no decoration: It was a plain, grey stone house

austere: The church was austere and simple

bare: bare wooden floors

spartan: her spartan home in a tiny village

stark: a stark white, characterless fireplace

2 obvious and easy to recognize or understand: It was plain to him that I was having a nervous breakdown

clear: The book is clear and readable

comprehensible: a comprehensible manual

distinct: a distinct smell of burning coal

evident: His footprints were clearly evident in the heavy dust

obvious: an obvious injustice

unmistakable: His voice was unmistakable

see also **blank, clear, common, evident, frank, manifest, obvious, simple, straight, straightforward, ugly, visible**

plan noun **1** a way thought out to do something: a plan to amalgamate the two parties

method: He did it by his usual method

proposal: The proposals need careful study

scheme: The scheme was an abject failure

strategy: What should our marketing strategy achieve?

system: the advantages of the new system over the old one

2 a detailed diagram of something that is to be made: a detailed plan of the prison

blueprint: a blueprint for a new bathroom

diagram: a circuit diagram

layout: He tried to recall the layout of the farmhouse

scale drawing: scale drawings of locomotives

▷ verb **3** to decide in detail what is to be done: when we plan road construction

arrange: We arranged a social event once a year

design: He approached me to design the restaurant

devise: We devised a plan

draft: The legislation was drafted by the committee

formulate: He formulated his plan for escape

see also **aim, arrange, contemplate, course, design, idea, intend, layout, mean, organize, pattern, plot, suggestion**

plane see **level**

planet see **earth**

planned see **calculated**

planning see **organization**

plant see **factory, place**

plaster see **spread**

plausible see **believable, convincing, logical, probable**

play verb **1** to take part in games or use toys: Polly was playing with her teddy bear

amuse oneself: He amused himself by rollerskating round the building

entertain oneself: I used to entertain myself by building model planes

frolic: Tourists sunbathe and frolic in the ocean

have fun: having fun with your friends

2 to take part in a sport or game: Alain was playing cards with his friends

compete: Eight entrants competed for the prize

participate: Sixteen teams participated in the tournament

take on: Scotland take on South Africa at Murrayfield

take part: The teams taking part in cricket's bitterest enemies

vie with: Arsenal are vying with Leeds for second spot in the league

▷ **noun 3** a piece of drama performed on stage, radio, or television: Chekhov's best play

comedy: a romantic comedy

drama: He also wrote radio dramas and film scripts

pantomime: He regularly performs in Christmas pantomimes

show: a one-woman show

tragedy: Shakespeare's tragedies

see also **act, appeal, perform**

play a part see **appear**

play a part in see **take part in**

play a trick on see **dupe**

play the part of see **act**

play up see **emphasize**

player see **figure**

plea see **appeal, defence, request**

plead verb to beg someone for something: She pleaded with her daughter to come home

appeal: The United Nations appealed for aid from the international

community

ask: I've asked you time and again not to do that

beg: We are not going to beg for help any more

beseech literary: She beseeched him to show mercy

implore: Opposition leaders implored the president to break the deadlock

see also **appeal, ask, beg, press, urge**

plead with see **implore**

pleasant adjective **1** enjoyable or attractive: I've got a pleasant little flat

agreeable: workers in more agreeable and better paid occupations

delightful: It was the most delightful garden I'd ever seen

enjoyable: an enjoyable meal

lekker South African slang: a lekker little town

lovely: He had a lovely voice

nice: It's nice to be here together again

pleasurable: He found sailing more pleasurable than skiing

2 friendly or charming: an extremely pleasant and obliging man

affable: He is an affable and approachable man

amiable: She had been surprised at how amiable and polite he had seemed

charming: He can be charming to his friends

friendly: She has a friendly relationship with her customers

likable or **likeable**: He's an immensely likable man

nice: He's a nice fellow, very quiet and courteous

see also **agreeable, lekker, lovely, warm**

please verb to give pleasure to: I was tidying my bedroom to please mum

amuse: The thought seemed to amuse him

charm: He charmed all of us

delight: music that has delighted audiences all over the world
entertain: Children's TV not only entertains but also teaches
see also **appeal, delight, entertain, satisfy, suit**

pleased adjective happy or satisfied: I'm pleased with the way things have been going
contented: She had a contented smile on her face
delighted: I know he will be delighted to see you
glad: I'm glad he changed his mind in the end
happy: She's a confident and happy child
satisfied: satisfied customers
see also **glad, proud, satisfied**

pleasing see **beautiful**
pleasurable see **agreeable, pleasant**
pleasure noun a feeling of happiness and satisfaction: Everybody takes pleasure in eating
amusement: Her impersonations provided great amusement
enjoyment: his enjoyment of the countryside
happiness: My happiness helped to erase the bad memories
joy: tears of joy
satisfaction: job satisfaction
see also **delight, entertainment, fun, happiness, pride**

pleat see **fold**
plebiscite see **vote**
pledge see **bond, guarantee, oath, promise, word**
plentiful adjective existing in large amounts: a plentiful supply
abundant: Birds are abundant in the tall vegetation
ample: The design created ample space for a large kitchen
bountiful: a bountiful harvest of

fruits and vegetables
copious: He attended the lectures and took copious notes
infinite: an infinite variety of landscapes
see also **abundant, generous, handsome, rich**

plenty noun a lot of something: There's plenty to go round
enough: Have you had enough?
great deal: I've spent a great deal of time on this project
heaps informal: You have heaps of time
lots informal: He has made lots of amendments to the script
plethora: a plethora of new products
see also **a lot or lots, abundance, heaps, many, wealth**

plenty of see **ample**
plethora see **plenty**
pliable see **flexible, soft**
plight see **jam, situation, state**
plot noun **1** a secret plan made by a group of people: the plot to assassinate Martin Luther King
conspiracy: a conspiracy to steal nuclear missiles
intrigue: political intrigues
plan: a secret government plan to build a nuclear waste dump
scheme: an elaborate scheme to dupe the police
2 the story of a novel or play: The film has a ludicrously complicated plot
narrative: a fast-moving narrative
scenario: The movie's scenario is nonsensical
story: I doubt the appeal of cinematic sex without a story
story line: It sounds like a typical story line from a soap opera
▷ verb **3** to plan something secretly with others: Prosecutors allege the defendants plotted to overthrow the government

conspire: The countries had secretly conspired to acquire nuclear weapons
hatch: He hatched a plot to murder his wife
plan: I suspect they are secretly planning to raise taxes
ploy see **manoeuvre, trick**
pluck see **bravery, courage, pick, tug**
plucky see **brave**
plug noun **1** a small, round object for blocking a hole: She put the plug in the sink and filled it with water
bung: Remove the bung from the barrel
cork: the sound of popping champagne corks
stopper: a bottle sealed with a cork stopper
▷ verb **2** to block a hole with something: working to plug a major oil leak
block: When the shrimp farm is built it will block the stream
fill: Fill small holes with wood filler
seal: She filled the containers and sealed them with a cork
see also **advertise, advertisement, block, promote, publicity, publicize**
plummet see **decline, descend, drop, fall**
plump adjective rather fat: a plump, fresh-faced young woman
beefy informal: beefy bodyguards
burly: burly shipyard workers
chubby: I was quite chubby as a child
fat: I could eat what I liked without getting fat
stout: He was a tall, stout man of sixty
tubby: He's a bit on the tubby side
see also **tubby**

plunder see **loot, raid**
plunge see **fall**
plus see **virtue**
plush see **luxurious**
poach see **cook**
podgy see **tubby**
poignant see **moving, sad, touching**
point noun **1** the purpose or meaning something has: Cutting costs is not the point of the exercise
aim: The aim of this book is to inform you
goal: The goal is to raise a lot of money
intention: It was never my intention to injure anyone
object: It was his object in life to find the island
purpose: He did not know the purpose of Vincent's visit
2 a quality or feature: Tact was never her strong point
attribute: Cruelty is a regrettable attribute of human behaviour
characteristic: their physical characteristics
feature: They're one of my best features
quality: mature people with leadership qualities
side: the dark side of his character
trait: Creativity is a human trait
3 the thin sharp end of something: the point of a needle
nib: the nib of my pen
prong: the prongs of a fork
tip: the tip of my scissors
see also **aspect, consideration, detail, item, location, message, moment, place, position, purpose, question, spot, stage, subject, use**
point of view see **attitude, feeling, opinion, view, viewpoint**
point out see **comment**
point-blank see **straight**
pointed see **sharp**
pointer see **hint**

pointless see **hopeless, unnecessary**

poise see **grace**

poison noun a substance that can kill people or animals: *Mercury is a known poison*

toxin: *the liver's ability to break down toxins*

venom: *the cobra's deadly venom*

see also **pollute**

poisonous adjective containing something that causes death or illness: *a large cloud of poisonous gas*

noxious: *Many household products give off noxious fumes*

toxic: *The cost of cleaning up toxic waste*

venomous: *The adder is Britain's only venomous snake*

poke verb 1 to jab or prod someone or something: *She poked a fork into the turkey skin*

dig: *His companions were digging him in the ribs*

elbow: *As I tried to get past him he elbowed me in the face*

jab: *Somebody jabbed an umbrella into his leg*

nudge: *She nudged me awake after I dozed off*

prod: *He prodded Murray with the shotgun*

stab: *He stabbed at Frank with his forefinger*

▷ noun 2 a jab or prod: *She gave Richard a playful poke*

dig: *She silenced him with a sharp dig in the small of the back*

jab: *a quick jab of the brakes*

nudge: *She slipped her arm under his and gave him a nudge*

prod: *He gave the donkey a mighty prod in the backside*

see also **dig, stick**

poke fun at see **mock**

poke your nose in see **pry**

pole see **bar, stick**

police see **guard**

policy see **course, procedure**

polish verb 1 to make smooth and shiny by rubbing: *He polished his shoes every morning*

buff: *He was already buffing the car's hubs*

shine: *Let him dust and shine the furniture*

wax: *a Sunday morning spent washing and waxing the car*

2 to improve a skill or technique: *Polish up your writing skills*

brush up: *She spent the summer brushing up on her driving*

improve: *I want to improve my golf game*

perfect: *We perfected a hand-signal system*

refine: *Surgical techniques are constantly being refined*

▷ noun 3 elegance or refinement: *The opera lacks the polish of his later work*

class informal: *For sheer class, Mark Waugh is the best batsman of the World Cup*

elegance: *The furniture combined practicality with elegance*

finesse: *It's good but it lacks the finesse of vintage champagne*

grace: *Ballet classes are important for learning poise and grace*

refinement: *a girl who possessed both dignity and refinement*

style: *Paris, you have to admit, has style*

see also **finish, gloss, perfect, practise**

polished see **glossy, perfect, smooth**

polite adjective 1 having good manners: *It's not polite to point at people*

civil: *I have to force myself to be*

civil to him

courteous: Her reply was courteous but firm

respectful: Their children are always respectful to their elders

well-behaved: well-behaved little girls

well-mannered: a very pleasant and well-mannered student

2 cultivated or refined: Certain words are not acceptable in polite society

cultured: He is immensely cultured and well-read

genteel: two ladies with genteel manners and voices

refined: His speech and manner are very refined

sophisticated: Recently her tastes have become more sophisticated

urbane: She describes him as charming and urbane

see also **refined**

politeness noun the quality of being civil to someone: She listened to him but only out of politeness

civility: Handle customers with tact and civility

courtesy: He did not even have the courtesy to reply to my fax

decency: He should have had the decency to inform us

etiquette: the rules of diplomatic etiquette

see also **courtesy**

polls see **vote**

pollute verb to contaminate with something harmful: Heavy industry pollutes our rivers with noxious chemicals

contaminate: Have any fish been contaminated in the Arctic Ocean?

infect: a virus which is spread mainly by infected blood

poison: Drilling operations have poisoned the Nile delta

taint: blood tainted with the hepatitis

viruses

see also **soil**

pomp see **ceremony**

pompous adjective behaving in a way that is too serious and self-important: a pompous man with a high opinion of his own capabilities

arrogant: an air of arrogant indifference

grandiose: grandiose plans which never got off the ground

ostentatious: an ostentatious wedding reception

pretentious: His response was full of pretentious nonsense

puffed up: He is puffed up with own importance

see also **pretentious**

ponder verb to think about something deeply: I'm continually pondering how to improve the team

brood: I guess everyone broods over things once in a while

consider: You have to consider the feelings of those around you

contemplate: He lay in bed contemplating his future

mull over: I'll leave you alone here so you can mull it over

reflect: I reflected on the child's future

think: I have often thought about this problem

see also **consider, contemplate, deliberate, think, wonder**

ponderous see **slow**

pong see **smell, stink**

pony see **horse**

pooch see **dog**

pool see **fund**

poor adjective **1** having little money: They see the government ignoring poor people

broke informal: He was broke when I married him

destitute: destitute people living on the streets

hard up informal: Her parents were very hard up

impoverished: one of the most impoverished suburbs of Rio de Janeiro

penniless: a penniless refugee

poverty-stricken: a teacher of poverty-stricken kids

2 of a low quality or standard: He was a poor actor

feeble: a feeble attempt to save Figo's shot

inferior: The cassettes were of inferior quality

mediocre: His school record was mediocre

second-rate: Passengers are fed up using a second-rate service

shoddy: shoddy goods

unsatisfactory: questions to which he received unsatisfactory answers

see also **deficient, hopeless, inadequate, inferior, lame, low, pathetic, remote, rotten, sorry, unsatisfactory, worthless**

poorly see **crook, ill, sick, unhealthy, unwell**

populace see **public**

popular adjective **1** liked or approved of by a lot of people: These delicious pastries will be very popular

fashionable: fashionable wine bars

favourite: Britain's favourite soap opera

in demand: He was much in demand as a lecturer

in favour: He is now back in favour with the manager

sought-after: one of the most sought-after new names in Hollywood

well-liked: She was very sociable and well-liked by the other students

2 involving or intended for ordinary people: the popular press

common: Much of the countryside has fallen out of common ownership and into private hands

conventional: a respectable married woman with conventional opinions

general: general awareness about bullying

prevalent: Smoking is becoming increasingly prevalent among younger women

universal: universal health care

see also **common, fashionable, mass, public**

populate see **inhabit, settle**

population see **people**

pore over see **read, scrutinize, study**

porker see **pig**

pornographic see **dirty, obscene**

portable see **light**

portion noun a part or amount of something: I have spent a considerable portion of my life here

bit: I missed the first bit of the meeting

chunk: Cut the melon into chunks

helping: She gave them extra helpings of ice-cream

part: A large part of his earnings went on repaying the loan

piece: Do you want another piece?

segment: the middle segment of his journey

serving: Each serving contains 240 calories

see also **measure, part, piece, section, share**

portly see **tubby**

portrait see **picture**

portray see **act, describe, represent**

pose verb **1** to ask a question: When I finally posed the question, "Why?" he merely shrugged

ask: I wasn't the only one asking questions

put: Some workers may be afraid to put questions publicly

submit: Passengers are invited to submit questions

2 to pretend to be someone else: The

team posed as drug dealers to trap the ringleaders
impersonate: He was once jailed for impersonating a policeman
masquerade as: He masqueraded as a doctor and fooled everyone
pass oneself off as: He frequently passed himself off as a lawyer
pretend to be: We spent the afternoon pretending to be foreign tourists
see also **show**

poser see **puzzle**

posh adjective **1** informal smart, fashionable and expensive: a posh hotel
classy informal: expensive cars with classy brand names
elegant: an elegant society ball
exclusive: a member of Britain's most exclusive club
fashionable: fashionable restaurants
smart: smart London dinner parties
stylish: stylish décor
up-market: an up-market agency aimed at professional people
2 upper-class: He sounded very posh on the phone
aristocratic: a wealthy, aristocratic family
genteel: two ladies with genteel manners and voices
upper-class: upper-class speech formal
see also **exclusive**

position noun **1** the place where someone or something is: The ship's name and position were reported to the coastguard
location: She knew the exact location of their headquarters
place: The pain is always in the same place
point: The pain originated from a point in his right thigh
whereabouts: Finding his whereabouts proved surprisingly easy
▷ verb **2** to put something somewhere: Position trailing plants near the edges
arrange: Arrange the books in neat piles
lay out: Grace laid out the knives and forks at the table
locate: the best city in which to locate a business
place: Chairs were placed in rows for the parents
put: She put the photograph on her desk
see also **appointment, attitude, fit, job, location, place, put, set, spot, state, status**

positive adjective **1** completely sure about something: I was positive he'd known about that money
certain: It wasn't a balloon – I'm certain about that
confident: My Ryan is confident of success
convinced: He was convinced that I was part of the problem
sure: It is impossible to be sure about the value of the land
2 providing definite proof of the truth or identity of something: positive evidence
clear: a clear case of mistaken identity
clear-cut: The issue is not so clear-cut
conclusive: Research on the matter is far from conclusive
concrete: He had no concrete evidence
firm: There is no firm evidence to prove this
3 tending to emphasize what is good: I anticipate a positive response
constructive: We welcome constructive criticism
helpful: Camilla's helpful comments
see also **certain, confident, definite, favourable, optimistic, sure**

possess verb 1 to have something as a quality: *He possesses both stamina and great technique*

be blessed with: *She was blessed with a photographic memory*

be born with: *Mozart was born with perfect pitch*

enjoy: *I have always enjoyed good health*

have: *They have talent in abundance* 2 to own something: *He was said to possess a huge fortune*

acquire: *I have acquired a new car*

control: *He now controls the entire company*

hold: *He does not hold a firearm certificate*

occupy: *US forces now occupy part of the country*

seize: *Troops have seized the airport and railway terminals*

take over: *They plan to take over another airline*

see also **have, own**

possession noun ownership of something: *How did this picture come into your possession?*

control: *The restructuring involves his giving up control of the firm*

custody: *She will have custody of their two children*

ownership: *the growth of home ownership*

tenure: *his 28-year tenure of the house*

possessions plural noun the things owned by someone: *People had lost all their possessions*

assets: *The group had assets worth over 10 million dollars*

belongings: *He was identified only by his personal belongings*

effects: *His daughters were collecting his effects*

estate: *She left her entire estate to a charity*

property: *the rightful owner of the property*

things: *She told him to take all his things and not to return*

see also **property, things**

possessor see **owner**

possibility noun something that might be true or might happen: *the possibility of a ban*

chance: *There's no chance of that happening*

hope: *We had absolutely no hope of raising the money*

likelihood: *the likelihood of infection*

odds: *What are the odds of that happening?*

prospect: *There is little prospect of peace*

risk: *It reduces the risk of heart disease*

see also **chance**

possible adjective 1 likely to happen or able to be done: *I am grateful to the staff for making this work possible*

attainable: *I always thought promotion was attainable*

feasible: *Whether such cooperation is feasible is a matter of doubt*

practicable: *It was not reasonably practicable for Mr Tyler to attend*

viable: *commercially viable products*

workable: *This isn't a workable solution in most cases*

2 likely or capable of being true or correct: *It's possible there's an explanation for all this*

conceivable: *It is just conceivable that a survivor might be found*

imaginable: *a place of no imaginable strategic value*

likely: *Experts say a 'yes' vote is still the likely outcome*

potential: *the channel's potential audience*

see also **believable, likely, potential**

possibly see **maybe, perhaps**

post see **appointment, base, job,**

support
poster see **notice**
posterior see **bottom**
postpone verb to put off to a later time: The visit has been postponed until tomorrow
  adjourn: The proceedings have been adjourned until next week
  defer: Customers often defer payments for as long as possible
  delay: I wanted to delay my departure until June
  put back: The news conference has been put back a couple of hours
  put off: The Association has put off the event until October
  shelve: Sadly, the project has now been shelved
  see also **delay**, **put off**
posy see **bunch**
potency see **strength**
potential adjective **1** possible but not yet actual: potential sources of finance
  likely: A draw is the likely outcome
  possible: Her family is discussing a possible move to America
  probable: A bomb was the accident's most probable cause
  ▷ noun **2** ability to achieve future success: Denmark recognized the potential of wind energy early
  ability: You have the ability to become a good pianist
  aptitude: more aptitude for academic work than the others
  capability: We experience differences in mental capability depending on the time of day
  capacity: people's creative capacities
  power: the power of speech
  wherewithal: She didn't have the financial wherewithal to do it
  see also **capacity**, **in the making**, **possible**
pothole see **pit**
pound see **bang**, **beat**

pour verb to flow quickly and in large quantities: Blood was pouring from his broken nose
  course: The tears coursed down her cheeks
  flow: compressor stations that keep that gas flowing
  gush: Piping-hot water gushed out
  run: Water was running down the walls
  spout: a fountain that spouts water 40 feet into the air
  stream: She came in, rain streaming from her clothes and hair
  see also **gush**, **rain**
poverty noun the state of being very poor: Garvey died in loneliness and poverty
  destitution: refugees living in destitution
  hardship: Many people are suffering economic hardship
  insolvency: Several companies are on the brink of insolvency
  want: We are fighting for freedom from want
poverty-stricken see **poor**
powdery see **fine**
power noun **1** control over people and activities: a position of great power and influence
  ascendancy: The extremists in the party are gaining ascendancy
  control: He has been forced to give up control over the company
  dominion: They truly believe they have dominion over us
  sovereignty: the resumption of Chinese sovereignty over Hong Kong in 1997
  supremacy: The party has re-established its supremacy
  2 authority to do something: The police have the power of arrest
  authority: The judge had no authority to order a second trial

authorization: I don't have the authorization to make such a decision
licence: He has given me licence to do the job as I see fit
privilege: the ancient powers and privileges of parliament
right: the right to vote
3 physical strength: Power and bulk are vital to success in rugby
brawn: He's got plenty of brains as well as brawn
might: The might of the army could prove a decisive factor
strength: He threw it forward with all his strength
vigour: His body lacks the vigour of a normal two-year-old
see also **capacity, control, drive, force, grip, influence, mana, potential, strength**

powerful adjective **1** able to control people and events: Russia and India, two large, powerful countries
commanding: We're in a more commanding position than we've been in for ages
dominant: He was a dominant figure in the Italian film industry
influential: He had been influential in shaping economic policy
2 physically strong: It's such a big powerful dog
mighty: a mighty river
strapping: He was a bricklayer – a big, strapping fellow
strong: I'm not strong enough to carry him
sturdy: The camera was mounted on a sturdy tripod
vigorous: He was a vigorous, handsome young man
3 having a strong effect: a powerful argument
compelling: a compelling reason to leave
convincing: convincing evidence

effective: Antibiotics are effective against this organism
forceful: forceful action to stop the suffering
persuasive: Mr. Knight made a persuasive case for removing the tax
telling: He spoke reasonably, carefully, and with telling effect
see also **convincing, important, impressive, intense, violent**

powerless adjective unable to control or influence events: I was powerless to save her
helpless: Many people felt helpless against the violence
impotent: The West is impotent to influence the Balkan war
incapable: He is incapable as a manager
see also **helpless, weak**

practicable see **possible**

practical adjective **1** involving experience rather than theory: practical suggestions for healthy eating
applied: plans to put more money into applied research
pragmatic: a pragmatic approach to the problems of Latin America
2 likely to be effective: The clothes are lightweight and practical for holidays
functional: The design is functional but stylish
sensible: sensible footwear
3 able to deal effectively with problems: the practical common sense essential in management
accomplished: an accomplished cook
experienced: a team packed with experienced professionals
proficient: A great number of them are proficient in foreign languages
seasoned: The author is a seasoned academic

skilled: *amateur but highly skilled observers of wildlife*
veteran: *a veteran broadcaster*
see also **handy, realistic, sensible, useful**

practically *see* **almost, nearly**

practice *noun* **1** something that people do regularly: *a public inquiry into bank practices*

custom: *I have tried to adapt to local customs*
habit: *a survey on eating habits*
method: *her usual method of getting through the traffic*
routine: *We had to change our daily routine and lifestyle*
way: *a return to the old ways of doing things*

2 regular training or exercise: *I need more practice*

drill: *The teacher ran them through the drill again*
exercise: *Lack of exercise can lead to feelings of exhaustion*
preparation: *Behind any successful event lie months of preparation*
rehearsal: *rehearsals for a concert tour*
training: *her busy training schedule*
see also **convention, custom, habit, procedure, routine, way**

practise *verb* **1** to do something repeatedly so as to gain skill: *Lauren practises the piano every day*

polish: *They just need to polish their technique*
rehearse: *She was in her room rehearsing her lines*
train: *He was training for the new season*

2 to take part in the activities of a religion, craft, or custom: *Acupuncture has been practised in China for thousands of years*

do: *I used to do karate*
follow: *Do you follow any particular*

religion?
observe: *American forces are observing Christmas quietly*

practised *see* **experienced**

pragmatic *see* **practical**

praise *verb* **1** to express strong approval of someone: *Many others praised Sanford for taking a strong stand*

admire: *All those who knew him will admire him for his work*
applaud: *He should be applauded for his courage*
approve: *Not everyone approves of the festival*
congratulate: *I must congratulate the organizers for a well run event*
pay tribute to: *He paid tribute to his captain*

▷ *noun* **2** something said or written to show approval: *She is full of praise for the range of services available*

accolade: *the ultimate international accolade, the Nobel Peace Prize*
approval: *an obsessive drive to gain her mother's approval*
commendation: *They received a commendation from the Royal Society of Arts*
congratulation: *I offered her my congratulations*
tribute: *We marched past in tribute to our fallen comrades*
see also **approval, approve, credit, glory, honour, tribute, worship**

prank *see* **joke**

prattle *see* **babble**

pray to *see* **worship**

precarious *see* **critical, serious, unsteady**

precaution *noun* an action intended to prevent something from happening: *It's still worth taking precautions against accidents*

insurance: *Farmers grew a mixture of crops as an insurance against* crop failure

preventative measure: *a preventative measure against heart disease*

protection: *protection against damage to buildings*

provision: *People need to make decent provision for their old age*

safeguard: *legislation that offers safeguards against discrimination*

preceding see **last, previous**

precious adjective of great value and importance: *precious jewels*

expensive: *an expensive new coat*

invaluable: *I was to gain invaluable experience over that year*

priceless: *his priceless collection of Chinese art*

prized: *These shells were very highly prized by the Indians*

valuable: *valuable books*

see also **beloved, dear, valuable**

precise adjective exact and accurate: *We may never know the precise details*

accurate: *an accurate description of his attackers*

actual: *The actual number of victims is higher than statistics suggest*

correct: *This information was correct at the time of going to press*

exact: *The exact number of protest calls has not been revealed*

particular: *a very particular account of events*

specific: *I asked him to be more specific*

very: *Those were his very words*

see also **accurate, careful, correct, exact, fine, formal, particular, right, strict**

precisely see **exactly, prompt**

preconception see **prejudice**

predetermined see **set**

predicament noun a difficult situation: *The decision will leave her in a peculiar predicament*

fix informal: *The government has really got itself into a fix*

hot water informal: *His antics keep landing him in hot water with officials*

jam informal: *We are in a real jam now*

scrape informal: *He's had his fair share of scrapes with the law*

tight spot: *This was one tight spot he couldn't get out of*

see also **fix, hole, jam, problem, state**

predict verb to say that something will happen in the future: *The opinion polls are predicting a very close contest*

forecast: *He forecasts that house prices will rise by 5% this year*

foresee: *He did not foresee any problems*

foretell: *prophets who have foretold the end of the world*

prophesy: *She prophesied a bad ending for the expedition*

prediction noun something that is forecast in advance: *He was unwilling to make a prediction for the coming year*

forecast: *a forecast of heavy weather to come*

prophecy: *the interpreters of Biblical prophecy*

predominant see **main**

predominantly see **mainly**

pre-eminent see **supreme, top**

preface see **introduction**

prefer verb to like one thing more than another thing: *Does he prefer a particular sort of music?*

be partial to: *I'm quite partial to mussels*

favour: *Both sides favour a diplomatic solution*

go for: *They went for a more up-market approach*

incline towards: *The majority are inclined towards a forgiving attitude*

like better: *I like the flat shoes better*

see also **favour**

preferred see **favourite**

prejudice noun **1** an unreasonable or unfair dislike or preference: *prejudice against workers over 45*

bias: *Bias against women permeates every level of the judicial system*

partiality: *She is criticized for her one-sidedness and partiality*

preconception: *preconceptions about the sort of people who did computing*

2 intolerance towards certain people or groups: *racial prejudice*

bigotry: *religious bigotry*

chauvinism: *the growth of Russian chauvinism*

discrimination: *sex discrimination*

racism: *the fight to rid sport of racism*

sexism: *sexism in the workplace*

see also **bias, colour, injustice**

prejudiced see **biased, narrow-minded**

premature see **early**

prematurely see **early**

premeditated see **deliberate**

premier see **top**

premise see **basis**

premium see **payment**

premonition noun a feeling that something unpleasant is going to happen: *He had a premonition that he would die*

foreboding: *His triumph was overshadowed by an uneasy sense of foreboding*

funny feeling informal: *I have a funny feeling something unpleasant is about to happen*

omen: *Her appearance at this moment is an omen of disaster*

sign: *a sign of impending doom*

see also **warning**

preoccupation see **complex, obsession**

preoccupied adjective totally

involved with something or deep in thought: *I am preoccupied with my tennis career*

absorbed: *They were completely absorbed in each other*

engrossed: *Tom didn't notice because he was too engrossed in his work*

immersed: *He's becoming really immersed in his studies*

oblivious: *When he was in his car he was totally oblivious to everybody else*

wrapped up: *She's wrapped up in her new career*

preparation see **practice**

prepare see **brief**

prepared see **agreeable, ready, willing**

preposterous see **daft, ridiculous, unbelievable**

prerequisite see **condition**

prerequisites see **essentials**

prescribed see **formal**

presence see **company**

present adjective **1** being at a place or event: *He had been present at the birth of his son*

at hand: *Having the right equipment at hand will be very useful*

here: *He was here a minute ago*

in attendance: *Police and several fire engines are in attendance*

there: *The group of old buildings is still there today*

to hand: *I haven't got the instructions to hand*

▷ noun **2** something given to someone: *a birthday present*

bonsela South African: *your kind bonsela to the museum*

donation: *Employees make regular donations to charity*

gift: *a Christmas gift*

offering: *Hindus kill turtles ritually as an offering to their gods*

▷ verb **3** to give something to someone: *The Mayor presented* the prizes

award: For his dedication he was awarded a medal of merit

bestow: The Queen bestowed on him a knighthood

donate: He frequently donates large sums to charity

give: She gave me a pen for my birthday

grant: France has agreed to grant him political asylum

hand out: One of my jobs was to hand out the prizes

see also **current, gift, give, modern, perform, submit**

presentation see **lecture, show**

present-day see **current, modern, recent**

presently see **soon**

preservation see **upkeep**

preserve see **keep, safeguard, save**

preside see **oversee**

president see **head**

press verb **1** to apply force or weight to something: Press the blue button

compress: Poor posture compresses the body's organs

crush: Peel and crush the garlic

mash: Mash the bananas with a fork

push: She pushed the door open

squeeze: He squeezed her arm reassuringly

2 to try hard to persuade someone to do something: Trade Unions are pressing him to stand firm

beg: I begged him to come back with me

implore: "Tell me what to do!" she implored him

petition: All the attempts to petition the government had failed

plead: I pleaded to be allowed to go

pressurize: He thought she was trying to pressurize him

urge: He had urged her to come to Ireland

see also **clasp, insist, push, rush, urge**

press on see **advance**

pressing see **serious, urgent**

pressure see **force, strain, stress**

pressurize see **bully, force, press, rush**

prestige see **glory, status**

presumably see **probably**

presume see **believe, expect, suppose**

presumed see **supposed**

pretence see **show**

pretend verb to claim or give the appearance of something untrue: Sometimes the boy pretended to be asleep

counterfeit: the coins he is alleged to have counterfeited

fake: He faked his own death last year

falsify: He was charged with falsifying business records

feign: The striker was accused of feigning injury

pass oneself off as: She tried to pass herself off as an actress

see also **fake**

pretend to be see **pose**

pretended see **mock**

pretentious adjective making unjustified claims to importance: Many critics thought her work and ideas pretentious and empty

affected: She passed along with an affected air and a disdainful look

conceited: I thought him conceited and arrogant

ostentatious: an ostentatious wedding reception

pompous: He's pompous and has a high opinion of his own capabilities

snobbish: a snobbish dislike for their intellectual inferiors

see also **ostentatious, pompous**

pretext see **excuse**

pretty adjective **1** attractive in a

delicate way: *She's a very charming and very pretty girl*
attractive: *She has a round attractive face*
beautiful: *a beautiful child*
cute: *a cute little baby*
lovely: *his lovely wife*
▷ adverb **2** informal quite or rather: *He spoke pretty good English*
fairly: *Both ships are fairly new*
kind of informal: *I was kind of embarrassed about it*
quite: *It was quite hard*
rather: *She's rather vain*
see also **attractive, cute, lovely, rather**

prevail see **triumph, win**

prevailing see **chief, common, fashionable**

prevalent see **common, popular, widespread**

prevent verb to stop something from happening: *the most practical way of preventing crime*
avert: *A fresh tragedy was narrowly averted yesterday*
foil: *The plot was foiled by policemen*
hinder: *Research is hindered by lack of cash*
impede: *Fallen rocks are impeding the progress of the rescue workers*
stop: *a new diplomatic initiative to try to stop the war*
thwart: *Her ambition to become an artist was thwarted by failing eyesight*
see also **bar, prohibit, stop**

preventative measure see **precaution**

previous adjective happening or existing before something else: *the previous year*
earlier: *His earlier works include impressive still lifes*
former: *A former president of Mexico*
one-time: *the country's one-time military rulers*

past: *a return to the turbulence of past centuries*
preceding: *This is examined in detail in the preceding chapter*
prior: *I can't make it. I have a prior engagement*
see also **last, past**

previously see **before**

price noun **1** the amount of money paid for something: *a sharp increase in the price of petrol*
amount: *I was asked to pay the full amount*
charge: *an annual management charge of 1.25%*
cost: *the cost of a loaf of bread*
fee: *the annual membership fee*
figure: *A figure of £2000 was mentioned*
value: *The company's market value rose to 5.5 billion dollars*
▷ verb **2** to fix the price or value of something: *I just can't imagine why it has been priced at this level*
cost: *We hope it won't cost too much*
estimate: *His personal riches were estimated at $368 million*
put a price on: *The company has refused to put a price on its bid*
value: *I had my jewellery valued for insurance purposes*
see also **charge, cost, rate, value**

priceless see **precious**

pricey see **dear, expensive**

pride noun **1** a feeling of satisfaction about your achievements: *We take pride in offering you the highest standards*
delight: *Haig took obvious delight in proving his critics wrong*
pleasure: *Our first win gave me great pleasure*
satisfaction: *His success was a great source of satisfaction to him*
2 an excessively high opinion of yourself: *His pride may still be his*

downfall

arrogance: He has a swaggering arrogance

conceit: He knew, without conceit, that he was considered a genius

egotism: typical showbiz egotism

smugness: a trace of smugness in his voice

snobbery: intellectual snobbery

vanity: her vanity about her long hair
see also **conceit, pick**

prim adjective behaving very correctly and easily shocked by anything rude: We tend to assume the Victorians were very prim and proper

proper: He was very pompous and proper

prudish: I'm not prudish but I think those photos are obscene

puritanical: He has a puritanical attitude towards sex

strait-laced: He very strait-laced and narrow-minded

primarily see **mainly**

primary see **chief, main, principal**

prime adjective **1** main or most important: a prime cause of brain damage

chief: The job went to one of his chief rivals

leading: a leading industrial nation

main: the city's main tourist attraction

principal: our principal source of foreign exchange earnings

2 of the best quality: prime beef

best: He'll have the best care

choice: our choicest chocolates

first-rate: He's a first-rate officer

select: With that historic win he now joins a select band of golfers

superior: superior coffee beans
see also **brief, chief, first, foremost, main, principal, select, top**

primed see **ready**

primeval see **early, first**

primitive adjective very simple or

basic: a very small primitive cottage

crude: crude stone carvings

rough: a rough wooden table

rude: He constructed a rude cabin for himself

rudimentary: The bomb was rudimentary but lethal

simple: a simple shelter
see also **crude, early**

principal adjective main or most important: Their principal concern is that of winning the election

chief: his chief reason for withdrawing

first: The first duty of this government is to tackle poverty

foremost: one of the world's foremost scholars of classical poetry

main: What are the main differences between them?

major: the major factor in her decision

primary: the primary cause of his problems

prime: Police will see me as the prime suspect!
see also **chief, essential, first, foremost, head, leader, leading, main, prime, supreme, top**

principally see **mainly**

principle noun **1** a set of moral rules guiding personal conduct: a woman of principle

conscience: the law on freedom of conscience and religious organizations

integrity: He has always been a man of integrity

morals: public morals

scruples: a man with no moral scruples

sense of duty: He did it out of a sense of duty to his men

2 a general rule or scientific law: the basic principles of Marxism

axiom: the long-held axiom that education leads to higher income

canon: the canons of political economy

doctrine: *Christian doctrine*
fundamental: *the fundamentals of astronomy*
law: *the laws of motion*
see also **basis, belief, ideal**
principles *see* **conscience, standards**
print *see* **publish**
prior *see* **previous**
prison *noun* a building where criminals are kept in captivity: *a high-security prison*
dungeon: *The castle's dungeons haven't been used for years*
jail: *Three prisoners escaped from the jail*
nick *British, Australian, New Zealand slang*: *I was banged up in the nick for six months*
penal institution: *Thirty years in a penal institution is indeed a harsh penalty*
see also **jail**
prisoner *noun* someone kept in prison or captivity: *top-security prisoners*
captive: *the difficulties of spending four months as a captive*
convict: *convicts serving life sentences*
hostage: *negotiations to release the hostages*
privacy *see* **solitude**
private *adjective* **1** for few people rather than people in general: *a private bathroom*
exclusive: *Many of our cheeses are exclusive to our shops in Britain*
individual: *Divide the vegetables among four individual dishes*
personal: *It's for my own personal use*
special: *her own special problems*
2 taking place among a small number of people: *He was buried in a private ceremony*
clandestine: *He had a clandestine*

meeting with his lover
confidential: *confidential information about her private life*
secret: *a secret love affair*
see also **own, personal**
privilege *see* **power**
prize *noun* **1** a reward given to the winner of something: *He won first prize at the Leeds Piano Competition*
accolade: *the ultimate international accolade, the Nobel Peace Prize*
award: *the Booker Prize, Britain's top award for fiction*
honour: *He was showered with honours – among them an Oscar*
trophy: *They haven't won a trophy since 1991*
▷ *adjective* **2** of the highest quality or standard: *a prize bull*
award-winning: *an award-winning restaurant*
first-rate: *a first-rate thriller writer*
outstanding: *an outstanding horse*
top: *Holland's top striker*
▷ *verb* **3** to value highly: *These ornaments are prized by collectors*
cherish: *We cherish our independence*
esteem: *one of Europe's most esteemed awards*
treasure: *She treasures her memories of those joyous days*
value: *I value the work he gives me*
see also **appreciate, reward, treasure, value**
prized *see* **dear, precious, valuable**
probability *noun* the likelihood of something happening: *the probability of a serious earthquake*
chances: *The chances of success for the product are good*
likelihood: *the likelihood of infection*
odds: *The odds are that you are going to fail*
prospect: *the prospect for peace in Rwanda*
see also **chance**

probable adjective likely to be true or to happen: *a misunderstanding about the probable cost*

apparent: *There is no apparent reason for the crime*

feasible: *Whether this is feasible is a matter of doubt*

likely: *Further delays are likely*

on the cards: *A promotion is definitely on the cards for you*

plausible: *a plausible explanation*

see also **believable, likely, potential**

probably adverb in all likelihood: *The wedding's probably going to be in late August*

doubtless: *He will doubtless try to change my mind*

in all probability: *Victory will, in all probability, earn France the title*

likely: *The entire surplus will most likely be handed over*

presumably: *The spear is presumably the murder weapon*

probe see **investigate, question**

problem noun **1** an unsatisfactory situation causing difficulties: *the economic problems of the inner city*

difficulty: *This company is facing great difficulties*

predicament: *the once great club's current predicament*

quandary: *We're in a quandary over our holiday plans*

trouble: *I had trouble parking this morning*

2 a puzzle that needs to be solved: *a mathematical problem*

conundrum: *an apparently insoluble conundrum*

puzzle: *The data has presented astronomers with a puzzle*

riddle: *the riddle of the birth of the universe*

see also **business, complex, difficulty, drawback, issue, puzzle, snag, trouble**

problematic see **tricky**

procedure noun the correct or usual way of doing something: *He did not follow the correct procedure in applying for a visa*

method: *new teaching methods*

policy: *It is our policy to prosecute shoplifters*

practice: *a public inquiry into bank practices*

process: *the production process*

strategy: *a strategy for controlling malaria*

system: *an efficient filing system*

see also **course, measure, method, process, routine, system, way**

proceed verb **1** to start doing or continue to do something: *I had no idea how to proceed*

begin: *He stood up and began to move about the room*

carry on: *"Can I start with a couple of questions?" – "Carry on."*

continue: *I need some advice before I can continue with this task*

get under way: *The court case got under way last autumn*

go on: *Go on with your work*

start: *I started to follow him up the stairs*

2 formal to move in a particular direction: *She proceeded along the hallway*

advance: *I advanced slowly, one step at a time*

continue: *He continued rapidly up the path*

go on: *They went on through the forest*

make your way: *He made his way to the marketplace*

progress: *He progressed slowly along the coast in an easterly direction*

travel: *You can travel to Helsinki tomorrow*

see also **advance, go, journey, start**

proceedings see case
proceeds see profit
process noun **1** a method of doing or producing something: The building process was spread over three years
  course of action: It is important that we take the right course of action
  means: The move is a means to fight crime
  method: new teaching methods
  procedure: the correct procedure for applying for a visa
  system: an efficient filing system
▷ verb **2** to deal with or treat something: Your application is being processed
  deal with: the way that banks deal with complaints
  dispose of: They disposed of the problem quickly
  handle: She didn't know how to handle the problem
  take care of: They left it to me to try and take care of the problem
  see also **action, manufacture, procedure**
processed see refined
procession see parade
proclaim see announce, declare
proclamation see statement
procure see acquire, buy, get, obtain, secure
prod see dig, poke
produce verb **1** to make something: a white wine produced mainly from black grapes
  construct: an inner frame constructed from timber
  create: It was created from odds and ends
  invent: He invented the first electric clock
  make: One of my jobs was to make the tea
  manufacture: They manufacture plastics

2 to bring out something so it can be seen or discussed: To hire a car you must produce a driving licence
  advance: Many new theories have been advanced recently
  bring forward: We will bring forward new proposals for legislation
  bring to light: new evidence brought to light by the police
  put forward: He has put forward new peace proposals
  see also **breed, bring, bring about, cause, compose, lead to, make, manufacture, occasion, product, provoke**
product noun something that is made to be sold: Many household products give off noxious fumes
  commodity: basic commodities such as bread and milk
  goods: imported goods
  merchandise: The club sells a wide range of merchandise
  produce: locally grown produce
  see also **result**
production see making, manufacture
productive adjective **1** producing a large number of things: Training makes workers highly productive
  fertile: a product of his fertile imagination
  fruitful: a landscape that was fruitful and lush
  prolific: She is a prolific writer of novels and short stories
2 bringing favourable results: I'm hopeful that the talks will be productive
  constructive: constructive criticism
  useful: We made some progress during a useful exchange
  valuable: The experience was very valuable
  worthwhile: It had been a worthwhile discussion
  see also **economic, efficient, fertile**

profess see **claim, declare**

profession noun a job that requires advanced education or training: *Harper was a teacher by profession*
  business: *May I ask you what business you're in?*
  career: *a career in journalism*
  occupation: *her new occupation as an author*
  see also **job, trade, work**

professional see **expert, skilled**

professionally see **well**

professor see **teacher**

proficiency see **skill**

proficient adjective able to do something well: *They tend to be proficient in foreign languages*
  able: *an able young rider*
  accomplished: *an accomplished fundraiser*
  adept: *an adept guitar player*
  capable: *a very capable speaker*
  competent: *a competent civil servant*
  efficient: *a team of efficient workers*
  skilful: *He is skilful at managing people*
  skilled: *a network of amateur but highly skilled observers of wildlife*
  see also **capable, expert, practical, skilful, skilled**

profit noun 1 money gained in business or trade: *The bank made pre-tax profits of $3.5 million*
  earnings: *his earnings as an accountant*
  proceeds: *The proceeds from the concert will go to charity*
  revenue: *tax revenues*
  surplus: *Japan's trade surplus*
  takings: *the pub's weekly takings*
  ▷ verb 2 to gain or benefit from something: *They profited shamefully at the expense of my family*
  capitalize on: *The rebels are trying to capitalize on the public's discontent*
  exploit: *They are trying to exploit the troubles to their advantage*
  make the most of: *Happiness is the ability to make the most of what you have*
  take advantage of: *She took advantage of him even after their divorce*
  see also **benefit, gain**

profitable see **economic, helpful, successful**

profits see **income**

profound see **deep, extreme, heavy, intense, serious**

programme noun 1 a planned series of events: *a programme of official engagements*
  agenda: *This is sure to be an item on the agenda again next week*
  schedule: *We both have such hectic schedules*
  timetable: *We've finally managed to agree on a timetable for formal talks*
  2 a broadcast on radio or television: *local news programmes*
  broadcast: *a broadcast by the President*
  show: *my favourite TV show*
  see also **routine**

progress noun 1 improvement or development: *progress in the fight against cancer*
  advance: *dramatic advances in road safety*
  breakthrough: *a breakthrough in their research*
  headway: *The police are making little headway in the investigation*
  improvement: *considerable room for improvement in facilities for patients*
  ▷ verb 2 to become more advanced or skilful: *His reading is progressing well*
  advance: *Japan has advanced from a rural society to an industrial power*
  blossom: *In just a few years it has blossomed into an international event*

develop: workshops designed to develop acting skills

improve: Their French has improved enormously

see also **advance, develop, improve, improvement, proceed**

progression see **sequence, spread**

progressive see **gradual**

prohibit verb to forbid something or make it illegal: a law which prohibited trading on Sundays

ban: The country will ban smoking in all offices this year

forbid: The country's constitution forbids the military use of nuclear energy

outlaw: In 1975 gambling was outlawed

prevent: Residents may be prevented from leaving the islands

see also **ban, forbid, veto**

prohibited see **illegal**

prohibition see **ban, veto**

project see **enterprise, extend, undertaking**

proliferate see **multiply, spread**

proliferation see **spread**

prolific see **fertile, productive**

prologue see **introduction**

prolong see **lengthen**

prolonged see **continuous**

prominence see **emphasis, fame**

prominent adjective 1 important: the children of very prominent or successful parents

eminent: an eminent scientist

famous: England's most famous modern artist

important: an important figure in the media

notable: the notable linguist, Henriette Walter

noted: a noted Hebrew scholar

renowned: Sir William Crookes, the renowned chemist

well-known: He liked to surround himself with well-known people

2 very noticeable, or sticking out a long way: a prominent feature of the landscape

conspicuous: a conspicuous landmark

eye-catching: I outlined it in black to make it more eye-catching

jutting: a jutting chin

noticeable: Squeezing spots only makes them more noticeable

obvious: His cultural roots are most obvious in his poetry

pronounced: The exhibition has a pronounced Scottish theme

striking: a striking aspect of these statistics

see also **leading**

promiscuous adjective having many casual sexual relationships: a promiscuous teenager

loose: If you wear a short skirt in here you're considered a loose woman

wanton: A woman with many sexual partners is still considered wanton

promise verb 1 to say that you will definitely do or not do something: I promise not to be back too late

assure: She assured me that she would deal with the problem

give your word: He had given us his word he would join the club

guarantee: Most countries guarantee the right to free education

pledge: They have pledged to support the opposition

vow: I vowed that someday I would return to live in Europe

2 to show signs of: This promised to be a very long night

hint at: One finding hints at support for this theory

indicate: His early work indicates talent

show signs of: Already she shows signs of beauty

▷ noun **3** an undertaking to do or not do something: *If you make a promise, you should keep it*

assurance: *He gave written assurance that he would start work at once*

guarantee: *They can give no guarantee that they will fulfil their obligations*

pledge: *a pledge to step up cooperation between the two countries*

undertaking: *an undertaking that he would be a responsible parent*

vow: *I kept my marriage vows*
see also **bond, guarantee, oath, prospect, word**

promote verb **1** to encourage the progress or success of something: *All attempts to promote a ceasefire have failed*

back: *She backed the new initiative enthusiastically*

support: *He thanked everyone who had supported the strike*

2 to encourage the sale of a product by advertising: *She's in Europe promoting her new film*

advertise: *She is contracted to advertise their beauty products*

plug *informal*: *He was on the show to plug his latest film*

publicize: *I was publicizing the film in London*

3 to raise someone to a higher rank or position: *He has been promoted twice in two years*

elevate: *He was elevated to the post of Prime Minister*

upgrade: *He was upgraded to supervisor*
see also **advertise, advocate, back, champion, publicize, support**

promotion *see* **publicity**

prompt verb **1** to make someone decide to do something: *Falling rates of pay have prompted consumers to*

stop buying new cars

cause: *What caused you to change your mind?*

induce: *Many teachers were induced to take early retirement*

inspire: *These herbs will inspire you to try out all sorts of dishes*

motivate: *How do you motivate people to work hard?*

spur: *Is it the money that spurs these firefighters to risk their lives?*

2 to encourage someone to say something: *"What was that you were saying about a guided tour?" he prompted her*

coax: *"Tell us what happened next," he coaxed me*

remind: *"You stopped in the middle of your story," I reminded mother*

▷ adverb **3** exactly at the time mentioned: *The invitation specifies eight o'clock prompt*

exactly: *He arrived at exactly five o'clock*

on the dot: *At nine o'clock on the dot, they have breakfast*

precisely: *The meeting began at precisely 4.00 pm*

sharp: *She planned to get up at 8.00 sharp*

▷ adjective **4** done without any delay: *a serious condition which needs prompt treatment*

immediate: *These incidents had an immediate effect*

instant: *He took an instant dislike to this woman*

instantaneous: *This would result in his instantaneous dismissal*

quick: *hoping for a quick end to the dispute*

rapid: *their rapid response to the situation*

swift: *make a swift decision*
see also **drive, hasty, instant, motivate, occasion, provoke,**

punctual, quick, swift
promptly see **immediately**
prone adjective **1** having a tendency to be affected by or do something: She is prone to depression
  disposed: I might have been disposed to like him in other circumstances
  given: I am not very given to emotional displays
  inclined: Nobody felt inclined to argue with Smith
  liable: equipment that is liable to break
  susceptible: She's very susceptible to colds and flu
  2 lying flat and face downwards: We were lying prone on the grass
  face down: He was lying face down on his bed
  prostrate: The injured jockey lay prostrate on the ground
prong see **point**
pronounce see **declare, issue**
pronounced see **prominent, significant**
proof noun evidence that confirms that something is true or exists: You have to have proof of residence in the state of Texas
  confirmation: further confirmation that house prices are no longer falling
  evidence: To date there is no evidence to support this theory
  testimony: His testimony was an important element of the prosecution case
  verification: verification of her story
prop see **support**
prop up see **support**
propagate see **breed, circulate**
propel see **drive**
propensity see **tendency**
proper adjective **1** correct or most suitable: the proper course of action
  appropriate: a smart outfit appropriate to the job

  apt: an apt title for the book
  correct: the correct way to do things
  fitting: His address was a fitting end to a bitter campaign
  right: He's the right man for the job
  suitable: She had no other dress suitable for the occasion
  2 accepted or conventional: She wanted a proper wedding
  accepted: the accepted way of doing things
  conventional: conventional surgical methods
  orthodox: orthodox police methods
  see also **appropriate, correct, decent, fair, fitting, prim, respectable, suitable**
property noun **1** the things that belong to someone: her personal property
  assets: The company has assets of 3.5 billion francs
  belongings: I collected my belongings and left
  effects: After the funeral he sorted his father's personal effects
  estate: His estate was valued at $150,000
  possessions: People had lost their homes and all their possessions
  2 a characteristic or quality: Mint has powerful healing properties
  attribute: a normal attribute of human behaviour
  characteristic: their physical characteristics
  feature: a feature of the local culture
  hallmark: The killing had the hallmarks of a professional assassination
  quality: mature people with leadership qualities
  trait: Creativity is a human trait
  see also **attribute, characteristic, feature, land, possessions, quality**
prophecy see **prediction**

prophesy see predict

proportion noun part of an amount or group: *a tiny proportion of the population*

percentage: *It has a high percentage of protein*

quota: *Britain's fishing quota has been cut*

segment: *a fast-growing segment of the market*

share: *I pay a share of the phone and gas bills*

see also **measure**

proportions see size

proposal see plan, suggestion

propose see aim, intend, nominate, submit, suggest, vote

proposition see offer, suggestion

proprietor see owner

prospect noun expectation or something anticipated: *There was no prospect of going home*

expectation: *The hotel was being renovated in expectation of a tourist boom*

hope: *There is little hope of improvement now*

outlook: *Officials say the outlook for next year is gloomy*

promise: *New Year brought the promise of better things to come*

see also **chance, possibility, probability**

prospective see future

prospects see outlook

prosper see flourish, succeed, thrive

prosperity see success, wealth

prosperous see rich, wealthy

prostrate see prone, worn-out

protect verb to prevent someone or something from being harmed: *Cash dispensers are protected by thick steel and glass*

defend: *I had to defend myself against the attack*

guard: *Soldiers guarded homes near the airport*

safeguard: *action to safeguard the ozone layer*

shelter: *a wooden house, sheltered by a low pointed roof*

shield: *He shielded his head from the sun with a newspaper*

see also **defend, guard, safeguard, save, shelter, take care of**

protected see immune, safe, secure

protection noun something that protects: *a diet believed to offer protection against some cancers*

barrier: *a flood barrier*

buffer: *Keep savings as a buffer against unexpected cash needs*

cover: *air cover for ground operations*

safeguard: *a safeguard against weeds*

shelter: *an air-raid shelter*

see also **defence, precaution, safeguard, safety, shelter**

protector see champion

protest verb **1** to disagree with someone or object to something: *She protested that she was a patriot, not a traitor*

complain: *People always complain that the big banks are unhelpful*

disagree: *I disagree with the drug laws in general*

disapprove: *Her mother disapproved of her working in a pub*

object: *We objected strongly but were outvoted*

oppose: *Many parents oppose bilingual education in schools*

▷ noun **2** a strong objection: *The council has ignored their protests by backing the scheme*

complaint: *the way that banks deal with complaints*

objection: *I questioned the logic of his objections*

outcry: *The incident caused an international outcry*

see also **agitate, complaint, grumble, object, objection**

protestation see **declaration**

protocol see **ceremony**

prototype see **example, ideal**

protrude see **bulge, extend**

protrusion see **bulge**

proud adjective feeling pleasure or satisfaction: *I was proud of our players today*
   gratified: *He was gratified by the audience's response*
   honoured: *I am honoured to work with her*
   pleased: *I was pleased to call him my friend*
   see also **haughty, stuck-up, vain**

prove verb to provide evidence that something is definitely true: *History will prove him to have been right all along*
   ascertain: *They had ascertained that he was not a spy*
   confirm: *X-rays confirmed that he had not broken any bones*
   demonstrate: *You have to demonstrate that you are reliable*
   establish: *The autopsy established the cause of death*
   verify: *I can verify that it takes about thirty seconds*
   see also **confirm, show**

prove false see **disprove**

proverb see **saying**

provide verb to make something available to someone: *I'll be glad to provide a copy of this*
   contribute: *NATO agreed to contribute troops and equipment*
   equip: *proposals to equip all officers with body armour*
   furnish: *They'll be able to furnish you with the rest of the details*
   outfit: *They outfitted him with artificial legs*
   supply: *the blood vessels supplying*

oxygen to the brain
   see also **equip, give, issue, supply**

providence see **fate**

province see **field, land, range, territory**

provision see **condition, precaution**

provisional see **temporary**

provisions see **food, kai, supplies, terms**

proviso see **condition, terms**

provoke verb 1 to try to make someone angry: *I didn't want to do anything to provoke him*
   anger: *It's important not to anger her*
   annoy: *You're just trying to annoy me*
   enrage: *He enraged the government by going back on the agreement*
   goad: *My little brother was always goading me*
   insult: *I didn't mean to insult you*
   irritate: *If you go on irritating that dog, it'll bite you*
   tease: *I'm sorry, I shouldn't tease you like that*
   2 to cause an unpleasant reaction: *His comments have provoked a shocked reaction*
   cause: *These policies are likely to cause problems*
   evoke: *The programme has evoked a storm of protest*
   produce: *The decision produced a furious reaction among fans*
   prompt: *The allegations prompted an indignant response from the accused*
   rouse: *This roused a feeling of rebellion in him*
   set off: *The arrival of the supply van set off a minor riot among waiting villagers*
   spark off: *a political crisis sparked off by religious violence*
   see also **bring about, cause, excite, incite, motivate, occasion**

proxy see **replacement, representative, substitute**

prudence see **caution, common sense, economy**

prudent see **careful, economical, sensible, thrifty**

prudish see **prim**

pry verb to try to find out about someone else's private business: *We do not want people prying into our business*

interfere: *I wish everyone would stop interfering and just leave me alone*

intrude: *The press were intruding into my personal life*

poke your nose in informal: *Who asked you to poke your nose in?*

snoop informal: *He was snooping around Kim's hotel room*

prying see **nosy**

psyche see **mind, personality**

pub noun a place where alcoholic drinks are served: *He goes to the pub most nights*

bar British: *He works in a bar*

boozer British, Australian, New Zealand informal: *the local boozer*

inn: *a village inn*

lounge: *the hotel lounge*

public house: *a robbery at a public house in New Milton*

saloon: *a Wild West saloon*

tavern: *an old country tavern*

public noun **1** people in general: *the public's confidence in the government*

masses: *a quest to bring the Internet to the masses*

nation: *The President spoke to the nation*

people: *the will of the people*

populace: *a large proportion of the populace*

society: *a menace to society*

▷ adjective **2** relating to people in general: *public support for the idea*

civic: *a sense of civic pride*

general: *The project should raise general awareness about bullying*

popular: *Popular anger has been expressed in demonstrations*

universal: *the universal outrage at the deaths*

▷ adjective **3** provided for everyone to use or open to anyone: *public transport*

communal: *a communal dining room centre*

community: *a village community centre*

open to the public: *Part of the castle is now open to the public*

universal: *universal health care*

see also **people**

public house see **pub**

publication see **book**

publicity noun information or advertisements about an item or event: *government publicity campaigns*

advertising: *tobacco advertising in women's magazines*

plug informal: *The whole interview was an unashamed plug for her new book*

promotion: *They've spent a lot of money on advertising and promotion*

publicize verb to advertise something or make it widely known: *The author appeared on TV to publicize her book*

advertise: *The product has been much advertised in specialist magazines*

plug informal: *another celebrity plugging their latest book*

promote: *a tour to promote his second solo album*

see also **advertise, promote**

publish verb to make a piece of writing available for reading: *We publish a range of titles*

bring out: *The newspapers all brought out special editions*

print: *a letter printed in the Times yesterday*

put out: *a statement put out by the Iraqi news agency*
see also **release**

puerile *see* **childish, frivolous**

puff *see* **gasp**

puffed up *see* **pompous**

puke *verb informal* to vomit: *They got drunk and puked*

be sick: *She got up and was sick in the handbasin*

chunder *Australian, New Zealand slang*: *the time you chundered in the taxi*

spew *informal*: *He's really drunk. I hope he doesn't start spewing*

throw up *informal*: *She threw up after reading reports of the trial*

vomit: *Anything containing cow's milk made him vomit*
see also **vomit**

puku *see* **stomach**

pull *verb* **1** to draw an object towards you: *a wooden plough pulled by oxen*

drag: *He dragged his chair towards the table*

draw: *He drew his chair nearer the fire*

haul: *A crane was used to haul the car out of the stream*

tow: *They threatened to tow away my van*

tug: *She kicked him, tugging his thick hair*

yank: *She yanked open the drawer*
▷ *noun* **2** the attraction or influence of something: *The pull of Mexico was too strong*

attraction: *The attraction of Hollywood began to pall*

lure: *The lure of rural life is as strong as ever*

magnetism: *the sheer magnetism of his presence*
see also **attract, draw, lure, tug**

pull back *see* **retreat**

pull out *see* **extract, withdraw**

pull through *see* **survive**

pull together *see* **cooperate, unite**

pull up *see* **halt**

pulse *see* **rhythm**

pump *see* **drain**

punctual *adjective* arriving or leaving at the correct time: *The most punctual airline last year was Swissair*

in good time: *It is now 5am and we are in good time*

on time: *I'm generally early or on time for an appointment*

prompt: *We expect you to be prompt for all your classes*

puncture *see* **burst, leak, pierce**

pungent *see* **sour**

punish *verb* to make someone suffer a penalty for some misbehaviour: *I got punished for insolence*

discipline: *He was disciplined by his company but not dismissed*

penalize: *Bad teaching is not penalized in a formal way*

rap someone's knuckles: *The company got its knuckles rapped for this advertisement*

sentence: *He has admitted the charge and will be sentenced later*

throw the book at: *The football authorities seem certain to throw the book at him*

punishment *noun* a penalty for a crime or offence: *The punishment must always fit the crime*

penalty: *One of those arrested could face the death penalty*

retribution: *He didn't want any further involvement for fear of retribution*

puny *adjective* very small and weak: *He's always been a puny lad*

feeble: *He was old and feeble*

frail: *She lay in bed looking frail*

sickly: *He has been a sickly child*

skinny: *a skinny little boy*

weak: *His arms and legs were weak*
see also **weak**

pupil noun a student taught at a school: *She is a model pupil*
  scholar South African: *a bunch of rowdy scholars*
  schoolboy or **schoolgirl**: *a group of ten-year-old schoolboys*
  schoolchild: *The bus was packed with schoolchildren*
  student: *The students are sorted into three ability groups*

purchase see **buy**

purchaser see **customer**

pure adjective **1** clean and free from harmful substances: *The water is pure enough to drink*
  clean: *Tiled kitchen floors are easy to keep clean*
  germ-free: *chlorine gas used to keep water germ-free*
  pasteurized: *The milk is pasteurized to kill bacteria*
  spotless: *She kept the kitchen spotless*
  sterilized: *sterilized surgical equipment*
  2 complete and total: *a matter of pure luck*
  absolute: *You're talking absolute nonsense*
  complete: *complete and utter rubbish*
  outright: *an outright rejection of the deal*
  sheer: *acts of sheer desperation*
  unmitigated: *Last year's crop was an unmitigated disaster*
  utter: *This, of course, is utter nonsense*
  see also **absolute, innocent, neat, refined, sheer, utter**

purely see **only**

purified see **clean, refined**

puritanical see **prim**

purple noun or adjective

purpose noun **1** the reason for something: *What is the purpose of this meeting?*
  aim: *the aim of the policy*
  function: *Their main function is to raise capital for industry*
  intention: *The intention of the scheme is to encourage faster sales*
  object: *the object of the exercise*
  point: *I don't see the point of it*
  reason: *What is the real reason for the delay?*

on purpose adverb deliberately: *Did you do that on purpose?*
  by design: *The pair met often – at first by chance but later by design*
  deliberately: *It looks as if the fire was started deliberately*
  intentionally: *I've never hurt anyone intentionally*
  knowingly: *He said that he'd never knowingly taken illegal drugs*
  purposely: *They are purposely withholding information*
  see also **function, goal, intention, object, point, reason, use, will**

purposeful see **determined**

purposely see **on purpose**

pursue see **chase, follow**

pursuit see **activity, interest**

push verb **1** to apply force to something in order to move it: *She pushed the door open*
  press: *He pressed his back against the door*
  ram: *He rammed the key into the lock*
  shove: *He shoved her aside*
  thrust: *They thrust him into the back of the jeep*
  2 to persuade someone into doing something: *His mother pushed him into auditioning for a part*
  encourage: *She encouraged me to stick to the diet*
  persuade: *They persuaded him to moderate his views*
  press: *Trade unions are pressing him to stand firm*

urge: He had urged her to come to Ireland

see also **advertise, agitate, campaign, drive, press, rush, stick, stuff**

pushy adjective informal unpleasantly forceful and determined: a confident and pushy young woman

aggressive: a very aggressive business executive

ambitious: You have to be ambitious to make it in this business

assertive: Women have become more assertive over the last ten years

bossy: She remembers being a rather bossy little girl

forceful: Sarah is notorious for her forceful and quarrelsome nature

obtrusive: "You are rude and obtrusive, Mr Smith," said Tommy

puss see **cat**

pussy see **cat**

pussycat see **cat**

put verb 1 to place something somewhere: She put the photograph on the desk

deposit: On his way out he deposited a glass in front of me

lay: Lay a sheet of newspaper on the floor

place: He placed it in the inside pocket of his jacket

position: Plants were carefully positioned in the alcove

rest: He rested his arms on the back of the chair

2 to express something: I think you put that very well

phrase: I would have phrased it quite differently

word: You misinterpreted his letter, or else he worded it poorly

see also **express, insert, lay, place, pose, position, set, stick**

put across see **express**

put back see **postpone, put off**

put by see **reserve, save**

put down verb 1 to criticize someone and make them appear foolish: Racist jokes come from wanting to put down other people

belittle: She's always belittling her husband in public

criticize: She rarely criticized any of her children

find fault: I wish you wouldn't find fault with me in front of the kids

humiliate: His teacher continually humiliates him

2 to kill an animal that is ill or dangerous: Magistrates ordered the dog to be put down immediately

destroy: The horse had to be destroyed

kill: Animals should be killed humanely

put out of its misery: The bird was so badly injured I decided to put it out of its misery

put to sleep: Take the dog to the vet's and have her put to sleep

see also **attack, criticize, crush, deposit, humiliate, insult**

put forward see **produce, submit**

put off verb to delay something: Ministers have put off making a decision until next month

defer: Customers often defer payment for as long as possible

delay: She wants to delay the wedding

postpone: The visit has been postponed indefinitely

put back: The news conference has been put back a couple of hours

put on ice: The decision has been put on ice until October

reschedule: Since I'll be away, I'd like to reschedule the meeting

see also **delay, discourage, postpone**

put on see **perform, wear**

put out see **eliminate, publish, release, trouble**

put through see **subject**

put to sleep see **hypnotize, put down**

put together see **assemble, construct**

put up see **accommodate, construct**

put up with verb to tolerate something disagreeable: They won't put up with a return to the bad old days

abide: I can't abide arrogant people

bear: He can't bear to talk about it

stand: She cannot stand her boss

stand for: We won't stand for it any more

stomach: He could not stomach violence

tolerate: She can no longer tolerate the position she is in
see also **tolerate**

puzzle verb 1 to perplex and confuse: There was something about her that puzzled me

baffle: An apple tree producing square fruit is baffling experts

bewilder: His silence bewildered her

confuse: German politics surprised and confused him

mystify: The audience were mystified by the plot

stump: I was stumped by an unexpected question

▷ noun 2 a game or question that requires a lot of thought to solve: a crossword puzzle

brain-teaser informal: It took me ages to solve that brain-teaser

poser: Here is a little poser for you

problem: a mathematical problem

riddle: See if you can answer this riddle
see also **confuse, mystery, problem, wonder**

puzzled see **confused**

puzzling see **confusing, funny, hard, tricky**

q

quack see **fraud**

quail see **cower**

quake see **shake**

qualification noun 1 a skill or achievement: His qualifications are impressive

ability: a man of considerable abilities

accomplishment: Carl was proud of his son's accomplishments

achievement: the highest academic achievement

capability: Her capabilities were not fully appreciated

quality: Colley's leadership qualities

skill: a skill you can use

2 something added to make a statement less strong: The argument is not true without qualification

condition: You can make any conditions you like

exception: a major exception to this general argument

modification: to consider modifications to his proposal

reservation: men whose work I admire without reservation
see also **condition**

qualify verb to pass the tests necessary for an activity: I qualified as a doctor 30 years ago

become licensed: You can only become licensed by doing an accredited course
gain qualifications: the opportunity to gain medical qualifications
get certified: They wanted to get certified as divers
graduate: She graduated as a physiotherapist in 1960
see also **pass**

quality noun **1** the measure of how good something is: The quality of food is very poor
calibre: a man of your calibre
distinction: a chef of great distinction
grade: high grade meat and poultry
merit: a work of real merit
value: He set a high value upon their friendship
worth: a person's true worth
2 a characteristic of something: These qualities are essential for success
aspect: every aspect of our lives
characteristic: their physical characteristics
feature: the most striking feature of his work
mark: the mark of a great composer
property: the magnetic properties of iron
trait: the young Ms Rankine's personality traits
see also **attribute, characteristic, feature, point, property, qualification, standard**

qualm see **doubt**
quandary see **fix, jam, problem**
quantities see **a lot** or **lots**
quantity noun **1** an amount you can measure or count: a large quantity of alcohol
amount: a small amount of mayonnaise
number: There are a limited number of seats available

part: the greater part of his wealth
sum: a large sum of money
2 the amount of something that there is: emphasis on quality rather than quantity
extent: the extent of the damage
measure: The government has had a fair measure of success
size: He gauged the size of the audience
volume: the sheer volume of traffic and accidents
see also **amount, lot**

quarrel noun **1** an angry argument: I had a terrible quarrel with my brother
argument: an argument about money
disagreement: My instructor and I had a brief disagreement
dispute: Brand eavesdropped on the petty dispute
feud: a two-year feud between neighbours
fight: It was a silly fight about where we parked the car
row: Maxine and I had a terrible row
squabble: minor squabbles about phone bills
▷ verb **2** to have an angry argument: My brother quarrelled with my father
argue: They were still arguing later
bicker: They bickered endlessly over procedure
clash: She had clashed with Doyle in the past
fall out informal: Mum and I used to fall out a lot
fight: The couple often fought with their son
row: He had rowed with his girlfriend
squabble: The children were squabbling over the remote control
see also **argue, clash, disagreement, row, squabble**
quarrelsome see **aggressive**
quarry see **dig**

quarter see region

quarters see accommodation

quash see cancel, suppress

queasy adjective feeling slightly sick: He already felt queasy

ill: I was feeling ill

nauseous: The medication may make you feel nauseous

queer: Twenty minutes later, he began to feel queer

sick: The very thought of food made him feel sick

unwell: He felt unwell this afternoon
see also **crook, ill, sick, unwell**

queer see bizarre, odd, peculiar, queasy, strange, weird

quell see crush, subdue, suppress

query noun **1** a question: If you have any queries, please contact us

inquiry: I'll be happy to answer all your inquiries, if I can

question: The President refused to answer further questions on the subject

▷ verb **2** to question something because it seems wrong: No one queried my decision

challenge: The move was challenged by two countries

dispute: He disputed the allegations

object to: A lot of people objected to the plan

question: It never occurred to me to question the doctor's decisions
see also **ask, dispute, doubt, question**

quest see search

question noun **1** a problem that needs to be discussed: Can we get back to the question of the car?

issue: What is your view on this issue?

motion: The conference is now debating the motion

point: There is another point to consider

subject: He raised the subject of money

topic: the topic of where to go on holiday

▷ verb **2** to ask someone questions: A man is being questioned by police

examine: Lawyers examined the witnesses

interrogate: I interrogated everyone even slightly involved

probe: tabloid journalists probing us for details

quiz: She quizzed me quite closely for a while

3 to express doubts about something: He never stopped questioning his own beliefs

challenge: Rose convincingly challenged the story

dispute: Nobody disputed that Davey was clever

distrust: I distrusted my ability to keep quiet

doubt: Nobody doubted his sincerity

query: No one queried my decision

suspect: Do we suspect the motives of our friends?
see also **affair, ask, business, challenge, contest, dispute, doubt, interrogate, issue, matter, query, subject**

questionable see doubtful, dubious, suspect, suspicious

queue see line, row

quick adjective **1** moving with great speed: You'll have to be quick to catch the flight

brisk: a brisk walk

fast: a very fast driver

hasty: He spoke in a hasty, nervous way

rapid: a rapid rise through the company

speedy: a speedy recovery

swift: She is as swift as an arrow

2 lasting only a short time: a quick chat

brief: a brief meeting

cursory: *a cursory glance inside the van*
hasty: *a hasty meal of bread and soup*
hurried: *He ate a hurried breakfast*
perfunctory: *With a perfunctory smile, she walked past Jessica*
3 happening without any delay: *a quick response*
hasty: *This is no hasty decision*
prompt: *Prompt action is needed*
sudden: *this week's sudden cold snap*
see also **acute, astute, brief, fast, intelligent, keen, prompt, sharp, sudden, swift**

quicken see **accelerate, hurry**

quickly adverb with great speed: *Stop me if I'm speaking too quickly*
fast: *How fast were you driving?*
hastily: *sheltering in hastily erected tents*
hurriedly: *students hurriedly taking notes*
rapidly: *moving rapidly across the field*
speedily: *She speedily recovered herself*
swiftly: *They had to act swiftly to save him*
see also **fast**

quick-witted see **sharp**

quiet adjective **1** making very little noise: *The children were quiet and contented*
hushed: *Tales were exchanged in hushed tones*
inaudible: *a tiny, almost inaudible squeak*
low: *I spoke in a low voice to Sullivan*
silent: *He could speak no English and was silent*
soft: *There was some soft music playing*
2 peaceful and calm: *a quiet evening at home*
calm: *The city seems relatively calm today*

mild: *The night was mild*
peaceful: *a peaceful old house*
restful: *a restful scene*
serene: *the beautiful, serene park*
tranquil: *a tranquil lake*
▷ noun **3** silence or lack of noise: *The teacher called for quiet*
calmness: *the calmness of this area*
peace: *I enjoy peace and quiet*
serenity: *the peace and serenity of a tropical sunset*
silence: *There was a silence around the table*
stillness: *the stillness of the summer night*
tranquillity: *the tranquillity of village life*
see also **calm, easy, peace, peaceful, silence, silent, sleepy, soft**

quieten see **calm, silence**

quip see **joke**

quirky see **eccentric**

quit verb to leave a place or stop doing something: *Leigh quit his job as a salesman*
discontinue: *Do not discontinue the treatment without seeing your doctor*
give up: *She gave up smoking last year*
leave: *He left school with no qualifications*
resign: *Scott resigned from the firm*
retire: *Littlejohn was forced to retire from the race*
stop: *I stopped working last year to have a baby*
see also **leave, resign, stop**

quite adverb **1** fairly but not very: *He is quite old*
fairly: *Both ships are fairly new*
moderately: *a moderately attractive man*
rather: *I made some rather bad mistakes*
reasonably: *I can dance reasonably*

well
somewhat: *He's somewhat deaf*
2 completely and totally: *Jane lay quite still*
absolutely: *I absolutely refuse to get married*
completely: *something completely different*
entirely: *an entirely new approach*
fully: *He has still not fully recovered*
perfectly: *They are perfectly safe to eat*
totally: *The fire totally destroyed the house*
see also **exactly, pretty, rather**
quiver *see* **shake**
quiz *see* **ask, interrogate, question**
quota *see* **proportion, share**
quotation *see* **passage**
quote *verb* **1** to repeat the exact words someone has said: *She quoted a great line from Shakespeare*
cite: *She cites a favourite poem by George Herbert*
extract: *This material has been extracted from the handbook*
recite: *They recited poetry to one another*
repeat: *Could you repeat the whole interview word for word?*
see also **estimate**

rabid *see* **fanatical**
race *noun* **1** a group of human beings with similar physical characteristics: *Discrimination on the grounds of race is illegal*
ethnic group: *Ethnic group and nationality are often different*
nation: *a mature and cultured nation*
people: *an address to the American people*
▷ *verb* **2** to move very quickly: *Her heart raced uncontrollably*
dash: *He dashed upstairs*
fly: *I must fly or I'll miss my train*
hurry: *They hurried down the street*
run: *The gunmen escaped by running into the woods*
speed: *speeding along as fast as I could*
tear: *The door flew open and she tore into the room*
see also **dash, fly, rush, speed, tear**
racism *see* **prejudice**
racket *noun* **1** a lot of noise: *The racket went on past midnight*
clamour: *She could hear a clamour in the road*
commotion: *He heard a commotion outside*
din: *make themselves heard over the*

din of the crowd
hubbub: His voice was drowned out by the hubbub of the fans
noise: There was too much noise in the room
row: "Whatever is that row?" she demanded
rumpus: There was such a rumpus, she had to shout to make herself heard
2 an illegal way of making money: a drugs racket
enterprise: A money-laundering enterprise
fraud: tax frauds
scheme: a quick money-making scheme
see also **noise, sound**

radiance see **light**
radiant see **bright, brilliant, shining**
radiate see **shine**
radical see **drastic, extreme, left-wing**

rage noun **1** a feeling of very strong anger: trembling with rage
anger: She felt deep anger at what he had said
frenzy: Their behaviour drove her into a frenzy
fury: Her face was distorted with fury and pain
wrath: He incurred the wrath of the referee
▷ verb **2** to be angry or speak angrily about something: He was raging at their lack of response
be furious: He is furious at the way his wife has been treated
fume: I was still fuming over her remark
lose your temper: They had never seen me lose my temper before
rave: She cried and raved for weeks
storm: "It's a disaster", he stormed
3 to continue with great force: The fire raged out of control
be at its height: when the storm was

at its height
rampage: a mob rampaging through the town
storm: armies storming across the continent
surge: The flood surged through the village
see also **anger, frenzy, rampage, rave**

ragged see **irregular, scruffy, shabby**
raging see **furious, violent, wild**

raid verb **1** to attack something by force: Soldiers raided the capital
assault: Their stronghold was assaulted by pirates
attack: We are being attacked!
break into: No-one saw them break into the warehouse
invade: The invading army took all their food supplies
plunder: plundering the homes of the inhabitants
▷ noun **2** an attack on something: a bank raid
attack: a surprise attack on the house
break-in: The break-in occurred last night
foray: Guerrillas made forays into the territory
see also **attack, loot**

rail see **bar**

rain noun **1** water falling from the clouds: A spot of rain fell on her hand
deluge: homes damaged in the deluge
downpour: A two-day downpour swelled water levels
drizzle: The drizzle had stopped and the sun was shining
rainfall: four years of below average rainfall
showers: bright spells followed by scattered showers
▷ verb **2** to fall from the sky in drops: It rained the whole weekend
drizzle: It was starting to drizzle

when I left

pour: We drove all the way in pouring rain

teem: It teemed the entire day

rainfall see **rain**

rainy see **wet**

raise verb **1** to make something higher: a drive to raise standards of literacy

elevate: Emotional stress can elevate blood pressure

heave: He heaved his crippled leg into an easier position

hoist: He climbed on the roof to hoist the flag

lift: She lifted the last of her drink to her lips

2 to look after children until they are grown up: the house where she was raised

bring up: She brought up four children single-handed

nurture: the best way to nurture a child to adulthood

rear: He reared his sister's family as well as his own

3 to mention or suggest something: He had raised no objections at the time

advance: Some important ideas were advanced at the conference

bring up: I hesitate to bring up this matter with you, but I have no choice

broach: Eventually I broached the subject of her early life

introduce: always willing to introduce a new topic

moot: The project was first mooted last year

suggest: one possibility that might be suggested

see also **breed, collect, lift**

rally see **gathering, hui, revive**

ram see **drive, jam, push, stick, stuff**

ramble noun **1** a long walk in the countryside: They went for a ramble through the woods

excursion: They organized an excursion into the hills

hike: a long hike along the valley floor

stroll: The next day we took a stroll along the river bank

walk: We often go for walks in the country

▷ verb **2** to go for a long walk: freedom to ramble across the moors

amble: ambling along a country lane

stray: You mustn't stray across the border

stroll: whistling as he strolled along the road

walk: We finished the evening by walking along the beach

wander: He loved to wander in the woods

3 to talk in a confused way: He started rambling and repeating himself

babble: She babbled on and on about the visitors

chatter: I was so nervous that I chattered away like an idiot

see also **walk, wander**

rambling see **indirect**

ramp see **slope**

rampage verb **1** to rush about angrily or violently: children rampaging round the garden

go berserk: The crowd went berserk at the sight of him

rage: His shop was stormed by a raging mob

run amok: He was arrested after running amok with a gun

run riot: The prisoners ran riot after the announcement

on the rampage adjective rushing about in a wild and violent way: a bull on the rampage

amok: The gunman ran amok and killed several people

berserk: The fans went berserk and mobbed the stage

wild: They just went wild after he left

see also **rage, riot**

rancid *see* **sour**

rancorous *see* **bitter**

rancour *see* **resentment**

random *adjective* **1** not based on a definite plan: *random violence against innocent victims*
  aimless: *after several hours of aimless searching*
  arbitrary: *Arbitrary arrests and detention without trial were common*
  haphazard: *He had never seen such a haphazard approach to writing*
  indiscriminate: *the indiscriminate use of fertilisers*
  spot: *picked up in a spot check*
at random *adverb* without any definite plan: *chosen at random*
  aimlessly: *wandering around aimlessly for hours*
  arbitrarily: *The questions were chosen quite arbitrarily*
  haphazardly: *The books were stacked haphazardly on the shelves*
  indiscriminately: *This disease strikes indiscriminately*
  randomly: *a randomly selected sample*
  see also **absent-minded, accidental, irregular**

randomly *see* **at random**

range *noun* **1** the maximum limits of something: *Tactical nuclear weapons have shorter ranges*
  bounds: *the bounds of good taste*
  extent: *the full extent of my knowledge*
  field: *The subject covers a very wide field*
  limits: *outside the city limits*
  province: *This doesn't fall within our province*
  scope: *He promised to widen the scope of their activities*
  2 a number of different things of the same kind: *a wide range of colours*

assortment: *There was a good assortment to choose from*
  class: *Cars in this class are expensive*
  gamut: *I experienced the whole gamut of emotions*
  selection: *a wide selection of delicious meals*
  series: *a completely new model series*
  variety: *The shop stocks a variety of local craft products*
▷ *verb* **3** to vary between two extremes: *goods ranging between the everyday and the exotic*
  extend: *The reclaimed land extends from here to the river*
  go: *Their sizes go from very small to enormous*
  run: *Accommodation runs from log cabins to high-standard hotels*
  stretch: *with interests that stretched from chemicals to sugar*
  vary: *The cycle of sunspots varies between 8 to 15 years*
  see also **area, choice, variety, wander**

rank *noun* **1** someone's level in a group: *He rose to the rank of captain*
  class: *relationships between social classes*
  echelon: *the upper echelons of society*
  grade: *Staff turnover is high among the junior grades*
  level: *various levels of the judiciary system*
  standing: *a woman of wealth and social standing*
  station: *a humble station in life*
  status: *promoted to the status of foreman*
  2 a row of people or things: *ranks of police in riot gear*
  column: *a column of figures*
  file: *They walked in single file to the top*
  line: *He waited in a line of slow-moving vehicles*

row: *She lived in the middle of a row of pretty cottages*
▷ *adjective* **2** complete and absolute: *It was rank stupidity to go there alone*
absolute: *not intended for absolute beginners*
complete: *her complete ignorance*
downright: *That was just downright rudeness*
sheer: *his sheer stupidity*
unmitigated: *an unmitigated villain*
utter: *his utter disregard for other people*
see also **class, classify, level, line, rate, row, status**

ransack *see* **loot**

rant *see* **rave**

rap *see* **blame, hit**

rap someone's knuckles *see* **punish**

rapid *see* **fast, hasty, prompt, quick, swift**

rapidity *see* **speed**

rapidly *see* **fast, quickly**

rapport *see* **relationship**

rapture *see* **delight, ecstasy, heaven, joy**

rare *adjective* not common or frequent: *a rare species of bird*
exceptional: *in exceptional circumstances*
few: *Genuine friends are few*
scarce: *Jobs are becoming increasingly scarce*
sparse: *Information about the tests is sparse*
sporadic: *occurring at only sporadic intervals*
uncommon: *The disease is uncommon in younger women*
unusual: *an unusual variety but a very attractive one*
see also **exceptional, scarce, singular, uncommon, unusual**

raring to go *see* **eager**

rarity *see* **curiosity**

rash *adjective* **1** acting in a hasty and foolish way: *It would be rash to act on such flimsy evidence*
foolhardy: *Some described his behaviour as foolhardy*
hasty: *This is no hasty decision*
impetuous: *As usual, he reacted in a heated and impetuous way*
impulsive: *He is too impulsive to take this responsibility*
reckless: *his reckless driving*
▷ *noun* **2** an irritated area on your skin: *I noticed a rash on my leg*
eruption: *an unpleasant skin eruption*
outbreak: *an outbreak of blisters around his mouth*
3 a large number of events happening together: *a rash of strikes*
epidemic: *A victim of the recent epidemic of shootings*
flood: *a flood of complaints about the programme*
plague: *Last year there was a plague of burglaries*
spate: *a spate of attacks on horses*
wave: *the current wave of violent attacks*
see also **unwise**

rasp *see* **scrape**

rasping *see* **hoarse**

rate *noun* **1** the speed or frequency of something: *appearing at the rate of one a week*
frequency: *She phoned with increasing frequency*
pace: *at an accelerated pace*
speed: *moving at the speed of light*
tempo: *They wanted to speed up the tempo of change*
velocity: *changes in wind velocity*
2 the cost or charge for something: *phone calls at cheap rates*
charge: *An annual charge will be made for this service*
cost: *a low-cost mortgage*

fee: The work will be invoiced at the usual fee

price: falling share prices

tariff: How much you pay depends on your tariff

▷ verb **3** to give an opinion of someone's qualities: He was rated as one of the best

appraise: She gave me an appraising glance

class: classed as one of the top ten athletes

consider: I considered myself to be quite good at maths

count: That would be counted as wrong

rank: The hotel was ranked as one of the world's best

regard: a highly regarded member of staff

see also **class, consider, cost, count, grade, judge**

rate highly see **appreciate, value**

rather adverb to a certain extent: We got along rather well

fairly: Both ships are fairly new

pretty informal: I'm pretty tired now

quite: The cottage looks quite ordinary from the road

relatively: I think I'm relatively easy to get on with

slightly: slightly startled by his sudden appearance

somewhat: He said, somewhat unconvincingly, that he would pay

see also **pretty, quite**

ration see **limit, share**

rational adjective using reason rather than emotion: to arrive at a rational conclusion

enlightened: enlightened companies who take a pragmatic view

logical: There must be a logical explanation for it

reasonable: a perfectly reasonable decision

sensible: The sensible thing is to leave them alone

see also **logical, reasonable, sane, sensible, wise**

rationality see **reason**

rations see **kai, supplies**

rattle see **shake**

ratty see **irritable**

rave verb **1** to talk in an uncontrolled way: He started raving about being treated badly

babble: She babbled on and on about her plans

rage: He was raging at their lack of response

rant: She started ranting about her boss's attitude

2 informal to be enthusiastic about something: She raved about the facilities there

be wild about informal: He was just wild about the play

enthuse: She enthused about the local architecture

gush: "It was brilliant," he gushed

see also **rage**

ravenous see **hungry**

raving see **hysterical**

raw see **cold, inexperienced, sore, tender**

raze see **destroy**

razor-sharp see **sharp**

reach verb **1** to arrive somewhere: He did not stop until he reached the door

arrive at: to arrive at an erroneous conclusion

attain: She worked hard to attain a state of calm

get as far as: If we get as far as the coast we will be quite satisfied

get to: You must get to the end before noon

make: They didn't think they would make the summit

2 to extend as far as something: Her cloak reached to the ground

extend to: The boundaries extend to the edge of the lake

go as far as: Try to make the ball go as far as the trees

touch: I could touch both walls with my arms extended

3 to arrive at a certain stage or level: Unemployment has reached record levels

arrive at: They planted a flag when they arrived at the top

attain: He was close to attaining his personal best

climb to: Attendance climbed to a record level this year

fall to: Profits are expected to fall to their lowest level

rise to: She rose rapidly to the top of her profession

see also **contact**, **extend**, **stretch**

reaction noun **1** a person's response to something: Reaction to the visit was mixed

acknowledgment: She made no acknowledgment of my question

answer: In answer to speculation in the press, she declared her interest

feedback: Continue to ask for feedback on your work

response: in response to a request from the members

2 a response to something unpopular: a reaction against religious leaders

backlash: the male backlash against feminism

counterbalance: an organization set up as a counterbalance to the official group

reactionary see **right-wing**

read verb **1** to look at something written: I love to read in bed

glance at: He just glanced briefly at the article

look at: She was looking at the evening paper

pore over: poring over a dictionary

scan: There's only time to scan through it quickly

study: I'll study the text more closely later

2 to understand what someone means: as if he could read her thoughts

comprehend: Her expression was difficult to comprehend

decipher: She was still no closer to deciphering the code

interpret: You have to interpret their gestures, too

read out see **issue**

read up see **study**

reading see **extract**

ready adjective **1** prepared for action or use: The plums are ready to eat now

organized: Everything is organized for the party tomorrow

prepared: He was prepared for a tough fight

primed: The other side is primed for battle

ripe: Are those strawberries ripe yet?

set: We'll be set to go in five minutes

2 willing to do something: She was always ready to give interviews

agreeable: We can go ahead if you are agreeable

eager: Children are eager to learn

happy: always happy to help

keen: He wasn't keen to get involved

willing: questions which they were not willing to answer

3 easily produced or obtained: ready cash

accessible: The system should be accessible to everyone

available: Food is available round the clock

convenient: a convenient excuse

handy: Keep a pencil and paper handy

see also **agreeable**, **fluent**, **willing**

real adjective **1** actually existing and

not imagined: *You're dealing with real life now*

actual: *She was the actual basis for the leading character*

authentic: *containing authentic details of what happened*

concrete: *I don't have any concrete evidence*

factual: *a factual account*

genuine: *His worries about the future were genuine ones*

legitimate: *These are legitimate concerns*

tangible: *I cannot see any tangible benefits from these changes*

true: *the true story of his life*

2 genuine and not imitation: *Is that a real gun?*

authentic: *an authentic French recipe*

bona fide: *We are happy to donate to bona fide charities*

dinkum *Australian, New Zealand informal: a place which serves dinkum Aussie tucker*

genuine: *It's a genuine Rembrandt, all right*

honest: *It was an honest attempt to set things right*

sincere: *His remorse was completely sincere, not just an act*

rightful: *the rightful heir to the throne*

true: *He is a true believer in human rights*

unaffected: *her genuine and unaffected sympathy for the victims*

see also **authentic, genuine, natural, sincere, true**

realism see **reality**

realistic adjective **1** accepting the true situation: *It's only realistic to admit that things will go wrong*

down-to-earth: *We welcomed her down-to-earth approach*

level-headed: *a sensible, level-headed approach*

matter-of-fact: *He sounded matter-of-fact and unemotional*

practical: *a highly practical attitude to life*

sensible: *I'm trying to persuade you to be more sensible*

sober: *a more sober assessment of the situation*

2 true to real life: *His novels are more realistic than his short stories*

authentic: *They have to look authentic*

faithful: *faithful copies of old household items*

lifelike: *almost as lifelike as a photograph*

true: *It gave a true picture of how things were*

see also **actual**

reality noun something that is true and not imagined: *Fiction and reality were increasingly blurred*

authenticity: *The film's authenticity impressed the critics*

fact: *No-one knew how much of what he said was fact*

realism: *His stories had an edge of realism*

truth: *I must tell you the truth about this situation*

see also **fact, truth**

realize verb to become aware of something: *People don't realize how serious it is*

appreciate: *He appreciates the difficulties we face*

comprehend: *They do not comprehend the nature of the problem*

grasp: *She still couldn't grasp what had really happened*

recognize: *Of course I recognize that evil exists*

understand: *I didn't understand what he meant until later*

see also **appreciate, discover, find, fulfil, grasp, see, sense,** understand

really adverb **1** very or certainly: *I've had a really good time*

absolutely: *feeling absolutely exhausted*

certainly: *I am certainly getting tired of hearing about it*

extremely: *My mobile phone is extremely useful*

remarkably: *They have been remarkably successful*

terribly: *I'm terribly sorry to bother you*

truly: *a truly splendid man*

very: *learning very quickly*

2 in actual fact: *He didn't really love her*

actually: *I pretended I was interested, but I was actually half asleep*

in fact: *It sounds simple, but in fact it's very difficult*

in reality: *He came across as streetwise, but in reality he was not*

truly: *I truly never minded caring for Rusty*

see also **very**

reappear see **return**

rear see **back, bottom, breed, raise**

reason noun **1** the cause of something that happens: *for a multitude of reasons*

cause: *The true cause of the accident may never be known*

grounds: *some grounds for optimism*

incentive: *There is no incentive to adopt these measures*

motive: *Police have ruled out robbery as a motive*

purpose: *the purpose of their visit*

2 the ability to think: *a conflict between emotion and reason*

intellect: *good health and a lively intellect*

judgment: *His judgment was impaired*

rationality: *We live in an era of rationality*

reasoning: *a lack of sound reasoning and logic*

sense: *He should have had more sense*

▷ verb **3** to try to persuade someone of something: *It's better to reason with them than to use force*

bring round *informal*: *We'll try to bring you round to our point of view*

persuade: *I had to persuade him of the advantages*

win over: *They still hoped to win him over to their way of thinking*

see also **argue, cause, excuse, grounds, purpose, sense, wisdom**

reasonable adjective **1** fair and sensible: *a reasonable sort of chap*

fair: *You can be sure she will be fair with you*

moderate: *an easygoing man of very moderate views*

rational: *Please try to be rational about this*

sane: *No sane person wishes to see a war*

sensible: *She was a sensible girl and did not panic*

sober: *We are now more sober and realistic*

steady: *a politician who was steady almost to the point of being boring*

wise: *You're a wise old man: tell me what to do*

2 based on good reasoning: *It seems reasonable to expect rapid urban growth*

justifiable: *Our violence was justifiable on the grounds of political necessity*

legitimate: *That's a perfectly legitimate fear*

logical: *There was a logical explanation*

sensible: *a sensible solution*

sound: *sound advice*

understandable: *His unhappiness*

was understandable

3 not too expensive: *His fees were quite reasonable*

cheap: *She said she'd share a flat if I could find somewhere cheap enough*

competitive: *homes offered for sale at competitive prices*

fair: *It's a fair price for a car like that*

inexpensive: *an inexpensive divorce settlement*

low: *The low prices and friendly service made for a pleasant evening*

modest: *a modest charge*

see also **cheap, decent, logical, moderate, rational, respectable, sane, sound, tolerable**

reasonably see **quite**

reasoned see **logical**

reasoning see **argument, reason**

reassure verb to make someone feel less worried: *She reassured me that everything was fine*

bolster: *measures intended to bolster morale*

cheer up: *I wrote it just to cheer myself up*

comfort: *He tried to comfort her as far as he could*

encourage: *Investors were encouraged by the news*

see also **comfort, encourage, satisfy**

reassured see **secure**

rebel verb to fight against authority and accepted values: *I rebelled against everything when I was young*

defy: *It was the first time she had defied her mother*

mutiny: *Sailors mutinied against their officers*

resist: *activists convicted of resisting apartheid*

revolt: *The islanders revolted against the prince*

rebellion noun an organized opposition to authority: *the ruthless*

suppression of the rebellion

insurrection: *They were plotting to stage an armed insurrection*

mutiny: *convicted of mutiny and high treason*

revolt: *The revolt ended in failure*

revolution: *after the French Revolution*

uprising: *Isolated attacks turned into a full-scale uprising*

rebuff see **reject**

rebuild see **reconstruct, restore**

rebuke see **scold**

recall see **memory, remember**

recapitulate see **sum up**

recapture see **recover, recovery**

recede see **disappear, vanish**

receive verb **1** to accept something from someone: *Did they receive my letter?*

accept: *They accepted the parcel gratefully*

be given: *We were all given presents*

get: *She got some lovely things*

pick up: *He picked up an award for his performance*

take: *Will you take this parcel for your neighbour?*

2 to experience something: *We received a very warm welcome*

encounter: *He encountered some unexpected opposition*

suffer: *He suffered some bangs and bumps*

sustain: *She had sustained a cut on her arm*

undergo: *You may have to undergo a bit of teasing*

3 to welcome visitors: *You must be there to receive your guests*

entertain: *She loved to entertain friends at home*

greet: *They greeted the visitors at the door*

meet: *I'll come down to meet you*

take in: *The country took in many*

refugees

welcome: Several people came by to welcome me

see also **admit, get, greet**

recent adjective happening a short time ago: his most recent acquisition

current: a sound knowledge of current affairs

fresh: fresh footprints in the snow

new: the subject of a new film

present-day: Even by present-day standards these were large aircraft

up-to-date: the most up-to-date computers

see also **modern**

reception see **function, party**

receptive see **impressionable, passive**

recess see **break, holiday**

recession noun a decline in economic conditions: companies which survived after the recession

decline: signs of economic decline

depression: the Great Depression of the 1930s

downturn: due to a sharp downturn in the industry

slump: Many jobs were lost during the slump

see also **decline**

recite see **quote**

reckless see **irresponsible, rash**

recklessness see **abandon**

reckon verb 1 informal to think or believe something is the case: I reckon he's still fond of her

assume: If mistakes occurred, they were assumed to be my fault

believe formal: "You've never heard of him?" "I don't believe so."

consider: Barbara considers that people who sell these birds are acting illegally

judge: I would judge that my earnings are considerably below those of my sister

suppose: I suppose I'd better do some homework

think: I think there should be a ban on tobacco advertising formal formal

2 to calculate an amount: The figure is now reckoned to be 15%

calculate: We calculate that the average size farm in the county is 65 acres

count: The years before their arrival in prison are not counted as part of their sentence

estimate: Analysts estimate its current popularity at around ten per cent

figure out: I roughly figured out the total

work out: It is proving hard to work out the value of their assets

see also **calculate, conclude, expect, figure, guess, think**

reckoning see **count, estimate, guess**

reclamation see **recovery**

recline see **lie**

recognition see **credit, gratitude, honour**

recognize verb 1 to know who or what someone or something is: I recognized him at once

identify: She tried to identify the perfume

know: You'd know him if you saw him again

place: He couldn't place my voice immediately

spot: I spotted the house quite easily

2 to accept or acknowledge something: He was recognized as an outstanding pilot

acknowledge: Her great bravery was acknowledged

appreciate: In time you'll appreciate his good points

honour: achievements honoured with the Nobel Prize

salute: We salute your great courage
see also **appreciate, distinguish, identify, know, realize, remember**

recommence see **continue, renew**

recommend see **advise, advocate, nominate, suggest, vote**

recommendation see **idea, suggestion**

reconcile see **settle**

reconcile oneself see **resign oneself**

recondition see **renovate**

reconstruct verb 1 to rebuild something that has been damaged: The city centre has been completely reconstructed
rebuild: The task of rebuilding would be very expensive
recreate: They try to recreate the atmosphere of former times
regenerate: the ability to regenerate damaged tissues
renovate: The hotel was being renovated
restore: experts who specialize in restoring old furniture
2 to build up from small details: The police reconstructed the scene of the crime
build up: They built up an image of him from several different descriptions
deduce: The date can be deduced from other documents
piece together: It was easy to piece together the shattered fragments
see also **restore**

record noun 1 a stored account of something: medical records
account: The company keeps detailed accounts
archives: Earlier issues are stored in the archives
file: the right to inspect company files
journal: He kept a journal while he was travelling
minute: Did you read the minutes of the last meeting?

register: a register of births, deaths and marriages
2 what someone has done in the past: You will be rejected if you have a criminal record
background: His background was in engineering
career: His career spoke for itself
curriculum vitae: I must update my curriculum vitae
track record informal: Her track record as a teacher was impeccable
▷ verb 3 to note and store information: Her diary records her daily life in detail
document: All these facts were well documented
enter: All the names are entered in this book
log: They log everyone who comes in or out
note: I must note your birthday
register: We registered his birth straight away
write down: If I don't write it down, I'll forget it
see also **entry, list, note, trace, write**

recoup see **recover**

recover verb 1 to get better again: He has still not fully recovered
convalesce: those convalescing from illness or surgery
get better: He never really got better again
get well: Get well soon!
improve: The condition of your hair will soon improve
recuperate: recuperating from a serious injury
revive: Business soon revived once he came back
2 to get something back again: They took legal action to recover the money
get back: We got everything back after the burglary

recapture: *trying to recapture the atmosphere of our holiday*

recoup: *trying to recoup their losses*

regain: *It took him a while to regain his composure*

retrieve: *I retrieved my bag from the back seat*

recovery noun **1** the act of getting better again: *He made a remarkable recovery after his illness*

healing: *Adams claims that humour is an integral part of healing*

improvement: *Germany is showing a perceptible improvement*

recuperation: *great powers of recuperation*

revival: *little chance of a revival of interest*

2 the act of getting something back: *a reward for the recovery of the painting*

recapture: *An offensive was launched for the recapture of the airbase*

reclamation: *the reclamation of dry land from the marshes*

restoration: *She owed the restoration of her sight to this remarkable technique*

retrieval: *electronic storage and retrieval systems*

recreate see **reconstruct**

recreation see **entertainment, fun, leisure, pastime**

recruit verb **1** to persuade people to join a group: *He helped to recruit volunteers*

draft: *drafted into the armed forces*

enlist: *I had to enlist the help of six people to move it*

enrol: *She enrolled me on her evening course*

muster: *trying to muster support for the movement*

▷ noun **2** someone who has recently joined a group: *the latest batch of recruits*

beginner: *The course is suitable for beginners*

convert: *a recent convert to their religion*

novice: *I'm a novice at these things*

trainee: *My first job was as a graduate trainee with a bank*

recruitment see **employment**

rectify see **correct, reform**

recuperate see **recover**

recuperation see **recovery**

recurrent see **continual, frequent**

red tape see **bureaucracy**

redeem see **save**

red-faced see **embarrassed**

reduce verb **1** to make something smaller in size or amount: *Gradually reduce the dosage*

curtail: *His powers will be severely curtailed*

cut: *The first priority is to cut costs*

cut down: *Try to cut down your coffee consumption*

decrease: *The government plans to decrease interest rates*

diminish: *to diminish the prestige of the monarchy*

lessen: *a diet that would lessen the risk of disease*

lower: *a commitment to lower taxes*

shorten: *taking steps to shorten queues*

2 to bring to a weaker or inferior state: *The village was reduced to rubble*

degrade: *I wouldn't degrade myself by going out with him*

demote: *The Soviet team have been demoted to second place*

downgrade: *The female role has been downgraded in the drive foreguality*

drive: *an old woman driven to shoplifting to survive*

force: *The men were so hungry they were forced to eat grass*

see also **cut, decline, decrease,**

diminish, lessen, lower, weaken
reduced see low
reduction see cut, decrease, fall
redundant see idle, unemployed
reek see smell, stink
reeking see smelly
re-establish see renew, restore
refer verb **1** to mention something: *In his speech, he referred to a recent trip to Canada*
   allude: *She alluded to his absence in vague terms*
   bring up: *Why are you bringing that up now?*
   cite: *She cites a favourite poem by George Herbert*
   mention: *She did not mention her mother's illness*
   2 to look at to find something out: *I had to refer to the manual*
   consult: *He had to consult a dictionary*
   look up: *I looked up your file to get your address*
refer to see consult, mention
referee see judge
reference see mention
referendum see vote
refine see perfect, polish
refined adjective **1** polite and well-mannered: *His speech and manner are very refined*
   civilized: *the demands of civilized behaviour*
   genteel: *two ladies with genteel manners and voices*
   gentlemanly: *Sopwith behaved in his usual gentlemanly manner*
   ladylike: *They are models of ladylike decorum*
   polite: *polite and correct behaviour*
   2 processed to remove impurities: *refined sugar*
   distilled: *distilled water*
   filtered: *two pints of spring or filtered water*

processed: *a diet high in processed foods*
   pure: *crisp pure air*
   purified: *freshly purified drinking water*
   see also **fine, polite, sophisticated**
refinement see polish
reflect see consider, deliberate, ponder, think
reflect on see contemplate
reflection see thought
reflective see thoughtful
reflex see automatic
reform noun **1** a major change or improvement: *radical economic reforms*
   amendment: *an amendment to remove the ban on divorce*
   correction: *a correction of social injustice*
   improvement: *She is pressing for improvements to education*
   rehabilitation: *the rehabilitation of young offenders*
   ▷ verb **2** to make major changes or improvements to something: *his plans to reform the economy*
   amend: *They want to amend the current system*
   better: *industrial action to better their working conditions*
   correct: *keen to correct injustices*
   rectify: *measures suggested to rectify the financial situation*
   rehabilitate: *a loan for Bulgaria to rehabilitate its railway system*
   see also **change, correct, transform**
refrain see abstain
refrain from see avoid
refresh verb to make you feel more energetic: *A glass of fruit juice will refresh you*
   brace: *a bracing walk*
   enliven: *Music can enliven the spirit*
   rejuvenate: *He was told that the Italian climate would rejuvenate him*

revive: The cold water revived me a bit

stimulate: a toner to stimulate the skin

refreshing see **cool**

refreshment see **food**

refrigerate see **food**

refuge noun a place where you go for safety: a mountain refuge

asylum: political asylum

harbour: Patches of gorse were a great harbour for foxes

haven: The island is a haven for international criminals

sanctuary: a sanctuary from the outside world

shelter: an underground shelter
see also **retreat, shelter**

refund see **compensate, repay, return**

refurbish see **renovate, restore**

refuse verb 1 to say you will not do something: He refused to speculate about the contents of the letter

abstain: people who abstain from eating meat

decline: He declined to comment on the story

withhold: Financial aid for Britain has been withheld

2 to say you will not allow or accept something: He offered me a drink, which I refused

decline: He declined their invitation

reject: The court rejected their petition

spurn: You spurned his last offer

turn down: He has turned down the job

▷ noun 3 rubbish or waste: a weekly collection of refuse

garbage: rotting piles of garbage

junk: informal: What are you going to do with all that junk?

litter: If you see litter in the corridor, pick it up

rubbish: They had piled most of their rubbish into yellow skips

trash: I forgot to take out the trash

waste: a law that regulates the disposal of waste
see also **decline, deny, garbage, junk, reject, resist, rubbish, trash**

refute see **deny, disprove**

regain see **recover**

regal see **royal**

regard verb 1 to have particular views about someone or something: I regard creativity as a gift

consider: I consider activities such as jogging a waste of time

judge: This may or may not be judged as reasonable

look on: A lot of people looked on him as a healer

see: I don't see it as my duty to take sides

think of: We all thought of him as a father

view: They view the United States as a land of opportunity

2 literary to look at someone in a particular way: She regarded him curiously for a moment

contemplate: He contemplated her in silence

eye: We eyed each other thoughtfully

gaze: gazing at herself in the mirror

look: She looked at him earnestly

scrutinize: She scrutinized his features to see if he was to be trusted

watch: Chris watched him sipping his brandy
see also **admiration, esteem, rate, respect, view**

regard as see **consider**

regarding see **about**

regardless of see **despite, in spite of**

regenerate see **reconstruct**

region noun a large area of land: a remote mountainous region of Afghanistan

area: The area is renowned for its cuisine

district: *I drove around the business district*
land: *a land permanently cloaked in mist*
locality: *All other factories in the locality went on strike*
quarter: *We wandered through the Chinese quarter*
sector: *the northeast sector of Bosnia*
territory: *the disputed territory of Kashmir*
tract: *They cleared large tracts of forest*
zone: *a different time zone*
see also **area, land**
regional see **local**
register see **list, note, record**
regret verb **1** to be sorry something has happened: *I gave in to him, and I have regretted it ever since*
be sorry: *I'm sorry you feel that way about it*
grieve: *grieving over the death of his wife*
lament: *We lament the loss of a fine novelist*
mourn: *to mourn the loss of a loved one*
repent: *He repents his past sins*
▷ noun **2** the feeling of being sorry about something: *He expressed regret that he had caused any offence*
grief: *his guilt and grief over the failed relationship*
pang of conscience: *He need not feel any pangs of conscience over his decision*
penitence: *an abject display of penitence*
remorse: *He expressed remorse over his own foolishness*
repentance: *an apparent lack of genuine repentance*
sorrow: *I feel real sorrow that my dad did this*
see also **disappointment, sorrow**

regretful see **guilty, sorry**
regular adjective **1** even or equally spaced: *soft music with a regular beat*
consistent: *a consistent heart-rate*
constant: *a constant temperature*
even: *an even level of sound*
periodic: *Periodic checks are carried out*
rhythmic: *the rhythmic beating of the drum*
steady: *a steady pace*
uniform: *The Earth rotates on its axis at a uniform rate*
2 usual or normal: *I was filling in for the regular bartender*
customary: *her customary place at the table*
everyday: *part of everyday life*
habitual: *habitual practices*
normal: *a normal day*
ordinary: *It was just an ordinary weekend*
routine: *a routine knee operation*
typical: *My typical day begins at 8.30*
usual: *In a usual week I watch about 15 hours of television*
see also **average, constant, continual, conventional, even, formal, normal, orderly, ordinary, routine, standard, steady, typical, usual**
regularity see **order**
regulation see **law, restriction, rule**
regulations see **bureaucracy**
regurgitate see **vomit**
rehabilitate see **reform**
rehabilitation see **reform**
rehearsal see **practice**
rehearse see **practise**
reheat see **heat**
reign see **rule**
reinforce see **augment, strengthen, supplement, support**
reinstate see **restore**
reintroduce see **restore**
reiterate see **repeat**

reject *verb* to refuse to accept
or agree to something: *We reject
any suggestion that the law needs
amending*

decline: *They declined his proposal*

deny: *He denied our offer of assistance*

rebuff: *She rebuffed his advances*

refuse: *He offered me a drink, which
I refused*

renounce: *She renounced her parents'
religion*

say no to: *Just say no to drugs*

spurn: *He spurned the advice of
management consultants*

turn down: *She turned down his offer
of marriage*
see also **boycott, deny, refuse,
renounce**

rejoice *verb* to be very happy about
something: *Today we can rejoice in
our success*

be overjoyed: *I was overjoyed to
see him*

celebrate: *We should celebrate our
victory*

delight: *He delighted in her success*

glory: *glorying in the achievement
of his troops*
see also **celebrate**

rejuvenate see **refresh**

relate see **connect**

relate to see **identify with**

relating to see **about**

relation *noun* **1** a connection
between two things: *This theory
bears no relation to reality*

bearing: *Diet has an important
bearing on your general health*

bond: *the bond between a mother
and child*

connection: *a possible connection
between BSE and human disease*

correlation: *the correlation between
unemployment and crime*

link: *a link between obesity and heart
problems*

relationship: *the relationship
between success and effort*

2 a member of your family: *I was
staying with relations in Atlanta*

kin: *She has gone to live with her
husband's kin*

kinsman or **kinswoman**: *the prince
who murdered his father and kinsmen*

relative: *Get a relative to look after
the children*
see also **bond, connection**

relations see **family, kin**

relationship *noun* **1** the way
people act towards each other: *He
has a friendly relationship with his
customers*

affinity: *the natural affinity between
the female members of the community*

association: *the association between
the two countries*

bond: *The experience created a bond
between us*

connection: *He felt a personal
connection with her*

rapport: *He has a terrific rapport
with kids*

2 a close friendship, especially
a sexual one: *I found myself in a
relationship I couldn't handle*

affair: *an affair with a married man*

liaison: *Nobody knew of their brief
liaison*

3 the connection between two
things: *the relationship between
humans and their environment*

connection: *the connection between
age and ill-health*

correlation: *the correlation between
unemployment and crime*

link: *the link between smoking and
lung cancer*

parallel: *the parallel between
painting and music*
see also **affair, association,
connection, link, relation, tie**

relative see **relation**

relatively see **rather**

relatives see **family, kin**

relax verb to be calm and become less worried: I never have any time to relax
laze: I'm just going to laze around and do nothing
rest: Try to rest as much as you can
take it easy: the chance to just take it easy for a week or so
unwind: It helps them to unwind after a busy day at work
see also **calm, ease, lift, moderate, outspan, rest**

relaxation see **ease, leisure, rest**

relaxed adjective **1** calm and not worried or tense: As soon as I made the decision, I felt more relaxed
at ease: It is essential to feel at ease with your therapist
calm: Diane felt calm and unafraid as she entered the courtroom
comfortable: He liked me and I felt comfortable with him
cool: He was marvellously cool, smiling as if nothing had happened
easy: By then I was feeling a little easier about the situation
serene: that serene smile of his
unflustered: He has a calm, unflustered temperament
2 calm and peaceful: The atmosphere at lunch was relaxed
calm: The city appears relatively calm today
casual: We have a very casual relationship
comfortable: a comfortable silence
informal: an informal occasion
peaceful: Sundays are usually quiet and peaceful in our house
see also **calm, casual, comfortable, cool, cosy, easy, informal, leisurely, secure**

relaxing see **comfortable**

release verb **1** to set someone or something free: negotiations to release the hostages
deliver: I thank God for delivering me from that pain
discharge: He may be discharged from hospital today
extricate: They managed to extricate the survivors from the wreckage
free: Israeli is set to free more Lebanese prisoners
let go: They held him for three hours and then let him go
liberate: liberated under the terms of the amnesty
set free: birds set free into the wild
2 to make something available: The new album is released next week
issue: He has issued a press statement
launch: The company has just launched a new range of products
publish: His latest book will be published in May
put out: putting out a series of novels by Nobel prize winners
▷ noun **3** the setting free of someone or something: his release from prison
discharge: a discharge from the army
emancipation: the emancipation of slaves in the 19th century
freedom: Hinckley campaigned for his freedom
liberation: their liberation from a Nazi concentration camp
liberty: her television appearances pleading for his liberty
see also **discharge, emit, free, freedom, issue**

relentless adjective never stopping or becoming less intense: The pressure was relentless
incessant: incessant rain
nonstop: nonstop background music
persistent: in the face of persistent criticism
sustained: a sustained attack
unrelenting: unrelenting protests

unremitting: *the unremitting demands of duty*
see also **constant, fierce**

relevant *adjective* connected with what is being discussed: *We have passed on all relevant information*
  applicable: *These fees are not applicable to mortgages in Scotland*
  apposite: *He could not think of anything apposite to say*
  appropriate: *The name seemed very appropriate*
  apt: *an apt comment*
  pertinent: *She had asked some pertinent questions*

reliable *adjective* able to be trusted: *You have to demonstrate that you are reliable*
  dependable: *dependable information*
  faithful: *a faithful friend*
  safe: *It's all right, you're in safe hands*
  sound: *sound advice*
  staunch: *a staunch supporter*
  sure: *a sure sign of rain*
  true: *a true account*
  trustworthy: *a trustworthy and level-headed leader*
  see also **responsible, sound, sure, trusty**

reliance see **confidence**
relic see **souvenir**
relics see **remains**
relief see **comfort, escape**
relieve see **ease**
relieve from see **spare**
religious *adjective* **1** connected with religion: *religious worship*
  devotional: *an altar covered with devotional pictures*
  divine: *a request for divine guidance*
  doctrinal: *their doctrinal differences*
  holy: *To Tibetans, this is a holy place*
  sacred: *Bach's sacred music*
  scriptural: *scriptural and theological references*
  spiritual: *We've got no spiritual values*

  theological: *theological studies*
  2 having a strong belief in a god or gods: *They are both very religious*
  devout: *She is a devout Catholic*
  God-fearing: *They brought up their children to be God-fearing Christians*
  godly: *a learned and godly preacher*
  pious: *He was brought up by pious female relatives*
  righteous: *struggling to be righteous and chaste*
  see also **holy**

relinquish see **renounce, surrender**
relish see **enjoy, glory, like, love**
relocate see **move**
reluctant *adjective* unwilling to do something: *He was reluctant to ask for help*
  averse: *I'm not averse to going along with the idea*
  disinclined: *He was disinclined to talk about himself*
  hesitant: *His advisers are hesitant to let the United States enter the conflict*
  loath: *The finance minister is loath to cut income tax*
  slow: *The world community has been slow to respond to the crisis*
  unwilling: *For months I had been unwilling to go through with it*
  see also **hesitant, unwilling**

rely on see **depend, expect**
rely upon see **trust**
remain *verb* **1** to stay somewhere: *You'll have to remain in hospital for the time being*
  be left: *He was left in the car*
  linger: *I lingered for a few days until he arrived*
  stay behind: *I was told to stay behind after the class*
  wait: *Wait here until I come back*
  2 to stay the same: *The men remained silent*
  continue: *This state of affairs cannot*

continue

endure: *Somehow their friendship endures*

go on: *The debate goes on*

last: *Nothing lasts forever*

stay: *They could stay afloat without swimming*

survive: *companies which survived after the recession*

see also **continue, endure, last, stay, wait**

remainder *noun* the part that is left of something: *He gulped down the remainder of his coffee*

balance: *pay the balance on delivery*

last: *He finished off the last of the wine*

others: *She took one and put the others back*

remnants: *The remnants of the force were fleeing*

remains: *tidying up the remains of their picnic*

rest: *I'm going to throw a party, then invest the rest of the money*

see also **difference, rest**

remains *plural noun* the parts of something left over: *the remains of an ancient mosque*

debris: *screws, bolts and other debris from a scrapyard*

dregs: *Colum drained the dregs from his cup*

leftovers: *Refrigerate any leftovers*

relics: *a museum of war relics*

remnants: *Beneath the present church were remnants of Roman flooring*

residue: *Discard the milky residue left behind*

scraps: *the scraps from the dinner table*

vestiges: *an attempt to destroy the last vestiges of evidence*

see also **body, remainder, ruin**

remark *verb* **1** to mention or comment on something: *She had remarked on the boy's improvement*

comment: *So far, he has not commented on these reports*

mention: *I mentioned that I didn't like jazz*

observe: *"You're very pale," he observed*

say: *"Well done," he said*

state: *We stated that he had resigned*

▷ *noun* **2** something you say: *a vulgar remark*

comment: *his abrasive wit and caustic comments*

observation: *a few general observations*

statement: *That statement puzzled me*

utterance: *admirers who hung on her every utterance*

word: *No-one had an unkind word to say about him*

see also **comment, expression, note, observe, word**

remarkable *see* **exceptional, marvellous, singular, uncommon, wonderful**

remarkably *see* **really**

remedy *see* **correct, cure, medicine**

remember *verb* to bring to mind something from the past: *I do not remember the exact words*

call to mind: *He invited the congregation to call to mind their sins*

recall: *He tried to recall the layout of the farmhouse*

recognize: *I don't recognize that name*

retain: *information which can be retained in the memory*

remembrance *see* **memory**

remind *verb* to make someone remember something: *He reminds me of myself at that age*

bring back to: *Talking about the accident brought it all back to me*

jog someone's memory: See if this picture helps jog your memory

make someone remember: Your article made me remember my own traumas

put in mind: His eagerness to please put her in mind of a puppy

refresh someone's memory: I read through the list to refresh my memory
see also **prompt**

reminder see **note**, **souvenir**

remission see **forgiveness**

remit see **function**, **send**

remittance see **payment**

remnant see **trace**

remnants see **remainder**, **remains**

remorse see **regret**

remorseful see **guilty**, **sorry**

remote adjective 1 far off in distance or in the past: a remote farm in the hills

distant: in that distant land

far-off: She has entirely forgotten those far-off days

inaccessible: people living in inaccessible parts of the country

isolated: Many of the refugee villages are in isolated areas

lonely: It felt like the loneliest place in the world

outlying: Tourists can visit outlying areas by jeep

2 not wanting to be friendly: She looked beautiful, but at the same time so remote

aloof: He seemed aloof, standing watching the others

cold: What a cold, unfeeling woman she was

detached: He tries to remain emotionally detached from the prisoners

distant: He is courteous but distant

reserved: She's quite a reserved person

withdrawn: Her husband had become withdrawn and moody

3 not very great: The chances of his surviving are pretty remote

poor: The odds of it happening again are very poor

slender: There is a slender possibility that the plan might work

slight: Is there even a slight hope that she might change her mind?

slim: There's still a slim chance that he may become Prime Minister

small: There was still a small possibility that he might phone
see also **distant**, **far**, **impersonal**, **lonely**, **slender**

removal see **transport**

remove verb to take something off or away: I removed the splinter from her finger

delete: He deleted files from the computer system

detach: Detach and keep the bottom part of the form

eject: He was ejected from the restaurant

eliminate: Eliminate dairy products from your diet

erase: She had erased the message

extract: She is having a tooth extracted today

get rid of: to get rid of raw sewage by pumping it out to sea

take away: She took away the tray

take off: I won't take my coat off, I'm not staying

take out: Take that dog out of here

withdraw: She withdrew her hand from Roger's
see also **banish**, **eliminate**, **extract**, **get rid of**, **lift**, **withdraw**

rendezvous see **appointment**, **meeting**

renew verb to begin something again: Syria renewed diplomatic relations with Egypt

begin again: The audience began the

slow handclap again

recommence: He recommenced work on his novel

re-establish: He had re-established his close friendship with Anthony

reopen: It is feared that this issue could re-open the controversy

resume: Rebels have refused to resume peace talks

renounce verb formal to reject something or give it up: She renounced terrorism

disown: The comments were later disowned by an official spokesman

give up: He did not want to give up his right to the title

reject: children who reject their parents' political and religious beliefs

relinquish: He does not intend to relinquish power formal

see also **deny, reject, surrender**

renovate verb to repair an old building or machine: They spent thousands renovating the house

do up: his father's obsession with doing up old cars

modernize: plans to modernize the refinery

recondition: The company specializes in reconditioning photocopiers

refurbish: This hotel has been completely refurbished

repair: He has repaired the roof to make the house more windproof

restore: The old town square has been beautifully restored

revamp: plans to revamp the airport

see also **decorate, mend, reconstruct, repair, restore**

renown see **fame, reputation**

renowned see **famous, prominent**

rent see **hire, let**

renunciation see **sacrifice**

reopen see **renew**

repair noun 1 something you do to mend something that is damaged:

The landlord carried out the repairs himself

darn: a sock with a big darn in it

mend: Spray the area with paint to make the mend invisible

patch: jackets with patches on the elbows

restoration: the restoration of a war-damaged building

▷ verb 2 to mend something that is damaged: The money will be used to repair faulty equipment

fix: If something is broken, get it fixed

mend: They mended it without charge

patch: They patched the barn roof

patch up: Patch up those holes

renovate: They spent thousands renovating the house

restore: experts who specialize in restoring ancient parchments

see also **fix, mend, piece together, renovate, restore**

repay verb to give back money which is owed: It will take me years to repay the loan

pay back: I'll pay you back that money tomorrow

refund: Any extra that you have paid will be refunded to you

settle up: If we owe you anything we can settle up when you come

see also **compensate, return**

repeal see **cancel**

repeat verb to say or write something again: Since you didn't listen, I'll repeat that

echo: "Are you frightened?" "Frightened?" she echoed. "Of what?"

reiterate: The lawyer could only reiterate what he had said before

say again: "I'm sorry," she said again

see also **quote, stress**

repeated see **continual, frequent**

repeatedly see **often**

repel verb 1 to horrify and disgust: The thought of spiders repels me

disgust: He disgusted everyone with his boorish behaviour
offend: viewers who are easily offended
revolt: The smell revolted him
sicken: What he saw there sickened him
2 to fight and drive back enemy forces: troops along the border ready to repel an enemy attack
drive off: They drove the guerrillas off with infantry and air strikes
repulse: Cavalry and artillery were sent to repulse the enemy forces
resist: The tribe resisted the Spanish invaders
see also **disgust**
repellent see **disgusting, nasty**
repent see **regret**
repentance see **regret**
repentant see **sorry**
replace verb to take the place of something else: the man who replaced him as England skipper
succeed: He was succeeded by his son
supersede: Horses were superseded by cars
supplant: Anger supplanted all other feelings
take over from: the man taking over from Mr Berry as chairman
take the place of: Debit cards are taking the place of cash and cheques
see also **change, substitute, succeed**
replacement noun a person or thing that takes the place of another: He has nominated Adams as his replacement
proxy: They must nominate a proxy to vote on their behalf
stand-in: He was a stand-in for my regular doctor
substitute: an artificial substitute for silk
successor: He recommended him as

his successor
surrogate: They had expected me to be a surrogate for my sister
see also **substitute**
replica see **copy, model**
reply verb **1** to give someone an answer: He did not even have the courtesy to reply to my fax
answer: He avoided answering the question
counter: "It's not that simple," he countered in a firm voice
respond: "Mind your manners, lady!" I responded
retort: "Nobody asked you," he retorted
return: "I can manage," she returned coldly
▷ noun **2** an answer given to someone: There was a trace of irony in his reply
answer: She could not give him a truthful answer
response: His response was brusque
retort: His sharp retort clearly made an impact
see also **answer**
report verb **1** to tell about or give an official account of something: He reported the theft to the police
cover: The US news media will cover the trial closely
describe: His condition was described as "improving"
inform of: Inform the police of any suspicious activity
notify: The skipper notified the coastguard of the tragedy
state: The police stated that he had been arrested
▷ noun **2** an account of an event or situation: reports of serious human rights violations
account: a dishonest account of events
description: a detailed description

of the match

statement: *a deliberately misleading statement*

see also **announcement, feature, item, review, statement**

represent *verb* **1** to stand for something else: *This rune represents wealth and plenty*

mean: *This tarot card means the death of your present situation*

stand for: *The olive branch stands for peace*

symbolize: *a scene which symbolizes the movie's message*

2 to describe something in a particular way: *The popular press tends to represent him as a hero*

depict: *Children's books usually depict farm animals as lovable*

describe: *She was always described as an intellectual*

picture: *In the American press she was pictured as a heroine*

portray: *She was portrayed as a heartless, terrible woman*

show: *He was shown as an intelligent and courageous man*

representation *noun* **model, symbol**

representative *noun* **1** a person who acts on behalf of another or others: *Employees from each department elect a representative*

agent: *You are buying direct, rather than through an agent*

delegate: *a union delegate*

deputy: *I can't make it so I'll send my deputy*

proxy: *They must nominate a proxy to vote on their behalf*

spokesman or **spokeswoman**: *the party's education spokesman*

▷ *adjective* **2** typical of the group to which it belongs: *fairly representative groups of adults*

characteristic: *a characteristic feature*

illustrative: *an illustrative example*

typical: *a typical Italian menu*

see also **official, substitute, typical**

repress *see* **contain, suppress**

repressed *see* **pent-up**

reprimand *see* **caution, lecture, scold**

reprisal *see* **revenge**

reproach *see* **censure**

reproduce *see* **breed, copy**

reproduction *see* **copy, fake**

republic *see* **state**

repulse *see* **repel**

repulsion *see* **disgust**

repulsive *see* **unpleasant**

reputable *see* **honest, respectable**

reputation *noun* the opinion that people have of a person or thing: *The college has a good reputation*

character: *a man of good character*

name: *I have disgraced the family's name*

renown: *a singer of great renown*

repute: *a writer and scholar of some repute*

standing: *This has done nothing to improve his standing*

stature: *his stature as the world's greatest cellist*

see also **fame, name**

repute *see* **reputation**

reputed *see* **supposed**

request *verb* **1** to ask for something politely or formally: *She requested that the door be left open*

ask: *The government is being asked to consider the plan*

beg: *May I beg a favour of you?*

seek: *You should seek a medical opinion*

▷ *noun* **2** the action of asking for something politely or formally: *France had agreed to his request for political asylum*

appeal: *an appeal for witnesses to come forward*

application: *Their application was vetoed*

call: *calls to decrease income tax*

plea: *his plea for help in solving the killing*

see also **appeal**

require verb **1** to need something: *A baby requires warmth and security*

be in need of: *The house was in need of modernization*

demand: *The task of reconstruction would demand patience and hard work*

depend on: *I depend on this money to survive*

need: *He desperately needed money*

want: informal: *The windows wanted cleaning*

2 to say that someone must do something: *The rules require employers to provide safety training*

compel: *legislation that would compel cyclists to wear a helmet*

demand: *This letter demands an immediate reply*

direct: *a court order directing the group to leave the area*

instruct: *They have instructed their solicitor to sue for compensation*

oblige: *This decree obliges unions to delay strikes*

order: *The court ordered him to pay the sum in full*

see also **demand, expect, involve, need, take, want**

required see **compulsory, necessary, supposed**

requirement noun something that you must have or do: *The products met all legal requirements*

demand: *the demands and challenges of his new job*

essential: *the basic essentials for bachelor life*

necessity: *food and other daily necessities*

need: *special nutritional needs*

specification: *These companies will have to meet new European specifications* formal formal

see also **condition, standard**

requisite see **compulsory, condition**

reschedule see **put off**

rescue see **save**

research noun **1** the act of studying and finding out about something: *funds for research into AIDS*

analysis: *They collected blood samples for laboratory analysis*

examination: *a framework for the examination of these topics*

exploration: *an exploration of classical myths*

investigation: *Further investigation was hindered by the loss of all documentation*

study: *The study demonstrated a link between obesity and heart problems*

▷ verb **2** to find out about something: *I'm researching for an article on New England*

analyse: *We haven't had time to analyse those samples yet*

examine: *The spacecraft will examine how solar wind affects the Earth's magnetic field*

explore: *I would probably be wise to explore the matter further*

investigate: *Gas officials are investigating the cause of the explosion*

study: *She's been studying chimpanzees for thirty years*

see also **investigate, study**

resemblance noun a similarity between two things: *I can see a resemblance between you*

analogy: *the analogy between racism and homophobia*

correspondence: *There's little correspondence between our lifestyles*

likeness: *These myths have a startling likeness to one another*

parallel: *There were parallels between*

the two murders
similarity: similarities between mother and son
see also **similarity**

resemble verb to be similar to something else: *Venison resembles beef in flavour*

bear a resemblance to: *She bears a resemblance to Marilyn Monroe*

be like: *The ground is like concrete*

be similar to: *The gun was similar to an air pistol*

look like: *He looks like his father*

parallel: *His fate paralleled that of his predecessor*

take after: *You take after your grandmother*

resent verb to feel bitter and angry about something: *I resent the slur on my integrity*

be angry about: *I was angry at the way he spoke to me*

be offended by: *She was offended by his comments*

dislike: *I dislike his patronizing attitude*

object to: *I object to being treated like an idiot*

take offence at: *She took offence at the implied criticism*
see also **envy**

resentful adjective bitter about something that has happened: *a sullen and resentful workforce*

aggrieved: *He is still aggrieved at the size of the fine*

angry: *I was angry that I wasn't consulted*

bitter: *a forsaken and bitter man*

embittered: *He had grown into an embittered, hardened adult*

huffy: *He's so huffy if he doesn't get his own way*

indignant: *They were indignant that they had not been consulted*

offended: *He was offended at being*

left out
see also **bitter, jealous, sulky**

resentment noun a feeling of anger and bitterness: *There is growing resentment against newcomers*

anger: *Perhaps anger had clouded his vision*

animosity: *The animosity between the two men grew*

bitterness: *I feel bitterness towards the person who knocked medown*

grudge: *It was an accident and I bear no grudges*

huff: *She went off in a huff*

indignation: *He could hardly contain his indignation*

rancour: *There was no trace of envy or rancour in her face*
see also **animosity, envy, hostility**

reservation see **qualification**

reserve verb 1 to keep for a particular person or purpose: *Hotel rooms have been reserved for us*

hoard: *They've begun to hoard food and petrol*

hold: *The information is held in a database*

keep: *Grate the lemon zest and keep it for later*

put by: *She had enough put by for her fare*

save: *Save me a seat*

set aside: *funds set aside for education*

stockpile: *People are stockpiling food for the coming winter*

store: *potatoes stored for sale out of season*

▷ noun **2** a supply kept for future use: *a drain on the cash reserves*

cache: *a cache of weapons and explosives*

fund: *a pension fund*

hoard: *a hoard of food and petrol*

stock: *stocks of paper and ink*

stockpile: *stockpiles of chemical*

weapons

store: a secret store of sweets

supply: food supplies

see also **bank, book, fund, hoard, save, stock, stockpile, store, supply**

reserved see **cold, distant, remote, secretive**

reservoir see **fund, stock, store**

reside see **inhabit, live**

residence see **home, house**

resident see **inhabitant, local**

residue see **remains**

resign verb 1 to leave a job: Scott resigned from the firm

abdicate: The King abdicated to marry an American divorcee

hand in your notice: I handed in my notice on Friday

leave: I am leaving to become a teacher

quit: He quit his job as an office boy

step down informal: He headed the government until he stepped down in 1990

resign oneself verb to accept an unpleasant situation: She had resigned herself to losing her home

accept: You've got to accept the fact that he's left you

bow: He bowed to the inevitable and allowed her to go

reconcile oneself: She had reconciled herself to never seeing him again

see also **quit**

resigned see **passive**

resilient see **tough**

resist verb to refuse to accept something and try to prevent it: They resisted our attempts to modernize

defy: arrested for defying the ban on street trading

fight: He vigorously fought the proposal

oppose: Many parents oppose

bilingual education in schools

refuse: The patient has the right to refuse treatment

struggle against: nations struggling against Communist takeovers

see also **oppose, rebel, repel**

resistance see **defence, opposition**

resistant see **immune**

resolute see **determined, firm, serious, steadfast**

resolution see **decision, determination, resolve, will**

resolve verb 1 to decide firmly to do something: She resolved to report the matter

decide: She decided to quit smoking

determine: He determined to rescue his two countrymen

intend: I intended to teach him a lesson he wouldn't forget

make up your mind: Once he made up his mind to do it, there was no stopping him

2 to find a solution to a problem: We must find a way to resolve these problems

clear up: The confusion was soon cleared up

find a solution to: the ability to find an effective solution to the crisis

overcome: Find a way to overcome your difficulties

solve: These reforms did not solve the problem of unemployment

sort out: The two countries have sorted out their trade dispute

work out: It seems like a nightmare, but I'm sure we can work it out

▷ noun 3 absolute determination: He doesn't weaken in his resolve

determination: the expression of fierce determination on her face

resolution: "I'm going on a diet," she said with sudden resolution

tenacity: Hard work and sheer tenacity are crucial to career success *see also* **decide, determination, determine, intend, settle, solve, will, work out**

resolved *see* **serious**

resonate *see* **ring**

resounding *see* **loud**

respect verb **1** to have a good opinion of someone: *I want him to respect me as a career woman*
admire: *I admire him for his honesty*
have a good opinion of: *Nobody seems to have a good opinion of him*
have a high opinion of: *He had a very high opinion of Neil*
honour: *the Scout's promise to honour God and the Queen*
look up to: *He looks up to his dad*
think highly of: *His boss thinks very highly of him*
venerate: *My father venerated General Eisenhower*
▷ noun **2** a good opinion of someone: *We have no respect for him at all*
admiration: *I have always had the greatest admiration for him*
esteem: *We have to win the trust and esteem of our clients*
regard: *I hold him in high regard*
reverence: *We did it out of reverence for the dead*
see also **admiration, admire, appreciate, approval, approve, consider, consideration, detail, esteem, value**

respectable adjective **1** considered to be acceptable and correct: *respectable families*
decent: *They married after a decent interval*
good: *He comes from a good family*
honourable: *His colleagues were honourable people*
proper: *It was not proper for women to go on the stage*
reputable: *a reputable firm*

upright: *an upright and trustworthy man*
worthy: *worthy citizens*
2 adequate or reasonable: *a respectable rate of economic growth*
appreciable: *making appreciable progress*
considerable: *a considerable amount*
decent: *a decent standard of living*
fair: *She had a fair command of English*
reasonable: *He couldn't make a reasonable living from his writing*
see also **decent**

respectful *see* **polite**

respite *see* **break, rest**

respond *see* **answer, reply**

respond to *see* **identify with**

response *see* **answer, reaction, reply**

responsibility noun **1** the duty to deal with or take care of something: *The garden is your responsibility*
duty: *My duty is to look after the animals*
obligation: *You have an obligation to help him*
onus: *The onus was on him to make sure he didn't fail*
2 the blame for something which has happened: *We must all accept responsibility for our mistakes*
blame: *I'm not going to take the blame for this*
fault: *This is all your fault*
guilt: *He was not completely free of guilt*
liability: *He admitted liability for the crash*
see also **blame, concern, duty, fault, function, job**

responsible adjective **1** being the person in charge of something: *The Cabinet is collectively responsible for policy*
in charge: *I wish someone else was in*

charge of this inquiry

in control: *Who is in control of the operation?*

2 being to blame for something: *I hold you responsible for this mess*

at fault: *I was not at fault as my vehicle was stationary*

guilty: *I still maintain that I am not guilty*

to blame: *Television is possibly to blame for this*

3 sensible and dependable: *He had to show that he would be a responsible parent*

dependable: *a dependable, trustworthy teacher*

level-headed: *a sensible, level-headed approach*

reliable: *You have to demonstrate that you are reliable*

sensible: *She's a sensible girl, if a bit headstrong*

sound: *sound advice*

trustworthy: *He is a trustworthy leader*

rest noun **1** the remaining parts of something: *Take what you want and leave the rest*

balance: *You pay half now and the balance on delivery*

others: *She took one and put the others back*

remainder: *He gulped down the remainder of his coffee*

surplus: *Coat with seasoned flour, shaking off the surplus*

2 a period when you relax and do nothing: *I'll start again after a rest*

break: *He needs to take a break from work*

holiday: *I could really do with a holiday*

leisure: *We get no leisure, no time off, no overtime pay*

relaxation: *Make time for a bit of relaxation*

respite: *a respite from the rush of everyday life*

▷ verb **3** to relax and do nothing for a while: *He rested briefly before going on*

have a break: *Paul felt he had to have a break*

idle: *He sat idling in his room*

laze: *lazing on the beach*

put your feet up: *Nobody's home, so I can put my feet up for a while*

relax: *Guests can relax in the cosy bar*

sit down: *I'll have to sit down for a minute*

take it easy: *the chance to just take it easy for a couple of weeks*

see also **break, outspan, pause, put, relax, remainder, set**

restful see **comfortable, quiet**

restless adjective unable to sit still or relax: *She had been restless and irritable all day*

edgy: *She was nervous and edgy, still chain-smoking*

fidgety: *bored, fidgety youngsters*

fretful: *The whole family was fretful and argumentative*

jumpy: *If she can't smoke she gets jumpy and irritable*

on edge: *She's been on edge for weeks*

unsettled: *The staff were unsettled and demoralized*

see also **active, busy, impatient**

restoration see **recovery, repair**

restore verb **1** to cause something to return to its previous state: *He was anxious to restore his reputation*

re-establish: *an attempt to re-establish diplomatic relations*

reinstate: *the failure to reinstate the ceasefire*

reintroduce: *the plan to reintroduce wolves to the Highlands*

return: *their attempts to return the country to an agrarian economy*

2 to clean and repair something: *experts who specialize in restoring* *ancient parchments*

fix up: *It took us months to fix this house up*

mend: *They finally got round to mending the roof*

rebuild: *plans to rebuild the opera house*

reconstruct: *reconstructing paintings by old masters*

refurbish: *The city is refurbishing the cathedral's facade*

renovate: *The hotel was being renovated in expectation of a tourist boom*

repair: *The money will be used to repair faulty equipment*

see also **mend, piece together, reconstruct, renovate, repair**

restrain *verb* to hold someone or something back: *He had to be restrained by his friends*

contain: *He could hardly contain his rage*

control: *She tried to control her excitement*

curb: *You must curb your extravagant tastes*

hamper: *I was hampered by a lack of information*

hinder: *Research is hindered by lack of cash*

hold back: *He could no longer hold back his laughter*

inhibit: *factors which inhibit growth*

see also **check, contain, curb, restrict, suppress**

restraint see **curb, economy, patience, restriction**

restrict *verb* to limit the movement or actions of someone or something: *laws to restrict foreign imports*

confine: *Keep your dog confined to the house*

contain: *The curfew had contained the violence*

hamper: *I was hampered by a lack of information*

handicap: *handicapped by the terms of the contract*

impede: *Their work was being impeded by shortages of supplies*

inhibit: *factors which inhibit growth*

limit: *He limited payments on the country's foreign debt*

restrain: *the need to restrain wage rises*

see also **confine, hamper, handicap, limit**

restriction *noun* a rule or situation that limits what you can do: *a speed restriction*

constraint: *financial constraints*

control: *a call for stricter gun control*

curb: *support for a curb on migration from neighbouring countries*

limitation: *A slipped disc causes severe limitation of movement*

regulation: *regulations outlawing child labour*

restraint: *new restraints on trade unions*

stipulation: *The only dress stipulation was "no jeans"*

result *noun* **1** the situation that is caused by something: *the result of lengthy deliberation*

consequence: *This could have disastrous consequences for industry*

effect: *the intended effect of the revised guidelines*

outcome: *The ultimate outcome will be different*

product: *the product of five years' work*

upshot: *The upshot is that our employees are all unhappy*

▷ *verb* **2** to be caused by something: *The crash resulted from a defect in the aircraft*

arise: *the publicity that arises from incidents of this kind*

derive: *Poor health often derives*

from poverty

develop: *a determination which has developed from his new-found confidence*

ensue: *If the system collapses, chaos will ensue*

follow: *the consequences which followed his release from prison*

happen: *What will happen if the test proves positive?*

stem: *Her hatred of cars stems from her mother's death in a crash*

see also **develop**, **effect**, **happen**

result in verb to cause something to happen: *50% of road accidents result in head injuries*

bring about: *The Suez crisis brought about petrol rationing*

cause: *The play caused a stir here*

lead to: *brain damage which leads to paralysis*

see also **bring**

resume see **continue**, **renew**

resuscitate see **revive**

retain see **remember**

retaliate verb to do something to someone in return for what they did: *The militia said it would retaliate against any attacks*

get back at: *a desire to get back at our enemies*

get even with informal: *He wanted to get even with his former employers*

get your own back informal: *the opportunity to get your own back on your husband*

hit back: *In this article he hits back at his critics*

pay someone back: *I'll pay him back for what he's done*

take revenge: *taking revenge for his father's murder*

see also **revenge**

retaliation see **revenge**

reticence see **silence**

reticent see **secretive**

retire see **quit**, **withdraw**

retiring see **shy**

retort see **answer**, **reply**

retract see **reverse**

retreat verb 1 to move away from someone or something: *damage inflicted by the rebels as they retreated from the town*

back away: *He put up his hands in protest and began to back away*

back off: *I stood up for myself and they backed off*

draw back: *They drew back in fear*

pull back: *Their forces have pulled back in all areas*

withdraw: *Troops withdrew from the country last month*

▷ noun 2 the action of moving away from someone or something: *the long retreat from Moscow*

departure: *the departure of all foreign forces from the country*

evacuation: *the evacuation of British troops from Dunkirk*

flight: *my panicked flight from London*

withdrawal: *French withdrawal from Algeria*

3 a quiet place you can go to: *He spent the day hidden away in his country retreat*

haven: *The hotel is a haven of tranquillity*

refuge: *a refuge from the harsh realities of the world*

sanctuary: *a sanctuary located on an island*

see also **withdraw**

retribution see **punishment**, **revenge**

retrieval see **recovery**

retrieve see **recover**

return verb 1 to go back to a place: *The plane failed to return at the scheduled time*

come back: *He said he'd come back later*

go back: I love going back home

reappear: He reappeared two nights later

turn back: We've come too far now to turn back

2 to give something back: They guarantee to return your original investment

give back: He is refusing to give the dog back

pay back: You have to pay back the loan, plus an arrangement fee

refund: The company will refund the full cost

repay: I can afford to repay the loan
see also **reply, restore, vote**

reunion see **meeting**

revamp see **renovate, revise**

reveal verb **1** to tell people about something: They were not ready to reveal any of the details

announce: She was planning to announce her engagement

disclose: He will not disclose the name of his patient

divulge: I do not want to divulge where the village is

get off your chest informal: I feel it's done me good to get it off my chest

let on: She never let on that anything was wrong

2 to uncover something that is hidden: The carpet was removed to reveal the original pine floor

bring to light: The truth is unlikely to be brought to light

lay bare: His real motives were laid bare

uncover: Auditors said they had uncovered evidence of fraud

unearth: Quarry workers have unearthed the skeleton of a mammoth

unveil: The statue will be unveiled next week
see also **announce, betray, expose, indicate, show, uncover**

revel see **glory**

revel in see **enjoy, like**

revelation see **surprise**

revenge noun **1** vengeance for wrongs or injury received: acts of revenge

reprisal: Witnesses are unwilling to testify through fear of reprisals

retaliation: The attack was in retaliation for his murder

retribution: They did not want their names used for fear of retribution

vengeance: He swore vengeance on everyone involved in the murder
▷ verb **2** to take vengeance on someone: to revenge himself on the press

avenge: He was trying to avenge the death of his friend

get even: I'm going to get even with you for this

get your own back informal: I simply want to get my own back on him

hit back: He hit back at those who criticized him

pay someone back: Some day I'll pay you back for this

retaliate: I was sorely tempted to retaliate

revenue see **profit**

reverence see **esteem, respect**

reverse verb **1** to change into something different or contrary: They won't reverse the decision to increase prices

change: They should change the law to make this practice illegal

invalidate: A contract signed now might be invalidated at a future date

overrule: In 1998 the Court of Appeal overruled the decision

overturn: When the parliament overturned his decision, he backed down

retract: He was asked to retract his comments but refused

▷ noun **2** the opposite of what has just been said or done: *The reverse seldom applies*
  contrary: *I'm not a feminist, quite the contrary*
  converse: *In fact, the converse is true*
  opposite: *When I told him to do something he always did the opposite*
  see also **back, opposite, overrule, overturn**

review noun **1** a critical assessment of a book or performance: *We've never had a good review in the music press*
  commentary: *He'll be writing a weekly commentary on American culture*
  criticism: *literary criticism*
  notice: *Richards's solo work received good notices*
  2 a general survey or report: *a review of safety procedures*
  analysis: *an analysis of American trade policy*
  examination: *an examination of the top 250 companies*
  report: *the committee's annual report*
  study: *a recent study of treatments for back pain*
  survey: *a survey of 250 businessmen*
  see also **summary**

revise verb to alter or correct something: *The second edition was completely revised*
  amend: *They voted unanimously to amend the constitution*
  correct: *time spent correcting his students' work*
  edit: *We have the right to edit this book once it's finished*
  revamp: *It is time to revamp the system*
  update: *He was back in the office, updating the work schedule*

revival *see* **recovery**

revive verb to make or become lively or active again: *an attempt to revive the Russian economy*
  rally: *Markets began to rally worldwide*
  resuscitate: *a bid to resuscitate the weekly magazine*
  see also **recover, refresh**

revoke *see* **cancel**

revolt *see* **disgust, rebel, rebellion, repel**

revolting *see* **disgusting**

revolution *see* **rebellion**

revolutionize *see* **transform**

revolve *see* **centre, spin**

revulsion *see* **disgust, hatred, horror**

reward noun something given in return for a service: *As a reward for good behaviour, treat your child to a new toy*
  bonus: *We don't get a Christmas bonus any more*
  bounty: *They paid bounties to people to give up their weapons*
  payment: *Players now expect payment for interviews*
  prize: *He won first prize*
  see also **compensate**

rewarding *see* **successful**

rhythm noun a regular movement or beat: *His body twists and sways to the rhythm*
  beat: *the thumping beat of rock music*
  pulse: *the repetitive pulse of the drum beat*
  tempo: *Elgar supplied his works with precise indications of tempo*
  time: *A reel is in four-four time*
  see also **beat**

rhythmic *see* **regular**

rich adjective **1** having a lot of money and possessions: *You're going to be a very rich man*
  affluent: *an affluent neighbourhood*
  loaded slang: *Of course he can afford it. He's loaded*
  opulent: *his opulent lifestyle*

prosperous: *the youngest son of a relatively prosperous family*

wealthy: *a wealthy international businessman*

well off: *My grandparents were quite well off*

2 abundant in something: *Bananas are rich in vitamin A*

abundant: *the Earth's most abundant natural resources*

fertile: *a fertile imagination*

plentiful: *a plentiful supply of vegetables*

see also **colourful, fertile, wealthy**

riches *see* **wealth**

rickety *see* **shaky, unsteady**

ricochet *see* **bounce**

rid get rid of *verb* to remove or destroy something: *a senior manager who wanted to get rid of him*

dispose of: *He disposed of the murder weapon*

dump: *We dumped our bags at the hotel*

eject: *Officials used guard dogs to eject the protestors*

jettison: *The crew jettisoned excess fuel*

remove: *Most of her fears had been removed*

weed out: *We must weed these people out as soon as possible*

riddle *see* **mystery, problem, puzzle**

ride *see* **drive**

ridge *see* **top**

ridicule *see* **make fun of, mock, mockery**

ridiculous *adjective* very foolish: *It is ridiculous to suggest we are having a romance*

absurd: *absurd claims to have met big stars*

laughable: *He claims the allegations are "laughable"*

ludicrous: *It's a completely ludicrous idea*

preposterous: *their preposterous claim that they had unearthed a plot*

see also **absurd, crazy, daft, silly**

rife *see* **widespread**

rift *see* **breach, fissure, split**

right *adjective* **1** in accordance with the facts: *That clock never tells the right time*

accurate: *an accurate record of events*

correct: *The correct answers can be found at the bottom of the page*

exact: *That clock never tells the exact time*

factual: *His version of events is not strictly factual*

genuine: *a genuine eyewitness account*

precise: *Officials did not give precise figures*

strict: *He has never been a playboy in the strict sense of the word*

true: *The true cost often differs from that*

valid: *Your point is a valid one*

2 most suitable: *The time is right for our escape*

acceptable: *This was beyond the bounds of acceptable behaviour*

appropriate: *an appropriate outfit for the occasion*

desirable: *This goal is neither achievable nor desirable*

done: *It just isn't done to behave like that in public*

fit: *a subject which is not fit for discussion*

fitting: *a fitting end to an exciting match*

okay or **ok** *informal*: *Is it okay if I bring a friend with me?*

proper: *It was not thought proper for a woman to appear on the stage*

seemly: *the rules of civility and seemly conduct*

suitable: *the most suitable man for the job*

▷ noun **3** what is just and fair: *At least he knew right from wrong*
fairness: *a decision based not on fairness but on expediency*
equity: *Income should be distributed with some sense of equity*
honour: *His whole life was dominated by his sense of honour*
integrity: *They always strove to maintain a high level of integrity*
justice: *He has no sense of justice or fair play*
legality: *They are expected to observe the principles of legality*
morality: *standards of morality and justice in society*
virtue: *Virtue is not confined to the Christian world*
see also **accurate, correct, fitting, immediately, power, proper, suitable**

right away *see* **immediately**
right now *see* **now**
righteous *see* **religious**
rightful *see* **legal, real**
right-hand man *see* **assistant, helper**
righting *see* **correction**
right-wing *adjective* believing in capitalist policies: *some right-wing politicians*
conservative: *the conservative manifesto*
reactionary: *reactionary army people*
Tory British: *a senior Tory peer*
rigid *adjective* **1** unchangeable and often considered severe: *Hospital routines for nurses are very rigid*
fixed: *fixed laws*
inflexible: *Workers said the system was too inflexible*
set: *They have very set ideas about how to achieve this*
strict: *a strict diet*
stringent: *stringent rules*
2 not easy to bend: *rigid plastic containers*
firm: *a firm platform*
hard: *Something cold and hard pressed into his back*
solid: *The concrete will stay as solid as a rock*
stiff: *Her fingers were stiff with cold*
see also **firm, hard, stiff, strict, tense, tight**

rigorous *see* **firm, strict, strict**
rigorously *see* **well**
rim *see* **border, edge**
ring *verb* **1** to make a loud clear sound: *He heard the school bell ring*
chime: *The clock chimed three o'clock*
clang: *A little later the church bell clanged*
peal: *Church bells pealed at the stroke of midnight*
resonate: *a strap hung with bells and resonating gongs*
toll: *The pilgrims tolled the bell*
▷ noun **2** an object or group of things in the shape of a circle: *a ring of blue smoke*
band: *a black arm-band*
circle: *Cut out four circles of pastry*
hoop: *a steel hoop*
loop: *a loop of garden hose*
round: *small fresh rounds of goats' cheese*
3 a group of people involved in an illegal activity: *a drug-trafficking ring*
band: *a small band of plotters*
cell: *a cell of neo-Nazis*
clique: *A small clique of people is trying to take over the party*
syndicate: *a major crime syndicate*
see also **sound**

ringleader *see* **leader**
rinse *see* **wash**
riot *noun* **1** a disturbance made by an unruly mob: *a prison riot*
anarchy: *a decade of civil war and anarchy*
disorder: *mass public disorder*

disturbance: Three fans were injured in a violent disturbance outside a pub
mob violence: last week's mob violence in Bucharest
strife: communal strife in Los Angeles
▷ verb **2** to take part in a riot: They rioted in protest against the Government
go on the rampage: Rock fans went on the rampage after a concert
rampage: A curfew was imposed as gangs rampaged through the streets
run riot: hooligans running riot in the streets
take to the streets: Workers and students took to the streets in protest

rip see **split, tear**

rip off see **cheat**

ripe see **ready**

ripple see **wave**

rise verb **1** to move upwards: Wilson watched the smoke rise from his cigar
ascend: He held her hand as they ascended the steps
climb: We climbed up the steps on to the bridge
go up: He went up the ladder quickly
move up: They moved up to second place after their win
2 to increase: House prices are expected to rise this year
go up: Life expectancy has gone up from 50 to 58
grow: The Chinese economy continues to grow
increase: the decision to increase prices
intensify: The conflict is bound to intensify
mount: For several hours the tension mounted
▷ noun **3** an increase in something: a rise in prices
improvement: a major improvement in standards
increase: a substantial increase in workload
upsurge: an upsurge of interest in books
see also **gain, increase, jump, slope**

rise to see **reach**

risk noun **1** a chance that something unpleasant might happen: That's a risk I'm happy to take
danger: the dangers of smoking
gamble: Booking a holiday can be a gamble
peril: the perils of starring in a TV commercial
pitfall: the pitfalls of working abroad
▷ verb **2** to do something knowing that something unpleasant might happen: If he doesn't play, he risks losing his place in the team
chance: No assassin would chance a shot from amongst that crowd
dare: Few people dared go anywhere on foot
gamble: gambling his life savings on the stock market
jeopardize: The talks may still be jeopardized by disputes
put in jeopardy: A series of setbacks have put the whole project in jeopardy
see also **danger, dare, endanger, gamble, possibility, threat**

risky see **dangerous**

rite see **ceremony**

ritual see **ceremony, custom**

rival noun **1** the person someone is competing with: He is well ahead of his nearest rival
adversary: political adversaries
antagonist: Greece's key rival and chief antagonist, Turkey
challenger: his only challenger for the presidency
opponent: He's a tough opponent but I'm too good for him
▷ verb **2** to be the equal or near equal of: As a holiday destination, South Africa rivals Kenya for weather

be a match for: On our day we are a match for anyone

equal: The victory equalled Portugal's best in history

match: I think we matched them in every department

see also **competitor**

rivalry see **competition**

road noun a route used by travellers and vehicles: There was very little traffic on the roads

motorway: Britain's first motorway, the M1

route: the most direct route to the town centre

street: He walked briskly down the street

track: a rough mountain track

see also **passage, route, way**

roam see **wander**

roar see **shout**

roast see **cook**

rob verb to take something from a person illegally: He was beaten senseless and robbed of all his money

burgle: He admitted that he was trying to burgle the surgery

con informal: The businessman had conned him of $10,000

defraud: charges of conspiracy to defraud the government

loot: thugs who have looted shops

steal from: trying to steal from a woman in the street

swindle: two executives who swindled their employer

robber see **thief**

robbery see **theft**

robe see **dress**

robot see **automatic**

robust see **fit, healthy, sound, sturdy, tough, well**

rocket see **bomb, explode**

rocky see **rough**

rod see **bar, stick**

rogue see **crook**

role see **duty, function, job, part**

roll see **flow**

romance see **affair**

romantic adjective connected with sexual love: a romantic relationship

amorous: The object of his amorous intentions is Wendy

loving: a loving husband

passionate: a passionate love affair

tender: They embraced and kissed. It was a tender moment

room noun 1 a separate section in a building: You can stay in my spare room

chamber: the council chamber

office: I'm in the office at the end of the corridor

2 unoccupied space: There wasn't enough room for his gear

capacity: a seating capacity of 17,000

elbow room: There wasn't too much elbow room in the cockpit

space: the high cost of office space

see also **capacity, space**

rooms see **flat**

root see **cause, origin**

rope see **tie**

rot verb 1 to become rotten: The grain started rotting in the silos

decay: The bodies buried in the fine ash slowly decayed

decompose: The debris slowly decomposes into compost

fester: The wound is festering and gangrene has set in

spoil: Fats spoil by becoming rancid

▷ noun 2 the condition that affects things when they rot: The timber frame was not protected against rot

decay: tooth decay

deterioration: gum deterioration

mould: He scraped the mould off the cheese

see also **eat away, nonsense, rubbish**

rotate see **spin, turn**

rotten adjective **1** decayed and no longer of use: *The front bay window is rotten*
bad: *That milk in the fridge is bad*
decayed: *teeth so decayed they need to be pulled*
decomposed: *The body was too badly decomposed to be identified at once*
mouldy: *mouldy bread*
sour: *sour milk*
2 informal of very poor quality: *It's a rotten idea*
inferior: *overpriced and inferior products*
lousy slang: *The menu is limited and the food is lousy*
poor: *The wine was very poor*
unsatisfactory: *if you have obtained unsatisfactory goods or services*
see also **shabby, terrible**

rough adjective **1** uneven and not smooth: *My bicycle bumped along the rough ground*
bumpy: *bumpy cobbled streets*
craggy: *craggy mountains*
rocky: *a bleak and rocky shore*
rugged: *a remote and rugged plateau*
uneven: *The ball bobbled awkwardly on the uneven surface*
2 difficult or unpleasant: *Teachers have been given a rough time*
difficult: *It's been a difficult month for us*
hard: *I've had a hard life*
tough: *She had a pretty tough childhood*
unpleasant: *The last few weeks here have been very unpleasant*
3 only approximately correct: *At a rough guess it is five times more profitable*
approximate: *The times are approximate only*
estimated: *There are an estimated 90,000 gangsters in the country*

sketchy: *a sketchy account of the incident*
vague: *She could only give a vague description of the intruder*
see also **approximate, broad, crude, jagged, primitive, uneven, violent, wild**
roughly see **about**

round adjective **1** shaped like a ball or a circle: *She has a round attractive face*
circular: *a circular hole twelve feet wide*
cylindrical: *a cylindrical container*
rounded: *a low rounded hill*
spherical: *gold spherical earrings*
▷ noun **2** one of a series of events: *After round three, two Americans shared the lead*
lap: *the last lap of the race*
period: *the second period of extra time*
session: *The World Champion was ahead after the first two sessions*
stage: *the second stage of the Tour de France*
see also **ring**

round off see **conclude**
round up see **gather**
roundabout see **indirect**
rounded see **blunt, round**
rouse see **provoke, wake**
rousing see **exciting**
rout see **defeat, vanquish**
route noun a way from one place to another: *the direct route to the town centre*
channel: *a safe channel avoiding the reefs*
course: *The ship was on a course that followed the coastline*
itinerary: *The next place on our itinerary was Silistra*
path: *We followed the path along the clifftops*
road: *The coastal road is longer, but more scenic*
way: *I'm afraid I can't remember the way*

see also **course, direction, line, passage, path, road, way**

routine adjective **1** ordinary, and done regularly: *a series of routine medical tests*

everyday: *an everyday occurrence*

normal: *The hospital claimed they were following their normal procedure*

ordinary: *It was just an ordinary weekend for us*

regular: *one of the regular checks we carry out*

standard: *It was standard practice for untrained clerks to do this work*

typical: *This was a fairly typical morning scene in our house*

usual: *The usual methods were not effective*

▷ noun **2** the usual way or order someone does things: *The players had to change their daily routine*

order: *Babies respond well to order in their daily lives*

pattern: *All three attacks followed the same pattern*

practice: *a public inquiry into bank practices*

procedure: *The White House said there would be no change in procedure*

programme: *It is best to follow some sort of structured programme*

schedule: *He has been forced to adjust his schedule*

system: *an efficient filing system*

see also **custom, everyday, habit, normal, ordinary, practice, regular, stock, straightforward, system**

row noun **1** several things arranged in a line: *He was greeted by a row of glum faces*

bank: *a bank of video screens*

column: *a column of figures*

line: *a sparse line of spectators*

queue: *a queue of shoppers*

rank: *a rank of taxis*

2 a serious disagreement: *This could provoke a major diplomatic row with France*

altercation: *He had an altercation with the umpire*

argument: *an argument about money*

quarrel: *I had a terrible quarrel with my brother*

squabble: *There have been minor squabbles about phone bills*

see also **argue, argument, disagreement, dispute, fight, line, noise, quarrel, racket, rank, squabble**

rowdy adjective rough and noisy: *He complained to the police about rowdy neighbours*

boisterous: *Most of the children were noisy and boisterous*

noisy: *My neighbours are a noisy bunch*

unruly: *a mother accompanied by her ghastly unruly child*

wild: *They loved fast cars and wild parties*

see also **wild**

royal adjective concerning a king or a queen or their family: *the royal yacht*

imperial: *the Imperial palace in Tokyo*

regal: *Never has she looked more regal*

sovereign: *the Queen's sovereign authority*

rub see **wear**

rub out see **delete**

rubbish noun **1** unwanted things or waste material: *tons of rubbish waiting to be dumped*

garbage: *I found all kinds of garbage left behind by the tide*

litter: *fines for dropping litter*

refuse: *The Council made a weekly collection of refuse*

trash: *The yards are overgrown and covered with trash*

waste: *the safe disposal of toxic waste*

2 foolish words or speech: *Don't talk rubbish!*

drivel: mindless drivel
garbage: I personally think this is complete garbage
hot air informal: His justification was just hot air
nonsense: all that poetic nonsense about love
rot: What a load of pompous rot!
see also **garbage, junk, nonsense, refuse, trash**

rude adjective **1** not polite: He is rude to her friends
disrespectful: They shouldn't treat their minister in this disrespectful way
impertinent: I don't like being asked impertinent questions
impudent: his rude and impudent behaviour
insolent: a defiant, almost insolent look
2 unexpected and unpleasant: a rude awakening
abrupt: The recession brought an abrupt end to his happiness
unpleasant: an unpleasant surprise
violent: violent mood swings
see also **abrupt, abusive, cheeky, common, dirty, indecent, primitive, unpleasant, vulgar**

rudeness see **cheek**
rudimentary see **crude, primitive**
rudiments see **essentials**
ruffle see **irritate, upset**
rugged see **rough, tough**

ruin verb **1** to destroy or spoil something: The crops have been ruined
break: He's broken all his toys
damage: This could damage our chances of winning
destroy: a recipe for destroying the economy
devastate: A fire had devastated large parts of the castle
impair: The flavour is impaired by overcooking
mar: The celebrations were marred by violence
mess up: He's messed up his whole career
spoil: Don't let a stupid mistake spoil your life
undo: He intends to undo everything I have fought for
wreck: He wrecked the garden
▷ noun **2** the state of being destroyed or spoiled: The vineyards were falling into ruin
decay: The house fell into a state of decay
destruction: the destruction caused by the rioters
devastation: A bomb brought chaos and devastation to the city centre yesterday
disrepair: Many of the buildings had fallen into disrepair
downfall: His lack of experience led to his downfall
fall: the fall of the Roman empire
3 the remaining parts of a severely damaged thing: the burnt-out ruins of houses
remains: the remains of an ancient mosque
shell: the shells of burned buildings
wreck: We thought of the house as a wreck and doing it up
see also **crash, destroy, downfall, harm, spoil**

ruined see **derelict**

rule noun a statement of what is allowed: This was against the rules
decree: a decree lifting sanctions against China
guideline: Are there strict guidelines for animal experimentation?
law: inflexible moral laws
order: He was sacked for disobeying orders
regulation: new safety regulations
as a rule adverb **1** usually or generally: As a rule, I eat my meals in

front of the TV

generally: It is generally true that the darker the fruit the higher its iron content

mainly: Mainly I work alone

normally: Normally, the transport system carries 50,000 passengers a day

on the whole: Their wines are, on the whole, of a very high standard

usually: She is usually a calm and diplomatic woman

▷ **verb 2** to govern people: For four centuries, he says, foreigners have ruled Angola

administer: calls for the UN to administer the country until the election

be in power: They were in power for eighteen years

govern: The citizens are thankful they are not governed by a dictator

lead: He led the country between 1949 and 1984

reign: Henry II reigned from 1154 to 1189
see also **control, law, line**

rule out see **exclude**

ruler noun a person who rules or commands: He was a weak-willed and indecisive ruler

commander: He is commander of the US Fifth Fleet

governor: He was governor of the province in the late 1970s

head of state: the heads of state of all the countries in the European Union

leader: the leader of the German Social Democratic Party

monarch: the coronation of the new monarch

sovereign: the first British sovereign to set foot on Spanish soil

rules see **standards**

ruling see **decision, judgment**

rummage see **fossick**

rumour noun a story which may or may not be true: persistent rumours of quarrels within the movement

gossip: We spent the first hour exchanging gossip

hearsay: Much of what was reported to them was hearsay

whisper: I've heard a whisper that the Bishop intends to leave

word: What's the latest word from Washington?

rumoured see **supposed**

rumpus see **racket**

run verb **1** to move on foot at a rapid pace: I excused myself and ran back to the telephone

bolt: The pig rose, squealing, and bolted

gallop: The horses galloped away

jog: He could scarcely jog around the block that first day

sprint: She sprinted to the car

2 to manage: He ran a small hotel

administer: the authorities who administer the island

be in charge of: He is in charge of public safety

control: He now controls a large retail development empire

direct: Christopher will direct day-to-day operations

look after: I look after his finances for him

manage: Within two years he was managing the store

see also **administer, conduct, dash, direct, drive, flow, function, head, manage, pour, race, range, rush, series, stretch, supervise**

run across see **meet**

run amok see **rampage**

run around see **associate**

run away see **bolt, escape, flee**

run into see **hit, meet**

run off see **bolt, escape**

run riot see **rampage, riot**

run through see **exhaust**

rundown see **outline, summary**

runner see **messenger**

running see **management, upkeep**

runny see liquid, thin

rupture see burst, division, tear

ruse see manoeuvre, trick

rush verb 1 to move fast or do something quickly: *Someone rushed out of the building*
  dash: *She dashed in from the garden*
  fly: *I must fly or I'll miss my train*
  gush: *Piping-hot water gushed out*
  hasten: *One of them hastened towards me*
  hurry: *She had to hurry home to look after her son*
  race: *He raced across town to her house*
  run: *I excused myself and ran to the door*
  scurry: *Reporters scurried to get to the phones*
  shoot: *The car shot out of a junction and smashed into them*
  2 to force into immediate action without sufficient preparation: *Ministers won't be rushed into a response*
  hurry: *I don't want to hurry you*
  hustle: *You won't hustle me into making a commitment*
  press: *attempting to press me into making a statement*
  pressurize: *Do not be pressurized into making your decision immediately*
  push: *Don't be pushed into signing anything*
  ▷ noun 3 a state of hurrying: *the rush not to be late for school*
  bustle: *the bustle of modern life*
  dash: *a 160-mile dash to the hospital*
  hurry: *Eric left the house in a hurry*
  race: *a race to get the work finished before the deadline*
  scramble: *the scramble to get a seat on the early morning flight*
  stampede: *There was a stampede for the exit*
  see also **bolt, burst, bustle, charge, dash, flood, fly, hurry, speed, wave**

ruthless see harsh, merciless

S

sack verb 1 informal to dismiss from a job: *sacked for punching his boss*
  discharge: *discharged from the army*
  dismiss: *the power to dismiss employees*
  fire informal: *He was fired for poor timekeeping*

the sack noun informal dismissal from a job: *He got the sack after three months*
  discharge: *He plans to appeal his discharge*
  dismissal: *the case for his dismissal*
  termination of employment: *wrongful termination of employment*
  see also **discharge, fire**

sacred see holy, religious

sacrifice verb 1 to give something up: *She sacrificed her family life for her career*
  forego: *If we forego our summer holiday we can afford a car*
  forfeit: *The company is forfeiting safety for the sake of profit*
  give up: *I gave up my job to be with you*
  surrender: *We have surrendered our political authority for economic gain*
  ▷ noun 2 the action of giving something up: *He was willing to*

make any sacrifice for peace

renunciation: religious principles of renunciation and dedication

self-denial: an unprecedented act of self-denial

sacrosanct see holy

sad adjective **1** feeling unhappy about something: The loss of our friendship makes me sad

blue: I don't know why I'm feeling so blue today

dejected: Everyone has days when they feel dejected

depressed: She's depressed about this whole situation

dismal: What are you all looking so dismal about?

down: The old man sounded really down

downcast: a downcast expression

glum: a row of glum faces

gloomy: Don't look so gloomy, Mr Todd. I'll do my best for you

grief-stricken: comforting the grief-stricken relatives

low: He used to listen when I was feeling low

melancholy: melancholy thoughts

mournful: the mournful expression on his face

unhappy: I hate to see you so unhappy

wistful: I found myself feeling wistful at the memory of him

2 making you feel unhappy: a sad song

depressing: a depressing film

dismal: a dark, dismal day

gloomy: a gloomy tale of a poor orphan

harrowing: a harrowing documentary about drug addicts

heart-rending: heart-rending pictures of the victims

melancholy: the melancholy music used throughout the film

mournful: a mournful ballad

moving: a deeply moving account of her life

pathetic: the pathetic sight of oil-covered sea birds

poignant: a poignant love story

tragic: his tragic death

upsetting: I'm afraid I have some upsetting news for you

see also gloomy, miserable, pathetic, sorry, unhappy

sadden see distress, grieve, hurt

saddened see disappointed

saddening see painful

sadistic see cruel

sadness noun the feeling of being unhappy: I said goodbye with a mixture of sadness and joy

dejection: a feeling of dejection and despair

depression: plunged into the deepest depression

despondency: Deep despondency set in again

melancholy: Dean had shaken off his melancholy

unhappiness: His unhappiness shows in his face

see also grief, misery, sorrow

safe adjective **1** not causing harm or danger: This is not a safe place for a woman on her own

harmless: harmless substances

innocuous: Both mushrooms look innocuous but are in fact deadly

wholesome: fresh, wholesome ingredients

2 not in any danger: I felt warm and safe with him

all right: I'll be all right on my own

in safe hands: It's all right, you're in safe hands

okay or **OK** informal: Could you check that the baby's okay?

out of danger: We were not out of danger yet

out of harm's way: I'm keeping him well out of harm's way

protected: Keep the plants dry and protected from frost

safe and sound: I'm hoping he will come home safe and sound

secure: I would like to feel financially secure

see also **harmless, immune, reliable, secure**

safe and sound see **safe**

safeguard verb 1 to protect something: international action to safeguard the ozone layer

defend: his courage in defending religious and civil rights

guard: He closely guarded her identity

look after: People tend to look after their own property

preserve: We need to preserve the forest

protect: What can we do to protect ourselves against heart disease?

save: This machine could help save babies from cot death

shield: They moved to shield their children from adverse publicity

▷ noun 2 something that protects people or things: adequate safeguards for civil liberties

barrier: a barrier against the outside world

cover: Airlines are required to provide cover against such incidents

defence: The immune system is our main defence against disease

protection: Innocence is no protection from the evils in our society

see also **defence, defend, guard, precaution, protect, protection, save**

safety noun the state of being safe from harm or danger: I was very anxious about her safety

immunity: natural immunity to the disease

protection: protection from harmful rays

security: a false sense of security

see also **shelter**

sagging see **flabby**

sail see **fly**

saintly see **holy**

salary see **income, pay**

sallow see **pale**

saloon see **pub**

salted see **salty**

salty adjective tasting of or containing salt: a good rasher of salty bacon

brak South African: the brak shallow water near the dam wall

briny: the flow of the briny water

salted: 8 ounces of slightly salted butter

salute see **recognize**

salvage see **save**

same adjective exactly like one another: The two words sound the same but have different spellings

alike: No two families are alike

equal: Mix equal quantities of soy sauce and rice vinegar

equivalent: One unit is roughly equivalent to a glass of wine

identical: Nearly all the houses were identical

indistinguishable: symptoms indistinguishable from those of AIDS

see also **like**

sameness see **similarity**

sample see **example, try**

sanction verb 1 to officially approve of or allow something: He is ready to sanction the use of force

allow: I cannot be seen to allow violence on school premises

approve: The parliament has approved a programme of economic reforms

authorize: We are willing to authorize a police raid

back: persuading the government to back the plan

endorse: policies endorsed by the voting public

permit: Will he let the court's decision stand and permit the execution?

support: The party is under pressure to support the ban

▷ noun **2** official approval of something: The king could not enact the law without the sanction of parliament

approval: The chairman has given his approval

authorization: You will need the authorization of a parent or guardian

backing: He said the president had the backing of his government

blessing: With the blessing of the White House, the group is meeting to identify more budget cuts

permission: Finally she gave permission for him to marry

support: The prime minister gave his support to the reforms formal

see also **approval**, **approve**, **let**, **permit**

sanctions noun penalties for countries which break the law: The United States is considering imposing sanctions against the regime

ban: After four years, he lifted the ban

boycott: the lifting of the economic boycott against the country

embargo: They called on the government to lift its embargo on trade with the country

penalties: legally binding penalties against treaty violators

sanctuary see **refuge**, **retreat**, **shelter**

sands see **beach**

sane adjective **1** having a normal healthy mind: This was not the act of a sane person

lucid: She was lucid right up until her death

normal: the question of what constitutes normal behaviour

rational: He seemed perfectly rational to me

2 showing good sense: a sane and practical policy

judicious: the judicious use of military force

level-headed: a sensible, level-headed approach

rational: a rational analysis

reasonable: a reasonable course of action

sensible: the sensible thing to do

sound: sound advice

see also **reasonable**

sanguine see **optimistic**

sanitation see **hygiene**

sap see **drain**, **tax**, **undermine**, **weaken**

sarcastic adjective saying the opposite of what you mean to make fun of someone: A sarcastic remark was on the tip of her tongue

caustic: his abrasive wit and caustic comments

ironic: an ironic remark

sardonic: a sardonic sense of humour

satirical: a satirical TV show

sarcophagus see **tomb**

sardonic see **sarcastic**

satire see **parody**

satirical see **sarcastic**

satisfaction see **comfort**, **delight**, **happiness**, **pleasure**, **pride**

satisfactorily see **well**

satisfactory adjective acceptable or adequate: a satisfactory explanation

acceptable: The air pollution exceeds acceptable levels

adequate: One in four people are without adequate homes

all right: The meal was all right, but nothing special

good enough: He's not good enough

for you

passable: She speaks passable French

sufficient: One teaspoon of sugar should be sufficient

see also **acceptable, adequate, decent, suitable**

satisfied adjective happy because you have got what you want: We are not satisfied with these results

content: I'm perfectly content where I am

contented: She led a quiet, contented life

happy: I'm not happy with the situation

pleased: He seemed pleased with the arrangement

see also **certain, confident, pleased, sure**

satisfy verb 1 to give someone as much of something as they want: a solution which I hope will satisfy everyone

gratify: He was gratified by the audience's response

indulge: I don't believe in indulging children

please: Our prime objective is to please our customers

2 to convince someone of something: He had to satisfy the doctors that he was fit to play

convince: trying to convince the public that its product is safe

persuade: I had to persuade him of the advantages

put someone's mind at rest: He has done his best to put my mind at rest

reassure: I tried to reassure them, but they knew I was lying

3 to fulfil a requirement: Candidates must satisfy the conditions for admission

fulfil: All the minimum requirements were fulfilled

meet: The current arrangements are inadequate to meet their needs

see also **convince, fulfil, meet, suit**

saturated see full, wet

savage adjective 1 cruel and violent: a savage attack

barbarous: the barbarous customs of earlier times

barbaric: a particularly barbaric act of violence

brutal: a very brutal murder

cruel: the cruel practice of bullfighting

ferocious: the most ferocious violence ever seen on the streets of London

inhuman: the inhuman slaughter of these beautiful creatures

vicious: a vicious blow to the head

violent: violent crimes

▷ noun **2** a violent and uncivilized person: They really are a bunch of savages

barbarian: Our maths teacher was a complete barbarian

beast: You beast! Let me go!

brute: He was a brute and he deserved his fate

lout: a drunken lout

monster: These men were total monsters

▷ verb **3** to attack and bite someone: He was savaged to death by the animal

attack: A lion attacked him when he was a child

bite: Every year thousands of children are bitten by dogs

maul: The dog went berserk and mauled one of the girls

see also **violent**

savagery see cruelty, violence

save verb 1 to rescue someone or something: come to someone's rescue: His uncle came to his rescue

deliver: I thanked God for delivering me from the pain

redeem: to redeem souls from

purgatory

rescue: *rescued from the flames*

salvage: *salvaging equipment from the wreckage*

2 to keep someone or something safe: *a new machine which could save babies from cot death*

keep safe: *to keep my home safe from germs*

preserve: *preserving old buildings*

protect: *What can we do to protect ourselves from heart disease?*

safeguard: *measures to safeguard the ozone layer*

3 to keep something for later use: *They are saving for a house*

hoard: *They've begun to hoard food and petrol*

keep: *Grate the lemon zest and keep it for later*

put by: *He's putting his money by in a deposit account*

reserve: *Drain the fruit and reserve the juice*

set aside: *£130 million would be set aside for repairs to schools*

see also **but, except, hoard, reserve, safeguard, stockpile, store**

save from *see* **spare**

saving *see* **cut**

say *verb* **1** to speak words: *She said they were very impressed*

see word studies **say**

▷ *noun* **2** a chance to express your opinion: *voters who want a say in the matter*

voice: *parents are given a voice in decision-making*

vote: *Every employee felt he had a vote in the company's future*

see also **choice, comment, observe, remark, state**

say again *see* **repeat**

say no to *see* **reject**

say sorry *see* **apologize**

saying *noun* a well-known sentence or phrase: *the saying, "charity begins at home"*

adage: *the old adage, "the show must go on"*

axiom: *the long-held axiom that education leads to higher income*

maxim: *I believe in the maxim, "If it ain't broke, don't fix it"*

proverb: *an old Chinese proverb*

scalding *see* **hot**

scale *see* **climb, extent**

scale drawing *see* **plan**

scan *see* **glance, inspect, read, scrutinize**

scandal *see* **disgrace, shame, slander**

scandalous *see* **disgraceful, notorious**

scant *see* **insufficient, low, meagre**

scanty *see* **few**

scarce *adjective* rare or uncommon: *Jobs are becoming increasingly scarce*

few: *Our options are few*

rare: *Puffins are now rare in this country*

uncommon: *an extreme but by no means uncommon case*

unusual: *To be appreciated as a parent is quite unusual*

see also **few, inadequate, rare, uncommon**

scarcely *see* **barely, hardly**

scarcity *see* **lack, shortage, want**

scare *verb* **1** to frighten someone: *You're scaring me*

alarm: *We could not see what had alarmed him*

frighten: *He knew that Soli was trying to frighten him*

give someone a fright: *The snake moved and gave everyone a fright*

intimidate: *Jones had set out to intimidate and dominate Paul*

startle: *Sorry, I didn't mean to startle you*

terrify: *Flying terrifies him*

terrorize: *pensioners terrorized by anonymous phone calls*
unnerve: *We were unnerved by the total silence*
▷ noun **2** a short period of feeling very frightened: *We got a bit of a scare*
fright: *the last time I had a real fright*
shock: *It gave me quite a shock to see his face on the screen*
start: *The sudden noise gave me quite a start*
3 a situation where people worry about something: *Despite the health scare there are no plans to withdraw the drug*
alert: *a security alert*
hysteria: *Everyone was getting carried away by the hysteria*
panic: *the panic over GM foods*
see also **alarm, frighten**
scared *see* **afraid, frightened**
scary *adjective informal* frightening: *Prison is going to be a scary thing for him*
alarming: *an alarming report on the rise of street crime*
chilling: *a chilling account of the accident*
creepy *informal*: *places that are really creepy at night*
eerie: *the eerie dark path*
frightening: *a very frightening experience*
hair-raising: *a hair-raising encounter with a wild boar*
spooky: *The whole place has a slightly spooky atmosphere*
terrifying: *I find it terrifying to be surrounded by a crowd of people*
unnerving: *It is very unnerving to find out that someone you know is carrying the virus*
see also **creepy, spooky**
scathing *see* **abusive, critical, scornful**
scatter *verb* to throw or drop things

all over an area: *She scattered the petals over the grave*
shower: *The bomb exploded, showering shrapnel over a wide area*
sow: *Sow the seeds in a warm place*
sprinkle: *Sprinkle a tablespoon of sugar over the fruit*
throw about: *They started throwing food about*
see also **distribute**
scenario *see* **plot, situation**
scene *noun* **1** a picture or view of something: *a village scene*
landscape: *Arizona's desert landscape*
panorama: *a panorama of fertile valleys*
view: *a view of the lake*
2 the place where something happens: *the scene of the crime*
location: *filmed in an exotic location*
place: *Can you show me the place where the attack happened?*
setting: *Rome is the perfect setting for romance*
site: *the site of the battle*
spot: *the ideal spot for a picnic*
3 an area of activity: *the music scene*
arena: *the political arena*
business: *the potential to revolutionize the publishing business*
environment: *the Japanese business environment*
world: *the fashion world*
see also **sight, spot, view**
scenery *noun* the things you see in the countryside: *drive slowly down the lane enjoying the scenery*
landscape: *Arizona's desert landscape*
panorama: *admiring the distant mountain panorama*
surroundings: *a holiday home in beautiful surroundings*
terrain: *The terrain changed from arable land to desert*
view: *The view from our window was spectacular*

scent see fragrance, smell

sceptical see cynical, dubious, suspicious

scepticism see doubt, suspicion

schedule see arrange, book, programme, routine, time

scheduled see set

scheme see idea, plan, plot, racket

scheming see crafty, devious, sly

schism see split

scholar see pupil

scholarly see learned

scholarship see knowledge

school see instruct, teach, train

schoolboy see boy, pupil

schoolchild see pupil

schoolgirl see pupil

schooling see education

scoff at see mock

scold verb to tell someone off: She scolded her daughter for being cheeky

chide: Cross chided himself for worrying

lecture: My mother always used to lecture me about not eating properly

rebuke: I turned to him and sharply rebuked him

reprimand: reprimanded for talking in the corridor

tell off informal: The teacher really told her off

tick off informal: ticked off for being late

see also abuse

scolding see lecture

scope see freedom, range

scorch see burn

scorching see hot

score see line

scores see a lot or lots, many

scorn noun 1 great contempt felt for something: The proposal was greeted with scorn

contempt: I treated this remark with the contempt it deserved

derision: shouts of derision

disdain: Janet looked at him with disdain

mockery: his mockery of all things English

▷ verb 2 to treat with great contempt: Eleanor scorns the work of others

despise: She secretly despises him

disdain: He disdained politicians

look down on: I wasn't successful so they looked down on me

slight: He felt slighted by this treatment

see also belittle, contempt

scornful adjective showing contempt for something: He is deeply scornful of his rivals

contemptuous: She gave a contemptuous little laugh

disdainful: He is disdainful of politicians

scathing: He made some scathing comments about the design

sneering: a sneering tone

supercilious: His manner is supercilious and arrogant

withering: Her mother gave her a withering look

scoundrel see crook

scour see clean, scrape, search

scourge see pest

scowl see frown, glare

scramble see rush

scrap see bit, junk

scrape verb 1 to rub a rough or sharp object against something: We had to scrape the frost from the windscreen

graze: He had grazed his knees a little

scour: Scour the pans

scratch: The branches scratched my face and hands

scuff: scuffed shoes

skin: I found that I had skinned my knuckles

2 to make a harsh noise by rubbing: his shoes scraping across the ground

grate: His chair grated as he got to his feet

grind: Blocks of ice ground against each other

rasp: The blade rasped over his skin

scratch: He scratched his knife over the worktop
see also **graze, predicament**

scraps see **remains**

scratch see **graze, scrape, tear**

scrawny see **skinny**

scream verb **1** to shout or cry in a high-pitched voice: If he says that again, I shall scream
cry: a crying baby
howl: He howled like a wounded animal
screech: "Get me some water!" I screeched
shout: I shouted at mother to get the police
shriek: She shrieked and leapt from the bed
squeal: Jennifer squealed with delight
yell: I pushed him away, yelling abuse
▷ noun **2** a loud, high-pitched cry: Hilda let out a scream
cry: a cry of horror
howl: a howl of rage
screech: The figure gave a screech
shriek: a shriek of joy
squeal: the squeal of piglets
yell: Something brushed Bob's face and he let out a yell
see also **shout**

screech see **scream**

screen see **cover, obscure**

screw up see **crumple, twist**

scriptural see **religious**

scrounge verb informal to get something by asking rather than working for it: He's always scrounging lifts
beg: They managed to beg a lift from a passing fisherman
bludge Australian, New

Zealand informal: They've come here to bludge food and money
cadge: Can I cadge a cigarette?
sponge informal: I got tired of him sponging off me and threw him out

scrub see **clean, wash**

scruffy adjective dirty and untidy: four scruffy youths
ragged: a ragged band of men
seedy: his seedy clothes
shabby: a shabby, tall man with dark eyes
tatty: a tatty old cardigan
unkempt: His hair was unkempt and filthy
see also **shabby**

scruples see **conscience, principle, standards**

scrupulous see **thorough**

scrutinize verb to examine something very carefully: She scrutinized his features
examine: He examined her passport
inspect: Cut the fruit in half and inspect the pips
pore over: We spent hours poring over the files
scan: She kept scanning the crowd for Paul
search: Her eyes searched his face
study: Debbie studied the document for a moment
see also **observe, regard**

scuff see **scrape**

sculpt see **carve, model**

scungy adjective Australian, New Zealand slang dirty: living in some scungy flat on the outskirts of town
dirty: He was wearing a dirty old mac
filthy: This flat is so filthy I can't possibly stay here
foul: foul polluted water
seedy: a seedy hotel
sleazy: sleazy bars
sordid: sordid little rooms
squalid: a squalid bedsit

scurry see bustle, hurry, rush

scuttle see bustle

seal see close, glue, plug

sealed see shut

search verb 1 to look for something:
*The security forces are searching for the
missing men*

comb: *Police combed the woods for
the murder weapon*

forage: *foraging for food*

fossick *Australian, New Zealand*: to
help Gaston fossick for food around
the hut

hunt: *hunting for a job*

look: *He's looking for a way out of
this situation*

scour: *They had scoured the
intervening miles of moorland*

seek: *the man he had been seeking
for weeks*

sift: *sifting through the wreckage
for clues*

▷ noun 2 the action of looking for
something: *Police will resume the
search today*

hunt: *the hunt for my lost boy*

quest: *his quest to find true love*
see also **fossick, look for, scrutinize**

search for see seek

seashore see beach

seaside see beach, coast

seasoned see experienced,
practical

secluded see lonely

seclusion see solitude

second see instant, minute,
moment, support

secondary see inferior, minor

second-class see inferior

second-rate see cheap, inferior,
poor

secret *adjective* known about by only
a few people: *a secret location*

closet *informal*: *a closet Fascist*

confidential: *a confidential report*

covert: *She gave him a covert glance*

furtive: *furtive meetings*

hidden: *a hidden camera*

undercover: *undercover FBI agents*

underground: *the underground
communist movement*
see also **private**

secrete see hide

secretive *adjective* hiding your
feelings and intentions: *Jake was very
secretive about his family affairs*

cagey *informal*: *He is cagey about
what he was paid for the business*

reserved: *He was unemotional and
reserved*

reticent: *She is very reticent about
her achievements*
see also **mysterious**

section *noun* one of the parts into
which something is divided: *this
section of the motorway*

division: *the company's sales division*

instalment: *Payment can be made
in instalments*

part: *the upper part of the body*

piece: *The equipment was taken down
the shaft in pieces*

portion: *I had learnt a portion of
the Koran*

segment: *the third segment of the
journey*
see also **compartment,
department, division, extract,
part, passage**

sector see division, region

secure *verb* 1 *formal* to manage to
get something: *His achievements
helped him to secure the job*

acquire: *General Motors recently
acquired a 50% stake in the company*

gain: *Hard work may not be enough to
gain a place at university*

get: *I got a job at the sawmill*

obtain: *He tried to obtain a false
passport*

procure *formal*: *trying to procure the
release of the hostages*

2 to make something safe: *We need to secure the building against attack*

fortify: *British soldiers are working to fortify the airbase*

make impregnable: *Their intention was to make the old fort impregnable*

make safe: *Crime Prevention Officers will suggest ways to make your home safe*

strengthen: *In the 14th century they strengthened this wall against raiders*

3 to fasten or attach something firmly: *The frames are secured by rails to the wall*

attach: *The gadget can be attached to any vertical surface*

bind: *Bind the ends of the cord together with thread*

fasten: *Her long hair was fastened by an elastic band*

fix: *He fixed a bayonet to the end of his rifle*

lock: *Are you sure you locked the front door?*

moor: *She moored her barge on the river bank*

tie up: *They dismounted and tied up their horses*

▷ *adjective* **4** tightly locked or well protected: *Make sure your home is as secure as possible*

fortified: *The door is fortified against flooding*

impregnable: *The old castle was completely impregnable against raids*

protected: *the right of women to be protected from sexual harassment*

safe: *We want to go to a football match knowing we are safe from hooliganism*

shielded: *The company is shielded from takeover attempts*

5 firmly fixed in place: *Shelves are only as secure as their fixings*

fastened: *Make sure the safety belt is fastened*

firm: *If you have to climb up, use a firm platform*

fixed: *Check the holder is fixed in its place on the wall*

locked: *Leave doors and windows locked*

solid: *I yanked on the bracket to see if it was solid*

stable: *The structure must be stable*

tight: *He kept a tight hold of her arm*

6 feeling safe and happy: *She felt secure when she was with him*

confident: *In time he became more confident*

protected: *It's good to have a place in which you feel protected and loved*

reassured: *I feel much more reassured when I've been for a health check*

relaxed: *There are very few people he feels relaxed with*

safe: *He kissed me and I felt warm and safe*

see also **acquire, close, confident, fasten, fix, gain, get, obtain, safe, steady, tie, tight, win**

securely *see* **fast**

security *see* **defence, safety**

seduce *see* **tempt**

seductive *see* **sexy**

see *verb* **1** to look at or notice something: *Did you see what happened?*

behold: *She looked into his eyes and beheld madness*

discern: *We could just discern the outline of the island*

glimpse: *She glimpsed the man's face briefly*

look: *He turned to look at him*

notice: *She noticed a bird sitting on the roof*

observe: *He observed a reddish spot on the planet's surface*

perceive: *Infants start to perceive objects at a very early age*

sight: *A fleet of French ships was*

sighted
spot: I think he spotted me but didn't
want to be seen

2 to realize or understand
something: I see what you mean
appreciate: He appreciates the
difficulties
comprehend: They do not
comprehend the nature of the problem
follow: Do you follow what I'm
saying?
get: You don't seem to get the point
grasp: They have not grasped the
seriousness of the crisis
realize: They realized too late that
they were wrong
understand: I'm not sure I
understand

3 to find something out: I'll see
what's happening outside
ascertain: Ascertain what services
your bank provides
determine: The investigation will
determine what really happened
discover: Try to discover what you
are good at
find out: Watch the next episode to
find out what happens
see also **comprehend, discern,
know, note, notice, observe,
picture, regard, sight, spot, tell,
understand, watch, witness**

see eye to eye see **agree**
see to see **deal, take care of**
seedy see **scruffy, scungy, shabby**
seek verb **1** to try to find something:
The police were still seeking
information
be after: At last I found what I
was after
hunt: Police are hunting for clues
look for: I'm looking for a lost child
search for: searching for answers

2 to try to do something: De Gaulle
sought to reunite the country
aim: We aim to raise funds for charity

aspire to: He aspired to work in music
journalism
attempt: He was forever attempting
to arrange deals
endeavour: They are endeavouring to
protect trade union rights
strive: The school strives to treat
pupils as individuals
try: We are trying to bring about a
better world
see also **ask, attempt, look for,
request, search, strive, try**

seem verb to appear to be: He seemed
such a quiet man
appear: She appeared intoxicated
give the impression: He gave
the impression of being the perfect
husband
look: The cottage looks quite ordinary
from the road
look like: You look like a nice guy
see also **look**

seem to be see **look**
seemly see **correct, right**
seep see **drain, leak**
segment see **portion, proportion,
section**
segregate see **divide**
seize verb **1** to grab something
firmly: He seized the phone
grab: I grabbed him by the neck
grasp: He grasped both my hands
snatch: Mick snatched the cards from
Archie's hand

2 to take control of something:
Rebels have seized the airport
annex: the plan to invade and annex
Kuwait
appropriate: The land was
appropriated by Communists
confiscate: The police confiscated
weapons and ammunition
hijack: Almost 250 trucks were
hijacked
impound: The ship was impounded
under the terms of the trade embargo

see also **arrest, capture, grab, grasp, kidnap, possess**

seizure see **arrest, capture**

select verb **1** to choose something: *They selected only the brightest pupils*

choose: *Houston was chosen as the site for the conference*

decide on: *I'm still trying to decide on an outfit for the wedding*

opt for: *You may wish to opt for one method straight away*

pick: *He had picked ten people to interview for the jobs*

settle on: *I finally settled on the estate car because it was so roomy*

single out: *His boss has singled him out for a special mission*

take: *"I'll take the grilled tuna," she told the waiter*

▷ adjective **2** of good quality: *a select band of top-ranking sportsmen*

choice: *We use only the choicest ingredients*

exclusive: *Britain's most exclusive club*

first-class: *a first-class hotel*

first-rate: *The first-rate cast includes many famous names*

hand-picked: *a hand-picked series of timeless classics*

prime: *one of the City's prime sites, with a view of several historic buildings*

special: *a special group of government officials*

superior: *a superior range of products*
see also **choose, exclusive, nominate, pick, prime**

selection see **appointment, choice, range**

self-assurance see **confidence**

self-assured see **confident**

self-centred see **selfish**

self-conscious see **embarrassed, shy, uncomfortable**

self-consciousness see **embarrassment**

self-denial see **sacrifice**

self-evident see **obvious**

self-importance see **conceit**

self-important see **conceited**

selfish adjective caring only about yourself: *his greedy and selfish behaviour*

egoistic or **egoistical**: *egoistic motives*

egotistic or **egotistical**: *an intensely egotistic streak*

greedy: *greedy bosses awarding themselves big rises*

self-centred: *He was self-centred, but he wasn't cruel*

self-possessed see **confident**

self-possession see **confidence**

self-propelled see **automatic**

self-satisfied see **smug**

self-sufficient see **independent**

sell verb to let someone have something in return for money: *a tobacconist that sells stamps*

deal in: *They deal in antiques*

hawk: *vendors hawking trinkets*

peddle: *arrested for peddling drugs*

stock: *The shop stocks a variety of local craft products*

trade in: *They trade in spices and all kinds of grain*
see also **stock**

sell at see **cost**

selling price see **value**

semblance see **illusion, look, show**

send verb **1** to arrange for something to be delivered: *He sent a basket of fruit and a card*

dispatch: *He dispatched a telegram of congratulation*

forward: *A letter was forwarded from the clinic*

remit: *Many immigrants regularly remit money to their families*

2 to transmit a signal or message: *The pilot was trying to send a distress signal*

broadcast: to broadcast a message to a whole group of people at once

transmit: the most efficient way to transmit data

send in see submit

send out see emit

send to prison see imprison

senior adjective the highest and most important in an organization: senior jobs

best: These officers have traditionally taken the best jobs

better: Well-qualified women are now attaining better positions

high-ranking: a high-ranking officer in the medical corps

superior: negotiations between crew members and their superior officers

see also superior

sensation see feeling, success

sensational see incredible, melodramatic

sense noun 1 a feeling you have about something: an overwhelming sense of guilt

consciousness: a consciousness of tension

feeling: It gave me a feeling of satisfaction

impression: The music creates an impression of menace

2 the ability to think and behave sensibly: He had the good sense to call me at once

brains informal: At least I had the brains to keep quiet

common sense: completely lacking in common sense

intelligence: He didn't have the intelligence to understand what was happening

judgment: I respect his judgment

reason: a conflict between emotion and reason

wisdom: the wisdom that comes of old age

▷ verb 3 to become aware of something: She sensed he wasn't telling her the whole story

be aware of: He was aware of her anger

feel: Suddenly, I felt a presence behind me

get the impression: I get the impression he's lying

have a hunch: Lowe had a hunch he was on to something

realize: We realized something was wrong

see also feeling, impression, intelligence, meaning, reason

sense of duty see principle

sense of right and wrong see conscience

senseless see foolish, idiotic, unconscious, unwise

sensible adjective showing good sense and judgment: a sensible, level-headed approach

down-to-earth: the most down-to-earth person I've ever met

judicious: the judicious use of military force

practical: practical suggestions

prudent: It is prudent to start any exercise programme gradually

rational: a rational decision

sound: sound advice

wise: a wise move

see also logical, practical, rational, realistic, reasonable, responsible, sane, sound, wise

sensitive adjective easily upset about something: He was sensitive about his height

easily offended: I am not a feminist, nor am I easily offended

easily upset: He remained deeply neurotic and easily upset

thin-skinned: I'm too thin-skinned – I want everyone to like me

touchy: She is very touchy about

her weight
see also **fine, impressionable, sore,
tactful, tender, touchy, tricky,
understanding, vulnerable**

sensitivity see **tact**

sensual see **sexy**

sensuous see **sexy**

sentence see **condemn, punish**

sentiment see **feeling**

sentimental adjective expressing
exaggerated sadness or tenderness:
sentimental love stories

   maudlin: Jimmy turned maudlin after
three drinks

   mushy informal: I go completely
mushy when I see a baby

   nostalgic informal: nostalgic for the good
old days

   sloppy informal: I hate sloppy
romantic films

   slushy informal: slushy ballads
see also **corny**

sentry see **guard**

separate adjective **1** not connected
to something else: The question
muddles up two separate issues

   detached: a detached house

   disconnected: sequences of
disconnected events

   discrete: two discrete sets of nerves

   divorced: speculative theories
divorced from reality

   isolated: He lives as if isolated from
the rest of the world

   unconnected: The two murders are
unconnected

▷ verb **2** to end a connection
between people or things: Police
moved in to separate the two groups

   detach: Three of the carriages on the
train became detached

   disconnect: Make sure supply plugs
are disconnected from the mains

   divide: This was a ruse to divide them

3 to end a relationship or marriage:
Her parents separated when she was

very young

break up: She hadn't used his name
since they broke up

divorce: We divorced ten years ago

part: He is parting from his Swedish-
born wife Eva

split up: I split up with my boyfriend
last year

see also **alone, different, divide,
independent, individual, single,
sort, split**

separation see **division**

sepulchre see **grave, tomb**

sequence noun **1** a number of
events coming one after another: an
unbroken sequence of victories

   chain: the chain of events leading to
the assassination

   course: a course of injections

   cycle: the cycle of birth, growth,
decay, and death

   progression: The story of American
freedom is anything but a linear
progression

   series: a series of explosions

   string: a string of burglaries

   succession: He took a succession of
jobs that stood him in good stead

2 a particular order in which things
are arranged: the colour sequence:
yellow, orange, purple, blue

   arrangement: a simple arrangement
of coloured tiles

   order: Music shops should arrange
their recordings in alphabetical order

   pattern: a systematic pattern of
behaviour

   progression: the natural progression
of the seasons

   structure: The bricks had been
arranged in a regular structure
see also **series**

serene see **cool, patient, peaceful,
quiet, relaxed**

serenity see **calm, quiet**

series noun a number of things

coming one after the other: *a series of loud explosions*
chain: *a bizarre chain of events*
run: *The England skipper is haunted by a run of low scores*
sequence: *a sequence of novels*
string: *a string of burglaries*
succession: *He had a succession of jobs*
see also **range, sequence, set**

serious adjective **1** very bad and worrying: *They survived their serious injuries*
acute: *an acute attack of appendicitis*
alarming: *the alarming increase in drug abuse*
bad: *a bad bout of flu*
critical: *He remains in a critical condition in hospital*
dangerous: *His wound proved more dangerous than it seemed at first*
extreme: *the most extreme case doctors have ever seen*
grave: *We are all in grave danger*
grievous: *grievous wounds*
grim: *Our situation is grim indeed*
intense: *Intense fighting has broken out in the capital*
precarious: *He is in a very precarious position*
severe: *a severe shortage of drinking water*
worrying: *It is a worrying situation*
2 important and deserving careful thought: *I regard this as a serious matter*
crucial: *Negotiations were at a crucial stage*
deep: *This novel raises deep questions about the nature of faith*
difficult: *The government faces even more difficult problems*
far-reaching: *His actions will have far-reaching consequences*
grave: *a grave situation*
important: *We've got more important*

things to worry about now
momentous: *the momentous decision to go to war*
pressing: *a pressing problem*
profound: *a man who thinks about the more profound issues of life*
significant: *the most significant question of all*
urgent: *He is not equipped to deal with an urgent situation like this*
weighty: *a weighty problem*
3 sincere about something: *I was not quite sure whether he was serious*
earnest: *It is my earnest hope that we can work things out*
genuine: *a genuine offer*
heartfelt: *a full and heartfelt apology*
honest: *He looked at me in honest surprise*
in earnest: *I can never tell if he is in earnest or not*
resolute: *He was resolute about his ideals*
resolved: *They are quite resolved about their decision*
sincere: *He's sincere in his views*
4 quiet and not laughing much: *He's quite a serious person*
earnest: *She looked up at me with an earnest expression*
grave: *He was looking unusually grave*
humourless: *a dour, humourless Scotsman*
pensive: *We're both in a pensive mood today*
sober: *sad, sober faces*
solemn: *His solemn little face broke into a smile*
staid: *bored with her marriage to a staid country doctor*
stern: *a stern headmaster feared by all the pupils*
see also **acute, critical, deep, grave, heavy, important, severe, solemn**

sermon see **lecture, talk**

serrated see jagged

serve as see form

service see ceremony, favour

serving see portion

session see round, term

set noun 1 a group of things that belong together: *a set of tools*

batch: *the latest batch of recruits*

kit: *I forgot my gym kit*

outfit: *She was wearing a brand new outfit*

series: *a series of books covering the history of aviation*

▷ verb 2 to put or place something somewhere: *He set his case down on the floor*

deposit: *Imagine if you were suddenly deposited on a desert island*

lay: *Lay a sheet of newspaper on the floor*

locate: *The restaurant is located near the cathedral*

place: *She placed a mug of coffee in front of him*

position: *Plants were carefully positioned in the alcove*

put: *He put the photograph on the desk*

rest: *He rested one of his crutches against the rail*

stick: *Just stick your bag down anywhere*

▷ adjective 3 fixed and not varying: *a set charge*

arranged: *We arrived at the arranged time*

established: *the established order*

firm: *a firm booking*

fixed: *a fixed rate of interest*

predetermined: *His destiny was predetermined from the moment of his birth*

scheduled: *The plane failed to return at the scheduled time*

see also **bunch, category, class, firm, group, harden, insert, lay,**

lot, ready, rigid, thicken, time

set about see begin, start

set against one another see divide

set aside see allow, reserve, save

set back see delay

set down see lay

set free see discharge, release

set loose see free

set off see explode, fire, flatter, go, provoke, sound

set on adjective determined to do something: *She was set on going to the States*

bent: *He's bent on suicide*

determined: *His enemies are determined to ruin him*

intent: *an actress who was intent on making a comeback*

set out see lay

set upon see attack

setback see blow, delay, disappointment

setting see scene, surroundings

settle verb 1 to put an end to an argument or problem: *The dispute has been settled*

clear up: *Eventually the confusion was cleared up*

decide: *None of the cases had been decided*

dispose of: *the way in which you disposed of that problem*

put an end to: *I just want to put an end to this situation*

reconcile: *urging the two parties to reconcile their differences*

resolve: *They hoped the crisis could be resolved peacefully*

straighten out: *doing their best to straighten out this confusion*

2 to decide or arrange something: *Let's settle where we're going tonight*

agree: *Have you agreed a date yet*

arrange: *Have you arranged our next appointment?*

decide on: *They decided on an*

evening to meet
determine: The final wording had not
yet been determined
fix: He's going to fix a time when I
can see him
3 to make your home in a place:
refugees settling in Britain
make your home: those who had
made their homes in China
move to: His family moved to New
Zealand when he was 12
people: The plateau was peopled by
nomadic tribes
populate: The island was populated
by Native Americans
see also **confirm, determine,
lay, pay**

settle on see **pick, select**

settle up see **repay**

settled see **definite**

settlement see **agreement, colony**

set up verb to make arrangements
for something: setting up a system of
communication
arrange: We have arranged a series
of interviews
establish: We have established links
with industry and commerce
install: I'm having cable installed
next week
institute: to institute better levels of
quality control
organize: a two-day meeting
organized by the UN
see also **organize, start**

several adjective indicating a small
number: several boxes filled with
albums
assorted: overnight stops in assorted
hotels
some: some cheers from the gallery
sundry: He has won sundry music
awards
various: a dozen trees of various sorts
see also **numerous**

severe adjective **1** extremely bad or

unpleasant: severe cash flow problems
acute: an acute economic crisis
critical: if the situation becomes
critical
deep: We will be in deep trouble if
this goes on
dire: This would have dire
consequences for domestic peace
extreme: people living in extreme
poverty
grave: He said the situation was
very grave
intense: A number of people collapsed
in the intense heat
serious: The government faces very
serious difficulties
terrible: terrible injuries
2 stern and harsh: This was a
dreadful crime and a severe sentence
is necessary
disapproving: Janet gave him a
disapproving look
grim: Her expression was grim and
unpleasant
hard: His father was a hard man
harsh: the cold, harsh cruelty of her
husband
stern: He said stern measures would
be taken
strict: My parents were very strict
see also **acute, drastic, extreme,
grim, harsh, intense, serious,
simple, violent**

severity see **violence**

sexism see **prejudice**

sexy adjective sexually attractive or
exciting: a sexy voice
erotic: an erotic film
seductive: I love dressing up to look
seductive
sensual: a wide, sensual mouth
sensuous: his sensuous young
mistress
voluptuous: a voluptuous figure

shabby adjective **1** ragged and worn
in appearance: a shabby overcoat

dilapidated: *a dilapidated old building*

ragged: *dressed in a ragged coat*

scruffy: *a scruffy basement flat in London*

seedy: *his seedy clothes*

tatty: *a tatty old cardigan*

threadbare: *a square of threadbare carpet*

worn: *a worn corduroy jacket*

2 behaving meanly and unfairly: shabby treatment

contemptible: *contemptible behaviour*

despicable: *a despicable thing to do*

dirty: *That was a dirty trick*

mean: *It was mean of you to hurt her like that*

rotten *informal*: *That's a rotten thing to say!*

see also **scruffy**

shade *see* colour, cover

shadow *see* blot out

shadowy *see* dark, dim

shady *see* corrupt, crooked, suspicious

shaft *see* bar

shake *verb* **1** to move something from side to side or up and down: *You have to shake the bottle before use*

agitate: *Gently agitate the water*

brandish: *He appeared brandishing a knife*

flourish: *He flourished his glass to make the point*

wave: *The crowd were waving flags and cheering*

2 to move from side to side or up and down: *The whole building shook with the force of the blast*

jolt: *The train jolted again*

quake: *The whole mountain quaked*

quiver: *Her bottom lip began to quiver*

shiver: *shivering with fear*

shudder: *Elaine shuddered with cold*

tremble: *The leaves trembled in the breeze*

vibrate: *The engine began to vibrate alarmingly*

3 to shock and upset someone: *The news shook me quite a bit*

distress: *Her death had profoundly distressed me*

disturb: *dreams so vivid that they disturb me for days*

rattle *informal*: *He was obviously rattled by events*

shock: *Pictures of emaciated prisoners shocked the world*

unnerve: *unnerved by the sight*

upset: *I was too upset to speak*

see also disturb, shock, wave

shaky *adjective* weak and unsteady: *threatening an already shaky economy*

rickety: *Mona climbed the rickety wooden stairway*

tottering: *the baby's first tottering steps*

trembling: *She held out one frail, trembling hand*

unstable: *an unstable lamp on top of an old tea-chest*

unsteady: *His voice was unsteady*

wobbly: *I'm sorry, this table's a bit wobbly*

see also **unsteady**

sham *see* fake, mock, phoney

shame *noun* **1** a feeling of guilt or embarrassment: *She felt a deep sense of shame*

embarrassment: *He turned red with embarrassment*

humiliation: *the humiliation of discussing her husband's affair*

ignominy: *the ignominy of being made redundant*

2 something that makes people lose respect for you: *I don't want to bring shame on the family*

discredit: *It was to his discredit that he did nothing*

disgrace: He had to resign in disgrace
dishonour: his sense of dishonour at his brother's conduct
scandal: They often abandoned their children because of fear of scandal
▷ verb **3** to make someone feel ashamed: Her son's affair had shamed her
disgrace: I have disgraced my country
embarrass: It embarrassed him that he had no idea of what was going on
humiliate: His teacher continually humiliates him in maths lessons
see also **disgrace, embarrass, embarrassment, humiliate, pity**
shameful see **disgraceful**
shameless adjective behaving badly without showing any shame: shameless dishonesty
barefaced: a barefaced lie
brazen: a brazen theft
flagrant: a flagrant violation of the law
unabashed: an unabashed egotist
unashamed: blatant, unashamed hypocrisy
wanton: a wanton woman
shampoo see **wash**
shape noun **1** the outline of something: a round shape
contours: the contours of the mountains
figure: a trim figure
form: the form of the human body
lines: The belt spoilt the lines of her long dress
outline: the dim outline of a small boat
▷ verb **2** to make something in a particular form: Shape the dough into a loaf
fashion: buttons fashioned from bone
form: The polymer is formed into a thin sheet
make: gold made into wedding rings
model: She began modelling animals

from clay
mould: Mould the cheese into small ovals
see also **body, build, condition, design, determine, fashion, figure, form, health, model, outline, state**
share verb **1** to divide something between two or more people: We shared a bottle of champagne
divide: The prize money was divided between the two winners
split: We split the bill between us
▷ noun **2** a portion of something: a share of the profits
allotment: a daily allotment of three ounces of bread
portion: his portion of the inheritance
quota: a quota of four tickets per person
ration: their daily ration of water
see also **proportion**
share out see **distribute**
shares see **stock**
shark see **crook**
sharp adjective **1** having a fine cutting edge or point: a sharp knife
jagged: jagged rocks
keen: a keen edge
pointed: pointed teeth
razor-sharp: the razor-sharp blade
2 quick to notice or understand things: a sharp intellect
alert: She is alert and sprightly despite her 85 years
astute: He made a series of astute business decisions
bright: an exceptionally bright child
observant: an observant eye
perceptive: a perceptive gaze
quick: His quick mind soon grasped the situation
quick-witted: He is very alert and quick-witted
3 sudden and significant: a sharp rise in prices
abrupt: Her idyllic world came to an

abrupt end when her parents died
marked: *a marked increase in crimes against property*
sudden: *a sudden change in course*
see also **acute, astute, bitter, brilliant, intelligent, perceptive, prompt, shrewd, shrill, sour**

shatter see **dash**

shattered see **broken**

shed see **discard**

sheen see **gloss**

sheepish see **ashamed, embarrassed**

sheer *adjective* **1** complete and total: *acts of sheer desperation*
absolute: *I think it's absolute nonsense*
complete: *He shook his head in complete bewilderment*
pure: *To have an uninterrupted night's sleep was pure bliss*
total: *This is total madness!*
unqualified: *It has been an unqualified disaster*
utter: *a look of utter confusion* formal
2 vertical: *There was a sheer drop just outside my window*
perpendicular: *the perpendicular wall of sandstone*
steep: *a narrow valley with steep sides*
vertical: *The climber inched up a vertical wall of rock*
3 very light and delicate: *sheer black tights*
delicate: *delicate fabric*
fine: *a fine, pale grey material*
lightweight: *lightweight materials with Lycra*
thin: *the thin silk of her blouse*
see also **absolute, fine, perfect, pure, rank, steep, transparent, utter**

sheet see **layer**

sheila see **female, woman**

shell see **bomb, ruin**

shelter *noun* **1** a place providing protection: *a bus shelter*
hostel: *She spent two years living in a hostel*
refuge: *a mountain refuge*
sanctuary: *His church became a sanctuary for people fleeing the civil war*
2 protection from bad weather or danger: *the hut where they were given food and shelter*
asylum: *refugees who sought political asylum*
cover: *They ran for cover from the storm*
harbour: *Patches of gorse were a great harbour for foxes*
haven: *The island is a haven for international criminals*
protection: *Riot shields acted as protection against the attack*
refuge: *They took refuge in an old barn*
safety: *the safety of one's own home*
sanctuary: *Some of them sought sanctuary in the church*
▷ *verb* **3** to stay somewhere in order to be safe: *a man sheltering in a doorway*
hide: *They hid behind a tree*
huddle: *She huddled inside the porch*
take cover: *Shoppers took cover behind cars as the shots rang out*
4 to hide or protect someone: *A neighbour sheltered the boy for seven days*
harbour: *He was accused of harbouring terrorist suspects*
hide: *They hid me until the coast was clear*
protect: *A purple headscarf protected her against the wind*
shield: *He shielded his head from the sun with a sack*
see also **accommodate, defend, guard, protect, protection, refuge**

shelve see **delay, postpone**

shield see **defend, guard, protect, safeguard, shelter**

shielded see **secure**

shimmer see **shine, sparkle**

shimmering see **shining**

shine verb to give out a bright light: *The sun is shining*
  beam: *The spotlight beamed down on the stage*
  gleam: *The moonlight gleamed on the water*
  glow: *The lantern glowed softly in the darkness*
  radiate: *the amount of light radiated by an ordinary light bulb*
  shimmer: *The lake shimmered in the sunlight*
  sparkle: *Diamonds sparkled on her wrists*
  see also **finish, gloss, glow, polish**

shining adjective giving out or reflecting light: *shining stainless steel tables*
  bright: *a bright star*
  brilliant: *brilliant sunshine*
  gleaming: *gleaming headlights*
  luminous: *the luminous dial on the clock*
  radiant: *He saw a figure surrounded by a radiant light*
  shimmering: *a shimmering gold fabric*
  sparkling: *elegant cutlery and sparkling crystal*

shiny see **glossy**

ship see **transport**

shipment see **load, transport**

shirk see **avoid, dodge**

shiver see **shake**

shock noun **1** a sudden upsetting experience: *The extent of the damage came as a shock*
  blow: *It was a terrible blow when he was made redundant*
  bombshell: *His departure was a*

bombshell for the team
  distress: *She wanted to save her mother all the distress she could*
  trauma: *the trauma of losing a parent*
  ▷ verb **2** to make you feel upset: *I was shocked by his appearance*
  numb: *numbed by suffering and terror*
  paralyse: *He stood paralysed with horror*
  shake: *The news of her death has shaken us all*
  stagger: *The judge said he was staggered by the defendant's callousness*
  stun: *Audiences were stunned by the film's violent ending*
  traumatize: *My wife was traumatized by the experience*
  3 to offend because of being rude or immoral: *She is very easily shocked*
  appal: *I was appalled by her rudeness*
  disgust: *He disgusted everyone with his boorish behaviour*
  offend: *Many people are offended by strong swearwords*
  outrage: *They were outraged by his racist comments*
  see also **amaze, amazement, blow, horrify, scare, shake, surprise**

shocking see **disgraceful**

shoddy see **inferior, poor**

shoot see **fire, rush, tear**

shoot up see **explode**

shop noun a place where things are sold: *I had to race round the shops*
  boutique: *He owns a jewellery boutique*
  market: *He sold fruit on a small market stall*
  store: *Within two years he was managing the store*
  supermarket: *Most of us do our food shopping in the supermarket*

shoplifter see **thief**

shopper see **customer**

shore noun

short *adjective* **1** not lasting very
long: *a short break*
brief: *a brief meeting*
fleeting: *a fleeting glimpse*
momentary: *a momentary lapse
of reason*
short-lived: *a short-lived craze*
2 small in height: *a short, elderly man*
see **word studies short**
3 not using many words: *a short
speech*
brief: *a brief description*
concise: *a concise summary*
succinct: *a succinct account*
terse: *a terse comment*
see also **abrupt, brief, concise,
deficient, inadequate,
insufficient, low**

shortage *noun* a lack of something:
a shortage of funds
dearth: *the dearth of good fiction by
English authors*
deficiency: *tests for vitamin
deficiency*
lack: *I was hampered by a lack of
information*
scarcity: *a scarcity of water*
shortfall: *a shortfall in income*
want: *a want of manners and charm*
see also **lack, want**

shortcoming see **defect, failure**

shorten *verb* to make something
shorter: *Smoking can shorten your life*
abbreviate: *He abbreviated his
name to Alec*
cut: *The film was cut to two hours*
trim: *I need to get my hair trimmed*
see also **reduce**

shortfall see **shortage**

short-lived see **short**

shortly see **soon**

shot see **attempt, go, try**

shoulder see **assume, bear**

shoulder to shoulder see **together**

shout *noun* **1** a loud call or cry: *I heard
a distant shout*
bellow: *a bellow of rage*
cry: *She gave a cry of horror*
roar: *a roar of approval*
scream: *screams of terror*
yell: *He let out a yell of delight*
▷ *verb* **2** to call or cry loudly: *He
shouted something to his brother*
bawl: *Laura and Peter were bawling
at each other*
bellow: *He bellowed orders down
the phone*
call: *He could hear them calling
his name*
cry: *"You're under arrest!" he cried*
roar: *"I'll kill you for that!" he roared*
scream: *screaming at them to get out
of my house*
yell: *She pushed him away, yelling
abuse*
see also **call, cry, scream**

shove see **push, stick, stuff**

show *noun* **1** to prove something:
*Tests show that smoking can cause
cancer*
demonstrate: *The study
demonstrated a link between obesity
and heart problems*
prove: *History will prove him to
be right*
▷ *verb* **2** to do something in order to
teach someone else: *I'll show you how
to set the video timer*
demonstrate: *She demonstrated
how to make ice cream*
instruct: *He instructed us on how to
give first aid*
teach: *She taught me how to ride*
3 to display a quality or
characteristic: *Her sketches showed
artistic promise*
demonstrate: *He has demonstrated
his ability*
display: *He displayed remarkable
courage*
indicate: *Her choice of words*

indicated her real feelings
manifest: *Fear can manifest itself in many ways*
reveal: *His reaction revealed a lack of self-confidence*
4 a public exhibition: *a fashion show*
display: *a gymnastics display*
exhibition: *an art exhibition*
presentation: *Julie's successful presentation to the board*
5 a display of a feeling or quality: *a show of affection*
air: *an air of indifference*
display: *a display of remorse*
pose: *a pose of injured innocence*
pretence: *They have given up all pretence of neutrality*
semblance: *trying to maintain a semblance of order*
see also **betray, expose, fair, front, indicate, play, programme, represent**
show signs of see **promise**
show up see **appear, come, expose, uncover**
shower see **hail, scatter**
showers see **rain**
showery see **wet**
show-off see **braggart**
showy see **flashy, gaudy, ostentatious**
shred see **tear**
shrewd *adjective* showing intelligence and good judgment: *a shrewd businessman*
astute: *an astute judge of character*
canny: *He was far too canny to give himself away*
crafty: *He is a clever man and a crafty politician*
perceptive: *a perceptive analysis of the situation*
sharp: *He is very sharp, and a quick thinker*
smart: *a very smart move*
see also **acute, astute, clever, keen,**

smart, wise
shriek see **scream**
shrill *adjective* high-pitched and piercing: *the shrill whistle of the engine*
penetrating: *a penetrating voice*
piercing: *a piercing squawk*
sharp: *the sharp cry of a vixen*
shrink *verb* to become smaller: *All my jumpers have shrunk in the wash*
contract: *The ribcage expands and contracts as you breathe*
diminish: *The threat of nuclear war has diminished*
dwindle: *The factory's workforce has dwindled from 4000 to 200*
get smaller: *Electronic systems are getting smaller*
narrow: *The gap between the two parties has narrowed*
see also **cower, decrease, diminish, flinch, lessen**
shrinkage see **decline**
shrivel see **burn, wither**
shroud see **obscure**
shudder see **shake**
shun see **avoid**
shunned see **unpopular**
shut *verb* **1** to close something: *Someone had forgotten to shut the door*
close: *If you are cold, close the window*
fasten: *He fastened the diamond clasp of the necklace*
slam: *He slammed the gate shut behind him*
▷ *adjective* **2** closed or fastened: *A smell of burning came from behind the shut door*
closed: *All the exits were closed*
fastened: *The pockets are fastened with buttons*
sealed: *a sealed envelope*
see also **close**
shut up see **confine**

shy adjective nervous in the company of other people: *a shy, quiet-spoken girl*

bashful: *Offstage, he is bashful and awkward*

retiring: *He was the quiet, retiring type*

self-conscious: *I felt a bit self-conscious in my swimming costume*

timid: *a timid little boy*

see also **timid**

sick adjective **1** unwell or ill: *a ward full of very sick people*

ailing: *She tenderly nursed her ailing mother*

poorly informal: *I called Julie and she's still poorly*

under par informal: *The flu has left me feeling under par*

under the weather: *Are you still a bit under the weather?*

unwell: *She had been unwell for some time*

2 feeling as if you are going to vomit: *The very thought of food made him sick*

ill: *The smell of curry always makes me ill*

nauseous: *These drugs may make you feel nauseous*

queasy: *The motion of the ship was already making him queasy*

sick of adjective informal tired of something: *I'm sick of your complaints*

bored: *I'm getting bored with the whole business*

fed up: *He is fed up with this country*

tired: *I am tired of this music*

weary: *She was weary of being alone*

see also **crook, ill, queasy, unhealthy, unwell**

sick person see **patient**

sicken see **disgust, horrify, repel**

sickening see **disgusting**

sickly see **puny, weak**

sickness see **illness**

side noun **1** the edge of something: *Her head hung over the side of the bed*

edge: *She fell over the edge of the balcony*

verge: *He parked on the verge of the road*

2 one of two groups involved in a dispute or contest: *Both sides began to prepare for battle*

camp: *Most of his supporters had now defected to the opposite camp*

faction: *leaders of the warring factions*

party: *the candidates for the three main parties*

team: *Both teams played well*

see also **aspect, bank, face, point, team**

side by side see **together**

sidestep see **avoid, dodge**

side with verb to support someone in an argument: *Louise always sided with her sister*

agree with: *She's bound to agree with her husband*

stand up for: *I was the one who always stood up for my mother*

support: *a fellow prisoner who supported her*

take the part of: *Why do you always take his part?*

see also **support**

sidle see **edge, sneak**

sift see **investigate, search**

sight noun **1** the ability to see: *My sight is so bad now that I can't read any more*

eyesight: *He suffered from weak eyesight*

visibility: *Visibility was very poor*

vision: *It can cause blindness or serious loss of vision*

2 something you see: *It was a ghastly sight*

display: *These flowers make a colourful display in spring*

scene: a bizarre scene

spectacle: an impressive spectacle

▷ verb **3** to see something or someone: He had been sighted in Cairo

see: I saw a deer in the woods today

spot: I drove round till I spotted her

see also **see, spot**

sign noun **1** a mark or symbol: The negative number is preceded by a minus sign

character: the characters used in the hallmarking system

emblem: a small yellow hammer-and-sickle emblem

logo: the company's logo

mark: Put a tick mark against the statements you agree with

symbol: the chemical symbol for mercury

2 a notice put up to give a warning or information: a sign saying that the highway was closed

board: He studied the destination board on the front of the bus

notice: a notice saying "no entry"

placard: The protesters sang songs and waved placards

3 evidence of something: the first signs of recovery

clue: the only real clue that something was wrong

evidence: there has been no evidence of criminal activity

hint: He showed only the slightest hint of emotion

indication: All the indications suggest that he is the murderer

symptom: typical symptoms of stress

token: a token of goodwill

trace: No traces of violence were found on the body

see also **indication, notice, omen, premonition, signal, symbol, trace**

sign up see **hire, join**

signal noun **1** something which

is intended to give a message: a distress signal

beacon: an emergency beacon

cue: He gave me my cue to speak

gesture: She made a menacing gesture with her fist

sign: They gave him the thumbs-up sign

▷ verb **2** to make a sign as a message to someone: He was frantically signalling to her to shut up

beckon: I beckoned her over

gesticulate: He was gesticulating at a hole in the ground

gesture: I gestured towards the house, and he went in

motion: He motioned to her to go behind the screen

nod: They nodded goodnight to the security man

sign: She signed to me to come near

wave: He waved the servants out of the tent

see also **indicate, indication**

signal to see **hail**

significance see **meaning**

significant adjective large or important: This drug seems to have a significant effect on the disease

considerable formal: Doing it properly makes considerable demands on our time

important: The strike represents an important challenge to the government

impressive: an impressive achievement

marked: a marked increase in crimes against property

notable: With a few notable exceptions, doctors are a pretty sensible lot

pronounced: The exhibition has a pronounced Scottish theme

striking: The most striking feature of these statistics is the rate of growth

see also **important, major, serious,**

special

signify see count, indicate, mean

silence noun **1** an absence of sound: There was a momentary silence

calm: He liked the calm of the evening

hush: A hush fell over the crowd

lull: a lull in the conversation

peace: I love the peace of the countryside

quiet: The quiet of the flat was very soothing

stillness: An explosion shattered the stillness of the night air

2 an inability or refusal to talk: breaking his silence for the first time about the affair

dumbness: a woman traumatized into dumbness

muteness: He retreated into stubborn muteness

reticence: Fran didn't seem to notice my reticence

speechlessness: He was shy to the point of speechlessness

▷ verb **3** to make someone or something quiet: The shock silenced her completely

deaden: We hung up curtains to try to deaden the noise

gag: I gagged him with a towel

muffle: You can muffle the sound with absorbent material

quiet: A look from her husband quieted her at once

quieten: She tried to quieten her breathing

stifle: He put his hand to his mouth to stifle a giggle

still: He raised a hand to still Alex's protest

suppress: She barely suppressed a gasp

see also **peace, quiet**

silent adjective **1** not saying anything: The class fell silent as the teacher entered

dumb: We were all struck dumb for a moment

mute: a mute look of appeal

speechless: speechless with rage

taciturn: a taciturn man with a solemn expression

wordless: They exchanged a wordless look of understanding

2 making no noise: The room was silent except for the ticking of the clock

hushed: the vast, hushed space of the cathedral

quiet: a quiet engine

soundless: My bare feet were soundless on the carpet

still: The room was suddenly still

see also **dumb, quiet**

silhouette see figure, outline

silky see smooth

silliness see stupidity

silly adjective foolish or ridiculous: I know it's silly to get so upset

absurd: He found fashion absurd

daft: That's a daft question

foolish: It is foolish to risk injury

idiotic: What an idiotic thing to say!

inane: He stood there with an inane grin on his face

ridiculous: a ridiculous suggestion

stupid: a stupid mistake

see also **daft, foolish, frivolous, unwise**

similar adjective like something else: an accident similar to Hakkinen's

alike: You two are very alike

analogous: a ritual analogous to those of primitive tribal cultures

comparable: paying the same wages for work of comparable value

like: They're as like as two peas in a pod

uniform: droplets of uniform size

see also **alike, like**

similarity noun the quality of being like something else: the similarity of our backgrounds

analogy: the analogy between racism and homophobia

likeness: These myths have a startling likeness to one another

resemblance: I could see the resemblance to his grandfather

sameness: He grew bored by the sameness of the speeches
see also **resemblance**

similarly see **alike**

simple adjective **1** easy to understand or do: a simple task

easy: This ice cream maker is cheap and easy to use

elementary: elementary computer skills

straightforward: It was a straightforward question

uncomplicated: an uncomplicated story

understandable: He writes in a clear, understandable style

2 plain in style: a simple but stylish outfit

classic: classic designs which will fit in anywhere

clean: the clean lines of Shaker furniture

plain: Her dress was plain but hung well on her

severe: hair scraped back in a severe style
see also **crude, easy, homely, humble, primitive, straightforward**

simplicity see **ease, innocence**

simplify verb to make something easier to do or understand: measures intended to simplify the procedure

make simpler: restructuring the tax system to make it simpler

streamline: an effort to cut costs and streamline operations

simply see **only**

simulate see **fake, imitate**

simulated see **false**

simultaneously see **together**

sin noun **1** wicked and immoral behaviour: preaching against sin

crime: a life of crime

evil: You can't stop all the evil in the world

offence: an offence which can carry the death penalty

wickedness: a sign of human wickedness

wrong: I intend to right that wrong
▷ verb **2** to do something wicked and immoral: I admit that I have sinned

do wrong: They have done wrong and they know it
see also **evil, wrong**

since see **because**

sincere adjective saying things that you really mean: my sincere apologies

genuine: a display of genuine emotion

heartfelt: heartfelt sympathy

real: the real affection between them

wholehearted: a wholehearted and genuine response
see also **dinkum, real, serious**

sinful see **evil, wicked**

singe see **burn**

single adjective **1** only one and no more: A single shot was fired

lone: A lone policeman guarded the doors

one: I just had one drink

only: My only regret is that I never knew him

sole: the sole survivor of the accident

solitary: There is not one solitary scrap of evidence

2 not married: I'm surprised you're still single

unattached: I only know two or three unattached men

unmarried: an unmarried mother

3 for one person only: a single room

individual: an individual portion

separate: *separate beds*
see also **alone**, **individual**

single out see **favour**, **select**

single-minded see **determined**

singular *adjective formal* unusual and remarkable: *a smile of singular sweetness*

exceptional: *children with exceptional ability*

extraordinary: *The task requires extraordinary patience and endurance*

rare: *a leader of rare strength and instinct*

remarkable: *a remarkable achievement*

uncommon: *She read Cecilia's letter with uncommon interest*

unique: *a woman of unique talent and determination*

unusual: *He had an unusual aptitude for mathematics*

see also **curious**, **extraordinary**, **odd**, **particular**, **weird**

sinister *adjective* seeming harmful or evil: *There was something cold and sinister about him*

evil: *an evil smile*

forbidding: *a huge, forbidding building*

menacing: *His dark eyebrows gave him a menacing look*

ominous: *A dark and ominous figure stood in the doorway*

threatening: *his threatening appearance*

see also **creepy**, **ominous**

sink see **descend**, **drive**, **drop**, **fail**

sip see **drink**, **taste**

siren see **alarm**

sit down see **rest**

site see **location**, **place**, **scene**, **spot**

sited see **located**

situate see **place**

situated see **located**

situation *noun* what is happening: *a serious situation*

case: *a clear case of mistaken identity*

circumstances: *I wish we could have met in happier circumstances*

plight: *the plight of Third World countries*

scenario: *a nightmare scenario*

state of affairs: *This state of affairs cannot continue*

see also **affair**, **location**, **matter**, **state**

sixth sense see **instinct**

sizable see **handsome**

size *noun* how big or small something is: *the size of the audience*

bulk: *Despite his bulk, he moved gracefully*

dimensions: *He considered the dimensions of the problem*

extent: *the extent of the damage*

immensity: *The immensity of the universe is impossible to grasp*

proportions: *In the tropics, plants grow to huge proportions*

see also **area**, **capacity**, **extent**, **quantity**

sizeable see **handsome**

skelm see **criminal**

sketch see **draw**, **outline**, **picture**

sketchy see **rough**

skilful *adjective* able to do something very well: *the country's most skilful politician*

able: *a very able businessman*

accomplished: *an accomplished pianist*

adept: *an adept diplomat*

competent: *a competent and careful driver*

expert: *He is expert at handling complex negotiations*

masterly: *a masterly performance*

proficient: *proficient with computers*

skilled: *a skilled wine maker*

see also **capable**, **expert**, **proficient**, **skilled**

skilfully see **well**

skill noun the ability to do something well: *This task requires great skill*
ability: *a man of considerable abilities*
competence: *his high professional competence*
dexterity: *Reid's dexterity on the guitar*
expertise: *the expertise to deal with these problems*
facility: *a facility for languages*
knack: *the knack of getting on with people*
proficiency: *basic proficiency in English*
see also **ability, qualification**

skilled adjective having the knowledge to do something well: *skilled workers, such as plumbers*
able: *an able craftsman*
accomplished: *an accomplished pianist*
competent: *a competent and careful driver*
experienced: *lawyers who are experienced in these matters*
expert: *It takes an expert eye to see the symptoms*
masterly: *the artist's masterly use of colour*
professional: *professional people like doctors and engineers*
proficient: *He is proficient in several foreign languages*
skilful: *the artist's skilful use of light and shade*
trained: *Our workforce is highly trained*
see also **able, expert, perfect, practical, proficient, skilful**

skim *see* **glance**
skin *see* **coat, graze, hide, scrape**
skinny adjective extremely thin: *a skinny little boy*
bony: *a long bony finger*
emaciated: *television pictures of emaciated prisoners*
lean: *a tall, lean figure*
scrawny: *the vulture's scrawny neck*
thin: *He is small and very thin with white skin*
underfed: *Kate still looks pale and underfed*
undernourished: *undernourished children*
see also **puny**

skip *see* **omit**
skirmish *see* **clash, fight**
skite *see* **boast, brag, braggart**
skiter *see* **braggart**
slack *see* **flabby, lazy, limp, loose**
slacken *see* **ease, loosen**
slag *see* **insult**
slam *see* **bang, dash, shut**
slander noun **1** something untrue and malicious said about someone: *He is now suing the company for slander*
libel: *defendants seeking damages for libel*
scandal: *She loves spreading scandal*
slur: *a vicious slur on his character*
smear: *He called the allegation "an evil smear"*
▷ verb **2** to say untrue and malicious things about someone: *He has been charged with slandering the Prime Minister*
libel: *The newspaper which libelled him had to pay compensation*
malign: *He claims he is being unfairly maligned*
smear: *an attempt to smear their manager*

slant *see* **colour, slope, tilt**
slanted *see* **biased**
slap *see* **hit**
slash *see* **cut, lower**
slate *see* **abuse**
slaughter *see* **kill, murder**
slave *see* **labour, work**
slay *see* **kill, murder**
slaying *see* **murder**

sleazy see scungy
sleek see glossy, smooth
sleep noun **1** the natural state of rest in which you are unconscious: *They were exhausted from lack of sleep*
  doze: *I had a doze after lunch*
  hibernation: *Many animals go into hibernation during the winter*
  kip British slang: *Mason went home for a couple of hours' kip*
  nap: *I might take a nap for a while*
  slumber: *He had fallen into exhausted slumber*
  snooze informal: *a little snooze after dinner*
  ▷ verb **2** to rest in a natural state of unconsciousness: *The baby slept during the car journey*
  doze: *He dozed in an armchair*
  hibernate: *Dormice hibernate from October to May*
  kip British slang: *He kipped on my sofa last night*
  slumber: *The girls were slumbering peacefully*
  snooze informal: *Mark snoozed in front of the television*
  take a nap: *Try to take a nap every afternoon*
sleepy adjective **1** tired and ready to go to sleep: *Do you feel sleepy during the day?*
  drowsy: *This medicine may make you feel drowsy*
  lethargic: *He felt too lethargic to get dressed*
  sluggish: *I was still feeling sluggish after my nap*
  2 not having much activity or excitement: *a sleepy little village*
  dull: *a dull town*
  quiet: *a quiet rural backwater*
  see also **tired**
slender adjective **1** attractively thin: *a tall, slender woman*
  lean: *Like most athletes, she was lean*

and muscular
  slight: *She is small and slight*
  slim: *Jean is pretty, with a slim build*
  2 small in amount or degree: *He won, but only by a slender majority*
  faint: *They now have only a faint chance of survival*
  remote: *a remote possibility*
  slight: *There is a slight improvement in his condition*
  slim: *a slim hope*
  small: *a small chance of success*
  see also **minute, narrow, remote**
slice see piece
slide see flow
slight adjective small in amount or degree: *a slight dent*
  insignificant: *an insignificant amount*
  minor: *a minor inconvenience*
  negligible: *The strike will have a negligible impact*
  small: *It only makes a small difference*
  trivial: *trivial details*
  see also **insult, light, minor, remote, scorn, slender, trivial, unimportant**
slightest see least
slightly see rather
slim see narrow, remote, slender, thin
sling see throw
slip verb **1** to go somewhere quickly and quietly: *Amy slipped downstairs and out of the house*
  creep: *I crept up to my room*
  sneak: *Sometimes he would sneak out to see me*
  steal: *They can steal away at night to join us*
  ▷ noun **2** a small mistake: *There must be no slips*
  blunder: *an embarrassing blunder*
  error: *a tactical error*
  mistake: *Many people are anxious about making mistakes in grammar*

see also **error, mistake, sneak, steal**

slippery see **crafty, sneaky**

slit see **cut**

slog away see **work**

slogan noun a short easily-remembered phrase: *a poster with the slogan, "Your country needs you"*
  jingle: *a catchy advertising jingle*
  motto: *"Who Dares Wins" is the motto of the Special Air Service*

slope noun **1** a flat surface with one end higher than the other: *The street is on a slope*
  gradient: *a steep gradient*
  incline: *The car was unable to negotiate the incline*
  ramp: *There is a ramp allowing access for wheelchairs*
  ▷ verb **2** to be at an angle: *The bank sloped sharply down to the river*
  fall: *The road fell steeply*
  rise: *The climb is arduous, rising steeply through thick bush*
  slant: *His handwriting slanted to the left*
  see also **tilt**

sloppy see **careless, inefficient, loose, sentimental**

slot see **opening**

slow adjective **1** moving or happening with little speed: *slow, regular breathing*
  gradual: *Losing weight is a gradual process*
  leisurely: *He walked at a leisurely pace*
  lingering: *a lingering death*
  ponderous: *His steps were heavy and ponderous*
  sluggish: *a sluggish stream*
  unhurried: *She rose with an unhurried grace*
  2 not very clever: *He got hit in the head and he's been a bit slow ever since*
  dense: *He's not a bad man, just a bit dense*
  dim: *He is rather dim*
  dumb informal: *too dumb to realise what was going on*
  obtuse: *It should be obvious even to the most obtuse person*
  stupid: *He can't help being a bit stupid*
  thick: *I can't believe I've been so thick*
  see also **dim, gradual, reluctant**

slow (down) verb to go or cause to go more slowly: *The car slowed (down) and then stopped*
  check: *attempts to check the spread of AIDS*
  decelerate: *He decelerated when he saw the warning sign*

slowly adverb not quickly or hurriedly: *He turned and began to walk away slowly*
  by degrees: *By degrees, the tension passed out of him*
  gradually: *Their friendship gradually deepened*
  unhurriedly: *The islanders drift along unhurriedly from day to day*

sluggish see **sleepy, slow**

slumber see **sleep**

slump see **decline, drop, fall, recession**

slur see **slander**

slushy see **sentimental**

sly adjective cunning and deceptive: *She is devious, sly and manipulative*
  crafty: *a crafty villain*
  cunning: *Some of these kids can be very cunning*
  devious: *an extremely dangerous, evil and devious man*
  scheming: *You're a scheming little rat, aren't you?*
  underhand: *underhand tactics*
  wily: *a wily politician*
  see also **crafty, cunning, sneaky**

smack see **blow, hit**

small adjective **1** not large in size, number or amount: *a small child*

2 not important or significant: *small changes*
see **word studies small**
see also **fine, low, minute, modest, remote, slender, slight**
smallest see **least**
small-minded see **petty**
smart adjective **1** clean and neat in appearance: *a smart navy blue outfit*
chic: *chic Parisian women*
elegant: *Patricia looked beautiful and elegant, as always*
neat: *a neat grey flannel suit*
spruce: *Chris was looking spruce in his uniform*
stylish: *stylish white shoes*
2 clever and intelligent: *a smart idea*
astute: *a series of astute business decisions*
bright: *She is not very bright*
canny: *He was far too canny to give himself away*
clever: *Nobody disputed that Davey was clever*
ingenious: *an ingenious plan*
intelligent: *Dolphins are an intelligent species*
shrewd: *a shrewd businessman*
see also **astute, bright, brilliant, clever, intelligent, neat, posh, shrewd**
smarting see **sore**
smash see **crash, dash**
smash into see **hit**
smashed see **broken**
smear see **slander, soil, spread**
smell noun **1** the quality of something which you sense through your nose: *a smell of damp wood*
aroma: *the aroma of fresh bread*
fragrance: *the fragrance of his cologne*
odour: *a disagreeable odour*
perfume: *enjoying the perfume of the lemon trees*
pong British, Australian informal:

What's that horrible pong?
reek: *the reek of whisky*
scent: *flowers chosen for their scent*
stench: *a foul stench*
stink: *the stink of stale beer on his breath*
▷ verb **2** to have an unpleasant smell: *Do my feet smell?*
pong British, Australian informal: *She said he ponged a bit*
reek: *The whole house reeks of cigar smoke*
stink: *His breath stinks of garlic*
3 to become aware of the smell of something: *I could smell liquor on his breath*
scent: *The dog had scented something in the bushes*
sniff: *He opened his window and sniffed the air*
see also **fragrance**
smelly adjective having a strong unpleasant smell: *smelly socks*
foul: *His breath was foul*
reeking: *poisoning the air with their reeking cigars*
stinking: *piles of stinking rubbish*
smile verb **1** to move the corners of your mouth upwards because you are pleased: *When he saw me, he smiled and waved*
beam: *She beamed at him in delight*
grin: *He grinned broadly*
smirk: *The two men looked at me, nudged each other and smirked*
▷ noun **2** the expression you have when you smile: *She gave me a big smile*
beam: *a strange beam of satisfaction on his face*
grin: *She looked at me with a sheepish grin*
smirk: *a smirk of triumph*
smirk see **smile**
smitten see **crazy**
smooth adjective not rough or

bumpy: *a smooth wooden surface*

glassy: *glassy green pebbles*

glossy: *glossy dark fur*

polished: *He slipped on the polished floor*

silky: *The sauce should be silky in texture*

sleek: *her sleek, waist-length hair*

see also **easy, even, flat, level**

smoothly *see* **well**

smother *see* **spread, suppress**

smoulder *see* **glow**

smudge *see* **mark, spot**

smug *adjective* pleased with yourself: *They looked at each other in smug satisfaction*

complacent: *an aggravating, complacent little smile*

conceited: *They had grown too conceited and pleased with themselves*

self-satisfied: *a self-satisfied little snob*

superior: *He stood there looking superior*

smuggle *see* **sneak**

smugness *see* **pride**

snag *noun* a small problem or disadvantage: *The snag was that he had no transport*

catch: *It sounds too good to be true – what's the catch?*

difficulty: *The only difficulty may be the price*

disadvantage: *The disadvantage is that this plant needs frequent watering*

drawback: *The flat's only drawback was its size*

problem: *The only problem about living here is the tourists*

see also **catch, difficulty, drawback, stick**

snap *see* **crack**

snare *see* **catch, trap**

snatch *see* **extract, grab, grasp, seize**

sneak *verb* **1** to go somewhere quietly: *Sometimes he would sneak out to see me*

lurk: *I saw someone lurking outside*

sidle: *He sidled into the bar, trying to look inconspicuous*

slip: *Amy slipped downstairs and out of the house*

steal: *They can steal out and join us later*

2 to put or take something somewhere secretly: *I sneaked the books out of the library*

slip: *He slipped me a note*

smuggle: *We smuggled a camera into the concert*

spirit: *treasures spirited away to foreign museums*

see also **slip, steal**

sneak a look *see* **peek**

sneaky *adjective* doing things secretly or being done secretly: *He only won by using sneaky tactics*

crafty: *the crafty methods used by salesmen to get people to sign up*

deceitful: *They claimed the government had been deceitful*

devious: *He was devious, saying one thing to me and another to her*

dishonest: *It would be dishonest to mislead people in that way*

mean: *That was a mean trick*

slippery: *She's a slippery customer, and should be watched*

sly: *He's a sly old beggar*

untrustworthy: *His opponents say he's untrustworthy*

sneering *see* **scornful**

snide *see* **spiteful**

sniff *see* **smell**

snigger *see* **laugh**

snippet *see* **extract**

snobbery *see* **pride**

snobbish *see* **haughty, pretentious, stuck-up, superior**

snoop *see* **greedy, mean**

snoop *see* **pry**

snooper noun a person who interferes in other people's business: *a tabloid snooper*
  meddler: *a meddler in the affairs of state*
  stickybeak Australian, New Zealand informal: *She's just an old stickybeak*
snooze see **sleep**
snub see **insult**
snug see **cosy, tight**
so see **therefore**
soak verb to make something very wet: *The water had soaked his jacket*
  bathe: *Bathe the infected area in a salt solution*
  permeate: *The water had permeated the stone*
  steep: *green beans steeped in olive oil*
  wet: *Wet the hair and work the shampoo through it*
  see also **steep, wet**
soak up see **absorb**
soaked see **wet**
soar see **explode, fly**
soaring see **tall**
sober see **grave, realistic, reasonable, serious, solemn**
sociable adjective enjoying the company of other people: *She's usually outgoing and sociable*
  friendly: *The people here are very friendly*
  gregarious: *I'm not a gregarious person*
  outgoing: *He was shy and she was very outgoing*
socialist see **left-wing**
socialize see **associate**
society noun 1 the people in a particular country or region: *a major problem in society*
  civilization: *an ancient civilization*
  culture: *people from different cultures*
  2 an organization for people with the same interest or aim: *the school*

debating society
  association: *the Football Association*
  circle: *a local painting circle*
  club: *He was at the youth club*
  fellowship: *the Visual Arts Fellowship*
  group: *an environmental group*
  guild: *the Screen Writers' Guild*
  institute: *the Women's Institute*
  league: *the World Muslim League*
  organization: *student organizations*
  union: *the International Astronomical Union*
  see also **association, body, club, fellowship, public**
sodden see **damp, wet**
soft adjective 1 not hard, stiff or firm: *a soft bed*
  flexible: *a flexible material*
  pliable: *a pliable dough*
  squashy: *a squashy tomato*
  supple: *supple leather*
  yielding: *yielding cushions*
  2 quiet and not harsh: *a soft tapping at my door*
  gentle: *a gentle voice*
  low: *She spoke in a low whisper*
  mellow: *mellow background music*
  muted: *Their loud conversation became muted*
  quiet: *He always spoke in a quiet tone to which everyone listened*
  subdued: *His voice was more subdued than usual*
  3 not bright: *The bedside lamp cast a soft radiance over her face*
  dim: *The light was dim and eerie*
  faint: *The stars cast a faint light*
  light: *The walls were painted a light yellow*
  mellow: *Their colour schemes tend towards rich, mellow shades*
  pale: *dressed in pale pink*
  pastel: *delicate pastel hues*
  subdued: *subdued lighting*
  see also **gentle, limp, quiet**
soften see **moderate**

soggy see **damp**

soil noun **1** the surface of the earth:
*The soil is reasonably moist after
the rain*
  clay: *a thin layer of clay*
  dirt: *The bulldozers piled up huge
mounds of dirt*
  earth: *a huge pile of earth*
  ground: *a hole in the ground*
  ▷ verb **2** to make something dirty:
*He looked at her as though her words
might soil him*
  dirty: *He was afraid the dog's hairs
might dirty the seats*
  foul: *The cage was fouled with
droppings*
  pollute: *chemicals which pollute
rivers*
  smear: *The pillow was smeared with
makeup*
  spatter: *Her dress was spattered
with mud*
  stain: *Some foods can stain the teeth*
  see also **dirt, earth, ground, stain**

soiled see **dirty**

soldier see **fighter**

sole see **only, single**

solely see **only**

solemn adjective not cheerful or
humorous: *a taciturn man with a
solemn expression*
  earnest: *Ella was a pious, earnest
woman*
  grave: *He was looking unusually
grave*
  serious: *She looked at me with big,
serious eyes*
  sober: *sad, sober faces*
  staid: *It is boring, old fashioned
and staid*
  see also **grave, grim, heavy, serious**

solicitor see **lawyer**

solid adjective **1** hard and firm: *a block
of solid wax*
  firm: *a firm mattress*
  hard: *The snow was hard and slippery*

2 not likely to fall down: *a solid
structure*
  stable: *stable foundations*
  strong: *a strong fence*
  sturdy: *The camera was mounted on
a sturdy tripod*
  substantial: *The posts are made of
concrete and are fairly substantial*
  see also **firm, hard, rigid, secure,
sound, stiff, stocky, sturdy, tough,
trusty**

solitary see **single**

solitude noun the state of being
alone: *He went to the cottage for a few
days of solitude*
  isolation: *the isolation he endured
while in captivity*
  loneliness: *I have a fear of loneliness*
  privacy: *the privacy of my own room*
  seclusion: *She lived in seclusion with
her husband*

solution see **idea, liquid**

solve verb to find the answer to a
problem or question: *attempts to
solve the mystery*
  clear up: *During dinner the confusion
was cleared up*
  crack: *He finally managed to crack
the code*
  decipher: *trying to decipher the
symbols on the stone tablets*
  get to the bottom of: *The police
wanted to get to the bottom of the case*
  resolve: *Scientists hope this will
finally resolve the mystery*
  work out: *I've worked out where I'm
going wrong*
  see also **crack, resolve, work out**

sombre see **drab, dull, grave**

some see **several**

sometimes adverb now and
then: *Her voice was so low she was
sometimes mistaken for a man*
  at times: *She can be a little common
at times*
  every now and then: *He checks up*

on me every now and then
every so often: Every so often he does something silly
from time to time: I go back to see my mum from time to time
now and again: I enjoy a day out now and again
now and then: These people like a laugh now and then
occasionally: I know that I do put people down occasionally
once in a while: It does you good to get out once in a while
somewhat see **quite, rather**
sookie see **cowardly**
soon adverb in a very short time: You'll be hearing from us very soon
any minute now: Any minute now she's going to start crying
before long: Interest rates will come down before long
in a minute: I'll be with you in a minute
in the near future: The controversy is unlikely to be resolved in the near future
presently: I'll deal with you presently
shortly: The trial will begin shortly
sooner see **before**
soothe see **calm, comfort, pacify**
sophisticated adjective **1** having refined tastes: a charming, sophisticated companion
cosmopolitan: The family are rich and extremely cosmopolitan
cultivated: an elegant and cultivated woman
cultured: He is immensely cultured and well-read
refined: a woman of refined tastes
urbane: a polished, urbane manner
2 advanced and complicated: a sophisticated piece of equipment
advanced: the most advanced optical telescope in the world
complex: complex machines

complicated: a complicated voting system
elaborate: an elaborate design
intricate: intricate controls
refined: a more refined engine
see also **polite**
sophistication see **style**
sorcery see **magic**
sordid see **scungy**
sore adjective causing pain and discomfort: a sore throat
inflamed: Her eyes were red and inflamed
painful: a painful knock on the knee
raw: Her hands were rubbed raw by the rope
sensitive: the pain of sensitive teeth
smarting: My eyes were smarting from the smoke
tender: My stomach feels very tender
see also **painful, inflamed**
soreness see **pain**
sorrow noun **1** deep sadness or regret: a time of great sorrow
grief: Their grief soon gave way to anger
heartache: suffering the heartache of a divorce
melancholy: She has an air of melancholy
misery: All his money brought him nothing but misery
mourning: a day of mourning
pain: My heart is full of pain
regret: She accepted his resignation with regret
sadness: It is with a mixture of sadness and joy that I say farewell
unhappiness: I had a lot of unhappiness in my adolescence
woe formal: a tale of woe
2 things that cause deep sadness and regret: the joys and sorrows of family life
heartache: all the heartaches of parenthood

hardship: *One of the worst hardships is having so little time with my family*
misfortune: *She seems to enjoy the misfortunes of others*
trouble: *She told me all her troubles*
woe: *He did not tell his friends about his woes*
worry: *a life with no worries*
see also **distress, evil, grief, misery, regret**

sorry adjective **1** feeling sadness or regret: *I'm terribly sorry to bother you*
apologetic: *"I'm afraid I can't help," she said with an apologetic smile*
penitent: *He sat silent and penitent in a corner*
regretful: *Now I'm totally regretful that I did it*
remorseful: *He was genuinely remorseful*
repentant: *repentant sinners*
2 feeling sympathy for someone: *I was sorry to hear about your husband's death*
moved: *I'm moved by what you say*
sympathetic: *She gave me a sympathetic glance*
3 in a bad condition: *He was in a pretty sorry state when we found him*
deplorable: *living in deplorable conditions*
miserable: *a miserable existence*
pathetic: *the pathetic sight of oil-covered sea birds*
pitiful: *a pitiful creature*
poor: *the poor condition of the pitch*
sad: *a sad state of affairs*
wretched: *the wretched victims of war*
see also **ashamed, guilty, miserable, pathetic**

sort noun **1** one of the different kinds of something: *a dozen trees of various sorts*
brand: *his favourite brand of whisky*
category: *The topics were divided into six categories*
class: *a better class of restaurant*
group: *Weathermen classify clouds into several different groups*
kind: *different kinds of roses*
make: *a certain make of car*
species: *400 species of fungi have been recorded*
style: *Several styles of hat were available*
type: *What type of dog should we get?*
variety: *many varieties of birds*
▷ verb **2** to arrange things into different kinds: *He sorted the material into three folders*
arrange: *Arrange the books in neat piles*
categorize: *ways to categorize information*
classify: *Rocks can be classified according to their mode of origin*
divide: *The subjects were divided into four groups*
grade: *musical pieces graded according to difficulty*
group: *The fact sheet is grouped into seven sections*
separate: *His work can be separated into three main categories*
see also **arrange, category, class, classify, form, grade, group, kind, type, variety**

sort out see **resolve**
so-so see **tolerable**
sought-after see **popular**
soul see **essence, individual, person, spirit**
sound noun **1** something that can be heard: *the sound of gunfire*
din: *make themselves heard over the din of the crowd*
hubbub: *the hubbub of excited conversation*
noise: *the noise of bombs and guns*
racket: *the racket of drills and electric saws*

tone: the clear tone of the bell
▷ verb **2** to produce or cause to produce a noise: A young man sounded the bell

blow: A guard was blowing his whistle
chime: He heard the doorbell chime
clang: The church bell clanged
peal: Church bells pealed at the stroke of midnight
ring: She heard the school bell ringing
set off: Any escape sets off the alarm
toll: The pilgrims tolled the bell
▷ adjective **3** healthy, or in good condition: His body was still sound

all right: Does the roof seem all right?
fine: She told me her heart was perfectly fine
fit: Exercise is the first step to a fit body
healthy: His once healthy mind was deteriorating
in good condition: The timbers were all in good condition
intact: The boat did not appear damaged and its equipment seemed intact
robust: He is in robust health for a man of his age
4 reliable and sensible: a sound financial proposition
down-to-earth: Their ideas seem very down-to-earth
good: Give me one good reason why I should tell you
reasonable: a perfectly reasonable decision
reliable: It's difficult to give a reliable estimate
sensible: sensible advice
solid: good solid information
valid: Both sides made some valid points
see also **bay, logical, reasonable, reliable, responsible, sane, sensible, well**
soundless see **silent**

sour adjective **1** having a sharp taste: The stewed apple was sour even with sugar added
acid: The wine had an acid taste
bitter: a bitter drink
pungent: a pungent sauce
sharp: a clean, sharp flavour
tart: the tart qualities of citrus fruit
2 unpleasant in taste because no longer fresh: This cream's gone sour
curdled: curdled milk
off: This meat's gone off
rancid: rancid butter
3 bad-tempered and unfriendly: a sour expression
disagreeable: a shallow, disagreeable man
embittered: an embittered old lady
jaundiced: a jaundiced attitude
tart: a tart reply
see also **bitter, rotten, stale**

source noun the place where something comes from: the source of his confidence
beginning: the beginning of all the trouble
cause: the cause of the problem
derivation: The derivation of the name is obscure
origin: the origin of life
originator: the originator of the theory
see also **cause, head, origin**

souvenir noun something you keep as a reminder: a souvenir of our holiday
keepsake: a cherished keepsake
memento: a memento of the occasion
relic: the threadbare teddy bear, a relic of childhood
reminder: a permanent reminder of this historic event

sovereign see **king, royal, ruler**
sovereignty see **power**
sow see **scatter**

space noun **1** an area which is empty or available: *a car with plenty of interior space*

accommodation: *We have accommodation for six people*

capacity: *the capacity of the airliner*

room: *no room to manoeuvre*

2 the gap between two things: *the space between the two tables*

blank: *I've left a blank here for your signature*

distance: *the distance between the island and the mainland*

gap: *The wind was tearing through gaps in the window frames*

interval: *the intervals between the trees*

3 a period of time: *two incidents in the space of a week*

interval: *a long interval of silence*

period: *for a limited period only*

span: *The batteries have a life span of six hours*

time: *At 15 he left home for a short time*

while: *Sit down for a while*

see also **capacity, gap, length, opening, room, stretch**

spacious adjective having or providing a lot of space: *a spacious lounge*

ample: *the city's ample car parks*

broad: *a broad expanse of green lawn*

expansive: *an expansive play area*

extensive: *The palace stands in extensive grounds*

huge: *a huge apartment overlooking the park*

large: *a large detached house*

vast: *a vast chamber*

see also **extensive**

span *see* **cross, length, space**

spare adjective **1** in addition to what is needed: *Luckily I had a spare pair of glasses*

extra: *Allow yourself some extra time in case of emergencies*

free: *I'll do it as soon as I get some free time*

superfluous: *I got rid of all my superfluous belongings*

surplus: *They sell their surplus produce*

▷ verb **2** to make something available: *Can you spare some money for a cup of tea?*

afford: *It's all I can afford to give you*

give: *It's good of you to give me some of your time*

let someone have: *I can let you have some milk and sugar*

3 to save someone from an unpleasant experience: *I wanted to spare her that suffering*

let off *informal*: *I'll let you off this time*

pardon: *Relatives had begged authorities to pardon him*

relieve from: *a machine which relieves you of the drudgery of housework*

save from: *I was trying to save you from unnecessary worry*

see also **extra**

spark off *see* **provoke**

sparkle verb to shine with small bright points of light: *Diamonds sparkled on her wrists*

gleam: *sunlight gleaming on the water*

glisten: *The wall glistened with frost*

glitter: *A million stars glittered in the black sky*

shimmer: *In the distance the lake shimmered*

twinkle: *The old man's eyes twinkled*

see also **flash, shine**

sparkling *see* **brilliant, lively, shining, witty**

sparse *see* **few, meagre, rare, uncommon**

spartan *see* **bare, plain**

spate see **burst, flood, rash**

spatter see **soil**

speak verb to use your voice to say words: She turned to look at the person who was speaking
see also **lecture**

speak out against see **oppose**

special adjective 1 more important or better than others of its kind: You are very special to me
 exceptional: children with exceptional ability
 important: This is an important occasion
 significant: of significant importance
 unique: a unique talent
 2 relating to one person or group in particular: the special needs of the chronically sick
 characteristic: a characteristic feature
 distinctive: the distinctive smell of chlorine
 individual: Each family needs individual attention
 particular: Fatigue is a particular problem for women
 peculiar: This is not a problem peculiar to London
 specific: the specific needs of the elderly
 see also **different, exceptional, individual, particular, peculiar, personal, private, select**

specialist see **expert, fundi**

speciality see **field**

species see **breed, kind, sort, type**

specific see **particular, precise, special**

specification see **requirement**

specify verb to state or describe something precisely: Specify which size and colour you want
 be specific about: She was never very specific about her date of birth
 indicate: Please indicate your preference below
 name: The victims of the fire have been named
 spell out: He spelled out the reasons why he was leaving
 state: Please state your name
 stipulate: His duties were stipulated in the contract
 see also **state**

specimen see **example**

speck see **spot**

spectacle see **sight, view, wonder**

spectator noun a person who watches something: Spectators lined the route
 bystander: an innocent bystander
 eyewitness: Eyewitnesses say the police opened fire in the crowd
 observer: a disinterested observer
 onlooker: A small crowd of onlookers was there to greet her
 witness: There were scores of witnesses
 see also **witness**

spectre see **ghost, spirit, vision**

speculate see **guess, wonder**

speculation see **guess**

speech noun a formal talk given to an audience: He delivered his speech in French
 address: an address to the American people
 discourse: a lengthy discourse on strategy
 lecture: a series of lectures on art
 talk: a talk on Celtic mythology
 see also **lecture, talk**

speechless see **dumb, silent**

speechlessness see **silence**

speed noun 1 the rate at which something moves or happens: a top speed of 200 mph
 haste: the old saying "more haste, less speed"
 hurry: the hurry and excitement of the city

momentum: This campaign is gaining momentum

pace: He walked at a leisurely pace

rapidity: My moods alternate with alarming rapidity

swiftness: Time is passing with incredible swiftness

velocity: the velocity of light

▷ verb 2 to move quickly: The pair sped off when the police arrived

career: His car careered into a river

flash: The bus flashed past me

gallop: galloping along the corridor

race: He raced across town

rush: He rushed off, closely followed by Kemp

tear: Miranda tore off down the road

see also **fly, race, rate, tear**

speed up see **accelerate, hurry**

speedily see **quickly**

speedy see **fast, quick, swift**

spell see **influence, period, stretch, term, time**

spell out see **specify**

spew see **puke**

sphere see **ball**

spherical see **round**

spicy see **hot**

spill see **leak, upset**

spin verb to turn quickly around a central point: as the earth spins on its axis

pirouette: She pirouetted in front of the mirror

revolve: The satellite revolves around the planet

rotate: rotating propellers

turn: a turning wheel

whirl: The fallen leaves whirled around

see also **drive, turn**

spineless see **weak**

spiral see **coil**

spirit noun 1 the part of you that is not physical: His spirit had left his body

life force: the life force of all animate things

soul: praying for the soul of her dead husband

2 a ghost or supernatural being: a protection against evil spirits

apparition: an apparition of her dead son

ghost: the premise that ghosts exist

phantom: People claimed to have seen the phantom

spectre: a spectre from the other world

sprite: a water sprite

3 liveliness and energy: They played with spirit

animation: They both spoke with animation

energy: At 80 her energy is amazing

enthusiasm: They seem to be lacking in enthusiasm

fire: His performance was full of fire

force: She expressed her feelings with some force

vigour: We resumed the attack with renewed vigour

zest: He threw himself into the project with typical zest

see also **energy, essence, ghost, sneak**

spirited see **energetic, vital**

spirits see **alcohol, humour, mood**

spiritual see **religious**

spite in spite of preposition **1** even though something is the case: In spite of all the gossip, Virginia stayed behind

despite: They manage to enjoy life despite adversity

even though: They did it even though I warned them not to

notwithstanding: Notwithstanding his age, Sikorski had an important job

regardless of: He led from the front, regardless of the danger

though: I enjoy painting, though I am not very good at it

▷ noun **2** a desire to hurt someone:
He just did it out of spite
ill will: *He didn't bear anyone any
ill will*
malevolence: *a streak of
malevolence*
malice: *There was no malice in
her voice*
spitefulness: *petty spitefulness*
venom: *His wit had a touch of venom
about it*

spiteful adjective *saying or doing
nasty things to hurt people*: *a stream
of spiteful telephone calls*
bitchy informal: *It's not just women
who are bitchy*
catty informal: *She's always making
catty remarks*
cruel: *They gave him a cruel nickname*
malevolent: *a malevolent stare*
malicious: *spreading malicious
gossip*
nasty: *What nasty little snobs you
all are*
snide: *He made a snide comment
about her weight*
venomous: *a venomous attack*
vindictive: *How can you be so
vindictive?*
see also **malicious, unkind**

spitefulness *see* **spite**

spitting image *see* **lookalike**

splash *see* **dash, drip**

splendid adjective **1** *very good
indeed*: *I've had a splendid time*
cracking British, Australian, New
Zealand informal: *It's a cracking script*
excellent: *The recording quality is
excellent*
fantastic informal: *a fantastic
combination of colours*
fine: *a fine little fellow*
glorious: *a glorious career*
great informal: *a great bunch of guys*
marvellous: *a marvellous thing to do*
wonderful: *a wonderful movie*

2 *beautiful and impressive*: *a
splendid old mansion*
gorgeous: *a gorgeous Renaissance
building*
grand: *a grand hotel*
imposing: *imposing wrought-iron
gates*
impressive: *an impressive spectacle*
magnificent: *magnificent views
across the valley*
superb: *The hotel has a superb
isolated location*
see also **fine, first-rate, grand,
marvellous, superb**

splendidly *see* **well**

splendour *see* **glory**

split verb **1** *to divide into two or more
parts*: *The ship split in two*
diverge: *Their paths began to diverge*
fork: *Ahead of us, the road forked*
part: *For a moment the clouds parted*
separate: *Fluff the rice with a fork to
separate the grains*

2 *to have a crack or tear*: *His
trousers split*
burst: *A water pipe has burst*
come apart: *My jacket's coming
apart at the seams*
crack: *A gas main cracked*
rip: *I felt the paper rip as we pulled in
opposite directions*

▷ noun **3** *a crack or tear in
something*: *There's a split in my
mattress*
crack: *The larvae burrow into cracks
in the floor*
fissure: *Water trickled out of fissures
in the limestone*
rip: *the rip in her new dress*
tear: *the ragged edges of a tear*

4 *a division between two things*:
*the split between rugby league and
rugby union*
breach: *a serious breach in relations
between the two countries*
breakup: *the breakup of the Soviet*

Union in 1991

divergence: *a divergence between France and its allies*

division: *the conventional division between "art" and "life"*

rift: *There is a rift between us and the rest of the family*

schism: *the schism which divided the Christian world*

see also **breach, burst, divide, division, fissure, hole, share, tear**

split up see **divide, separate**

spoil verb 1 to damage or destroy something: *Don't let it spoil your holiday*

damage: *This could damage our chances of winning*

destroy: *His criticism has destroyed my confidence*

harm: *This product harms the environment*

impair: *The flavour is impaired by overcooking*

mar: *The celebrations were marred by violence*

mess up: *He's messed up his life*

ruin: *My wife was ruining her health through worry*

wreck: *the injuries which nearly wrecked his career*

2 to give someone everything they want: *Grandparents often spoil their grandchildren*

cosset: *We did not cosset our children*

indulge: *a heavily indulged youngest daughter*

pamper: *pampered pets*

see also **rot, ruin**

spoils see **loot**

spoilsport noun a person who spoils other people's fun: *They made me feel like a spoilsport for saying no*

misery British informal: *the miseries in the government*

wowser Australian slang: *a small group of wowsers*

spoken see **oral**

spokesman see **representative**

spokeswoman see **representative**

sponge see **clean, scrounge**

sponsor see **supporter**

spoof see **parody**

spooky adjective eerie and frightening: *The whole place had a slightly spooky atmosphere*

creepy: Informal: *a place that is really creepy at night*

eerie: *The wind made eerie noises in the trees*

frightening: *Whenever I fall asleep, I see these frightening faces*

ghostly: *The moon shed a ghostly light on the fields*

haunted: *a haunted house*

supernatural: *The blade glowed with a supernatural light*

scary: *a scary ruined castle*

uncanny: *The strange, uncanny feeling was creeping all over me*

see also **creepy, scary**

sporadic see **occasional, rare**

sport see **wear**

spot noun 1 a small round mark on something: *a navy blue dress with white spots*

blemish: *A small blemish spoiled the surface*

blot: *an ink blot*

blotch: *His face was covered in red blotches*

mark: *a little red mark on my neck*

smudge: *There was a dark smudge on his forehead*

speck: *a speck of dirt*

2 a location or place: *an out-of-the-way spot*

location: *The hotel is in a superb isolated location*

place: *Jerusalem is Christianity's most venerated place*

point: *the point where the river had burst its banks*

position: She moved the body to a position where it would not be seen

scene: He left a note at the scene of the crime

site: plans to construct a temple on the site

▷ verb **3** to see or notice something: Her drama teacher spotted her ability

catch sight of: I caught sight of an ad in the paper

detect: The test should enable doctors to detect the disease early

discern: I did not discern any change

observe: Can you observe any difference?

see: I can see a resemblance between you

sight: A fleet of French ships was sighted

see also **discern**, **location**, **notice**, **observe**, **random**, **recognize**, **scene**, **see**, **sight**, **stain**

spotless see **clean**, **innocent**, **pure**

spotlight see **feature**

spouse see **partner**

spout see **pour**

sprain see **twist**

sprawl see **lie**, **spread**

spray see **bunch**, **wet**

spread verb **1** to put or spread over an area: He spread his coat over the bed

extend: The new territory would extend over one-fifth of Canada's land mass

fan out: She spun, and her dress's full skirt fanned out in a circle

open: She opened her arms and gave me a big hug

sprawl: The recreation area sprawls over 900 acres

unfold: When the bird lifts off, its wings unfold to a six-foot span

unfurl: We began to unfurl the sails

unroll: I unrolled my sleeping bag

2 to put a thin layer on a surface: Spread the bread with the cream cheese

apply: Apply the preparation evenly over the wood's surface

coat: Coat the fish with the paste

cover: I covered the table with a cloth

overlay: The floor was overlaid with rugs

plaster: She plastered herself in sun lotion

smear: Smear a little oil over the inside of the bowl

smother: He likes to smother his bread with butter

3 to reach or affect more people gradually: The sense of fear is spreading in the neighbourhood

circulate: Rumours were circulating that the project was to be abandoned

grow: Opposition grew and the government agreed to negotiate

expand: The industry is looking for opportunities to expand into other countries

increase: The population continues to increase

proliferate: the free Internet services that are proliferating across the world

travel: News of his work travelled all the way to Asia

▷ noun **4** the extent or growth of something: the gradual spread of information

diffusion: the development and diffusion of ideas

expansion: the rapid expansion of private health insurance

extent: the growing extent of the problem

growth: the growth of nationalism

increase: an increase of violence along the border

progression: This drug slows the progression of HIV

proliferation: the proliferation of nuclear weapons

upsurge: the upsurge in interest in

these books
see also **circulate, communicate, distribute, lay, multiply, stretch**

spreading see **infectious**

sprightly see **active, agile, lively, vital**

spring see **develop, jump, leap**

sprinkle see **scatter**

sprinkling see **dash**

sprint see **dash, run**

sprite see **spirit**

sprout see **grow**

spruce see **neat, smart**

spruce up see **tidy**

spur see **drive, prompt**

spurn see **boycott, refuse, reject**

spurt see **gush**

squabble verb **1** to quarrel about something trivial: *Mum and Dad squabble all the time*
argue: *They went on arguing all the way down the road*
bicker: *The two women bickered constantly*
fall out: *Mum and I used to fall out a lot*
feud: *feuding neighbours*
fight: *Mostly, they fight about paying bills*
quarrel: *At one point we quarrelled over something silly*
row: *They rowed all the time*
wrangle: *The two sides spend their time wrangling over procedural problems*
▷ noun **2** a quarrel: *There have been minor squabbles about phone bills*
altercation: *an altercation with the referee*
argument: *a heated argument*
barney *British, Australian, New Zealand informal*: *We had such a barney that we nearly split up*
disagreement: *My instructor and I had a brief disagreement*
dispute: *a dispute between the two*

countries over farm subsidies
fight: *He had a big fight with his dad that night*
quarrel: *I had a terrible quarrel with my brother*
row: *A man had been stabbed to death in a family row*
tiff: *She was walking home after a tiff with her boyfriend*
see also **argue, argument, clash, disagreement, fight, quarrel, row**

squad see **party, team**

squalid see **scungy**

squander see **waste**

squandering see **waste**

square see **agree**

squash see **crush**

squashy see **soft**

squat see **crouch, low**

squeal see **scream**

squeeze see **clasp, cram, ease, hug, press, stuff**

squirm see **fidget**

stab see **attempt, effort, go, poke**

stabilize see **balance, steady**

stable see **constant, secure, solid, steady**

stack see **heap, load, pile**

stacks see **heaps**

staff noun the people who work for an organization: *She made little effort to socialize with other staff*
employee: *a temporary employee*
personnel: *An announcement was made to all personnel*
team: *The team worked well under his direction*
workers: *weekend and night-shift workers*
workforce: *a sullen and resentful workforce*

stage noun **1** a part of a process: *the closing stages of the race*
lap: *The first lap was clocked at under a minute*
period: *We went through a period of*

unprecedented change

phase: *a passing phase*

point: *a critical point in the campaign*

step: *the next step in the process*

▷ *verb* **2** to organize something:
*Workers have staged a number of
one-day strikes*

arrange: *We're arranging a surprise
party for her*

engineer: *He was the one who
engineered the merger*

mount: *a security operation mounted
by the army*

orchestrate: *a carefully orchestrated
campaign*

organize: *a two-day meeting
organized by the UN*

see also **level, perform, round**

stagger see **amaze, shock, surprise**

staggering see **amazing**

stagnant see **stale**

staid see **serious, solemn, stuffy**

stain noun **1** a mark on something:
grass stains

blot: *an ink blot*

mark: *I can't get this mark to come off*

spot: *brown spots on the skin caused
by the sun*

▷ *verb* **2** to make a mark on
something: *Some foods can stain
the teeth*

dirty: *Sheets can be reused until they
are damaged or dirtied*

mark: *the places where Steve's boots
had marked the wood*

soil: *a soiled white apron*

spot: *her coat was spotted with blood*

see also **colour, mark, soil**

stake see **gamble**

stale adjective no longer fresh: *a lump
of stale bread*

flat: *flat beer*

old: *mouldy old cheese*

sour: *sour milk*

stagnant: *stagnant water*

see also **corny, hackneyed, stuffy**

stalk see **follow**

stall see **jam**

stamina see **strength**

stamp out see **crush, eliminate,
suppress**

stampede see **charge, dash, rush**

stance see **attitude**

stand see **base, endure, put up with,
tolerate**

stand by see **wait**

stand for see **allow, put up with,
represent**

stand up for see **side with**

stand up to see **brave**

standard noun **1** a particular level of
quality or achievement: *There will be
new standards of hospital cleanliness*

calibre: *the high calibre of these
researchers*

criterion: *The most important
criterion for entry is excellence in your
chosen field*

guideline: *The accord lays down
guidelines for the conduct of
government agents*

level: *The exercises are marked
according to their level of difficulty*

norm: *the commonly agreed norms
of democracy*

quality: *Everyone can improve their
quality of life*

requirement: *These products meet
all legal requirements*

▷ *adjective* **2** usual, normal, and
correct: *It was standard practice for
them to consult the parents*

accepted: *It is accepted wisdom that
the state of your body impacts on your
state of mind*

correct: *the correct way to produce a
crop of tomato plants*

customary: *It is customary to offer a
drink or a snack to guests*

normal: *Some shops were closed, but
that's quite normal for a Thursday*

orthodox: *orthodox police methods*

regular: This product looks and tastes like regular lemonade

usual: It is usual to tip waiters
see also **average, common, conventional, ideal, level, normal, ordinary, routine, stock, typical, usual**

standards plural noun moral principles of behaviour: My father has always had high moral standards

ethics: the difference between our personal and social ethics

ideals: The party has drifted too far from its socialist ideals

morals: Western ideas and morals

principles: He refused to do anything that went against his principles

rules: They were expected to adhere to the rules of the convent

scruples: a man with no moral scruples

values: the values of liberty and equality

stand-in see **replacement**

standing see **mana, rank, reputation, status**

standstill see **halt**

star noun a famous person: a film star

celebrity: A host of celebrities attended the premiere

idol: the city's greatest soccer idol

luminary literary: The event attracted such pop luminaries as Madonna
see also **celebrity, feature, personality, success**

stare verb to look at something for a long time: He stared at the floor, lost in meditation

gaze: gazing at herself in the mirror

look: He looked at her with open hostility

ogle: ogling the girls as they went past

stark see **plain**

stark-naked see **naked**

start verb **1** to begin to take place:

School starts again next week

arise: A conflict is likely to arise

begin: A typical day begins at 8.30

come into being: The festival came into being in 1986

come into existence: a club that came into existence only 30 years ago

commence: The academic year commences at the beginning of October

get under way: The game got under way

originate: The disease originated in Africa

2 to begin to do something: Susie started to cry

begin: He began to groan with pain

commence: The hunter commenced to skin the animal

embark upon: He's embarking on a new career as a writer

proceed: He proceeded to get drunk

set about: How do you set about getting a mortgage?

3 to cause something to begin: a good time to start a business

begin: The US is prepared to begin talks immediately

create: Criticism will only create feelings of failure

establish: The school was established in 1899

found: Baden-Powell founded the Boy Scouts in 1908

get going: I've worked hard to get this business going

inaugurate formal: the company which inaugurated the first scheduled international flight

initiate: They wanted to initiate a discussion

instigate: The violence was instigated by a few people

institute: We have instituted a number of measures

introduce: The government has

introduced other money-saving
schemes
launch: *The police have launched an
investigation into the incident*
open: *We opened the service with
a hymn*
pioneer: *the man who invented and
pioneered DNA testing*
set in motion: *Several changes have
already been set in motion*
set up: *A committee was set up to
arbitrate in the dispute*
trigger: *Nuts can trigger an allergic
reaction in some people*

▷ **noun 4** the beginning of
something: *His career had an
auspicious start*
beginning: *the beginning of all the
trouble*
birth: *the birth of modern art*
commencement: *Applicants
should be at least 16 before the
commencement of the course*
dawn: *the dawn of a new age*
foundation: *the foundation of the
National Organization for Women*
inauguration: *the inauguration of
new exam standards*
inception *formal*: *Since its inception
the company has produced 53 different
aircraft designs*
initiation: *There was a year between
initiation and completion*
onset: *the onset of puberty*
opening: *the opening of the trial*
outset: *There were lots of problems
from the outset*
see also **begin, beginning, flinch,
head, opening, proceed, scare,
surprise**

starter *see* **beginner**
startle *see* **alarm, frighten, scare**
startled *see* **frightened**
startling *see* **amazing**
starving *see* **hungry**
stash *see* **hide, stockpile, store**

state noun **1** the condition or
circumstances of something: *the
pathetic state of the rail network*
circumstances: *He's in desperate
circumstances*
condition: *He remains in a critical
condition in hospital*
plight: *the plight of Third World
countries*
position: *We are in a privileged
position*
predicament: *the once great club's
current predicament*
shape: *Her finances were in terrible
shape*
situation: *a precarious situation*
2 a country: *the state of Denmark*
country: *a country where alcohol is
prohibited*
kingdom: *The kingdom's power
declined*
land: *in that distant land*
nation: *a leading nation in world
politics*
republic: *In 1918, Austria became
a republic*

▷ verb **3** to say something, especially
in a formal way: *Please state your
occupation*
affirm: *a speech in which he affirmed
his policies*
articulate: *an attempt to articulate
his feelings*
assert: *He asserted his innocence*
declare: *He declared that he would
fight on*
express: *He expressed regret that he
had caused any offence*
say: *The police said he had no
connection with the security forces*
specify: *Please specify your
preferences below*
see also **condition, country, declare,
observe, remark, report, specify,
territory**

state of affairs *see* **situation**

state of mind see mood

statement noun a short written or spoken piece giving information: *He was depressed when he made that statement*

account: *He gave a detailed account of what happened that night*

announcement: *He made his announcement after talks with the President*

bulletin: *A bulletin was released announcing the situation*

declaration: *a public declaration of support*

explanation: *They have given no public explanation for his dismissal*

proclamation: *The proclamation of independence was broadcast over the radio*

report: *A press report said that at least six people had died*

testimony: *His testimony was an important part of the prosecution case*
see also **announcement, bill, comment, declaration, remark, report, word**

station see base, rank

stationary see still

statistic see figure

stature see mana, reputation

status noun a person's social position: *the status of children in society*

position: *a privileged position*

prestige: *to diminish the prestige of the monarchy*

rank: *He was stripped of his rank*

standing: *This has done nothing to improve his standing*
see also **level, mana, rank**

statute see law

staunch see faithful, firm, loyal, reliable, steadfast, trusty

stay verb to remain somewhere: *She stayed in bed till noon*

hang around informal: *I can't hang around here all day*

linger: *I lingered on for a few days until he arrived*

loiter: *We loitered around looking in shop windows*

remain: *You'll have to remain in hospital for the time being*

tarry: *The shop's aim is to persuade you to tarry and spend*

wait: *I'll wait here till you come back*
see also **live, remain, visit, wait**

stay afloat see float

stay behind see remain

steadfast adjective refusing to change or give up: *He remained steadfast in his belief*

constant: *He has been her constant companion for the last four months*

faithful: *this party's most faithful voters*

firm: *He held a firm belief in the afterlife*

immovable: *On one issue, however, she was immovable*

resolute: *a decisive and resolute international leader*

staunch: *a staunch supporter of these proposals*

steady: *He was firm and steady, unlike many men she knew*

unshakeable: *his unshakeable belief in the project*

steady adjective **1** continuing without interruptions: *a steady rise in profits*

consistent: *consistent support*

constant: *under constant pressure*

continuous: *Japanese-style programmes of continuous improvement*

even: *an even level of sound*

nonstop: *nonstop background music*

regular: *a regular beat*

uninterrupted: *28 years of uninterrupted growth*

2 not shaky or wobbling: *O'Brien*

held out a steady hand
firm: Make sure the tree is securely mounted on a firm base
secure: Check joints are secure and the wood is sound
stable: stable foundations
▷ verb **3** to prevent something from shaking or wobbling: Two men were steadying a ladder
brace: the old timbers which braced the roof
secure: The frames are secured by horizontal rails
stabilize: gyros which stabilize the platform
support: Thick wooden posts support the ceiling
see also **balance, constant, even, gradual, reasonable, regular, steadfast**

steal verb **1** to take something without permission: He was accused of stealing a tin of pineapple chunks
appropriate: Several other companies have appropriated the idea
nick British, Australian, New Zealand slang: I nicked that money from the till
pilfer: Staff were pilfering behind the bar
pinch informal: Someone's pinched my wallet
swipe slang: Did you just swipe that book?
take: The burglars took anything they could carry
2 to move somewhere quietly and secretly: They can steal out and join us later
creep: We crept away under cover of darkness
slip: I wanted to duck down and slip past but they saw me
sneak: Sometimes he would sneak out to see me
tiptoe: She slipped out of bed and

tiptoed to the window
see also **slip, sneak**

steal from see **rob**
stealing see **theft**
steam see **cook**
steamy see **humid**
steep adjective **1** rising sharply and abruptly: a steep hill
sheer: a sheer drop
vertical: The slope was almost vertical
2 larger than is reasonable: steep prices
excessive: excessive charges
extortionate: an extortionate rate of interest
high: high loan rates
unreasonable: unreasonable interest charges
▷ verb **3** to soak something in a liquid: green beans steeped in olive oil
immerse: Immerse the gammon in cold water to remove the salt
marinate: Marinate the chicken for at least four hours
soak: Soak the beans overnight
see also **sheer, soak**

steer see **drive, lead, manoeuvre**
steer clear of see **avoid**
stem see **result**
stench see **smell, stink**
stencil see **pattern**
step see **advance, measure, stage**
step down see **resign**
stereotyped see **corny, stock**
sterile adjective **1** free from germs: Protect the cut with a sterile dressing
antiseptic: an antiseptic hospital room
germ-free: Keep your working surfaces germ-free
sterilized: a sterilized laboratory
2 unable to produce: He found out he was sterile
barren: a barren mare
unproductive: 70 million acres of

unproductive land
see also **barren**

sterilized see **clean, pure, sterile**

stern see **back, grim, harsh, serious, severe, strict**

stew see **cook**

stick noun 1 a long, thin piece of wood: crowds armed with sticks and stones

bat: a baseball bat

cane: He wore a grey suit and leaned heavily on his cane

mace: a statue of a king holding a golden mace

pole: He reached up with a hooked pole to roll down the shutter

rod: a witch-doctor's rod

truncheon: a policeman's truncheon

twig: the sound of a twig breaking underfoot

wand: You can't wave a magic wand and make everything okay

▷ verb 2 to thrust something somewhere: They stuck a needle in my back

dig: She dug her spoon into the moussaka

insert: He inserted the key into the lock

jab: A needle was jabbed into my arm

poke: He poked his finger into the hole

push: She pushed her thumb into his eye

put: Just put it through my letter-box when you're finished with it

ram: He rammed the jacket under the seat

shove: We shoved a copy of the newsletter beneath their door

stuff: I stuffed my hands in my pockets

thrust: A small aerial thrust up from the grass verge

3 to attach or become attached: Stick down any loose bits of flooring

adhere: Small particles adhere to the seed

attach: We attach labels to things before we file them away

bond: Strips of wood are bonded together

cling: His sodden trousers were clinging to his shins

fix: Fix the photo to the card using double-sided tape

fuse: The flakes fuse together and produce ice crystals

glue: Glue the fabric around the window

paste: The children were busy pasting stars on to a chart

4 to jam or become jammed: The dagger stuck tightly in the silver scabbard

catch: His jacket buttons caught in the net

jam: Every few moments the machinery became jammed

lodge: The car has a bullet lodged in the passenger door

snag: The fishermen said their nets kept snagging on underwater objects
see also **club, fix, glue, jam, set**

stick out see **bulge, extend**

stick up for see **champion, defend**

sticker see **label**

sticky adjective covered with a substance that sticks to other things: She thrust her hand into the sticky mess

adhesive: adhesive tape

tacky: covered with a tacky resin
see also **humid**

stickybeak see **snooper**

stiff adjective 1 firm and not easily bent: stiff metal wires

firm: a firm mattress

hard: the hard wooden floor

rigid: a rigid plastic container

solid: a block of solid wax

taut: He lifted the wire until it was taut

2 not friendly or relaxed: the rather

stiff and formal surroundings of the Palace
cold: Sharon was very cold with me
forced: a forced smile
formal: His voice was grave and formal
stilted: Our conversation was stilted and polite
unnatural: a strained and unnatural atmosphere
wooden: a wooden performance
3 difficult or severe: a stiff exam
arduous: an arduous undertaking
difficult: a difficult job
exacting: exacting standards
formidable: a formidable task
hard: a hard day's work
rigorous: rigorous military training
tough: a tough challenge
see also **firm, formal, hard, rigid**
stiffen see **harden, strengthen**
stifle see **contain, silence, suppress**
stifling see **stuffy**
still adjective not moving: The air was still
calm: the calm waters of the harbour
inert: He covered the inert body with a blanket
motionless: He stood there, motionless
stationary: The train was stationary for 90 minutes
tranquil: a tranquil lake
see also **calm, peaceful, silence, silent**
stillness see **calm, peace, quiet, silence**
stilted see **stiff**
stimulant see **drug**
stimulate see **interest, refresh**
stimulating see **exciting, interesting**
stimulus see **incentive**
stink verb **1** to smell very bad: His breath stinks of garlic
pong British, Australian informal: She

said he ponged a bit
reek: The whole house reeks of cigar smoke
▷ noun **2** a very bad smell: the stink of stale beer on his breath
pong British, Australian informal: What's that horrible pong?
stench: a foul stench
see also **smell**
stinking see **smelly**
stint see **stretch**
stipulate see **specify**
stipulation see **condition, restriction**
stipulations see **terms**
stir see **fuss, touch, wake**
stir up see **excite**
stirring see **impressive, moving**
stock noun **1** shares bought in an investment company: the buying of stocks
bonds: the recent sharp decline in bond prices
investments: Earn a rate of return of 8% on your investments
shares: He was keen to buy shares in the company
2 a supply of something: The shop withdrew a quantity of stock from sale
goods: Are all your goods on display?
merchandise formal: 25% off selected merchandise
reserve: 65% of the world's oil reserves
reservoir: the body's short-term reservoir of energy
stockpile: treaties to cut stockpiles of chemical weapons
store: my secret store of chocolate biscuits
supply: What happens when food supplies run low?
3 an animal or person's ancestors: We are both from working-class stock
ancestry: a family who can trace their ancestry back to the sixteenth

century
descent: All the contributors were of
African descent
extraction: Her father was of Italian
extraction
lineage: a respectable family of
ancient lineage
parentage: She's a Londoner of mixed
parentage
origin: people of Asian origin
▷ verb **4** to keep a supply of goods
to sell: The shop stocks a wide range
of paint
deal in: They deal in kitchen
equipment
sell: It sells everything from hair
ribbons to oriental rugs
supply: We supply office furniture and
accessories
trade in: He had been trading in
antique furniture for 25 years
▷ adjective **5** commonly used:
National security is the stock excuse for
government secrecy
hackneyed: It may be an old
hackneyed phrase, but it's true
overused: an overused catch phrase
routine: We've tried all the routine
methods of persuasion
standard: the standard ending for a
formal letter
stereotyped: stereotyped ideas
about women
typical: the typical questions
journalists ask celebrities
usual: He came out with all the usual
excuses
see also **bank, breed, fill, origin,
reserve, sell, stockpile, store,
supply, typical**
stockpile verb **1** to store large
quantities of something: People are
stockpiling food for the winter
accumulate: Some people get rich by
accumulating wealth very gradually
amass: It is best not to enquire how

he amassed his fortune
collect: Two young girls were
collecting firewood
gather: We gathered enough wood to
last the night
hoard: They've begun to hoard food
and petrol
save: Scraps of material were saved
for quilts
stash informal: He had stashed
money in an offshore account
store up: Investors were storing up
cash in anticipation of disaster
▷ noun **2** a large store of something:
stockpiles of fuel
arsenal: a formidable arsenal of guns
and landmines
cache: a cache of weapons and
explosives
hoard: a hoard of silver and jewels
worth $40m
reserve: The country's reserves of food
are running low
stash informal: her mother's stash of
sleeping pills
stock: Stocks of ammunition were
being used up
store: his secret store of sweets
see also **gather, hoard, reserve,
stock, store, supply**

stocky adjective short but solid-
looking: a stocky, middle-aged man
chunky: the chunky South African
tennis player
solid: a solid build
sturdy: a short, sturdy woman in her
early sixties

stomach noun the front part of the
body below the waist: Breathe out
and flatten your stomach
belly: the enormous belly of the Italian
foreign minister
paunch: Nicholson surveyed his
spreading paunch
puku New Zealand: a pain in my puku
tummy informal: I'd like a flatter

tummy, but then who wouldn't?
see also **bear, put up with**

stony *see* **cold**

stoop *see* **bend**

stop verb **1** to cease doing
something: *I stopped working last
year to have a baby*
cease: *A small number of firms have
ceased trading*
cut out *informal*: *Will you cut out
that racket?*
desist: *boycotting Norwegian
products until they desist from whaling*
discontinue: *Do not discontinue the
treatment without seeing your doctor*
end: *public pressure to end the
embargo*
quit: *He's trying to quit smoking*
2 to come to an end: *He prayed for
the blizzard to stop*
cease: *At one o'clock the rain ceased*
come to an end: *An hour later, the
meeting came to an end*
conclude: *The evening concluded
with dinner and speeches*
end: *The talks ended in disagreement*
finish: *The teaching day finishes at
around 4 pm*
halt: *Discussions have halted again*
3 to prevent something: *measures to
stop the trade in ivory*
arrest: *trying to arrest the bleeding*
check: *a policy to check fast
population growth*
prevent: *the most practical way of
preventing crime*
see also **block, cease, check, end,
halt, prevent, quit, suppress, visit**

stop working *see* **fail**

stoppage *see* **blockage, halt, pause**

stopper *see* **plug, top**

store noun **1** a supply kept for
future use: *I have a store of food and
water here*
cache: *a cache of weapons and
explosives*

fund: *an extraordinary fund of energy*
hoard: *a hoard of supplies*
reserve: *the world's oil reserves*
reservoir: *the body's short-term
reservoir of energy*
stock: *stocks of paper and ink*
stockpile: *stockpiles of nuclear
warheads*
supply: *food supplies*
2 a place where things are kept: *a
grain store*
depot: *a government arms depot*
storeroom: *a storeroom filled with
furniture*
warehouse: *a carpet warehouse*
▷ verb **3** to keep something for
future use: *The information can be
stored in a computer*
hoard: *They've begun to hoard food
and petrol*
keep: *Grate the lemon zest and keep
it for later*
save: *His allotment of gas had to be
saved for emergencies*
stash *informal*: *He had stashed
money away in a secret offshore
account*
stockpile: *People are stockpiling food
for the coming winter*
see also **bank, collection, fund,
hoard, keep, reserve, shop, stock,
stockpile, supply, wealth**

store up *see* **stockpile**

storeroom *see* **store**

stores *see* **supplies**

storm *see* **attack, charge, hail, rage**

stormy *see* **wild**

story noun a tale told or written
to entertain people: *a poignant
love story*
account: *a true account*
anecdote: *her store of theatrical
anecdotes*
legend: *an old Scottish legend*
narrative: *a fast-moving narrative*
tale: *a fairy tale*

yarn: *a children's yarn about giants*
see also **article, feature, plot**

story line see **plot**

stout see **overweight, plump, sturdy, tubby**

straight *adjective* **1** upright or level: *Keep your arms straight*

erect: *The upper back and neck are held in an erect position*

even: *to ensure an even hem*

horizontal: *a horizontal line*

level: *a completely level base*

perpendicular: *Position your body perpendicular with the slope*

upright: *He sat upright in his chair*

vertical: *Keep the spine vertical*

2 honest, frank and direct: *They wouldn't give me a straight answer*

blunt: *She is blunt about her personal life*

candid: *I haven't been completely candid with you*

forthright: *a forthright reply*

frank: *a frank discussion*

honest: *Please be honest with me*

outright: *This was outright rejection*

plain: *plain talking*

point-blank: *a point-blank refusal*
see also **direct, neat, straightforward**

straightaway see **immediately, now**

straighten see **stretch, tidy**

straighten out see **settle**

straightforward *adjective* **1** easy and involving no problems: *The question seemed straightforward enough*

basic: *The film's story is pretty basic*

easy: *The shower is easy to install*

elementary: *elementary computer skills*

routine: *a fairly routine procedure*

simple: *simple advice on filling in your tax form*

uncomplicated: *good British*

cooking with its uncomplicated, natural flavours

2 honest, open, and frank: *I liked his straightforward, intelligent manner*

candid: *I haven't been completely candid with you*

direct: *He avoided giving a direct answer*

forthright: *He was known for his forthright manner*

frank: *They had a frank discussion about the issue*

honest: *I was totally honest about what I was doing*

open: *He had always been open with her*

plain: *I believe in plain talking*

straight: *He never gives a straight answer to a straight question*
see also **blunt, candid, direct, easy, frank, simple**

strain *noun* **1** worry and nervous tension: *the stresses and strains of a busy career*

anxiety: *Her voice was full of anxiety*

pressure: *the pressure of work*

stress: *the stress of exams*

tension: *Laughing relieves tension and stress*

▷ *verb* **2** to make something do more than it is able to do: *You'll strain your eyes reading in this light*

overwork: *Too much food will overwork your digestive system*

tax: *He is beginning to tax my patience*
see also **breed, burden, difficulty, stress, struggle, tax, variety**

strained see **tense**

strains see **tune**

strait-laced see **prim, stuffy**

straits see **distress**

strand see **beach, coast**

strange *adjective* **1** unusual or unexpected: *A strange thing happened*

abnormal: *an abnormal fear of*

spiders
bizarre: *a bizarre scene*
curious: *a curious mixture of ancient and modern*
extraordinary: *an extraordinary occurrence*
funny: *a funny feeling*
odd: *There was something odd about her*
peculiar: *It tasted very peculiar*
queer: *I think there's something a bit queer going on*
uncommon: *A 15-year lifespan is not uncommon for a dog*
weird: *He's a really weird guy*
2 new or unfamiliar: *alone in a strange country*
alien: *transplanted into an alien culture*
exotic: *filmed in an exotic location*
foreign: *This was a foreign country, so unlike his own*
new: *I'm always open to new experiences*
novel: *a novel idea*
unfamiliar: *visiting an unfamiliar city*
see also **bizarre, curious, eccentric, extraordinary, funny, odd, peculiar, unfamiliar, weird**
strapping see **powerful**
strategy see **plan, procedure**
stratum see **layer**
stray see **ramble**
streak see **line, mark**
stream see **flood, flow, gush, pour**
streamline see **simplify**
street see **road**
strength noun **1** physical energy and power: *an astonishing display of physical strength*
brawn: *He's got plenty of brains as well as brawn*
might: *the full might of the army*
muscle: *demonstrating both muscle and skill*

stamina: *The race requires a lot of stamina*
2 the degree of intensity: *an indication of the strength of feeling among parents*
force: *the force of his argument*
intensity: *the intensity of their emotions*
potency: *the extraordinary potency of his personality*
power: *the overwhelming power of love*
vehemence: *I was surprised by the vehemence of his criticism*
vigour: *We resumed the attack with renewed vigour*
see also **character, energy, force, merit, power, virtue**
strengthen verb **1** to give something more power: *This move will strengthen his political standing*
consolidate: *to consolidate an already dominant position*
encourage: *encouraged by the shouts of their supporters*
harden: *evidence which hardens suspicions about their involvement*
stiffen: *This only stiffened his resolve to quit*
toughen: *new laws to toughen police powers*
2 to support the structure of something: *The builders had to strengthen the joists with timber*
bolster: *steel beams used to bolster the roof*
brace: *tottering pillars braced by scaffolding*
fortify: *citadels fortified by high stone walls*
reinforce: *They had to reinforce the walls with exterior beams*
support: *the thick wooden posts that supported the ceiling*
see also **build, secure**
strenuous see **hard**

stress noun **1** worry and nervous tension: *the stresses and strains of a busy career*

anxiety: *Her voice was full of anxiety*

hassle *informal*: *I don't think it's worth the money or the hassle*

pressure: *I felt the pressure of being the first woman in the job*

strain: *She was tired and under great strain*

tension: *Laughing relieves tension*

worry: *It was a time of worry for us*

▷ verb **2** to emphasize something: *The leaders have stressed their commitment to the talks*

accentuate: *make-up which accentuates your best features*

emphasize: *He flourished his glass to emphasize the point*

repeat: *We are not, I repeat not, in the negotiating process*

underline: *The report underlined his concern about falling standards*

see also **beat, burden, care, emphasize, strain**

stressful *see* **tense**

stretch verb **1** to extend over an area or time: *an artificial reef stretching the length of the coast*

continue: *The road continued into the distance*

cover: *The oil slick covered a total area of seven miles*

extend: *The caves extend for some 18 kilometres*

go on: *The dispute looks set to go on into the new year*

hang: *The branches hang right down to the ground*

last: *His difficulties are likely to last well beyond childhood*

reach: *a caravan park which reached from one end of the bay to the other*

spread: *The estuary spreads as far as the eye can see*

2 to reach out with part of your

body: *She arched her back and stretched herself*

extend: *Stand straight with your arms extended at your sides*

reach: *He reached up for an overhanging branch*

straighten: *Point your toes and straighten both legs slowly*

▷ noun **3** an area of land or water: *It's a very dangerous stretch of road*

area: *extensive mountainous areas of Europe and South America*

expanse: *a huge expanse of grassland*

extent: *a vast extent of fertile country*

sweep: *The ground fell away in a broad sweep down the river*

tract: *They cleared large tracts of forest for farming*

4 a period of time: *He would study for eight hour stretches*

period: *a long period of time*

run: *The show will transfer to the West End, after a month's run in Birmingham*

space: *They've come a long way in a short space of time*

spell: *a long spell of dry weather*

stint: *He is coming home after a five-year stint abroad*

term: *She worked the full term of her pregnancy*

time: *doing very little exercise for several weeks at a time*

see also **extend, lengthen, period, range, tax, term, time**

strict adjective **1** very firm in demanding obedience: *My parents were very strict*

authoritarian: *He has an authoritarian approach to parenthood*

firm: *the guiding hand of a firm father figure*

rigid: *a rigid hospital routine*

rigorous: *rigorous military training*

stern: *Her mother was stern and hard to please*

stringent: stringent rules

2 precise and accurate: *He has never been a playboy in the strict sense of the word*

accurate: *an accurate record of events*

exact: *I do not remember the exact words*

meticulous: *meticulous attention to detail*

particular: *very particular dietary requirements*

precise: *precise instructions*

true: *a true account*

see also **accurate, faithful, right, rigid, severe**

stride see **walk**

strident see **loud, noisy**

strife see **conflict, riot, war**

strike see **beat, bump, occur**

striking see **bold, impressive, memorable, prominent, significant**

string see **sequence, series**

stringent see **rigid, strict**

stripe see **line**

stripped see **bare**

strive verb to make a great effort to achieve something: *He strives hard to keep himself fit*

attempt: *He attempted to smile, but found it difficult*

do your best: *I'll do my best to find out*

do your utmost: *She was certain he would do his utmost to help her*

endeavour *formal*: *They are endeavouring to protect trade union rights*

make an effort: *He made no effort to hide his disappointment*

seek: *We have never sought to impose our views*

try: *He tried to block her advancement in the Party*

see also **aim, attempt, seek,**

struggle, try

stroke see **feel, hit**

stroll see **ramble, walk, wander**

strong adjective **1** having powerful muscles: *a strong, robust man*

2 able to withstand rough treatment: *a strong casing, which won't crack or chip*

3 great in degree or intensity: *Despite strong opposition, she was victorious*

see **word studies strong**

see also **bold, fierce, hard, healthy, passionate, powerful, solid, sturdy, tough, violent, well**

strong point see **merit**

structure noun **1** the way something is made or organized: *the structure of this molecule*

arrangement: *an intricate arrangement of treadles, rods and cranks*

construction: *The chairs were light in construction but very strong*

design: *The shoes were of good design and good quality*

make-up: *the chemical make-up of the oceans and atmosphere*

organization: *the organization of the economy*

2 something that has been built: *The museum is an impressive structure*

building: *an ugly modern building*

construction: *an impressive steel and glass construction*

edifice: *historic edifices in the area*

see also **building, form, sequence, system**

structuring see **organization**

struggle verb **1** to try hard to do something: *They had to struggle to make ends meet*

strain: *straining to lift heavy weights*

strive: *He strives hard to keep himself fit*

toil: *toiling to make up for lost time*

work: I had to work hard for everything I've got
▷ noun **2** something that is hard to achieve: Life became a struggle for survival

effort: It was an effort to finish in time
labour: weary from their labours
toil: another day of toil and strife
work: It's been hard work, but rewarding
see also **clash, competition, contest, effort, fight**

struggle against see **resist**

stubborn adjective determined not to change or give in: a stubborn character who is used to getting his own way
dogged: his dogged insistence on his rights
inflexible: His opponents viewed him as dogmatic and inflexible
obstinate: a wicked and obstinate child
tenacious: a tenacious and persistent interviewer
wilful: a headstrong and wilful young lady
see also **obstinate**

stuck-up adjective informal proud and conceited: She was famous, but she wasn't a bit stuck-up
arrogant: He was so arrogant, he never even said hello to me
conceited: He's a very conceited young man
disdainful: She cast a disdainful glance at me
haughty: She looks haughty, but when you get to know her, she's very friendly
proud: He's too proud to use public transport
snobbish: I'd expected her to be snobbish, but she was warm and welcoming

see also **haughty, superior, vain**

student see **pupil**
studied see **deliberate**

study verb **1** to spend time learning about something: He is studying History and Economics
learn: I'm learning French
read up: She spent a year reading up on farming techniques
swot British, Australian, New Zealand informal: swotting for their finals
2 to look at something carefully: He studied the map in silence
contemplate: He contemplated his hands, frowning
examine: He examined her passport and stamped it
pore over: We spent hours poring over travel brochures
▷ noun **3** the activity of learning about a subject: the serious study of medieval architecture
lessons: He was lagging behind in his lessons
research: funds for research into AIDS
school work: She buried herself in school work
swotting British, Australian, New Zealand informal: She put her success down to last-minute swotting
see also **consideration, examination, examine, investigate, observe, piece, read, research, review, scrutinize**

stuff noun **1** a substance or group of things: "That's my stuff," he said, pointing to a bag
apparatus: all the apparatus you'll need for the job
belongings: I collected my belongings and left
equipment: outdoor playing equipment
gear: fishing gear
kit: I forgot my gym kit

material: *organic material*
substance: *The substance that's causing problems comes from barley*
tackle: *Martin kept his fishing tackle in his room*
things: *Sara told him to take all his things and not to return*
▷ *verb* **2** to push something somewhere quickly and roughly: *He stuffed the newspapers into a litter bin*
cram: *I crammed her hat into a waste-basket*
force: *I forced the key into the ignition*
jam: *Pete jammed his hands into his pockets*
push: *Someone had pushed a tissue into the keyhole*
ram: *He rammed his clothes into a drawer*
shove: *We shoved a newsletter beneath their door*
squeeze: *I squeezed everything into my rucksack*
thrust: *She thrust a stack of photos into my hands*
3 to fill something with a substance or objects: *He stood there, stuffing his mouth with popcorn*
cram: *I crammed my bag full of clothes and set off*
fill: *I filled the box with polystyrene chips*
load: *They loaded all their equipment into backpacks*
pack: *a lorry packed with explosives*
see also **cram**, **equipment**, **fill**, **jam**, **material**, **matter**, **stick**, **substance**, **things**

stuffy *adjective* **1** formal and old-fashioned: *his lack of stuffy formality*
dull: *They are nice people but rather dull*
formal: *an austere and formal family*
old-fashioned: *She was condemned as an old-fashioned prude*
staid: *He is boring, old-fashioned and staid*
strait-laced: *She is very strait-laced and narrow-minded*
2 not containing enough fresh air: *It was hot and stuffy in the classroom*
close: *The atmosphere was close*
heavy: *The air was heavy, moist and sultry*
muggy: *It was muggy and overcast*
oppressive: *The little room was windowless and oppressive*
stale: *A layer of smoke hung in the stale air*
stifling: *the stifling heat of the room*

stumble see **trip**
stumble on see **discover**
stump see **puzzle**
stun see **amaze**, **numb**, **shock**, **surprise**
stunned see **dazed**, **unconscious**
stunner see **beauty**
stunning see **amazing**
stunted see **low**
stupendous see **unbelievable**

stupid *adjective* lacking intelligence or good judgment: *How could I have been so stupid?*
absurd: *absurd ideas*
daft *informal*: *That's a daft question*
dim: *He is rather dim*
foolish: *It is foolish to risk injury*
idiotic: *What an idiotic thing to say!*
inane: *She's always asking inane questions*
obtuse: *It should be obvious even to the most obtuse person*
thick: *I must have seemed incredibly thick*
see also **daft**, **dim**, **dumb**, **idiotic**, **mad**, **silly**, **slow**, **unwise**

stupidity *noun* lack of intelligence or good judgment: *I was astonished by his stupidity*
absurdity: *the absurdity of the suggestion*
folly: *the danger and folly of taking*

drugs
foolishness: He expressed remorse over his own foolishness
inanity: The inanity of the conversation
silliness: He sounded quite exasperated by my silliness

sturdy adjective strong and unlikely to be damaged: The camera was mounted on a sturdy tripod
durable: Fine china is surprisingly durable
hardy: He looked like a farmer, round-faced and hardy
robust: very robust, simply-designed machinery
solid: The car feels very solid
substantial: Jack had put on weight – he seemed more substantial
stout: a stout oak door
strong: a strong casing which won't crack or chip
well-built: Mitchell is well-built and of medium height
see also **powerful, solid, stocky, tough**

style noun 1 the way in which something is done: a dictatorial management style
approach: his blunt approach
manner: a satire in the manner of Dickens
method: a new method of education
mode: a cheap and convenient mode of transport
technique: his driving technique
way: He had a strange way of talking
2 smartness and elegance: She has not lost her grace and style
chic: French designer chic
elegance: Princess Grace's understated elegance
flair: dressed with typical Italian flair
sophistication: to add a touch of sophistication to any wardrobe
taste: impeccable taste

see also **design, fashion, language, manner, name, polish, sort, type, way**

stylish see posh, smart, trendy

subdue verb to bring people under control by force: The government have not been able to subdue the rebels
crush: ruthless measures to crush the revolt
defeat: an important role in defeating the rebellion
overcome: working to overcome the enemy forces
overpower: The police eventually overpowered him
quell: tough new measures to quell the disturbances
vanquish: his vanquished foe

subdued see dull, soft

subject noun 1 the thing or person being discussed: They exchanged views on a wide range of subjects
issue: an issue that had worried him for some time
matter: I don't want to discuss the matter
object: the object of much heated discussion
point: There is another point to consider
question: the difficult question of unemployment
theme: The book's central theme is power
topic: The weather is a constant topic of conversation
▷ verb **2** to make someone experience something: He was subjected to constant interruptions
expose: people exposed to high levels of radiation
put through: My husband put me through hell
submit: The old woman was submitted to a terrifying ordeal
see also **affair, business, issue,**

matter, question

submerge see dive, flood

submission see surrender, tender

submissive see meek, obedient, passive

submit *verb* **1** to accept or agree to something unwillingly: *I submitted to their requests*

agree: *Management has agreed to the union's conditions*

bow: *Some shops are bowing to consumer pressure and stocking the product*

capitulate: *He capitulated to their ultimatum*

comply: *The commander said his army would comply with the ceasefire*

give in: *Officials say they won't give in to the workers' demands*

surrender: *We'll never surrender to these terrorists*

yield: *She yielded to her mother's nagging and took the child to a specialist*

2 to formally present a document or proposal: *They submitted their reports to the Chancellor*

hand in: *I'm supposed to hand in my dissertation on Friday*

present: *The group intends to present this petition to the parliament*

propose: *He has proposed a bill to abolish the House of Commons*

put forward: *He has put forward new peace proposals*

send in: *Applicants are asked to send in a CV and covering letter*

table: *They've tabled a motion criticizing the Government for its actions*

tender: *She tendered her resignation*
see also **give in, nominate, pose, subject, surrender**

subordinate see inferior, junior

subsequent see next

subsequently see after, next

subservient see obedient

subside see abate, fall

subsidize see fund

subsidy see grant

substance *noun* a solid, powder, liquid or gas: *Poisonous substances should be labelled as such*

element: *a chart of the chemical elements*

fabric: *Condensation will rot the fabric of the building*

material: *an armchair of some resilient plastic material*

stuff: *the stuff from which the universe is made*
see also **material, matter, stuff, wealth**

substantial see solid, sturdy

substantiate see confirm

substitute *verb* **1** to use one thing in place of another: *You can substitute honey for the sugar*

exchange: *exchanging one set of problems for another*

interchange: *Meat can be interchanged with pulses as a source of protein*

replace: *We dug up the concrete and replaced it with grass*

swap: *Some hostages were swapped for convicted prisoners*

switch: *They switched the tags on the cables*

▷ *noun* **2** something used in place of another thing: *an artificial substitute for silk*

deputy: *I can't make it so I'll send my deputy*

proxy: *They must nominate a proxy to vote on their behalf*

replacement: *He has nominated Adams as his replacement*

representative: *Employees from each department elect a representative*

surrogate: *They had expected me to be a surrogate for my sister* see also **change, replacement**

subtle see **fine**

subtract verb **1** to take one number away from another: *If you subtract 3 from 5 you get 2*

deduct: *Marks will be deducted for spelling mistakes*

take away: *Take the number you first thought of*

take from: *Take the 5% discount from the total amount due*

subvert see **undermine**

succeed verb **1** to achieve the result you intend: *To succeed, you must learn to overcome obstacles*

be successful: *We must help our clubs to be successful in Europe*

do well: *Their team did well*

flourish: *The business flourished*

make it informal: *It is hard for an English actress to make it in Hollywood*

prosper: *His team have always prospered in cup competitions*

thrive: *The company has thrived by selling cheap, simple products*

triumph: *a symbol of good triumphing over evil*

work: *The plan worked*

2 to be the next person to have someone's job: *David is almost certain to succeed him as chairman*

replace: *the man who replaced him as England skipper*

take over from: *Last year he took over from Bauman as chief executive*

see also **flourish, follow, pass, replace, triumph, win**

succeed in see **manage**

succeeding see **next**

success noun **1** the achievement of a goal, fame, or wealth: *Do you believe that work is the key to success?*

celebrity: *I never expected this kind of celebrity when I was writing my novel*

eminence: *a pilot who achieved eminence in the aeronautical world*

fame: *her rise to fame as a dramatist*

prosperity: *the country's economic prosperity*

triumph: *last year's Republican triumph in the elections*

victory: *Union leaders are heading for victory in their battle over workplace rights*

wealth: *His hard work brought him wealth and respect*

2 a person or thing achieving popularity or greatness: *Everyone who knows her says she will be a huge success*

celebrity: *At the age of 12, Dan is already a celebrity*

hit: *The song became a massive hit*

sensation: *the film that turned her into an overnight sensation*

star: *I always knew she would be a star*

triumph: *a triumph of modern surgery*

winner: *Selling was my game and I intended to be a winner*

see also **triumph, victory, win**

successful adjective having achieved what you intended to do: *Mr Singh was a highly successful salesman*

flourishing: *a flourishing business*

lucrative: *a lucrative career*

profitable: *a profitable exchange of ideas*

rewarding: *a rewarding investment*

thriving: *a thriving housebuilding industry*

top: *a top model*

successfully see **well**

succession see **sequence, series**

successor see **replacement**

succinct see **concise, short**

succumb see **develop, give in, surrender**

sudden adjective happening quickly and unexpectedly: *a sudden cry*

abrupt: *Her idyllic world came to an*

abrupt end when her parents died
hasty: his hasty departure
quick: I had to make a quick decision
swift: a swift blow to the stomach
unexpected: His death was totally unexpected
see also **abrupt, quick, sharp**

suffer verb to be affected by pain or something unpleasant: I knew he was suffering some discomfort
bear: He bore his trials with dignity and grace
endure: The writer endured a harsh life
experience: Widows seem to experience more distress than do widowers
go through: I wouldn't like to go through that again
sustain: He had sustained massive facial injuries
undergo: He had to undergo a body search
see also **bear, endure, feel, receive, undergo**

sufferer see **patient**
suffering see **distress**
suffice see **do**
sufficient adjective being enough for a purpose: He had sufficient time to prepare his speech
adequate: an adequate income
ample: an ample supply of petrol
enough: enough cash to live on
see also **adequate, ample, satisfactory**

sugary see **sweet**
suggest verb 1 to mention something as a possibility or recommendation: Clive suggested going out for tea
advise: I advise you to keep quiet
advocate: Mr Jones advocates longer school days
propose: And where do you propose building such a huge thing?

recommend: I have no qualms about recommending this approach
2 to hint that something is the case: Reports suggested the factory would close
hint: The President hinted that he might make some changes
imply: the tone of the report implied that his death was inevitable
indicate: She has indicated that she may resign
insinuate: an article which insinuated that he was lying
intimate: He did intimate that he is seeking legal action
see also **advise, hint, nominate, raise, vote**

suggestion noun 1 an idea mentioned as a possibility: practical suggestions
plan: The government is being asked to consider the plan
proposal: the proposal to do away with nuclear weapons
proposition: a business proposition
recommendation: a range of recommendations for change
2 a slight indication of something: a suggestion of dishonesty
hint: He showed only the slightest hint of emotion
indication: He gave no indication of remorse
insinuation: The insinuation is that I have something to hide
intimation: He did not give any intimation that he was going to resign
trace: No traces of violence were found on the body
see also **advice, hint, idea, indication, trace**

suit verb 1 to be acceptable: They will only move if it suits them
be acceptable to: The name chosen had to be acceptable to everyone
do: A holiday at home will do me

just fine

please: I'll leave when it pleases me and not before

satisfy: Nothing you can do will satisfy him

2 to match something else: The battery can be shaped to suit any device

agree: His statement agrees with those of the other witnesses

conform to: designed to conform to the new safety requirements

correspond: a number which corresponds to a horse running in the race

go with: Do these shoes go with this dress?

match: tan slacks with a safari jacket to match

see also **blend, flatter, match**

suitable adjective right or acceptable for a particular purpose: Conditions were not suitable for life to flourish

acceptable: a mutually acceptable new contract

appropriate: an appropriate outfit for the occasion

apt: an apt name

fit: the suggestion that she is not a fit mother

fitting: a fitting background for her beauty

proper: It was not thought proper for a woman to be on stage

right: He always said just the right thing

satisfactory: a satisfactory arrangement

see also **appropriate, favourable, fitting, proper, right**

sulky adjective showing annoyance by being silent and moody: a sulky adolescent

huffy: What are you being so huffy about?

moody: Her husband had become

withdrawn and moody

petulant: He's just being childish and petulant

resentful: a resentful workforce

sullen: He lapsed into a sullen silence

see also **grumpy, moody**

sullen see **grumpy, moody, sulky**

sum see **count, quantity, total**

sum total see **whole**

summarize see **outline, sum up**

summary noun a short account of something's main points: a summary of the report

outline: an outline of the proposal

review: a film review

rundown: Here's a rundown of the options

summing-up: The judge concluded his summing-up

synopsis: a brief synopsis of the book

see also **outline**

summing-up see **summary**

summit see **peak, top**

sumptuous see **luxurious**

sumptuousness see **luxury**

sum up verb to describe briefly: He summed up his weekend in one word: "Disastrous"

recapitulate: Let's just recapitulate the essential points

summarize: The article can be summarized in three sentences

sundry see **several, various**

sunken see **low**

sunny see **cheery**

superb adjective very good indeed: With superb skill, he managed to make a perfect landing

breathtaking: The house has breathtaking views

excellent: You've done an excellent job

exquisite: His photography is exquisite

magnificent: a magnificent country house

marvellous: *She is a marvellous cook*

outstanding: *an outstanding performance*

splendid: *a splendid Victorian mansion*

superior: *a superior blend of the finest coffee beans*

unrivalled: *He has an unrivalled knowledge of British politics*

wonderful: *The sun setting over the mountains was a wonderful sight*

see also **brilliant, excellent, first-rate, marvellous, outstanding, splendid, wonderful**

supercilious see **scornful, superior**

superfluous see **excess, spare, waste**

superior adjective **1** better than other similar things: *superior coffee beans*

better: *I'd like to move to a better area*

choice: *the choicest cuts of meat*

de luxe: *a de luxe model*

exceptional: *children with exceptional ability*

first-rate: *a first-rate thriller*

surpassing: *her surpassing achievements*

unrivalled: *colour printing of unrivalled quality*

2 showing pride and self-importance: *He stood there looking superior*

condescending: *I'm fed up with your condescending attitude*

disdainful: *She passed along with a disdainful look*

haughty: *He spoke in a haughty tone*

lofty: *lofty disdain*

patronizing: *his patronizing attitude to the homeless*

snobbish: *her snobbish dislike for their intellectual inferiors*

stuck-up *informal: She was a famous actress, but she wasn't a bit stuck-up*

supercilious: *His manner is supercilious and arrogant*

▷ noun **3** a person in a higher position than you: *his immediate superior*

boss *informal: Her boss was very supportive*

manager: *His plans found favour with his manager*

senior: *He was described by his seniors as a model officer*

supervisor: *Each student has a supervisor*

see also **prime, select, senior, smug, superb**

superiority see **advantage, victory**

superlative see **incomparable**

supermarket see **shop**

supernatural see **spooky**

supersede see **follow, replace**

superstar see **celebrity**

supervise verb to oversee a person or activity: *He supervised more than 400 volunteers*

be in charge of: *He is in charge of the whole project*

direct: *Christopher will direct day-to-day operations*

have charge of: *He has charge of a three-acre estate*

keep an eye on: *I told you to keep an eye on the children*

manage: *I manage a small team of workers*

oversee: *an architect to oversee the work*

run: *Each teacher will run a different workshop*

see also **administer, command, direct, guard, handle, lead, oversee**

supervision see **watch**

supervisor see **superior**

supplant see **replace**

supple see **agile, flexible, soft**

supplement verb **1** to add to something to improve it: *I suggest supplementing your diet with vitamin A*

add to: A good bathroom adds to the value of any house

augment: a way to augment the family income

complement: an in-work benefit that complements earnings

reinforce: measures which will reinforce their current strengths

top up: compulsory contributions to top up pension schemes

▷ noun **2** something added to something else: a supplement to their basic pension

addition: an addition to the existing system

appendix: The report includes a six-page appendix

complement: The photographs are a perfect complement to the text

extra: an optional extra

see also **add**, **addition**, **supplies**

supplies plural noun food or equipment for a particular purpose: I had only two pints of water in my emergency supplies

equipment: vital medical equipment

provisions: provisions for two weeks

rations: Aid officials said food rations had been distributed

stores: an important part of a ship's stores

supply verb **1** to provide someone with something: an agreement not to supply chemical weapons

equip: plans for equipping the island with water

furnish: They'll be able to furnish you with the details

give: We'll give you all the information you need

provide: They'll provide all the equipment

▷ noun **2** an amount of something available for use: a plentiful supply of vegetables

cache: a cache of weapons and explosives

fund: an extraordinary fund of energy

hoard: a hoard of food and petrol

reserve: The Gulf has 65% of the world's oil reserves

stock: stocks of paper and ink

stockpile: stockpiles of chemical weapons

store: I have a store of food and water here

see also **equip**, **fund**, **give**, **hoard**, **issue**, **provide**, **reserve**, **stock**, **store**

support verb **1** to agree with someone's ideas or aims: We supported his political campaign

back: a new witness to back his claim

champion: He passionately championed the cause

defend: He defended all of Clarence's decisions, right or wrong

promote: He continued to promote the idea of Scottish autonomy

second: The Prime Minister seconded the call for discipline

side with: accused of siding with terrorists

uphold: We uphold the capitalist free economy

2 to help someone in difficulties: Try to support each other when one of you is feeling down

encourage: When things aren't going well, he encourages me

help: He'd do anything to help a friend

3 to hold something up from underneath: Thick wooden posts support the ceiling

bolster: steel beams used to bolster the roof

brace: The roll-over bar braces the car's structure

hold up: Her legs wouldn't hold her up

prop up: Use sticks to prop the plants up

reinforce: They had to reinforce the

walls with exterior beams

▷ noun **4** an object that holds
something up: *the metal supports
which hold up the canvas*
brace: *He will have to wear a neck
brace for several days*
foundation: *the foundation on which
the bridge was built*
pillar: *the pillars supporting the roof*
post: *The device is fixed to a post*
prop: *a structural part such as a
beam or prop*
see also **advocate, back, bear,
blessing, champion, comfort,
defend, encourage, favour,
finance, fund, help, promote,
sanction, side with, steady,
strengthen**

supporter noun *a person who
agrees with or helps someone*: *He is
a strong supporter of the church*
adherent: *Communism was gaining
adherents in Latin America*
advocate: *a strong advocate of free
market policies*
ally: *a close political ally*
champion: *a champion of women's
causes*
fan: *fans of this football club*
follower: *followers of the Dalai Lama*
sponsor: *the first sponsor of
Buddhism in Japan*
see also **defender, fan, follower,
helper**

supportive see **helpful**

suppose verb *to think that
something is probably the case*:
Where do you suppose he has gone?
assume: *I assume you have
permission to be here?*
believe: *We believe them to be hidden
somewhere in the area*
expect: *I don't expect you've had
much experience in the job yet*
guess: *I guess you're right*
imagine: *We tend to imagine that the*

Victorians were prim and proper
presume: *I presume you're here on
business*
think: *Do you think she was
embarrassed?*
see also **assume, conclude, figure,
guess, imagine, reckon, suspect**

supposed adjective **1** planned,
expected, or required to do
something: *You're not supposed to
leave a child on its own*
expected: *You were expected to arrive
much earlier than this*
meant: *Parties are meant to be fun*
obliged: *He is legally obliged to
declare his interests*
required: *Will I be required to come to
every meeting?*

2 generally believed or thought to
be the case: *What is his son supposed
to have said?*
alleged: *The accused is alleged to
have killed a man*
assumed: *As usual, the mistakes
were assumed to be my fault*
believed: *He is believed to have
died in 1117*
meant: *They are meant to be one of
the top teams in the world*
presumed: *This area is presumed
to be safe*
reputed: *The monster is reputed to
live in the deep waters of a Scottish
loch*
rumoured: *They are rumoured to be
on the verge of splitting up*

supposition see **theory**

suppress verb **1** to prevent people
from doing something: *international
attempts to suppress drug trafficking*
crush: *a plan to crush the uprising*
quash: *It may help to quash these
rumours*
quell: *The army moved in to quell
the uprising*
stamp out: *steps to stamp out*

bullying in schools
stop: *measures to stop the trade in ivory*
2 to stop yourself from expressing a feeling or reaction: *She barely suppressed a gasp*
conceal: *Robert could not conceal his relief*
contain: *He could hardly contain his rage*
curb: *He curbed his temper*
repress: *people who repress their emotions*
restrain: *unable to restrain her anger*
smother: *I smothered a chuckle*
stifle: *Miller stifled a yawn and looked at his watch*
see also **curb, silence**

suppressed see **pent-up**
suppression see **ban**
supremacy see **control, power**
supreme *adjective* of the highest degree or rank: *They conspired to seize supreme power*
chief: *his chief rival*
foremost: *the world's foremost scientists*
greatest: *the city's greatest soccer idol*
highest: *the highest academic achievement*
leading: *the world's leading basketball players*
paramount: *a factor of paramount importance*
pre-eminent: *a pre-eminent political figure*
principal: *the principal reason*
top: *the president's top military advisers*
ultimate: *the ultimate international accolade, the Nobel Prize*
see also **absolute, ideal, incomparable, ultimate**

sure *adjective* **1** having no doubts: *She was no longer sure how she felt*

about him
certain: *certain of getting a place on the team*
clear: *He is not clear on how he will go about it*
convinced: *He is convinced it's your fault*
definite: *a definite answer*
positive: *I'm positive it will happen*
satisfied: *We must be satisfied that the treatment is safe*
2 reliable or definite: *a sure sign that something is wrong*
definite: *a definite advantage*
dependable: *dependable information*
foolproof: *a foolproof system*
infallible: *an infallible eye for detail*
reliable: *a reliable source*
trustworthy: *trustworthy reports*
undeniable: *a sad but undeniable fact*
see also **certain, confident, positive, reliable, yes**

surface see **appear, face, finish, outside**
surfeit see **excess**
surge see **burst, jump, rage, wave**
surly see **grumpy**
surmise see **conclude, theory**
surmount see **overcome**
surpass see **outdo, pass, top**
surpassing see **superior**
surplus see **excess, profit, rest, spare**
surprise *noun* **1** something unexpected: *The resignation came as a complete surprise*
bombshell: *His departure was a bombshell for the team*
jolt: *Henderson was jolted by the news*
revelation: *Degas's work had been a revelation to her*
shock: *I got a shock when I saw her*
start: *You gave me quite a start*
2 the feeling caused by something unexpected: *an exclamation of*

surprise
amazement: He stared in baffled amazement
astonishment: "What?" Meg asked in astonishment
incredulity: The announcement has been met with incredulity
wonder: Cross shook his head in wonder
▷ verb **3** to give someone a feeling of surprise: I was surprised by the vehemence of his criticism
amaze: Most of the cast were amazed by the play's success
astonish: I was astonished to discover his true age
astound: He was astounded at the result
stagger: I was staggered by his reaction
stun: Audiences were stunned by the film's tragic end
take aback: Derek was taken aback when a man answered the phone
see also **amaze, amazement**
surprising see **amazing, extraordinary, unexpected**
surrender verb **1** to agree that the other side has won: We'll never surrender to the terrorists
capitulate: They had no choice but to capitulate
give in: She gave in to him on everything
submit: I refuse to submit to their demands
succumb: The Minister said his country would never succumb to pressure
yield: The government had to yield to local opinion
2 to give something up to someone else: We have surrendered our political authority for economic gain
cede: After the war, Spain ceded the island to America

give up: She is loath to give up her hard-earned liberty
relinquish: He does not intend to relinquish power
renounce: He renounced his claim to the throne
yield: He was obliged to yield territory to France
▷ noun **3** a situation in which one side gives in to the other: unconditional surrender
capitulation: the German capitulation at the end of the First World War
submission: The army intends to starve the city into submission
see also **give in, sacrifice, submit**
surrogate see **replacement, substitute**
surround verb to be all around a person or thing: He was surrounded by bodyguards
encircle: A forty-feet-high concrete wall encircles the jail
enclose: The land was enclosed by a fence
encompass: the largest lake in Canada wholly encompassed by a town
envelop: The rich smell of the forest enveloped us
hem in: a valley hemmed in by mountains
see also **enclose**
surrounded by see **among**
surroundings plural noun the area and environment around a person or place: He felt a longing for familiar surroundings
background: a fitting background for her beauty
environment: a safe environment for marine mammals
location: filmed in an exotic location
neighbourhood: living in an affluent neighbourhood
setting: Rome is the perfect setting

for romance
see also **scenery**

surveillance see **watch**

survey see **inspect, measure, observe, review**

survive verb to live or exist in spite of difficulties: *companies which survived after the recession*

endure: *Somehow their friendship endures*

last: *Nothing lasts forever*

live: *having lived through the 1930s depression*

outlive: *They have outlived the horror of the war*

pull through: *He should pull through okay*

see also **continue, endure, last, remain**

susceptible see **impressionable, prone, vulnerable**

suspect verb 1 to think something is likely: *I suspect they are secretly planning to raise taxes*

believe: *Police believe the attacks were carried out by nationalists*

feel: *I somehow feel he was involved*

guess: *As you probably guessed, I don't like him much*

suppose: *The problem is more complex than he supposes*

2 to have doubts about something: *He suspected her motives*

distrust: *I don't have any particular reason to distrust them*

doubt: *Do you doubt my word?*

mistrust: *He mistrusts all journalists*
▷ adjective 3 not to be trusted: *a rather suspect holy man*

dodgy British, Australian, New Zealand informal: *a dodgy car dealer*

doubtful: *These details are of doubtful origin*

dubious: *dubious practices*

fishy informal: *There's something very fishy about it*

questionable: *the questionable motives of politicians*

see also **dubious, guess, imagine, question, suspicious**

suspend see **cease, delay, hang, interrupt**

suspicion noun 1 a feeling of mistrust: *I was always regarded with suspicion because of my background*

distrust: *an instinctive distrust of authority*

doubt: *I have my doubts about his ability to govern*

misgiving: *His first words filled us with misgiving*

mistrust: *a deep mistrust of banks*

scepticism: *The report was greeted with scepticism*

2 a feeling that something is true: *I have a strong suspicion they are lying*

hunch: *Lowe had a hunch he was on to something*

idea: *I had an idea that he joined the army later*

impression: *I get the impression he's hiding something*

see also **idea, trace**

suspicious adjective 1 feeling distrustful of someone or something: *He was rightly suspicious of their motives*

apprehensive: *She was apprehensive of strangers*

distrustful: *Voters are deeply distrustful of all politicians*

doubtful: *At first I was doubtful about their authenticity*

sceptical: *Other archaeologists are sceptical about his findings*

wary: *Many people are wary of lawyers*

2 causing feelings of distrust: *suspicious circumstances*

dodgy British, Australian, New Zealand informal: *He was a bit of a dodgy character*

doubtful: *selling something of doubtful quality*
dubious: *This claim seems to us rather dubious*
fishy *informal*: *There's something fishy going on here*
funny: *There's something funny about him*
questionable: *there was something questionable about his behaviour*
shady *informal*: *shady deals*
suspect: *The whole affair has been highly suspect*
see also **dubious, wary**
sustain *see* **have, receive, suffer**
sustained *see* **relentless**
swab *see* **clean**
swag *see* **loot**
swaggering *see* **boastful**
swallow *see* **believe**
swamp *see* **flood**
swap *verb* to replace one thing for another: *Some hostages were swapped for convicted prisoners*
barter: *bartering wheat for cotton and timber*
exchange: *exchanging one set of problems for another*
interchange: *Meat can be interchanged with pulses as a source of protein*
switch: *They switched the tags on the cables*
trade: *They traded land for goods and money*
see also **change, exchange, substitute**
swarm *see* **crawl, crowd**
swarthy *see* **dark**
sway *see* **hold, influence, persuade**
sweep *see* **blow, flourish, stretch**
sweep away *see* **wash**
sweeping *see* **broad, extensive**
sweet *adjective* **1** containing a lot of sugar: *a mug of sweet tea*
  cloying: *a cloying apricot chutney*

sugary: *a sugary meringue pie*
sweetened: *sweetened shortcrust pastry*
2 having a pleasant smell: *the sweet smell of roses*
aromatic: *a plant with aromatic leaves*
fragrant: *fragrant clover*
perfumed: *perfumed soaps*
sweet-smelling: *cottage gardens filled with sweet-smelling flowers and herbs*
3 pleasant-sounding and tuneful: *the sweet sounds of children's singing*
harmonious: *harmonious sounds*
mellow: *mellow background music*
melodious: *The melodious tones of the organ echoed around the great cathedral*
musical: *He had a soft, musical voice*
tuneful: *The band were noted for their tuneful backing vocals*
▷ *noun* **4** a sweet-tasting thing such as a toffee: *His sack was full of packets of sweets*
candy *American*: *We were sick after eating some syrupy candies she had made*
confectionery: *The company specializes in selling confectionery from all over the world*
lolly *Australian, New Zealand*: *avoid feeding him too many lollies*
sweetie: *She presented him with a jar of his favourite sweeties as a thank-you*
see also **lovable**
sweetened *see* **sweet**
sweetie *see* **sweet**
sweet-smelling *see* **fragrant, sweet**
swell *see* **bulge, expand, increase, wave**
swelling *see* **boil, bulge, bump, lump**
swerve *verb* to change direction suddenly to avoid hitting something: *He swerved to avoid*

a truck
swing: *The car swung off the road*
turn: *He turned sharply to the left*
veer: *The vehicle veered out of control*
see also **curve, dodge**

swift *adjective* happening or moving very quickly: *make a swift decision*
brisk: *walking at a brisk pace*
express: *a special express service*
fast: *The question is how fast the process will be*
hurried: *a hurried breakfast*
prompt: *Prompt action is needed*
quick: *The country has been developing at a very quick pace*
rapid: *Will the Tunnel provide more rapid transport than ferries?*
speedy: *We wish Bill a speedy recovery*
see also **brief, fast, hasty, prompt, quick, sudden**

swiftly *see* **fast, quickly**
swiftness *see* **speed**
swig *see* **drink**
swindle *see* **cheat, con, rob**
swindler *see* **crook**
swine *see* **pig**
swing *see* **swerve**
swipe *see* **steal**
switch *see* **exchange, substitute, swap**
swivel *see* **turn**
swoon *see* **faint**
swot *see* **study**
swotting *see* **study**

symbol *noun* a design or idea used to represent something: *the chemical symbol for mercury*
emblem: *His badge bore a small yellow hammer-and-sickle emblem*
figure: *the figure of a five-pointed star*
logo: *the company's logo*
mark: *a mark of identification*
representation: *This rune is a representation of a spearhead*
sign: *a multiplication sign*

token: *He gave her a ring as a token of his love*
see also **sign**

symbolize *see* **represent**
symmetry *see* **order**
sympathetic *see* **compassionate, favourable, sorry, understanding**
sympathize with *see* **pity**

sympathy *noun* kindness and understanding towards someone in trouble: *My heartfelt sympathy goes out to all the relatives*
compassion: *I was impressed by the compassion he showed for a helpless old woman*
empathy: *They displayed an admirable understanding of the crime and empathy with the victim*
pity: *He showed no pity for his victims*
understanding: *I'd like to thank you for your patience and understanding*
see also **pity**

symptom *see* **sign**
syndicate *see* **association, ring**
synopsis *see* **outline, summary**

system *noun* **1** an organized way of doing or arranging something: *the advantages of the new system over the old one*
arrangement: *an intricate arrangement of treadles, rods and cranks*
method: *the methods employed in the study*
procedure: *This is now the standard procedure*
routine: *his daily routine*
structure: *the structure of local government*
technique: *a new technique for processing sound*
see also **plan, procedure, process, routine**

table see **submit**

taciturn see **silent**

tackle see **equipment, stuff**

tacky see **flashy, gaudy, sticky, tasteless**

tact noun the ability not to offend people: *He has handled the affair with great tact*
  delicacy: *Both countries are behaving with rare delicacy*
  diplomacy: *It took all Minnelli's diplomacy to get him to return*
  discretion: *I appreciate your discretion*
  sensitivity: *The police treated the victims with great sensitivity*
  see also **consideration**

tactful adjective showing tact: *Sorry, that wasn't a very tactful question*
  diplomatic: *She is very direct. I tend to be more diplomatic*
  discreet: *They were gossip and not always discreet*
  sensitive: *his sensitive handling of the situation*

tactic see **manoeuvre**

tactless see **thoughtless**

tag see **label**

taint see **infect, pollute**

take verb **1** to require something: *He takes three hours to get ready*
  demand: *The task of rebuilding would demand much patience*
  require: *The race requires a lot of stamina*

2 to carry something: *I'll take these papers home and read them*
  bear formal: *They bore the hardwood box into the kitchen*
  bring: *He poured a brandy for Dena and brought it to her*
  carry: *She carried the shopping from the car*
  convey formal: *The minibus conveyed us to the city centre*
  ferry: *A plane arrives to ferry guests to the island*
  fetch: *Sylvia fetched a towel from the bathroom*
  transport: *They use tankers to transport the oil to Los Angeles*

3 to lead someone somewhere: *She took me to a Mexican restaurant*
  bring: *Come to my party and bring a girl with you*
  conduct formal: *He asked if he might conduct us to the ball*
  escort: *I escorted him to the door*
  guide: *a young Egyptologist who guided us through the tombs*
  lead: *She confessed to the killing and led police to his remains*
  usher: *I ushered him into the office*
  see also **accept, bear, bring, capture, carry, choose, demand, receive, select, steal**

take aback see **surprise**

take advantage of see **impose on, profit**

take after see **resemble**

take away see **remove, subtract**

take care of verb **1** to look after someone or something: *There was no-one to take care of the children*
  care for: *They hired a nurse to care for her*

look after: I love looking after the children

mind: Jim will mind the shop while I'm away

nurse: All the years he was sick, my mother had nursed him

protect: He vowed to protect her all the days of her life

tend: He tends the flower beds that he has planted

watch: Are parents expected to watch their children 24 hours a day?

2 to deal with a problem, task, or situation: "Do you need clean sheets?" "No, Mrs May took care of that."

attend to: We have business to attend to first

cope with: A new system has been designed to cope with the increased demand

deal with: the way that building societies deal with complaints

handle: She handled the president's travel arrangements during the campaign

manage: He expects me to manage all the household expenses on very little

see to: While Frank saw to the luggage, Sara took the children home
see also **deal, handle, look after, mind, process, tend, watch**

take down see **lower, write**

take for see **mistake**

take from see **subtract**

take in verb **1** to deceive someone: He was a real charmer who totally took me in

con informal: The British public has been conned by the government

deceive: He has deceived us all

dupe: Some offenders dupe the psychologists who assess them

fool: Art dealers fool a lot of people

mislead: It appears we were misled by a professional con artist

trick: He'll be upset when he finds out how you tricked him

2 to understand something: She seemed to take in all he said

absorb: It will take time for us to absorb the news

appreciate: She never really appreciated the bitterness of the conflict

assimilate: My mind could only assimilate one of these ideas at a time

comprehend: He failed to comprehend the significance of this remark

digest: They need time to digest the information they have learned

get: You just don't get what I'm saying, do you?

grasp: The Government has not yet grasped the seriousness of the crisis

understand: They are too young to understand what is going on
see also **absorb, admit, comprehend, deceive, grasp, involve, receive, trick, understand**

take into account see **consider**

take off see **remove**

take on see **assume, employ, play**

take out see **extract, remove, withdraw**

take over see **possess**

take over from see **replace, succeed**

take part see **participate, play**

take place see **come, happen, occur**

takeoff see **parody**

taking see **capture**

taking on see **employment**

takings see **income, profit**

tale see **story**

talent noun a natural ability: Both her children have a talent for music

ability: Her drama teacher spotted her ability

aptitude: Alan has no aptitude for music

capacity: people's creative capacities

flair: *a dentist with a flair for invention*
genius: *his genius for chess*
gift: *a gift for teaching*
knack: *He's got the knack of getting people to listen*
see also **ability, gift**
talented *see* **able, exceptional**
talk *verb* **1** to say things: *They were talking about American food*
▷ *noun* **2** a conversation: *We had a long talk about her father*
chat: *I had a chat with him*
chatter: *idle chatter*
conversation: *We had a long conversation*
3 an informal speech: *a talk about AIDS*
address: *an address to the American people*
discourse: *a lengthy discourse on strategy*
lecture: *a series of lectures*
sermon: *a church sermon*
speech: *He delivered his speech in French*
see also **chat, discussion, lecture, speech, word**
talk about *see* **discuss**
talk into *see* **coax, persuade**
talkative *adjective* talking a lot: *His eyes grew bright and he suddenly became very talkative.*
chatty: *She's quite a chatty person*
communicative: *She has become a lot more communicative*
long-winded: *I hope I'm not being too long-winded*
tall *adjective* higher than average: *tall buildings*
high: *a high wall*
lanky: *He was six foot four, all lanky and leggy*
lofty: *lofty ceilings*
soaring: *the soaring spires of churches like St Peter's*
towering: *towering cliffs of black granite*
tally *see* **agree, correspond, count, match**
tamper *see* **interfere**
tang *see* **taste**
tangible *see* **real**
tangle *noun* **1** a mass of long things knotted together: *a tangle of wires*
jumble: *a jumble of twisted wires*
knot: *Her hair was full of knots*
mass: *a flailing mass of arms and legs*
mat: *the thick mat of sandy hair on his chest*
muddle: *The back of the tapestry was a muddle of threads*
web: *a thick web of fibres*
▷ *verb* **2** to twist together or catch someone or something: *Dolphins can get tangled in fishing nets and drown*
catch: *a fly caught in a spider's web*
jumble: *The wires were all jumbled together and tied in a knot*
knot: *The kite strings had got knotted together*
twist: *Her hands began to twist the handles of the bag*
see also **muddle**
tangled *see* **complex**
target *see* **aim, focus, goal**
tariff *see* **duty, rate, tax**
tarry *see* **stay**
tart *see* **bitter, sour**
task *noun* a job that you have to do: *Walker had the task of breaking the bad news*
assignment: *written assignments and practical tests*
chore: *household chores*
duty: *I carried out my duties conscientiously*
job: *He was given the job of tending the fire*
mission: *Salisbury sent him on a diplomatic mission to North America*
undertaking: *Organizing the show*

has been a massive undertaking
see also **job, undertaking, work**

taste noun **1** the flavour of
something: I like the taste of wine
flavour: a crumbly texture with a
strong flavour
tang: the tang of lemon
2 a small amount of food or drink:
He swirled the brandy around before
taking another small taste
bite: Chew each mouthful fully before
the next bite
mouthful: She gulped down a
mouthful of coffee
sip: a sip of wine
3 a liking for something: a taste for
adventure
appetite: his appetite for success
fondness: I've always had a fondness
for jewels
liking: She had a liking for good
clothes
penchant formal: He had a penchant
for playing jokes on people
see also **style**

tasteless adjective **1** having little
flavour: The fish was mushy and
tasteless
bland: It tasted bland, like warmed
cardboard
insipid: a rather insipid meal
2 vulgar and unattractive: a house
crammed with tasteless ornaments
flashy: a flashy sports car
garish: garish bright red boots
gaudy: her gaudy floral hat
tacky informal: tacky holiday
souvenirs
tawdry: a tawdry seaside town
vulgar: a very vulgar house
see also **crude, flashy, vulgar**

tasty adjective having a pleasant
flavour: The food was very tasty
appetizing: a choice of appetizing
dishes
delicious: a wide selection of delicious

desserts
lekker South African slang: a lekker
meal
luscious: luscious fruit
palatable: some very palatable wines
see also **delicious, lekker**

tattered see worn-out

tattoo see parade

tatty see scruffy, shabby

taunt see make fun of, tease

taut see stiff, tense, tight

tavern see pub

tawdry see cheap, tasteless, vulgar

tax noun **1** money paid to the
government: the tax on new cars
duty: customs duties
excise: These products are excused
VAT and excise
levy formal: an annual motorway levy
on all drivers
tariff: America wants to eliminate
tariffs on items such as electronics
▷ verb **2** to make heavy demands on
someone: They must be told not to tax
your patience
drain: conflicts that drain your energy
exhaust: She has exhausted my
sympathy
sap: The illness sapped his strength
strain: The volume of flights is
straining the air traffic control system
stretch: The drought there is
stretching American resources to
their limits
see also **drain, duty, strain**

teach verb to instruct someone
how to do something: She taught
Julie to read
coach: He coached the basketball
team
drill: He drills the choir to a high
standard
educate: He was educated at
Haslingden Grammar School
instruct: He instructed family
members in nursing techniques

school: *He had been schooled to take over the family business*

train: *They train teachers in counselling skills*

tutor: *She was tutored at home by her parents*

see also **instruct, lecture, show, train**

teacher noun someone who teaches something: *a geography teacher*

coach: *her drama coach*

don: *a Cambridge don*

guru: *a religious guru*

instructor: *a driving instructor*

lecturer: *a lecturer in law*

master or **mistress**: *a retired maths master*

professor: *a professor of economics*

tutor: *He surprised his tutors by failing the exam*

see also **master**

team noun **1** a group of people: *the football team*

band: *a band of rebels*

crew: *the ship's crew*

gang: *a gang of workmen*

group: *The students work in groups*

side: *Italy were definitely the better side*

squad: *the England under-21 squad*

troupe: *troupes of travelling actors*

▷ verb **2** to work together: *A friend suggested that we team up for a working holiday*

collaborate: *The two men met and agreed to collaborate*

cooperate: *They would cooperate in raising their child*

join forces: *The groups joined forces to fight against the ban*

link up: *the first time the two armies have linked up*

pair up: *Men and teenage girls pair up to dance*

unite: *The two parties have been trying to unite*

work together: *We have always wanted to work together*

see also **party, side, staff**

team-mate see **partner**

tear noun **1** a hole in something: *I peered through a tear in the curtains*

hole: *the hole in my shoe*

ladder: *There was a ladder in her tights*

rip: *the rip in her new dress*

rupture: *a rupture in the valve*

scratch: *I pointed to a number of scratches in the tile floor*

split: *the split in his trousers*

▷ verb **2** to make a hole in something: *She nearly tore my overcoat*

ladder: *after she laddered her tights*

rip: *I tried not to rip the paper*

rupture: *a ruptured appendix*

scratch: *Knives will scratch the worktop*

shred: *They may be shredding documents*

split: *I'd split my trousers*

3 to go somewhere in a hurry: *He tore through busy streets in a high-speed chase*

charge: *He charged through the door*

dart: *Ingrid darted across the deserted street*

dash: *He dashed upstairs*

fly: *She flew to their bedsides when they were ill*

race: *He raced across town*

shoot: *Another car shot out of a junction*

speed: *A low shot sped past Lukic*

zoom: *We zoomed through the gallery*

see also **dash, fly, hole, race, speed, split**

tease verb to make fun of someone: *He used to tease me about wanting to act*

make fun of: *The kids at school made fun of me and my Cockney accent*

mock: *Don't mock me!*
needle *informal*: *He used to enjoy needling people*
taunt: *Other youths taunted him about his clothes*
see also **bully, joke, pick on, provoke**
technique see **method, style, system, way**
tedious see **boring, dreary, dull**
tedium see **boredom**
teem see **crawl, rain**
tell *verb* **1** to let someone know something: *They told us the dreadful news*
inform: *My daughter informed me that she was pregnant*
notify: *We have notified the police*
2 to give someone an order: *A passer-by told the driver to move his car*
command: *He commanded his troops to attack*
direct *formal*: *They have been directed to give special attention to the problem*
instruct: *The family has instructed solicitors to sue the company*
order: *He ordered his men to cease firing*
3 to judge something correctly: *I could tell he was scared*
discern: *It was hard to discern why this was happening*
see: *I could see she was lonely*
see also **announce, distinguish, inform, instruct, notify**
tell a lie see **lie**
tell apart see **distinguish**
tell off see **scold**
tell on see **inform on**
tell the difference see **distinguish**
telling see **convincing, powerful**
temper see **humour, moderate, mood**
temperament see **character**
temperamental see **moody**
temperate see **mild**

template see **pattern**
tempo see **rate, rhythm**
temporary *adjective* lasting a short time: *a temporary loss of memory*
ephemeral: *a reminder that earthly pleasures are ephemeral*
fleeting: *a fleeting glimpse*
interim: *an interim measure*
momentary: *a momentary lapse*
passing: *a passing phase*
provisional: *a provisional coalition government*
transient: *Modelling is a transient career*
transitory: *the transitory nature of political success*
tempt *verb* to persuade someone to do something: *Children not attending schools may be tempted into crime*
entice: *She resisted attempts to entice her into politics*
lure: *The company aims to lure smokers back to cigarettes*
seduce: *We are seduced into buying all these items*
see also **attract, lure**
temptation see **bait, lure**
tenacious see **determined, stubborn**
tenacity see **determination, resolve**
tend *verb* **1** to happen usually or often: *I tend to forget things*
be apt: *She was apt to raise her voice*
be inclined: *He was inclined to self-pity*
be liable: *equipment that is liable to break*
be prone: *We know males are more prone to violence*
have a tendency: *Shetland jumpers have a tendency to be annoyingly itchy*
2 to look after someone or something: *the way we tend our cattle*
care for: *They hired a nurse to care for her*

look after: I love looking after the children
nurse: In hospital they nursed me back to health
take care of: There was no one else to take care of the animals
see also **look after, take care of**

tendency *noun* behaviour that happens very often: *a tendency to be critical*
inclination: *his artistic inclinations*
leaning: *their socialist leanings*
propensity: *his propensity for violence*

tender *adjective* **1** showing gentle and caring feelings: *tender, loving care*
affectionate: *She gave him an affectionate smile*
caring: *He is a lovely boy, and very caring*
compassionate: *a deeply compassionate film*
gentle: *Michael's voice was gentle and consoling*
kind: *She is warmhearted and kind to everyone and everything*
loving: *He was a most loving husband and father*
sensitive: *He was always so sensitive*
warm: *She was a very warm person*
2 painful and sore: *My tummy felt very tender*
aching: *The weary holidaymakers soothed their aching feet in the sea*
bruised: *bruised legs*
inflamed: *Her eyes were inflamed*
painful: *Her glands were swollen and painful*
raw: *the drag of the rope against the raw flesh of my shoulders*
sensitive: *Ouch! I'm sorry, my lip is still a bit sensitive*
sore: *My chest is still sore from the surgery*
▷ *verb* **3** to offer something such

as an apology or resignation: *She tendered her resignation*
hand in: *All the opposition members have handed in their resignation*
offer: *May I offer my sincere condolences?*
▷ *noun* **4** a proposal to provide something at a price: *Builders will be asked to submit a tender for the work*
bid: *Sydney's successful bid for the 2000 Olympic Games*
estimate: *The firm is preparing an estimate for the work*
package: *We opted for the package submitted by the existing service provider*
submission: *A written submission has to be prepared*
see also **affectionate, compassionate, gentle, loving, offer, painful, romantic, sore, submit**

tenet see **belief**

tense *adjective* **1** nervous and unable to relax: *Never had she seen him so tense*
anxious: *She had become very anxious and alarmed*
edgy: *She was nervous and edgy, still chain-smoking*
jittery *informal*: *Investors have become jittery about the country's economy*
jumpy: *I told myself not to be so jumpy*
nervous: *It has made me very nervous about going out*
uptight *informal*: *Penny never got uptight about exams*
2 causing anxiety: *the tense atmosphere at the talks*
anxious: *They had to wait ten anxious days*
nerve-racking: *It was more nerve-racking than taking a World Cup penalty*

stressful: *a stressful job*
3 having tight muscles: *She lay, eyes shut, body tense*
rigid: *Andrew went rigid whenever he saw a dog*
strained: *His shoulders were strained with effort*
taut: *when muscles are taut or cold*
tight: *It is better to stretch the tight muscles first*
see also **nervous, tight**
tension see **strain, stress**
tentative see **cautious**
tenure see **possession**
tepid see **warm**
term *noun* **1** a fixed period of time: *a 12 month term of service*
period: *for a limited period only*
session: *The parliamentary session ends on October 4th*
spell: *a six-month spell of practical experience*
stretch: *He did an 18-month stretch in prison*
time: *He served the time of his contract and then left the company*
2 a name or word for a particular thing: *the medical term for a heart attack*
designation: *Level Four Alert is a designation reserved for very serious incidents*
expression: *She used some remarkably coarse expressions*
name: *The correct name for this condition is bovine spongiform encephalopathy*
word: *The word ginseng comes from the Chinese "Shen-seng"*
see also **expression, length, name, period, stretch**
terminal see **fatal**
terminate see **end, halt**
termination see **conclusion**
termination of employment see **the sack**

terms *plural noun* conditions that have been agreed: *the terms of the merger agreement*
conditions: *They may be breaching the conditions of their contract*
provisions: *the provisions of the Amsterdam treaty*
proviso: *He left me the house with the proviso that it had to stay in the family*
stipulations: *He left, violating the stipulations of his parole*
see also **condition**
terrain see **ground, scenery**
terrible *adjective* **1** serious and unpleasant: *a terrible illness*
appalling: *an appalling headache*
awful: *an awful crime*
desperate: *a desperate situation*
dreadful: *a dreadful mistake*
frightful *old-fashioned*: *He got himself into a frightful muddle*
horrendous: *horrendous injuries*
horrible: *a horrible mess*
horrid *old-fashioned*: *What a horrid smell!*
rotten: *What rotten luck!*
2 of very poor quality: *Paddy's terrible haircut*
abysmal: *The standard of play was abysmal*
appalling: *Her singing is appalling*
awful: *Jeans look awful on me*
dire: *Most of the poems were dire*
dreadful: *My financial situation is dreadful*
horrible: *a horrible meal*
rotten: *I think it's a rotten idea*
see also **awful, dreadful, severe**
terribly see **really, very**
terrific see **grand**
terrified see **frightened**
terrify see **frighten, scare**
terrifying see **frightening, horrible, scary**
territory *noun* the land that a person or country controls: *gangs*

fighting to defend their territories

area: They claim that the entire area belongs to Syria

country: He is an ambassador to a foreign country

district: Stick to your own district and stay out of ours

domain: He surveyed his domain from the roof of the castle

dominion: men who ruled their dominions with ruthless efficiency

land: New mines were discovered on what had been Apache land

province: debates about the political future of their province

state: This state remains suspended from the Commonwealth

see also **colony, field, habitat, land, region**

terror see **fear, horror, panic**

terrorism see **violence**

terrorize see **frighten, scare**

terse see **abrupt, concise, short**

test verb 1 to find out what something is like: travelling to Holland to test a British-built boat

assess: The test was to assess aptitude rather than academic achievement

check: It's worth checking each item for obvious flaws

try: Howard wanted me to try the wine

try out: London Transport hopes to try out the system in September

▷ noun 2 an attempt to test something: the banning of nuclear tests

assessment: He was remanded for assessment by doctors

check: regular checks on his blood pressure

trial: clinical trials

see also **check, exam, examine, try**

testimony see **declaration, proof, statement, tribute**

tether see **tie**

textbook see **book**

textiles see **cloth**

texture noun the way that something feels: Her skin is pale, the texture of fine wax

consistency: Mix the dough to the right consistency

feel: Linen raincoats have a crisp, papery feel

see also **finish**

thankful see **grateful**

thanks see **credit, gratitude**

thanks to see **by virtue of**

thaw see **melt, warm**

theatrical see **melodramatic**

theft noun the crime of stealing: the theft of classified documents

robbery: The man was serving a sentence for robbery

stealing: She was jailed for six months for stealing

thieving: an ex-con who says he's given up thieving

theme see **message, subject**

theological see **religious**

theory noun an idea that explains something: Darwin's theory of evolution

conjecture: That is a conjecture, not a fact

hypothesis: Different hypotheses have been put forward

supposition: As with many such suppositions, no one had ever tested it

surmise formal: His surmise proved correct

there see **present**

therefore adverb as a result: Muscles need lots of fuel and therefore burn lots of calories

as a result: I slept in, and, as a result, I was late for work

consequently: He's more experienced, and consequently earns a higher salary

for that reason: I'd never met my in-laws before. For that reason, I was a little nervous

hence formal: These products are all natural, and hence, better for you

so: I was worried about her, so I phoned to check how she was

thus: His men were getting tired, and thus, careless

thick adjective 1 measuring a large distance from side to side: a thick stone wall

fat: a fat book

wide: a desk that was almost as wide as the room

2 containing little water: thick soup

clotted: clotted cream

concentrated: a glass of concentrated orange juice

condensed: tins of condensed milk

3 grouped closely together: thick dark hair

bristling: a bristling moustache

dense: a large dense forest

lush: the lush green meadows

luxuriant: the luxuriant foliage of Young Island

see also **broad, dim, dumb, slow, stupid**

thicken verb to become thicker: The clouds thickened

clot: The patient's blood refused to clot

condense: Water vapour condenses to form clouds

congeal: The blood had started to congeal

set: as the jelly starts to set

thief noun someone who steals something: a car thief

burglar: Burglars broke into their home

crook informal: a petty crook

mugger informal: after being threatened by a mugger

pickpocket: a gang of pickpockets

robber: armed robbers

shoplifter: a persistent shoplifter

see also **crook**

thieving see **theft**

thin adjective 1 measuring a small distance from side to side: The material was too thin

fine: the fine hairs on her arms

narrow: a narrow strip of land

slim: a slim volume of verse

2 not carrying a lot of fat: a tall, thin man with grey hair

see **word studies thin**

3 containing a lot of water: thin soup

dilute or **diluted**: a dilute solution of bleach

runny: a runny soft cheese

watery: watery beer

weak: a cup of weak tea

see also **narrow, sheer, skinny**

thing noun a physical object: What's that thing doing here?

article: household articles

object: everyday objects such as wooden spoons

see also **article, complex, item, object, obsession**

things plural noun someone's clothes or belongings: Sara told him to take all his things with him

belongings: He was identified only by his personal belongings

effects: His daughters were collecting his effects

gear: They helped us put our gear back into the van

possessions: People had lost all their possessions

stuff: Where have you put all your stuff?

see also **possessions, stuff**

think verb 1 to consider something: Let's think what we can do next

consider: The government is being asked to consider the plan

contemplate: He cried as he contemplated his future

deliberate: She deliberated over the decision for a good few years

meditate: He meditated on the problem

mull over: I'll leave you alone so you can mull it over

muse literary: Many of the papers muse on the fate of the President

ponder: I'm continually pondering how to improve the team

reflect: I reflected on the child's future

2 to believe something: I think she has a secret boyfriend

believe: Experts believe that the drought will be extensive

consider: He considers that this is the worst recession this century

deem formal: Many people have ideas that their society deems to be dangerous

hold: The theory holds that minor events are the trigger for larger events

imagine: I imagine he was just showing off

judge: He judged that this was the moment to say what had to be said

reckon: Toni reckoned that it must be about three o'clock

see also **assume, consider, expect, feel, guess, ponder, reckon, suppose**

think about see **consider, contemplate**

think of see **contemplate, regard**

thinking see **thought**

thin-skinned see **sensitive**

thirst see **longing, wish**

thorough adjective careful and complete: a thorough examination

complete: a complete overhaul of the engine

comprehensive: a comprehensive guide to the region

exhaustive: exhaustive enquiries

full: Mr Primakov gave a full account of his meeting with the President

intensive: four weeks of intensive study

meticulous: A happy wedding day requires meticulous planning

painstaking: a painstaking search

scrupulous: Observe scrupulous hygiene when preparing and cooking food

see also **absolute, careful, complete, full, utter**

thoroughly see **well**

though see **but, in spite of**

thought noun **1** an idea or opinion: his thoughts on love

idea: his ideas about democracy

notion: We each have a notion of what kind of person we'd like to be

opinion: most of those who expressed an opinion

view: Make your views known to your MP

2 the activity of thinking: After much thought I decided to end my marriage

consideration: There should be careful consideration of the BBC's future role

contemplation: He was lost in contemplation of the landscape

deliberation: the result of lengthy deliberation

meditation: He stared at the floor, lost in meditation

reflection: after days of reflection

thinking: This is definitely a time for decisive action and quick thinking

see also **consideration**

thoughtful adjective **1** quiet and serious: He was looking very thoughtful

contemplative: a quiet, contemplative sort of chap

pensive: He looked unusually pensive before the start

reflective: I walked on in a reflective mood

2 showing consideration for others:

thoughtless | 534

a thoughtful and caring man

attentive: an attentive husband

caring: a caring son

considerate: the most considerate man I've ever known

kind: She is warmhearted and kind to everyone

see also **humane, kind**

thoughtless adjective showing a lack of consideration: It was thoughtless of her to mention it

insensitive: My husband is very insensitive about my problem

tactless: a tactless remark

see also **irresponsible, unkind**

thrash see **beat**

threadbare see **shabby, worn-out**

threat noun **1** a statement that someone will harm you: death threats

menace: demanding money with menaces

threatening remark: He was overheard making threatening remarks to the couple

2 something that seems likely to harm you: the threat of tropical storms

hazard: a health hazard

menace: a menace to the public

risk: a fire risk

see also **danger**

threaten verb **1** to promise to do something bad: He threatened her with a knife

make threats to: despite all the threats he'd made to harm her

menace: She's being menaced by her sister's latest boyfriend

2 to be likely to cause harm: The newcomers threaten the livelihood of the workers

endanger: Toxic waste could endanger lives

jeopardize: He has jeopardized the future of his government

put at risk: If they have the virus, they are putting patients at risk

put in jeopardy: A series of setbacks have put the whole project in jeopardy

see also **endanger**

threatening see **ominous, sinister**

threatening remark see **threat**

thrift see **economy**

thrifty adjective careful not to waste money or resources: Britain become a nation of thrifty consumers and bargain hunters

careful: He's very careful with his money

economical: a very economical way to travel

frugal: a frugal lifestyle

prudent: the need for a much more prudent use of energy

see also **economical**

thrill noun **1** a feeling of excitement: the thrill of waking up on Christmas morning

high informal: the high of a win over New Zealand

kick informal: I got a kick out of seeing my name in print

▷ verb **2** to cause a feeling of excitement: It thrilled me to see her looking so happy

excite: I only take on work that excites me

give a kick informal: It gave me a kick to actually meet her

see also **delight, excite, excitement**

thrilled see **excited**

thrilling see **exciting**

thrive verb to be successful: His company continues to thrive

do well: Connie did well at school

flourish: Racism and crime still flourish in the ghetto

prosper: His team have always prospered in cup competitions

see also **flourish, succeed**

thriving see **successful**

throng see crowd, jam, mass

throw verb to make something move through the air: *throwing a tennis ball against a wall*
  cast: *He cast the stone away*
  chuck informal: *I chucked the paper in the bin*
  fling: *Peter flung his shoes into the corner*
  hurl: *Groups of angry youths hurled stones at police*
  lob: *Thugs lobbed a grenade into the crowd*
  pitch: *Simon pitched the empty bottle into the lake*
  sling: *He took off his anorak and slung it into the back seat*
  toss: *She tossed her suitcase onto one of the beds*

throw about see scatter

throw away see discard, dispose of, dump, waste

throw out see discard, dump

throw up see puke

thrust see dig, drive, push, stick, stuff

thud see bump

thug noun a very violent person: *a gang of armed thugs*
  bandit: *terrorist acts carried out by bandits*
  hooligan: *severe measures against soccer hooligans*
  tough: *The neighbourhood toughs beat them both up*
  tsotsi South African: *Many are too terrified of local tsotsis to protest*

thump see bang, blow, bump

thunderous see loud

thus see therefore

thwart see block, dash, foil, frustrate, prevent

tick off see caution, scold

ticket see label, pass

ticking-off see lecture

tide see current, flow

tidings see news

tidy adjective **1** arranged in an orderly way: *a tidy desk*
  neat: *She put her clothes in a neat pile*
  orderly: *a beautiful, clean and orderly city*
  ▷ verb **2** to make something neat: *He tidied his garage*
  spruce up: *Many buildings have been spruced up*
  straighten: *straightening cushions and organizing magazines*
  see also **neat, orderly**

tie verb **1** to fasten something: *They tied the ends of the bag securely*
  bind: *Bind the ends of the cord together with thread*
  fasten: *instructions on how to fasten the strap to the box*
  knot: *He knotted the laces securely together*
  lash: *The shelter is built by lashing poles together*
  rope: *I roped myself to the chimney*
  secure: *He secured the canvas straps as tight as they would go*
  tether: *tethering his horse to a tree*
  truss: *She trussed him quickly with stolen bandage*
  2 to have the same score: *Rafferty tied with Nobilo*
  be level: *At the end of 90 minutes the teams were level*
  draw: *Holland and Ireland drew 1–1*
  ▷ noun **3** a connection with something: *I had very close ties with the family*
  affiliation: *They asked her what her political affiliations were*
  affinity: *He has a close affinity with the landscape*
  bond: *The experience created a special bond between us*
  connection: *The police say he had no connection with the security forces*
  relationship: *family relationships*

see also **association, attach, bond, fasten, join, link**

tie up *see* **secure**

tiff *see* **disagreement, squabble**

tight *adjective* **1** fitting closely: *The shoes are too tight*
  constricted: *His throat began to feel swollen and constricted*
  cramped: *families living in cramped conditions*
  snug: *a snug black T-shirt*
  2 firmly fastened: *a tight knot*
  firm: *He managed to get a firm grip of it*
  secure: *Check joints are secure and the wood is sound*
  3 not slack or relaxed: *Pull the elastic tight*
  rigid: *I went rigid with shock*
  taut: *The clothes line is pulled taut and secured*
  tense: *A bath can relax tense muscles*
  see also **mean, secure, tense**

tight spot *see* **hole, predicament**

tightly *see* **fast**

till *see* **dig**

tilt *verb* **1** to raise one end of something: *Leonard tilted his chair back on two legs*
  incline: *Jack inclined his head*
  lean: *Lean the plants against a wall*
  slant: *The floor slanted down to the window*
  slope: *The bank sloped down sharply to the river*
  tip: *She had to tip her head back to see him*
  ▷ *noun* **2** a raised position: *the tilt of the earth's axis*
  angle: *The boat is now leaning at a 30 degree angle*
  gradient: *a gradient of 1 in 3*
  incline: *at the edge of a steep incline*
  slant: *The house is on a slant*
  slope: *The street must have been on a slope*

time *noun* **1** a particular period: *I enjoyed my time in Durham*
  interval: *a long interval of silence*
  period: *a period of calm*
  spell: *a brief spell teaching*
  stretch: *an 18-month stretch in the army*
  while: *They walked on in silence for a while*
  ▷ *verb* **2** to plan when something will happen: *We had timed our visit for March 7*
  schedule: *The space shuttle had been scheduled to blast off at 04:38*
  set: *A court hearing has been set for December 16*
  see also **beat, chance, life, moment, occasion, period, rhythm, space, stretch, term**

time off *see* **holiday, leave, leisure**

timely *see* **lucky**

timetable *see* **programme**

timid *adjective* lacking courage or confidence: *a timid child*
  bashful: *Offstage, he is bashful and awkward*
  cowardly: *I was too cowardly to complain*
  diffident: *Helen was diffident and reserved*
  nervous: *a very nervous woman*
  shy: *a shy, quiet-spoken girl*
  see also **meek, shy**

tinge *see* **trace**

tint *see* **colour**

tiny *adjective* very small: *The living room is tiny*
  diminutive: *a diminutive figure standing at the entrance*
  microscopic: *a microscopic amount of the substance*
  miniature: *He looked like a miniature version of his brother*
  minute: *Only a minute amount is needed*
  negligible: *The pay that the soldiers*

received was negligible
wee *Scottish: a wee boy*
see also **minute**

tip see **hint, point, tilt**
tip over see **overturn**
tipple see **drink**
tipsy see **drunk**
tiptoe see **steal**
tire *verb* to use a lot of energy: *If driving tires you, take the train*
drain: *My emotional turmoil had drained me*
exhaust: *Walking in deep snow had totally exhausted him*
fatigue: *He is easily fatigued*
see also **wear out**
tire out see **exhaust**
tired *adjective* having little energy: *She was too tired to take a shower*
drained: *as United stalked off, stunned and drained*
drowsy: *He felt pleasantly drowsy*
exhausted: *She was too exhausted and distressed to talk*
fatigued: *Winter weather can leave you feeling fatigued*
sleepy: *I was beginning to feel sleepy*
tuckered out *Australian, New Zealand informal: You must be tuckered out after that bus trip*
weary: *a weary traveller*
worn out: *He's just worn out after the drive*
see also **sick of, bored, hackneyed, weary, worn-out**
tireless see **energetic, industrious**
tiresome see **boring**
titillate see **excite**
title see **book, name**
title holder see **champion**
titter see **laugh**
toast see **cook**
today's see **current**
toddler see **child**
to-do see **fuss**
toey see **nervous, touchy**

together *adverb* **1** with other people: *We went on long bicycle rides together*
collectively: *The Cabinet is collectively responsible for policy*
en masse: *The people marched en masse*
in unison: *Michael and the landlady nodded in unison*
jointly: *an agency jointly run by New York and New Jersey*
shoulder to shoulder: *They could fight shoulder to shoulder against a common enemy*
side by side: *areas where different nationalities live side by side*
2 at the same time: *Three horses crossed the finish line together*
as one: *The 40,000 crowd rose as one*
at once: *You can't do two things at once*
concurrently: *There were three races running concurrently*
simultaneously: *The two guns fired almost simultaneously*
with one accord: *They turned and walked back*
toil see **labour, struggle, work**
token see **sign, symbol**
tolerable *adjective* **1** able to be tolerated: *The pain was tolerable*
acceptable: *a mutually acceptable new contract*
bearable: *A cool breeze made the heat bearable*
2 fairly satisfactory: *a tolerable salary*
acceptable: *We've made an acceptable start*
adequate: *The level of service was adequate*
okay or **OK** *informal: For a fashionable restaurant like this the prices are okay*
passable: *Ms Campbell speaks passable French*

reasonable: *able to make a reasonable living from his writing*

so-so *informal: Their lunch was only so-so*

see also **acceptable, decent**

tolerance see **patience**

tolerant *adjective accepting of different views and behaviour: more tolerant attitudes to unmarried couples having children*

broad-minded: *a very fair and broad-minded man*

liberal: *She is known to have liberal views on divorce*

open-minded: *I am very open-minded about that question*

understanding: *Fortunately for John, he had an understanding wife*

tolerate *verb* **1** to accept something you disagree with: *We will not tolerate such behaviour*

accept: *Urban dwellers often accept noise as part of city life*

put up with: *You're late again and I won't put up with it*

2 to accept something unpleasant: *She can no longer tolerate the position that she's in*

bear: *He can't bear to talk about it*

endure: *unable to endure the pain*

stand: *He can't stand me smoking*

see also **allow, bear, put up with**

toll see **ring, sound**

tomb *noun* a burial chamber: *Carter discovered Tutankhamun's tomb*

grave: *They used to visit her grave twice a year*

mausoleum: *the elaborate mausoleums of the Paris cemetery*

sarcophagus: *an Egyptian sarcophagus*

sepulchre *literary: the ornate lid of the sepulchre*

vault: *the family vault*

see also **grave**

tome see **book**

tone see **note, sound**

tone down see **moderate**

tongue see **language**

tons see **heaps**

too *adverb* **1** also or as well: *You were there too*

as well: *She published historical novels as well*

besides: *Besides, you get to take lots of samples home*

in addition: *There are, in addition, other objections to the plan*

into the bargain: *The machine can play CDs into the bargain*

likewise: *She sat down and he did likewise*

moreover: *He didn't know, and moreover, he didn't care*

2 more than a desirable or acceptable amount: *You've had too many late nights*

excessively: *He had an excessively protective mother*

over-: *I didn't want to seem over-eager*

overly: *Most people consider him to be overly ambitious*

unduly: *She's unduly concerned with what people think of her*

unreasonably: *These prices seem unreasonably high to me*

see also **also**

tool *noun* a hand-held instrument for doing a job: *The best tool for the purpose is a pair of shears*

implement: *knives and other useful implements*

instrument: *instruments for cleaning and polishing teeth*

utensil: *cooking utensils*

see also **gadget**

top *noun* **1** the highest part of something: *I waited at the top of the stairs*

apex: *at the very apex of the pyramid*

brow: *the brow of the hill*

crest: *the crest of the wave*

crown: the crown of the head
culmination: the culmination of his career
head: A different name was placed at the head of the chart
height: at the height of his success
high point: the high point of his movie career
peak: at the peak of the morning rush hour
pinnacle: the pinnacle of sporting achievement
ridge: He died after falling from a ridge on Mount Snowdon
summit: the summit of the mountain
zenith literary: His career is now at its zenith

2 the lid of a container: a bottle top
cap: She unscrewed the cap of her water bottle
lid: the lid of the jar
stopper: a scent bottle with a stopper in blue frosted glass

▷ adjective **3** being the best of its kind: He was the top student in physics
best: the best pupil of his year
chief: one of the world's chief nuclear scientists
elite: the elite troops of the presidential bodyguard
foremost: the foremost urban painter of his age
head: He was head boy when he was at school
highest: He achieved one of the highest positions in the land
lead: She has landed the lead role in a major film
leading: a leading member of the community
pre-eminent: a pre-eminent political figure
premier: the country's premier theatre company
prime: The store will be built in a prime location
principal: the principal singer with the Royal Opera House

▷ verb **4** to be greater than something: The temperature topped 90 degrees
cap: He capped his display with two fine goals
exceed: Its research budget exceeds $700 million a year
go beyond: This goes beyond anything I've ever attempted before
outstrip: Demand is outstripping supply
surpass: He has surpassed the record of nine wins in one season

5 to be better than someone or something: You'll never manage to top that story
beat: Nothing beats a nice, long bath at the end of a day
better: As an account of adolescence, this novel cannot be bettered
eclipse: Nothing is going to eclipse winning the Olympic title
improve on: We need to improve on our performance against France
outdo: Both sides are trying to outdo each other
surpass: He was determined to surpass the achievements of his brothers
see also **foremost, head, leading, maximum, outdo, peak, prize, successful, supreme**

top up see augment, supplement
topic see issue, question, subject
topple see fall, overthrow, overturn
torment see bully, persecute, pick on
torpedo see bomb
torrent see burst, flood
tortuous see indirect
torture see ordeal, persecute
Tory see right-wing
toss see throw

tot see **child**

total noun **1** several things added together: *The companies have a total of 1776 employees*
- **aggregate**: *three successive defeats by an aggregate of 12 goals*
- **sum**: *the sum of all the angles*
- **whole**: *taken as a percentage of the whole*

▷ adjective **2** complete in all its parts: *a total failure*
- **absolute**: *absolute beginners*
- **complete**: *a complete mess*
- **out-and-out**: *an out-and-out lie*
- **outright**: *an outright rejection of the deal*
- **unconditional**: *unconditional surrender*
- **undivided**: *You have my undivided attention*
- **unmitigated**: *an unmitigated failure*
- **unqualified**: *an unqualified success*
- **utter**: *utter nonsense*

▷ verb **3** to reach the sum of: *Their debts totalled over 300,000 dollars*
- **add up to**: *Profits can add up to millions of dollars*
- **amount to**: *Spending on sports-related items amounted to £9.75 billion*
- **come to**: *That comes to over a thousand pounds*

see also **absolute, add, complete, figure, sheer, utter, whole**

totally see **quite**

tottering see **shaky, unsteady**

touch verb **1** to put your hand on something: *Don't touch that dial*
- **feel**: *The doctor felt his head*
- **finger**: *He fingered the few coins in his pocket*
- **handle**: *Wear rubber gloves when handling cat litter*

2 to come into contact with: *Annie lowered her legs until her feet touched the floor*
- **brush**: *Something brushed against her leg*
- **graze**: *A bullet had grazed his arm*
- **meet**: *when the wheels meet the ground*

3 to emotionally affect someone: *I was touched by his kindness*
- **affect**: *Jazza was badly affected by his divorce*
- **move**: *These stories surprised and moved me*
- **stir**: *She stirred something very deep in me*

see also **contact, feel, handle, move, note, reach, trace**

touch down see **land**

touch on see **mention**

touch upon see **mention**

touching adjective causing sadness or sympathy: *a touching tale*
- **affecting** literary: *an affecting memorial to Countess Rachel*
- **moving**: *It was a moving moment for Marianne*
- **poignant**: *a poignant love story*

see also **moving**

touchy adjective easily upset: *She is very touchy about her past*
- **easily offended**: *viewers who are easily offended*
- **sensitive**: *Young people are very sensitive about their appearance*
- **toey** Australian, New Zealand slang: *Don't be so toey*

see also **sensitive**

tough adjective **1** able to put up with hardship: *She is tough and ambitious*
- **hardened**: *hardened criminals*
- **hardy**: *a hardy race of pioneers*
- **resilient**: *a good soldier, calm and resilient*
- **robust**: *Perhaps men are more robust than women?*
- **rugged**: *Rugged individualism forged America's frontier society*
- **strong**: *Eventually I felt strong enough to look at him*

2 difficult to break or damage: *beans with a rather tough outer skin*
durable: *Fine bone china is both strong and durable*
hard-wearing: *hard-wearing cotton shirts*
leathery: *leathery skin*
resilient: *an armchair of some resilient plastic material*
robust: *very robust machinery*
rugged: *You need a rugged, four-wheel drive vehicle*
solid: *The car feels very solid*
strong: *a strong casing, which won't crack or chip*
sturdy: *The camera was mounted on a sturdy tripod*
3 full of hardship: *She had a pretty tough childhood*
arduous: *an arduous journey*
difficult: *We're living in difficult times*
exacting: *an exacting task*
hard: *a hard life*
see also **hard, hooligan, rough, stiff, thug**

toughen *see* **strengthen**
tour *see* **journey**
tournament *see* **competition, contest**
tow *see* **drag, pull**
towering *see* **tall**
town *see* **city**
towpath *see* **path**
toxic *see* **poisonous**
toxin *see* **poison**
trace *verb* **1** to look for and find something: *Police are trying to trace the owner*
locate: *We've simply been unable to locate him*
track down: *She had spent years trying to track down her parents*
▷ *noun* **2** a sign of something: *No trace of his father had been found*
evidence: *He'd seen no evidence of fraud*

hint: *I saw no hint of irony on her face*
indication: *He gave no indication of remorse*
record: *There's no record of any marriage or children*
sign: *Sally waited for any sign of illness*
suggestion: *a faint suggestion of a tan*
whiff: *Not a whiff of scandal has ever tainted his private life*
3 a small amount of something: *to write without a trace of sensationalism*
dash: *a story with a dash of mystery*
drop: *a drop of sherry*
remnant: *Beneath the present church were remnants of Roman flooring*
suspicion: *large blooms of white with a suspicion of pale pink*
tinge: *Could there have been a slight tinge of envy in Eva's voice?*
touch: *a touch of flu*
vestige: *the last vestige of a UN force that once numbered 30,000*
see also **draw, lead, note, sign, suggestion**

track *see* **follow, line, path, road**
track down *see* **find, locate, track**
track record *see* **record**
tract *see* **region, stretch**
trade *noun* **1** the buying and selling of goods: *foreign trade*
business: *a career in business*
commerce: *They have made their fortunes from industry and commerce*
2 the kind of work someone does: *He learnt his trade as a diver in the North Sea*
business: *the music business*
line: *Are you in the publishing line too?*
line of work: *In my line of work I often get home too late for dinner*
occupation: *her new occupation as an author*
profession: *Harper was a teacher by profession*

▷ *verb* **3** to buy and sell goods: *They had years of experience of trading with the West*
  deal: *They deal in antiques*
  do business: *the different people who did business with me*
  traffic: *those who traffic in illegal drugs*
  see also **business, change, exchange, job, swap**

trade in *see* **sell, stock**

trader *noun* someone who trades in goods: *a timber trader*
  broker: *a financial broker*
  dealer: *dealers in commodities*
  merchant: *a wine merchant*

trading *see* **business**

tradition *noun* a long-standing custom: *the rich traditions of Afro-Cuban music*
  convention: *It's just a social convention that men don't wear skirts*
  custom: *an ancient Japanese custom*
  see also **convention, custom, habit**

traditional *adjective* existing for a long time: *her traditional Indian dress*
  conventional: *conventional family planning methods*
  established: *the established church*
  see also **conservative, conventional**

traffic *see* **trade**

tragedy *see* **disaster, play**

tragic *adjective* very sad: *a tragic accident*
  distressing: *distressing news*
  heartbreaking: *a heartbreaking sight*
  heart-rending: *heart-rending pictures of refugees*
  see also **sad**

trail *see* **drag, lag, path**

train *verb* to teach someone how to do something: *We train them in bricklaying and other building techniques*
  coach: *He coached the basketball team*
  drill: *He drills the choir to a high standard*
  educate: *I was educated at the local grammar school*
  instruct: *All their members are instructed in first aid*
  school: *He has been schooled to take over the family business*
  teach: *This is something they teach us to do in our first year*
  tutor: *She decided to tutor her children at home*
  see also **instruct, practise, teach**

trained *see* **skilled**

trainee *see* **beginner, recruit**

training *see* **education, exercise, experience, practice**

trait *see* **attribute, characteristic, point, property, quality**

trajectory *see* **course, curve, line**

trance *see* **dream**

tranquil *see* **calm, peaceful, quiet, still**

tranquillity *see* **peace, quiet**

transaction *see* **business**

transfer *see* **transport**

transform *verb* to change something completely: *This technology has transformed our society*
  alter: *New curtains can completely alter the look of a room*
  change: *alchemists attempting to change base metals into gold*
  convert: *They have converted the church into a restaurant*
  reform: *He was totally reformed by this experience*
  revolutionize: *a device which will revolutionize the way you cook*
  see also **change, turn**

transformation *see* **change**

transient *see* **temporary**

transitory *see* **temporary**

translucent *see* **clear, transparent**

transmit *see* **communicate, send**

transparent adjective able to be seen through: a sheet of transparent plastic

clear: a clear glass panel

crystalline literary: crystalline lakes

sheer: a sheer black shirt

translucent: translucent corrugated plastic

see also **clear**

transport noun 1 the moving of goods and people: The prices quoted include transport costs

removal: the furniture removal business

shipment: transported to the docks for shipment overseas

transportation: the transportation of refugees

▷ verb 2 to move people or goods somewhere: They use tankers to transport the oil to Los Angeles

carry: The ship could carry seventy passengers

convey formal: a branch line to convey fish direct to Billingsgate

ship: the food being shipped to Iraq

transfer: She was transferred to another hospital

see also **banish, bring, carry, take**

transportation see **transport**

trap noun 1 a device for catching animals: a rabbit trap

net: a fishing net

snare: a snare for catching birds

▷ verb 2 to catch animals: The locals were encouraged to trap and kill the birds

catch: an animal caught in a trap

corner: like a cornered rat

snare: He'd snared shark earlier in the day

3 to trick someone: Were you trying to trap her into making some admission?

dupe: a plot to dupe stamp collectors into buying fake rarities

trick: His family tricked him into going to Pakistan

see also **catch**

trapping see **capture**

trash noun 1 waste material: He picks up your trash on Mondays

garbage: rotting piles of garbage

refuse: a weekly collection of refuse

rubbish: They had piled most of their rubbish into yellow skips

waste: a law that regulates the disposal of waste

2 something of poor quality: Don't read that awful trash

garbage informal: He spends his time watching garbage on TV

rubbish: He described her book as absolute rubbish

see also **garbage, junk, refuse, rubbish**

trauma see **shock**

traumatize see **shock**

travel verb to make a journey somewhere: You had better travel to Helsinki tomorrow

go: We went to Rome

journey formal: He intended to journey up the Amazon

make your way: He made his way home at last

take a trip: We intend to take a trip there sometime

see also **go, journey, proceed, spread**

traverse see **cross**

treacherous adjective 1 likely to betray someone: He denounced the party's treacherous leaders

disloyal: disloyal Cabinet colleagues

faithless: an oppressive father and faithless husband

unfaithful: his unfaithful wife

untrustworthy: Jordan has tried to brand his opponents as untrustworthy

2 dangerous or unreliable: treacherous mountain roads

dangerous: a dangerous stretch of road

hazardous: hazardous seas

perilous literary: The roads grew even steeper and more perilous

see also **dangerous, two-faced**

treasure verb to consider something very precious: He treasures his friendship with her

cherish: The previous owners had cherished the house

hold dear: forced to renounce everything he held most dear

prize: one of the gallery's most prized possessions

value: if you value your health

see also **appreciate, dear, prize, value**

treasured see **beloved, dear**

treasures see **valuables**

treat verb 1 to behave towards someone: Artie treated most women with indifference

act towards: the way you act towards other people

behave towards: He always behaved towards me with great kindness

deal with: in dealing with suicidal youngsters

2 to give someone medical care: the doctor who treated her

care for: They hired a nurse to care for her

nurse: All the years he was sick my mother had nursed him

see also **luxury**

treatment see **cure**

treaty see **agreement**

trek see **journey, walk**

tremble see **shake**

trembling see **shaky**

tremendous see **brilliant, enormous, wonderful**

trend see **craze, fashion, wave**

trendy adjective informal fashionable:

a trendy night club

fashionable: a very fashionable place to go on holiday

in slang: what's in and what's not

in fashion: Calf-length skirts are in fashion this season

in vogue: African art is in vogue at the moment

latest: the latest thing in camera technology

stylish: This city has got a lot more stylish in recent years

trespass see **breach, intrude**

trial see **case, ordeal, test**

tribulation see **difficulty, ordeal**

tribunal see **court**

tribute noun something that shows admiration: Police paid tribute to her courage

accolade formal: To play for your country is the ultimate accolade

compliment: We consider it a compliment to be called 'conservative'

honour: Only two writers are granted the honour of a solo display

praise: That is high praise indeed

testimony: a testimony to her dedication

see also **honour, praise**

trice see **instant, minute**

trick noun 1 something that deceives someone: We are playing a trick on a man who keeps bothering me

con informal: Slimming snacks that offer miraculous weight loss are a con

deception: the victim of a cruel deception

hoax: a bomb hoax

ploy: a cynical marketing ploy

ruse: This was a ruse to divide them

▷ verb **2** to deceive someone: They tricked me into giving them all my money

con informal: We have been conned for 20 years

deceive: He deceived me into thinking

the money was his
dupe: I was duped into letting them in
fool: They tried to fool you into coming after us
take in informal: I wasn't taken in for a minute
see also **con, deceive, dupe, fool, take in, trap**

trickery see **dishonesty, fraud**

trickle see **drip**

tricky adjective difficult to do or to deal with: This could be a very tricky problem
complex: the whole complex issue of crime and punishment
complicated: a complicated operation
delicate: This brings us to the delicate question of his future
difficult: It was a difficult decision to make
hard: That's a hard question to answer
problematic: It's a very problematic piece to play
puzzling: a puzzling case to solve
sensitive: The death penalty is a very sensitive issue

trifling see **insignificant, minor, petty, trivial, worthless**

trigger see **start**

trim see **border, fit, neat, shorten**

trinket see **ornament**

trip noun 1 a journey to a place: a business trip
excursion: a coach excursion to Trondheim
jaunt: a jaunt in the car
journey: the journey to Bordeaux
outing: a school outing
voyage: Columbus's voyage to the West Indies
▷ verb 2 to fall over: I tripped on the stairs
fall over: Plenty of top skiers fell over
lose your footing: He lost his footing and slid into the water

stumble: He stumbled and almost fell
see also **drive, fall, journey**

trite see **corny, hackneyed**

triumph noun 1 a great success: The championships proved to be a personal triumph for the coach
success: The jewellery was a great success
victory: a victory for common sense
▷ verb 2 to be successful: a symbol of good triumphing over evil
come out on top informal: The only way to come out on top is to adopt a different approach
prevail: I do hope he will prevail over the rebels
succeed: if they can succeed in America
win: The top four teams all won
see also **succeed, success, victory, win**

triumph over see **overcome**

trivial adjective not important: She doesn't concern herself with such trivial details
insignificant: The dangers are insignificant compared with those of smoking
minor: a minor inconvenience
negligible: The strike will have a negligible impact
paltry: They had no interest in paltry domestic concerns
petty: I wouldn't indulge in such petty schoolboy pranks
slight: It's only a slight problem
trifling: The sums involved were trifling
unimportant: Too much time is spent discussing unimportant matters
see also **insignificant, minor, petty, slight, unimportant, worthless**

trophy see **prize**

trouble noun 1 a difficulty or problem: financial troubles
bother: Vince is having a spot of

bother with the law

difficulty: economic difficulties

hassle informal: We had loads of hassles trying to find somewhere to rehearse

problem: The main problem is unemployment

▷ verb **2** to make someone feel worried: He was troubled by the lifestyle of his son

agitate: The thought agitates her

bother: Is something bothering you?

disturb: dreams so vivid that they disturb me for days

worry: I didn't want to worry you

3 to cause someone inconvenience: Can I trouble you for some milk?

bother: I don't know why he bothers me with this kind of rubbish

disturb: a room where you won't be disturbed

impose upon: I was afraid you'd feel we were imposing on us

inconvenience: He promised to be quick so as not to inconvenience them further

put out: I've always put myself out for others

see also **agitate, bother, burden, care, concern, difficulty, distress, disturb, drawback, effort, hassle, jam, pain, problem, sorrow, worry**

troubled see **anxious, upset, worried**

troublesome see **difficult**

trounce see **defeat, vanquish**

trouncing see **defeat**

troupe see **band, company, team**

truce see **peace**

true adjective **1** not invented: The film is based on a true story

accurate: an accurate assessment of the situation

correct: a correct diagnosis

factual: any comparison that is not strictly factual

2 real or genuine: She was a true friend

authentic: authentic Italian food

bona fide: We are happy to donate to bona fide charities

genuine: There was a risk of genuine refugees being returned to Vietnam

real: No, it wasn't a dream. It was real

see also **accurate, actual, authentic, correct, devoted, exact, faithful, loyal, real, realistic, reliable, right, strict, trusty**

truly see **really**

truncheon see **club, stick**

trunk see **box**

truss see **tie**

trust verb to believe that someone will do something: The president can't be trusted

count on: I can always count on you to cheer me up

depend on: You can depend on me

have confidence in: We have the utmost confidence in your abilities

have faith in: I have no faith in him any more

place your trust in: I would never place my trust in one so young

rely upon: I know I can rely on you to sort it out

see also **belief, believe, confidence, depend, faith**

trusting see **gullible**

trustworthy see **honest, reliable, responsible, sure, trusty**

trusty adjective considered to be reliable: a trusty member of the crew

dependable: a dependable and steady worker

faithful: his faithful black Labrador

firm: Betty became a firm friend of the family

reliable: the problem of finding reliable staff

solid: one of my most solid supporters

staunch: He proved himself a staunch ally
true: a true friend
trustworthy: trying to find a trustworthy adviser
see also **loyal**
truth noun the facts about something: Marcel is keen to get to the truth of what happened
fact: How much was fact and how much fancy no one knew
reality: Fiction and reality were increasingly blurred
see also **fact, reality**
truthful see **candid, honest**
try verb 1 to make an effort to do something: I tried hard to persuade him to stay
attempt: They are accused of attempting to murder British soldiers
endeavour formal: I will endeavour to arrange it
make an attempt: He made three attempts to break the record
make an effort: He made no effort to hide his disappointment
seek: We have never sought to impose our views
strive: The school strives to treat pupils as individuals
2 to test the quality of something: Howard wanted me to try the wine
check out: We went to the club to check it out
sample: We sampled a selection of different bottled waters
test: The drug was tested on rats
try out: London Transport hopes to try out the system in September
▷ noun 3 an attempt to do something: After a few tries he pressed the right button
attempt: a deliberate attempt to destabilize the defence
effort: his efforts to improve
endeavour formal: His first

endeavours in the field were wedding films
go informal: She won on her first go
shot informal: I have had a shot at professional cricket
see also **attempt, go, seek, strive, test**
try out see **test, try**
try your hand at see **attempt**
trying see **difficult**
tryst see **meeting**
tsotsi see **thug**
tubby adjective rather fat: He's a bit on the tubby side
chubby: She was very chubby as a child
fat: He was short and fat
overweight: Being overweight is bad for your health
plump: a plump, good-natured little woman
podgy: Eddie is a little podgy round the middle
portly: a portly gentleman
stout: His wife was a small, stout lady
see also **plump**
tuck see **fold**
tucker see **food, kai**
tuckered out see **tired, weary**
tug verb 1 to give something a quick, hard pull: A little boy tugged at her skirt excitedly
drag: He grabbed my ankle and dragged me back
draw: She took his hand and drew him along
haul: I gripped his wrist and hauled him up
heave: They heaved the last bag into the van
jerk: He jerked his hand out of mine angrily
pluck: The beggar plucked at her sleeve as she passed
pull: She pulled down the hem of her skirt over her knees

wrench: The horse wrenched its head free
yank: He grabbed my arm and yanked me out of the car
▷ noun **2** a quick, hard pull: He felt a tug at his arm
heave: With a mighty heave, she pulled herself away from him
jerk: He gave a sudden jerk of the reins
pull: Give the cord three sharp pulls
wrench: He lowered the flag with a quick wrench
yank: He gave the phone a savage yank
see also **pull**

tuition see **education**

tumble see **drop**

tummy see **stomach**

tumour see **boil**

tumultuous see **noisy**

tune noun a series of musical notes: She was humming a merry little tune
melody: a beautiful melody
strains: She could hear the tinny strains of a chamber orchestra

tuneful see **sweet**

tunnel see **dig**

turbulent see **violent, wild**

turmoil see **disorder, mess**

turn verb **1** to change the direction or position of something: She had turned the bedside chair to face the door
rotate: Take each foot in both your hands and rotate it
spin: He spun the wheel sharply and made a U-turn
swivel: She swivelled her chair round
twirl: Bonnie twirled her empty glass in her fingers
twist: She twisted her head sideways
2 to become or make something different: A hobby can be turned into a career
change: She has now changed into a happy, self-confident woman

convert: a table that converts into an ironing board
mutate: Overnight, the gossip begins to mutate into headlines
transform: the speed at which your body transforms food into energy
▷ noun **3** someone's right or duty to do something: Tonight it's my turn to cook
chance: All eligible people would get a chance to vote
go: Whose go is it?
opportunity: Now is your opportunity to say what you've always wanted
see also **bend, curve, get, grow, spin, swerve**

turn back see **return**

turn down see **decline, refuse, reject**

turn out see **work out**

turn red see **blush**

turn under see **fold**

turn up see **appear, come, find**

tutor see **adviser, instruct, master, teach, teacher, train**

tutoring see **lesson**

twice see **double**

twig see **stick**

twin see **double**

twine see **coil, twist**

twinge see **pain**

twinkle see **flash, sparkle**

twirl see **turn**

twist verb **1** to turn something round: Her hands began to twist the handles of the bag
bend: Bend the bar into a horseshoe
curl: She sat with her legs curled under her
twine: He had twined his chubby arms around Vincent's neck
weave: He weaves his way through a crowd
wring: after wringing the chicken's neck

2 to bend into a new shape: *The car was left a mess of twisted metal*

distort: *A painter may exaggerate or distort shapes and forms*

mangle: *the mangled wreckage*

screw up: *Amy screwed up her face*

3 to injure a part of your body: *I've twisted my ankle*

sprain: *He fell and sprained his wrist*

wrench: *He had wrenched his back badly from the force of the fall*

see also **bend, coil, misrepresent, tangle, turn**

twisted see **crooked**

twit see **idiot**

twitch see **fidget**

two-faced *adjective* not honest in dealing with other people: *a two-faced, manipulative woman*

deceitful: *a deceitful, conniving liar*

dishonest: *He's been dishonest in his dealings with us both*

disloyal: *I can't stand people who are disloyal*

false: *He had been betrayed by his false friends*

hypocritical: *a hypocritical and ambitious careerist*

insincere: *They are still widely seen as insincere and untrustworthy*

treacherous: *He has been consistently treacherous to both sides*

see also **insincere**

twofold see **double**

two-timing see **unfaithful**

type *noun* a group of things that have features in common: *There are various types of dog suitable as pets*

brand: *his favourite brand of whisky*

breed: *a rare breed of cattle*

class: *a better class of restaurant*

group: *Weather forecasters classify clouds into several different groups*

kind: *I don't like that kind of film*

make: *He'll only drive a certain make of car*

sort: *a dozen trees of various sorts*

species: *a rare species of moth*

style: *Several styles of hat were available*

variety: *Many varieties of birds live here*

see also **breed, category, class, form, kind, sort, variety**

typical *adjective* having the usual characteristics of something: *a typical American child*

average: *The average adult man burns 1500 to 2000 calories per day*

characteristic: *a characteristic feature of the landscape*

normal: *a normal day*

regular: *He describes himself as just a regular guy*

representative: *fairly representative groups of adults*

standard: *It was standard practice in cases like this*

stock: *He had a stock answer for all problems*

usual: *a neighborhood beset by all the usual inner-city problems*

see also **average, characteristic, natural, normal, regular, representative, routine, stock**

typically see on **average**

tyrannical see **absolute**

tyranny see **oppression**

ugly adjective having a very unattractive appearance: *She makes me feel dowdy and ugly*
plain: *a shy, plain girl with a pale complexion*
unattractive: *painted in an unattractive shade of green*
unsightly: *The view was spoiled by some unsightly houses*

ultimate adjective **1** being the final one of a series: *It is not possible to predict the ultimate outcome*
eventual: *Reunification is the eventual aim*
final: *the fifth and final day*
last: *This is his last chance to do something useful*
2 the most important or powerful: *the ultimate goal of any player*
greatest: *Our greatest aim was to take the gold medal*
paramount: *His paramount ambition was to be an actor*
supreme: *the supreme test of his abilities*
utmost: *This has to be our utmost priority*
▷ noun **3** the finest example of something: *This hotel is the ultimate in luxury*

epitome: *She was the epitome of the successful businesswoman*
extreme: *This was shyness taken to the extreme*
height: *the height of bad manners*
peak: *roses at the peak of perfection*
see also **extreme, final, last, limit, supreme**

umpire see **judge**
umpteen see **many**
unabashed see **shameless**
unable see **incompetent**
unacceptable see **unbearable, unsatisfactory, unsuitable**
unaccustomed see **inexperienced**
unadventurous see **conventional**
unaffected see **immune, natural, real**
unaided see **independent, on your own**
unappreciative see **ungrateful**
unashamed see **shameless**
unassuming see **humble, meek, modest**
unattached see **single**
unattractive see **ugly**
unavoidable see **necessary**

unaware adjective not knowing about something: *Many people are unaware of how much they eat*
ignorant: *They are completely ignorant of the relevant facts*
oblivious: *John appeared oblivious to his surroundings*
unconscious: *totally unconscious of my presence*
unsuspecting: *The cars were then sold to unsuspecting buyers*
see also **ignorant, unconscious**

unbearable adjective too unpleasant to be tolerated: *Life was unbearable for the remaining citizens*
intolerable: *The heat and humidity were intolerable*
oppressive: *An oppressive sadness weighed upon him*

unacceptable: She left her husband because of his unacceptable behaviour

unbeatable see **invincible**

unbelievable adjective **1** extremely great or surprising: He showed unbelievable courage

colossal: There has been a colossal waste of public money

incredible: You're always an incredible help on these occasions

stupendous: It cost a stupendous amount of money

2 so unlikely it cannot be believed: He came up with some unbelievable story

implausible: a film with an implausible ending

improbable: highly improbable claims

inconceivable: It was inconceivable that he'd hurt anyone

incredible: It seems incredible that anyone would want to do that

preposterous: The whole idea was preposterous

unconvincing: In response he was given the usual unconvincing excuses
see also **improbable**, **incredible**, **unlikely**

unbeliever see **heathen**

unbroken see **flat**

uncalled-for see **unnecessary**

uncanny see **spooky**

uncertain adjective **1** not knowing what to do: For a moment he looked uncertain as to how to respond

doubtful: He was a bit doubtful about starting without her

dubious: We were a bit dubious about it at first

unclear: I'm unclear about where to go

undecided: Even then she was still undecided about her future plans

2 not definite: facing an uncertain future

ambiguous: The wording of the contract was ambiguous

doubtful: The outcome of the match is still doubtful

indefinite: suspended for an indefinite period

indeterminate: a woman of indeterminate age
see also **doubtful**, **vague**

uncertainty see **doubt**

unchanging see **eternal**

unclean see **dirty**

unclear adjective confusing and not obvious: It is unclear how much popular support they have

ambiguous: in order to clarify the earlier ambiguous statement

confused: The situation remains confused, as no clear victor has emerged

vague: The description was pretty vague
see also **uncertain**, **vague**

unclothed see **naked**

uncomfortable adjective **1** feeling or causing discomfort: an uncomfortable bed

awkward: Its shape made it awkward to carry

cramped: living in very cramped conditions

disagreeable: designed to make flying a less disagreeable experience

ill-fitting: Walking was difficult because of her ill-fitting shoes

painful: a painful back injury

2 not relaxed or confident: Talking about money made him uncomfortable

awkward: Offstage, he is bashful and awkward

embarrassed: an embarrassed silence

ill at ease: I always feel ill at ease in their company

self-conscious: She was always self-conscious about her height

uneasy: He looked uneasy and refused to answer any more questions

uncommon adjective **1** not happening or occurring often: This type of cancer is uncommon among young women

exceptional: These are exceptional circumstances

extraordinary: an act of extraordinary generosity

few: Genuine friends are few

infrequent: one of the infrequent visitors to the island

out of the ordinary: My story is nothing out of the ordinary

scarce: places where jobs are scarce

sparse: Traffic is sparse on this stretch of road

rare: a rare occurrence

unusual: an unusual sight these days

2 unusually great: She had read Cecilia's last letter with uncommon interest

acute: He has an acute dislike of children

exceptional: a woman of exceptional beauty

extraordinary: a young player of extraordinary energy

extreme: regions suffering from extreme poverty

great: They share a great love of Bach's music

intense: intense heat

remarkable: a musician of remarkable talent

see also **particular, rare, scarce, singular, strange, unusual**

uncomplicated see **simple, straightforward**

unconcern see **neglect**

unconcerned see **uninterested**

unconditional see **total**

unconnected see **separate**

unconscious adjective **1** in a state similar to sleep: By the time the ambulance arrived, he was unconscious

asleep: They were fast asleep in their beds

senseless: He was beaten senseless and robbed of all his money

stunned: stunned by a blow to the head

2 not aware of what is happening: quite unconscious of their presence

oblivious: He seemed oblivious of his surroundings

unaware: He was unaware of the chaos he was causing

unknowing: unknowing accomplices in his crimes

unsuspecting: She was an unsuspecting victim of his deceit

see also **ignorant, unaware**

uncontaminated see **clean**

uncontrolled see **wild**

unconventional see **unusual**

unconvinced see **dubious**

unconvincing see **lame, unbelievable, unlikely**

uncoordinated see **clumsy**

uncouth see **vulgar**

uncover verb **1** to find something out: Auditors said they had uncovered evidence of fraud

bring to light: The truth is unlikely to be brought to light

expose: His lies were exposed in court

reveal: He will reveal the truth behind the scandal

show up: His true character has been shown up for what it is

unearth: a campaign to unearth supposed conspiracies

2 to remove the lid or cover from something: When the seedlings sprout, uncover the tray

expose: The wreck was exposed by the action of the tide

lay bare: Layers of paint and flaking plaster were laid bare

open: *I opened a new jar of coffee*

reveal: *His shirt was open, revealing a tattooed chest*

unearth: *Quarry workers have unearthed the skeleton of a mammoth*

unveil: *The statue will be unveiled next week*

unwrap: *unwrapping Christmas presents*

see also **expose, open, reveal**

uncovered *see* **bare, open**

uncultivated *see* **wild**

uncut *see* **whole**

undecided *see* **dubious, uncertain**

undeniable *see* **certain, sure**

undeniably *see* **certainly**

under *preposition* at a lower level than something: *a labyrinth of tunnels under the ground*

below: *The sun had already sunk below the horizon*

beneath: *the frozen grass crunching beneath his feet*

underneath: *people trapped underneath the wreckage*

see also **below**

under par *see* **sick**

under the weather *see* **crook, sick**

undercover *see* **secret**

underfed *see* **skinny**

undergo *verb* to have something happen to you: *He had to undergo major surgery*

be subjected to: *She was subjected to constant interruptions*

endure: *The company endured heavy losses*

experience: *They seem to experience more distress than the others*

go through: *I wouldn't like to go through that again*

suffer: *The peace process had suffered a serious setback*

see also **experience, feel, go through, have, receive, suffer**

underground *see* **secret**

underhand *see* **devious, sly**

underline *see* **emphasize, stress**

underling *see* **inferior**

undermine *verb* to make something less secure or strong: *You're trying to undermine my confidence again*

impair: *Their actions will impair France's national interests*

sap: *I was afraid the illness had sapped my strength*

subvert: *an attempt to subvert their culture from within*

weaken: *Her authority had been fatally weakened*

see also **weaken**

underneath *see* **below, under**

undernourished *see* **skinny**

understand *verb* **1** to know what someone means: *Do you understand what I'm saying?*

catch on *informal*: *I didn't catch on immediately to what he meant*

comprehend: *Whenever she failed to comprehend, she just laughed*

follow: *I don't follow you at all*

get: *Did you get that joke?*

grasp: *He instantly grasped that they were talking about him*

see: *"I see," she said at last*

take in: *too much to take in at once*

2 to know why or how something is happening: *too young to understand what was going on*

appreciate: *You must appreciate how important this is*

comprehend: *I just cannot comprehend your viewpoint*

fathom: *His attitude was hard to fathom*

grasp: *We immediately grasped the seriousness of the crisis*

realize: *People just don't realize how serious it could be*

3 to hear of something: *I understand she hasn't been well*

believe: *She's coming back tomorrow,*

I believe
gather: *We gather the report is critical of the judge*
hear: *I hear you've been having some problems*
learn: *On learning who he was, I wanted to meet him*
see also **appreciate, comprehend, gather, grasp, hear, know, learn, realize, see, take in**
understandable *see* **reasonable, simple**
understanding *noun* **1** a knowledge of something: *a basic understanding of computers*
appreciation: *some appreciation of the problems of consumers*
comprehension: *completely beyond our comprehension*
grasp: *a good grasp of foreign languages*
knowledge: *I have no knowledge of his business affairs*
perception: *Her questions showed a shrewd perception*
2 an informal agreement: *There was an understanding between us*
accord: *trying to reach an accord*
agreement: *A new defence agreement was signed last month*
pact: *an electoral pact between the parties*
▷ *adjective* **3** having a sympathetic nature: *Fortunately he had an understanding wife*
compassionate: *a deeply compassionate man*
considerate: *They should be more considerate towards the prisoners*
sensitive: *He was always sensitive and caring*
sympathetic: *a sympathetic listener*
see also **experience, grasp, intelligence, pity, sympathy, tolerant**
undertake *see* **assume, do**

undertaking *noun* a task which you have agreed to do: *Organizing the show has been a massive undertaking*
affair: *It's going to be a tricky affair to arrange*
business: *Livestock farming is an arduous and difficult business*
endeavour: *an endeavour that was bound to end in failure*
enterprise: *a risky enterprise such as horse breeding*
job: *What made you decide to take this job on?*
operation: *the man in charge of the entire operation*
project: *I can't take responsibility for such a huge project*
task: *a task I do not feel equipped to take on*
venture: *a venture that few were willing to invest in*
see also **act, enterprise, guarantee, promise, task**
undertow *see* **current**
undervalue *see* **belittle**
undesirable *see* **unpopular**
undivided *see* **complete, total, whole**
undo *see* **loosen, open, ruin**
undomesticated *see* **wild**
undone *see* **open**
undoubtedly *see* **certainly**
undressed *see* **bare, naked**
undue *see* **excessive**
unduly *see* **too**
unearth *see* **discover, expose, find, reveal, uncover**
unease *see* **anxiety, worry**
uneasy *adjective* worried that something may be wrong: *I was very uneasy about these developments*
agitated: *She seemed agitated about something*
anxious: *He admitted he was still anxious about the situation*
nervous: *Consumers say they are*

nervous about their jobs
perturbed: I am not too perturbed at this setback
worried: If you're worried about it, just ask for more details
see also **anxious, uncomfortable, worried**

uneconomical see **wasteful**

unemployed adjective not having a job: an unemployed mechanic
idle: He has been idle for almost a month
jobless: One in four people are now jobless
redundant: aid for the 30,000 redundant miners
see also **idle**

uneven adjective **1** having an unlevel or rough surface: I tripped and fell on an uneven pavement
bumpy: bumpy cobbled streets
not level: It was hard to walk because the road was not level
not smooth: The icing isn't smooth enough
rough: She picked her way across the rough ground
2 not the same or consistent: six lines of uneven length
fluctuating: a fluctuating temperature
inconsistent: Their performance was inconsistent over the whole season
irregular: at irregular intervals
patchy: Her career has been patchy
variable: The potassium content of food is very variable
see also **irregular, rough**

uneventful see **dreary**

unexpected adjective not considered likely to happen: His death was completely unexpected
astonishing: What an astonishing piece of good luck!
chance: a chance meeting
surprising: a most surprising turn

of events
unforeseen: The show was cancelled due to unforeseen circumstances
see also **abrupt, sudden**

unfair adjective without right or justice: It was unfair that he should suffer so much
unjust: an unjust decision
wrong: It would be wrong to allow the case to go any further
wrongful: his claim for wrongful dismissal
see also **wrong**

unfairness see **injustice**

unfaithful adjective not being faithful to your partner: He was unfaithful to her for years
adulterous: an adulterous relationship
two-timing informal: She called him a two-timing rat
see also **false, treacherous**

unfamiliar adjective not having been seen or heard of before: She grew many plants which were unfamiliar to me
alien: transplanted into an alien culture
exotic: filmed in an exotic location
foreign: This was a foreign country, so unlike his own
new: This was a new experience for me
novel: having to cope with many novel situations
strange: All these faces were strange to me
unknown: I'd discovered a writer quite unknown to me
see also **strange, unknown**

unfit see **inappropriate, unsuitable**
unflustered see **relaxed**
unfold see **spread**
unforeseeable see **unpredictable**
unforeseen see **abrupt, unexpected**
unforgettable see **memorable**
unfortunate see **unlucky**

unfriendly adjective not showing any warmth or kindness: *He can expect an unfriendly welcome*

aloof: *His manner was aloof*

antagonistic: *They were always antagonistic to newcomers*

cold: *She was a cold, unfeeling woman*

disagreeable: *He may be clever but he's most disagreeable*

hostile: *The prisoner eyed him in hostile silence*

unkind: *They're always unkind to newcomers*

see also **disagreeable**, **unpleasant**

unfurl see **spread**

unfurnished see **empty**

ungainliness see **clumsiness**

ungainly see **clumsy**

ungrateful adjective not appreciating the things you have: *the most miserable and ungrateful people on earth*

unappreciative: *He was unappreciative of our efforts*

unthankful: *mercenary players and unthankful supporters*

unhappiness see **grief, misery, sadness, sorrow**

unhappy adjective feeling sad or depressed: *He was a shy, sometimes unhappy man*

depressed: *She's depressed about this whole situation*

despondent: *After the interview John was despondent*

down: *They felt really down after they spoke to him*

miserable: *My job made me really miserable sometimes*

sad: *I felt sad to leave our little house*

see also **miserable, sad, upset**

unhealthy adjective 1 likely to cause illness: *an unhealthy lifestyle*

bad for you: *the argument that eating meat is bad for you*

harmful: *Try to avoid harmful habits like smoking*

insanitary: *the insanitary conditions of slums*

noxious: *factories belching out noxious fumes*

unwholesome: *an epidemic originating from the unwholesome food they ate*

2 not well: *an unhealthy looking man with a bad complexion*

ailing: *The President is said to be ailing*

crook Australian, New Zealand informal: *I'm sorry to hear you've been crook, mate*

ill: *He didn't look at all ill when I last saw him*

not well: *When I'm not well, she looks after me*

poorly British informal: *She's still poorly after that bout of pneumonia*

sick: *He's very sick and he needs treatment*

unwell: *an infection which could make you very unwell*

see also **ill, perverted**

unheard-of see **exceptional**

unhinged see **insane**

unhurried see **leisurely, slow**

unhurriedly see **slowly**

uniform see **constant, even, regular, similar**

uniformly see **alike**

unimaginable see **incredible**

unimportant adjective having little significance or importance: *The difference in their ages seemed unimportant at the time*

insignificant: *In 1949, Bonn was a small, insignificant city*

minor: *a minor inconvenience*

paltry: *They had little interest in paltry domestic concerns*

slight: *We have a slight problem*

trivial: *She waved aside the trivial details*

see also **insignificant, petty, trivial**
uninhabited see **empty, lonely**
unintelligent see **foolish**
unintelligible see **garbled**
uninterested adjective not interested in something: *I'm completely uninterested in anything you have to say*

apathetic: *apathetic about politics*
bored: *She looked bored with the whole performance*
impassive: *He remained impassive while she ranted on*
indifferent: *He is totally indifferent to our problems*
nonchalant: *"Suit yourself," I said, trying to sound nonchalant*
passive: *That passive attitude of his drives me mad*
unconcerned: *She is unconcerned about anything except herself*

see also **apathetic, bored**
uninteresting see **dull**
uninterrupted see **continual, continuous, direct, steady**
union noun 1 an organization of people or groups with mutual interests: *a trades union*

association: *a member of several different associations*
coalition: *governed by a coalition of three parties*
confederation: *a confederation of mini-states*
federation: *a federation of six separate agencies*
league: *the League of Nations*

2 the joining together of two or more things: *The majority voted for union with Russia*

amalgamation: *an amalgamation of two organizations*
blend: *a blend of traditional charm and modern amenities*
combination: *the combination of science and art*

fusion: *fusions of jazz and pop*
mixture: *a mixture of nuts, raisins, and capers*

see also **bond, club, society**
unique see **different, individual, peculiar, singular, special**
unit see **attachment, department, fitting, party**
unite verb to join together and act as a group: *We must unite to fight our common enemy*

collaborate: *They all collaborated on the project*
combine: *The companies have combined to form a multinational*
join: *People of all kinds joined to make a dignified protest*
join forces: *The two parties are joining forces*
link up: *the first time the two armies have linked up*
merge: *The media group hopes to merge with its rival company*
pull together: *The staff and management are pulling together to save the company*
work together: *industry and government working together*

see also **combine, team**
universal adjective relating to everyone or to the whole universe: *These programmes have a universal appeal*

common: *The common view is that it is a good thing*
general: *This project should raise general awareness about the problem*
unlimited: *destruction on an unlimited scale*
widespread: *Food shortages are widespread*
worldwide: *the fear of a worldwide epidemic*

see also **broad, common, general, mass, popular, public**
unjust see **unfair, wrong**

unkempt see **scruffy, untidy**

unkind adjective lacking in kindness and consideration: *It's very unkind to describe her in those terms*
 cruel: *Children can be so cruel*
 malicious: *spreading malicious gossip*
 mean: *I'd feel mean saying no*
 nasty: *What nasty little snobs you are!*
 spiteful: *How can you say such spiteful things about us?*
 thoughtless: *a small minority of thoughtless and inconsiderate people*
 see also **hostile, unfriendly**

unknowing see **unconscious**

unknown adjective not familiar or famous: *He was an unknown writer at that time*
 humble: *He started out as a humble fisherman*
 obscure: *an obscure Greek composer*
 unfamiliar: *There were several unfamiliar names on the list*
 unsung: *among the unsung heroes of our time*
 see also **obscure, unfamiliar**

unlawful see **criminal, illegal**

unlike adjective different from: *She was unlike him in every way*
 different from: *I've always felt different from most people*
 dissimilar to: *a cultural background not dissimilar to our own*
 distinct from: *Their cuisines are quite distinct from each other*
 divergent from formal: *That viewpoint is not much divergent from that of his predecessor*
 far from: *His politics are not all that far from mine*
 see also **different**

unlikely adjective probably not true or likely to happen: *a military coup seems unlikely*
 implausible: *a film with an implausible ending*

incredible: *an incredible pack of lies*
 unbelievable: *I know it sounds unbelievable, but I wasn't there that day*
 unconvincing: *He came up with a very unconvincing excuse*
 see also **improbable**

unlimited see **universal**

unload see **empty**

unlock see **open**

unlocked see **open**

unlucky adjective having bad luck: *He was unlucky not to score during the first half*
 cursed: *the most cursed family in history*
 hapless: *a hapless victim of chance*
 luckless: *the luckless parents of a difficult child*
 unfortunate: *Some unfortunate person nearby could be injured*
 wretched: *wretched people who had to sell or starve*

unmarked see **blank**

unmarried see **single**

unmistakable see **naked, noticeable, plain**

unmitigated see **perfect, pure, rank, total**

unnatural see **creepy, stiff**

unnecessary adjective completely needless: *He frowns upon unnecessary expense*
 needless: *causing needless panic*
 pointless: *pointless meetings*
 uncalled-for: *uncalled-for rudeness*

unnerve see **alarm, frighten, scare, shake**

unnerving see **scary**

unpaid see **free, outstanding**

unpalatable see **unpleasant**

unparalleled see **incomparable**

unpleasant adjective **1** causing feelings of discomfort or dislike: *It has a very unpleasant smell*
 bad: *I have some bad news*

disagreeable: *a disagreeable experience*
distasteful: *I find her gossip distasteful*
nasty: *This divorce could turn nasty*
repulsive: *repulsive fat white slugs*
unpalatable: *Only then did I learn the unpalatable truth*
2 rude or unfriendly: *a thoroughly unpleasant person*
disagreeable: *He may be clever, but he's a very disagreeable man*
horrid: *I must have been a horrid little girl*
objectionable: *His tone was highly objectionable*
obnoxious: *Clarissa's obnoxious brother James*
rude: *He was frequently rude to waiters and servants*
unfriendly: *spoken in a rather unfriendly voice*
see also **disagreeable, horrible, nasty, painful, rough, rude**
unpolluted see **clean**
unpopular *adjective* disliked by most people: *an unpopular idea*
detested: *The rebels toppled the detested dictator*
disliked: *one of the most disliked choices on offer*
shunned: *the shunned former minister*
undesirable: *all sorts of undesirable effects on health*
unpredictable *adjective* unable to be foreseen: *Britain's notoriously unpredictable weather*
chance: *A chance meeting can change your life*
doubtful: *The outcome remains doubtful*
hit and miss *informal*: *Farming can be a very hit and miss affair*
unforeseeable: *unforeseeable weather conditions*

see also **changeable**
unproductive see **sterile, useless, vain**
unprotected see **helpless**
unqualified see **sheer, total**
unquestionably see **certainly**
unreasonable see **excessive, extreme, steep**
unreasonably see **too**
unrelated see **independent**
unrelenting see **relentless**
unreliable see **deceptive, dubious**
unremitting see **relentless**
unrivalled see **incomparable, superb, superior**
unroll see **spread**
unruly see **rowdy**
unsafe see **unsteady**
unsatisfactory *adjective* not good enough: *His work was judged unsatisfactory*
disappointing: *The results were disappointing*
inadequate: *The problem goes far beyond inadequate staffing*
mediocre: *a mediocre string of performances*
poor: *Her school record was poor at first*
unacceptable: *The quality of his work was unacceptable*
see also **poor, rotten**
unscrupulous see **corrupt**
unsecured see **loose**
unseemly see **inappropriate**
unseen see **invisible**
unselfish see **kind**
unsettle see **disturb**
unsettled see **restless**
unshakable see **firm**
unshakeable see **steadfast**
unsharpened see **blunt**
unsightly see **ugly**
unsound see **faulty, irrational, wrong**
unstable see **changeable, shaky,**

unsteady

unsteady adjective not held or fixed securely and likely to fall over: *a slightly unsteady item of furniture*
precarious: *The beds are precarious-looking hammocks strung from the walls*
rickety: *She stood on a rickety old table*
shaky: *He climbed up the shaky ladder to the scaffold*
tottering: *a tottering pile of bricks*
unsafe: *That bridge looks decidedly unsafe to me*
unstable: *funds used to demolish dangerously unstable buildings*
wobbly: *cat-scratched upholstery and wobbly chairs*
see also **shaky**

unsuccessful see **futile, in vain**

unsuitable adjective not appropriate for a purpose: *Her shoes were unsuitable for walking any distance*
improper: *an improper diet*
inappropriate: *inappropriate use of the Internet*
unacceptable: *using completely unacceptable language*
unfit: *unfit for human habitation*
see also **inappropriate, useless**

unsung see **unknown**

unsure see **dubious, hesitant**

unsuspecting see **unaware, unconscious**

untamed see **wild**

unthankful see **ungrateful**

unthinkable see **impossible, incredible**

untidy adjective not neatly arranged: *The place quickly became untidy*
bedraggled: *My hair was a bedraggled mess*
chaotic: *the chaotic mess of papers on his desk*
cluttered: *There was no space on the cluttered worktop*

jumbled: *We moved our supplies into a jumbled heap*
messy: *She was a good, if messy, cook*
unkempt: *the unkempt grass in front of the house*
see also **confused**

untie see **loosen**

untimely see **early, inappropriate**

untold see **countless, extensive, infinite**

untrue adjective not true: *The allegations were completely untrue*
erroneous: *an erroneous description*
false: *He gave a false name and address*
fictitious: *the source of the fictitious rumours*
inaccurate: *the passing on of inaccurate or misleading information*
incorrect: *an incorrect account of the sequence of events*
misleading: *It would be misleading to say we were friends*
mistaken: *I had a mistaken idea of what had happened*
see also **false, wrong**

untrustworthy see **sneaky, treacherous**

untruthful see **lying**

unused see **waste**

unusual adjective not occurring very often: *many rare and unusual plants*
curious: *a curious mixture of ancient and modern*
exceptional: *exceptional circumstances*
extraordinary: *What an extraordinary thing to happen!*
rare: *one of the rarest species in the world*
uncommon: *It's a very uncommon surname*
unconventional: *produced by an unconventional technique*
see also **curious, exceptional, extraordinary, funny, rare, scarce,**

singular, uncommon

unveil see **reveal, uncover**

unwell adjective ill or sick: *He felt unwell and had to go home early*

  ailing: *The President is said to be ailing*

  crook Australian, New Zealand informal: *I'm sorry to hear you've been crook, mate*

  ill: *Payne was seriously ill with pneumonia*

  poorly British informal: *Julie is still poorly after her bout of flu*

  queasy: *I always feel queasy on boats*

  sick: *He's very sick and he needs treatment*

  see also **crook, ill, queasy, sick, unhealthy**

unwholesome see **unhealthy**

unwilling adjective not wanting to do something: *an unwilling participant in school politics*

  averse: *I'm not averse to going along with the suggestion*

  grudging: *a grudging acceptance of the situation*

  loath: *She is loath to give up her hard-earned liberty*

  reluctant: *They were reluctant to get involved at first*

  see also **reluctant**

unwind see **relax**

unwise adjective foolish or not sensible: *It would be unwise to expect too much of her*

  daft: *You'd be daft to get on the wrong side of him*

  foolish: *It was foolish to risk injury like that*

  idiotic: *What an idiotic thing to do!*

  irresponsible: *irresponsible plans for tax cuts*

  rash: *Don't panic or do anything rash*

  senseless: *It would be senseless to try and stop him now*

  silly: *You're not going to go and do something silly, are you?*

  stupid: *I've had enough of your stupid suggestions*

  see also **foolish**

unwrap see **uncover**

up see **over**

up to see **equal to**

up-and-coming see **in the making**

upbeat see **cheery**

upbringing see **background**

upcoming see **near**

update see **revise**

upgrade see **improve, promote**

upheaval see **hassle**

uphill see **difficult**

uphold see **advocate, champion, defend, support**

upkeep noun the process and cost of maintaining something: *The money will be used for the upkeep of the grounds*

  keep: *He does not contribute towards his keep*

  maintenance: *the regular maintenance of government buildings*

  overheads: *We must cut our overheads or we shall have to close*

  preservation: *the preservation of historical sites*

  running: *The running of the house took up all her time*

up-market see **exclusive, posh**

upper limit see **maximum**

upper-class see **posh**

upright see **fair, noble, respectable, straight**

uprising see **rebellion**

uproar see **noise**

upset adjective **1** feeling unhappy about something: *She was very upset when she heard the news*

  agitated: *in an excited and agitated state*

  distressed: *The animals were distressed by the noise*

  frantic: *frantic with worry*

hurt: *I was very hurt when they refused*

troubled: *He sounded deeply troubled*

unhappy: *The divorce made him very unhappy*

▷ **verb 2** to make someone worried or unhappy: *The whole incident upset me terribly*

agitate: *The thought agitates her*

bother: *Don't let his manner bother you*

distress: *The whole thing really distressed him*

disturb: *These dreams disturb me for days afterwards*

grieve: *deeply grieved by their suffering*

ruffle: *She doesn't get ruffled by anything*

3 to turn something over accidentally: *Don't upset that pile of papers*

capsize: *He capsized the boat through his carelessness*

knock over: *The kitten knocked over the vase*

overturn: *She overturned her glass of wine as she stood up*

spill: *The waiter spilled the drinks all over the table*

see also **agitate, blow, distress, disturb, grieve, hurt, overturn, shake**

upsetting see **sad**

upshot see **effect, result**

upsurge see **increase, rise, spread, wave**

uptight see **nervous, tense**

up-to-date see **modern, recent**

up-to-the-minute see **current, modern**

upturn see **improvement**

urbane see **polite, sophisticated**

urge noun **1** a strong wish to do something: *stifling the urge to scream*

compulsion: *a compulsion to write*

desire: *I had a strong desire to help and care for people*

drive: *a demonic drive to succeed*

impulse: *Peter resisted an impulse to smile*

longing: *his longing to return home*

wish: *She had a genuine wish to make amends*

▷ **verb 2** to try hard to persuade someone: *He urged the government to change the law*

beg: *I begged him to leave me alone*

beseech: *Her eyes beseeched him to show mercy*

implore: *He left early, although they implored him to stay*

plead: *kneeling on the floor pleading for mercy*

press: *The unions are pressing him to stand firm*

see also **advise, insist, instinct, press, push, whim, wish**

urgent adjective needing to be dealt with quickly: *an urgent need for food and water*

compelling: *There are compelling reasons to act swiftly*

immediate: *The immediate problem is transportation*

imperative: *It is imperative we end up with a win*

pressing: *one of our most pressing problems*

see also **serious**

usage see **use**

use verb **1** to perform a task with something: *Use a sharp knife to trim the edges*

apply: *The company applies this technology to solve practical problems*

employ: *the methods employed in the study*

operate: *Can you operate a fax machine?*

utilize: *The body utilizes many different minerals*

▷ **noun 2** the act of using something: *the use of force*

application: *Her theory was put into practical application*

employment: *the employment of completely new methods*

operation: *the operation of the computer mouse*

usage: *Parts of the motor wore out because of constant usage*

3 the purpose for which something is utilized: *of no practical use whatsoever*

end: *The police force was manipulated for political ends*

object: *the object of the exercise*

point: *I don't see the point of a thing like that*

purpose: *It is wrong to use it for military purposes*

see also **impose**, **benefit**, **employ**, **value**, **wear**

use up see **drain**, **exhaust**

used see **accustomed**

useful *adjective* something which helps or makes things easier: *a great deal of useful information*

beneficial: *It may be beneficial to study the relevant guidelines*

effective: *Antibiotics are effective against this organism*

helpful: *a number of helpful booklets*

practical: *practical suggestions for healthy eating*

valuable: *Here are a few valuable tips to help you to succeed*

worthwhile: *a worthwhile source of income*

see also **beneficial**, **convenient**, **handy**, **helpful**, **productive**, **valuable**

usefulness see **value**

useless *adjective* not suitable or useful: *We realized that our money was useless here*

futile: *It would be futile to make any*

further attempts

impractical: *A tripod is impractical when following animals on the move*

unproductive: *increasingly unproductive land*

unsuitable: *This tool is completely unsuitable for use with metal*

worthless: *The old skills are worthless now*

see also **futile**, **hopeless**, **inadequate**, **incompetent**, **vain**, **worthless**

usher see **accompany**, **lead**, **take**

usual *adjective* done or happening most often: *sitting at his usual table*

accustomed: *She acted with her accustomed shrewdness*

common: *the commonest cause of death*

customary: *It's customary to offer guests a drink*

habitual: *He soon recovered his habitual geniality*

normal: *That's quite normal for a Friday*

regular: *samples from one of their regular suppliers*

standard: *It was standard practice to put them outside*

see also **average**, **common**, **natural**, **normal**, **ordinary**, **regular**, **routine**, **standard**, **stock**, **typical**

usually see **as a rule**, **on average**

utensil see **tool**

utilize see **employ**, **use**

utmost see **limit**, **maximum**, **ultimate**

utter *adjective* complete or total: *scenes of utter chaos*

absolute: *This is absolute madness!*

complete: *a complete mess*

consummate: *a consummate professional*

out-and-out: *an out-and-out lie*

outright: *an outright rejection of the deal*

perfect: *a perfect stranger*
pure: *She did it out of pure malice*
sheer: *an act of sheer stupidity*
thorough: *She is a thorough snob*
total: *a total failure*
see also **absolute, complete, emit, perfect, pure, rank, sheer, total**
utterance *see* **remark, word**

vacant *see* **bare, blank, empty**
vacation *see* **holiday, leave**
vague *adjective* not clearly expressed or clearly visible: *vague promises about raising standards*
  hazy: *Many details remain hazy*
  indefinite: *at some indefinite time in the future*
  indistinct: *The lettering was worn and indistinct*
  loose: *a loose translation*
  uncertain: *Students are facing an uncertain future*
  unclear: *The proposals were sketchy and unclear*
  see also **broad, dim, faint, rough, unclear**
vain *adjective* **1** very proud of your looks or qualities: *I think he is shallow and vain*
  conceited: *They had grown too conceited and pleased with themselves*
  egotistical: *an egotistical show-off*
  ostentatious: *He was generous with his money without being ostentatious*
  proud: *She was said to be proud and arrogant*
  stuck-up *informal*: *She was a famous actress, but she wasn't a bit stuck-up*
  2 not successful in achieving what

was intended: *He made a vain effort to cheer her up*

abortive: *the abortive coup attempt*

fruitless: *It was a fruitless search*

futile: *their futile attempts to avoid publicity*

unproductive: *an unproductive strategy*

useless: *a useless punishment which fails to stop crime*

in vain adjective unsuccessful in achieving what was intended: *Her complaints were in vain*

fruitless: *Four years of negotiation were fruitless*

to no avail: *His protests were to no avail*

unsuccessful: *Previous attempts have been unsuccessful*

wasted: *Their efforts were wasted*
see also **conceited, fond, futile, hopeless**

valiant see **brave**

valid see **legal, logical, right, sound**

validate see **confirm**

valour see **bravery, courage**

valuable adjective **1** having great importance or usefulness: *The experience was very valuable*

beneficial: *Using computers has a beneficial effect on learning*

helpful: *a number of helpful booklets*

important: *Her sons are the most important thing in her life*

prized: *one of the gallery's most prized possessions*

useful: *a mine of useful information*

worthwhile: *a worthwhile source of income*

2 worth a lot of money: *valuable old books*

costly: *a small and costly bottle of scent*

expensive: *exclusive, expensive possessions*

precious: *rings set with precious jewels*
see also **precious, productive, useful**

valuables plural noun the things you own that cost a lot of money: *Leave your valuables in the hotel safe*

heirlooms: *family heirlooms*

treasures: *The house was full of art treasures*

valuation see **estimate**

value noun **1** the importance or usefulness of something: *Studies are needed to see if these therapies have any value*

advantage: *the great advantage of this method*

benefit: *They see no benefit in educating these children*

effectiveness: *the effectiveness of the new system*

importance: *They have always placed great importance on live performances*

merit: *the artistic merit of their work*

use: *This is of no use to anyone*

usefulness: *the usefulness of the Internet in disseminating new ideas*

virtue: *the great virtue of modern technology*

worth: *This system has already proved its worth*

2 the amount of money that something is worth: *The value of his house has risen by more than 100%*

cost: *the cost of a loaf of bread*

market price: *buying shares at the current market price*

price: *a sharp increase in the price of petrol*

selling price: *the average selling price of a new home*

worth: *He sold the car for less than half its worth*

▷ verb **3** to appreciate something and think it is important: *Do you value your friends enough?*

appreciate: I would appreciate your advice

cherish: Cherish every moment you have with your children

have a high opinion of: Your boss seems to have a high opinion of you

prize: These items are prized by collectors

rate highly: He is an excellent keeper and I rate him highly

respect: I respect his talent as a pianist

treasure: memories I will treasure for the rest of my life

4 to decide how much money something is worth: I have had my jewellery valued for insurance purposes

appraise: He was called in to appraise and sell the cottage

assess: Experts are now assessing the cost of the restoration

cost: an operation costed at around $649m

estimate: a personal fortune estimated at more than $400m

evaluate: The company needs to evaluate the cost of leasing the building

price: The property was priced at less than £1m

see also **admire, appreciate, ideal, merit, price, prize, quality, treasure**

valueless see **worthless**

values see **standards**

vandal see **hooligan**

vanish verb **1** to disappear: The moon vanished behind a cloud

become invisible: The plane became invisible in the clouds

be lost to view: They watched the ship until it was lost to view

disappear: The aircraft disappeared off the radar

fade: We watched the harbour fade into the mist

recede: Gradually Luke receded into the distance

2 to cease to exist: Dinosaurs vanished from the earth millions of years ago

become extinct: Without help, these animals will become extinct

cease: At one o'clock the rain ceased

cease to exist: Without trees, the world as we know it would cease to exist

die out: Britain's bear population died out about 2,000 years ago

dissolve: The crowds dissolved and we were alone

evaporate: All my pleasure evaporated when I saw him

fade away: Her black mood faded away

go away: All she wanted was for the pain to go away

melt away: All my cares melted away

pass: Breathe deeply and the panic attack will pass

see also **die out, disappear, melt**

vanished see **lost**

vanity see **conceit, pride**

vanquish verb to defeat someone completely: a happy ending in which the hero vanquishes the monsters

beat: the team that beat us in the finals

conquer: a great warrior who conquers the enemies of his people

crush: their bid to crush the rebels

defeat: His guerrillas defeated the colonial army in 1954

overcome: They overcame the opposition to win the cup

rout: the battle at which the Norman army routed the English

trounce: Australia trounced France by 60 points to 4

see also **beat, crush, defeat, overcome, subdue**

vapour see **cloud**

variable see **changeable, irregular, uneven**

variant see **form**

variation noun a change from the normal or usual pattern: *a variation of the same route*

alteration: *some alterations in your diet*

change: *a change of attitude*

departure: *Her new novel is a departure from her previous work*

deviation: *Deviation from the norm is not tolerated*

difference: *a noticeable difference in his behaviour*

diversion: *a welcome diversion from the daily grind*

see also **difference**

variety noun **1** a number of different kinds of things: *a wide variety of readers*

array: *an attractive array of bright colours*

assortment: *an assortment of pets*

collection: *a huge collection of books*

medley: *a medley of vegetables*

mixture: *a mixture of sweets*

range: *a range of sun-care products*

2 a particular type of something: *a new variety of celery*

category: *There are three broad categories of soil*

class: *several classes of butterflies*

kind: *different kinds of roses*

sort: *several articles of this sort*

strain: *a new strain of the virus*

type: *What type of guns were they?*

see also **breed, choice, form, kind, range, sort, type**

various adjective of several different types: *trees of various sorts*

assorted: *swimsuits in assorted colours*

different: *different brands of drinks*

disparate: *the disparate cultures of India*

diverse: *Society is more diverse than ever before*

miscellaneous: *a hoard of miscellaneous junk*

sundry: *sundry journalists and lawyers*

see also **several**

vary verb **1** to change to something different: *weather patterns vary greatly*

alter: *During the course of a day the light alters constantly*

alternate: *My moods alternate with alarming rapidity*

change: *My feelings haven't changed*

fluctuate: *Weight may fluctuate markedly*

2 to introduce changes in something: *Vary your routes as much as possible*

alternate: *Alternate the chunks of fish with chunks of vegetable*

diversify: *They decided to diversify their products*

modify: *The government refuses to modify its position*

see also **range**

vast adjective extremely large: *farmers who own vast stretches of land*

colossal: *a colossal statue*

enormous: *The main bedroom is enormous*

giant: *a giant meteorite heading for the earth*

gigantic: *a gigantic shopping mall*

great: *a great hall as long as a church*

huge: *a huge crowd*

immense: *an immense castle*

massive: *a massive theme park*

see also **broad, colossal, enormous, extensive, huge, immense, large, spacious**

vault see **jump, leap, tomb**

veer see **swerve**

vehemence see **heat, strength, violence**

vehement | 568

vehement see **intense**

vehicle see **automobile, car, medium**

velocity see **rate, speed**

venerate see **respect, worship**

venerated see **holy**

vengeance see **revenge**

venom see **poison, spite**

venomous see **poisonous, spiteful**

vent see **opening**

venture see **dare, enterprise, undertaking**

verbal see **oral**

verdict noun a decision or opinion on something: *The doctor's verdict was that he was fine*

conclusion: *I've come to the conclusion that she's lying*

decision: *The editor's decision is final*

finding: *The court announced its findings*

judgment: *My judgment is that things are going to get worse*

opinion: *You should seek a medical opinion*

see also **conclusion, decision, judgment**

verge see **side**

verification see **proof**

verified see **actual**

verify see **confirm, determine, prove**

vernacular see **language**

versed in see **familiar**

versus see **against**

vertical see **sheer, steep, straight**

very adverb to a great degree: *very bad dreams*

deeply: *I was deeply sorry to hear about your loss*

extremely: *My mobile phone is extremely useful*

greatly: *I was greatly relieved when he finally arrived*

highly: *Mr Singh was a highly successful salesman*

really: *I know her really well*

terribly: *I'm terribly sorry to bother you*

see also **precise, really**

very much see **far**

vessel see **container**

vestige see **trace**

vestiges see **remains**

veteran see **practical**

veto verb **1** to forbid something: *Treasury officials vetoed the plans*

ban: *The authorities have banned the advertisement*

forbid: *Most airlines forbid the use of mobile phones on their planes*

prohibit: *The government intends to prohibit all trade with the country*
▷ noun **2** the act of forbidding or power to forbid something: *Dr. Baker has the power of veto*

ban: *the arms ban on the Bosnian government*

prohibition: *a prohibition on nuclear testing*

see also **forbid**

vex see **annoy**

viable see **economic, possible**

vibrant see **colourful**

vibrate see **shake**

vice see **evil**

vicious see **cruel, malicious, savage, violent, wicked**

viciousness see **cruelty**

victor see **champion, winner**

victory noun a success in a battle or competition: *his 15th consecutive victory in a doubles final*

laurels: *a former British champion took the laurels in this event*

success: *league and cup successes*

superiority: *United Nations air forces won air superiority*

triumph: *last year's Republican triumph in the elections*

win: *eight wins in nine games*

see also **success, triumph, win**

vie see **compete**

vie with see **play**

view noun **1** a personal opinion: *his political views*

attitude: *other people's attitudes towards you*

belief: *people's beliefs about crime*

conviction: *a firm conviction that things have improved*

feeling: *It is my feeling that Klein is right*

opinion: *a favourable opinion of our neighbours*

point of view: *an unusual point of view on the subject*

2 the things you can see from a particular place: *There was a beautiful view from the window*

aspect: *the Yorkshire hills which give the cottage a lovely aspect*

landscape: *Arizona's desert landscape*

panorama: *a panorama of fertile valleys*

perspective: *the aerial perspective of St Paul's Cathedral*

scene: *Wright surveyed the scene from his chosen seat*

spectacle: *a sweeping spectacle of rugged peaks*

▷ verb **3** to think of something in a particular way: *They viewed me with contempt*

consider: *We consider them to be our friends*

deem formal: *His ideas were deemed unacceptable*

judge: *His work was judged unsatisfactory*

regard: *They regard the tax as unfair*

see also **belief, feeling, idea, judgment, observe, opinion, outlook, regard, scene, scenery, thought, watch**

viewpoint noun an attitude towards something: *We all have our own personal viewpoints*

attitude: *other people's attitudes towards you*

belief: *people's beliefs about crime*

conviction: *a very personal, political conviction*

feeling: *What are your feelings on this matter?*

opinion: *a favourable opinion of our neighbours*

point of view: *an unusual point of view on the subject*

see also **opinion**

vigilant see **alert, observant, wary**

vigorous see **energetic, powerful**

vigour see **drive, energy, power, spirit, strength**

vile see **disgusting, evil, nasty**

vilify see **attack**

villain see **criminal, crook**

vindicate see **justify**

vindictive see **spiteful**

violate see **break, disobey, intrude, invade**

violated see **broken**

violation see **breach, crime**

violence noun **1** behaviour which is intended to hurt people: *Twenty people were killed in the violence*

bloodshed: *The government must avoid further bloodshed*

brutality: *the brutality of the war in Vietnam*

cruelty: *Human beings are capable of such cruelty to each other*

force: *If you use any force, I shall inform the police*

savagery: *acts of vicious savagery*

terrorism: *political terrorism in the 19th century*

2 force and energy: *Amy spoke with sudden violence*

fervour: *views he had put forward with fervour*

force: *She expressed her feelings with some force*

harshness: the harshness of her words

intensity: His voice hoarsened with intensity

severity: the severity of her scoldings

vehemence: Tweed was taken aback by her vehemence

violent adjective **1** intending to hurt or kill people: violent criminals

bloodthirsty: a bloodthirsty monster

brutal: a brutal crime

cruel: He is cruel towards animals

murderous: a murderous bank-robber

savage: savage warriors

vicious: He was a cruel and vicious man

2 happening unexpectedly and with great force: violent storms

powerful: He was caught by a powerful blow

raging: a raging flood

rough: A wooden ship sank in rough seas

strong: strong winds and rain

turbulent: the turbulent events of the century

wild: the wild gales sweeping up from the channel

3 said, felt, or done with great force: the violent reaction to his plans

acute: pain which grew more and more acute

furious: a furious row

intense: a look of intense dislike

powerful: a powerful backlash against the government

severe: a severe emotional shock

strong: strong words

see also **rude, savage, wild**

VIP see **celebrity**

virginal see **innocent**

virtually see **nearly**

virtue noun **1** the quality of doing what is morally right: He is a paragon of virtue

goodness: He has faith in human goodness

integrity: He was praised for his fairness and integrity

morality: standards of morality and justice in society

2 an advantage something has: the virtue of neatness

advantage: the advantages of the new system

asset: The one asset the job provided was contacts

attribute: a player with every attribute you could want

merit: the merits of various football teams

plus informal: The nutrients in milk have pluses and minuses

strength: the strengths and weaknesses of our position

by virtue of preposition because of: The article stuck in my mind by virtue of one detail

as a result of: People will feel better as a result of their efforts

because of: She was promoted because of her experience

by dint of: He succeeds by dint of hard work

on account of: The city is popular with tourists on account of its many museums

thanks to: Thanks to recent research, new treatments are available

see also **merit, right, value**

virtuoso see **fundi, genius**

virtuous see **holy, honest, noble**

visibility see **sight**

visible adjective **1** able to be seen: The warning lights were clearly visible

clear: the clearest pictures ever of Pluto

conspicuous: He felt more conspicuous than he'd have liked

distinguishable: colours just distinguishable in the dark

in sight: There wasn't another vehicle in sight

observable: the observable part of the Universe

perceptible: Daniel gave a barely perceptible nod

2 noticeable or evident: There was little visible excitement

apparent: There is no apparent reason for the crime

evident: He ate with evident enjoyment

manifest: his manifest enthusiasm

noticeable: subtle but noticeable changes

obvious: There are obvious dangers

plain: It is plain a mistake has been made

see also **evident**

vision noun **1** a mental picture in which you imagine things: my vision of the future

conception: my conception of a garden

daydream: He learned to escape into daydreams

dream: his dream of becoming a pilot

fantasy: fantasies of romance and true love

ideal: your ideal of a holiday

image: an image in your mind of what you are looking for

2 the ability to imagine future developments: a total lack of vision and imagination

foresight: They had the foresight to invest in technology

imagination: He had the imagination to foresee dangers

insight: the development of insight and understanding

intuition: Her intuition told her something was wrong

3 an experience in which you see things others cannot: She was convinced her visions were real

apparition: One of the women was the apparition he had seen

hallucination: The drug can cause hallucinations

illusion: Perhaps the footprint was an illusion

mirage: The girl was a mirage, created by his troubled mind

phantom: People claimed to have seen the phantom

spectre: a spectre from the other world

see also **dream, imagination, sight**

visit verb **1** to go to see and spend time with someone: He wanted to visit his brother in Sydney

call on: Don't hesitate to call on me

go to see: I'll go to see him in the hospital

look up: She looked up friends she had not seen for a while

▷ noun **2** a trip to see a person or place: Helen had recently paid him a visit

call: He decided to pay a call on Tommy

stay: An experienced guide is provided during your stay

stop: The last stop in Mr Cook's tour was Paris

see also **frequent**

visualize see **imagine, picture**

vital adjective **1** necessary or very important: a blockade which cut off vital fuel supplies

central: He is central to the whole project

critical: This decision will be critical to our future

crucial: the man who played a crucial role in the negotiations

essential: It is essential that you see a doctor soon

important: the most important piece of evidence in the case

indispensable: an indispensable

piece of equipment
necessary: *the skills necessary for survival*
pivotal: *He played a pivotal role in the match*
2 energetic and full of life: *Old age has diminished a once vital person*
active: *an active youngster*
dynamic: *a dynamic and exciting place*
energetic: *She became a shadow of her happy, energetic self*
lively: *a beautiful, lively young girl*
spirited: *the spirited heroine of this film*
sprightly: *a sprightly old man*
vivacious: *She is vivacious and charming*
see also **basic, critical, crucial, essential, necessary**

vitality see **energy**

vivacious see **active, alive, lively, vital**

vivid see **bold, bright, brilliant, colourful**

vocabulary see **language**

vociferous see **noisy**

vogue see **craze, fashion**

voice see **express, say**

void see **abyss**

volatile see **changeable, moody**

volition see **will**

volley see **hail**

volume see **amount, book, capacity, quantity**

voluminous see **full**

voluptuous see **sexy**

vomit *verb* to have food and drink come back up through the mouth: *Any product made from milk made him vomit*
be sick: *She was sick in the handbasin*
bring up: *Certain foods are difficult to bring up*
chunder *Australian, New Zealand slang: the time you chundered*

in the taxi
heave: *He gasped and heaved and vomited again*
puke *informal: They got drunk and puked out of the window*
regurgitate: *swallowing and regurgitating large quantities of water*
see also **puke**

vote *noun* **1** a decision made by allowing people to state their preference: *Do you think we should have a vote on that?*
ballot: *The result of the ballot will be known soon*
plebiscite *formal: A plebiscite made Hitler the Chancellor*
polls: *In 1945, Churchill was defeated at the polls*
referendum: *Estonia planned to hold a referendum on independence*
▷ *verb* **2** to indicate a choice or opinion: *It seems that many people would vote for the opposition*
cast a vote: *90% of those who cast a vote*
go to the polls: *Voters are due to go to the polls on Sunday*
opt: *The mass of Spaniards opted for democracy*
return: *Members will be asked to return a vote for or against the motion*
3 to suggest that something should happen: *I vote that we all go to Holland*
propose: *I propose that we all try to get some sleep*
recommend: *I recommend that he be sent home early*
suggest: *I suggest we go round the table and introduce ourselves*
see also **say**

vow see **oath, promise**

voyage see **journey, trip**

vrou see **woman**

vulgar *adjective* **1** socially unacceptable or offensive: *vulgar*

language
coarse: *coarse humour*
crude: *crude pictures*
dirty: *dirty jokes*
indecent: *an indecent suggestion*
rude: *a rude gesture*
uncouth: *that oafish, uncouth person*
2 showing a lack of taste or quality: *I think it's a very vulgar house*
common: *She could be a little common at times*
flashy: *flashy clothes*
gaudy: *a gaudy purple-and-orange hat*
tasteless: *a house with tasteless decor*
tawdry: *a tawdry seaside town*
see also **common, crude, gaudy, indecent, low, naughty, tasteless**

vulnerability see **weakness**

vulnerable *adjective* **1** weak and without protection: *vulnerable old people*
exposed: *The west coast is very exposed to Atlantic winds*
sensitive: *Most people are highly sensitive to criticism*
susceptible: *an area that is susceptible to attack*
weak: *He spoke up for the weak and defenceless*
see also **helpless, impressionable**

waffle see **nonsense**

waft see **blow**

wages see **income, pay**

wail see **lament**

wait *verb* **1** to spend time before something happens: *Wait until we get there*
linger: *I lingered on for a few days until he arrived*
pause: *The crowd paused for a minute, wondering what to do next*
remain: *You'll have to remain in hospital for the time being*
stand by: *Ships are standing by to evacuate the people*
stay: *Stay here while I go for help*
▷ *noun* **2** a period of time before something happens: *They faced a three-hour wait before they could leave*
delay: *The accident caused some delay*
interval: *a long interval when no-one spoke*
pause: *There was a pause before he replied*
see also **pause, remain, stay**

wake *verb* to make or become conscious again after sleep: *It was still dark when he woke*
awake: *We were awoken by the doorbell*

come to: When she came to she found it was raining

rouse: We roused him at seven so he would be on time

stir: She shook him and he started to stir

waken: wakened by the thunder

waken see **wake**

walk verb **1** to go on foot: I walked slowly along the road

see **word studies walk**

▷ noun **2** a journey made by walking: We'll have a quick walk while it's fine

hike: a long hike in the country

march: a day's march north of their objective

ramble: They went for a ramble through the woods

stroll: After dinner we took a stroll around the city

trek: He's on a trek across the Antarctic

3 the way someone moves when walking: Despite his gangling walk he was a good dancer

carriage: her regal carriage

gait: an awkward gait

pace: moving at a brisk pace down the road

stride: He lengthened his stride to catch up with her

see also **ramble**

wall see **barrier**

wan see **pale**

wand see **stick**

wander verb to move about in a casual way: They wandered aimlessly around the village

cruise: A police car cruised by

drift: The balloon drifted slowly over the countryside

ramble: freedom to ramble across the moors

range: They range widely in search of food

roam: Barefoot children roamed the streets

stroll: We strolled down the street, looking at the shops

see also **ramble**

wandering see **indirect**

wane see **abate, fail, weaken**

want verb **1** to feel a desire for something: I want a red car for a change

covet: He coveted his boss's job

crave: Sometimes she still craved chocolate

desire: He could make them do whatever he desired

wish: I don't wish to know that

2 to need something: My hair wants cutting

be deficient in: Their diet was deficient in vitamins

demand: The task of reconstruction demanded much sacrifice

lack: training to give him the skills he lacked

need: My car needs servicing

require: He knows exactly what is required of him

▷ noun **3** a lack of something: becoming weak from want of rest

absence: a complete absence of evidence

deficiency: They did blood tests for signs of vitamin deficiency

lack: He got the job in spite of his lack of experience

scarcity: an increasing scarcity of water

shortage: A shortage of funds is holding them back

see also **deficiency, demand, desire, hardship, lack, need, poverty, require, shortage, wish**

wanting see **deficient**

wanton see **promiscuous, shameless**

war noun **1** a period of armed conflict between countries: The war dragged on for five years

combat: men who died in combat

conflict: The conflict is bound to intensify

fighting: He was killed in the fighting which followed the treaty

hostilities: in case hostilities break out

strife: The country was torn with strife

warfare: chemical warfare

▷ verb **2** to fight against something: The two countries had been warring with each other for years

battle: Thousands of people battled with the police

clash: The two armies clashed at first light

combat: measures to combat smuggling

fight: The tribe fought with its rivals see also **conflict**

warden see **guard**

wardrobe see **clothes**

warehouse see **store**

warfare see **war**

warm adjective **1** having some heat but not hot: a warm spring day

balmy: balmy summer evenings

heated: a heated swimming pool

lukewarm: Heat the milk until lukewarm

pleasant: After a chilly morning, the afternoon was very pleasant

tepid: a bath full of tepid water

2 friendly and affectionate: a warm and likable personality

affectionate: with an affectionate glance at her children

amiable: He was very amiable company

cordial: We were given a most cordial welcome

friendly: All her colleagues were very friendly

genial: a warm-hearted friend and genial host

loving: He is a loving husband and father

▷ verb **3** to heat something gently: The sun came out and warmed his back

heat: Heat the bread in the oven

heat up: The fire soon heated up the room

melt: He melted the butter in a small pan

thaw: Always thaw pastry thoroughly

warm up: You must begin gently to warm up the muscles

see also **cosy, hot, loving, tender**

warm up see **heat, warm**

warmth see **affection, enthusiasm, heat, passion**

warn verb to give advance notice of something unpleasant: I warned him about those looking tiles

alert: The siren alerted them to the danger

caution: Their reaction cautioned him against any further attempts

forewarn: We were forewarned of what to expect

notify: The weather forecast notified them of the coming storm

see also **alert, caution, notify**

warning noun something that tells people of possible danger: advance warning of the attack

alarm: They heard the fire alarm and ran to safety

alert: a security alert

caution: a note of caution

notice: three months' notice

premonition: He had a premonition of bad news

see also **alarm, indication, lecture, notice, omen**

warp see **bend**

warped see **crooked**

warrant see **deserve, justify, merit, permit**

warrigal see **wild**

warrior see **fighter**

wary adjective showing lack of trust in something: She was wary of marriage

cautious: His experience has made him cautious

distrustful: Voters are deeply distrustful of all politicians

guarded: The boy gave him a guarded look

suspicious: He was rightly suspicious of their motives

vigilant: He warned the public to be vigilant

see also **alert, cautious, suspicious**

wash verb **1** to clean something with water: He got a job washing dishes

bathe: She bathed her blistered feet

cleanse: the correct way to cleanse the skin

launder: freshly laundered shirts

rinse: Rinse several times in clear water

scrub: I was scrubbing the bathroom floor

shampoo: You must shampoo your hair first

2 to carry something by the force of water: washed ashore by the waves

carry off: The debris was carried off on the tide

erode: Exposed soil is quickly eroded by wind and rain

sweep away: The floods swept away the houses by the river

see also **clean**

wash away see **wear**
wash out see **fade**
washed see **clean**

waste verb **1** to use too much of something unnecessarily: I wouldn't waste my money on something like that

fritter away: He just fritters his time away

squander: He had squandered his chances of winning

throw away: You're throwing away a good opportunity

▷ noun **2** using something excessively or unnecessarily: What a complete waste of money!

extravagance: widespread tales of his extravagance

misuse: This project is a misuse of public funds

squandering: a squandering of his valuable time

▷ adjective **3** not needed or wanted: waste paper

leftover: leftover pieces of fabric

superfluous: She got rid of many superfluous belongings

unused: spoiled or unused ballot papers

see also **barren, garbage, refuse, rubbish, trash**

wasted see **in vain, weak**

wasteful adjective using something in a careless or extravagant way: wasteful duplication of effort

extravagant: an extravagant lifestyle

uneconomical: the uneconomical duplication of jobs

watch noun **1** a period of time when a guard is kept on something: Keep a close watch on the prisoners

observation: In hospital she'll be under observation night and day

supervision: A toddler requires close supervision

surveillance: kept under constant surveillance

▷ verb **2** to look at something for some time: I don't watch television very often

gaze at: gazing at herself in the mirror

look at: They looked closely at the insects

observe: Researchers observed the behaviour of small children

pay attention: Pay attention or you

liking: a liking for tripe and onions
passion: His other great passion was his motorbike
penchant: a stylish woman with a penchant for dark glasses
see also **defect, disadvantage, fault, love**

wealth noun **1** a large amount of money: Economic reform brought them wealth
  affluence: the trappings of affluence
  fortune: He made a fortune in the property boom
  means: a person of means
  money: All that money brought nothing but sadness and misery
  prosperity: Japan's economic prosperity
  riches: His Olympic medal brought him fame and riches
  substance: run by local men of substance
2 a lot of something: a wealth of information
  abundance: This area has an abundance of safe beaches
  bounty: autumn's bounty of fruits and berries
  plenty: He grew up in a time of plenty
  store: She dipped into her store of theatrical anecdotes
see also **success**

wealthy adjective having plenty of money: She came from a very wealthy background
  affluent: living in an affluent neighbourhood
  comfortable: from a stable, comfortable family
  opulent: Most of the cash went on supporting his opulent lifestyle
  prosperous: The place looks more prosperous than ever
  rich: I'm going to be very rich one day
  well-to-do: a rather well-to-do family in the shipping business

see also **rich**

wear verb **1** to be dressed in something: He was wearing a brown uniform
  be clothed in: She was clothed in a flowered dress
  be dressed in: The women were dressed in their finest attire
  don: The police responded by donning riot gear
  have on: I had my new shoes on that night
  put on: He had to put on his glasses to read the paper
  sport Informal: sporting a red tie
2 to become worse in condition with use or age: The old stone steps were worn in the middle
  corrode: The underground pipes were badly corroded
  erode: Exposed rock is quickly eroded by wind and rain
  fray: fraying edges on the stair carpet
  rub: The inscription had been rubbed smooth by generations of hands
  wash away: The topsoil had been washed away by the incessant rain
▷ noun **3** the type of use which causes something to be damaged: The tyres showed signs of wear
  corrosion: Zinc is used to protect other metals from corrosion
  deterioration: The building is already showing signs of deterioration
  erosion: erosion of the river valleys
  use: The carpet must be able to cope with heavy use
see also **clothes**

wear away see **eat away, erode**
wear down see **erode**
wearied see **bored**
weariness see **boredom**
wear out verb to make someone tired: The past few days have really worn me out
  exhaust: The long working day

exhausted him

tire: If driving tires you, take the train

weary: wearied by the constant demands on his time

see also **exhaust**

weary adjective very tired: She sank to the ground, too weary to walk another step

drained: He's always completely drained after a performance

exhausted: She was too exhausted and upset to talk

fatigued: Winter weather can leave you feeling fatigued

tired: He was too tired even to take a shower

tuckered out Australian, New Zealand informal: You must be tuckered out after that bus trip

worn out: He's just worn out after the long drive

see also **sick of, tired, wear out, worn-out**

weave see **twist**

web see **tangle**

wedge see **lump**

wedlock see **marriage**

wee see **tiny**

weed out see **get rid of**

weep see **lament**

weigh see **compare, count**

weight see **burden, emphasis, influence**

weighted see **biased**

weighty see **heavy, important, serious**

weird adjective strange or odd: I had such a weird dream last night

bizarre: his bizarre behaviour

curious: What a curious thing to say!

extraordinary: an extraordinary occurrence

funny: There's something funny about him

odd: an odd coincidence

singular formal: I can't think where

you got such a singular notion

strange: Didn't you notice anything strange about her?

peculiar: It tasted very peculiar

queer: I think there's something queer going on here

see also **bizarre, eccentric, odd, peculiar, strange**

weirdo noun informal a person who behaves in a strange way: All the other kids thought I was a weirdo

crank informal: He kept quiet in case people thought he was a crank

eccentric: a local eccentric who wears shorts all year round

freak informal: Barry's always been looked on as a bit of a freak

loony slang: I realize I must sound like a complete loony

nut slang: There's some nut out there with a gun

nutter British slang: She was being stalked by a real nutter

welcome see **greet, receive**

welcoming see **favourable, friendly, homely**

well adverb 1 in a satisfactory way: The interview went well

satisfactorily: The system should work satisfactorily

smoothly: So far, the operation is going smoothly

splendidly: They have behaved splendidly

successfully: The changeover is working successfully

2 with skill and ability: He draws well

ably: He was ably assisted by the other members of staff

admirably: dealing admirably with a difficult situation

adequately: He speaks French very adequately

competently: They handled the situation very competently

effectively: In the first half he

operated effectively in defence

efficiently: He works efficiently and accurately

expertly: Shopkeepers expertly rolled spices up in bay leaves

professionally: These tickets have been forged very professionally

skilfully: He skilfully exploited his company's strengths

3 fully and with thoroughness: They should be well washed and well dried

amply: I was amply rewarded for my trouble

closely: He studied the documents closely

completely: Make sure you defrost it completely

fully: The new system is now fully under way

highly: one of the most highly regarded authors

meticulously: He had planned his trip meticulously

rigorously: Their duties have not been performed as rigorously as they might have been

thoroughly: Add the oil and mix thoroughly

4 in a kind way: He treats his employees well

compassionately: He always acted compassionately towards me

considerately: I expect people to deal with me considerately and fairly

favourably: companies who treat men more favourably than women

humanely: They treat their livestock humanely

kindly: Children are capable of behaving kindly

with consideration: He was treated with consideration and kindness

▷ *adjective* **5** having good health: I'm not very well today

blooming: She felt confident, blooming, and attractive

fit: He keeps himself really fit

healthy: Most people want to be healthy and happy

in good condition: He's in good condition for his age

in good health: He seemed to be in good health and spirits

robust: He's never been a very robust child

sound: a sound body

strong: Eat well and you'll soon be strong again

see also **fit**, **healthy**

well off see **rich**

well-behaved see **polite**

wellbeing see **comfort**, **health**

well-built see **sturdy**

well-known see **prominent**

well-liked see **popular**

well-mannered see **polite**

well-to-do see **wealthy**

well-versed see **experienced**

wet *adjective* **1** covered in liquid: Don't get your feet wet

damp: Her hair was still damp

drenched: getting drenched by icy water

moist: The soil is reasonably moist after the September rain

saturated: The filter has been saturated with oil

soaked: soaked to the skin

sodden: We took off our sodden clothes

waterlogged: The game was called off because the pitch was waterlogged

2 in rainy weather conditions: It was a miserable wet day

humid: hot and humid weather conditions

misty: The air was cold and misty

rainy: The rainy season starts in December

showery: The day had been showery with sunny intervals

▷ *verb* **3** to put liquid onto

something: *Wet the edges and stick them together*

dampen: *You must dampen the laundry before you iron it*

irrigate: *irrigated by a system of interconnected canals*

moisten: *Take a sip of water to moisten your throat*

soak: *The water had soaked his jacket and shirt*

spray: *It can spray the whole field in half an hour*

water: *We have to water the plants when the weather is dry*

see also **damp, soak**

whack see **bang, blow**

whereabouts see **location, position**

wherewithal see **potential**

whiff see **trace**

while see **but, period, space, time**

whim noun a sudden fancy for something: *We decided to go more or less on a whim*

craze: *the latest fitness craze*

fad informal: *just a passing fad*

fancy: *I had a fancy for some strawberries*

impulse: *He resisted the impulse to buy a new one*

urge: *He had an urge to open a shop of his own*

whimsical see **eccentric**

whine see **complain, grumble, moan**

whinge see **complain, grumble, moan**

whip up see **incite**

whirl see **blow, spin**

whisper see **rumour**

whole adjective 1 indicating all of something: *We spent the whole summer abroad*

complete: *The list filled a complete page*

entire: *There are only ten in the entire country*

full: *a full week's notice*

total: *The evening was a total fiasco*

uncut: *the uncut version of the film*

undivided: *He has my undivided loyalty*

▷ noun 2 the full amount of something: *the whole of Asia*

aggregate: *the aggregate of the individual scores*

all: *All is not lost*

everything: *Everything that happened is my fault*

lot: *He lost the lot within five minutes*

sum total: *The small room contained the sum total of their possessions*

total: *The eventual total was far higher*

see also **complete, total**

wholehearted see **sincere**

wholesome see **beneficial, healthy, safe**

wicked adjective 1 very bad or evil: *That was a wicked thing to do*

atrocious: *He had committed atrocious crimes against the refugees*

bad: *Please forgive our bad behaviour*

depraved: *the work of depraved criminals*

evil: *the country's most evil terrorists*

sinful: *"This is a sinful world," he said*

vicious: *He was a cruel and vicious man*

2 mischievous in an amusing or attractive way: *She always felt wicked when eating chocolate*

impish: *an impish sense of humour*

mischievous: *like a mischievous child*

naughty: *little boys using naughty words*

see also **evil**

wickedness see **evil, sin**

wide adjective 1 measuring a large distance from side to side: *It should be wide enough to give plenty of working space*

2 extensive in scope: *a wide range*

of colours

▷ adverb **3** as far as possible: *Open wide!*

see **word studies** **wide**

see also **broad, extensive, thick**

widen see **extend**

wide-ranging see **broad**

widespread *adjective* existing over a large area: *Food shortages are widespread*

broad: *The agreement won broad support among the people*

common: *the common view that treatment is ineffective*

extensive: *The bomb caused extensive damage*

pervasive: *the pervasive influence of the army in national life*

prevalent: *Smoking is becoming more prevalent among girls*

rife: *Bribery and corruption were rife in the industry*

see also **common, extensive, general, mass, universal**

wife see **partner**

wild *adjective* **1** not cultivated or domesticated: *a meadow of wild flowers*

fierce: *Fierce hyenas scavenged for food after the kill*

free: *stunning pictures of wild and free animals*

natural: *In the natural state this animal is not ferocious*

uncultivated: *developed from an uncultivated type of grass*

undomesticated: *These cats lived wild and were completely undomesticated*

untamed: *the untamed horses of the Camargue*

warrigal *Australian literary*: *a warrigal mare*

2 in stormy conditions: *They were not deterred by the wild weather*

howling: *a howling gale*

raging: *The trip involved crossing a raging torrent*

rough: *The two ships collided in rough seas*

stormy: *a dark and stormy night*

violent: *That night they were hit by a violent storm*

3 without control or restraint: *wild with excitement*

boisterous: *Most of the children were noisy and boisterous*

rowdy: *The television coverage revealed their rowdy behaviour*

turbulent: *five turbulent years of rows and reconciliations*

uncontrolled: *His uncontrolled behaviour disturbed the entire group*

wayward: *wayward children with a history of emotional problems*

see also **crazy, fanatical, irresponsible, on the rampage, rowdy, violent**

wildness see **abandon**

wilful see **obstinate, stubborn**

will *verb* **1** to leave something to someone when you die: *He had willed his fortune to his daughter*

bequeath: *She bequeathed her collection to the local museum*

leave: *Everything was left to the housekeeper*

pass on: *He passed on much of his estate to his eldest son*

▷ *noun* **2** the strong determination to achieve something: *the will to win*

determination: *Determination has always been a part of his make-up*

purpose: *They are enthusiastic and have a sense of purpose*

resolution: *He began to form a resolution to clear his name*

resolve: *This will strengthen the public's resolve*

willpower: *succeeding by sheer willpower*

3 what someone wants: *the will of*

the people

choice: It's your choice

inclination: She showed no inclination to go

mind: You can go if you have a mind to do so

volition: a product of our volition

wish: done against my wishes

willing adjective ready and eager to do something: a willing helper

agreeable: We can go ahead if you are agreeable

eager: Children are eager to learn

game informal: He still had new ideas and was game to try them

happy: That's a risk I'm happy to take

prepared: I'm not prepared to take orders from her

ready: ready to die for their beliefs see also **agreeable, ready**

willpower see **will**

wilt see **wither**

wily see **crafty, cunning, devious, sly**

wimp see **coward**

win verb 1 to defeat your opponents: The top four teams all won

be victorious: Despite the strong opposition she was victorious

come first: They unexpectedly came first this year

prevail: the votes he must win in order to prevail

succeed: the skills and qualities needed to succeed

triumph: a symbol of good triumphing over evil

2 to succeed in obtaining something: moves to win the support of the poor

achieve: We have achieved our objective

attain: He's half-way to attaining his pilot's licence

gain: After three weeks the hostages finally gained their freedom

get: My entry got a commendation this year

secure: Her achievements helped secure her the job

▷ noun 3 a victory in a contest: a run of seven games without a win

success: his success in the Monaco Grand Prix

triumph: their World Cup triumph

victory: the 3-1 victory over Switzerland

see also **earn, gain, triumph, victory**

win over see **persuade, reason**

wince see **flinch**

wind see **coil**

wind up see **conclude**

winner noun a person who wins something: The winners will be notified by post

champion: a former Olympic champion

conqueror: This time they easily overcame their former conquerors

victor: He emerged as the victor by the second day

see also **champion, success**

wintry see **cold**

wipe see **clean**

wisdom noun judgment used to make sensible decisions: the wisdom that comes from experience

discernment: Her keen discernment made her an excellent collector

insight: a man of considerable insight and diplomatic skills

judgment: He respected our judgment on this matter

knowledge: the quest for scientific knowledge

reason: a conflict between emotion and reason

see also **knowledge, sense**

wise adjective able to make use of experience and judgment: a wise old man

informed: an informed guess at his wealth

judicious: the judicious use of military force

perceptive: the words of a perceptive political commentator

rational: You must look at both sides before you can reach a rational decision

sensible: The sensible thing is to leave them alone

shrewd: a shrewd deduction about what was going on

see also **logical**, **reasonable**, **sensible**

wisecrack see **joke**

wish noun **1** a desire for something: She was sincere in her wish to make amends

desire: her desire for a child of her own

hankering: She had always had a hankering to be an actress

hunger: a hunger for success

longing: He felt a longing for familiar surroundings

urge: He had an urge to open a shop of his own

want: Supermarkets respond to the wants of their customers

▷ verb **2** to want something: We wished to return

desire: He was bored and desired to go home

hunger: She hungered for adventure

long: I'm longing for the holidays

thirst: thirsting for knowledge

want: people who know exactly what they want in life

yearn: The younger ones yearned to be part of a normal family

see also **desire**, **urge**, **want**, **will**

wistful see **sad**

wit see **common sense**, **humour**, **intelligence**

witchcraft see **magic**

withdraw verb **1** to take something out: He withdrew some money from the bank

draw out: I'll have to draw out some of my savings

extract: She extracted another dress from the wardrobe

remove: I removed the splinter from her finger

take out: There was a fee for taking out money from the account

2 to back out of an activity: They withdrew from the conference

back out: He backed out of the agreement

leave: Davis left the game to go to hospital

pull out: The general pulled out of the talks after two days

retire: The jury retired three hours ago

retreat: retreating from the harsh realities of life

see also **leave**, **remove**, **retreat**

withdrawal see **retreat**

withdrawn see **distant**, **remote**

wither verb to become weaker and fade away: Will the company flourish or wither?

decline: The church's influence has declined

droop: plants drooping in the heat

fade: Prospects for peace have already started to fade

shrivel: They watched their crops shrivel and die in the drought

wilt: The roses wilted the day after she bought them

withering see **scornful**

withhold see **deny**, **refuse**

without charge see **free**

without delay see **now**

without doubt see **certainly**

witness noun **1** someone who has seen something happen: The police appealed for witnesses to come forward

bystander: Seven other innocent bystanders were injured

eyewitness: Eyewitnesses say the

soldiers opened fire on the crowd
observer: *A casual observer would not have noticed them*
onlooker: *a small crowd of onlookers*
spectator: *carried out in full view of spectators*
▷ verb **2** to see something happening: *Anyone who witnessed the attack should call the police*
be present at: *Many men are now present at the birth of their children*
observe: *We observed them setting up the machine gun*
see: *I saw him do it*
watch: *She had watched them drinking heavily before the accident*
see also **observe, spectator**

wits see **head**

witticism see **joke**

witty adjective amusing in a clever way: *He's so witty I could listen to him for hours*
amusing: *He provided an irreverent and amusing commentary to the film*
brilliant: *a brilliant after-dinner speaker*
clever: *He raised some smiles with several clever lines*
funny: *a film packed with incredibly funny dialogue*
humorous: *a satirical and humorous parody*
sparkling: *He's famous for his sparkling conversation*
see also **funny**

wizard see **expert**

wobbly see **loose, shaky, unsteady**

woe see **care, misery, sorrow**

wolf see **gobble**

woman noun an adult female human being: *women over 75 years old*
dame slang: *Who does that dame think she is?*
female: *The average young female is fairly affluent*
girl: *a night out with the girls*

lady: *Your table is ready, ladies, so please come through*
lass: *a lass from the country*
sheila Australian, New Zealand informal: *his role as a sheila in his own play*
vrou South African: *Have you met his vrou yet?*
see also **adult, female**

womanly see **female**

wonder verb **1** to think about something with curiosity: *I wondered what that noise was*
ask oneself: *You have to ask yourself what this really means*
ponder: *pondering how to improve the team*
puzzle: *Researchers continue to puzzle over the origins of the disease*
speculate: *He refused to speculate about the contents of the letter*
2 to be surprised and amazed: *He wondered at her anger*
be amazed: *Most of the cast were amazed by the play's success*
be astonished: *I was astonished to discover his true age*
boggle: *The mind boggles at what might be in store for us*
marvel: *We marvelled at her endless energy*
▷ noun **3** something that amazes people: *one of the wonders of nature*
marvel: *a marvel of high technology*
miracle: *It's a miracle no one was killed*
phenomenon: *a well-known geographical phenomenon*
spectacle: *a spectacle not to be missed*
see also **amazement, miracle, surprise**

wonderful adjective **1** extremely good: *It's wonderful to see you*
excellent: *The recording quality is excellent*

great *informal: a great bunch of guys*
marvellous: *What a marvellous time we had!*
superb: *The hotel has a superb isolated location*
tremendous: *I thought it was a tremendous book*
2 very impressive: *The sunset was a truly wonderful sight*
amazing: *containing some amazing special effects*
astounding: *The results are quite astounding*
incredible: *The intensity of colour was incredible*
magnificent: *magnificent views across the valley*
remarkable: *It was a remarkable achievement to complete the course*
see also **brilliant, grand, marvellous, splendid, superb**
wont see **custom**
woo see **court**
wooden see **stiff**
wool see **coat**
word noun **1**
2 a remark: *I'd like to say a word of thanks to everyone who helped me*
comment: *He left without any further comment*
remark: *Apart from that one remark, he stayed quiet all evening*
statement: *Verity issued a brief statement to the press*
utterance: *a crowd of admirers who hung on his every utterance*
3 a brief conversation: *James, could I have a quick word with you?*
chat: *We need to have a chat about the arrangements some time*
conversation: *He recalled his brief conversation with the Queen*
discussion: *We had a very short discussion about what to do*
talk: *I bumped into him yesterday and we had a quick talk*

4 a message: *Since then we've had no word from them*
announcement: *There has been no formal announcement from either government*
bulletin: *A spokesperson said no bulletin would be issued*
communication: *The ambassador brought a communication from the President*
information: *They will issue written information in due course*
intelligence: *He wanted to pass this intelligence on to her*
message: *Did he leave any message for me?*
news: *Is there any news from the embassy?*
5 a promise or guarantee: *He gave me his word that he would be there*
assurance: *Do I have your assurance that you'll take responsibility?*
oath: *She gave her solemn oath not to tell anyone*
pledge: *He gave his personal pledge that he would help*
promise: *I'll support you – you have my promise on that*
word of honour: *I want your word of honour that you'll respect my anonymity*
see also **bond, guarantee, information, message, news, put, remark, rumour, term**
word of honour see **word**
wording see **language**
wordless see **silent**
work verb **1** to do the tasks required of you: *I had to work twelve hours a day*
labour: *peasants labouring in the fields*
slave: *slaving over a hot stove*
slog away: *They are still slogging away at algebra*
toil: *Workers toiled long hours in*

the mills

▷ noun 2 someone's job: She's trying to find work

business: We have business to attend to first

craft: He learned his craft from an expert

employment: unable to find employment

job: I got at a job at the sawmill

livelihood: fishermen who depend on the seas for their livelihood

occupation: Please state your occupation

profession: a dentist by profession

3 the tasks that have to be done: Sometimes he had to take work home

assignment: written assignments and practical tests

chore: We share the household chores

duty: My duty is to look after the animals

job: It turned out to be a bigger job than expected

task: catching up with administrative tasks

yakka Australian, New Zealand informal: a decade of hard yakka on the land

see also **act, behave, book, drive, effort, exercise, fashion, function, go, labour, piece, struggle, succeed**

work together see **cooperate, team, unite**

workable see **possible**

worker noun a person who works: seeking a reliable research worker

craftsman: furniture made by a local craftsman

employee: Many of its employees are women

labourer: a farm labourer

workman: Workmen are building a steel fence

see also **employee**

workers see **labour, staff**

workforce see **labour, staff**

working see **busy**

workman see **employee, worker**

workmate see **associate, colleague**

work out verb 1 to find the solution to something: It took us some time to work out what was happening

calculate: First, calculate your monthly living expenses

figure out: You don't need to be a detective to figure that one out

resolve: They hoped the crisis could be quickly resolved

solve: We'll solve the case ourselves and surprise everyone

2 to happen in a certain way: Things didn't work out that way after all

develop: Wait and see how the situation develops

go: Did it all go well?

happen: Things don't happen the way you want them to

turn out: Sometimes life doesn't turn out as we expect

see also **calculate, comprehend, crack, reckon, resolve, solve**

works see **factory**

world see **earth, scene**

worldwide see **universal**

worn see **shabby, worn-out**

worn out see **tired, weary**

worn-out adjective 1 no longer usable because of extreme wear: a worn-out pair of shoes

broken-down: Broken-down cars lined the road

tattered: tattered clothes

threadbare: a square of threadbare carpet

worn: Worn tyres cost lives

2 extremely tired: You must be worn-out after the journey

exhausted: too exhausted to do any more

fatigued: Winter weather can leave

you feeling fatigued

prostrate: He lay prostrate with exhaustion

tired: I need to rest because I'm tired

weary: a weary traveller

worried adjective being anxious about something: His parents were worried about his lack of progress

anxious: I was very anxious about her safety

bothered: I'm not bothered about it at all

concerned: a phone call from a concerned neighbour

nervous: Consumers say they are nervous about their jobs

troubled: He was troubled by the lifestyle of his son

uneasy: an uneasy feeling that everything was going wrong

see also **anxious, nervous, uneasy**

worry verb 1 to feel anxious about something: Don't worry, it's bound to arrive soon

be anxious: They admitted they were still anxious about the situation

brood: constantly brooding about her family

feel uneasy: I felt very uneasy at the lack of response

fret: You mustn't fret about someone else's problems

2 to disturb someone with a problem: I didn't want to worry the boys with this

bother: I hate to bother you again so soon

hassle informal: Then my boss started hassling me

pester: I wish they'd stop pestering me for an answer

plague: I'm not going to plague you with more questions

trouble: Don't trouble me while I'm working

▷ noun **3** a feeling of anxiety: a major source of worry

anxiety: anxieties about money

apprehension: real anger and apprehension about the future

concern: growing concern for the environment

fear: His fears might be groundless

misgiving: She had some misgivings about what she was about to do

unease: a deep sense of unease about the coming interview

see also **agitate, anxiety, bother, burden, care, concern, distress, disturb, sorrow, stress, trouble**

worrying see **serious**

worsen verb to become more difficult: My relationship with my mother worsened

decline: Hourly output declined in the third quarter

degenerate: The whole tone of the campaign began to degenerate

deteriorate: The weather conditions are deteriorating

go downhill informal: Things have gone steadily downhill since he left

worship verb 1 to praise and revere something: People go to church to pray and worship their god

glorify: The monks devoted their days to glorifying God

honour: the Scout's promise to honour God

praise: She asked the church to praise God

pray to: They prayed to their gods to bring them rain

venerate: the most venerated religious figure in the country

2 to love and admire someone: She had worshipped him from afar for years

adore: an adoring husband

idolize: She idolized her father as she was growing up

love: He genuinely loved and cherished her

▷ **noun 3** a feeling of love and admiration for something: *the worship of the ancient Roman gods*

admiration: *Her eyes widened in admiration*

adoration: *He had been used to female adoration all his life*

adulation: *The book was received with adulation by the critics*

devotion: *flattered by his devotion*

homage: *The emperor received the homage of every prince*

praise: *singing hymns in praise of their god*

see also **love**

worth see **merit, quality, value**

worthless *adjective* having no real value or worth: *a worthless piece of junk*

meaningless: *their sense of a meaningless existence*

paltry: *a paltry amount*

poor: *a poor reward for his effort*

trifling: *We were paid a trifling sum*

trivial: *She would go to the doctor for any trivial complaint*

useless: *I felt useless and a failure*

valueless: *commercially valueless trees*

see also **empty, useless**

worthwhile see **productive, useful, valuable**

worthy see **noble, respectable**

would like see **fancy**

wound see **harm, hurt, injure, injury**

wounded see **hurt**

wowser see **spoilsport**

wrangle see **argue, clash, dispute, squabble**

wrap see **enclose**

wrapped up see **preoccupied**

wrapper see **cover**

wrath see **anger, rage**

wreak see **bring**

wreck see **crash, destroy, ruin, spoil**

wrench see **tug, twist**

wretched see **miserable, sorry, unlucky**

wring see **exact, twist**

wrinkle see **crumple, fold**

write *verb* to record something in writing: *Write your name and address on a postcard and send it to us*

compose: *Vivaldi composed many concertos*

correspond: *We corresponded for several years*

inscribe: *Their names were inscribed on the front of the pillar*

record: *Her letters record the domestic and social details of her life*

take down: *notes taken down in shorthand*

see also **compose**

write down see **record**

wrong *adjective* **1** not correct or truthful: *That was the wrong answer*

false: *We don't know if the information is true or false*

faulty: *His diagnosis was faulty from the outset*

incorrect: *a decision based on figures which were incorrect*

mistaken: *a mistaken view of the situation*

unsound: *The thinking is good-hearted, but muddled and unsound*

untrue: *The remarks were completely untrue*

2 morally unacceptable: *It's wrong to hurt people*

bad: *I may be a thief but I'm not a bad person*

crooked: *crooked business deals*

evil: *the country's most evil terrorists*

illegal: *It is illegal to intercept radio messages*

immoral: *Many would consider such practices immoral*

unfair: *It was unfair that he should suffer so much*

unjust: *unjust treatment*

▷ noun **3** an unjust action: *the wrongs of our society*
abuse: *controversy over human rights abuses*
crime: *crimes against humanity*
grievance: *He had a deep sense of grievance*
injustice: *A great injustice had been done to him in the past*
sin: *He admitted the many sins of his youth*
see also **crime, injustice, sin, unfair**
wrongful see **unfair**

y

ya see **yes**
yakka see **work**
yank see **pull, tug**
yarn see **story**
yawning see **deep**
yeah see **yes**
yearn see **desire, long, wish**
yearn for see **be dying for, miss**
yearning see **desire, longing**
yell see **call, cry, scream, shout**
yelp see **bay**
yen see **desire**
yes *interjection* an expression used to agree with something or say it is true: *"Are you a friend of his?" – "Yes."*
    aye *Scottish informal*: *"Can I borrow this?" – "Aye, but I want it back."*
    okay: *"Will we leave now?" – "Okay, if you like."*
    sure: *"Can I come too?" – "Sure."*
    ya *South African*: *"Are you a runaway?" – "Ya," the child replied*
    yeah *informal*: *Yeah, I think we've met once*
yet see **but**
yield see **give, give in, submit, surrender**
yielding see **soft**
yob see **hooligan**
yokel *noun* a person who lives in the

country: *a bunch of those yokels*

bushie or **bushy** *Australian, New Zealand informal: "I'm a bit of a bushie at heart," she said*

countryman: *They are true old-fashioned countrymen*

peasant: *In rural Mexico a peasant is rarely without his machete*

young adjective **1** not yet mature: *young people*

adolescent: *He spent his adolescent years playing guitar*

immature: *an immature female whale*

infant: *his infant daughter*

junior: *a junior member of the family*

juvenile: *a juvenile delinquent*

little: *What were you like when you were little?*

youthful: *the youthful stars of the film*

▷ plural noun **2** the babies an animal has: *The hen may not be able to feed its young*

babies: *animals making nests for their babies*

brood: *a hungry brood of fledglings*

family: *a family of weasels*

litter: *a litter of pups*

little ones: *a family of elephants with their little ones*

offspring: *female rats' offspring*

youngster see **boy**, **child**

youth see **boy**

youthful see **young**

Z

zany see **crazy**

zeal see **passion**

zealot see **fan, fanatic**

zealous see **fervent**

zenith see **peak, top**

zero noun nothing or the number 0: *I will now count from zero to ten*

nil: *They beat Argentina one-nil*

nothing: *Some weeks I earn nothing*

nought: *How many noughts are there in a million?*

zest see **spirit**

zone see **area, region**

zoom see **tear**

Word Studies ○

BAD

Bad is such a commonly-used word that it has come to lose much of its effectiveness. Depending on the sense and context of what you are saying, there are many other much more expressive substitutes which can be used instead.

having a harmful effect:
extremely **damaging** **destructive** effect **detrimental** impact **harmful** effects **unhealthy** lifestyle **unpleasant** side-effects

making someone feel upset or uneasy:
distressing images **disturbing** news **grim** time **painful** memories **traumatic** period **unsettling** atmosphere **upsetting** experience

causing physical pain:
acute attack **agonizing** death **excruciating** pain **intense** cramps **painful** back **serious** knee problems **severe** stomach pains **terrible** migraine

of poor quality:
defective products **deficient** diet **faulty** goods **imperfect** work **inadequate** work conditions **inferior** quality **pathetic** excuse **poor** housing **sorry** state of affairs **unsatisfactory** service

lacking skill:
incompetent managers **inept** performance **poor** judge **useless** at ...

having an evil character:
morally **corrupt** **criminal** actions **depraved** criminals **evil** man **immoral** act **sinful** act **villainous** characters **wicked** stepmother something **wrong**

of children behaving badly:
disobedient children **mischievous** little scamp **naughty** boy **undisciplined** pupils **unruly** kids

of food:
mouldy cheese This meat's **gone off** **rancid** butter **rotten** eggs **sour** milk

of language:
obscene lyrics **offensive** language **rude** words **vulgar**
expression

BADLY

Badly, like bad, can be avoided in favour of less commonly-used
and more expressive alternatives.

in an inferior way:
inadequately trained run **ineptly** **poorly** organized
shoddily built **unsatisfactorily** regulated system

seriously:
deeply hurt **desperately** unhappy **gravely** ill **seriously**
injured.

cruelly:
brutally assaulted **callously** treated **cruelly** tormented
savagely beaten struck **viciously**

BEST

There are a number of alternatives for the word best which will
make your writing more interesting.

of the highest standard:
the **finest** wines **first-rate** performance **foremost** painter
greatest film **leading** actors **outstanding** tennis players
pre-eminent pop act **principal** publishing houses
superlative products **supreme** achievement **top** athletes

most desirable:
correct thing **most desirable** outcome **most fitting** location
right person

the preferred thing:
the **cream** of Scottish artists the **elite** of the sporting world
the **finest** wine the **pick** of the crop

BETTER

Like **best**, the word better can be replaced with a number of synonyms to add variety and interest to your written and spoken English.

of higher quality or worth:
no **finer** place   much **grander** house   **greater** prize   **higher-quality** service   much **nicer** room   **preferable** to   far **superior** to yours   **surpassing** quality   **worthier** cause

of greater skill:
the **greater** writer   more **advanced** skiers   more **expert** at some things   more **skilful** player   more **talented** than he is

in improved health:
now I'm **cured**   fully **recovered**   much **healthier** not **improving**   **on the mend** now (informal)   she's **recovering** getting **stronger**   feeling **well** again

BIG

A cautionary tale: a teacher was trying to get her class to substitute more interesting words for very commonly-used ones in their writing. She noticed that one boy had described a castle as "big" in his essay, and asked him to write the sentence again in a more creative way. He came back with the following: "I saw a castle which was big, and when I say big, I mean *big*."

in size:
colossal statue   **enormous** building   **gigantic** creature   **great** commotion   **huge** cake   **immense** task   **large** map   **massive** display   **significant** difference   **vast** stadium

in importance:
eminent politician   **important** influence   **influential** figure **leading** screenwriters   **major** role   **powerful** businessman **principal** guest   **prominent** jazz musician   **significant** investor

of an issue or problem:

grave crisis **momentous** decision **serious** disadvantage
urgent need **weighty** problem

BREAK

The word **break** is often over-used. There are lots of more
descriptive words which you can use to give additional
information about how something breaks, so try to choose one
of them instead.

If something hard **cracks**, or you **crack** it, it becomes
slightly damaged, with lines appearing on its surface:
A gas main had **cracked** under my garden.
To get at the coconut flesh, **crack** the shell with a hammer.

If something **fractures**, or you **fracture** it, it gets a slight
crack in it:
One strut had **fractured** and had to be repaired.
You've **fractured** a rib.

If something **snaps**, or you **snap** it, it breaks suddenly,
with a sharp cracking noise:
A twig **snapped** under his foot.
She gripped the pipe in both hands, trying to **snap** it in half.

If something **splits**, or you **split** it, it breaks into two or
more parts:
In the severe gale, the ship **split** in two.
We **split** the boards down the middle.

If something **splinters**, or you **splinter** it, it breaks into
thin, sharp pieces:
The ruler **splintered** into pieces.
The stone hit the glass, **splintering** it.

If something **fragments**, or is **fragmented**, it breaks or
separates into small parts:
The rock began to **fragment** and crumble.

If something **crumbles**, or you **crumble** it, it breaks into many small pieces:
Under the pressure, the flint **crumbled** into fragments.
Crumble the cheese into a bowl.

If something **shatters**, it breaks into many small pieces:
safety glass that won't **shatter** if it's hit

If something **disintegrates**, it breaks into many pieces and is destroyed:
The car's windscreen **disintegrated** with the impact of the crash.

If you **smash** something, or it **smashes**, it breaks into many small pieces, often because it has been hit or dropped:
Someone had **smashed** a bottle.
Two glasses fell off the table and **smashed** into pieces.

If you **wreck** or demolish something, you completely destroy it:
The bridge was **wrecked** by the storms.
The hurricane **demolished** houses across the area.

CALL

Depending on which sense of **call** you are thinking of, there are a number of words which you can substitute for it to make your language more interesting.

to give a name:
christen their child   **designate** an area   the man **dubbed** "the world's greatest ..."   they **named** their child

to describe as:
I **consider** myself   I'm not what you'd **describe** as   do you **judge** this   He **referred** to her as   widely **regarded** as   **termed** as political   people will **think** us

to telephone:
Contact us immediately   **phone** me   I'll **ring** you   please **telephone**

to say loudly:
he **announced** she **cried** she **cried out** he **shouted** **yelled** over to

to send for someone:
please **fetch** **sent** for I was **summoned**

to bring together:
they **assembled** the group **convened** a council **gathered** together **muster** an army **summoned** to a meeting

to pay a visit:
drop in (informal) **pop in** (informal) **stop by**

CLOSE

Close is another over-used word. Depending on whether you are talking about people or things which are close in *distance* or in *time*, the closeness of *personal relationships*, a closeness in *resemblance* between two things, or you are referring to a *description or translation*, you can use various other words as substitutes.

in distance:
at hand **adjacent** buildings **adjoining** stall keep something **handy** quite **near** **nearby** shop **neighbouring** table

in relationships:
attached to one another **dear** companion deeply **devoted** couple too **familiar** very **friendly** **intimate** friends **loving** relationship.

in time:
My birthday is **approaching** the time is **at hand** is **coming** a deal is **imminent** **impending** disaster the day is **near**

of a resemblance:
distinct resemblance **marked** similarity **pronounced** similarities **strong** resemblance

of a description or translation:
accurate description **exact** translation **faithful** rendition **literal** interpretation **precise** detail **strict** account

CRY

There are a number of alternative words which you can use instead of **cry**, if you want to say a little more about how someone cries.

If you **weep**, you cry. This is quite a literary word:
The woman began to **weep** uncontrollably.

If you **whimper**, you make a low, unhappy sound as if you are about to cry:
He huddled in a corner, **whimpering** with fear.

If you **sob**, you cry in a noisy way, with short breaths:
Her sister broke down and began to **sob** into her handkerchief.

If you **blubber**, you cry noisily and in an unattractive way:
To our surprise, he began to **blubber** like a child.

If you **howl** or **wail**, you cry with a long, loud noise:
The baby was **howling** in the next room.
a mother **wailing** for her lost child

If you **bawl**, you cry very loudly:
One of the toddlers was **bawling**.

CUT

There are many useful synonyms for the word **cut**. Different words are appropriate substitutes, depending on what it is that is being cut, what is being used to do the cutting, and how deep or extensive the cutting is.

If you **nick** something, you make a small cut on its surface:
He **nicked** his chin while he was shaving.

If you **score** something, you cut a line or lines on its surface:
Lightly **score** the surface of the steaks with a cook's knife.

If you **pierce** something with a sharp object, or a sharp object pierces it, the object goes through it and makes a hole in it:
Pierce the skin of the potato with a fork.

If something **penetrates** an object, it goes inside it or passes through it:
a spider with fangs big enough to **penetrate** the skin

If you **slit** something, you make a long narrow cut in it:
He began to **slit** open each envelope.

If you **gash** or **slash** something, you make a long, deep cut in it:
He **gashed** his leg on the barbed wire.
She threatened to **slash** her wrists.

If you **clip** something, you cut small pieces from it in order to shape it:
I saw an old man out **clipping** his hedge.

If you **trim** something, you cut off small amounts of it to make it look neater:
I have my hair **trimmed** every eight weeks.

If you **pare** something, you cut off its skin or outer layer:
She was sitting **paring** her nails with a pair of clippers.

If you **prune** a tree or bush, you cut off some of its branches:
Apple trees can be **pruned** once they've lost their leaves.

If you **mow** grass, you cut it with a lawnmower:
He **mowed** the lawn and did various other chores.

If you **snip** something, you cut it with scissors or shears:
The hairdresser **snipped** off my split ends.

If you **split** or **divide** something, you cut it into two or more parts:
Split the planks down the middle.
Divide the pastry into four equal parts.

If you **sever** something, you cut it off or cut right through it:
He **severed** the tendon of his thumb in an industrial accident.

If you **saw** something, you cut it with a saw:
Your father is **sawing** wood in the garden.

If you **hack** something, you cut it using rough strokes:
Matthew desperately **hacked** through the straps.

If you **slice** something, you cut it into thin pieces:
I **sliced** the beef into thin strips.

If you **chop** something, you cut it into pieces with strong downward movements of a knife or axe:
You will need to **chop** the onions very finely.

If you **carve** an object, you make it by cutting it out of a substance such as wood or stone:
He **carves** these figures from pine.

If you **carve** meat, you cut slices from it:
Andrew began to **carve** the roast.

If you **hew** stone or wood, you cut it, perhaps with an axe. This is an old-fashioned word:
He felled, peeled and **hewed** his own timber.

If you **lop** something off, you cut it off with one quick stroke:
Somebody has **lopped** the heads off our tulips.

If you **dock** an animal's tail, you cut it off:
I think it is cruel to **dock** the tail of any animal.

EAT

There are a number of more descriptive words which you can use instead of the basic **eat**, to say something about the way in which a person eats.

If you **consume** something, you eat it. This is a formal word:
Andrew would **consume** nearly a pound of cheese a day.

When an animal **feeds**, or **feeds on** something, it eats:
After a few days the caterpillars stopped **feeding**.
Slugs **feed on** decaying plant material.

If you **swallow** something, you make it go from your mouth into your stomach:
Snakes **swallow** their prey whole.

If you **snack**, you eat things between meals:
Instead of **snacking** on crisps and chocolate, eat fruit.

If you **chew** something, you break it up with your teeth so that it is easier to swallow:
I pulled out a filling while I was **chewing** a toffee.

If you **nibble** food, you eat it by biting very small pieces of it, perhaps because you are not very hungry:
She **nibbled** at a piece of dry toast.

If you **munch** food, you eat it by chewing it slowly, thoroughly, and rather noisily:
Luke **munched** his sandwiches appreciatively.

If you **stuff** yourself, you eat a lot of food:
They'd **stuffed** themselves with sweets before dinner.

If you **gobble, guzzle, wolf (down)**, or **scoff** food, you eat it quickly and greedily. **Guzzle, wolf** (down), and **scoff** are all informal words:
Pete **gobbled** all the stew before anyone else arrived.
women who **guzzle** chocolate whenever they are unhappy
I was back in the changing room **wolfing** sandwiches.
She bought a hot dog from a stand and **wolfed** it down.
You greedy so-and-so! You've **scoffed** the lot!

If you **devour** something, you eat it quickly and eagerly:
She **devoured** half an apple pie.

END

End is a commonly over-used word. Depending on your context, you can use the following substitutes to add variety and interest to your writing.

of a period of time:
by the **close** of last year **ending** of a great era the **expiry** of his period nearing its **finish**

of an event:
the dramatic **climax** the **close** the **conclusion** of remarkable **culmination** tragic **ending** grand **finale** disappointing **finish**

the furthest part of something:
the boundaries of the paths beyond the **bounds edge** of the cliff western **extremity** city **limits** forest **margin**

the point of something long or sharp:
the southernmost **point** the **tip**

a leftover piece:
a cigarette **butt** trimmings and **leftovers remnants** of fabric **scraps** of spare material a ticket **stub** The **stump** of his left arm

the purpose of doing something:
united by a common **aim** working towards the same **goal** real **intentions** the stated **object** the **objective** of the true **purpose** business **reasons**

FAT

Some words used to describe a person who is overweight can be more hurtful or insulting than others. There are also words to describe varying degrees of being overweight.

Someone who is **overweight** weighs more than is considered healthy. However, you can be just a little overweight as well as very overweight:
Since having my baby, I feel slightly **overweight**.

If you say someone is **podgy**, you mean that they are slightly fat. This is an informal word:
Eddie's getting a little **podgy** round the middle.

If you describe someone as **fleshy**, you mean that they are slightly too fat:

He was well-built, but too **fleshy** to be an imposing figure.

A **chubby**, **tubby** or **stout** person is rather fat:

I was greeted by a small, **chubby** man.
He had been a short, **tubby** child who was taunted about his weight.
a tall, **stout** man with gray hair

A **portly** person is rather fat. This word is mostly used to describe men:

a **portly**, middle-aged man

You can use the word **plump** to describe someone who is rather fat or rounded, usually when you think this is a good quality:

Maria was a pretty little thing, small and **plump** with a mass of dark curls.

If you describe a woman's figure as **rounded** or **curvy** you mean that it is attractive because it is well-developed and not too thin:

a beautiful woman with blue eyes and a full, **rounded** figure
she's lovely and **curvy**

A **roly-poly** person is pleasantly fat and round. This is an informal word:

a short, **roly-poly** little woman with laughing eyes

If you describe a woman as **buxom**, you mean that she looks healthy and attractive and has a rounded body and big breasts:

Melissa was a tall, **buxom** blonde.

If you describe someone as **obese**, you mean that they are fatter than overweight, perhaps to the point of being unhealthy:

Obese people tend to have higher blood pressure than lean people.

If you describe someone as **gross**, you mean that they are extremely fat and unattractive. This is a very insulting

word to use:
He tried to raise his **gross** body from the sofa.

GOOD

Like bad, the word **good** is used in so many ways to describe so many things that it has lost a great deal of its effectiveness. A wide range of synonyms is available to you for every context in which you might be tempted to use good; try to vary your language and vocabulary by choosing these instead.

in quality:
acceptable standard **awesome** special effects (slang)
excellent meal **fine** wines **first-class** game **first-rate** service
great book **satisfactory** quality **splendid** hotel
super recipe(informal) **superb** selection

of an experience:
agreeable evening **delightful** few hours **enjoyable** trip
lovely time **pleasant** stay **satisfactory** season

having a beneficial effect:
advantageous changes **beneficial** effects **favourable**
conditions **positive** results

morally virtuous:
commendable character **decent** person **ethical** stance
honest citizens **honourable** person morally **righteous** people
morally **upright** **virtuous** life **worthy** causes

kind and thoughtful:
kindly and **benevolent** too **charitable** **considerate** to others
generous and **selfless** nature a **gracious** and genial host a
humane and caring woman **kind** of you **kind-hearted** colleagues
a **kindly** soul an **obliging** fellow **thoughtful** to offer.

skilled at something:
able student **accomplished** pianist **adept** at manipulating
very **capable** nanny **clever** at raising money careful and
competent worker **efficient** manager **expert** cyclists **first
rate** teacher **proficient** driver **skilled** carpenter

of behaviour:
disciplined behaviour meek and **docile** child **obedient** children
orderly behaviour polite and **well-behaved** **well-mannered**

of advice:
thoughtful and **constructive** input **helpful** suggestions
sound advice **practical** guidelines **useful** tips

of an idea:
judicious approach **practical** solution **prudent** strategy
sensible way **wise** plan

of a price, sum of money, amount or quantity:
ample supply **considerable** income **fair** bit over **large** profit
reasonable number **substantial** amount

of a person's mood:
buoyant spirits **cheerful** nature **genial** mood **happy**
disposition **optimistic** frame of mind **sunny** mood

GREAT

There are a number of ways in which the word **great** can be
used, depending on what you are referring to. But why not make
your language more interesting and use one of the following
instead?

in size:
big house **colossal** tomb **huge** marquee **large** pile **enormous**
hall **extensive** range **gigantic** theme park **immense** building
stupendous sum **tremendous** challenge **vast** area

in degree:
high degree of risk **excessive** speeds **extravagant** claims
extreme violence **tremendous** strength

in importance:
chief problems **important** question **main** competitor **major**
issue **momentous** occasion **principal** aim **serious**
deficiency **significant** step

in fame:
celebrated author **distinguished** baritone **eminent** scientists
famed actor **famous** artist **illustrious** ballerina **notable** chess
player **prominent** historian **renowned** surgeon

in skill:
excellent teacher **expert** skiers **masterly** display
outstanding cricketer **skilful** player **skilled** boxer **superb**
goalkeeper **superlative** writer **talented** management team

in quality:
a **beaut** place (Australian, New Zealand) good food and **fine**
wines **excellent** pasta sauce **superb** works of art **fantastic**
display **first-rate** service **marvellous** restaurant
outstanding works of art **superb** staircase **terrific** party
tremendous job **wonderful** time

HAPPY

Happy is another over-used word. You can vary your language
by choosing one of the alternatives shown here.

displaying a cheerful nature or mood:
cheerful disposition **cheery** face you're very **chirpy** (informal)
jolly fat man **merry** laugh **sunny** nature

feeling joy at something:
seem **delighted** I was **ecstatic** he was **elated** **euphoric** over his
success **glad** to be back **joyful** pride **jubilant** over their victory.
overjoyed to be reunited very **pleased** with the verdict **thrilled**
to be playing again **over the moon** with this result (informal)

causing joy:
agreeable task **blissful** marriage **festive** occasion **gratifying**
relationship **joyful** event **joyous** news **pleasurable** memory

willing to do something:
content just to sit **glad** to be of service **pleased** to take you
prepared to talk **ready** to help anyone **willing** to wait

lucky:
auspicious start **convenient** outcome **favourable** result
fortunate situation **lucky** chance **opportune** moment
timely arrival

HIGH

High is another word which has a number of meanings.
Depending on just what you are describing as high, you have a
whole range of substitutes to choose from to give your writing
some added variety and expressiveness.

of a building, ceiling or mountain:
elevated position **lofty** towers **soaring** spire **steep** hill **tall**
walls **towering** cliffs

of an amount or degree:
acute anxiety **excessive** speed **extraordinary** quantities
extreme pressure **great** level of interest **severe** penalties

of a cost or price:
costly premiums too **dear** **expensive** prices **steep** charges

of a wind:
blustery breezes **extreme** wind **squally** winds **strong** gusts
violent gales

important:
a **chief** position **most eminent** scientists **exalted** circles
important post **influential** place in the system **leading**
figure **powerful** men **pre-eminent** position **prominent**
political figures **superior** status

of a voice or sound:
high-pitched cry **penetrating** whistle **piercing** note **shrill**
scream **soprano** voice

of a person's spirits:
buoyant spirits **cheerful** spirits **elated** feeling **exhilarated**
frame of mind **exuberant** moods felt **joyful** **merry** mood

HIT

The word **hit** is often over-used. There are a number of more descriptive words which you can use to give additional information about the way in which something is hit, or how hard it is hit.

If you **strike** someone or something, you hit them deliberately. This is a formal word:
She stepped forward and **struck** him across the mouth.

If you **tap** something, you hit it with a quick light blow or series of blows:
Tap the egg gently with a teaspoon to crack the shell.

If you **pat** something or someone, you tap them lightly, usually with your hand held flat:
"Don't worry about it," he said, **patting** me on the knee.

If you **rap** something, or rap on it, you hit it with a series of quick blows:
rapping the glass with the knuckles of his right hand
He **rapped** on the door with his cane.
If you **slap** or **smack** someone, you hit them with the palm of your hand:
I **slapped** him hard across the face.
She **smacked** the child on the side of the head.

If you **swat** something such as an insect, you hit it with a quick, swinging movement using your hand or a flat object:
Every time a fly came near, I **swatted** it with a newspaper.

If you **knock** someone or something, you hit it roughly, especially so that it falls or moves:
She accidentally **knocked** the tin off the shelf.

If you **knock** something such as a door or window, you hit it, usually several times, to attract someone's attention:
She went to his apartment and **knocked** the door loudly.

If you **beat** something, you hit it hard, usually several
times or continuously for a period of time:
a circle of men **beating** drums

If you **hammer** something, you hit it hard several times to
make a noise:
We had to **hammer** the door and shout to attract their attention.

If you **pound** something, you hit it with great force,
usually loudly and repeatedly:
He **pounded** the table with both fists.

If you **batter** someone or something, you hit them very
hard, using your fists or a heavy object:
He **battered** her round the head with a club.

If you **bang** something, you hit it hard, making a loud noise:
We **banged** on the door and shouted to be let out.

If you **bang** a part of your body, you accidentally knock it
against something and hurt it:
She'd fainted and **banged** her head.

If you **belt** someone, you hit them very hard. This is an
informal word:
She drew back her fist and **belted** him right in the stomach.

If you **bash** someone or something, you hit them hard.
This is an informal word:
The chef was **bashed** over the head with a bottle.

If you **whack** someone or something, you hit them hard.
This is an informal word:
Someone **whacked** me with a baseball bat.

If you **wallop** someone or something, you hit them very
hard, often causing a dull sound. This is an informal word:
Once, she **walloped** me over the head with a frying pan.

If you **thump** someone or something, you hit them hard,
usually with your fist:
I'm warning you, if you don't shut up, I'll **thump** you.

If you **punch** someone or something, you hit them hard with your fist:
After **punching** him on the chin, she ran off.

LITTLE

Depending on what you are describing, you can choose from any of the following alternatives instead of the over-used word **little**.

of objects: in physical size:
dainty sandwiches **dwarf** tulips **mini** laptop **miniature** toy boats **minute** particles **pygmy** goats **skimpy** bikini **small** table **tiny** pieces **wee** bit of cake

of people: in height:
dainty girl **diminutive** stature **petite** women too **short** to reach up short, **squat** figure **tiny** woman **wee** guy

in duration:
brief pause **fleeting** glimpse **hasty** peek **momentary** lapse of memory **quick** smile **short** break

in quantity:
done **hardly any** work **not much** difference **meagre** pay increase **measly** ration **paltry** salary **scant** attention

in age:
baby sister **infant** son **small** kids **young** child

in importance:
insignificant detail **minor** squabble influence is **negligible** **petty** complaints **trifling** problem **trivial** matters **unimportant** event

a small amount:
bit of peace **dash** of bravado **fragment** of skin tissue **hint** of coriander **small** amount **spot** of milk **touch** of irritation **trace** of blood

LONG

Try to vary your language by using one of these substitutes for **long**.

in physical extent:
elongated body **extensive** list of products **lengthy** queues

in duration:
extended period **interminable** debate **lengthy** delay
lingering death **long-drawn-out** war **prolonged** labour
protracted negotiations **slow** process **sustained** run

LOOK

All of the following words mean to **look**, but each one has an extra shade of meaning which makes it a more expressive substitute for the word look in particular situations or contexts.

If you **glance**, **peek**, or **peep** at something, you look at it quickly, and often secretly:
He **glanced** at his watch as she spoke.
She **peeked** at him through the curtains.
He **peeped** at me to see if I was watching him.

If you **scan** something written or printed, you look at it quickly:
She **scanned** the advertisement pages of the newspapers.

If you **eye** or **regard** someone or something, you look at them carefully:
The waiters **eyed** him with suspicion.
He **regarded** me curiously.

If you **gaze** or **stare** at someone or something, you look at them steadily for a long time. Staring is often thought to be rude, but gazing is not:
She sat **gazing** into the fire for a long time.
They **stared** silently into each other's eyes.

If you **observe** or **watch** someone or something, you look at them for a period of time to see what they are doing or what is happening:

A man was **observing** him from across the square.

I hate people **watching** me while I eat.

If you **survey** or **view** someone or something, you look at the whole of them carefully:

He stood up and **surveyed** the crowd.

The mourners filed past to **view** the body.

If you **examine**, **scrutinize**, or **study** something, you look at it very carefully, often to find out information from it:

He **examined** all the evidence.

He **scrutinized** her passport and stamped it.

We **studied** the menu for several minutes.

If you glare, glower, or scowl at someone, you stare at them angrily:

He **glared** resentfully at me.

She stood **glowering** at me with her arms crossed.

She **scowled** at the two men as they came into the room.

If you **peer** or **squint** at something, you try to see it more clearly by narrowing or screwing up your eyes as you look at it:

He was **peering** at me through the keyhole.

She **squinted** at the blackboard, trying to read what was on it.

If you **gape** at someone or something, you look at them in surprise, usually with your mouth open:

She was **gaping** at the wreckage, lost for words.

If you **goggle** at someone or something, you look at them with your eyes wide open, usually because you are surprised by them:

He **goggled** at me in disbelief.

If you **ogle** someone, you look at them in a way that makes it very obvious that you find them attractive:

I hate the way he **ogles** every woman who goes by.

MARK

Mark is rather a vague word. Depending on what you are referring to, there are a number of more interesting synonyms which you can use in its place.

a stain:
an ink **blot** **line** of dirt lipstick **smudge** grease **spot** **stain** on his shirt **streak** of mud

a damaged area:
slight **blemishes** purple **blotches** cuts and **bruises** tiny **dent** little **nicks** jagged **scar** long **scratch**

a written or printed symbol:
Chinese **characters** company's **emblem** Papal **insignia** multiplication **sign** date **stamp** peace **symbol**

a characteristic of something:
essential **attributes** defining **characteristic** fundamental **features** **hallmark** of his films **measure** of change **symptom** of depression common **trait**

an indication of something:
gesture of goodwill **indication** of his regard **sign** of respect **symbol** of mourning **token** of our friendship

MOVE

Move is not a very expressive word. If you can use a more descriptive substitute to say something about the way in which a person or thing moves, it will give your writing variety and interest.

When a person **crawls**, they move forwards on their hands and knees:
As he tried to **crawl** away, he was kicked in the head.

When an insect **crawls** somewhere, it moves there quite slowly:
I watched the moth **crawl** up the outside of the lampshade.

If a person or animal **creeps** somewhere, they move quietly and slowly:
I tried to **creep** upstairs without being heard.

To **inch** somewhere means to move there very carefully and slowly:
He began to **inch** along the ledge.

If you **edge** somewhere, you move very slowly in that direction:
He **edged** closer to the telephone.

If a person or animal **slithers** somewhere, they move by sliding along the ground in an uneven way:
Robert lost his footing and **slithered** down the bank.
The snake **slithered** into the water.

If you **wriggle** somewhere, for example through a small gap, you move there by twisting and turning your body:
I **wriggled** through a gap in the fence.

When people or small animals **scamper** or **scuttle** somewhere, they move there quickly with small, light steps:
The children got off the bus and **scampered** into the playground.
The crabs **scuttled** along the muddy bank

When people or small animals **scurry** somewhere, they move there quickly and hurriedly, often because they are frightened:
The attack began, sending residents **scurrying** for cover.

If you **hurry**, **race**, or **rush** somewhere, you go there as quickly as you can:
Claire **hurried** along the road.
He **raced** across town to the hospital.
A schoolgirl **rushed** into a burning building to save a baby.

If you **hasten** somewhere, you hurry there. This is a literary word:
He **hastened** along the corridor to Grace's room.

If you **hare** off somewhere, you go there very quickly. This is an informal British word:
She **hared** off to ring the doctor.

If you **dash**, **dart**, or **shoot** somewhere, you run or go there quickly and suddenly:
She jumped up and **dashed** out of the room.
The girl turned and **darted** away through the trees.
They had almost reached the boat when a figure **shot** past them.

If you say that someone or something **flies** in a particular direction, you are emphasizing that they move there with a lot of speed and force:
I **flew** downstairs to answer the door.

If you **tear** somewhere, you move there very quickly, often in an uncontrolled or dangerous way:
Without looking to left or right, he **tore** off down the road.

When you **run**, you move quickly because you are in a hurry to get somewhere:
I excused myself and **ran** back to the telephone.

If you **jog**, you run slowly:
She **jogged** off in the direction he had indicated.

If you **sprint**, you run as fast as you can over a short distance:
The sergeant sprinted to the car.

If you **gallop**, you run somewhere very quickly:
They were **galloping** round the garden playing football.

If a person or animal **bolts**, they suddenly start to run very fast, often because something has frightened them:
I made some excuse and **bolted** towards the exit.

If a group of animals or people **stampede**, they run in a wild, uncontrolled way:
The crowd **stampeded** out of the hall.

NEW

Depending on the sense of **new** which you mean, there are a number of alternatives which you can use to vary your writing and make it more interesting.

recently discovered or created:
most **advanced** **current** gossip **fresh** footprints **ground-breaking** discovery **latest** films **modern** technology most **recent** novel **ultra-modern** shop most **up-to-date** computers **up-to-the-minute** information

not used or owned before:
brand new car **fresh** page **unused** dresses

unfamiliar:
completely **different** idea **novel** way **original** idea **strange** country **unaccustomed** experience **unfamiliar** places completely **unknown**

NICE

When you are writing or talking and you are going to use the word **nice**, try to think of a more descriptive and interesting word instead. Here are some ideas for words and phrases that you might use to describe different aspects of people and things.

of someone's appearance:
attractive man very **beautiful** very **cute** girl **dishy** guy **good-looking** man **gorgeous** woman **handsome** young man **lovely** woman **pretty** lady

of an object, place or view:
beautiful little antique shop **charming** little fishing village **delightful** place **lovely** old English garden **pretty** room

of clothing:
a **chic** look **elegant** dress **fetching** outfit **smart** navy-blue suit **stylish** clothes.

of an event or occasion:
agreeable evening **delightful** time more **enjoyable** than
fantastic party **lovely** holiday **pleasant** experience
pleasurable sensation

of someone's personality:
amiable man **considerate** towards others **friendly** to
strangers unfailingly **good-natured** **kind** to everyone **kindly**
old man immensely **likeable** chap **thoughtful** gesture

of food or drink:
appetizing smell **delectable** raspberries **delicious** food
luscious peaches **mouthwatering** dessert **tasty** dishes

of the weather:
beautiful morning **weather** is fine **glorious** day

of a room, flat or house:
comfortable home **cosy** parlour **homely** atmosphere
relaxing room

OLD

Depending on the sense of **old** that you mean, there are a
number of alternatives which you can use to vary your writing
and make it more interesting.

having lived for a long time:
aged parent **ancient** grandparents **elderly** man **venerable**
father-figure

in the past:
relics of **ancient** cultures rituals of a **bygone** civilization
children from an **earlier** marriage heroes of these **early** days
his **ex-wife** **former** lover **olden** times **one-time** president
past grievances **previous** tenants **prior** criminal convictions
remote days of glory

out of date:
antiquated methods **archaic** practices **behind the times**

quite **dated** **obsolete** equipment **old-fashioned** style **outmoded** equipment **out of date** car that music is **passè**

SAY

There are a number of more interesting or creative words you can use in place of the basic verbs **say**, **speak**, and **talk**, if you want to describe the way in which a person says something.

If someone **utters** sounds or words, they say them. This is a literary word:
They left without **uttering** a single word.

If you **comment** on something, you say something about it:
He has refused to **comment** on these reports.

If you **remark** that something is the case, you say that it is the case:
"I don't see you complaining," he **remarked**

If you **state** something, you say it in a formal or definite way:
Could you please **state** your name for the record?

If you **mention** something, you say something about it, usually briefly:
He never **mentioned** that he was married.

If you **note** something, you mention it in order to bring people's attention to it:
"It's already getting dark," he **noted**.

If you **observe** that something is the case, you make a comment about it, especially when it is something you have noticed or thought about a lot:
"He's a very loyal friend," Daniel **observed**.

If you **point out** a fact or mistake, you tell someone about it or draw their attention to it:
"You've not done so badly out of the deal," she **pointed out**.

If you **announce** something, you tell people about it publicly or officially:
"We're engaged!" she **announced**.

If you **affirm** something, you state firmly that it is the case:
"I'm staying right here," he **affirmed**.

If you **declare** that something is true, you say that it is true in a firm, deliberate way:
"I'm absolutely thrilled with the result," he **declared**.

If you **add** something when you are speaking, you say something more:
"Anyway, it serves you right," she **added** defiantly.

If you **interrupt**, you say something while someone else is speaking:
"I don't think you quite understand," James **interrupted**.

If you **put in** a remark, you interrupt someone or add to what they have said with the remark:
"Not that it's any of your business," Helen **put in**.

When people **chat**, they talk to each other in a friendly way:
We were just standing **chatting** in the corridor.

If you **converse** with someone, you talk to them. This is a formal word:
They were **conversing** in German.

When people **natter**, they talk casually for a long time about unimportant things:
Susan and her friend were still **nattering** when I left.

If you **gossip** with someone, you talk informally, especially about other people or events:
We sat and **gossiped** well into the evening.

If you **explain** something, you give details about it so that it can be understood:
"We weren't married at that point," she **explained**.

If you **ask** something, you say it in the form of a question because you want to know the answer:
"How is Frank?" he asked.

If you **inquire** about something, you ask for information about it. This is a formal word:
"Is something wrong?" he inquired.

To **query** or question means to ask a question:
"Can I help you?" the assistant queried.
"What if something goes wrong?" he questioned anxiously.

When you **answer** or **reply** to someone who has just spoken, you say something back to them:
"When are you leaving?" she asked. "Tomorrow," he answered.
"That's a nice outfit," he commented. "Thanks," she replied.

When you **respond** to something that has been said, you react to it by saying something yourself:
"Are you well enough to carry on?" "Of course," she responded scornfully.

If you **riposte**, you make a quick, clever response to something that someone has just said. This is a formal word:
"It's tough at the top," I said. "It's even tougher at the bottom," he riposted.

To **retort** means to reply angrily to someone. This is a formal word:
"I don't agree," James said. "Who cares what you think?" she retorted.

If someone **babbles**, they talk in a confused or excited way:
"I'm so excited I don't know what I'm doing," she babbled.

If you **chatter**, you talk quickly and excitedly about things which are not important:
Everyone was chattering away in different languages.

If you **gabble**, you say things so quickly that it is difficult for people to understand you:
Marcello sat on his knee and gabbled excitedly.

If you **prattle**, you talk a great deal about something unimportant:
She was **prattling** on about this guy she had met the night before.

If someone **rambles**, they talk but do not make much sense because they keep going off the subject:
an old man who **rambled** about his feud with his neighbours

If someone **breathes** something, they say it very quietly. This is a literary word:
"Oh, thank God you're here," he **breathed**.

When you **whisper**, you say something very quietly, using your breath rather than your throat:
"Keep your voice down," I **whispered**.

If you **hiss** something, you say it forcefully in a whisper:
"Stay here and don't make a sound," he **hissed**.

If you **mumble**, you speak very quietly and not at all clearly, so that your words are hard to make out:
"I didn't know I was meant to do it," she **mumbled**.

If you **murmur** something, you speak very quietly, so that not many people can hear you:
"How convenient," I **murmured**.

If you **mutter**, you speak very quietly, often because you are complaining about something:
"Oh great," he **muttered**, "That's all I need."

If you **croak** something, you say it in a low, rough voice:
"Water!" he **croaked**.

If you **grunt** something, you say it in a low voice, often because you are annoyed or not interested:
"Rubbish," I **grunted**, "You just didn't try hard enough."

If you **rasp** something, you say it in a harsh, unpleasant voice:
"Get into the car," he **rasped**.

If you **wheeze** something, you say it with a whistling sound, for example because you cannot get your breath:
"I'm really out of condition," I **wheezed**.

If you **gasp** something, you say it in a short, breathless way, especially because you are surprised, shocked, or in pain:
"What do you mean?" she **gasped**.

If you **pant** something, you say it while breathing loudly and quickly with your mouth open because you have been doing something energetic:
"Let me get my breath back," he **panted**, "I'm not as young as I used to be."

If you **groan** or **moan** something, you say it in a low voice, usually because you are unhappy or in pain:
"My leg - I think it's broken," Eric **groaned**.
"I can't stand it any longer," she **moaned**.

When someone **growls** something, they say it in a low, rough, and angry voice:
"I ought to kill you for this," Sharpe **growled**.

If you **snarl** something, you say it in a fierce, angry way:
"Get out of here," he **snarled**.

If you **snap** at someone, you speak to them in a sharp, unfriendly way:
"Of course you can't have it," he **snapped**.

SHORT

Some words used to describe a person who is **short** can be more hurtful or insulting than others.

A little or **small** person is not large in physical size:
She was too **little** to reach the books on the top shelf.
She is **small** for her age.

A **diminutive** person is very small:
a **diminutive** figure standing at the entrance

A **tiny** person is extremely small:
Though she was **tiny**, she had a loud voice.

If you describe a woman as **petite**, you are politely saying that she is small and not fat. This is a complimentary word:
a **petite** blonde woman

If you describe someone as **dumpy**, you mean they are short and fat. This is an uncomplimentary word:
a **dumpy** woman in a baggy tracksuit

If you describe someone as **squat**, you mean that they are short and thick, usually in an unattractive way:
Eddie was a short, **squat** fellow in his mid-forties.

SMALL

Depending on the sense of **small** which you mean, there are a number of alternatives which you can use to vary your writing and make it more interesting.

of things: in size:
little table **miniature** camera **minuscule** shorts **minute** amount **tiny** room

in area:
little distance **narrow** space **restricted** habitat

of a business:
humble corner shop **modest** beginnings **small-scale** industry **unpretentious** restaurant

of people: in size:
diminutive figure **dumpy** woman **little** person **petite** woman **small** for her age short, **squat** fellow **tiny** baby

of people: young:
baby sister **infant** prodigy **little** person **young** child

in importance:
inconsequential event **insignificant** village **little** thing **minor**

detail **negligible** impact **petty** things **slight** difference **trifling** objections **trivial** details **unimportant** event

STRONG

Strong is an over-used word. Depending on what you are referring to, there are many substitutes which you can use in its place to add variety and interest to your writing.

of a person: having powerful muscles:
tall and **athletic** **brawny** rugby player big, **burly** man she was lean and **muscular** powerful **bodybuilder** big, **strapping** fellow **well-built** runner

of a person: in good physical condition:
blooming with health **fit** again **healthy** child **good condition** **robust** child **sound** physical condition

of a person: confident and courageous:
brave girl **courageous** leader **plucky** schoolgirl have some **resilience** feisty, **self-confident** be **tough** to survive

of an object: able to withstand rough treatment:
durable plastic **hard-wearing** overalls **heavy-duty** canvas bag **reinforced** concrete supports **sturdy** tripod a **substantial** boat **tough** vehicle **well-built** fence

of feelings: great in degree or intensity:
acute feelings **ardent** admirer **deep** resentment **fervent** hope **fierce** loyalty **intense** dislike **keen** interest **passionate** believer **profound** distrust **vehement** criticism **violent** hostility **zealous** religious beliefs

of an argument: convincing or supported by a lot of evidence:
compelling case **convincing** theory **effective** arguments **persuasive** reasons a **sound** case **telling** condemnation

of a smell: very noticeable:
overpowering aftershave **powerful** smell **pungent** aroma

of food or drink: having a powerful flavour:
hot curry **overpowering** taste **piquant** sauce **powerful**
flavour **sharp** taste **spicy** foods

of a person's accent: very noticeable:
distinct American drawl **marked** West country accent
noticeable southern accent **unmistakeable** Latin accent

of colours: very bright:
bold colours **bright** reds and blues **brilliant** jewel colours
glaring red **loud** patterns.

THIN

Some words which you might use to describe someone who is
thin are complimentary, some are neutral, and others are
definitely uncomplimentary.

A **slender** person is attractively thin and graceful:
a tall, **slender** lady in a straw hat

A **slim** person has an attractively thin and well-shaped body:
a pretty, **slim** girl with blue eyes

A **slight** person has a fairly thin and delicate-looking body:
He is a **slight**, bespectacled, intellectual figure.

A **light** person does not weigh very much:
You need to be **light** to be a dancer.

Someone who is **spare** is tall and not at all fat. This is a
literary word:
She was thin and **spare**, with a sharp, intelligent face.

If you describe someone as **lean**, you mean that they are
thin but look strong and healthy:
Like most athletes, she was **lean** and muscular.

If you say someone is **lanky**, you mean that they are tall
and thin and move rather awkwardly:
He had grown into a **lanky** teenager.

A **skinny** person is extremely thin, in a way that you find unattractive. This is an informal word:
I don't think these **skinny** supermodels are at all sexy.

If you say a person is **scraggy** or **scrawny**, you mean that they look unattractive because they are so thin:
a **scraggy**, shrill, neurotic woman
a **scrawny** child of fifteen

Someone who is **bony** has very little flesh covering their bones:
a **bony** old woman dressed in black

If someone is **underweight**, they are too thin and therefore not healthy:
Nearly a third of the girls were severely **underweight**.

A person or animal that is **emaciated** is very thin and weak from illness or lack of food:
horrific television pictures of **emaciated** prisoners

WALK

There are a number of more interesting or creative words you can use in place of the basic verb **walk**, if you want to say something about the way in which a person walks.

If you **step** in a particular direction, you move your foot in that direction:
I **stepped** carefully over the piles of rubbish.

If you **tread** in a particular way, you walk in that way. This is rather a literary word:
She **trod** carefully across the grass.

If you amble or **stroll**, you walk in a slow, relaxed way:
We **ambled** along the beach hand in hand.
They **strolled** down the High Street, looking in shop windows.

If you **saunter**, you walk in a slow, casual way:
He was **sauntering** along as if he had all the time in the world.

If you **wander**, you walk around in a casual way, often without intending to go anywhere in particular:
Khachi was **wandering** aimlessly about in the garden.

If you **tiptoe**, you walk very quietly without putting your heels on the ground, so as not to be heard:
She slipped out of bed and **tiptoed** to the window.

If you **toddle**, you walk unsteadily, with short quick steps. This word is most often used of babies or small children:
My daughter **toddles** around after me wherever I go.

If you **mince**, you walk with quick, small steps in a put-on, effeminate way:
drag artists **mincing** around the stage in tight dresses and high heels

If you **pace**, you walk up and down a small area, usually because you are anxious or impatient:
As he waited, he **paced** nervously around the room.

If you **stride**, you walk with quick, long steps:
He turned abruptly and **strode** off down the corridor.

If you **march**, you walk quickly and in a determined way, perhaps because you are angry:
She **marched** into the office and demanded to see the manager.

If you **stamp**, you put your feet down very hard when you walk, usually because you are angry:
"I'm leaving!" he shouted as he **stamped** out of the room.

If you **flounce**, you walk quickly and with exaggerated movements, in a way that shows you are annoyed or upset about something:
She **flounced** out of the room in a huff.

If you **stalk**, you walk in a stiff, proud, or angry way:
He **stalked** out of the meeting, slamming the door.

If you **lurch**, you walk with sudden, jerky movements:
He **lurched** around the room as if he was drunk.

If you **stagger** or **totter**, you walk very unsteadily, often
because you are ill or drunk:
He **staggered** home from the pub every night.
I had to **totter** around on crutches for six weeks.

If you **reel**, you walk about in an unsteady way as if you are
going to fall:
He lost his balance and **reeled** back.

If you **stumble**, you trip while you are walking and almost fall:
I **stumbled** into the phone box and dialled 999.
If you **hike** or **ramble**, you walk some distance in the
countryside for pleasure:
They **hiked** along a remote trail.
a relaxing holiday spent **rambling** over the fells

If you **trek**, you make a journey across difficult country by
walking:
This year we're going **trekking** in Nepal.

You can also use **trek** to describe someone walking rather
slowly and unwillingly, usually because they are tired:
We **trekked** all round the shops looking for white shoes.

If you **plod**, **tramp**, or **trudge**, you walk slowly, with heavy
steps, often because you are tired:
He **plodded** about after me, looking bored.
They spent all day **tramping** through the snow.
We had to **trudge** all the way back up the hill.

WIDE

There are a number of ways in which the word **wide** can be used,
depending on what you are referring to. But you can make your
language more interesting by using one of the following instead.

measuring a large distance from side to side:
ample bosom **baggy** trousers **broad** shoulders **expansive** play area **extensive** grounds **full** skirt **immense** body of water **large** rivers and lakes **roomy** jacket **spacious** kitchen **sweeping** curve of the bay **vast** stretches of land **voluminous** trench coat

extensive in scope:
ample scope **broad** range **catholic** taste **comprehensive** guide **encyclopedic** knowledge **exhaustive** knowledge **extensive** press coverage **far-ranging** reforms **immense** range **inclusive** survey **large** selection **vast** range of products **wide-ranging** aims

as far as possible:
open **completely** **dilated** pupils extend **fully** fully **open** spread **right out**